Merging Lines

Merging Lines

American Railroads

1900–1970

Richard Saunders, Jr.

Northern

Illinois

University

Press

DeKalb

Library of Congress Cataloging-in-Publication Data

Saunders, Richard, 1940–

Merging lines: American railroads, 1900–1970/Richard Saunders, Jr.

   p.   cm.

Rev. ed. of: The railroad mergers and the coming of Conrail. 1978.

Includes bibliographical references and index.

ISBN 0-87580-265-6 (alk. paper)

1. Railroads and state—United States—History—20th century. 2. Railroads—
Mergers—United States—History—20th century. 3. ConRail—History—20th century.
I. Title: American railroads, 1900–1970. II. Saunders, Richard, 1940– Railroad
mergers and the coming of Conrail. III. Title.

HE2757 1978.S28 2001

385'.1—dc21   2001030354

Contents

List of Maps

List of Tables

Railroad Names

Abbreviations

ACL	Atlantic Coast Line Railroad
ARR	Alaska Railroad
B&M	Boston & Maine Railroad
B&O	Baltimore & Ohio Railroad
B&S	Buffalo & Susquehanna Railway
BN	Burlington Northern Railroad
C&EI	Chicago & Eastern Illinois Railway
C&NW	Chicago & North Western Railway (North Western)
C&O	Chesapeake & Ohio Railway (Chessie)
C&S	Colorado & Southern
CGW	Chicago Great Western Railroad
CMStP&P	Chicago, Milwaukee, St. Paul & Pacific Railroad (Milwaukee Road)
CN	Canadian National Railways
CNJ	Central Railroad of New Jersey (Jersey Central Lines)
CNO&TP	Cincinnati, New Orleans & Texas Pacific Railroad (a division of the Southern Railway)
CofG	Central of Georgia Railway
CP	Canadian Pacific Railway
CSX	(stands for) Chessie-Seaboard-Together
D&H	Delaware & Hudson Company

D&RGW	Denver & Rio Grande Western Railroad (Rio Grande)
DL&W	Delaware, Lackawanna & Western (Lackawanna)
DSS&A	Duluth, South Shore & Atlantic Railroad
DT&I	Detroit, Toledo & Ironton Railroad
EL	Erie Lackawanna Railroad (Railway after 1968)
FEC	Florida East Coast Railway
GM&N	Gulf, Mobile & Northern Railroad
GM&O	Gulf, Mobile & Ohio Railroad
GN	Great Northern Railway
GNP & BL	Great Northern Pacific & Burlington Lines
GTP	Grand Trunk Pacific Railway (Canada)
GTW	Grand Trunk Western
IC	Illinois Central Railroad
ICG	Illinois Central Gulf Railroad
KCS	Kansas City Southern Railway
L&N	Louisville & Nashville Railroad
L&NE	Lehigh & New England Railroad
LIRR	Long Island Railroad
LV	Lehigh Valley Railroad (Lehigh)
M&StL	Minneapolis & St. Louis Railway
MKT	Missouri-Kansas-Texas (Katy)
MP	Missouri Pacific Railroad (MoPac)
N&C	Nashville, Chattanooga & St. Louis Railway
N&W	Norfolk & Western Railway
NC&StL (or N&C)	Nashville, Chattanooga & St. Louis Railway
NH	New York, New Haven & Hartford Railroad
NP	Northern Pacific Railroad
NTR	National Transcontinental Railway (Canada)
NYC	New York Central Railroad (Central)
NYC&StL	New York, Chicago & St. Louis Railroad (Nickel Plate)
NYNH&H (or NH)	New York, New Haven & Hartford Railroad (New Haven)

O&W	New York, Ontario & Western Railway
P&LE	Pittsburgh & Lake Erie
P&WV	Pittsburgh & West Virginia Railway
PC	Penn Central Transportation Company
PM	Pere Marquette Railway
PRR	Pennsylvania Railroad (Pennsy)
QNS&L	Quebec, North Shore & Labrador
RI	Chicago, Rock Island & Pacific (Rock Island, or Rock)
SAL	Seaboard Air Line Railroad
SCL	Seaboard Coast Line Railroad
SP	Southern Pacific Railroad
SP&S	Spokane, Portland & Seattle
SR	Southern Railway
T&P	Texas & Pacific Railway
TC	Tennessee Central Railroad
TP&W	Toledo, Peoria & Western Railroad
TRRA	Terminal Railroad Association of St. Louis
UP	Union Pacific Railroad
Vgn	Virginian Railway
W&A	Western & Atlantic
W&LE	Wheeling & Lake Erie Railway
WM	Western Maryland Railway
WP	Western Pacific Railroad

Commonly Used Railroad Nicknames

Burlington Route, or Burlington	Chicago, Burlington & Quincy
Central	New York Central (locally in New Jersey, Central Railroad referred to the Jersey Central and locally in Georgia to the Central of Georgia)
Chessie	Chesapeake & Ohio
Cotton Belt	St. Louis Southwestern
Frisco	St. Louis–San Francisco

Jersey Central	Central Railroad of New Jersey
Katy	Missouri-Kansas-Texas
Lackawanna	Delaware, Lackawanna & Western
Lehigh	Lehigh Valley
Milwaukee Road	Chicago, Milwaukee, St. Paul & Pacific
Monon	Chicago, Indianapolis & Louisville (changed officially to Monon in 1956)
MoPac	Missouri Pacific
New Haven	New York, New Haven & Hartford
Nickel Plate	New York, Chicago & St. Louis
North Western	Chicago & North Western
Pennsy	Pennsylvania
Rio Grande	Denver & Rio Grande Western
Rock Island, or Rock	Chicago, Rock Island & Pacific
Santa Fe	Atchison, Topeka & Santa Fe
Soo Line, or Soo	Minneapolis, St. Paul & Sault Ste. Marie (changed officially to Soo Line in 1960)
West Point Route	Atlanta & West Point, Georgia Railroad and Western Railway of Alabama

A Word about the Dashes in Railroad Names

A very few railroads used dashes regularly in their proper names—the Missouri-Kansas-Texas (Katy) and the St. Louis–San Francisco (Frisco) are among them.

The hyphen is used in this book mostly to indicate two independent railroads that are presenting a joint case in order to merge (e.g., the Penn-Central or the Erie-Lackawanna). In general, after a merger was consummated, the hyphen was not used (e.g., the Penn-Central was referred to as the Penn Central after the merger). The Erie Lackawanna kept its hyphen for a time after its merger but dropped it in 1964. The Chesapeake & Ohio–Baltimore & Ohio used a slash after the C&O took control of the B&O to show their affiliation but also to denote that they remained two separate systems sharing a common upper management. That cumbersome appellation was dropped in favor of "Chessie System."

Preface

Much of the material in this book was first published in 1978 by Greenwood Press under the title *The Railroad Mergers and the Coming of Conrail*. That book was written as the Penn Central lay in bankruptcy and physical ruin. Headlines screamed about botched management, insider deals, phony accounting, laundered money, buckling morale, and customers leaving in droves. Operating losses ran a million dollars a day. Nationalization or liquidation loomed. Liquidation meant selling pieces of the railroad to the highest bidder, as junk or as cow pasture. It was the darkest hour of the American railroad.

The last chapter of that book, about the creation of Conrail out of the wreckage of Penn Central and other bankrupt roads in the Northeast, was written as events were unfolding. Conrail was struggling. Press accounts pronounced it dead at birth, at best a permanent ward of the government. Bankruptcy and pending liquidation spread to the Midwest, to the Rock Island and the Milwaukee Road. The conventional wisdom was that it was only a matter of time before railroads were nationalized. A lot of them would probably be abandoned. The original book was filled with that despair.

We know now that the early 1970s, where this volume ends, were the blackest midnight of American railroads. We know that the remainder of that decade was a difficult time, with the outcome in doubt. We know now that the seeds of the eventual turnaround were sown even in the 1960s, as the cataclysm approached. They took root in the 1970s thanks to wise but gutsy public policy that unleashed private energies and imagination. Sometime after 1980, a slimmed-down freight railroad system returned with resurgent health, productive, innovative, profitable—as revolutionary a facilitator of the division of labor as railroads were when they consolidated the industrial revolution in the mid–nineteenth century. By century's end, 12,000-ton monster trains roamed the rails on tight headway, and railroads struggled to reopen routes previously closed because they needed the capacity. But that is a story for another book.

The original book was generally well received when it came out. It was reviewed in sixteen journals in North America and Europe, mostly favorably, often enthusiastically. The American Trucking Association called me personally to get 25 copies immediately, as though they were already dancing on the grave. I am not sure if the Association of American Railroads ever bought a copy. *Forbes* sent its star transportation reporter, James Cook, and a photographer all the way to Clemson, South Carolina, to interview me (see the issue of October 30, 1978, p. 100). But the book became dated very quickly. It was the classic danger of writing history too soon after the fact. It is a rare privilege to be able to update a work such as this and to retell the story with a longer view.

Much of the work for this book was done at the now defunct Interstate Commerce Commission in Washington. I propose a toast in memory of the men and women of the ICC. Whatever one thinks of the agency or the importance of its work, its people were helpful and courteous to me. I know I annoyed the scores of truckers' lawyers who buzzed in and out of the dockets file room like hummingbirds while I was clacking away on my Royal manual portable. Perhaps the demise of the ICC is for the best; but a new agency, the Surface Transportation Board, takes its place, so I do not really see what purpose was served by getting rid of the ICC. I will always remember the time I spent there. The ICC library was a good library; it has been preserved at the University of Denver. And the cuisine at the GSA cafeteria at the ICC was precisely my cuisine—the best place to eat in Washington.

I want to apologize to the people at the Bureau of Railway Economics Library at the Association of American Railroads. In the 1978 edition of this book, I made some unkind remarks about them. The Bureau of Railway Economics Library is a private reference library for engineering, commercial, financial, statistical, regulatory, and legal matters that pertain to railroads. The library is not really meant for historical research, although, of course, materials accumulate over time and become historical. Unfortunately, when I went there they had just moved to new quarters and had taken the opportunity to cull out much of the old stuff. Items I expected to find had vanished. I should have been more understanding and should have recognized that it is not a public library. I thought I had observed proper protocol when I went there, but it was a very gray-suit environment, and I was probably wearing jeans and a hooded sweatshirt; in any event, I was asked to leave and never quite got over it. It was a misunderstanding. I hope we can turn a new leaf.

I want to thank Bob Sutton, professor emeritus of history at the University of Illinois, who was my guide and mentor for the 1970 dissertation that represents about a quarter of this book (even though it was 700 pages long). He loves trains as I do; I will always have a warm spot in my heart for him. Special thanks to Dick Overton, then dean of railroad historians, who took an interest in a young scholar and graciously offered to write a foreword to *Railroad Mergers and the Coming of Conrail*. His death in 1988 was a loss to railroad historical scholarship. Thanks also to Jim Sabin at Greenwood Press, who saw the merit in the work and agreed to publish the original book. Thanks to my colleague Don McKale and to Professor Alfred Mierzejewski at Athens State College who together gave important insight into the Deutsche Reichsbahn in the years after World War I. Thanks also to Roger Grant, then at the University of Akron, who suggested to Northern Illinois University Press that this would be a good book to republish. I owe a great debt to the excellent reporting of Robert Bedingfield in the *New York Times* from the 1950s to the 1970s and to James Cook for his accounts in *Forbes*.

I am also indebted to William K. Dozier, Jr., then with the Federal Reserve Bank of Atlanta, now in law school, who helped to prepare statistical analysis for some of the subjects in this book. Keith was one of my favorite students in 1994 and is one of my best friends now. Most of his work wound up on the cutting room floor. I understand things through stories, not figures. To explain what happened and why it happened, I think carefully told stories do a better job than numbers, though I know both techniques can be manipulated if one is so inclined. When I worked for the New York Central, I helped compile statistics for management, mostly for the morning report. For a mix of reasons, mostly to cover screwups, I was ordered to add a few cars here, a few cars there. The figures we sent up were not exactly lies; they bore a resemblance to reality. But they were not accurate, either. In later research, I found out that the figures were just a little phony everywhere. I am sure in a computer age, with all its cross-checking, they are much better. I agree that statistics are an important tool, but I have no faith in their precise accuracy. I will not embarrass Keith by misusing them here.

Thanks to Tom Wilcockson of Mapcraft for doing the maps.

Finally, thanks to friends who helped in the final preparation: my colleague, Dr. Mike Silvestri; T.J. Gaffney of Port Huron, Michigan, a master's student who completed an excellent thesis on railroads and the economy of the Thumb Region of Michigan; past graduate assistants Carole Hasson, Niles Illich, Grant Greenwood, and Paul Curry; and my present excellent team of assistants—Nate Plucker in my World Since World War II course and Brian Feltman and Sean "Stick" Simon in my Western Civilization course. Stick is also my good friend, business partner, and fellow Arctic explorer.

Merging Lines

Introduction

This book is not about generalizations. It is about individual railroads, individual executives, individual corporate strategies, and the political economy in which they existed. That is why it is so long.

This introduction is a primer on the American railroad system in the middle of the twentieth century. It includes definitions of the terms that describe how individual railroads functioned together as a system. It is meant to give readers who are not already familiar with those terms and that information a quick reference guide to the great railroad companies of yesterday, before the mergers of the second half of the twentieth century. A generation of rail enthusiasts call these the "fallen flags." Readers who are well versed in railroad knowledge—those who are a part of the rail and railfan communities and learned all this stuff poring over maps or old *Official Guides* as children—may go directly to Chapter 1.[1]

Newcomers getting ready to throw up their hands in despair should remember that the railroads were very important in their regions once upon a time. Their names were familiar to millions. Their emblems were familiar trademarks. Many people kept these railroads' timetables in their desk drawers for handy reference. Such familiarity declined with the decline of the passenger train across the 1960s and ended abruptly after private railroads stopped operating passenger trains with the creation of Amtrak in 1971. By century's end, railroads in general, and certainly individual railroads, were quite unfamiliar to most ordinary people. A few historic names like the Santa Fe or the Union Pacific might ring a bell, but that was about all. In order to understand what happened and why it happened, one needs to learn the names of the old railroads.

The American railroad network was made up of independent private

companies, each with its distinct problems, traditions, and business strategies. To function as a system, to get a shipment from a customer on railroad A to one on railroad B, these independent companies had to cooperate with each other as no other industry needed to. Even competitors had
to do business with each other on a day-to-day basis. The most basic
mechanisms of their cooperation were worked out at the end of the nineteenth century, including the standardization of track gauge and the
adoption of procedures of interchange by which one railroad allowed its
cars to operate on the tracks of another railroad so that goods did not
have to be unloaded and reloaded at every junction. These are described
in a short but important book by George Rogers Taylor and Irene D. Neu,
The American Railroad Network, 1861–1890 (Cambridge: Harvard University
Press, 1956).

The railroad companies themselves grew without much planning. Each
was conceived as a money-making scheme. The strong ones acquired less
successful ones as they became available. The result was that, although
railroads could be roughly grouped into regions (the East, the South, the
Midwest, the West), there was overlap, there were gaps, there was duplication among sometimes four or more railroads on a given route, and there
were nuisance railroads spiked down parallel to existing ones just to make
trouble. It was not utter chaos, but it certainly can look like chaos to
someone approaching it for the first time.

To make sense out of it, let us first define some terms. Until well into
the twentieth century, most traffic stayed within a region. Before the railroads goods were grown or made locally, or people did without. Few goods
could absorb the cost of a long overland haul. The railroad changed that,
but did not change it all at once, and so deep into the twentieth century
the idea of independent railroads operating locally within a region made
sense. As the economy became more interdependent among the regions,
the powerful incentive for railroads to consolidate lines under a single
management became evident. By the end of the twentieth century, the
walls dividing Northeast from Southeast came tumbling down, although
the wall between East and West remained intact. The North American Free
Trade Agreement of 1993 made the economy of the entire continent more
integrated. It is not surprising, therefore, that Canada's two railroad giants, the Canadian National (CN) and the Canadian Pacific (CP), acquired
parts of the U.S. rail network and that a U.S. road, the Kansas City Southern (KCS), gained big chunks of the Mexican network. But when our story
begins, railroads for the most part found it advantageous to stay within a
region; and as traffic moved between regions, they were on equally good
terms with the connecting lines in the other regions.

Much traffic moved interline, meaning it originated on one road but
would be delivered by another. The process of transferring traffic from one
line to another was called *interchange,* and by the twentieth century, the

mechanisms for it were smooth as silk. Interchange normally passed through *gateways,* those junction points at which through rates were quoted. Not every junction was a gateway, although it could become one if both railroads at the junction wanted to make it one. Shippers called the local railroad of their choice, and the whole procedure was handled from there. They received a single bill no matter how many railroads handled their shipment. Shippers could pick every railroad they wanted to handle their shipment and specify every junction point along the way, and often they did. But traffic normally moved over established routes, frequently chosen by the originating carrier. Shippers were usually content with this because the service was good and the traffic moved on through rates. By the mid-1960s, *run-through* trains were common; those were whole trains that passed from one railroad to another intact, sometimes changing crews at the transfer point but often not changing locomotives.

Railroads that originated traffic had a great deal of influence over routes. Those that terminated traffic had the expense of collecting the money from the customer and dividing the revenue among the railroads that had participated in the movement. Terminating roads usually had to deal with the bulk of customer complaints.[2] Ideally, origination and termination should balance each other, but they seldom did on any given railroad. The preponderant flow of traffic in the United States was west to east and south to north, meaning that railroads in the Northeast had a disproportionate share of terminal expense.

Often in between lay another kind of railroad, the *bridge carrier.* Bridge carriers received traffic from the railroad that originated it and delivered it to the railroad that terminated it. Being a bridge carrier was lucrative, at least if the haul was long enough, because there was no switching expense at either end. It was straight line-haul revenue. But the bridge carrier was vulnerable if its principal connections merged into hostile railroad camps. Thus, for example, when the Denver & Rio Grande Western's (D&RGW, or Rio Grande) major connection from the west, the Western Pacific (WP), and its major connection to the east, the Missouri Pacific (MP, or MoPac), were both merged into the Union Pacific (UP) in 1982, its lucrative bridge traffic dried up quickly.

No railroad wanted to *short-haul* itself, meaning it wanted to get the longest possible mileage for itself and not turn over traffic to a connecting line any sooner than it had to. The Chicago & North Western's (C&NW, or North Western) main line, for example, went only as far west as Omaha (actually Fremont, Nebraska), and so it turned traffic over to the Union Pacific at that point. But the Chicago, Burlington & Quincy (Burlington) and the Chicago, Rock Island & Pacific (RI, Rock Island, or Rock), which went to Omaha, also went on to Denver. Because they would short-haul themselves if they turned traffic over at Omaha, they preferred to turn traffic over to the Rio Grande at Denver. Lines that connected without either road short-hauling itself were called *friendly connections*. It was important for railroads to have friendly connections, and when a merger threatened to eliminate one, it was a matter of great concern.

There were, in the 1950s, several hundred different railroad companies. Only 134 of those were Class I carriers, which in those days meant they had annual gross revenues of more than a million dollars. Only about half of those were of national significance, and of that half, only a portion are of concern to us here. The United States was divided into three railroad territories. The East, called Official Territory for rate-making purposes, extended south to the Potomac and Ohio Rivers and west to a line between Chicago and St. Louis. The Southern Territory extended from the Potomac through the Deep South and west to the Mississippi. The Western Territory was everything west of Chicago and the Mississippi River.

On the borders between the regions lay the major junction points, or gateways, where traffic funneled on through rates from one region to another. Between East and West, the principal gateways were Chicago and St. Louis, with Peoria playing a lesser role; between South and West the gateways were Memphis and New Orleans; and between North and South, Alexandria, Virginia, on the Potomac and Cincinnati on the Ohio River.

The East: The Official Territory

Astride the East lay four railroads called trunk lines that extended all the way from the Atlantic to the western gateways. Two, the New York Central (NYC, or Central) and the Pennsylvania (PRR, or Pennsy), were railroad supergiants of their day. More than just railroad supergiants, they were corporate supergiants, for many years the bluest of Wall Street's blue chips. They headed out of New York in opposite directions, but they turned west, the Central at Albany and the Pennsylvania at Philadelphia, to blanket the entire region that in days gone by was the heartland of American manufacturing. Each of them served Buffalo, Rochester, Pittsburgh, Cleveland, Columbus, Cincinnati, Detroit, Indianapolis, St. Louis, Peoria, and Chicago.

The NYC and the PRR carried on one of the most historic rivalries in American business. Travelers who knew their way around chose the Central when they could, for the famous breakfast run, the final sprint of the great overnight expresses from the Midwest, along the Hudson River from Albany to New York. It was one of the great train rides of the world. But the Pennsylvania had an edge on the Central as the bulk mover, of people along the New York–Washington corridor and of heavy freight to the steel districts. It was always a little bigger. Both were aristocrats of business.

The Pennsylvania Railroad paid a dividend every year since 1847 (until the Penn Central's [PC] bankruptcy in 1970), and its management was self-perpetuating. Each generation of top officers selected the next generation. The Central had a managerial revolution in 1954 that severed all connection with the founding Vanderbilt family (see chapter 3). After that, the two railroads developed very different philosophies of how to run a railroad and how to price its services.

There were two other trunks, much smaller than the Central or the Pennsy, connecting the Atlantic ports to the midwestern gateways. One was the Baltimore & Ohio (B&O), for years one of the country's oldest surviving railroad corporate structures, having been chartered on February 28, 1827, at the dawn of the railroad age. It might have rivaled the Central and the Pennsy, but it was stunted at a critical moment of its development by the Civil War. Its main line lay astride the border between the North and the South. Its trains were commandeered by the Union armies and stolen, or blown up, by the Confederates. It recovered, though clearly set back, and eventually concentrated on hauling raw materials to the steel district. It had lines to Washington, Baltimore, and Philadelphia in the East; Pittsburgh, Buffalo, Cleveland, Detroit, Cincinnati, and Louisville in the middle; and Chicago and St. Louis in the West, but these were often circuitous and hampered by heavy mountain grades.

The other, the Erie, was a good, mostly double-tracked, freight line between New York and Chicago, but it missed just about every major city in between except over branches (to Rochester, Buffalo, Cleveland, and Cincinnati). It was the only trunk that did not reach St. Louis. It concentrated mostly on forwarding trainloads of western perishables to the East. The Erie was best remembered for its seedy financial past, when nineteenth-century railroad barons manipulated its stock and loaded it with debt, a burden that reached out a dead hand as late as 1976 to crush it.

In the eastern district there were railroads that were not trunks because they did not go all the way from the Atlantic to the western gateways. First, there were the New England roads. New England was like a laboratory for all that was troubled in railroading in the second half of the twentieth century. Distances were short. Long distance meant that the railroad's cost advantage ruled; short distance meant that door-to-door service by trucks was more important. Two lines in northern New England, the Bangor & Aroostook and the Maine Central, carried mostly raw materials to markets farther south and earned regular, if modest, profits. The two major lines in southern New England, the Boston & Maine (B&M) and the New York, New Haven & Hartford (NYNH&H, NH, or New Haven), were burdened with extensive branchlines, heavy money-losing passenger and commuter traffic (which the New Haven carried on expensive four-track high-speed lines), and short hauls, which meant a lot of their freight was lost to trucks.

Getting heavy freight trains into New England was more of a problem than it may seem from a glance at a map. There were no railroad bridges across New York Harbor; transfer had to be made by tug and barge (lighters) because freights could not negotiate the clearance of the passenger tunnels through Penn Station. Lots of railroad lighters plied New York Harbor. North of New York was the Hudson River, a formidable barrier both because it was a big river and because of the steep Palisades on its banks.

South of Albany, only two railroad bridges crossed the Hudson. The Poughkeepsie Bridge brought the New Haven into Maybrook Yard in New York State, where the Erie and several odd bridge carriers funneled freight into southern New England. The Poughkeepsie Bridge is burned now, and there is hardly a trace of Maybrook Yard or those odd little railroads that once went there. Further north, the New York Central's Boston & Albany connected those two cities, making the Central the only trunk line to enter New England. The Boston & Maine crossed the Hudson at its headwaters north of Albany. Its double-tracked Fitchburg Division across Massachusetts, with its Hoosac Tunnel under the Berkshire Mountains, rolled a lot of fast freight, though not enough of it far enough to make the B&M a strong carrier. To the north of that was Lake Champlain, and the next railroad entry into New England was at the Quebec border.

There was another group of eastern railroads called the anthracite roads. It is hard to imagine, in these days when homes are heated with oil or gas, how important anthracite (hard coal) once was. It was used for space heating, and without it northerners froze in the winter. Five major railroads were built to carry hard coal from the anthracite fields in northeastern Pennsylvania. The Central Railroad of New Jersey (CNJ, or Jersey Central) sent it east to New Jersey and New York City. The Reading carried it south to Philadelphia. The Delaware & Hudson (D&H) took it north to New England and Montreal. The Lehigh Valley (LV, or Lehigh) and the Delaware, Lackawanna & Western (DL&W, or Lackawanna), carried it both east to New York and west to Buffalo, where it went on to Canada or the American Midwest.

All the anthracite roads carried general traffic as well—lots of it—the D&H carried wood pulp from Canada, for example; the Reading, bituminous coal to the industrial complex of the lower Delaware Valley; the Lehigh and the Lackawanna, traffic between Buffalo and New York from the Great Lakes to the sea (traffic shortly to be hit by the opening of the St. Lawrence Seaway). All of them ran famous passenger trains, and the Lackawanna, the Jersey Central, and the Reading carried commuters— thousands of them—into New York and Philadelphia each day. But when anthracite was replaced by other fuels, the rug was pulled out from under these railroads. After the late 1950s, only the D&H, a line that carried bridge traffic to New England and that was not burdened with extensive passenger operations, was able to preserve a semblance of prosperity.

A third subgroup of eastern railroads was known as the Pocahontas roads. On the borderlands between the eastern and southern districts lay what was called the Pocahontas Region. There, two principal east-west roads—the Norfolk & Western (N&W) and the Chesapeake & Ohio (C&O, or Chessie)—and a smaller but important one—the Virginian Railway (Vgn)—carried bituminous (soft) coal east to the Atlantic and west to midwestern industry. West Virginia coal was not much of a factor when the twentieth century began, but these railroads helped make it competitive for steelmaking and for generating electricity. Though they had branches extending even into North Carolina, their traffic was so intimately a part of the northern economy that their interests were generally with the North. People gave up on anthracite to heat their homes, but the demand for steel and electricity kept growing and so did the demand for Appalachian coal. Hauling coal was something railroads could do very well, and they could make a lot of money doing it. It should be no surprise that the two Pocahontas roads (the Virginian was later absorbed by the N&W) were the railroad Rocks of Gibraltar on which two of the latter-day super-railroads were built—the Norfolk & Western the nucleus of the modern Norfolk Southern, and the Chesapeake & Ohio of the Chessie-Seaboard-Together (CSX).

A fourth subgroup in the Eastern District was the midwestern bridge lines that connected western roads at Chicago and/or St. Louis to the anthracite (and other) roads at Buffalo/Niagara Falls. The two that were best known in this category were the New York, Chicago & St. Louis (NYC&StL, or Nickel Plate Road), and the Wabash. Both served Chicago and St. Louis, the Wabash going all the way to Kansas City and Omaha. This was the same area as the western halves of the trunks. If Wabash and Nickel Plate were matched up with Great-Lakes-to-the-sea anthracite roads, the Lackawanna, and the Lehigh Valley, they formed trunk lines. It was no surprise that these two anthracite roads regarded the midwestern bridges as very friendly connections, the Lackawanna and Nickel Plate exchanging traffic at Buffalo and the Wabash and Lehigh Valley at Suspension Bridge (Niagara Falls), New York.[3]

Like the Pocahontas roads, the midwestern bridges were a little wobbly early in the century. But as the national economy became more inter-regional, they could haul a growing volume of traffic from the midwestern gateways to eastern connections over long distances and flat lands, and with hardly any terminal expense to themselves. It was quite lucrative. Nickel Plate's strength was its single-track Buffalo–Chicago main line that became a freight hauler of formidable efficiency. Wabash had a problem in that all its traffic had to be ferried across the Detroit River at Detroit. Its strength was down St. Louis way, and the fact that it connected directly with the Union Pacific at Kansas City. These roads were too small to become railroad giants on their own, but they were prime pawns in the consolidation game to come.

Two other roads are often overlooked as midwestern bridges because they are better known for other things. The Pere Marquette (PM) concentrated mostly on traffic local to Michigan or that moved into or out of Michigan to the south. But it also connected Chicago with Suspension Bridge (over trackage rights on the New York Central's Michigan Central–Canada Southern Division from St. Thomas, Ontario). It merged with the Chesapeake & Ohio in 1947. The Grand Trunk Western (GTW) was a subsidiary of the Canadian National Railways. It was the U.S. portion of the original Montreal–Chicago main line of the British Empire's Grand Trunk Railroad. Grand Trunk Western is known mostly as a funnel for traffic to and from Canada, and a very busy railroad in its own right in Michigan. But with its parent CN, it also connected Chicago with Suspension Bridge, and so part of its role as a U.S. carrier was as a midwestern bridge. Since GTW was already a part of a super railroad, the CN, it will play only a small role in the story to come.

The Southern Territory

The major railroads of the South grew steadily in traffic and financial health as the region industrialized and urbanized and came to be called the Sunbelt in the years after World War II. On the coastal plain, the Atlantic Coast Line (ACL) and the Seaboard Air Line (SAL) competed mile for mile for both freight and passengers between Florida, the Carolinas, and the North. The ACL was traditionally the larger and stronger of the two, but the Seaboard possessed two of the most famous passenger trains in all of railroad lore, the Cotton States Special and the Orange Blossom Special. In the 1920s, the Seaboard and the ACL largely created Florida as a prime tourist destination and were probably best known for the streamliners they ran at incredibly high speeds between the North and Florida. Those trains remained popular long after passenger traffic fell off elsewhere; they were still playing to packed houses at the end of private operation (when Amtrak took over in 1971). But the money was in freight, and they forwarded a lot of it, over long distances, very profitably in the years after World War II.

To their west, in the Piedmont and mountain regions, extending as far west as the Mississippi River, were the Southern Railway (SR) and the Louisville & Nashville (L&N). Both shared in the prosperity that came to the region with the building of the Tennessee Valley Authority. Both hauled Kentucky coal. Both served burgeoning Atlanta. Both were steeped in southern tradition. The Southern ran the famous Royal Palm from Cincinnati to Florida and the Crescent from New York to New Orleans.[4] The L&N ran the Pan American, which was made famous in the early days of radio when its daily passage was blasted to the world by a trackside microphone of Nashville's clear-channel radio station WSM. WSM was the home of the Grand Ole Opry, and needless to say, this was where trains met country music. To Hank Williams, the Pan American was the soul of the South:

She's the beauty of the Southland,
Listen to that whistle scream.
It's the *Pan American*
On her way to New Orleans.
She leaves Cincinnati
Headin' down that Dixie Line.
When she passes the Nashville tower,
You can hear that whistle whine.
Stick your head out the window
And feel that southern breeze.
You're on the *Pan American*
On her way to New Orleans.[5]

The L&N controlled the Nashville, Chattanooga & St. Louis (NC&StL; known locally as the N&C) a busy route that, despite its name, ran between Memphis, Nashville, and Atlanta. Some regard the merger of the NC&StL into the L&N in 1957 as the beginning of the merger movement. Others do not, because it simply tidied up a corporate relationship that had existed since 1880.

The Southern was the larger of the two trans-Appalachian haulers. But the L&N was controlled by the Atlantic Coast Line, and although they operated as separate companies, together they were bigger than the Southern. The ACL-L&N family also controlled the Georgia RR–West Point Route between Augusta, Atlanta, and Montgomery as well as the Clinchfield, a line from Elkhorn City, Kentucky, to Spartanburg, South Carolina. It was part of a through route between the steel belt and the Piedmont–coastal plain. The Clinchfield was (and still is, as part of CSX) a busy freight railroad, with long, heavy trains that traverse some of the most difficult mountain terrain in the world.

Two other southern roads of importance to this story are the Central of Georgia (CofG) and the Florida East Coast (FEC). Both wrote significant chapters in railroad labor relations in the 1960s (for their stories, see chapter 11).

Along the Mississippi River, from the Delta cotton lands of Mississippi to Chicago and then west across Iowa to Sioux City and Sioux Falls, was the Illinois Central (IC). It dominated the state of Mississippi so is included here as a southern carrier; it was just as much a midwestern granger road. In a country where the dominant flow of traffic was east and west, or at least crisscrossing east and west, the IC ran straight north and south. It fit in no category except with the parallel, and remarkably weaker, Gulf, Mobile & Ohio (GM&O), with which it merged in 1972. The IC stayed out of the emerging supersystems of the 1980s until 1998, when the Canadian National bought it for an outlet to the warm-water Gulf.

In the Southwest (Arkansas, Oklahoma, and Texas) were a group of railroads that were mostly starved for traffic in the old days, when the region was poor and dusty. After World War II, that area became a vibrant part of the rising Sunbelt. Its railroads, most of them, prospered along with it. Two lines became jewels in the consolidation game. The Missouri Pacific was the largest. It fanned out in a quadrant to the west and south of St. Louis. It shared in—in fact helped create—the industrial rise of Texas. It controlled the Texas & Pacific (T&P) between New Orleans, Dallas, and El Paso. Although the T&P had deep roots in Texas and once dreamed of being a mighty transcontinental, it is treated here as a part of the MoPac. The MoPac was also part of a transcontinental route, connecting with the Rio Grande at Pueblo, Colorado, which in turn connected with the Western Pacific. This route had been the heart of Jay Gould's drive for a truly coast-to-coast railroad, which included the Wabash and other lines to the East, an overextended empire that collapsed after 1912. In the streamliner era, MoPac was known for a classy fleet of blue and silver trains known as the Eagles, but in the heavyweight era, its famous train was the Sunshine Special from St. Louis and Memphis to Dallas, Fort Worth, Houston, San Antonio, and El Paso, with through cars to Los Angeles and Mexico City. Its name will live forever in the lore of railroading.

> See that engine rollin', she's ballin' the jack,
> Her wheels hummin' *Dixie* and her headlight on the track.
> Watch that engine swayin' while she's comin' down the line.
> *Sunshine Special,* she'll be right on time.[6]

The other major southwestern road was the St. Louis–San Francisco (Frisco). It ran in an X pattern southwest from St. Louis to Oklahoma City and Dallas and southeast from Kansas City to Memphis, Birmingham, and (via subsidiaries) Mobile and Pensacola, with the fulcrum at Springfield, Missouri.

Two smaller southwesterns were also jewels, prospering as the Sunbelt prospered. The Kansas City Southern ran straight south from Kansas City to the Gulf of Mexico at Port Arthur and New Orleans (by acquiring the wobbly Louisiana & Arkansas between New Orleans and Dallas in 1939). It stumbled badly in the 1970s but got a grip on itself and became a busy, vibrant line poised to take advantage of the NAFTA treaty with subsidiaries in Mexico and a deepening friendship with Canadian roads. The St. Louis–Southwestern (Cotton Belt) ran from St. Louis and Memphis to Texas. It was a subsidiary of the Southern Pacific (SP).

In the Southwest only the Missouri-Kansas-Texas (MKT, or Katy) remained untouched by Sunbelt success. The pioneer line into Texas, it helped open up the Indian Territory (Oklahoma) to white settlement. Katy set its sights on Creek lands first, then on the Choctaw, and then on the

Cherokee. It pulled stunts like charging admission to watch two locomotives crash head-on at full speed. That was in 1896. The boilers exploded and several onlookers were skewered with metal shards. The Eleven O'Clock Katy was a Texas institution, leaving Houston every night with sleepers to most other Texas cities. Katy was a sad, poorly managed road (see chapter 4). In the merger era, nobody who was anybody knocked on Katy's door until finally, in 1988, the Union Pacific was persuaded to take it in.

The Western Territory

In the West there were two distinct categories of railroads—the grain-carrying grangers and the transcontinentals. In the nineteenth century, in good years, farmers could expect between 60 cents and a dollar a bushel for wheat. That was paid at the railhead, so the cost to transport it by wagon over dirt country roads to the railroad was the farmer's expense. Since it ran around one-half cent per mile per bushel, a journey of 40 miles or more cut heavily into profits. But in the nineteenth century, railroads were cheap to build on the flat lands. The result was a dense network of criss-crossing lines, many of which had an appalling lack of traffic except at harvesttime when the grain began to move. In the twentieth century, farmers bought farm trucks and could haul their crops much farther, and a lot of those lines became unnecessary. Grain was once shipped in boxcars with a capacity of about 20 tons; after the 1960s, it was much more productive to ship it in covered hoppers that held 80 tons or more, but the bridges and trestles on the old granger branches could not handle cars that heavy. So the story of midwestern railroads, more than that of any other region, has been one of retrenchment and abandonment. For example, in 1995, Iowa had barely half the railroad mileage it had in 1970.

Four major railroads served the region almost exclusively, and their strength depended largely on how well they connected with transcontinental routes. The Burlington was part of James J. Hill's Great Northern–Northern Pacific empire. It had good routes and was well run. The Chicago & North Western was the prime connection for the Union Pacific at Omaha.

The Chicago, Milwaukee, St. Paul & Pacific (CMStP&P; known in the twentieth century as the Milwaukee Road) was the most important of seven routes between Chicago and the Twin Cities. It was exceptionally well engineered. Its Hiawatha fleet of fast trains was very popular when it was introduced in the 1930s, and the cars on those trains, built mostly in the Milwaukee's own shops, rode more smoothly than anything else on rails. In 1909 the Milwaukee completed its own route to Puget Sound, making it the only granger to own a transcontinental route. But its Pacific Extension was a disappointment. There will be much more to say about that.

The Rock Island served more of the southern plains than the other grangers. It was the first railroad to bridge the Mississippi, but its routes were circuitous. Its transcontinental connection, the Southern Pacific, treated it like a stepchild. It was devoid of geographic integrity, with routes running north into South Dakota and south, deep into Louisiana. It reached key gateways—Kansas City and Denver—over trackage rights, both on the Union Pacific. Its north-south route through Oklahoma followed the old Chisholm Trail and thus missed Oklahoma City. Its Rocket fleet of streamlined passenger trains was very popular; it had the second highest passenger revenues of the grangers, slightly behind the North Western in 1951. But it was strangely weak. It played a major role in the drama recounted here and was the first major American railroad to go out of business entirely.

Three other railroads in the granger region need to be mentioned. The Chicago Great Western (CGW) connected Chicago and Omaha and St. Paul and Kansas City, with its hub at Oelwein, Iowa. It was poorly engineered with poor routes. There were not many hills in Iowa, but it found them. This railroad was not needed in the first place. In the merger era, it had horrible labor relations and provided horrible service. It plays a bit part in the railroad drama. Most of it is abandoned and would be forgotten except for Roger Grant's most excellent history of it, *The Corn Belt Route*, published by Northern Illinois University Press.

The Minneapolis, St. Paul & Sault Ste. Marie Railway (Soo Line) was a true grain-hauling granger of the northern high plains, built originally by Minneapolis interests to break the rate-making stranglehold of Chicago-based lines, first to a connection with the Canadian Pacific at Sault Ste. Marie, Ontario, across Michigan's Upper Peninsula (1883), then westward to another connection with the CP at Portal, North Dakota (1904). The Canadian Pacific, Canada's great privately owned railway, controlled the Soo Line during the nineteenth century, although that line was never as integral a part of the CP as the Grand Trunk was of the CN. Together with the CP, the Soo Line operated one of North America's last great heavy-weight (nonstreamlined) transcontinental passenger trains, the Mountaineer, to the Canadian Rockies, a favorite with tour groups that often operated in two sections as late as 1959. But Soo was not especially well engineered. Its locomotives were small; its trains were slow; it was modestly busy, modestly profitable, and rather dull, a railroad that survived but never set the world on fire. Finally in this category, the Minneapolis & St. Louis (M&StL) was also conceived by Minneapolis interests as a gigantic bypass around Chicago to Peoria and a connection with eastern roads there. It was bought by the C&NW in 1960, but it was important enough that large segments remain as part of the modern Union Pacific.

The second group of western carriers comprised the transcontinentals. These were the long-haul railroads that crossed mighty mountains and parched deserts to reach the Pacific. They had long hauls of diversified freight and, except for the Pacific Extension of the hapless Milwaukee Road, made lots of money.

The Union Pacific was the eastern half of the first transcontinental. The Southern Pacific owned the western half, and together it was known as the Overland Route. The Union Pacific also reached directly to Seattle and Los Angeles. It was, and is, a mighty thing. The Southern Pacific had its own line from San Francisco to New Orleans known as the Sunset Route, and it had a transcontinental connection with the Rock Island known as the Golden State Route. The SP had a practical monopoly of north-south traffic on the West Coast. It built California and once dominated California with a power that no private enterprise was ever intended to have: before 1910, it was a matter of indifference to the railroad whether the Republicans or the Democrats won the statehouse because it owned them both. But it was a busy railroad and was, despite its sins, the heart and soul of historic California.

The Atchison, Topeka & Santa Fe (Santa Fe) ran from Chicago to California and fanned out across Kansas, Oklahoma, and Texas. It may have been America's quintessential railroad, famous in the lore of the Old West, serving such points as Dodge City, Kansas, made famous in the *Gunsmoke* radio and television series and for its famous trains, the Chief and the Super Chief. It was famous in the diesel age for its red and silver "warbonnet" locomotives that symbolized railroading to more Americans than probably anything else (partly because the Lionel Corporation made models of them that were the single most popular toy for boys in the early 1950s). The Santa Fe was famous for Johnny Mercer's 1945 hit from the MGM musical *The Harvey Girls:*

> Do you hear that whistle down the line?
> I reckon that it is engine number forty nine.
> She's the only one that'll sound that way,
> On the Atchison, Topeka and the Santa Fe.[7]

Since the Santa Fe was such a perfect railroad, it will be absent from most of the stories that follow. There has to be a problem for there to be a story, and the Santa Fe had few problems until the 1980s. That is quite a tribute to business success.

In the far north were the "Hill Lines," the competing Great Northern (GN) and Northern Pacific (NP), brought under common control by the empire builder himself, James J. Hill, only to be forcibly broken up in the opening story of this book. Smaller than the other transcontinentals, they were both well run, busy, and profitable. They had loyal customers and were beloved in the territory they served—the best of what private industrial capitalism had to offer. But their role in the story that follows is not wholly uplifting.

Two others need to be mentioned. The Denver & Rio Grande Western (D&RGW, or Rio Grande) ran from Denver to Salt Lake City, and the Western Pacific ran from Salt Lake City to San Francisco. They were late bloomers. Their prosperity awaited the solving of technical problems so that they could run enough trains over their mountain routes to be profitable. But when they did, they were bantam-weight gems and operators of the California Zephyr—the postwar era's most talked-about train, at least according to their advertising, which was probably accurate. It had plenty of Vista-Domes to view the mountains but tried to provide cruise ship luxury at common carrier prices. People flocked to it while it lasted.

one

The Ambiguous Legacy of the Era of Reform
1893–1920

Did railroad builder James J. Hill suspect that a depression was coming in November of 1892? His Great Northern Railway was finished except for a gap over the high Cascades of Washington State. Winter was coming, but he ordered construction to go forward. Winter must not delay it. Hill's Great Northern was the new route from the Mississippi at St. Paul to the Pacific at Seattle. It grew from a local route from St. Paul to Winnipeg built in the years just after the Civil War. In 1887, it struck west over the North Dakota prairie, following the Missouri River across Montana to Great Falls. There it linked up with a new local line, the Montana Central, into Helena, the territorial capital, and across the mountains to Butte. Montana was a boom state. A bright future appeared to lie ahead. Railroads were going to build that future.

The Last Spike at Stevens Pass

In 1889 John Stevens was heading up a railroad scouting party exploring the land west of Fort Assiniboine (near present-day Havre, Montana), when he found Marias Pass. At 5,214 feet above sea level, it was an amazingly easy crossing of the Continental Divide. Hill, with financial backing from J. P. Morgan, decided to build through the pass and on to the Pacific. The line was built in a hurry, but carefully, with sound bridges and good alignments.

In the autumn of 1892, there remained only the gap over the Cascades. Winter was no time for railroad building in these mountains. Pacific storms bring glowering skies and deep snow. A good railroad was going to require a tunnel at the summit of Stevens Pass; but, uncharacteristically,

Hill was in too big a hurry. Instead of a tunnel, he turned to the expedi-
ence of switchbacks: trains would move forward, then backward, forward,
then backward, as though climbing a stair up the mountain. It would be
costly to operate once the line opened.

Winter was brutal. Rains came first, with flash floods. Then came sleet
and snow. One of the workers wrote home, "The only tracks made today
were our tracks in the snow."[1] On January 6, 1893, high atop Stevens Pass,
crews from the west met crews from the east. Amid the snowdrifts, they
paused for a brief ceremony as the last spike was driven home. A new line
to the Pacific was open. When the weather got better in June, Minneapolis
and St. Paul honored the last spike with a big celebration, and Seattle dedicated most of its Fourth of July festivities to it.

The Great Northern's rival, the Northern Pacific, was only ten years old
at that time. It was built with massive government subsidy and land
grants bigger than the state of Nebraska, three-quarters the size of Italy,
and including all of what would become Yellowstone Park. It had too
many circuitous miles, too many heavy grades, and too much debt. Hill
built his line with no subsidy and no land grant. In 1884, the year after
the Northern Pacific was completed to Seattle, the Union Pacific finished

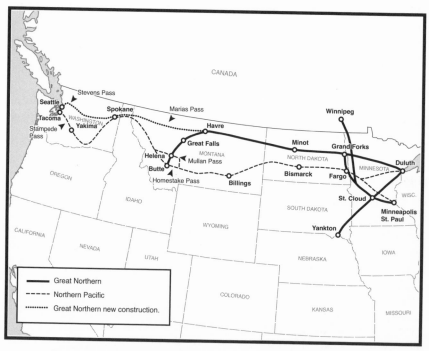

The Great Northern Completes a Second Route to Puget Sound

its Oregon Short Line down the south bank of the Columbia River to Portland. On August 25, 1893, just months after Hill finished the Great Northern, Minneapolis's Soo Line Railroad reached Portal, on the North Dakota–Saskatchewan border, connecting with the Canadian Pacific for a through route from St. Paul to Vancouver. So in a very short time, the Northwest filled with railroads—perhaps too many railroads.

But it was the ill financial winds that spooked Hill. The British investment house of Baring Brothers collapsed; frantic British investors were selling their American securities (for gold, of course—it was the high tide of the gold standard). Gold was fleeing the United States. If the Great Northern were not completed before the storm, it might never be completed at all.

On May 5, 1893, the stock market plunged. On June 27, it collapsed, setting off what would be known as the Panic of 1893. Writer Matthew Josephson wrote, "businessmen who yesterday were affluent, tear up the day's paper and fall sobbing at the feet of their wives, crying, 'we are ruined.'" Thus began five years of severe depression. Thousands of investors lost everything, businesses went under, farmers lost their land, hundreds of thousands were unemployed. More than half the nation's railroads were plunged into bankruptcy. The new "yellow" press reported daily fresh revelations of mismanagement, wasted capital, and falsely inflated securities that had been palmed off on the public and were now worthless.

A strike at George M. Pullman's sleeping-car plant in Chicago, in which workers lost not only their jobs but their homes as well, mushroomed into a general railroad strike (the Pullman Boycott). The strike was called by the American Railway Union, a renegade union that was not one of the established brotherhoods. It was led by the socialist Eugene Debs. Troops were deployed along the rail lines, ostensibly to protect the mails but really to break the strike. Rag-tag "armies" of the unemployed sprang up all over the country in what appeared to be general anarchy. One of them in 1894, led by "General" Jacob Coxey of Massillon, Ohio, began a march on Washington and threatened to bring the anarchy to the capital itself. Revolution was in the wind.

Before the Panic of 1893, new railroad routes were opening all the time. New lines were built and older ones combined on the whims of their promoters or the demands of the bankers who financed them. It was a growing industry in a growing country. But by 1893, the network already connected every major point to every other major point. Most river valleys and mountain passes had railroads. There were ominous signs that the system was overbuilt—six routes from the Great Lakes to New York Harbor, seven from Chicago to the Twin Cities, six from Chicago to Omaha.

After the panic prosperity did return for the nation and the railroads. Railroads counted the years from the end of the panic (1898) to the beginning of World War I as mostly good years. A few new routes were even built, some extensions, some cutoffs, some new connections to the West Coast, but the era of new routes was coming to an end. In the decade of prosperity that opened the twentieth century, railroads were more interested in the technological improvement of routes that were already built than in building new ones. Those routes that were well situated to begin with—the ones that had secure access to capital, that could afford to reduce curves and ruling grades, buy heavier locomotives, and install signals to increase the number of trains on a given track—began to stand out as the routes that would survive. There was already a sense that sooner or later there would be a great weeding out.

Probably no one who witnessed the driving of the Great Northern's last spike in Stevens Pass in 1893 sensed that this was anything more than a hasty ceremony for a semifinished line. Railroads were the future. The railroad-building frenzy would go on. There would be more ceremonies— bigger ones, grander ones. William Gilpin, Colorado's former governor, had just published a 400-page book on his vision for a railroad from Denver to Paris (by way of the Bering Strait), with spurs to Valparaiso, Singapore, St. Petersburg, Capetown, and Dakar.[2] *That* was grand.

The ceremony at Stevens Pass was not the beginning of the end of the American railroad. Railroad's biggest triumphs were yet to come. The short trains behind teakettle locomotives on frail track over spindly trestles did not compare to the 12,000-ton monsters that would roam the rails a century later. But it was the end of the age of construction when new railroads were built, and more were dreamed of as if there never could be enough. The age of consolidation was about to begin.

The *Northern Securities* Case

In the midst of the panic, Hill's banker J. P. Morgan saw the bankruptcy of the Great Northern's rival, the Northern Pacific, as an opportunity to buy it cheaply and bring all transportation in the Northwest under his control, along with all the land the government had given to the Northern Pacific. Most of the NP's bonds were held by German investors, so Morgan's negotiations had the aura of high diplomacy—meetings in London, talks with the Deutchesbank. Morgan did not turn the NP over to Hill right away; but by 1900, he decided common control of the GN and the NP was a good idea.

That same year, Hill and Morgan set their sights on the mighty Burlington road as an entrance into Chicago. The Burlington blanketed much of Iowa and Nebraska, had routes from Chicago to Denver and from Kansas City to Billings, and was profitable. What interested Hill was its route from St. Paul to Chicago, much of it along the very bank of the Mississippi River. But E. H. Harriman of the Union Pacific, who also coveted the Burlington, challenged Hill and Morgan. This battle set off what came to be known as

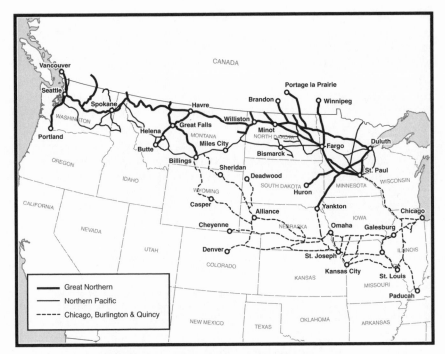

Morgan's and Hill's Northern Securities Empire

the Panic of 1901. Technically, it was not over Burlington shares but over Northern Pacific shares, because Harriman decided that was the part of the Morgan-Hill empire that was the most vulnerable. A lot of small-scale investors were ruined when NP shares hit dizzying highs and then fell to the subbasement. The financial markets shook because a few powerful individuals made them shake, and the public was not amused.

Hill and Morgan won the battle for the Burlington and created the Northern Securities Company to bring the Great Northern, the Northern Pacific, and the Burlington under common control, which many readers will recognize as the latter-day Burlington Northern. Harriman sold his NP shares to the Northern Securities. There were no other through railroads in the area from Minneapolis to Seattle, approximately a quadrant of U.S. territory. Because there was no other economical means of transportation, Northern Securities was a monopoly. Under Hill's management, it would probably be a reasonably efficient one. It was not necessarily going to be a bad one.

The purpose of Morgan and Hill was not to put the Northwest at their mercy and extract obscene profits. There were easier ways to steal money than to build fine railroads. Their purpose was to make sure that competition did not drive rates down to ruinous levels, making it impossible to repay the money already borrowed to build the railroads or to borrow more money to improve them, maybe even making it impossible to sustain them as functioning railroads.

They also wanted to make their railroads a corporate entity large enough to be a player against the emerging trusts in other industries and the emerging Harriman railroad empire of the Union Pacific–Southern Pacific to the south. This was not retrenchment or contraction; it was a kind of circling the wagons. A lot of money was sunk into these railroads, and it could not be easily withdrawn and put somewhere else if things did not work out. A truck could go down a different highway, or an airplane could fly to a different city, but the railroad lived or died where it was. Large size and limiting its exposure to ruinous competition gave it some control over the many variables.

By 1901, when Northern Securities was conceived, the depression of the 1890s was long past. The economy was looking robust. Farm prices were rising, and the rural radicalism of the 1890s gave way to a more traditional rural conservatism. But the middle class fretted about trusts and monopolies, which were daily news, coming in a wave after the *E. C. Knight* decision of 1895; that event virtually set aside the Sherman Antitrust Act, which the public thought was supposed to put a stop to them. The Sherman Act remained an effective tool to bust labor unions, but it was gutted as a tool against big business. It seemed that almost all industry came under the domination of huge trusts, some of them with names that would echo throughout American business in the next century—American Tobacco, American Telephone & Telegraph, General Electric, International Harvester, National Biscuit. No theory of the free market had foreseen such market control by so few individuals. The middle class, not yet over its fright of the 1890s, believed, perhaps irrationally but nevertheless deeply, that if the trend toward trusts continued, there would be no more middle class, just owners and lackeys.

This is important to understand. The push to break up the trusts came from the middle class and the party that represented it, the Republican Party. Socialists and an even more flamboyant expression of radicalism, the Industrial Workers of the World (IWW)—formed in 1905 and known popularly as the "Wobblies"—dreamed of bringing down the capitalist system, not reforming it to make it work a little longer. The middle class felt cornered between the giant interests and the radicals. The stunner was the announcement on April 1, 1901, of the creation of the steel trust, United States Steel—the biggest corporate entity on the face of the earth—by J. P. Morgan. Still recovering from the panic set off by the battle between Hill and Harriman for the Burlington, the middle class wanted action.

In September 1901 Teddy Roosevelt—a Republican, the son of old money, a hero of the Battle of San Juan Hill, and former governor of New York—became president following the assassination of William McKinley.

He was 42 years old, the father of five, full of life, and immensely popular. He recognized a hot political issue. On the advice of Philander Knox, his attorney general, Roosevelt decided that Northern Securities was a more vulnerable target than U.S. Steel for a reversal of the *E. C. Knight* decision. He ordered a suit brought against Northern Securities. Morgan came to visit Roosevelt and uttered the words that became a cliche: "If we have done anything wrong, send your man to my man and they can fix it up."[3]

Roosevelt, a progressive who believed the flaws in the American system could be reformed and the whole made perfect, was not going to settle for a deal with Morgan. He went on a tour of New England and the Midwest to explain the trust problem, calling for a "Square Deal" for the American people. "We do not intend to destroy our corporations," he said, "but we do wish to make them subserve the public good."[4]

A lot of eyes were on this case. For fear it could cause a market upheaval, the Supreme Court took pains not to reveal ahead of time the date the decision would be rendered. But the hall was packed the morning of March 14, 1904, when it was handed down, with what the *New York Times* called an "expectant crowd." A divided (5-4) Court decided in favor of the government, against Northern Securities.[5] Northern Securities was held to be a combination in restraint of trade, in violation of the Sherman Act. The Great Northern and the Northern Pacific were ordered to be separated, even to be physically separated in their common headquarters building in St. Paul. Rep. Sereno Payne, chairman of the House Ways and Means Committee, jubilantly proclaimed that all the credit went to Teddy Roosevelt, and he expected the Republican Party to reap big gains from the decision. Gov. Van Sant of Minnesota said it meant more to the country than any event since the Civil War. But the *New York Times* was not so sure. Its headline the next day read "Supreme Court Wrecks Merger."

This was the first time any arm of government had given a firm no to any of the huge industrial enterprises that had emerged in the latter half of the nineteenth century. The railroads opened a vast inland empire to agriculture and fostered new industries. But now, millions were dependent on them. Rail services and the price charged for them were coming to be seen as too important to too many people and too many businesses to be left to financiers with no public accountability.

Honest people had honest differences over the issues posed by *Northern Securities*. One side argued that the railroads comprising Northern Securities had not actually *done* anything to restrain trade and that, furthermore, those who owned private property ought to be able to do with it as they pleased. The other side insisted that the potential for harm was too threatening, remedies would be too slow, and a republic of free people did not need to be held hostage to unaccountable power. Besides, it was hardly private property in the classic sense. Those railroads represented the pooled capital of thousands of investors. Such pooling existed only because the people said it could, as governed by corporate charters. Railroads could be built only because the people were willing to grant them the right of eminent domain. And some railroads, including components of Northern Securities, represented massive gifts of land and resources from the public domain.

Frank Wilner, in his book *Railroad Mergers,* dismisses Teddy Roosevelt as a populist trying to please an emotional, poorly informed electorate. Most historians see the *Northern Securities* decision as a reasonable solution under the law. The people perceived a problem, their elected representatives passed a law, and the court upheld that law. The decision against Northern Securities did not lead to the destruction of private enterprise, obviously, because the American economy went on to greater and greater triumphs.

As for the railroads directly involved in *Northern Securities,* the Great Northern and the Northern Pacific were each allowed to retain a 48 percent interest in the Burlington, and they cooperated a few years later to build the Spokane, Portland & Seattle Railway (SP&S) along the tortuous north bank of the Columbia River for an entrance into Portland. So despite the ruling, the components of Northern Securities continued to have a linkage; they were known in railroading as the "Hill Lines" or "the Northerns." All of them went on to be successful railroads notwithstanding predictions of imminent calamity if business was not allowed to have its way. The crowning jewel of the Great Northern, the eight-mile Cascade Tunnel underneath Stevens Pass (an engineering masterpiece in the true tradition of Hill), was opened January 12, 1929. It required the electrification of 72 miles of line between Skykomish and Wenatchee. President Hoover hailed it as a victory for all Americans, and it was proof that enforcing antitrust did not destroy capitalism.

The Last Additions to the North American Railroad Network

If Morgan and Hill had not decided to make the Burlington their chosen midwestern connection for both the Great Northern and the Northern Pacific, a basic railroad stability might have worked itself out west of the Mississippi. The Santa Fe was a transcontinental with its own granger lines in the Midwest. The Union Pacific's favored connection came to be the Chicago & North Western. The Southern Pacific's favored connection was more or less the Rock Island, after the extension of the Rock Island to Tucumcari in 1902, which created what would be known as the Golden State Route after the most famous passenger train to ply it. This left one major midwestern granger road with no transcontinental connection—the Chicago, Milwaukee & St. Paul, known then as the St. Paul and known to later generations as the Milwaukee Road.

In 1901, as soon as the Hill Lines' link with the Burlington became clear, fearing that it was going to be encircled and forever cut off from transcontinental traffic, Pres. Albert Earling of the St. Paul sent surveyors to look for a new route to the Pacific Northwest. The NP had the valley of the Yellowstone and the GN the valleys of the Missouri and its tributary, the Milk. There was no easy passage for a new railroad. But in 1905, urged on by William Rockefeller, John D.'s brother, and William's son Percy, the St. Paul's directors authorized a Pacific Extension.

Construction began immediately at the town of Bowdle, South Dakota, west of Aberdeen, the westernmost point on the road's line west from the Twin Cities. The Missouri River was bridged at a point named Mobridge, South Dakota, in 1906, and the line reached Miles City in 1907. It opened new wheat lands across northern South Dakota, western North Dakota, and eastern Montana. It platted new towns, and the Milwaukee Land Company set up offices in the East and in Europe to recruit settlers. The company was most successful in the Ukraine and among the Volga Germans, giving its lands a Catholic stamp just as Hill's efforts in Scandinavia gave Great Northern lands a Lutheran stamp.

Settlers poured into the new towns, which were so numerous that it seemed they could not think up names for them fast enough. Some names were quite impromptu: towns were named for roadmasters on the railroad

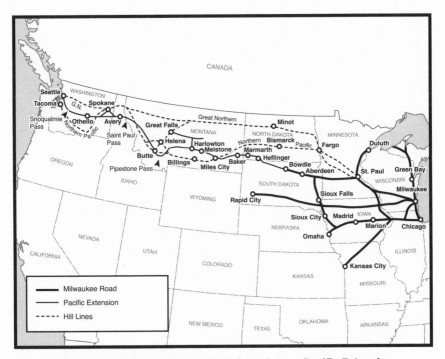

The Chicago, Milwaukee & St. Paul Completes a Pacific Extension

and for roadmasters' daughters. President Earling asked a young man sitting next to him on one of the immigrant trains crossing Montana, "Who are you?" "A reporter for the *Chicago Tribune.*" "What's your name?" "Melvin Stone, sir." Moments later, Earling got off the train and said, "I pronounce the name of this town Melstone."[6] Stone went on to become head of the Associated Press. As for Melstone, the land was gorgeous. The rains came in those first few years after the Milwaukee Road was built, and the crops grew, and all seemed well.

The line breached the Big Belt Mountains through spectacular Sixteen Mile Canyon. It crossed the Continental Divide by tunneling under Pipestone Pass and descended a steep grade into Butte. Butte was rich with copper developed by John D. Ryan and the mighty Anaconda. The new age of electricity meant high prices for copper, and Butte was certain it was going to be a metropolis. Geography forced the Milwaukee Road to be almost parallel to the Northern Pacific through here, but the land was growing; there was plenty for all.

The NP and the GN filled the narrow strip along Lake Pend Oreille that formed the only gash between the Selkirk and the Bitterroot Mountains. The Milwaukee was forced to "short cut" through the Bitterroots, cresting them at St. Paul Pass between Montana and Idaho. Through the Bitterroots, it was a dazzling "Swiss Alp" railway of tunnels and spidery trestles, like those over Kelly Creek and Turkey Creek in Idaho, that seemed to launch trains into space. Across Washington, the Milwaukee was 19 miles shorter than the GN and 86 miles shorter than the NP, but it paid a price by crossing the Saddle Mountains. It crossed the Columbia River at Beverly, Washington, on a breathtaking span. Its passage over the Cascades through Snoqualmie Pass was an engineering masterpiece, almost 300 feet lower than either the NP or the GN. In later years, the Milwaukee developed the Snoqualmie Snow Bowl as a ski resort, running special trains out of Seattle. It built a yard and an ocean terminal at Tide Flats in Tacoma, on the waters of Puget Sound, where steamers from the Orient could pull directly alongside waiting boxcars.

More than 600 miles of the line were electrified with a GE three-phase, 3,000-volt direct current system, with locomotives built by GE at Erie, Pennsylvania, and electric wire by Anaconda. It was the first use of electric power on long-distance lines involving heavy freight trains over difficult grades.[7] This was the newest of the new when it was installed in 1918–1919, the technology of the new century. All railroads were watching.

The Northwest was growing. America was fascinated with the Orient. Missionaries were already there, and investment was not far behind. There could not be enough railroads to serve the Pacific ports. But the Milwaukee Road's golden spike ceremonies at Garrison, Montana, on May 19, 1909, were muted—invited guests only. Trade through the Port of Tacoma never came up to expectations. Many blamed the opening of the Panama Canal in 1914. The dry years of the Montana high plains began in 1917. Only 11 inches of rain fell at Baker, Montana, that year. Of the thousands of settlers who came west with the Milwaukee, thousands were wiped out and moved on west to Washington. During the depression, things got worse.[8]

The Hill Lines closed all gateways to the Milwaukee Road west of the Twin Cities: even business it solicited in the Midwest or the East had to be turned over to the GN or the NP at St. Paul for the long haul west if it was bound for a siding on their lines. Across 1,600 miles, not a single major railroad exchanged cars with the Milwaukee Road except the Union Pacific at Butte and in Washington State. The Pacific Extension was financed not with equity but by borrowing, to the profit of bankers Kuhn, Loeb & Company and the Rockefellers' National City Bank. Interest on this debt easily could have been paid if things had worked out but constituted a fatal burden when they did not. William Rockefeller sat on the board of Anaconda Copper. Anaconda's president, John D. Ryan, sat on the railroad's board. Ryan helped push the railroad into electrification—copper consisted of 18 percent of the project's cost—and then signed it up for a 99-year contract with his Montana Power Company, which required it to buy power whether it used it or not. Ryan and William Rockefeller also pushed the railroad to buy two dubious lines into the southern Indiana coalfields that proved to be worthless. Once a solid dividend payer, the Milwaukee Road crashed into bankruptcy in 1925, an ominous financial thud on the eve of the Great Bull Market.[9] It reorganized in 1928 but fell back into bankruptcy in 1935 and did not emerge from that until 1945. If it was not clear before, it was now: the nation had too many railroads.

The Union Pacific completed its Los Angeles & Salt Lake line across the Mojave Desert in 1907. The Western Pacific was completed from Salt Lake City to Oakland, over Beckwourth Pass and down the Feather River Canyon of California on November 1, 1909, just months after the Milwaukee Road's Pacific Extension. The WP was financially shaky until after World War II. The Florida East Coast entered Key West in 1912, but that extension was a failure and was not rebuilt south of Homestead after the hurricane of 1935. The Seaboard Air Line Railroad entered Miami on January 8, 1927. The Illinois Central finished its "Edgewood Cutoff" through southern Illinois and western Kentucky in 1928, to expedite traffic from the Great Lakes to the Gulf around the hills and dales of its original line. In 1931 the Great Northern built south into California, to a connection with the Western Pacific, creating a new route from the Northwest to California. It was a modest success. In 1934 the Denver & Rio Grande built a 40-mile cutoff in central Colorado to a connection with the Denver & Salt Lake, creating for the first time a through route west from Denver. In the 1950s, the Burlington and Santa Fe railroads built new shortcuts into Kansas City and Dallas, respectively.

In Canada construction continued at a frenetic pace right up to World

War I, but like the late additions in the United States, much of this was of marginal usefulness and zero profitability for years to come. Following the completion of the Canadian Pacific in 1885, William MacKenzie and Donald Mann (later Sir William and Sir Donald) pieced together a second transcontinental route, though one that geography forced to dip into U.S. territory south of Lake-of-the-Woods in northern Minnesota. That was the Canadian Northern, begun in 1899. It entered Vancouver in 1916 on a line from Edmonton through Yellowhead Pass and was digging its way into Montreal through the Mount Royal Tunnel when it went bankrupt in 1918. In 1903 a third transcontinental was begun, in the west as the Grand Trunk Pacific (GTP), in the east as the National Transcontinental Railway (NTR). Together, they were to create a line as straight as possible from St. John on the Atlantic to Prince Rupert on the Pacific. This is country that remains largely unpopulated even in 1999. The NTR collapsed financially in 1915 and the GTP in 1919, and all of this, including the Canadian Northern, was folded into the Canadian National Railways.

Accountability through Trustbusting

Two other giant railroad combinations with overtones of monopoly were in the works at the time of the *Northern Securities* decision. One was E. H. Harriman's combination of his Union Pacific with the Southern Pacific, when, in 1900, he put the two big western roads under common management. The other was an odd arrangement called community-of-interest that would bring "order" to the eastern railroads.

Harriman put a lot of money into the Southern Pacific. He finished the Coast Line in 1901 as a second route between Los Angeles and San Francisco along the Pacific surf for 100 miles, one of the great train journeys of the world. He built the Bayshore Cutoff down the peninsula from San Francisco and the Montalvo Cutoff west out of Burbank over Santa Susana Pass. He built the Lucin Cutoff, which carried the railroad on a causeway over the Great Salt Lake and directly into Ogden. He began work on the Cascade low-grade line in Oregon. He began a major realignment of track in the Imperial Valley after an irrigation dam burst, flooding Colorado River water into the Salton Sink, creating what is now the Salton Sea and wiping out the original railroad. Harriman was very proud of how the SP handled the San Francisco earthquake of 1906, running evacuation trains and supply trains and working with civil and military authorities to restore a semblance of normalcy to the stricken city.

But in 1906 the Interstate Commerce Commission (ICC) launched an investigation of Harriman's empire. The tone of its final report was hostile, and his control of the two western giants (plus the Illinois Central) was found to be harmful to the public interest. The report asked Congress to make any combination that might reduce competition illegal.[10] In 1913

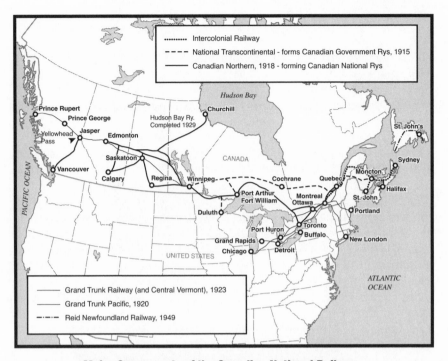

Major Components of the Canadian National Railways

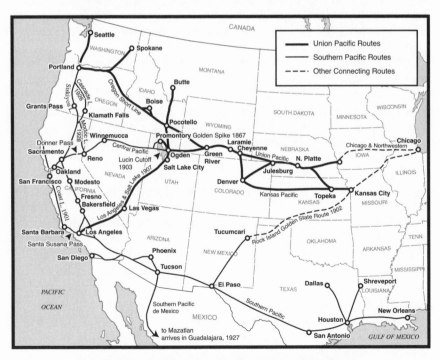

E. H. Harriman's Union Pacific–Southern Pacific Empire

the Supreme Court ordered the Harriman empire broken up, much as it had the Northern Securities. The Southern Pacific was the octopus of Frank Norris's novel *The Octopus*. It made enemies in California even though, probably more than any other institution, it also made modern California possible. At the time, the Union Pacific and the Southern Pacific served mostly different routes. They had not yet made the acquisitions that would make their eventual merger in 1996 a cause of major antitrust concern. Separating them was not going to restore competition. The message of the Court seemed to be that bigness was badness.

In the East plans were under way for the greatest trustlike creation of all. Neither a merger nor a holding company, it was called community-of-interest. It was a cartel, and the purpose was to end rate competition. The Pennsylvania Railroad and the New York Central—the two superpowers of eastern railroading—and their bankers sought to control all the lines in the East, either by stock control or through interlocking directors. The Pennsylvania bought control of the Baltimore & Ohio and the Norfolk & Western. The New York Central bought into the Lackawanna. Together, they bought into the Jersey Central, the Reading, the Chesapeake & Ohio, and the New England roads. Their bankers sat on the boards of each, to make sure no one tried to injure anyone else. At the pinnacle, between the NYC and the PRR there was a kind of diplomatic understanding, as there was when the world powers divided up Europe at the Congress of Vienna. They had no formal arrangement, but their very size and power seemed to ensure that everyone would behave.[11]

At the time of the Panic of 1901, community-of-interest was still in its formative stages. But the *Northern Securities* decision rang down the curtain on old-style, private trust agreements. The message was clear to the promoters of community-of-interest: break up now voluntarily, on your own terms, or have it done for you by the courts.

Two high-speed wrecks on the New Haven Railroad turned the spotlight on J. P. Morgan's role in all of this and brought the wrath of reformers down upon him. Morgan's New Haven tried to take over the Boston & Maine. Morgan and his New England lieutenant, Charles Mellen, intended to build a total monopoly of all New England transportation, even seeking to control the coastwise steamship lines. They admitted that their purpose was to control rates. What was best for the House of Morgan was best for New England, they said, because otherwise, the trunk lines such as the Pennsylvania or the New York Central would dominate the smaller New England roads to New England's disadvantage. Of course, Morgan was already the banker to the New York Central. Morgan's technique was to force the New Haven to buy the securities of the other New England roads at inflated prices. Morgan made his money selling securities, not by running fine railroads.

Weighted down by debt, the New Haven did not have the cash even for routine maintenance; that led, rather directly, to the crashes. They were grisly, and the Hearst newspapers wallowed in every lurid detail. Louis Brandeis made his debut as a national figure by his relentless pursuit of Mellen in what became a classic progressive-style attack on monopoly. By 1914, he had succeeded: Mellen was out, and the New Haven, unable to pay dividends, acquired the cadaver-like quality it would retain to the end of its days. New England was left with neither the advantages of healthy competition nor those of a single integrated unit.[12]

For a curtain call, the ICC exposed how the once prosperous Cincinnati, Hamilton & Dayton line (later the B&O's route between Cincinnati and Toledo) was financially broken by the manipulations of J. P. Morgan (although the ICC put the blame on the Pere Marquette Railway). "This sordid tale has been told without adjectives," said the outraged commissioners in their final report. "The facts speak for themselves, and have been told in all their nakedness."[13]

With the trustbusters in power in government, community-of-interest faded away. The dismantling was done quietly, and a few of the new relationships remained. The New York Central kept the Boston & Albany, for example, and integrated it into its system, making it the only trunk line with a route in New England. The Pennsylvania kept its interest in the Norfolk & Western. The West Virginia coal that it hauled was just becoming competitive in eastern markets. The N&W was going to be a valuable asset.

Sometimes stabs at solutions only cause more problems, and antitrust very much falls in this category; that is why it has periodically waxed and waned in the American political economy. For the railroads, it stopped the rise of megagiants with probable rate-setting power in an age before there was competition from other modes. But it froze the railroads into a miscellaneous collection of units that was neither natural nor ideal. Some were big and well entrenched, with good routes and terminals, while others were excluded from lucrative traffic and left to feed on the scraps. Some could earn a respectable return, which meant they could raise more capital for more investment to make themselves better and better. Others were condemned to a slow death, unable to amass the capital to pay for the improvements that would make them competitive. If the industry could not be restructured by the bankers, it would have to be restructured by someone else. For the time being, no one had an answer.

Accountability through Regulation

Busting trusts was one way to get a handle on the power of railroads. It can be argued that it was the free market way, that is, if one assumes there can be no free market if the price is set by monopolies rather than the market. Another way was to regulate. If one decided that large railroad combinations with access to capital could provide better railroad service, then fair but firm regulation offered the possibility of combining efficient size and accountability.

The original Act to Regulate Commerce of 1887 set up the Interstate Commerce Commission to try to oversee reasonably equitable access to markets for shippers, a noble aspiration. But the law had loopholes, the railroads found them, and the ICC was, until 1906, ineffectual. The Hepburn Act of 1906 plugged the loopholes of the original act and gave the commission power to set maximum rates. The Mann-Elkins Act of 1910 plugged two remaining loopholes. It restored the long-haul–short-haul clause of the original act, which had been rendered unenforceable by the *Alabama Midlands* case of 1897.[14] Long haul–short haul made it illegal to charge more to ship goods a shorter distance from a noncompetitive point than to ship the same goods a longer distance from a competitive point. Mann-Elkins also allowed the ICC to suspend a rate for a maximum of 120 days before it went into effect, while it determined whether the rate was just and reasonable. The Hepburn Act had allowed a rate to go into effect while the ICC deliberated; and if the rate was found to be unjust, the customer was reimbursed, except that by that time, some shippers had already passed on the cost to their customers, and others would have been driven out of business entirely.

So it was not until after 1910 that the ICC had effective power to set maximum rates. It flexed its new muscle in the railroads' request for rate increases amounting to about 15 percent in 1910. The railroads faced inflation that was driving up their costs. If they were to continue to make physical improvements, they had to attract capital. To attract capital, they had to show a fair rate of return. Just about everyone agreed up to this point. To show a return, the railroads said they needed the increase. There the disagreement began.

The "public" presented its case mainly through the lawyer Louis Brandeis, who was hired to represent the Traffic Committee of the Commercial Associations of the Atlantic Seaboard, which meant shippers. There should be no mistaking that "the public" in these matters was generally not "average folks like you and me," but shippers with a vested interest. Sometimes these were farmers or farm associations and small businesses; some were giant corporations. There was nothing sinister about this—strong shippers meant jobs and a strong economy and were good for everyone— but there was an edge of vested interest.

Brandeis dragged out the railroads' past sins—there were plenty, and there had just been fresh revelations of kickbacks on the Illinois Central. But his main point was that railroads were inefficient. If they shaped up, maybe using the principles of scientific management advanced by Frederick Taylor that were then the rage of progressive thinking, they would not need a rate increase. A new generation of techno-expert management on the railroads (Daniel Willard of the B&O was probably the most famous) was beginning to focus on these very problems of efficiency and productivity.

The railroads presented an absolutely stumbling case. They had no idea about their costs or their return on investment. They had overall figures, but they could not pinpoint anything, and railroad executives' testimony about guesses and inner feelings withered under Brandeis's cross-examination. Of course, modern cost accounting was in its infancy, but the railroads knew they had put on a poorly supported case and so established the Bureau of Railway Economics Library so that next time they would have the figures they needed. As for the 15 percent rate hike, the ICC said no.

When the railroads asked for 5 percent in 1913, the ICC took 19,000 pages of testimony and heard horrendous stories of scandalous mismanagement of Rock Island, Frisco and Alton roads. It hesitantly allowed increases in some areas, denying them in others. It did not make its ruling until the end of July 1914. Three days later, German armies were in Belgium. The United States was not officially in the war until 1917, but it supplied the British. American railroads began to clog with war traffic by early 1915. Their operating costs went up as the price of coal and other supplies went up. They came back again for a rate increase, and again, after a mountain of testimony, only a few hesitant increases were allowed.

It is the thesis of historian Albro Martin in *Enterprise Denied* that the reformers and regulators crippled the railroads. Railroads had to earn enough to attract capital. They had begun the century full of optimism and had borrowed and invested on the basis of that optimism. But after 1910, their rate of investment fell off. The economy was roaring up to 1914, but the railroads seemed to grow timid and pessimistic. They arrived at World War I shorn of their confidence, though not always of their arrogance, and expressed their lack of confidence through decreased investment. When the war came, they had neither the equipment nor the capacity to handle the crushing load. This was before there was any meaningful competition from trucks or airplanes, so competition from newer modes was not the cause of the railroads' decline. Martin blames regulation, specifically the reformers he calls the "archaic progressives." The timing of the rise of regulation and of railroad decline, too coincidental to ignore, is what gives the thesis its power.[15] The major glitch is that ton miles fell in 1913–1915. This is hard to explain if the ICC were forcing the railroads to charge rates that were too low—perhaps explaining why the railroads were caught short of equipment when war traffic began to surge in 1916.

Ari and Olive Hoogenboom in their *History of the ICC* suggested that, just as some railroads had talented executives and others did not, so the effectiveness of the ICC depended on the talent and industriousness of the people on it at any given time.[16] So, for example, in 1912, when the commission was presented with a case involving the express companies, it found they had a rate structure that was a mass of conflict, confusion, and discrimination. The commissioners then sitting rolled up their sleeves, absorbed the minute details of rates and costs, and handed the express companies a streamlined rate structure that worked. It worked so well that the Post Office adopted it verbatim when it inaugurated parcel post the following year. Regulation, in other words, could be effective. It could even be creative, more than just a referee blowing a whistle and saying no. But there was no guarantee it would be effective; it depended on the mix of personalities on the ICC at any given moment.

In a later day, in a different context with an entirely different competitive situation for the railroads, regulation was generally looked on as a bad thing; it was mostly abandoned in 1980. The ICC itself was abandoned in 1995. Whether it was a mistake at the time it was put in place is another matter. It freed the railroads from ruinous rate competition, their old bugaboo. Not long before, ruinous competition had put a ceiling on their ability to borrow. If there was blame to pass out for the refusal to allow rate increases, shippers certainly have to share it with reformers and progressives. They were the ones who paid the lawyers' fees to mount the case that stopped the rate increase.

Perhaps most important, the national economy was roaring. Maybe stimulating the whole economy by keeping freight rates low helped to make it roar. It is possible that readers of this book, like the author, are prone to confuse the welfare of railroads, or of a favorite railroad, with the general welfare. But railroads, and transportation, constitute only a single phase in the production of goods. The real measure of success may not be the profitability of railroads but the health of the national economy. After all, most other countries of the world deliberately choose to juice their national economy with rail transportation run at or below cost. It may be too much to expect every single phase of the productive process to produce a profit. This neither justifies nor condemns the concept of regulation but suggests that, whatever its effect on the railroads, it arrived simultaneously with a booming, blossoming national economy.

The early regulators did not have all the answers. They were individuals of honest intent who accepted the progressive notion that a perfect balance was out there, that it was possible to find a level of rates that both fostered the growth of the national economy and left the railroads with profits sufficient to attract capital. They were groping toward solutions just as the railroads were. A situation had arisen for which there was little precedent. An industry, privately owned, had suddenly arrived at the nexus of an interdependent national economy. It had to raise capital, and if it was to remain privately owned, it had to earn profits. But producers had to have equitable access to markets. They had to have accountability from their railways. Nobody had a perfect answer.

Government Operation in World War I

American railroads reached their peak of operating mileage in 1916 (at 259,211 miles of track). From that point on, miles abandoned exceeded miles built. The first abandoned were often the last built, such as the Buffalo & Susquehanna (B&S) line to Buffalo, one too many railroads in a region that was grotesquely overbuilt. The B&S, built in 1906, was ripped up in 1916 and sold to Imperial Russia, spikes and all. Russia was then at war with Germany. Some say the B&S actually got to Russia; others say it lies at the bottom of the White Sea, the victim of a German sub.[17] The Colorado Midland was abandoned in 1918, because it was foolish to attempt a railroad over Hagerman Pass west of Leadville, although in a later decade it might have been a glorious tourist attraction raking in Japanese yen and German marks. The tide that began to turn in the snows of Stevens Pass in 1893 was now a rushing ebb, and there were not even hard-surfaced roads yet, let alone trucks.

Even before the United States formally entered World War I in April 1917, railroad traffic began to surge, especially at the Atlantic ports. Traffic backed up because German subs took a toll on shipping and there were not enough ships. Rail cars waiting to be unloaded were not available for

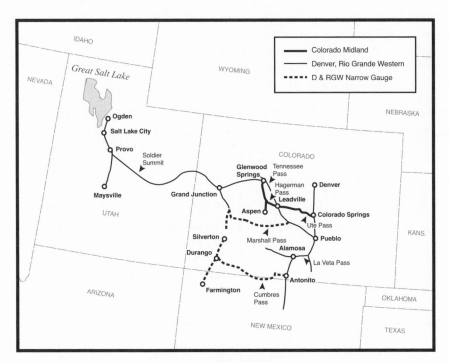

Colorado Midland Railway

reloading at the mine or the mill. Railroad executives sensed that the only way to keep the lines fluid was to coordinate, and this meant calling a truce in corporate rivalries. In a few cases, even the bitterest of rivals worked out emergency agreements. When the Baltimore & Ohio ran short of locomotives to double-head over the heavy grades between Pittsburgh and New Castle, and the bottleneck threatened to shut down the entire railroad, rival Pittsburgh & Lake Erie let B&O use its low-grade line along the Monongahela River. A crisis was averted. Between November 1916, when munitions shipments first began to clog eastern terminals, and December 1917, railroads set up five different voluntary committees to try to unsnarl operations. For this, they might have been hauled up on antitrust violations.

Only the last of these committees, the so-called Railroad War Board, was given any real authority by its constituent companies. For example, in order to redistribute rail cars, it ordered the Lackawanna to dispatch 1,100 empty hoppers westward in a single day for delivery to connecting lines. The B&O was ordered to send nine solid trains of empty boxcars from Baltimore to St. Louis, regardless of owner or routing, to ease car shortages in the West. The board received hourly reports on the location of trains and the availability of cars, with the power to reroute if necessary to avoid bottlenecks. After the fact, the board was accused of mismanagement, though its failings were not necessarily its fault. For example, it ordered trains away from badly congested Cleveland, but Ohio Governor Cox defied the direction, commandeered the trains, and ordered them to Cleveland anyway, where they clogged the terminal.[18] Bravely, Daniel Willard of the Baltimore & Ohio said every railroad man and every locomotive would do its duty.

If the railroads had been more extensively consolidated when the war began, coordination might have succeeded. As it was, voluntary efforts did not work for these were competitors trying to cooperate, and when all was said and done, they were not able to. Trains of war materials rolled into congested eastern ports while southern ports remained idle, yet what mighty eastern trunk, congested or not, would turn its traffic over to a southern route? Coal roads solicited their own special customers, which meant that coal was frequently cross-hauled: Pennsylvania coal might go to customers in the West while Illinois or Kentucky coal moved east. But what railroad would let a rival serve its customers? Beyond practical matters, the men involved could never quite put aside loyalty to their team. A casual remark by a New York Central executive on the Railroad War Board showed the mindset: "I've always wanted to issue *orders* to the Pennsylvania Railroad, and now I have my chance."[19]

Winter came early in 1917, and it came with a vengeance. The cold snap was one burden too many for railroads already buckling under the load of war traffic. Switches froze and trains stalled. Loaded hopper cars of coal had to be thawed before they could be unloaded. It was the bad break in the weather that finally plunged everything into chaos. The first alarm came over fuel supplies in the cities. The cities were going to run out of coal if the railroads broke down. At Toledo and Columbus, trains on the Chesapeake & Ohio were stalled for lack of terminal space. Back at the mines, production stopped for lack of hopper cars. At the Drop Forge Company at Alliance, Ohio, and at war industries all across the state, production ceased for lack of fuel.[20] The public demanded that something be done.

On December 29, 1917, President Wilson ordered that the operation of the railroads be taken over by the government. Ownership would remain in private hands, but operations would be conducted by the U.S. Railroad Administration (USRA). Some thought this smacked dangerously of socialism, but the men selected to run the new system were hardly socialists. There was Hale Holden of the Burlington and Henry Walters of the Atlantic Coast Line; Walker Hines of the Santa Fe and Alfred H. Smith of the New York Central; and John Williams, who was serving as comptroller of the currency, was formerly of the Seaboard. These men were all from that techno-expert new breed of railroad executive. As chief administrator, Wilson chose William Gibbs McAdoo, his son-in-law, frequently cited as the most able man in the cabinet. Congress held hearings in January and readily approved the president's action, for the good of the country and for victory.

Under the new administration, the railroads retained their separate identities and their own operating officers, but all routes and operations might be integrated, whether or not previously competing carriers were involved. Efficiency was the only criterion; the very competition the progressives thought was paramount was tossed out the window. That was of little consequence, for by 1917 the only real support for old-fashioned railroad busting came from a hard core of railroad haters from the farm states of the South and the West. The more sophisticated element of the reform movement had long since adopted new ideas of productivity and scientific management, and the new USRA was a giant laboratory.[21]

As an experiment in the new doctrine of productivity, the USRA was a mixed disappointment. It kept the war trains rolling and never broke supply lines on the home front. McAdoo and his successor, Hines, thought this was significant. Wartime was not a good time to experiment with untried procedures and operations. Even so, car and locomotive design was standardized. The highly individualized locomotives of the various roads could never wander far from their supplies of parts and so could not roam around the country like ordinary boxcars. Standardization was a prerequisite for truly unified operation. But only a few services were actually coordinated. Baltimore & Ohio passenger trains on the Royal Blue Line were brought into Penn Station in New York instead of ending their runs in Jersey City, and since that was the only coordinated project readily visible to the public, the USRA made the most out of publicizing it.[22]

Less visible was the fact that 1.9 percent more ton miles were performed by 2.1 percent fewer train miles, which meant that more trains were operating as solid units to their destinations. A number of circuitous routes, all of them in the West, were eliminated, and the bottleneck at Cincinnati was eased by coordinating traffic over the Ohio River bridges. The accuracy and completeness of statistics were improved by adopting the procedures of scientific management; this was essential for good managerial decisions.[23] Nevertheless, this was hardly the sweeping coordination that had been anticipated; besides, the operation incurred a serious financial loss, mostly as a result of substantial wage increases that were forced by inflation and by the fear that a strike would bring everything to a halt.

The Weak Road–Strong Road Problem

At the end of the war, there was some support for continued government operation, but not among the Republican majority in Congress. Debate focused on the conditions by which the lines would be returned to private control. The legislation being drawn up for that purpose became known as the Esch-Cummins Act or the Transportation Act of 1920. The chairman of the House Committee on Interstate Commerce, John J. Esch, a conservative from Wisconsin, wanted to re-create the prewar status. His counterpart in the Senate, Albert Cummins of Iowa, was more ready to experiment with new ideas.

Albert Cummins was once a believer in old-fashioned trustbusting and regulation. As a freshman in the Iowa legislature in the 1890s, he listened to the antirailroad diatribes of the populists, even though he was not one of them. Later, he was twice defeated for the Senate by the railroads' political machines. When he was elected governor in 1902 as an insurgent Republican, it was on a militantly antirailroad platform.

In three terms as governor, he guided a series of measures through the legislature giving Iowa comprehensive railroad regulation. There was an increased assessment on railroad land and a maximum passenger fare of two cents a mile. A two-way demurrage law made railroads subject to penalty for failure to furnish shippers with cars, and there was a law against free passes (even though Cummins himself regularly accepted passes until 1905). A complicated rate law forced substantial rate reductions. Antilobbying and primary election laws were intended to destroy the railroads' political machines.[24] These were immensely popular measures, for they curbed giant out-of-state corporations to the benefit of local farmers and small businesses, people to whom men like Cummins, a young lawyer from a moderately well-to-do background, were usually responsive. Railroad men thought it was a vendetta that smacked of pathological hatred.

When Cummins was elected to the Senate in 1908, his reputation as an expert in railroad matters was well established, and he quickly assumed a leading role on the Commerce Committee, where he sat for hearings on the Mann-Elkins Act. Albro Martin, in *Enterprise Denied,* singles him out as the arch villain of the progressive clique that destroyed the railroads. Until 1917, he never veered from the notion that bigness was badness, especially when it came to railroads. He voted enthusiastically for the Clayton Act in 1914, which tightened the antitrust laws.

But in 1917 he accepted the USRA without qualms, even though the railroads were going to be operated by their old executives as a monopoly. He never asked himself if the policies he had previously sponsored created the crisis of 1917. Nevertheless, his switch to the new doctrine of productivity was complete. In the long debate on what to do with the railroads after the war, Albert Cummins became the principal spokesman for large, consolidated railways. For better or for worse, he was the architect of the latter-day consolidation policy.

He now identified the heart of the railroad problem as the fact that some roads were financially strong, strong enough to attract more capital to make them stronger, and some roads were weak, starving for capital and dying. He took his examples from back home in Iowa, where the Chicago Great Western earned a meager 1.7 percent return while its competitor, the mighty Chicago & North Western, earned a handsome 6.13 percent. Of 118 Class I railroads in 1919, only 18 earned as high a return as 6 percent. Rates adequate for the North Western would starve the Great Western. Cummins assumed that rates high enough for the Great Western would give the North Western excess profits—heaven forbid—even though the actual effect would probably be to make some commodities unshippable.

A purely private-enterprise solution would be to let the weak roads die. If they were so unnecessary that nobody wanted to ship or travel on them, or if they were so poorly built that they could not move traffic at a competitive cost, or if they were so poorly managed that the competition ran circles around them, or if their security holders were so greedy that they had skimmed all the profits, then those lines deserved to die. The railroad system as a whole would be better off without them, for they did, after all, siphon off traffic and divide the pie.

Besides that, the industrial economy was built on change. Before the century was very old, lines in New England and New York and Michigan built to carry tourists to ninteenth-century resorts were going to be redundant. Eventually, so were all those granger lines in the Midwest, built before farmers had farm trucks and hard-surfaced roads. A purely market-driven railroad system would adjust. Freezing the system to preserve weak roads and redundant lines would only burden the whole system.

That free market model was powerful, but it oversimplified a complex problem. A road could be weak for a number of reasons having to do with its history, its management, or its luck. It might be weak merely because its route went through the mountains, but mountain people needed railroads.

Just because a road was weak did not mean it was unnecessary. Some weak roads were very busy hauling people and goods, which meant that a lot of people, a lot of local businesses, and employees of and investors in those businesses needed that railroad. If a community lost its railroad, it lost its future. No one should be surprised that, if the marketplace dictated that they would lose their railroad and with it everything they had built, the community would turn to the government to protect them.

Besides that, yesterday's weak railroad could be tomorrow's strong road. In this book we will meet the Nickel Plate Road and the Western Pacific, two ugly ducklings that eventually became swans, the first one now a busy component of the Norfolk Southern, the second of the Union Pacific. The market solution would have jettisoned these vital lines.

It occurred to many that rational human beings ought to be able to figure out a way to have efficient railroads and at the same time not make millions of honest people the victims of a bad roll of the dice. The railroad system could be rationalized. Truly unnecessary lines might be phased out in an orderly way. But lines that were weak by some luck of the draw might be strengthened, by combining them with other weak lines to make a strong one or by combining them with a road that was already strong.

Cummins's initial thinking would allow the planning to be done by the railroad industry itself, with management and security holders having appropriate input. This would require statesmanship from railroads and their security holders. But if the planning was left strictly to the industry, the strongest roads would probably arrange things for their own short-run interest. That was not necessarily the long-term public good. Because the government represented all the people, not just the interests, Cummins thought the government should have the final word in consolidation and a veto over the interests. Ultimately, when a plan that would do maximum good and minimum harm was found, government would have the power to compel, even though that could result in short-term pain for some people— for some local communities, for some railroad executives, and for some stockholders and bondholders. But Cummins did not mean this as a government takeover. He saw it as a win-win way to go. The railroad industry as a whole would come out strengthened, and its securities would be better secured. The public would be protected from being wiped out by either railroads that were too strong or railroads that were too weak.

The idea accepted that the market was a powerful mechanism that settled many accounts fairly and efficiently but could crush an individual in an instant. Just as people buy insurance against fire or theft, people looked to government to secure them against a spin of the market dice. Transportation was too important to be left solely to market forces. That was why every other country, with governments ranging from Bolshevik to democratic to monarchical, was moving to bring transportation under some kind of public accountability.

In the United States, in 1919, Albert Cummins wrestled with the idea of planned consolidation. On a trip home, this Republican son of Iowa told the legislature, "I look upon transportation by rail as a government function. I believe it is as much the duty of government to provide people with adequate transportation at low cost as it is to provide them with adequate highways, water supplies and courts of justice."[25]

The Plumb Plan

The first people to be hurt by consolidation—or even worse, by the liquidation of the weak roads—were the men and women who worked for the railroads. Jobs would be eliminated. With consolidation or liquidation appearing to be inevitable, labor thought it would be wise to have a plan of its own. Glenn Plumb, a railroad labor lawyer, devised labor's plan.

Plumb never regarded himself as a radical, only as a pragmatist who saw problems and tried to find solutions that were fair to all. To him, "all" included labor, and in the atmosphere of 1919, that was enough to make him seem like a radical to many. When Plumb was a young lawyer, Chicago's Mayor Dunne chose him to lead the city's fight against the street railways, whose ironclad franchises made them bastions of privilege. It was one of urban progressivism's classic fights, which Plumb carried all the way to the Supreme Court. In 1916 the railway brotherhoods asked him to be their general counsel. It was in that capacity that he addressed a militant labor rally in Atlantic City in June 1919, putting forth what came to be known as the Plumb Plan. Brotherhood leadership was dubious of it, but the crowd cheered and applauded, and the fight for the Plumb Plan became a fight of the rank and file. Soon there was a Plumb Plan League, which held rallies, sang anthems, and cheered wildly in support. Capital—the interests—denounced it as the foulest dropping from the bowels of Bolshevism.[26]

In Plumb's analysis capital, labor, and the public all had vested interests in the management of railways, yet only capital was represented on the boards of directors. Excluded from all decision making, labor turned to unions and the public to government regulation. This created a system in which management, unions, and regulatory agencies worked at cross-purposes and with every incentive to be irresponsible. No one was happy: management said it could not earn a fair return, labor said wages were too low, and the public said rates were too high.

Plumb saw no reason why capital had the right to be the sole manager of railroad property. The sweat of workers and the sweat and investment in the businesses that were the railroads' customers were other kinds of capital and deserved representation. He thought it would be much wiser for capital, labor, and the public to share in the responsibility. He suggested that it be done in the following way:

—The government would acquire all railroad property, paying prices based on fair valuation. To pay for it, the government would issue its own securities at the lowest obtainable rate. Once the debt was paid off, old investors would have no further claim on railroad profits, except as holders of government securities.

—The government should lease its newly acquired railroads to a federally chartered corporation.

—The corporation would have a nominal stock issue, with the primary capital being operating skill. The stock would be trusteed for the benefit of its employees. Workers would be divided into two categories: class A would be managerial employees, and class B, wage earners.

—One-third of the board of directors would represent the public, appointed by the president, with the advice and consent of the Senate. One-third would represent class A employees, and one-third class B.

—The corporation would pay all operating expenses and arrange for capital improvements, provide a sinking fund to extinguish government bonds, and divide any net income equally between the government and its own stockholders (up to a total return of 5 percent, after which the ICC would order a reduction in rates).

—Half the dividends would go to the smaller number of class A employees and half to the larger number of class B employees. The stock would give the employees a vested interest in efficient operation. The possibility that employees might use their dominant position on the board to vote themselves higher wages would be precluded by their conflicting dividend desires, since class A employees would benefit more from higher dividends than higher wages. The 5 percent limit on profits would guarantee the lowest possible rates to the public.[27]

Before writing this plan off as silly, recall that the government was poised to build a huge national highway system. Why should it be so natural that the government build and operate highways, but not railroads?

Nevertheless, this was 1919. Bolshevism was consolidating its power in Russia, creating the new Soviet Union, and seemed on the verge of power in Hungary and Germany. In victorious Britain, France, and the United States, boys who had gone off to war were in no mood to be treated by business like expendable dirt when they went back to their jobs. The war had created terrible inflation, and wages had not kept up, so for those who had stayed at the production lines and had won the war, their thanks was a lower standard of living. It was the year of the Great Steel Strike and general strikes in Seattle and Winnipeg. In a general strike all workers walked out, and rich people had no water, no electricity, and no groceries on their shelves and found out the power of an angry working class. The Industrial Workers of the World still sounded its fury. Red flags still waved at socialist rallies. In Russia, Lenin said this was the moment of world revolution that Marx had predicted, when the underprivileged everywhere would refuse to "take it" anymore.

By fall the United States was gripped by a Red Scare. The middle and upper classes were afraid that their privileged life, which depended on a docile workforce, might shortly come to a fiery end. It was funny that a war intended to preserve a way of life had unleashed all this. Troops were called out to fire on striking workers.

The hysteria killed any idea supported by the underprivileged. The campaign against the Plumb Plan was never a debate of its merits. It was shrill and emotional. Hoke Smith of Georgia called it "simon-pure Bolshevism," and John Esch called it "sovietism." To the Guaranty Trust Company, it was "class rule and class profiteering," something it abhorred, at least in others.[28] Ironically, more than it resembled Bolshevism, the Plumb Plan was akin to the concept of corporatism that would soon be promoted by Mussolini's Fascist Party in Italy, generally considered a movement of the right, although "fascism" was an amalgam of often contradictory ideas from left and right.

More devastating than the opposition of bankers was the opposition of Samuel Gompers of the American Federation of Labor (AFL), for this doomed a united front by labor. The plan violated his theory of industrial relations, which held that labor and management must always be separate, adversarial, and free to bargain to their best advantage. As for Plumb, he was engulfed by the movement he spawned. In August, he presented it to the Esch committee, which listened politely and then denounced him publicly. Plumb spent the next two years in an arduous speaking campaign. He had always been the heart and soul of the movement, a tireless speaker, not fiery but sincere and persuasive. The Plumb Plan League and its publicity organ, the newspaper *Labor*, tried to keep the flame alive. Plumb, exhausted, died in 1922.

None of the other Western democracies found ideas like the Plumb Plan too radical. Faced with problems that were similar though not identical, they all turned to solutions that would bring labor and the public in on managerial decisions:

1. In Canada, the Canadian National Railways was created in 1918 to assume operations of all government-owned lines. A crown corporation owned by the government, it was free to run its own affairs (and compete with the privately owned Canadian Pacific). It was a monumental consolidation project that eventually created a single operating unit of 23,000 miles spanning six time zones.
2. The British Railways Act of 1921 provided that all railroads be amalgamated into four regional systems. If railroads could not agree on terms voluntarily, they would be determined by an amalgamation

tribunal. A minister of transport would supervise the standardization of operations and services. A railroad rates tribunal would set rates, and a central wages board would determine wage scales.

3. In France, the six regional systems (five of them private; one, the Ouest, public) would continue as separate corporations, but they would be managed as a single unit by the Comité de Direction, composed of the managements of the six companies. Above the comité, serving as an advisory board to the government, was the Conseil Supérieur des Chemins de Fer, a body of 71 members, including 21 delegates from the railroad companies, 4 from the labor unions, 13 from the government, and 23 from agricultural and industrial associations. The conseil was to supervise the standardization of rates, operations, equipment, and wages.[29]

4. In Germany, railways previously owned by the individual states were taken over by the new German (Weimar) Republic. A new ministry created in 1919, the Reichsverkehrsministirium, directed the new Deutsche Reichsbahn or German National Railway. It immediately absorbed a huge number of veterans into its payroll.

This was to forestall a social revolution that many expected in the chaotic months after the war if these men remained unemployed. This was an example of how other countries saw railroads as a mechanism to solve a variety of social and political problems, not just in terms of profit and loss like the Americans. However, many in the bloated workforce had to be let go as the economy recovered. In the Dawes Plan of 1924 to restructure and manage the payment of Germany's reparations (war indemnities) to France and Britain, and French and British war debts to the United States, the national railway was restructured as a private corporation owned by the government, much like the Canadian National Railways, or later Conrail in the United States. This Deutsche Reichsbahngesellschaft was built into an efficient super railroad marked by high-speed passenger operations and reliable, precisely scheduled freight service. Both the Weimar government and the Nazi regime that followed regularly called it Germany's "most valuable asset."[30]

What was good for other countries, however, was not necessarily good for the United States. Every railroad executive before the Cummins committee was asked whether regional consolidation was desirable, and they all said no. Their reasons were partly personal, no doubt. Too many executives would lose their jobs. But they all said it was impractical. The American network was too complex and too busy to be managed in monopolistic units. Even the USRA had maintained the identity of the separate lines.[31]

As flawed as the Plumb Plan may have been, it died a victim of hysteria and class intolerance. It was a bold proposal for a new order of industrial relations that was ill suited to an era that craved "normalcy." It had tried to come to grips with the fact that regulation was not working and that the three-way antagonism between capital, labor, and the public was destructive. The railroad plans of other democracies underscored, even at this early date, how isolated the United States was in its rigid defense of the right of capital alone to make decisions that affected everyone.

Esch-Cummins, the Transportation Act of 1920

Albert Cummins had a plan. He would set rates at a level that would produce a fair return, which he determined was 6 percent. This "rule of rate making" was a significant departure from previous regulatory philosophy, for it recognized the paramount need not to keep rates low to give shippers a short-term boost, but to set them high enough to attract capital to the railroads. The 6 percent return was meant for railroads in general, not for any one railroad in particular. It was to be based on a fair valuation of the property, rather than merely the face value of securities that happened to be outstanding. Any earnings in excess of 6 percent were to go into a special fund, from which the money thus "recaptured" would be distributed to roads that failed to earn 6 percent. The law also gave the ICC power to regulate minimum rates. The purpose was to stop ruinous competition, although as the fledgling trucking industry got under way, it was used more to keep railroad rates high enough to give the truckers a chance. By the 1950s, railroads came to see minimum rate setting as the deadliest feature of rate regulation. The law also gave the ICC the power to regulate new railroad construction.[32]

Cummins figured that recapture could never give the weak roads more than a little short-term help. The ultimate solution to their problem lay in consolidation. His thinking on this had now sharpened. He wanted a new agency, a transportation board, free of the past record of the ICC, to draw up a plan for general consolidation. There were to be not less than 20 and not more than 25 operating companies. Competition was to be preserved, along with existing routes and channels of trade. Weak roads were to be absorbed by strong roads so that the surviving companies would have roughly equal earning power. Once the plan was drawn up, railroads would have seven years to consolidate on their own terms according to the plan; after that, consolidation would be compulsory.

Did the government have the constitutional power to compel? Was this not confiscation of private property? Cummins said the state had the power of eminent domain, and that was all the authority it needed. The Cummins Plan would give the government a creative role in economic engineering, a role that was a new departure from the nay-saying regulation of the past.

The Cummins Plan was the basis of the Senate version of the new legislation. Had it been enacted as he envisioned it, it might have worked. But

John Esch and his fellow conservatives in the House tore the heart out of the plan and thus guaranteed its failure, proving to some that government plans never work. First, instead of Cummins's rate-making principle, which was meant to produce a fair return, the plan reiterated the old progressive nostrum of "fair and reasonable" rates, to be determined by a strengthened ICC. This was so open-ended as to be meaningless—"fair and reasonable" for whom? Second, although consolidation was deemed desirable, it was not to be compulsory. The ICC could draw up a plan for consolidation, but the railroads would be free to accept or reject it as they chose.

Cummins knew that this gutted his whole scheme. He knew railroad executives rather liked the idea of consolidation, except the compulsory part. He had heard them all—Carl Gray of the Union Pacific, Julius Kruttschnitt of the Southern Pacific, Samuel Rea of the Pennsylvania, Howard Elliott of the Northern Pacific. They gave nearly identical testimony on why they should be freed of the Clayton Act without further obligation. They wanted to be free to take what they wanted and strengthen their own strong companies.[33] Cummins knew, as they did, that consolidation would divvy up a lot of good things, but eventually there were the bitter pills, and without compulsion no one would swallow them.

The railroads thought they had a pretty good deal. Rate regulation freed them from having to compete. Rates were supposed to be sufficient to earn them 6 percent, at least if they ran a tight ship. And they were not compelled to do anything they did not want to do. The watered-down version became law. It is an old dilemma of democracy: does the debate and compromise that free democracy requires make a good idea better, or does it just wreck a good idea? Cummins never thought the watered-down version would amount to much. The final bill was only a gesture in the direction of productivity progressivism, all the more dangerous because it looked like the real thing. Perhaps the ICC could draw up a plan so suitable, so wonderful, that everyone would rush to consolidate and the problems would be solved. But it was not likely.

two

The Legacy of the Transportation Act of 1920
1920–1940

The Transportation Act of 1920 charged the ICC with the responsibility for drawing up a plan for railroad consolidation but gave it no power to enforce its plan. The idea was not really to save money for the railroads; no duplicate mileage to speak of would be eliminated. The purpose was to create units that were roughly equal in terms of size, traffic volume, return on investment, and most of all borrowing power.

Without any power to compel, here was what was likely to happen: weak roads might be combined with other weak roads in the hope of creating a strong one. If the underlying problems that caused them to be weak were not remedied, however, the result would be a bigger weak road. Strong roads had no incentive to see weak roads rise up as strong competitors. A strong road might be willing take in a smaller road that gave it access to this or that market, so long as the small road did not burden the big road with debt. But strong roads were not going to take in big weak roads with a lot of debt. Even if managements of strong roads could be persuaded, their security holders would never permit it. In a few corporate charters, even a single class of minority stockholders could veto a deal that everyone else agreed to (see chapter 3). So well-meaning plans without any power to compel would not be likely to amount to much. Cummins knew this. The Pennsylvania Railroad knew this. A little compulsion could have gone a long way. It might never have had to be used; the threat of it might have been enough to get the strong roads to belly up, take responsibility, and work out combinations of equal earning power. But with no compulsion, well-meaning plans would go nowhere.

The ICC seemed to move with gusto into its new role as a planning agency. It engaged Prof. William Ripley of Harvard to draw up a tentative plan that would be the basis for discussion in future hearings. He was the author of treatises on rates, regulation, and finance and seemed as qualified for the job as anyone could be. But the law specified that all railroads must be combined into 25 or 30 systems of equal size and earning power that preserved competition and existing routes and channels of trade. Ripley found that this was easier said than done.

The only plan he could devise that met all the criteria rested on two controversial expedients. First, he wanted to dismember certain existing systems. It was the only way to achieve balance, particularly in the West, where there were not enough transcontinental lines to match with all the granger roads of the Midwest. Second, he wanted to create monopolies in geographic subregions, namely Michigan and New England, where there were not enough independent lines to give one to each major system. Whether or not this was good railroading, it was terrible politics. A lot of people who were now very important had once led the attack on Morgan for creating monopolies—what the expert now said was the right thing to do.

At first, the difficulties seemed minor. Ripley's plan was a tour de force that grouped all the railroads in the United States into 24 systems. The ICC held brief hearings on it in the summer of 1921, made enough modifications to muddy up the water, and labeled it its Tentative Plan. The New England monopoly was too hot to handle and was thrown out, although the one for Michigan was retained. The idea of forced dismemberment was also thrown out, except for the Wabash, one of only two major railroads that straddled the invisible line dividing western territory from other regions. (The other was the Frisco.)

Hearings on the Tentative Plan went on for 21 months in cities coast to coast. Out of them was supposed to come a Final Plan, as directed by Congress. But even at this stage, something seemed to go wrong. The hearings would get stuck on this or that specific proposal, of interest to whatever private party wanted to make an issue of it. They rarely examined industrywide or even regional implications. In the East, for example, most of the time was spent on an inconclusive debate between the Baltimore & Ohio and the New York Central over who should get the Jersey Central and the Reading. In the West, where the plan combined the Northern Pacific with the Burlington and the Great Northern with the Milwaukee Road, the GN and the NP each made impassioned explanations as to why the other was more suited to be paired with the Milwaukee Road, which both regarded as a loser. The Milwaukee's president, Harry Byram, thought these were great arguments and was ready to sign the merger papers on the spot. Harvard Prof. William Cunningham thought this episode was the most entertaining show of the whole affair.[1] When the hearing was over, it was assumed that a Final Plan would soon be forthcoming. Instead, there was silence from the commission, which had evidently split over what to do. Three years later, the commission notified Congress that it was unable to devise a plan and asked to be relieved of the duty.[2]

Congress considered the matter in 1926. Albert Cummins was discouraged and repeated that, without compulsion, consolidation would come to naught. He introduced a bill that would excuse the commission from making a final plan for five years, during which time the railroads might consolidate voluntarily. After that, the commission was to go ahead with a compulsory final plan, and from that point permit no deviations from it.[3] The bill failed, and Cummins's death later that year frustrated efforts to revive it. Two years later, Sen. Simeon Fess of Ohio introduced similar legislation, more friendly to the railroads, but it failed as well.[4] It is clear in retrospect that the concept of planning was dead the moment the commission announced it could not come up with a plan. After that, all meaningful initiative came from the railroads.

The Four Powers of the East

The northeastern United States was crisscrossed with railroads. It had railroad superpowers; it had busy, double-tracked bantam weights; it had nuisance railroads, built parallel to established lines for speculative purposes; it had interesting failures—the Erie and the B&O, for example, too important to be thrown away but never quite filled out as viable systems. There were too many railroads, most notably in western New York, where lines were built up the valley of just about every stream. The East, needing consolidation, was a good laboratory for the functioning or malfunctioning of the Transportation Act of 1920.

In the rough-and-tumble days before planned consolidation, the powerful could expect to get more powerful. Planning meant the powerful were held in check while the weak were brought up to a rough equality. Planning was not a matter of government versus the railroads. It was a matter of strong railroads who could take care of themselves versus weaker roads who needed help, as well as the shippers, the employees, and the on-line communities of those weaker roads. The nation's most powerful railroad, the Pennsylvania, deeply resented any plan in which it did not remain the most powerful. The PRR, therefore, was going to present the concept of planning with a severe test. The B&O, in contrast, looked forward to planning as a way to strengthen itself.

Planned consolidation offered the B&O an expedient way to do what it could not do on its own—develop its extremities. Its middle portions were healthy enough, but its lines to the eastern seaboard and the Midwest reached out like dangling strings, devoid of branches or friendly feeders. Since the New York Central or the Pennsylvania could outbid it for any acquisition that might remedy this, the B&O needed strong government. By adding the Reading and the Jersey Central, it would get lucrative anthracite and passenger traffic, an entrance to one of the nation's most intensely industrialized areas, and port facilities at New York and along the Delaware River. The addition of the Western Maryland (WM) could bring a rich bituminous coal traffic plus an eastbound gradient over the Alleghenies more favorable than its own main line. The addition of the Alton would help it get a share of the midwestern grain traffic, whereas the Alton line to Kansas City would give it the longest haul of any eastern trunk line.

The B&O dreamed. It dreamed "I-80" dreams, of a route running straight west from New York toward Cleveland, roughly parallel to the later Interstate 80. It would consist of Jersey Central and Reading routes from New York Harbor to central Pennsylvania. Across western Pennsylvania, it bought the Buffalo, Rochester & Pittsburgh in 1930 and the remnants of the Buffalo & Susquehanna in 1932. That narrowed the gap to about 50 miles in north central Pennsylvania, but it was never filled. Still, a strong B&O was always crucial to balance in the East, and Ripley and the ICC treated it well. No road stood to gain as much and lose as little from planned consolidation as the B&O.

The New York Central, the Vanderbilt Road, more powerful than the B&O, was less powerful than the Pennsylvania but fully capable of protecting its own interests. The Tentative Plan offered it little, so it was hardly enthusiastic. But on the surface, it seemed strangely compliant. Its strategy was to contrive a stalemate, which would discredit the whole concept of planning. It demanded the Virginian Railway as an entrance to the West Virginia coalfields, which neither Ripley nor the ICC offered to give it. The Virginian was little more than a conveyor belt for coal from the mines of southern West Virginia to tidewater at Sewall's Point, near Norfolk. It was built by Standard Oil magnate Henry Rogers and completed in 1909. The Central knew the PRR coveted the Virginian and knew the PRR would fight the Central over it. The Central mounted a frontal assault on the B&O by demanding the Jersey Central and the Reading. It claimed that its main line was congested and it wanted an alternate route between Cleveland and New York through the Clearfield District of Pennsylvania— another "I-80" scheme. It was unlikely that the Central would actually divert trains from its water-level main line and send them over a single-track mountain railroad.[5] But all this served to frustrate the plan.

Neither Professor Ripley nor the ICC calculated on the emergence of the Van Sweringen brothers as a dynamic force in eastern railroading. The Vans were real estate developers from Cleveland. Before World War I, they developed land known as Shaker Heights, a planned suburb outside Cleveland. To get the right-of-way for a rapid transit line to downtown, they bought the entire Nickel Plate Road from the New York Central. The Nickel Plate was one of those nuisance railroads, built parallel to the Central's Lake Shore route for 500 miles between Buffalo and Chicago. The Vanderbilts had bought it as soon as it was completed in 1882, just as the

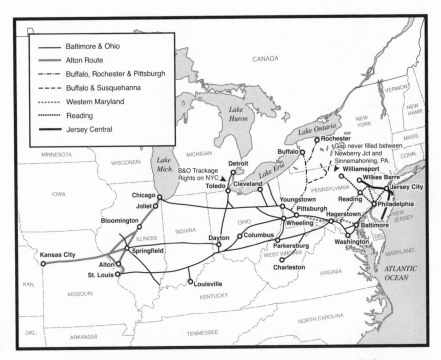

Baltimore & Ohio with Ripley and Tentative Plan Recommendations

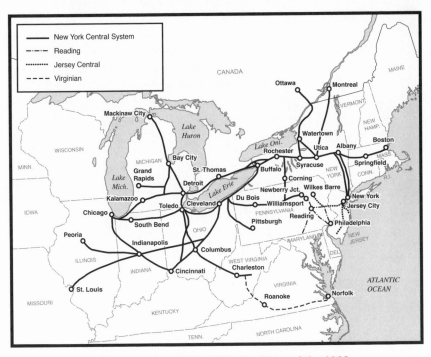

New York Central's Wish List in the Plans of the 1920s

speculators who built it had figured they would. Presumably, the threat of an antitrust suit induced the Central to sell, and since the Vans cared about only seven of the Nickel Plate's 500 miles, it was doubtful they would ever do much to hurt the Central. Besides, J. P. Morgan & Company was the banker for both the Central and the Vans, which gave rise to rumors (never proven) that they were merely the Central's stalking horses.

The Vans took advantage of the Nickel Plate's one great asset, its high-level crossing of the Cuyahoga Valley in Cleveland, much superior to the Central's heavily graded line to the valley floor. They built the Cleveland Union Terminal (CUT) beside it, on four acres of land they had purchased on Public Square. It was an early urban renewal project, and it became the focus of rail and rapid transit lines in the city. The Central cooperated enthusiastically, sending its trains into the new CUT. But the project was expensive: bonds were still outstanding on the terminal even after the last Central passenger train departed in 1971.[6]

A taste of big-time railroading whetted the Vans' appetite for more. By their astute use of the holding company, they were able to collect and control a number of railroads with a minimum investment and without the need for ICC approval. Even as the hearings on the Tentative Plan

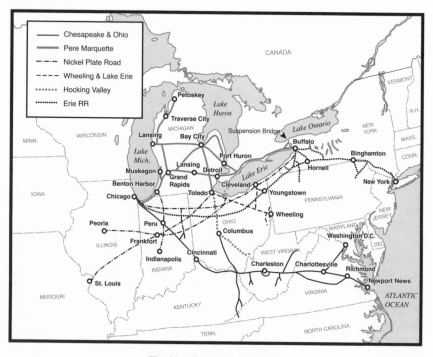

The Van Sweringen Roads

were in progress, the Vans acquired the Lake Erie & Western and the Toledo, St. Louis & Western (the Clover Leaf Route). In 1923 they merged them into the Nickel Plate, providing it with valuable feeder lines and entrances into the important midwestern gateways of Peoria and St. Louis. This was consistent with the Ripley Report and the ICC's tentative plan, and so there should have been no objection.

But instead of requesting approval under the consolidation provisions of the 1920 act (paragraph 6 of section 5), they applied under paragraph 18 of section 1 for permission to operate constituent railroads and under section 20A to issue stock in exchange for the stock of constituent roads. Thus, if the ICC approved this transaction, which it acknowledged was in the public interest, it would set a precedent on method that could open the door to future consolidation that did not conform to a plan. The commission subjected the Nickel Plate Unification to intense scrutiny but finally gave its approval. Ironically, it was the only significant consolidation of the 1920s.[7]

It was their later acquisitions that gave the Vans their clout in eastern railroading. The Erie, the Pere Marquette, the Hocking Valley, the Wheeling & Lake Erie (W&LE), and the big, coal-rich Chesapeake & Ohio all came under their control through holding companies. On two occasions they tried to merge all these properties into a unified system. The first attempt failed because of the opposition of certain C&O stockholders, who did not want their equity in a strong road diluted by the weaker ones. The second failed because the ICC, though professing not to care whether this would ruin its five-system plan, said the holding company was too shaky a structure on which to base a major trunk line. The Vans had given the holding company substance, however. They may have been speculators themselves, but they hired experts. For example, they established the Advisory Mechanical Committee for the roads under their control to coordinate and standardize mechanical design. At the end of the 1920s, this body introduced on the Van Sweringen roads the first super steam power, the 2-8-4 Berkshire-type locomotive. A formidably efficient freight-hauling machine, it was the first of the last generation of steam power in the United States.

But as long as the Erie and the Nickel Plate remained under Van control, a five-system East was a practical impossibility. One could be built out of the Wabash, but a trunk line that had to ferry all its traffic across the Detroit River probably was not going to stand for long against the likes of the New York Central or the Pennsylvania. Therefore, unless the commission was willing to break up the holding companies, which it clearly was not, the only plan that could work was to ratify what the railroads had already done.

Finally, there was the Pennsylvania, large, powerful, profitable, and content to remain, as it fancied itself, "the standard railroad of the world." Both the Ripley Report and the Tentative Plan tried to impose five major systems on the East, when in fact there were only four railroad powers to

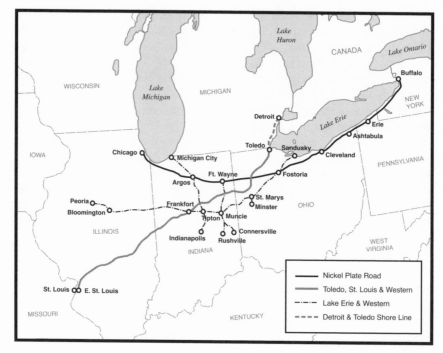

Nickel Plate Unification

begin with. The Pennsylvania suspected that the fifth system was going to be created from its own ribs, and it was not happy. So it set out to use the planning process for its own purposes. All efforts to plan consolidation in the East would fail as a result of the scheming of the Pennsylvania Railroad.

The PRR was not about to have a meddling government hold it in check while lesser lines were strengthened. It thought if there was a feast, the largest should get the most. It demanded trackage along the south shore of Lake Erie (which the New York Central would never tolerate) and an an-thracite road—either the Lackawanna or the Lehigh Valley would do. It wanted a route between Chicago and St. Louis—either the Wabash, the Al-ton, or the Chicago & Eastern Illinois (C&EI). And it made it very clear it would not gracefully give up its interest in the Norfolk & Western.[8]

Furthermore, the PRR had something in its favor that none of the oth-ers could match—an articulate spokesman for its cause. Albert J. County was officially the vice president of accounting; unofficially, he was the secretary of state to deal with other railroad powers. Born in Dublin, he began his ca-reer on the Irish Railways, graduated from the Wharton School, and went di-rectly to the secretary's office of the PRR. He was present at all the public and private consolidation conferences of the 1920s. He was the rock upon which the plans of the planners and the dreams of the underdogs crashed.

County raised fundamental questions about consolidation that had evaded Cummins, Ripley, and Joseph Eastman. Eastman was planning's most articulate defender on the ICC. County turned out to be more perceptive than any of them. First, he said that no one, certainly not the congressmen who wrote the law, knew whether consolidation would solve the weak road problem or provide cheaper transportation; they only guessed it. Studies were needed, and he was not at all sure they would show what the planners wanted them to show. Second, he said no one really asked whether the weak lines were essential. He thought the motor truck was about to open a new era of intermodal transportation. In place of weak, underutilized railroads, trucks would feed the traffic to the strong roads. Finally, repeating forcefully what railroad men had been saying all along, he said the need was for capital, not for plans, and if government really wanted to help, it would supply capital at low rates. There was no reason why it should not do this. It supplied capital to build highways, and railroads served as much a public purpose as roads. This point, he hastened to add, was just a helpful observation about the weak road problem. The Pennsylvania was capable of raising all the capital it needed.[9] Meanwhile, another phase of the railroad problem took center stage.

The Shopmen's Strike of 1922

Industrial efficiency fascinated Louis Brandeis and many of the progressives at the time of the *Fifteen Percent* case in 1910. They considered it one of the keys to better wages. The other was capital investment in machines. Workers who produced more, because they worked more effectively or because machines did more of the work, were worth more and could be paid more without bankrupting their employers and without causing inflation. Nothing in this equation required the employer to pay out the benefits in better wages, but only if there was more output per man hour was there even a possibility of better standards of living. The word for this was productivity. In the nineteenth century, industrial capitalism appeared to produce a small class of the industrial superrich and a large class of the impoverished masses (though we know now that this is oversimplified). By the end of the twentieth century, capitalism seemed to have distributed the good things of life more widely (though far from evenly or equally). Productivity was what made the difference. Railroads, like all other transportation industries, were labor intensive, and so efficiency was of more than passing interest; certainly this was so by the 1920s as the industry began to contract.

The apostle of efficiency was an engineer named Frederick Winslow Taylor—Speedy Fred—who devised the techniques for time and motion study that gave job managers precise knowledge of the cost and benefit from each (often minute) change in production arrangements. Fundamental to pure Taylorism was the concept of piecework, according to which wages were based directly on output (per piece of finished product). All manufacturers were fascinated, and they sent armies of efficiency experts into their plants with stopwatches to time precisely how long it took to perform each individual procedure. Much of Taylorism was not of immediate use to the railroads. Out on the line, productivity in the 1920s meant longer trains with more cars of larger payload, and this depended on the limits of technology and the amount of capital investment.

But Taylor's techniques did apply in one critical area on the railroad—the shops that built and repaired locomotives and cars. They were not as applicable as in straight assembly-line production, because very little railroad equipment was standardized, certainly not the steam locomotives, which were built in many different types for precisely the kind of traffic they would haul and the operating conditions they would face. In the shops, many different crafts were required to maintain them—machinists, blacksmiths, electricians, boilermakers, and sheet-metal workers. Shops were alive with mammoth machinery—cranes that could hoist locomotives off their wheels, fiery smelters, drop forges, air hammers, air guns—and were often sprawling operations, located all over the country. In otherwise nonindustrial areas, these shops were the only industrial operations around. In the years before World War I, the railroads began introducing piecework in many shops.

The pace for Taylor's piecework was set by the fastest, most compulsive worker—the classic workaholic that normal people liked to think lived a constipated life before dropping, unloved, into an early grave. Was that the standard that "scientific" management demanded of everyone? Taylor said no, he took a "good average man." Something as unquantifiable as a "good average man" compromised the premise that there was anything "scientific" about this at all. By some lights Taylor's brave new world of efficiency looked like a living hell. Labor saw Taylorism and his piecework as a speedup—a way to extract more work for less pay, and a way to rob work of any pride or pleasure.[10]

To the good-hearted progressive, there had to be a golden mean where the benefits of productive labor perfectly balanced the surrender of personal control. But perfect balances were hard to come by and had eluded progressives on matters like railroad rates and regulation. Despite efficiency's benefits, there was a price to pay and treacherous times ahead.

Piecework put the workers on edge. It affected different crafts in different ways and was not instantly condemned by all crafts or by all shops, but an explosive issue was on the table. During the war, there was plenty of work for everyone, but inflation made it difficult to support a family. Wage increases allowed by the U.S. Railroad Administration during the war shocked the railroads but still did not keep pace with inflation, and so they satisfied no one. Congress was aware of the growing tension and knew that a rail strike would paralyze the national economy. It therefore created the Railway Labor Board (RLB) as part of the Transportation Act of 1920 to mediate labor disputes, although the board had no power to enforce a decision beyond the "power of public opinion."

After the war there was a sharp economic downturn, which turned a labor shortage into a labor surplus. Prices fell, prompting the railroads to demand an immediate reduction in wages. Some railroad management—not all—thought the time was ripe to break the unions and gain authoritarian control over their employees. A Pennsylvania Railroad pamphlet of 1920 said, "Men are now seeking jobs instead of jobs seeking men. The swanking and swaggering will soon be on the wane. Workers will pay more attention to their jobs and less attention to the agitators who fill no pay envelopes but fill their followers only with wind."[11] The Republican Party that won the 1920 election was quite changed from Teddy Roosevelt's day; then a party of reform, it now believed that what was good for business was good for the country. Harding's appointment to head the RLB was Ben Hooper, the former governor of Tennessee, who said strikes ought to be banned on the railroads, and if there was no law to that effect already, there ought to be. The public craved normalcy, so railroad management figured public opinion would be on its side if push came to shove.

In 1920 the Pennsylvania Railroad, with plenty of shop capacity of its own, contracted out some of its locomotive repair to the Baldwin Locomotive Works in Philadelphia, paying Baldwin more than the cost of doing the repairs in its own shops. Other railroads, notably the Erie, followed suit. This was intended to put pressure on its own shop workers. In June 1922, the railroads persuaded the RLB to allow a 7 percent reduction in shop workers' wages. This was the last straw. The day the reduction went into effect, July 1, the shop workers walked. The day shift joined the night shift as it came off work, and they marched together through the streets of shop towns in a grand show of solidarity. The Great Railroad Shopmen's Strike of 1922 had begun.

At the very beginning, the walkout was orderly. But three days into it, Hooper at the RLB issued what came to be known by the strikers as the "outlaw resolution." It not only gave the railroads a green light to hire strikebreakers but promised strikebreakers "the protection of every department and branch of the Government, state and national." Strikebreakers were hired. To house and feed them, railroads threw up dormitories and commissaries inside barbed-wire stockades, protected by towers and posted with armed guards. Local business usually sided with the strikers, posting signs such as "If You Are a Scab, Your Business Is Not Wanted." Local police, often the brothers, lodge brothers, neighbors, or fellow parishioners of strikers, were usually on the strikers' side.[12]

The barbed-wire barricades at the scab compounds became the flashpoint.

At first it was heckling. Here, the striking unions' ladies' auxiliaries were critical. These were the mothers, wives, and sweethearts of the strikers. A male heckler could be popped in the jaw or jabbed with a rifle butt, but the women hecklers posed a more delicate problem. But after hecklers began to be shot and killed, beginning on July 8 with one dead in Buffalo and another in Cleveland, with reports coming in of strikers being shot all over the country, the stakes were raised. "Chain gangs" or "wrecking crews" of strikers beat up scabs, or whipped them, or put them through mock lynchings, or dumped them disoriented and buck naked outside of town. There were drive-by shootings.

Asserting that the unions were conspiracies in restraint of trade, the government responded with injunctions under the Sherman Antitrust Act. These made support of the strike a criminal offense, even to the little sign that William Allen White, then editor of a small Kansas newspaper, the *Emporia Gazette*, displayed in the paper's window. Federal marshals were dispatched to enforce the injunctions, with orders to make arrests first and ask questions later. Some of them became a local gestapo. The extreme case was at Eagle Grove, Iowa, where a marshal by the name of Daniel Phelan ordered businesses closed and citizens off the streets and decreed, "I am the law. I will be obeyed."[13] Strikers began stoning marshals. There were acts of sabotage of moving trains at Gary, Indiana, and Treverton, Pennsylvania. Many more acts of sabotage and bombings were reported. Signal wires were cut on the Boston & Maine. One of the union leaders told the union's lawyer, Donald Richberg, "There's no use shutting your eyes, Don. A strike ain't no pink tea."[14]

The man behind the injunctions was Harry Daugherty, attorney general for the Harding administration. Daugherty wanted union leaders arrested, and he sent his assistant, Hiram Todd, to get them, frame them, do whatever it took. Eight were arrested, convicted, and jailed. When Gov. Pat Neff of Texas pleaded for time to let tempers cool in the shop town of Denison, Texas, Secretary of War John Weeks declared martial law and ordered in federal troops; when this succeeded, he dispatched troops to ten other Texas shop towns.

Within the industry, President Daniel Willard of the B&O led a faction of railroads, including most prominently the Seaboard, that sought a settlement that would leave the strikers with at least a fig leaf of pride, including their seniority. Seniority, the just reward for a lifetime spent in difficult and dangerous work, on call night and day, often far from home, meant everything to a railroad worker. But the Pennsylvania Railroad, for one, wanted the unions broken; PRR president W. W. (William Wallace) Atterbury denounced Willard and his notions of a just settlement. With the arrogance that characterized the PRR even to its dying day, it sneered that Willard's willingness to deal with the unions was all one could expect from a man who had worked himself up from the ranks of labor. From within the Harding administration, Secretary of Commerce Herbert Hoover embarked on a mission of conciliation, over the fierce objection of Daugherty and Weeks. This mission was backed by Harding, who, despite his friendship with Daugherty, thought government should be an honest broker. But Hoover's mission foundered on the obstinacy of the railroads' bankers, specifically Benjamin Strong of the Federal Reserve Bank of New York. Harding himself tried twice more, his efforts rebuffed by the unions over the issue of seniority.

By August 1922 violence was escalating. In Sacramento, James Mero, the shopcraft unions' leader, was assassinated by railroad guards as he was getting off a trolley near his home. Locomotives and cars were in dangerous states of disrepair but were ordered out on the road anyway by the desperate railroads. The operating brotherhoods sporadically refused to operate unsafe trains and were threatening to shut down everything. Daugherty again got the president's ear. His solution was a sweeping injunction that invoked the commerce clause and the Sherman Act and zeroed in on the railroads' role in moving the mails. It would be a criminal offense to interfere with trains or equipment repair, to encourage anyone else to do so, to intimidate others, including jeering or using epithets, to congregate in the vicinity of railroad facilities, or to ask anyone to ever stop work "in any manner, by letter, printed or other circulars, telegrams, telephones, word of mouth, oral persuasion or suggestion."[15] Presumably with Harding's OK, though without the knowledge of Secretary Hoover, Daugherty got Judge James Wilkerson of the U.S. District Court in Chicago to issue the injunction. It was one of the most extreme pronouncements in American history, violating any number of constitutional guarantees of free speech, free press, and free assembly. It effectively broke the strike.

The B&O offered a settlement that preserved seniority but incorporated some of the Taylorite principles of scientific management. The NYC, the Milwaukee Road, the Chicago & North Western, the Southern, and the Seaboard, later joined by the Grand Trunk, the Rock Island, and the Rio Grande, were the larger roads that joined the B&O. Reluctant to break ranks, but with little other choice, the unions accepted. Elsewhere, the strike continued. But with unions unable to pay strike benefits and community support on the wane, one by one strikers either took other jobs, became scabs themselves on other railroads, or went back to their old jobs stripped of seniority. Road by road, the unions called it off and the mighty strike came to a whimpering end. It finally ended on the Pennsylvania Railroad in 1928. By that time, it had no effect on the railroad or its operations.

Four years after the strike began, and with the strike very much in mind, Congress passed the Railway Labor Act of 1926, which, in its 1934 modified form, was the governing labor law for the remainder of the century. Its premise was that railroad transportation was too important to be disrupted. To this end, the right of workers to organize and the requirement that both sides bargain in good faith was written clearly into the law. It required an elaborate procedure of mediation to postpone and hopefully head off strikes. The most obvious result was that future labor disputes were argued by lawyers, and not by taunting mobs, mayhem, and murder. The Shopmen's Strike of 1922 was the last of the violent railroad strikes.

The problem of labor and productivity had not gone away, however. For the railroads, work had to be made efficient. They were going to face a greater competitive onslaught than they could have dreamed of in 1922, and there would be no choice but to make work productive. Although railroad workers had extraordinary loyalty to their jobs, almost as though railroad work were a calling, railroad labor was going to face technological changes that would render whole crafts obsolete, and there were going to be bitter tears. For the nation, the railroads stood at the nexus of the national economy. If they shut down, virtually everything else shut down. Assembly lines and utilities all required transportation that only the rails could provide. Farmers would be bankrupted, grocery shelves would empty out, the electricity would go off. Everyone had a stake in this, and there was trouble ahead.

Fifth Systems and the Scramble of 1929

As long as there was no official consolidation plan, each of the Big Four hoped to influence the shape of the final plan in its favor. If they could agree on a plan to divide the pie among them, they could present a united front to the commission. Failing this, they could each hasten to grab what they wanted and present each other with done deals. A series of more or less secret great power conferences pitted the PRR against the other three. The other three wanted four systems in the East, which they saw as natural. The PRR wanted a fifth system. It remained in the shadows on this, keeping much of its activity secret. Its purpose was to make sure the fifth system was too weak to work. When it failed, the PRR would inherit the pieces.

One of these fifth-system schemes rested on the dynamic personality of Leonor Loree, once a rising young executive of the PRR, who became president of the independent Delaware & Hudson. He tried to combine the D&H with other medium-sized lines, notably the Lehigh Valley and the Wabash. The combination would have been a circuitous trunk line with little chance of success against the established routes. Loree, nonetheless, was a formidable presence. He was a big man and handsome, a football star at Rutgers, articulate and forceful. Many remembered having been awestruck in his presence, and because of this the fifth-system scheme always seemed more substantive than it was. It was odd that when Loree's career was over, he had done little but run the middling D&H reasonably well. The PRR watched his fifth-system maneuvers with a wary eye and

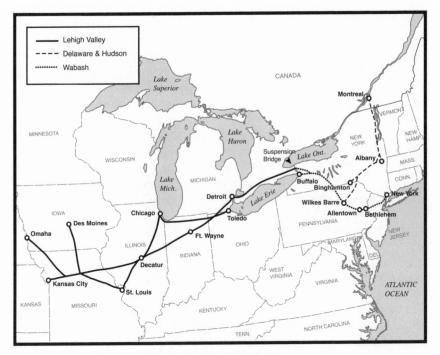

Leonor Loree's Fifth System

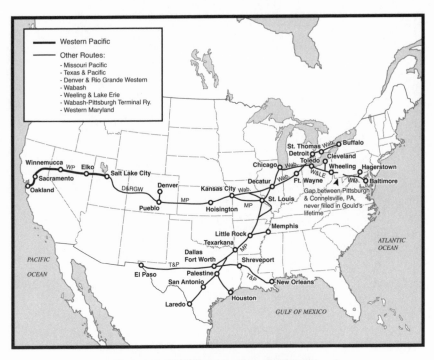

George Gould's Transcontinental Empire

then decided to nurture them for their nuisance value. Loree, despite his past association with the PRR, was never entirely in its pocket. He attended the great power conferences as a full-fledged spokesman for the fifth system. But he narrowly failed to win a proxy fight for the Lehigh Valley, after which his sizable chunks of Lehigh and Wabash stock fell to the PRR.[16]

A second scheme, to which the PRR was attracted in its later stages, was the ambitious plan of the Taplin brothers to create a new lakes-to-the-sea system. The Taplins owned coal mines along the Pittsburgh & West Virginia Railway (P&WV), a sixty-mile line from southeastern Ohio to the Pittsburgh industrial area. It was the remnant of the old Wabash-Pittsburgh Terminal Railway, which George Gould intended as the final link in his ill-starred transcontinental system, one of the last swashbuckling gambles of the robber-baron age. The line was built to elaborate specifications, some of it double- and quadruple-tracked, with grades superior to those of the competing St. Louis line of the PRR. The Taplins hoped to win control of the Wheeling & Lake Erie, itself a coal hauler of vast potential, which would extend their railroad to Lake Erie at Cleveland and Toledo. Then they wanted to build 40 miles of new line, the 40 miles that had defeated Gould, from Pittsburgh to a connection with the Western Maryland Railway at Con-

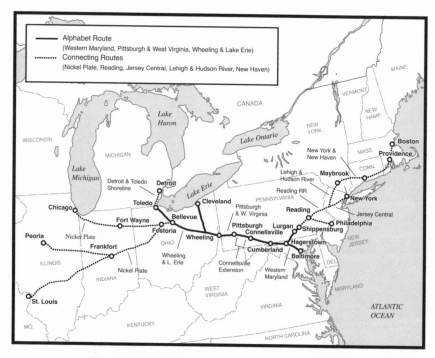

The Alphabet Route and Its Principal Connections

nellsville, Pennsylvania. If they could get control of the Western Maryland, they would own a potentially formidable east-west service route.

Since the B&O already owned enough stock to control the Western Maryland, the project was in trouble from the start. Nevertheless, three of the big powers (the B&O, the Central, and the Vans) were sufficiently frightened to snap up joint control of the Wheeling & Lake Erie. At first, the PRR thought the Taplins were stalking horses for the other three, and it threatened to cut off all interchange with the Pittsburgh & West Virginia if the Connellsville Extension went through. But it did go through (in 1928) and the PRR, unable to stop it, decided to use it for its own purposes. When the Taplins found their empire beyond their grasp and grew tired of the whole scheme, the PRR paid them handsomely for the P&WV. Although a unified Wheeling-P&WV-WM system never materialized, and although various segments belonged to rival camps, it did become an important freight service route, nicknamed the Alphabet Route for the extraordinary number of railroad initials that went into the routing. All a shipper had to say was "Alphabet." It won a lot of loyal customers and was a factor in developments to come.[17]

When the buffer schemes collapsed, some less subtle tactics were in order. The PRR tried to lease the Norfolk & Western but was rebuffed by the ICC.[18] Then the N&W tried to merge with the Virginian, but this was also refused.[19] Next the Virginian extended its lines across the Kanawha River at Deepwater, West Virginia, to a strategic connection with the New York Central, a liaison with significance for the future.[20] The PRR hung securely onto the Wabash and the Lehigh Valley, but the Central also began to buy Lehigh stock, then sold it and bought Lackawanna instead.

Congress refused to relieve the ICC of the duty to make a plan. By 1928, as fifth-system plans collapsed, with vital segments of the eastern network falling into the hands of the PRR, it was soon going to be impossible to consolidate anything except under the railroads' own terms. To undo some of the damage, the ICC instigated a number of Clayton Act proceedings to break these newly acquired holds and at the same time intimated that it was going ahead with a final plan.[21] Within a year, the Central, the B&O, and the Vans had to give up the Wheeling, and the B&O had to quit the Western Maryland.[22] The PRR was ordered to sell the Wabash and the Lehigh, but it appealed and kept the case in litigation through the crucial years that followed. In 1934 the Supreme Court, in a 4–4 decision (sustaining a lower court ruling) found for the PRR.[23] So the result of these proceedings was to strengthen the strongest (PRR) and strip the roads that needed to expand.

In the short run this unleashed a new acquisition binge by the great powers known as the scramble of 1929. Each tried to grab and hang onto anything it could. It was the year of the Great Bull Market, and some of the roads were speculating as everyone else was. Most of the purchases were on money borrowed at 6 percent or more, and when the crash came, they constituted a fearful overextension of credit. The New York Central bought heavily into the Lackawanna; the B&O increased its hold on the Reading. The Vans formed a new holding company, the Alleghany Corporation, to control all their railroad enterprises, which then bought blocks of the Missouri Pacific, the Kansas City Southern, and the Chicago Great Western.

None used the holding company device more skillfully than the PRR. It feared the final plan more than the others and had the most to lose if it did not checkmate the ICC with strategic stock purchases of its own. The venerable (1870) Pennsylvania Company, wholly owned by the railroad and with identical officers, owned the Wabash and Lehigh Valley stocks that were under litigation. But its principal vehicle of expansion was the new Pennroad Company, formed in 1928 and owned by the railroad's stockholders, not the railroad itself. By selling stock to stockholders, the railroad was able to tap a new source of capital, and since all that stock was trusteed for ten years, there would be no loss of control. The PRR's record for astute stock purchases was so good that Pennroad was quickly oversubscribed. Many of its acquisitions were strictly for investment, but they strengthened the PRR's hold on the Wabash and the Lehigh and made Pennroad the

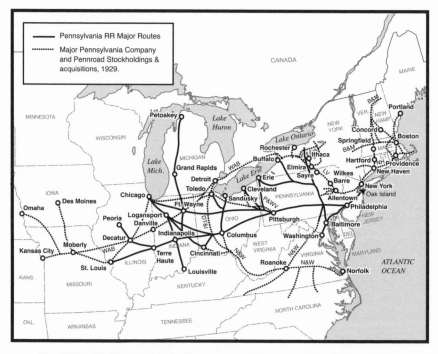

The PRR with Pennsylvania Company and Pennroad Stock Purchases

dominant force on the Detroit, Toledo & Ironton (DT&I), which it purchased from Henry Ford. Most significantly, in the summer of 1929 it bought large blocks of the New Haven and the Boston & Maine (whereupon the PRR named a vice president for New England affairs).[24]

The "Final" Plan

Since the ICC's announcement of a final plan triggered the scramble, publication of such a plan might end it, but through most of 1929 no plan was forthcoming. It was known that the commission was divided between those who wanted a four-system East (which would ratify what the great powers had already done) and those who favored a five-system East (which would require divestitures). No attempt was made to bring the 1923 hearings up to date, even though the situation had changed.

Then in December, the ICC released a final plan that shocked everyone. It called for a five-system East, with none of the five having an entrance to New England. The PRR was to be stripped of everything but the Long Island Railroad (LIRR); the New York Central was to get the Virginian; the B&O was to have everything it wanted; the Vans' empire was to remain intact. The ICC proposed the following restructuring:

System 1. The Boston & Maine, including the Bangor & Aroostook, the Delaware & Hudson, the Maine Central, and the Rutland

System 2. The New Haven, including the Lehigh & Hudson River; the Lehigh & New England; and the New York, Ontario & Western

System 3. The New York Central, including the Pittsburgh & Lake Erie and the Virginian Railway

System 4. The Pennsylvania, including the Long Island

System 5. The Baltimore & Ohio, including the Buffalo, Rochester & Pittsburgh; the Chicago & Alton; the Jersey Central; and the Reading

System 6. The Chesapeake & Ohio, including the Bessemer & Lake Erie, the Chicago & Illinois Midland, the Erie, the Hocking Valley, the Lackawanna, the Nickel Plate, and the Pere Marquette

System 7. The Wabash-Seaboard, including the Lehigh Valley; the Norfolk & Western; the Pittsburgh & West Virginia; the Seaboard Air Line; the Toledo, Peoria & Western; the Wabash; the Western Maryland; and the Wheeling & Lake Erie

System 8. The Atlantic Coast Line, including the Atlanta, Birmingham & Coast; the Clinchfield; the Gulf, Mobile & Northern; the Louisville & Nashville; and the Nashville, Chattanooga & St. Louis

System 9. The Southern Railway, including the Florida East Coast, the Georgia & Florida, and the Norfolk Southern

System 10. The Illinois Central, including the Central of Georgia, the Minneapolis & St. Louis, and the St. Louis Southwestern

System 11. The Chicago & North Western, including the Chicago & East-
ern Illinois and the Mobile & Ohio
System 12. The Great Northern, including the Northern Pacific and the
Spokane, Portland & Seattle
System 13. The Milwaukee, including the Duluth, Missabe & Iron Range
System 14. The Burlington, including the Colorado & Southern, the Fort
Worth & Denver City, the Green Bay & Western, the Missouri-
Kansas-Texas, and the Oklahoma City–Ada–Atoka
System 15. The Union Pacific, including the Kansas City Southern
System 16. The Southern Pacific
System 17. The Santa Fe, including the Chicago Great Western
System 18. The Missouri Pacific, including the Denver & Rio Grande West-
ern, the Texas & Pacific, and the Western Pacific
System 19. The Rock Island, including the St. Louis–San Francisco
System 20. All Canadian National properties in the United States, includ-
ing the Central Vermont; the Duluth, Winnipeg & Pacific; the Grand
Trunk (Maine); and the Grand Trunk Western
System 21. All Canadian Pacific properties in the United States, including
the Duluth, South Shore & Atlantic; the Soo Line, and the Wisconsin
Central

The plan left established subsidiaries attached to their parent
companies—for example, the Michigan Central to the New York Central,
the Oregon Short Line to the Union Pacific, the Omaha Road to the
Chicago & North Western. It parceled out all short lines, but terminal railroads remained neutral. Some trackage rights were ordered to fill in gaps
for some systems. A few properties were divided. The Tennessee Central
(TC) was chopped into pieces, as it eventually was anyway. The ICC did
not know who to give the Monon (Chicago, Indianapolis & Louisville before 1956) to, so it gave a half interest to the B&O, a quarter to the Southern, and a quarter to the Atlantic Coast Line.

The Great Northern and the Northern Pacific rather liked the plan. Pair-
ing them seemed to affirm the logic of James J. Hill back at the time of the
Northern Securities case. The GN's president, Ralph Budd, convinced the
Northern Pacific and the Burlington that the time was ripe to make another try for merger. The ICC agreed to a GN-NP merger, but the price was
to give up all interest in the Burlington (in which, it will be recalled, each
owned a 48 percent beneficial interest, as part of the *Northern Securities* settlement). This was too steep, and there was no merger.

The shocker of the Final Plan was system 7, the Wabash-Seaboard System. It was based on the financial strength of the Lehigh Valley and the
Norfolk & Western, both torn from the PRR, and the Alphabet Route torn
from the others. It would run from Omaha to Miami via Buffalo and did
not appear to have much geographic cohesion (except that, in an odd

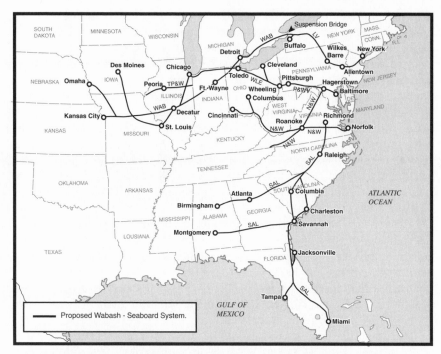

The Proposed Wabash–Seaboard System of the ICC's Final Plan

way, it resembled the later CSX and Norfolk Southern systems). Henry Sturgis of the First National Bank of New York recalled how he used to kid friends on the Lehigh Valley that they would probably wind up with the dubious honor of caring for the weak Wabash. "I intended it as a joke," he said, "I'm afraid the joke has gone a little far."[25]

The Final Plan terrorized the great powers of the East into settling their differences. The secret conferences reopened. The PRR made it clear that it would not give up the Norfolk & Western. The Wabash-Seaboard fifth system was parceled out among them. In the settlement presented by the eastern railroads to the commission, there was not a single word about economy or coordinated service. It had nothing to do with public interest. It was a paper plan that served the railroads' private interests, just in case consolidation should ever become compulsory.[26]

The Prince Plan and the Washington Agreement

With the onset of the Great Depression, consolidation came to be seen as a mechanism to shrink the railroad system: not only to solve the weak road–strong road problem, but to get rid of duplicate lines and terminals.

In 1930 Herbert Hoover, now president, was desperate to stimulate capital investment. He thought consolidation might provide a stimulus for railroads. Railroad security owners were tired of management's evasions and wanted action. They had come to see consolidation as a path to operating economy, including the elimination of duplicate executives. Once again, Professor Ripley was summoned, this time to shuttle between the railroads and the White House in search of commitments. Recognizing the signals from the White House, the ICC modified its "Final Plan" to suit the whims of the great powers, thereby indicating that nothing was ever final and that the railroads could manipulate the process if they presented a reasonably united front. This revision was called the Revised Final Plan, and it was seldom heard of again.

Hoover was so hopeful that the new plan would pave the way for consolidation that he announced it himself on December 30, 1930. He said the purpose of the consolidation legislation of 1920 was to provide more adequate service, a simplified rate structure, and lower operating costs, which was wrong. In 1920 Congress worried about weak roads–strong roads, not operating efficiency.[27] Efficiency was the reason consolidation was needed in 1930. Walker Hines and the scientific management crowd of the USRA seemed to be vindicated.

The downside was that jobs would be eliminated. Easing the depression with measures that were likely to cause more unemployment did not seem like a good idea to everyone. Labor took careful note of this new enthusiasm for economy and surmised that it was going to be the victim. On labor's behalf, Sen. James Couzzens of Michigan introduced legislation to have the consolidation provisions of the 1920 act repealed and to subject the railroads to the same antitrust legislation as everyone else. Hearings on his Railroad Unification Act of 1931 indicated that it had become a political issue, with owners in favor of general consolidation and labor and management united in opposition (since management jobs were on the line, too). The debate went to fundamentals: should prosperity be revived by helping business—in this case by encouraging consolidation—or by preventing consolidation and preserving jobs? The problem was passed to the Roosevelt administration.

Franklin Roosevelt's campaign speech on transportation, delivered at Salt Lake City in September 1932, repeated the Hoover policy of encouraging consolidation to stimulate investment. Between then and Roosevelt's inauguration, Frederick H. Prince, a Boston banker and past president of the Pere Marquette Railway, speaking as the president of the Association of Railroad Security Owners, published a plan for consolidation more sweeping than anything since the Plumb Plan.

The Prince Plan's greatest attribute was that it concentrated maximum traffic on minimum trackage and still preserved competition. A radical contraction of the railroads was essential, said John Barriger (the young engineer who did most of the work on the plan), because the downward trend of commodity prices was going to make many commodities unshippable. Railroads would have to economize so that they could reduce rates to hold on to their traffic.

Prince divided the entire network into seven systems: two in the East, two in the South, and three in the West. Each system would be a new corporation that would acquire railroads by leasing them and paying rent to their owners. The Reconstruction Finance Corporation would buy the new companies' 4.5 percent debenture bonds at par, the funds to be used as needed, even for buying the stock of leased lines when offered at a discount. For two years, all wage earners displaced by the plan would receive a protection allowance of one-half to two-thirds of their previous salaries.[28] The plan attracted considerable attention from President Roosevelt. Raymond Moley explained that it was novel, and Roosevelt liked anything that was novel.[29]

Congress had the Prince Plan in mind when it passed the Emergency Transportation Act in 1933. This established the office of federal coordinator of transportation to encourage the carriers to reduce duplication and to reorganize their finances. Consolidation was one way to reach that goal, but not the only way. The law was vague, and the coordinator's power to coerce was doubtful. Joseph Eastman seemed to be a good choice for the job, but he was probably too confident of his ability to persuade and too reluctant to risk a showdown in the courts. Ultimately, the act failed to bring about any consolidation, and when it failed, it was easy to forget how hard Eastman worked to get it.

Eastman's tenure began with promise. He appointed William B. Poland, an experienced railroad engineer, to test the findings of the Prince Plan. In the East, the Prince Plan envisioned two systems—the northern, including the New York Central, the Van Sweringen Lines, and all of northern New England; and the southern, including the PRR, the B&O, the N&W, and the New Haven. Poland found no quarrel with these groupings, but he questioned the extent to which they could produce the savings the plan said they would. For example, Barriger calculated that, between Pittsburgh and Chicago, the Pennsylvania would carry all the traffic, and the B&O could be ripped up as a main line. Poland felt not only that the traffic warranted two lines but also that the B&O was the superior route anyway, a judgment that proved correct in the 1980s.[30] Between Washington and New York, Barriger put all traffic on the Pennsylvania and anticipated the elimination of the B&O–Reading–Jersey Central Royal Blue line. Again, Poland questioned the ability of the Pennsylvania to handle the traffic. Poland reduced Barriger's anticipated savings from $743 million a year to $218 million a year, which was still a substantial amount in those days.

The first annual report of the coordinator contained the Poland Report.

It also contained an opinion by Leslie Craven, law professor at Duke, that the government did have the constitutional power to compel consolidation. It could use its power under the commerce clause to create federal corporations and direct them to acquire railroad property. Existing companies that did not accede could then be forbidden to engage in interstate commerce.[31] Despite this ammunition, Eastman could find no support in any quarter. When he wrote his fourth and last report, he was disillusioned and put the blame on the railroad executives.

> Their habit of mind is intensely individualistic and suspicious of collective action. When such action is proposed—notwithstanding that it may be for the good of the industry as a whole—the normal executive will at once seek to determine how it will affect his railroad in comparison to others. . . . He is particularly wary of any collective proposal which has a nationwide aspect, for he sees in it what he regards as a tendency toward nationalization of the railroads, and at all events, a decrease in the importance of local managements.[32]

Railroad managements, wary that they might be pushed into something they did not like, responded by creating their own coordinating agency, the Association of American Railroads (AAR). It was similar to the cartel-like structures being created in other industries as part of the Blue Eagle recovery program. It took over such functions as car reporting and establishing technical standards; it absorbed the Bureau of Railway Economics and its library; and it consolidated all the railroads' lobbying activities in Washington. Following the Poland Report, the association released its own studies on locomotive and car supplies, which concluded that no coordination efforts were needed or desirable.[33]

Labor was even more wary. Earl Latham, author of a study of the Emergency Act, said that labor thought it was the "typical right-wing remedy for the ills of industry—deflation without regard to social cost."[34]

But in case mass consolidation, labor and management negotiated what was called the Washington Labor Protection Agreement of 1936. The agreement represented labor's view that it was unfair for the benefits of consolidation to go to capital alone, leaving nothing but mass unemployment for workers. It provided protection payments for all workers displaced by consolidation at 60 percent of their prior wages. These payments would last for five years beginning the day the workers were actually laid off. This was a lifeline, especially for workers in small railroad towns across rural America where there were no other jobs. For management, the agreement meant that if consolidation did come to pass, management could count on labor going along, grumbling perhaps, but going along. Most Class I railroads outside the South signed the agreement, and the southerners came on board later.

The Washington Agreement was an important document that remained in force for the remainder of the century. But the Emergency Transportation Act that spawned the agreement was a faulty piece of legislation that aroused strong opposition and failed to produce the results anticipated. It was temporary and was not renewed when it expired in 1936.

Roosevelt appointed a Committee of Three to make recommendations. He chose three of the ICC's most progressive commissioners—Charles Mahaffie, Eastman, and Walter M. W. Splawn. They suggested that all railroads be consolidated into a single unit under private management and ownership. The idea was breathtaking, and the president said he liked it. On May 8, 1938, he hinted publicly that sweeping, compulsory consolidation might be in the offing.

But Roosevelt knew that labor and management feared consolidation almost equally, so he appointed another committee, the Committee of Six, three from labor and three from management, to make its recommendation. The committee suggested nothing stronger than voluntary consolidation on company initiative, and with heavy restrictions on that. Security owners denounced this handiwork of the hired men before a Senate committee headed by Burton K. Wheeler of Montana. Wheeler was conducting hearings on new transportation legislation that would become the Transportation Act of 1940.[35]

The Transportation Act of 1940 was the governing law for all the mergers up to 1996; it largely embodied the recommendations of the Committee of Six. Consolidation was to be supervised by the ICC. The ICC was to look favorably on proposals that were consistent with the public interest. They did not have to promote the public interest, only to be consistent with it. There was to be no compulsion. Most labor leaders were content with the Washington Agreement and wanted no statutory provisions, although Congressman Vincent Harrington of Iowa, at the request of the Brotherhood of Railroad Trainmen, achieved an amendment that guaranteed four years' protection for displaced employees at 100 percent of wages starting the day the consolidation was approved.[36] Some thought this would reduce the benefit to owners so drastically that consolidation would be a dead letter.

Recounting the failure of Albert Cummins's inspiration for planned consolidation, economist William Leonard blamed three parties. First there were the strong railroads, which were determined to remain strong and did not want to see weaker roads strengthened. Second, the ICC fumbled, perhaps deliberately, since many of its members were Harding appointees who were ideologically opposed to the idea of government's making business do anything it did not want to do. Finally, the law was faulty. Instead of emphasizing efficiency and economy, as the technocrats said it should, it was offered as a panacea for the weak road problem, which it could not solve. Leonard himself was convinced that planned compulsory consolidation was possible and desirable.

The railroads thought it proved that consolidation could not be planned by so-called experts. In fact, no such thing had been proved. What had been shown was that a poorly devised plan based on ill-conceived and watered-down legislation, administered by an indecisive commission and targeting a troubled but nonetheless powerful industry, would not work.

The Railway Labor Act and the Electro-Motive FT

Remembering the Shopmen's Strike of 1922, Congress was frightened enough to want to try to head off future strikes. The majority in the 1920s was none too sympathetic to labor but understood that, if the aim was to keep the channels of commerce open, neither a bloody showdown nor military intervention, nor any suspension of basic constitutional rights, was the way to do it. Collective bargaining and mediation were more likely to avoid catastrophe. The result was the Railway Labor Act of 1926, which was substantially modified in 1934. Even its original version said unequivocally that employees had a right to organize. The act required both sides to bargain in good faith. In case bargaining reached an impasse, the act established a National Mediation Board, appointed by the president and confirmed by the Senate, that would try to find a compromise both sides could accept. If the National Mediation Board's efforts failed, incentives were provided for both sides to submit to arbitration. If they did not submit, the president could appoint a Presidential Emergency Board to make a fact-finding recommendation. All this machinery could take six months or more, during which time a settlement was likely. By the time the matter got to a Presidential Emergency Board, public opinion would be engaged, and it was hoped that this would force both sides to accept the findings of the Presidential Emergency Board. If they did not, 30 days after the Presidential Emergency Board's report, both sides were free to pursue their economic interests as they saw them.

The purpose was not to enhance the welfare of the railroads or of the railroad unions but to avoid a nationwide strike. The stakes for the national economy were too high, but how this would affect the railroad industry, no one knew. A number of laws had tried to deal with the problem and failed—the Act of 1888, the Erdman Act of 1898, the Newlands Act of 1913, the Adamson Act of 1916, and the Transportation Act of 1920. The Railway Labor Act of 1926, as modified in 1934, worked well enough to avert most nationwide strikes and remained the basic law for the remainder of the century. The most obvious result was that instead of the chain gangs and wrecking crews that characterized the Shopmen's Strike of 1922, along with the marshals and the assassinations, railway labor disputes became a matter for lawyers and mediators. Another result was that, in the drawn-out, multitiered process, tough issues usually got postponed. In sheer exhaustion, the two sides would agree on what they could and postpone the rest.[37]

Railroads required the services of just about every craft. Each was represented by its own union, all of them organized along tight craft lines—the Brotherhood of Locomotive Engineers (1863), the Order of Railway Conductors and Brakemen (1863), the Brotherhood of Locomotive Firemen and Enginemen (1873), the Switchmen's Union of North America (1877), the Brotherhood of Railroad Trainmen (1883), the Brotherhood of Maintenance of Way Employees (1886), the Order of Railway Telegraphers (1886), the Brotherhood of Railway and Steamship Clerks, Express Agents, and Station Handlers (1899), the Brotherhood of Railroad Signalmen (1908), the American Train Dispatchers Association (1917), the Railroad Yardmasters Association (1910), the Brotherhood of Sleeping Car Porters (1925). Electrical workers, machinists, sheet metal workers, boilermakers, and workers in other crafts were represented separately. This extraordinary division of craft unions was peculiar to railroads. By the 1930s, steelworkers, coal miners, autoworkers, and teamsters were organizing whole industries with a single union, but not the railroad workers. A dispute involving any one of these crafts could set the whole mediation machinery in motion. If changing technology threatened the existence of any one of these crafts, the union would use all the machinery at its disposal to save itself. This would be the kind of intractable issue that was likely to get postponed.

On May 26, 1934, the Burlington's Zephyr, a little stainless steel streamlined and diesel-powered train, made a historic run from Denver to Chicago in a single day—dawn to dusk—arriving in Chicago just in time for the opening of the Century of Progress Exhibition, where it promptly went on display. Thousands came to see it whiz by. This was not the first diesel to pull a train, but it was the first to grab public attention, and it grabbed it with a vengeance. (It was not the first streamliner, either. That honor went to the Union Pacific M-10000, but that train was gasoline-powered. It was the reason the UP had proprietary rights to the word *streamliner*. Others had to be content with *streamlined train*.)

These first diesels were operated without firemen, because they had no fire. But in 1937 the Brotherhood of Locomotive Firemen and Enginemen made this an intractable bargaining issue. It was the depression, and the crying need was for jobs, not job displacement. Public opinion sided with the firemen. The railroads themselves had little idea how important the diesel was going to be. Steam men, who dominated railroad mechanical departments, assumed that the diesel's use would be limited to certain kinds of passenger trains, and rather gimmicky ones at that.

But on November 25, 1939, after a brief shakedown on the B&O, the Electro-Motive Division of General Motors sent its new FT model 5,400-horsepower diesel touring on American railroads. It climbed the Front

Range on the Rio Grande; it crested Mullan Pass on the Northern Pacific and Snoqualmie Pass on the Milwaukee Road. It doubled the tonnage of double-heading Mikado steam engines over the tortuous section of the Southern's "Rathole" Division between Danville, Kentucky, and Oakdale, Tennessee, and took a full hour off the normal running time over the whole distance between Cincinnati and Chattanooga. It whisked tonnage across the New York Central's Water Level Route and over the high plains on both the Missouri Pacific and the Rock Island. It snubbed helper engines and water towers; it was ready to roll after no more than a simple brake test. Old-time mechanical officers knew steam, had spent their life with steam, had mastered steam, could sense an engine's capability by its feel. They regarded the fancy painted diesels of the first streamliners as dainty and frail, but the FT left them in awe. A new technology was born, and big labor problems lay ahead.[38]

Radio communication was right around the corner. This would enable an engineer to talk to his conductor in the caboose, which meant that back-up and coupling operations could be done without trainmen's waving lanterns. Union Switch & Signal installed centralized traffic control (CTC) on the Denver line of the Burlington in 1937; it was not the first installation but was the best laboratory test to date of that technology. All trains were controlled from a central board, from which all switches and all signals were set. Someday, nobody at all would be needed at the rear of the train to throw switches.

All this technology was coming on fast. None of it was in universal use, but it was clear that the railroad of tomorrow would need only a fraction of the manpower it needed in 1940, and whether the Railway Labor Act could handle this was yet to be seen.

The DC-3 and the Pennsylvania Turnpike

Technology in other areas was going to have an impact on the railroads. In 1935 Douglas Aircraft went to work expanding its DC-2 aircraft to meet a specific request from American Airlines for a plane with 14 sleeper berths to fly coast to coast. The result was the Douglas Sleeper Transport, better known in its day coach version as the DC-3. It could seat 21 passengers. In the spring of 1936, American Airlines began DC-3 service between New York and Chicago. At last a plane had enough payload to make a profit. The DC-3 was the first aircraft large enough to make money hauling passengers alone, without help from a mail contract or mail subsidy. A war was coming in which air power would play a major role, and the government would underwrite huge developmental costs for aircraft design and manufacture. When the war was over, the airplane was no longer just a novelty.

At the automobile's first appearance early in the century, it was a toy for the rich because, first, most people could not afford one and, second, there were no roads to drive them on. Henry Ford's assembly line lowered the cost of a car. Rising productivity throughout the 1920s, thanks to the assembly line, meant that many workers could afford to buy one. Now at the end of the 1930s, a war was coming in which American productive capacity would be the wonder of the world; because of strong unions, some of the fruits of that productivity would show up in better paychecks. The result was that when World War II was over, the nation was ready to buy cars as never before.

Several tentative efforts to build better roads culminated in the creation in 1916 of the Bureau of Public Roads, which had a small budget at first. Seen primarily as a builder of farm-to-market roads, it was put under the Department of Agriculture. It had poor leadership in its early days. But after World War I, General Pershing returned home convinced that the wars of the future would be on wheels, and that the United States needed roads. To test American roads, he ordered a convoy of 300 soldiers on 29 trucks to navigate the Lincoln "Highway" from Washington to San Francisco. The trip took 56 days. A young lieutenant who went along was Dwight Eisenhower.

In 1919 Thomas MacDonald arrived at the Bureau of Public Roads. He took over an agency that had built only twelve and a half miles of road, had spent only a fraction of the money appropriated to it, and was sinking in bureaucratism. In his documentary film and book *Divided Highways,* Tom Lewis suggests that MacDonald was as much responsible for putting Americans behind the wheel as Ford or Alfred Sloan (who built General Motors).[39]

Under MacDonald's leadership, the bureau's budget was increased tenfold, and it laid out a network of national roads. In 1926 it brought state highway directors to a meeting at Pinehurst, North Carolina, where they signed off on the final routes. Both the Hoover and the Roosevelt administrations found highway construction an expedient and noncontroversial way for government to spend money and put people to work during the depression.

Less than a year after the last stretches of pavement were poured on the Lincoln Highway (Route 30) to San Francisco and Route 66 to Los Angeles, General Motors' "Futurama" Pavilion opened at the 1939 New York World's Fair. It was a vision of far-off 1960, a breathtaking diorama of "Magic Motorways" connecting bucolic farmland with the "Metropolis." Cars moved on controlled-access highways on autopilot, at scale speeds of 50, 75, and 100 mph. As visitors left, they were given a pin proclaiming, "I have seen the future."

On October 10, 1938, the New Deal's Public Works Administration began the construction of the Pennsylvania Turnpike. Its chief engineer was

Samuel Marshall. It employed an army of 30,000 workers who bulldozed and dynamited through six mountain ranges to build a four-lane, divided, controlled-access highway of reinforced concrete. Curves and gradients were engineered for a steady speed of 70 mph. Marshall wrote, "It was the fastest moving, hardest hitting engineering organization with which I have ever been associated." The highway opened October 1, 1940. The future was here.

Railroads at War

In the bleak depression years, the streamliners gave railroad morale a boost. The Hiawathas were streaking over the Milwaukee Road. Trackside signs on curves warned engineers, "Slow to 100." The Rockets rolled on the Rock Island and the 400 fleet on the North Western. The first streamliner to Florida was the Seaboard's Silver Meteor. Its first departure on February 2, 1939, was broadcast on WOR New York. All-coach streamliners brought luxury to average folks, the El Capitan on the Santa Fe, the Challenger on the Union Pacific, the Trail Blazer on the Pennsylvania, and the Pacemaker on the New York Central.

But the depression years had taken a toll. More than a third of all railroad mileage was owned by carriers that were in receivership, among them the Wabash, the Seaboard, the Chicago & North Western, the Missouri Pacific, the Erie, the Frisco, and the Rio Grande. Some roads had scraped together the money for new high-power locomotives (2-8-4 Berkshire, 4-8-4 Northern, or 2-10-4 Texas types), but many trains were still handled by smaller, wheezing Ten Wheelers or Mikados or light Pacifics from the World War I era. As the Nazis stormed through Europe and the Japanese through China, it was clear that if America went to war, it would be the arsenal of democracy. This would require transportation on an unprecedented scale.

On December 7, 1941, the New York Central proudly introduced its new Empire State Express, a stainless steel streamliner on the daylight run from New York to Rochester, Buffalo, Cleveland, and Detroit. It chose a Sunday for the inaugural run, hoping it would grab headlines in the New York papers. As everyone knows, another story stole the headlines that Sunday.

The war brought major changes to the American railroads: railroads carried 234 billion ton miles of freight in depression 1932, 373 billion on the eve of the war in 1940, and 737 billion in wartime 1944. They ran 16 billion passenger miles in depression 1932, 24 billion in 1940, and 96 billion in wartime 1943. All this was done with precious few new cars or locomotives and with thousands of their skilled men and women in military service—11,000 from the Southern Pacific alone, many of them operating railroads overseas.

During the war, there were solid trains of oil tank cars for east coast refineries because Nazi subs were sinking coastwise shipping. Somewhere in the United States every six minutes, a special troop train started on its way to a port of embarkation. Every four seconds, a train of war goods or foodstuffs set off. The 201st Armored Division moved out by rail, the tanks and the trucks rolling onto flatcars, the band playing as the men marched aboard the sleepers, two to a lower berth, one to an upper.

The most emotional moments of war for many Americans involved trains. On station platforms, people said goodbyes to husbands, sons, daughters, brothers, and sisters, trying to be brave, but hugging them harder than they ever hugged them before. On station platforms, they welcomed them home—the long anxiety usually giving way to the most intense surge of joy they would feel in their lifetimes, but sometimes to silence as the coffins were unloaded from the baggage car.

Southern Pacific's timetable for May 3, 1943, noted that "in our dining cars, we are rationed much as you are at home and we can't always get the supplies in our allotment. That means only two meals will be served, breakfast until noon, and dinner, starting at 3 in the afternoon, and only one cup of coffee with dinner. When your turn comes in the diner, please remember other people are probably waiting for your seat. No need to bolt your meal, but please don't linger over it. If blackouts are in effect at the time of departure, trains will leave after a two hour delay or until the all-clear." And it added: "shhhhhh! Do not discuss what you see on passing trains"—the enemy must not know about the tanks, trucks, and troops rolling to ports.

The New Haven Railroad honored the young men going to war. They displayed a picture of the "Kid in Upper 4" as he lay awake, two of his buddies asleep in the berth below, as their train rolled toward a waiting convoy. "Next time you are on the train, remember the kid in upper 4. If you have to stand, it is so he can have a seat. If there is no berth for you, it is so he may sleep. If you have to wait in the diner, it is so he may have a meal he won't forget in the days to come. For to treat him as our most honored guest is the least we can do to pay a mighty debt of gratitude."

In tribute to its fallen, the Pennsylvania Railroad had a statue created. The Walter Hancock statue of a 37-foot bronze statue of the Archangel Michael bearing a fallen GI into heaven stands today in the 30th Street Station in Philadelphia. It is inscribed with the words "in memory of the 1,307 men and women of the Pennsylvania Railroad who gave their lives for their country, 1941–1945," and the names of all.

It was the railroads' finest hour. When it was over, there was hope for a bright future. But there was also a shadow and a shiver that, for the railroads, the best might be done and gone.

three

Dead Ends
with Pennroad
and Robert R. Young
1940–1954

During the hearings on the Transportation Act of 1940, the railroads said, essentially, "Get rid of plans, stop threatening us with compulsion, and we will consolidate." Congress wanted to encourage consolidation that was in the public interest, but it kept the Clayton Antitrust Act in place in case the railroads' proposals were not in the public interest. Whatever conflict there was between the two laws was resolved in the *McLean* case of 1944. The McLean Trucking Company claimed that the ICC had paid insufficient attention to the antitrust statutes when it allowed a number of small-scale truckers to merge into Associated Transport. The Supreme Court held that, when the advantages of consolidation outweighed the disadvantages of reduced competition, Congress intended that consolidation should take place.[1]

So now it was up to the railroads. They had a law that encouraged consolidation without compulsion. They had a Supreme Court ruling that encouraged consolidation. They said they were ready to consolidate. The result was that almost no consolidation took place in the next 15 years.

The Pennsylvania Railroad and Pennroad

No railroad used the planning experience of the 1920s to its advantage better than the Pennsylvania Railroad. It wrapped its tentacles around a number of lines, among them the Norfolk & Western, the Lehigh Valley, the Wabash, and the New Haven. This gave the PRR an effective veto over restructuring in the East unless the government was willing to move forcefully against it, and it was not. However, the PRR took two bad spills as the 1940s began, one over its Pennroad holding company and one over the New Haven.

In the heady days of the 1929 Bull Market, everything the PRR touched seemed to turn to gold. Investors eagerly bought shares in its Pennroad holding company just to get in on a good thing. The railroad took that money to make its strategic purchases of the New Haven, the Boston & Maine, the Detroit, Toledo & Ironton, and the Pittsburgh & West Virginia. The purchaser of a Pennroad share received only a trust certificate, without voting rights, to be exchanged for the actual share after ten years. It did not seem to matter; the stock was immediately oversubscribed.[2]

By May Day of 1939, the day Pennroad shares could be exchanged, a lot had changed for the PRR and for the railroad securities market. The certificates had been actively traded, and many of them were now in hands not friendly to the railroad. Most of Pennroad's holdings were purchased on the Bull Market at speculative prices; and after the market collapsed, Pennroad never paid a dividend. So many of those who gathered at the Pennroad stockholders' meeting that May Day bore a grudge—a grudge that turned to rage when old A. J. County told them Pennroad was going to write off $84 million of its holdings as a dead loss. When the pandemonium quieted and management beat back a motion by dissident stockholders for an investigation, four lawsuits were filed charging the officers of Pennroad and the Pennsylvania Railroad with mismanagement and moral turpitude. The charges were serious enough that the Pennroad officers resigned and were replaced by nominees of the dissidents. At that point, the PRR lost control of Pennroad.[3]

The railroad insisted that everyone who put their money in Pennroad knew, or should have known, that this investment was for strategic, not beneficial, purposes. Pennroad had not paid exorbitant prices, it said; its only fault was not to foresee the depression. PRR's main defense, though, was that time had expired under the statute of limitations. Judge Walsh exonerated the officers but held the company liable for $25 million in damages. On appeal, the judgment was reversed solely because of the statute of limitations. Pennroad threatened further appeal, and the railroad finally settled out of court for $15 million, still proclaiming its innocence.[4]

The Pennroad affair left scars; the stockholders lost $15 million, management barely avoided conviction for moral turpitude, and plans for expansion were set back so severely they remained dormant for nearly a decade. The affair strained relations between the railroad and its principal banker, Kuhn, Loeb & Company, for it had paid Kuhn, Loeb a fee of $4.75 million for the bright idea of establishing Pennroad in the first place.[5] The affair demonstrated that the holding company was a fragile and dangerous structure on which to build a sound railroad.

The PRR got kicked out of New England. The New Haven entered receivership in 1937, and when it reorganized in 1941, its old common stock was written off as worthless. PRR wanted to keep its leverage in New England, and its lawyers did their best to convince the federal district court in

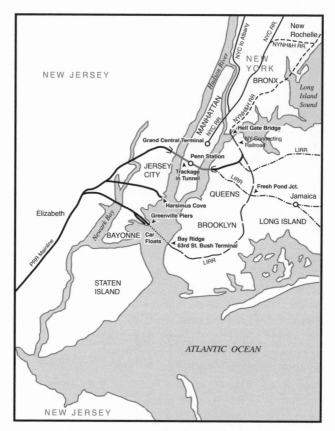

**New York Connecting and the Trans-Bay Car Float Freight Connection
between the Pennsylvania and the New Haven**

Connecticut that the old stock had value. Most New Englanders wanted
the PRR out. A committee of New England governors and the Boston Port
Authority argued that the PRR controlled New England traffic to the region's disadvantage. It forced traffic over the Hell Gate Bridge Route to the
New Haven's Bay Ridge Yard on Long Island, where it had to be transferred
by lighter to the PRR on the New Jersey shore. It was a slow and expensive
route that did not compare to the service of all-rail routes. The PRR was furious that it should be kicked out of New England when the New York Central was allowed to remain (with its Boston & Albany), but the court's decision was final and the New England adventure came to an end.[6]

The PRR managed to hang on to the Wabash, barely. It paid $77 a
share for 119,000 Wabash shares in 1927, then saw their price drop to
one-tenth of that four years later. The Wabash, never a strong earner, was
the second major railroad insolvency of the depression. For a moment in

1937, reorganization seemed around the corner, but earnings fell again and action was postponed until 1941. Even then, it was unlikely that the old common stock would have any value at all, and the PRR stood to lose its influence as well as its investment.[7]

The PRR set out to persuade other Wabash creditors that the old common stock did have value. The company presented a reorganization plan based on the premise that former bondholders would not be interested in new common stock. They would have first claim on it, but they would have only 90 days to withdraw it from escrow. After that, former stockholders could purchase stock at $12.75 a share in amounts proportional to the number of old shares they owned. If, after all this, the PRR was still not the largest stockholder, it offered to buy stock from others at $12.75 a share. For $7 million, it thought it could retain its dominant position.[8] The PRR also asked the ICC for permission to control.

The PRR did not make a strong enough case that control was a good thing. It made much of the Detroit Arrow service, a joint passenger operation between Detroit and Chicago via Fort Wayne. But the Detroit Arrow was already in place, so control was not necessary in order for it to exist, and it was such a marginal service that it was one of the first name-train

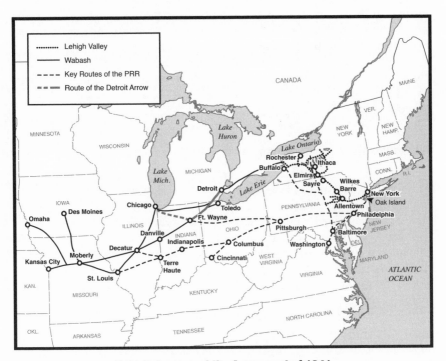

Detroit Arrow and the Agreement of 1941

runs to be discontinued (in 1949). The PRR touted a number of joint yards and joint services that control would make possible, but none of them came to pass.[9] Control was not going to mean better transportation. The two systems did not fit together, unless the purpose was to join Wabash with another piece of the PRR empire, the Lehigh Valley. This would create a Chicago–Buffalo–New York route that clearly threatened the New York Central. This was why neither Professor Ripley nor the ICC had combined the two in the plans of the 1920s.

It was rare for the two great trunk lines to confront each other directly before the ICC, but the New York Central could not abide the PRR's domination of the Wabash, which it saw as an invasion of the Central's Detroit enclave, from which it dispatched a million cars a year. The Central would defend the traffic against all comers. It was not about to see the PRR create a Wabash–Lehigh Valley trunk line that served all the same points as its own main line. The Central had fought this fight before, and it told the ICC it was ready to subpoena all the PRR's private papers into the public record, if need be, to stop it. The time had come for the superpowers to make a deal; if the PRR would put its Lehigh stock in trust, the Central would withdraw.[10] This was the Agreement of 1941. Years later, when the PRR did take control of the Lehigh, the Central claimed it had been betrayed.

In July 1941 the Wabash—which *Business Week* called "one of the biggest chips in the great consolidation poker game" of the 1920s—came under the control of the PRR. No attempt was made to integrate operations. The Wabash traffic department continued to solicit as it always had, in active competition with the PRR. There were no savings and no efficiencies. Control merely denied the Wabash to anyone else who might wish to consolidate it legitimately—anyone, that is, who did not have the approval of the PRR.

Robert Young Comes to Alleghany

Like Pennroad, the Van Sweringen brothers' empire fell on evil days. The Vans' last super–holding company, the Alleghany Corporation, had to be propped up by massive loans from the Reconstruction Finance Corporation (RFC); and when even that was not enough, creditors, notably J. P. Morgan & Company, demanded that the whole thing be auctioned off. The auction was a strange affair, conducted in a loft over 30 Vesey Street in New York. One of the brothers, Mantis James, was mortally ill, and the other, Otis Paxton, wept and said, "I would rather have paid my bills." Within a year, they were both dead.

Robert Young, a Wall Street upstart from Texas, bid at the Vesey Street auction, but the prize went to George Ball, the glass jar manufacturer from Muncie, Indiana, a friend of the brothers and a major Nickel Plate shipper. After the brothers were gone and Ball had made his money manipulating

Alleghany through his tax-free foundation, he sold it to Young, whom he remembered from the auction. Thus the man who would be the most aggressive figure in consolidation in the 1940s came to railroading. Young, a colorful individual, had only a slender grasp of transportation economics. Some called him a gadfly. Latter-day railroad executives dismissed him as an embarrassment. But he was bold enough to try to break out of the stalemate the railroads had created for themselves.

Young was a speculator. He quit the University of Virginia in his sophomore year, worked his way up from statistician to assistant treasurer for General Motors in the 1920s, hobnobbed with the DuPonts at General Motors (GM), and met Jacob Raskob, GM's chief financial officer and the manager of Gov. Al Smith's 1928 presidential campaign. In 1929 he became Raskob's personal financial advisor but left in 1931 to join his GM friend Frank Kolbe in speculating ventures. They invited some other GM friends to help them swing the Alleghany deal. The group tried to dump Young and buy control without him. The plot might have succeeded had it not been for Senator Wheeler, who was conducting the hearings on what would become the Transportation Act of 1940. Wheeler found out that men connected with GM were about to buy railroads on which GM was a major shipper, and he warned them off. Young went to another friend—the silent Allan P. Kirby, conservative heir to the Woolworth fortune—and together they gave Ball a promissory note for a controlling interest in Alleghany. Both Young and Kirby were seated on the board of Alleghany's most important subsidiary, the Chesapeake & Ohio.[12]

Young's early days at Alleghany were difficult: he could not quite keep the empire intact. As a result of reorganization, Alleghany's holdings in the Erie and the Chicago & Eastern Illinois were so drastically reduced that both stocks were sold. His greatest obstacle was the bankers. Before the Wheeler Committee, he faced New Dealers of a populist/progressive variety who were hostile to speculators. Young was the crassest speculator of them all, but he knew how to please an audience. He treated them to a stump speech on the need for competitive bidding in railroad security issues. It was not customary practice, but he said it was necessary if the power of the big investment banking houses was ever to be broken. The Wheeler Committee liked his speech, and it seemed to ease his difficulties with them. The bankers were not pleased, and they plotted to get rid of him once and for all.

When the Van Sweringens were trying to make their faltering securities more salable, they wrote a clause into the C&O's indentures that said that, if any C&O security ever fell below 150 percent of par, voting power would go to a trustee. Morgan, Stanley & Company and Guaranty Trust were the trustees, and C&O securities were selling below 150 percent of par. But when Morgan and Guaranty tried to invoke this provision to get Young off the board, he sued and got an injunction on the grounds that the bankers had engineered the unreasonable contract in the first place. Then he began a campaign against bankers and absentee control to win the support of C&O management and thousands of small-scale C&O shareholders, people who came to be known as Young's "Aunt Janes." By accident, he, an absentee controller (from his home in Newport, Rhode Island), became the champion of plain people against the banker-insider clique that had manipulated railroads since the days of the robber barons. Before this business was settled, the promissory note to George Ball came due and could not be paid. Young picked up a tip that the Securities and Exchange Commission (SEC) was about to investigate Ball for the manipulation of Alleghany stock, and so he got another injunction, eventually settled with Ball out of court, and by the narrowest of margins hung on to Alleghany.

All of this aroused the curiosity of the ICC, which launched one of its rare independent investigations. The report by Examiner Charles E. Boles in 1945 concluded that though the Alleghany roads were well managed, permission to control them had never been sought. It recommended forced divestiture. Desperate, and furious that the ICC held him to a higher standard than the bankers, Young worked out a compromise. All railroad stocks other than the C&O would go into a voting trust administered by Guaranty.[13]

In 1938, while recovering from something resembling a nervous breakdown, Young had penned a few lines:

> Until today, it seemed my path led ever upward.
> But now, I find myself upon a constant downward slope
> Which gains in pitch until I see
> Dim, distantly, a void,
> From which departed friends have turned their tired faces,
> The quest of fortune ended,
> While none but liars house the halls of state.[14]

But he held on. By 1945, all his railroads were sound and making money. The time was right.

The Alleghany Merger That Never Was

Of the four railroads that remained in Alleghany, two were financially strong and two had to be made strong. The two coal haulers, the C&O and the Wheeling & Lake Erie, were historically sound. The C&O, the core of the empire, became a prime money earner in World War I, when West Virginia coal became competitive in eastern markets. The C&O never looked back. Dependence on a single commodity was not healthy for any railroad, but profits were dependable even in the depression. The C&O was a rock upon which a mighty system could be built. The Wheeling was much smaller, but it had a lively coal traffic and was a vital link in the Alphabet Route. More than 3,000 cars a month were using the Alphabet now, five times as many as in 1929. The public knew little of the Wheeling. It never bought a new passenger car after 1904, and all passenger service ended in 1938. But it was a freight line whose star was rising.

The Nickel Plate and the Pere Marquette were the weak components, but both were on the threshold of greatness. The Nickel Plate failed to cover its fixed charges in the depression and was forced three times to postpone payment of a $10 million bond issue originally due in 1932. Its only liquid asset was the Wheeling trust certificates it held on its own account. In 1941, when the Nickel Plate could not meet that $10 million obligation and receivership seemed inevitable, the C&O bought the certificates to keep the Wheeling in Alleghany hands and to keep the Nickel Plate out of the courts.[15] Despite the Nickel Plate's financial problems, the road had excellent management; and in the late 1930s, it began a capital improvement program to upgrade its engineering standards.

On the eve of World War II, the Nickel Plate found its niche in eastern railroading. Behind the new Berkshire-type (2-8-4) steam locomotives, the Nickel Plate dispatched frequent fast freights and rolled them at a steady 60 mph over the flat lands. Shippers responded with enthusiasm. Most traffic was overhead (received from connections and delivered to connections), which meant the Nickel Plate received the full mileage rate with virtually no terminal expense. Unlike its archrival, the New York Central, it had no costly multiple tracks or passenger congestion. In short, the Nickel Plate was ideally suited to do what railroads could do best in the latter half of the twentieth century. It was destined to become rich and important, and it was never financially embarrassed again after 1941.[16]

The Pere Marquette ran a dense network of lines on Michigan's lower peninsula. It was built to carry lumber and tourists. When the timber was gone and the vacationers found other ways to get to the Michigan lakes, the future of the PM was grim. It was saved by the development of the automobile industry in Michigan, of General Motors in particular—it served GM plants in Saginaw, Flint, Lansing, and Detroit. But the PM's profits were dissipated in improvident dividends that the Vans forced it to pay their holding companies (which shows precisely why holding companies were a bad idea). In 1929 the PM did not have a single creosoted tie or a piece of rail heavier than 90 pounds per yard. It floated bond issues that year to finance improvements and then could not meet the fixed charges. It was kept afloat by short-term loans from the RFC. In 1938 it had to borrow just to meet midyear taxes. The banks lost confidence, and the Pere Marquette was saved only by a loan from the C&O.

In 1942 Young ended an old Van Sweringen practice of maintaining common officers on the PM and the C&O. PM vice president Robert Bowman was put in full command, with orders to bring his railroad up to

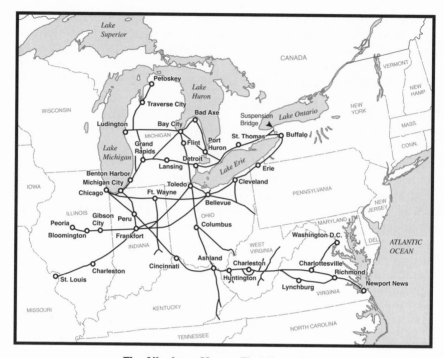

The Alleghany Merger That Never Was

C&O standards. He abandoned many of the unused branches in the cut-over timber districts and began systematic reduction of debt and a program of physical rehabilitation. The PM was being groomed for inclusion in the C&O.[17]

In 1943 a terse statement from Alleghany said that a committee had been formed "to consider ways and means to bring about full or partial unification." Nothing more was heard for the next two years. Then, shortly after V-J Day, Young called a meeting of the four railroads' presidents. Young himself did not attend, but they were told that the time was ripe and merger would proceed immediately. After a long recess, the C&O men, accompanied by an "expert" from Standard & Poor (whom no one but the C&O people seemed to know), presented a stock exchange ratio and demanded that the others accept it. This ratio, the amount of C&O stock that would be exchanged for the stock of the other companies, meant a lot of money to a lot of people. Calculations were based on the closing market prices of the previous day, which did not necessarily reflect a fair price over time.[18]

In the last week of September 1945, representatives from each of the roads conferred with Young. The Pere Marquette was granted certain modifications, but no agreement could be reached on the demands of certain

Nickel Plate preferred stockholders.[19] Between then and the Nickel Plate's October 30 board meeting, those Nickel Plate preferred holders formed a protective committee and promised to fight the terms offered before the ICC and before the courts. Under Ohio law (the Nickel Plate was chartered in that state), these minority stockholders had the power to block a merger. Nickel Plate president John Davin informed Young that the situation was hopeless. The Nickel Plate could not join, and without it there was no point to bring in the Wheeling because none of its lines connected with the C&O.[20]

This was a stunning development. A merger that had been expected since the early 1920s just collapsed, for reasons most people never understood. Some thought it was Young's fault. Had he tried to force the merger too soon? Apparently he feared that though the four roads stood at about equal financial strength in August 1945, the situation might not last long, for a postwar depression was generally anticipated. For years afterward, he would tell the story of how the C&O saved the Nickel Plate and its preferred stockholders from certain receivership in 1941. They were ungrateful and unwise, he said, and the C&O would "never again bend its knee to the Nickel Plate Road."[21]

The C&O, the Nickel Plate, and the *Schwabacher* Ruling

Some important developments came out of the wreckage. The first was a merger of the C&O and the Pere Marquette. Two months after the Alleghany merger collapsed, C&O offered to take in the PM on the same terms as before. There were complications with Michigan law, and the legislature showed signs of resistance. The lawmakers wondered if the C&O would be as interested in serving the branches of the forested interior as it was in the auto plants of Flint and Saginaw. But the governor wanted the merger, and enabling legislation was secured. Before the ICC, the C&O claimed that its own good credit would allow the PM to refinance its debt and reduce its fixed charges. The commission wondered if the PM's auto traffic might go the way of lumber and tourists, because the auto industry was already beginning to decentralize out of Michigan. The ICC also questioned the stability of Young's management on the C&O, particularly as shown by the rapid turnover of presidents.[22]

Preferred stockholders could be a problem, especially when their guaranteed dividends were in arrears and their rights were protected by state laws. Michigan law, for example, provided that when a company was going to "wind up its affairs," preferred stockholders were to be paid the full value of their shares before the common stockholders got anything. Since the owners of PM common stock were going to get C&O stock, the preferred holders said they were entitled to $100 a share par value plus $72.50 in accrued arrearage.[23] The commission said stockholders with complaints of this nature would have to seek redress in a Michigan court, and it approved the merger.

The preferred stockholders did not go to a Michigan court; they went to a federal court to have the whole merger set aside. The suit made its way to the Supreme Court, which handed down a sweeping decision. The ICC had erred, the decision said, in its implication that Michigan law superseded the Interstate Commerce Act. Under the commerce clause, federal law superseded all state laws in the matter of railroad consolidation.[24] For the C&O and for all other railroads, this *Schwabacher* decision swept away all hindrances from state law, including charter restrictions. Few Supreme Court decisions were as important as this one to the future structure of railroading.

On May 20, 1947, the Pere Marquette became the Pere Marquette District of the Chesapeake & Ohio. Unlike the Norfolk & Western, its Pocahontas twin, the C&O was now more than just a coal road. It had access to one of the nation's most industrialized areas. It also got some pocket streamliners, the Pere Marquettes, that ran between Detroit and Grand Rapids and between Grand Rapids and Chicago. They were lemon yellow and blue and very classy.

The second development from the Alleghany wreckage was the combi-

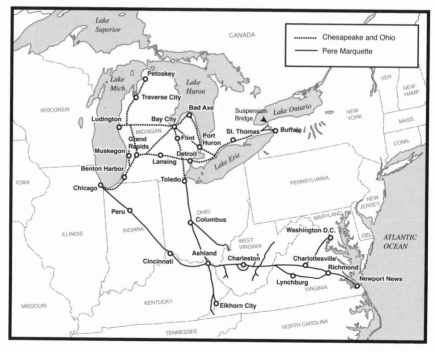

Chesapeake & Ohio–Pere Marquette

nation of the Wheeling and the Nickel Plate. On the same day that the C&O sent its offer to the Pere Marquette, it announced it would dispose of its Wheeling common stock. The C&O had kept the stock in a kind of trust for the Nickel Plate; but no favors were owed now, and the C&O wanted a lot more money than it had paid. The Nickel Plate was already embarked on another capital improvement program, but it had no choice but to come up with the $5.5 million requested. Only the troublesome preferred stockholders were opposed; if the railroad had $5.5 million for an old coal road, they said, it could pay their dividends that were in arrears.[25]

If the Nickel Plate did not get the Wheeling, the PRR probably would, for the C&O had already asked the PRR for a bid and PRR officers had gone to Cleveland to talk to Young in person.[26] If the Alphabet Route should fall to the PRR, it would be a disaster for the Nickel Plate. So the preferred holders were strong-armed, the money was paid, and the Nickel Plate was granted first permission to control the Wheeling and then permission to lease it. A full merger would require the seating of Mrs. Taplin (widow of one of the Taplin brothers who had tried to wrest control of the Wheeling in the 1920s and whose estate still had a large block of shares) and someone from Pennroad on the Nickel Plate board, and that was more than the preferred holders would stand for.

The Lackawanna–Nickel Plate: What Might Have Been

In the fall of 1947, the C&O distributed its Nickel Plate stock as a very handsome dividend to its own shareholders. The Nickel Plate was, not unexpectedly, being expelled from Alleghany. More than once the C&O hinted that, since the merger was off, it had no intention of being an investment trust for 4 percent securities. Since the Nickel Plate was cast out, its ownership was scattered to the wind, into thousands of independent portfolios, making it a truly independent railroad for the first time in its history. Then, for the next two months, the price of its common stock inched up steadily, a sign that someone was buying systematically and for a purpose. Who? The Pennsylvania? Perhaps. Nickel Plate president John Davin just said he would "stick to his knitting" and serve the stockholders to the best of his ability, whoever they turned out to be.[27]

The mystery was solved shortly before Christmas by a letter to Davin from William White of the Lackawanna. The Lackawanna had nearly 10 percent of Nickel Plate's common stock and planned to seek control with intent to merge. It was the most natural merger in the East. The two roads were each other's best connections, interchanging whole trains daily at Buffalo. Their traffic departments solicited together, and their operating departments maintained joint schedules. It was an old relationship that had seemed to grow stronger with the years. Robert Young always said that if the Alleghany consolidation had gone through, the Lackawanna

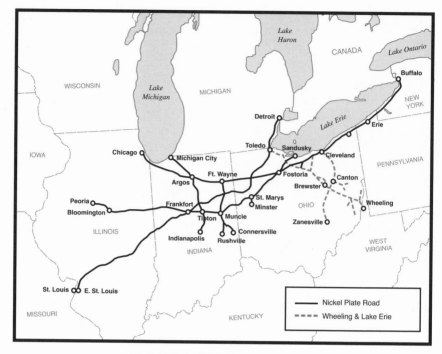

Nickel Plate–Wheeling & Lake Erie

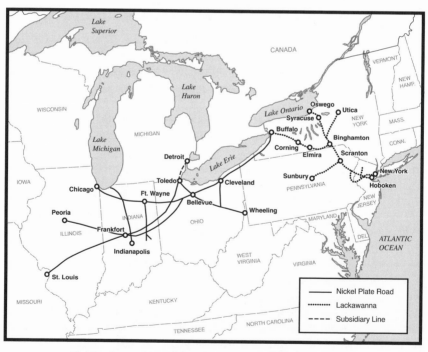

The Lackawanna–Nickel Plate Merger That Never Was

would have been the most natural addition, and Professor Ripley had paired the Lackawanna and the Nickel Plate back in 1921.

Back then, the Lackawanna was paying 7 percent dividends, among the highest in the nation. It had turned the Nickel Plate down cold, saying it would be impossible to bring the Nickel Plate up to Lackawanna standards.[28] Now things were the other way around. Anthracite was no longer black gold. The Lackawanna crossed the mountains with double tracks, hauled lots of passengers and commuters, and served congested terminals that required expensive lighterage operations in New York Harbor. Everything about the Lackawanna was a liability, and unless it could pull off this Nickel Plate deal quickly, time would work against it. The Lackawanna had wasted its years of wealth and greatness when it could have named its partner. The Nickel Plate, in contrast, was just coming into its greatness. No matter how right, how logical this combination might be, there would surely be those same preferred stockholders at Nickel Plate who would not let their securities fall to what they saw as a stuffy has-been.

William White invited Nickel Plate's officers and directors to a joint meeting with the Lackawanna board in January 1948. The Nickel Plate men were ushered into Lackawanna's sumptuous boardroom, seated politely, and told to resign. One Nickel Plate director said later, "It took me some time to recover from my surprise."[29] The meeting ended in a stalemate. By the next May, a group of Nickel Plate directors representing minority stock interests made it clear that they were opposed to any kind of affiliation with the Lackawanna. White, disastrously unheeding of these people, told them they could not dictate what the Lackawanna would do. They were human, he said, and would die, but the Lackawanna was a corporation that would survive them all, and it could wait for a propitious time.[30]

Recognizing the trouble the Lackawanna was in—though its beautiful new streamliner, the Phoebe Snow, was making a daily dash from New York to Buffalo—White retreated from his demand for common officers and said he would be content if two Lackawanna directors were seated on the Nickel Plate board. They would be forceful railroad men and would give Lackawanna effective control. No agreement could be reached on that, either, and litigation began that lasted seven years. By 1957, the Lackawanna could ill afford a forced divestiture of its dividend-paying Nickel Plate stock, which by then was its last liquid asset. It put the stock in trust rather than risk being forced to divest it.[31] The Lackawanna had lost its last chance for independent greatness.

Robert Young and the New York Central

Young did not conceal his disappointment over the collapse of the Alleghany consolidation. One day shortly afterward, Robert Bowman, his lieutenant at the Pere Marquette, came into his office and said it was a good thing the Nickel Plate had turned them down, because there was a much bigger prize waiting to be won—the New York Central. This railroad was an aristocrat of American business, and its showy passenger trains were favored by celebrities. Young loved fast silvery trains. Young loved celebrities. From that day on, he said, he could think of nothing but the New York Central.[32]

Perhaps as early as October 1, 1946, he asked Merrill Lynch to buy Central common stock for Alleghany as quietly as possible. No one at the C&O and only a few at Alleghany knew. There were rumors on Wall Street, one report naming the financial backers as Young's celebrity friends the Duke and Duchess of Windsor.[33] Central common was low—$16 in the fall of 1946, down from $30 in 1945. Even at the height of Alleghany's buying in the fall of 1946, it rose only to $18.

Young and Bowman asked for seats on the Central's board, a body made up mostly of the same bankers that Young had defeated in the fight for Alleghany back in 1938. They detested Robert Young and everything he stood for, but they offered the seats as long as the ICC would allow it. They had read the Boles Report and knew what the ICC thought of Young. And when Young went to the ICC to ask for permission, who else but C. E. Boles was appointed to conduct the hearings?[34]

Young's ambitions, and his tactics for realizing them, became more bizarre with the passing months. He tried to buy the Pullman sleeping-car service and was frustrated by a consortium of railroads. He carried that campaign to the public with the same method he had used to win the support of small-scale C&O stockholders back in the 1930s. He sponsored an advertisement pointing out that hogs could travel across the country without changing trains but humans could not.[35] It was a nonissue. Nobody wanted to sit in a roomette for four days without a walk in the station or a meal in a restaurant. Not that many people even traveled from New York to Los Angeles each day: they went from countless intermediate points to countless other intermediate points. To get from where they were to where they were going, they had to pass through gateways, just as airline passengers passed through hubs in a later day. A coast-to-coast sleeper was an empty gesture. But it was intended to catch the public imagination, and it did, and it made Young a celebrity.

Some even thought he should run for president of the United States. Then he went off to Georgia to confer with Governor Arnall about that state's litigation against the eastern railroads over rate fixing. He said he was trying to negotiate a settlement for all; other railroads said it was to make a deal for the C&O.[36] They pushed their rate-fixing bill, the Reed-Bulwinkle Act, through Congress, and Young denounced them for it and yanked the C&O and the Nickel Plate out of the Association of American Railroads. At the time of the New York Central affair, the C&O was still outside the AAR, heading up its own Federation for Railway Progress and hoping others would join.

Young became preoccupied with passenger trains. He ordered a new train for the C&O, the Chessie, to be built by the Budd Company in shimmering stainless steel, an eye-popping dream train for the Washington-Cincinnati run, with movie theaters, dancing lounges, scenic domes, movies, children's playrooms, and aquariums. He established a central reservations bureau, a no-tipping policy, and credit cards, each with appropriate fanfare, and his credit cards were introduced long before credit cards were common anywhere.

Then he pushed his board into ordering an astounding 200 more streamlined cars from Pullman-Standard—sleepers, coaches, diners, lounges. The C&O, which served a region with very limited passenger potential, would never conceivably need a fleet of cars like that. It was not only a terrible business decision but also indicated a slender grasp on reality. His board sensed this and forced him to scale back the order.

After the hog ads he was a folk hero with a name that was recognized nationally. He now fancied himself a David against the Goliath of the "damnbankers," and he liked to taunt them in public. "How can slave railroads serve the public?" he asked in one of his more controversial advertisements, which portrayed a dull-eyed steam locomotive held on a leash held by a fat, pompous banker.[37] Yet within his own Alleghany, there were rumors of monumental confrontations between Young and other C&O directors over the Chessie, over the mediocre performance of C&O's securities, over the cheap publicity about "goddamn bankers," and over foulmouthed temper tantrums by Allan Kirby. Company lawyers were beside themselves over the ads, which were insulting and maybe even libelous.[38] Such was the world of Robert Young when he arrived in Washington in September 1947 to testify before the ICC on why he should sit on the board of the New York Central.

His outward opposition before the commission came from Chrysler, Packard Motors, and the Virginian Railway. One sensed that behind them was the "establishment." Chrysler and Packard did not want the Central under the domination of a railroad (the Pere Marquette) that was known as a General Motors road. The PM had recently sponsored a rate schedule for new automobiles that was highly favorable to GM. Young said he was not familiar with such minor details as freight rates on automobiles.[39] The Virginian feared that it would lose its valuable role as the Central's connection to the coalfields. Young said the Virginian was merely a tool of Morgan and other "damnbankers." The Central was not present, although some thought the Virginian Railway, in its ruthless cross-examination, was speaking on the Central's behalf.[40]

Young only wanted a seat on the Central board, yet his plans for modeling the Central in his own image were certainly ambitious. How could

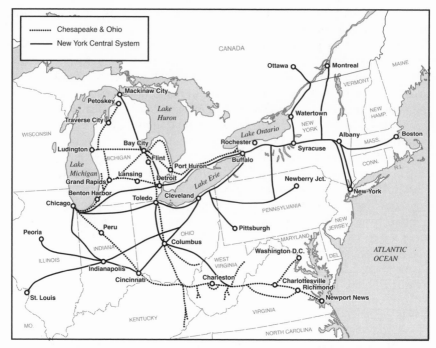

Chesapeake & Ohio–New York Central Combination That Never Was

he do all this if he were only a director? Historically, his opponents pointed out, interlocking directorates only reduced competition and never led to innovative programs. Robert Bowman tried to explain: forceful directors, experienced in railroad affairs, would have a great deal of influence, especially beside the Central's present directors, who were mostly bankers and knew little about the technicalities of railroad operations.

To support this, renowned professors of transportation Julius Grodinsky and William Leonard, both authors of important books on railroad consolidation, were brought in to testify on the theoretical desirability of interlocking directorates as a first step toward merger. Grodinsky's testimony was shredded by a withering cross-examination. After pontificating on how we must "strive to achieve a golden mean between competition and cost control," he was exposed as having only the most rudimentary knowledge of commodity rates and movements in the Northeast and no concept whatever of how interlocking directorates might affect them. He barely avoided trick questions meant to trap him, but his credibility as an "expert witness" was demolished.[41] Professor Leonard did somewhat better, but it was an embarrassing reminder that academics' generalizations did not go far in a high-stakes court fight.

The star witness was Robert Young himself. What he delivered was not testimony but a performance. About bankers, he said:

> And what did they do about [the depression]? Come down here and oppose everything Mr. Roosevelt tried to do to take care of their employees, and ended up paying ten times more through the tax route than if they had spent it in a constructive way rehabilitating the rundown railroad system. I say it would have been a lot more constructive if the unemployed had been reducing curves and building sleeping cars rather than chasing starlings around the sidewalks of Washington. The railroads couldn't spend because the bankers loaded them down with debt, so they could sell and resell their bonds and make their five points, and it's going to happen again if people like Chrysler come down here and oppose the railroads making a 2 percent return on their investment.[42]

About Chrysler and Packard:

> As a matter of fact, it appears that a lot of steel can go to Chrysler and Packard so they can make a 30 percent or 40 percent return and the railroad car builders who need steel and stuff to relieve the suffering abroad, they cannot get steel, but it's going to Mr. Chrysler and Mr. Packard. It reminds me of Doris Duke intervening in a wage proceeding to see that her footman doesn't get a raise.[43]

About railway progress:

> Yes, New York Central uses diesels and the C&O uses steam on passenger trains, but we are not reactionary as some people say, because we are experimenting with steam turbines . . . and I say further that railroads are using up oil at a rapid rate and should not use diesels, and some government agency ought to investigate and see that they go back to coal.[44]

On the New York Central:

> The first thing is to improve the passenger service. Coal you just haul one way, but people, if you treat them well, you can haul them back and forth two or three times a month. I look at the Central with envy, and just dream of what I could do if I had their kind of opportunities.
>
> Let's talk about sleeping cars . . . I came down here and laid $75 million on a silver platter and said I will put it in this dead duck and I will replace every damn one of them, and we will get some people seeing this great country of ours instead of locking them up and treating them so miserably on trains they hope the planes and the highways do take their business away from them. But the railroads turned me down. They said I was a sucker and they wouldn't take my sucker money.[45]

On why he should go on the Central board:

> If one man can never serve on the boards of directors of two railroads, you will never get any railroad consolidation. It is something that goes to the key of the national defense. It goes to the key of the national economy, and it's at the root of the present spiral of inflation and living costs.

> Q [by the examiner]: Your going on the board of the Central is the key to all these problems?
> A: I think the railroad industry is the key to the national defense and if it goes along at this 2 percent starvation diet that Mr. Chrysler and others want it to operate on, I say that at the first sign of a depression in this country, tens of thousands, hundreds of thousands of men are going to be laid off by the railroads out of sheer necessity.
> Q: And the cure for all that is Robert Young on the board of the New York Central?
> A: It will go a damn long way in the direction of curing it . . . for a little fellow.[46]

At the very end of the hearing, the Virginian Railway put on its star witnesses, the officers of the Central. Although they were under subpoena, they talked freely of their opposition to Young and the C&O, knowing, they said, that such talk would probably cost them their jobs if Young won. The Central did have problems, and they were trying to solve them. Flashy streamliners were not the answer. Their testimony was devastating to Young's cause.[47] Examiner Boles was quick to recommend against seating Young. The official reason was the effect on competition; the real reason was a lack of confidence in Young. "The applicants have given only the most general consideration to the problems with which they would be confronted." And that was that.[48]

Young thought the deck was stacked, and he was furious. "It's difficult for us to take the Commission's two-faced justice," he said. "Harry Hagerty of the Metropolitan Life Insurance Company was quietly granted the right, without a hearing, to sit on the boards of the New Haven and the Erie, at the very time we were required to appear before the Commission."[49] Then he launched a series of peculiar advertisements headlined "Memo to the New York Central." There were five of them altogether, and they challenged the Central to imitate the C&O's progressive passenger train innovations.[50] *Trains,* in an imitation of the ads, urged Young to "get off the branchline and onto the mainline" and worry about the Central's real problems, such as the low rate of return and intermodal freight competition.[51]

On May 10, 1948, the full commission said no to Robert Young. After that, all was quiet. There were rumors that Young was trying to work out a three-way deal to include the Virginian, but little came of it. Then there was a rumor that Alleghany purchases of the Seaboard and the Rock Island anticipated a Young-controlled transcontinental, but nothing came of that, either. Alleghany continued to buy Central common, until by 1950 it had doubled its holdings since the end of the hearing. In 1951 there was a wild rumor that Young was about to resign from the C&O and seek control of the Central independently. It was denied, and all was silent, except at the Central; they were preparing for the onslaught.[52]

The New York Central Proxy Fight

The announcement came on January 19, 1954. Young was ready to give up the C&O and wage a proxy fight for the New York Central. He used all the persuasive techniques that he had mastered in the fights against the bankers in the 1930s to appeal to thousands of "Aunt Jane" small-scale stockholders and the public. He promised to end banker domination and put both an employee (retired engineer William E. Landers) and a woman (*Readers' Digest* copublisher Lila Belle Acheson Wallace) on the Central's new board. There was national publicity—lots of it—including a debate between Young and Central president William White on *Meet the Press*.

White was a worthy adversary. He liked streamliners, too. Before he went to the Central, he pushed his board on the Lackawanna to buy the Phoebe Snow. But he had little respect for Young's preoccupation with the flashy side of railroading. "If we should get licked in this fight," he said, "I want to see Mr. Young up there on the 32nd floor [of the New York Central Building] meeting our day-to-day problems. I'd just like to see him sit down, by God, and stick it out for five years."[53]

The crux of the case was the 800,000 Central shares owned by the C&O in trust at the Chase National Bank. The Chase would almost surely vote them against Young. So Young got his millionaire friends, Texas oilmen Sid Richardson and Clint Murchison, to buy them. The Central tried legal maneuvers to block this but failed. On May 26, 1954, both Young and White rode the Stockholders' Special to Albany to the annual meeting. They rode in different cars and did not speak to each other. They solicited proxies all the way. It took two breathless weeks to count the votes; Young won—by 1,026,000 shares—just a little more than the Murchison-Richardson block of shares.[54]

The change at the Central was complete. Not one of the Vanderbilts would serve on the Young slate, so all connection with the company's founding family was severed. Young chose Alfred Perlman of the Denver & Rio Grande Western Railroad to be his president and chief operating officer. Perlman had taken a second-rate mountain railroad and turned it into a first-class competitor of the Union Pacific. Hopefully, the same magic would work at the Central. Perlman had a no-nonsense temperament. He did not share Young's fascination with fancy passenger trains or hobnobbing with celebrities. There was public speculation on how they would get along.

Perlman and his wife arrived in New York by train the night the final proxy count was announced. At Grand Central, with flashbulbs popping, he pledged to serve Young and the Central. The next day, Young, Perlman, Mrs. Wallace, and others made a triumphal march from Alleghany headquarters in the Woolworth Building to the New York Central Building on Park Avenue. So began the Young era on the road of the Vanderbilts.

According to Young's biographer, Joseph Borkin, White and his directors were in possession of a terrifying fact—the Central was bankrupt. Perlman toured the line and was heartsick. The road was even more passenger-oriented than he had imagined. The property was littered with stations that were marble echo chambers, that cost boodles in heating bills, upkeep, and taxes before a passenger ever got on a train. The four-track main line was a millstone. The passenger tracks were signaled for 80 mph, useless for freight, and the freight tracks were signaled for 30 mph, useless for a service that needed to compete. West of Buffalo, where the New York Central and the Nickel Plate raced neck and neck right beside each other, the short, fast Nickel Plate freights darted past the Perlman inspection train in a dazzling display of technological superiority. To add to the humiliation, the Nickel Plate was doing it with steam locomotives.

Young and Perlman were lucky for a while; 1955 and 1956 were good years. Net income was up. Perlman found enough cash to install centralized traffic control on the main line between Buffalo and Cleveland, the first real application of CTC in multiple-track, high-speed, high-density territory. The installation began operation on January 16, 1957. Freights could now operate at 60 mph. It was a great success. A few weeks later, Perlman opened a laboratory in Cleveland to test everything on the railroad, from signal relays to track bolts. In March 1957, the first of the electronic freight classification yards opened, Frontier Yard in Buffalo, that would vastly speed up and simplify the regrouping of incoming cars into outgoing trains. It cost over $10 million but was expected to save $4 million annually.

Young found enough cash to play with his dream trains, no longer the rolling cruise ships like the Chessie but low-slung articulated models, christened the Ohio Xplorer and the Great Lakes Aerotrain. They had the riding quality of the Cyclone at Coney Island and caused some patrons to vomit. Both were immediate and dismal failures. The "travel-tailored" timetable in the fall of 1956, the penultimate effort to achieve a super passenger service, resulted in a $52 million out-of-pocket loss. After that, the fight seemed to go out of Young. Stock that soared to $49 a share in the heady days after the Young victory, now sank to $13. With the onset of recession in the fall of 1957, everything went sour, and this apparently sparked the first merger talks with the PRR. The first quarter dividend in 1958 was omitted.

After breakfast on the morning of January 26, 1958, at his home in Palm Beach, Robert Young shot himself to death. His body was taken by train to Newport, where he was buried beside his daughter. He had sold all of his Central holdings in the weeks before. His friends, who had bought stock to help in the proxy fight, had taken terrible losses. Facing them must have been unbearable, although Allan Kirby remained steadfastly loyal.

There were stories of a letter that lay before him on his desk, from a disillusioned "Aunt Jane" stockholder who had bought shares on Young's promise of better things and had lost everything. Borkin and others discount this as a cause of his death. It was not certain he even read it. It was quite obviously in the same hand as other crank mail he had received. The Central and Alleghany denied that the state of their fortunes had anything to do with his death, and the only man who could verify this was silent. Everyone recalled those disturbing lines of poetry he had penned just as his career was beginning and speculated that, beneath the optimistic exterior, there lay a will for self-destruction: "I see dim, distantly, a void, from which departed friends have turned their tired faces."

At Elkhart, Indiana, a new electronic classification yard was named in Young's honor, one of the few reminders on the latter-day Central of his colorful association with it. Perlman, in full command, immediately began the transformation of the New York Central from a four-track passenger line into a double-track, high-capacity, high-speed freight line. This was far removed from Robert Young's dreams of streamliners, celebrities, fame, and the New York Central he had coveted with the anticipation of a little boy who dreams of a Lionel train at Christmas time.

four

Troubles

1945–1964

The Golden Glow Years, 1945–1955

Instead of a postwar depression, there was a postwar boom. Once postwar inflation ran its course, this boom was probably the soundest and happiest the country ever had, because real per capita income advanced at a solid 2.25 percent a year. One wage earner could support a family in a middle-class style, and expectations were rising. The railroads shared in the boom. Their share of the transportation pie was shrinking, but the pie was getting so much bigger that railroads were busier than ever except for the war years. Ton miles, for example, were 597 billion in 1950, down from a wartime high of 735 billion in 1943 but far above the 379 billion of prewar 1940. The rate of return on investment for the industry as a whole stayed around 4.25 percent through 1955, down from the wartime peak of 5.78 percent in 1943 but far above 1940's 2.95 percent. All but one of the major roads forced into receivership in the depression were able to reorganize. For the exception, the Missouri Pacific, it was not for lack of net income.

Basking in the glow of their World War II performance, railroads set out to showcase the modern, vital role they expected to play in the postwar era. Many of them made films to show off how modern they were, and a number of those survived to be put on video as snapshots of a golden but fleeting moment. Many roads were coming up on their centennials and proudly invited the public to their celebrations. With its *Wheels-a-Rollin'* pageant, produced by Edward Hungerford, the Chicago Railroad Fair drew two and half million spectators in the summers of 1948 and 1949 and echoed self-confidence.

Railroad traffic in the golden glow years was much as it had been for a century. There were still lots of little boxcars from lots of little shippers go-

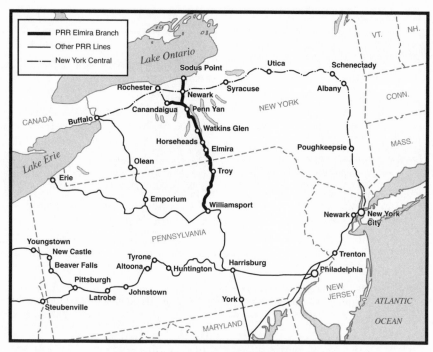

Pennsylvania Railroad's Elmira Branch

ing to lots of little places. Take the Elmira Branch of the Pennsylvania Railroad, for example. On a map of the mighty PRR system, it did not look like much. It was the line that branched off the Buffalo route at Williamsport, Pennsylvania, and headed straight north to Elmira, New York, then to Watkins Glen and Penn Yan, finally ending on the shores of Lake Ontario at Sodus Point, New York. With its single track, it was far from the Pennsy's main line.

But the Elmira Branch was a busy railroad.[1] Coal of all sorts—some anthracite, mostly bituminous—went to a number of customers, including a joint coal movement with the New York Central in which locomotives were pooled. A Niagara Mohawk power plant at Oswego, New York, was the biggest single customer. The ice business was gone. Electric refrigeration brought that to an end in the 1930s. The milk business was on its way out, although there were some active creameries through the mid-1950s, particularly a big Borden facility at Troy, Pennsylvania, that produced about 150,000 pounds of milk products a day. There was still a lot of agricultural movement by rail, some of it fresh vegetables (beets, onions, potatoes, and cabbages), some of it fresh fruits (cherries, grapes, peaches, and apples); and there were roses from the Jackson & Perkins Greenhouses in Newark, New York. These were called the cabbage trains.

Processed foods were shipped from several canneries and sauerkraut plants, from the Block & Guggenheim pickle factory at Seneca Castle, New York, and a major Bird's Eye frozen vegetable and frozen turkey plant at Marion, New York. Among the industrial shippers were Preston Brothers and Swayze Folding Box at Canton, Pennsylvania; Troy Engine, F. P. Case, and Cummings Lumber at Troy, Pennsylvania; American LaFrance (fire engine equipment), Thatcher Glass, Westinghouse, General Electric, Bendix, and American Bridge at Elmira and Horseheads, New York; Shepard Niles Crane & Hoist at Montour Falls, New York; and International Salt and Sinclair Refining at Watkins Glen, New York. About 20 cars of raw material a day for Corning Glass were turned over to the Erie or the Lackawanna at Elmira. Traffic passed on and off the branch from the PRR at Williamsport, of course, and from five other railroads through 12 different junction points. The Elmira branch even fed traffic to other railroads' branches.

The Elmira branch was a last bastion for steam. The last steamer, a Class II 2-10-0 Decapod of behemoth proportions, was dispatched south from Elmira on September 13, 1957. Four passenger trains each way in 1930 became two in 1940, then one in 1950, a night train with a through sleeper from Washington to Rochester (picked up by the New York Central at Canandaigua, New York, for the run into Rochester). That was discontinued on January 2, 1956.

It was coincidence, perhaps, but the demise of the whole operation was not far behind the passing of the passenger train and the passing of steam. Across the next decade, plants closed or shifted their business to trucks or converted from coal to oil; and shipper by shipper, the traffic fell away. When Hurricane Agnes destroyed much of the line in 1972, there was no reason to rebuild it. Only a few short segments remained in service in 1999.

In a similar vein but based on a more agricultural setting, historian Thomas J. Gaffney tells about the railroads of Michigan's bucolic Thumb, for which sugar beets and dry beans earned a living. They were a Grand Trunk Western branch to Caseville called the Polly-Ann and a rambling, arch-shaped branch of the old Pere Marquette through Bad Axe. Until the 1940s these lines even carried fresh Lake Huron whitefish for the tables of fine restaurants as far away as New York. The Thumb was surrounded by a ring of fire, the big auto plants at Saginaw, Flint, and Detroit, where double-track railroads hauled important freight to important destinations. Thumb branches might as well have been on the other side of the moon. They picked up a carload of beets at this station, a carload at that, and hauled them a few miles down the line to the processing plant, then hauled some fertilizer and farm implements back up the line. After the station agent filled out the paperwork in multiple carbon copies, he went outside and helped load up the beets himself. These railroads were the economic veins and arteries even to very local economies, to farmers and local elevators.[2] There were Polly-Anns and Elmira Branches all over the

United States, metaphors for that last twilight of the railroad Americans had known since the nineteenth century.

The Golden Glow was buoyed by the advent of the diesel locomotive. Steam hauled 78 percent of freight in 1946, 31 percent in 1951, and less than 0.5 percent in 1959. Savings from the diesel were real and immediate. A big saving was reduced shop time; this allowed locomotives to spend more time on the road earning money, and fewer locomotives could do a bigger job. But these one-time savings papered over fundamental problems.

As many a steam lover can wistfully point out, diesels won the war but did not win all the battles. The now famous New York Central tests of 1946 pitted diesels against the most technologically advanced steam power, namely the Central's new 4-8-4 Niagaras. When all costs were factored— initial investment, labor, maintenance, fuel consumption, and pulling power (earning capacity)—the difference between steam and diesel was not that great. But most roads were buying diesels to replace steam engines built before the depression, sometimes long before, that were technologically obsolete. Diesels had a higher initial cost and an economic life of only about 15 years, but steam engines required more labor, exponentially more labor, to keep them repaired and running. Labor was the cost factor that would rise the most in the years to come. In other words, if new steam and new diesels under ideal main-line conditions were neck-and-neck in 1946, they were not going to be neck-and-neck for long.[3]

Steam power that could hope to compete with diesels was big steam power, 2-8-4 Berkshires and 4-8-4 Northerns (the Niagaras on the New York Central), or the 4-6-6-4 Challengers and 4-8-8-4 Big Boys on the Union Pacific. These machines were too heavy for the light rail and light bridges of weaker roads and branches. If the diesel had not come along when it did, a number of routes would have been phased out right then, including whole railroads, and the entire system might have been stronger for it. The diesel was going to give marginal routes the chance to wheeze along for another generation, until heavier diesels and jumbo freight cars spelled an end for routes with "dirt" ballast, light rail, and light structures.

Even as the diesel reprieved marginal routes, other new railroad technology did not auger well for duplicate lines and light branches. Centralized traffic control, which involved controlling all signals and switches on a given line from a central control panel, speeded service and vastly increased the productivity of a piece of track. Al Perlman's installation of it on the New York Central between Buffalo and Cleveland in 1957, the first in high-speed, high-density, multitrack territory, showed conclusively that it was possible to run more trains on two tracks, faster and more efficiently, than were previously carried on four. That was wonderful. But CTC was too expensive to install on multiple parallel railroads connecting the same points. If CTC was the railroads' future (and it was), traffic would have to be consolidated on fewer routes.

Who Shot the Passenger Train?

On a July day in 1953, the New England States, the New York Central's crack train from Chicago to Boston and a proud entry in its Great Steel Fleet, awaited its 2:30 departure from LaSalle Street Station. Its augmented consist at the peak of the summer travel season was sold out—280 people in five coaches and 216 in ten sleepers, two of them with lounges; there were also two diners. It was visually striking in shimmering stainless steel. The trip was exciting: once past the South Side stop at 63rd Street and Englewood, the train moved fast, a no-nonsense fast, past farms and factories and towns, not stopping in Cleveland at all, and barely pausing at Buffalo a little past midnight.

This was common carrier travel, meaning it was crowded to the point where civility required a degree of effort. It was not the *Ile de France* on a luxury cruise with promenade decks and grand salons. It was quite utilitarian by comparison. The high point was dinner in the diner, where there were five sittings of an hour each starting at five o'clock. Place settings were hotel-grade crockery. Utensils were heavy, hotel-grade silverplate. Tablecloths were sturdy, launderable starched cotton. The food was satisfying but not gourmet. The meal was memorable because the passing American scene outside the window was endlessly entertaining, and there was always the sense of relentless speed, high speed, hurtling speed. The experience was more than memorable; it was a thrill. Those who remember it ache for it. Those who missed it can not imagine how speeding steel-on-steel, the panorama of industry and agriculture, the splendid engineering of the four-lane steel highway, the hospitality and professionalism of waiters and stewards, the flash of signal lights out the window, and the rush of mighty trains in the opposite direction all permanently imprinted the souls of those who experienced it. No plodding "dinner train" nor even Amtrak can re-create it.

But was the New England States making money? On peak-season days like that one, the answer was a guarded yes, depending on what fixed costs were charged to it. The train had a chance since it was full and most of its passengers got on in Chicago and went all the way—a few got off in Springfield, a few in Worcester, a few in Framingham, but most went through to Boston, either to the Back Bay Station or to the South Station downtown. On most trains, a full load all the way was rare. Add in the locals and "accommodation" runs, and the railroads were losing a lot of money. Much of the revenue was penny-ante—$4.52 for a round trip between Hornell and Olean, New York, on the Erie for my grandmother in 1954, or $1.66 for a 40-quart can of sour cream "for churning only" from Addison, New York, to the Mayfair Creamery in Buffalo on the Erie Lackawanna (EL) on October 15, 1962. The paperwork for $1.66 in revenue was dutifully filled out with four carbons. Included in passenger revenue was all the mail, express, newspapers, and fresh milk carried in baggage cars at the front of the train—called "head-end" business.

The service was labor-intensive, and the cost of labor was going up. It required too many expensive facilities. It was too seasonal. It lost money because trains could not deliver enough paying cargo fast enough per unit of labor and per unit of capital investment at a price people would pay. The economic principles were no different than for freight, except that for freight the equations worked out more favorably. Trains could move a lot of people when they were packed in like sardines—as on the New York subway or on commuter trains—hence the term *mass transit*. Even those services lost money, although they were probably more cost-effective than building highways. For long-distance travel, people were willing to be squeezed like sardines for a short while on an airplane, but not for a 72-hour transcontinental haul by train.

In 1953 the operating ratio for all railroads in freight service was 69.13, meaning that costs absorbed 69 percent of revenue. In passenger service the operating ratio was 138.16, meaning that for every dollar the railroad earned it spent $1.38. There were only two exceptions. One was the Long Island Railroad, a commuter line that packed people like cattle, day in and day out; it had a passenger ratio of 89 in 1959. The other was the New Haven Railroad, which did little better than break even (a 1959 ratio of 98.3); again, it did this well because of the sheer volume of traffic every day. A ratio of 98.3 left nothing for capital investment, so it cannot be regarded as profitable.

The big, bad bottom line was this: in an industry where overall earnings were not large, passenger deficits consumed an enormous proportion of those earnings—39 percent in 1953, 43 percent in 1954. For the New York Central alone, the loss for the entire passenger service was $52 million in 1956. This left a net railway operating income of $24 million, which then had to cover fixed charges (interest on borrowed money). This was a company, and an industry, where earnings were so low that borrowing for fixed plant was nearly impossible. Money could be borrowed for rolling stock—locomotives and cars—because they could be sold to another railroad if the original borrower was not able to pay. But fixed plant—track, structures, signals, and yards—represented sunken investment, and the state of railroad earnings made this too risky for most banks. The maintenance and improvement of the physical plant therefore had to come out of earnings. If passenger deficits ate up most of these earnings, the situation was more than serious. It was a death warrant. If the railroad could not keep its physical plant in state-of-the-art condition, it would die.

After World War II, with visions of packed wartime trains dancing in their heads, railroads hoped they would play a vital role in postwar passenger travel. That was when they ordered beautiful streamliners like the

New England States. When the 1950s began, there were already signs of trouble, but there was still hope, and still a great sense of pride that this was important work the railroads must do. When the 1950s were over, the question was how quickly and how gracefully could railroads get out of the business. Trains might continue to operate as long as the postwar equipment was still usable, but before 1960 replacing it was out of the question.

The conventional wisdom on what went wrong was the assertion that the public preferred the convenience of the automobile and the speed of the airplane. This is a part of the story, but it is too convenient to be the whole story. As late as the eve of Pearl Harbor, in the still photographs and snippets of film that survive, we can see platforms jammed with eager and curious people who have chosen to spend what was probably their only free time that week to inspect the new Zephyr, Rocket, Hiawatha, or City streamliners as they went on inspection tours. Carpet had to be replaced three times in the original Zephyr before it even went into service because of the hundreds of thousands of feet that tromped through it. On July 8, 1938, for example, far from the Pennsylvania's main line, 8,000 people in Elmira, New York, came out to see a new Pennsy K-4 locomotive streamlined by industrial designer Raymond Loewy. People could hardly wait to see what the railroads of the future would be like; trains were still a vital part of their lives and dreams.

What appeared to be a purely market choice in favor of air and auto transportation was helped along immensely by the huge developmental and capital investment costs that were covered by the government to make these modes economic and attractive: on June 29, 1956, Eisenhower signed the Federal-Aid Highway Act, creating the National System of Interstate and Defense Highways, commonly known as the interstates. Ike was in the hospital when he signed it and did not want cameras around. Uprisings in Poland upstaged it anyway. Probably no one had an inkling of how profoundly this would forever alter transportation, energy consumption, land use, urban development, commercial development, and living styles.

General Lucius Clay, hero of the Berlin Airlift, chaired the committee that drafted the plan. Presenting the project as a military requirement quieted criticism of the vast expense. The roads would be engineered for military convoys and the evacuation of cities in a national emergency. They would be paid for through a Highway Trust Fund, which earmarked a new gasoline tax specifically for highway construction, thus creating an amazing endowment that no kind of rail service could hope to match. The night Ike signed the law, it was not the military that celebrated but the contractors, the oil companies, the auto makers, the tire makers, the truckers, and all their unions. It was the biggest construction project in history. Really big economic breakthroughs require a public-private cooperation, and this was a big one.

On the air side, at the beginning of the war the military piggybacked on civilian air design. The civilian DC-3 became the military C-47 transport and was made by the thousands. But the great planes of civil aviation after the war were largely military designs. The Lockheed Super Constellation was the old C-69 transport. The Boeing Stratocruiser was cobbled from the B-29 bomber and the C-97 cargo-tanker. The bomb bay area was converted to a cocktail lounge reached from the main cabin by a spiral staircase, one of the glamorous thrills of postwar air travel. Development of the Boeing 707 jetliner began in 1954 when the Air Force underwrote developmental costs by agreeing to buy the first production run as KC-135 Stratotankers. On October 16, 1955, a test run of a prototype 707 flew from Seattle to Washington, D.C., in three hours and 58 minutes. Commercial service began in October 1957, by Pan American on the North Atlantic run.

Cities built airports. The three major airports of the New York metropolitan area occupied 13.5 square miles of land, acquired by public bodies and tax free. The tab for air traffic control was picked up by the federal government. Railroads installed their own signals at private expense, and they paid taxes on their railroad stations. It was no wonder that air travel became as attractive as it did as soon as it did.

In days gone by, the railroad had moved the masses, with 70 to 85 people in a coach. Sleepers were upper and lower berths, heavy green curtains offering the only privacy. Travelers had to wriggle in and out of their clothes while lying on their berth. It was not comfortable, but it was often remembered fondly as a shared experience. After the war, since planes and buses had to pack people in pretty tight, railroads decided their draw would be luxury and privacy. So they bought sleeping cars with all private rooms, lounges and diners, and most intriguing of all, vista-domes. These were Plexiglas bubbles above the cars for viewing the scenery and meeting other travelers. Most long-distance trains became absolutely delightful, rolling cruise ships, on which, to borrow a phrase from the Cunard Steamship Company, getting there was meant to be half the fun. These trains did draw the crowds for a while, but at a cost.

One could not roll restaurants and cocktail lounges and private bedrooms, with extra-wide berths and snowy sheets, up and down the Rocky Mountains for free. Private-room sleepers carried 22 to 24 paying customers. Some luxury coaches carried a mere 46. These cars were expensive pieces of equipment. It took a lot of fuel to roll them around the countryside. This was not cost effective, not at common carrier fares.[4]

In hindsight the railroads might have been wiser to concentrate on medium-distance and intermediate-stop traffic, which the airlines could not do well, perhaps with youth-oriented budget bunk sleepers like the European couchettes and family-style table d'hote diners, finger-lickin' but not fancy. Of course, when the postwar streamliners were conceived in all their five-star glory, no one foresaw how efficiently the interstates and the jumbo jets would move the masses. Once the money was sunk into domes and lounges and private-room sleepers, the railroads were stuck with them. But the fact was that these land cruises could not move enough people fast enough to make money.

No train captured the postwar imagination of luxury travel as much as the California Zephyr. Inaugurated in 1949 between Chicago and San Francisco on the Burlington, Rio Grande, and Western Pacific Railroads, it had a diner serving full-course meals, a cocktail lounge, an observation lounge, a coffee shop, and five Plexiglass domes to view the gorgeous mountain scenery. It was scheduled to cross both the Rockies and the Sierras in daylight. There were few travel experiences in the world to compare with descending the Feather River Canyon on the westbound California Zephyr or breaking through the Front Range going east, with Denver still 30 miles away but its lights twinkling on the Great Plains below.

But the train could accommodate only 250 passengers, 150 in coach, 100 in sleepers. When it began operation in 1949, a DC-3 carried only 21 passengers and made about four round trips to the train's one. A DC-6 of the mid-1950s could accommodate 86 and make six round trips. The Boeing 707 could accommodate 176 and make eight round-trips. Then came the jumbo jets. The Zephyr required 77 people—engineers, conductors, stewardesses, porters, bartenders, waiters, cooks—to get it across the country. They earned an average of $1.92 an hour in 1950. By 1965, that was $3.52 an hour. The 707 required a crew of seven.

In metropolitan areas, on commuter trains with the passengers packed like sardines, the railroad moved the masses. But on the long hauls, the economics of jet aircraft was formidable. The California Zephyr had an average occupancy rate of nearly 80 percent (that would make any airline envious) right up to its last trip on March 22, 1970. People liked it. But even before the 1950s were over, the productivity equation was clear.

The railroad unions refused to contemplate the productivity equation. Crews were paid on a mileage basis rather than by the hour, and they received a full day's pay for every 100 miles (150 miles for some of the onboard crew). It was 366 miles between Jacksonville and Miami, and the Florida East Coast had to pay three crews a full day's wage to forward a train between them. An engineer on the Pennsylvania could run a 450-mile round-trip between New York and Washington in a calendar day and collect four and a half days' pay, or about $92 in 1962. It took eight crews to forward the Burlington's Denver Zephyr the 1,034 miles between Denver and Chicago, a feat done in 16.5 hours, or a day's pay for a little over two hours' work. In fairness, it took a crewman most of a career to work up to plush assignments like the Denver Zephyr, much of it spent on 24-hour call, and this in the days before beepers. But the rigidity of these work rules were killing productivity and before long were going to kill the jobs as well.

State governments did their best to kill the trains they said they needed. Still dominated by small towns in the days before redistricting, many states required useless locals to ply their lonely way up every branch. Suppose new state authorities had worked with the railroads to set up high-speed hub-and-spoke services centered on the state capital and state university towns. This would have required public money to get branchline track up to speed and to buy equipment. But it would have made the state capital (rather than an out-of-state big city) a destination for retail shopping. It would have permitted all kinds of school and civic group movements for field trips, athletics, and performing arts and would have facilitated statewide specialty schools and hospitals. It would have fed traffic into hub airports and the long-distance trains. Countries in Europe and Asia acknowledged that rail passenger transportation lost money by itself but was a cost-effective way to solve a number of other economic, social, political, and urban problems, and so they thought nothing of a government subsidy. But in the United States, such state involvement would have smacked of nationalization, and the railroads would not have allowed it, even if state administrations had been imaginative enough to suggest it.

The Transportation Act of 1958 gave the ICC jurisdiction over passenger discontinuances, which short-circuited the state public service commissions and brought an end to the useless locals. But except in Wisconsin, where Ben Heineman of the Chicago & North Western convinced state authorities to let him substitute two medium-distance streamliners for a number of locals, no alternative was provided to feed traffic to and from the main lines. Downtown stations, once an asset, became a liability as commercial and recreational activity shifted out of city centers.

In December 1958, with fewer than 350 people a day riding all of its trains combined, the Lehigh Valley petitioned to end all passenger service. The Black Diamond, its once famous but now shabby New York–Buffalo day train, made its last run on May 11, 1959. Forced to retain a skeleton service until January 1961, the Maine Central actually beat the Lehigh out the door as the first reasonably major carrier to exit the business entirely. The Milwaukee Road's Olympian Hiawathas departed Chicago and Seattle for the last time on May 22, 1961, the first of the truly flashy postwar streamliners to end service. An era was passing.

The passenger problem was not irrelevant. It cast a pall over all railroading. It was the passenger train that linked the railroad to the public at large, to excitement and glamour and moments of passage in people's lives. It was what set the railroads apart from other, mundane industries. As the passenger train faded, the railroad itself began to fade from the public consciousness. Watching beautiful trains depart half empty took a toll on railroad people, as if they had given a beautiful party and nobody came. One by one in the 1960s, railroad managements that had once tended flagship trains with loving care became realistic, which meant hardnosed, which meant run the public off and get rid of the damn things. Deep in their hearts, they knew something irretrievable was slipping away. As the crowds thinned and the upholstery went threadbare and the paint began to peel, railroad morale crumbled.

More than pride was at stake. The precision on-time railroading required by the passenger train had a halo effect that carried over to the great redball[5] fast freights. There had been a time when the streamliners rolled into the night at the appointed nanosecond with a wave of the lantern, a notch of the throttle, a blast of the horn, and a high-pitched whine of the diesel's electric motors. As the tight discipline of passenger operations waned into sloppiness, so did all precision and discipline, and the freight operation got sloppy as well. That was just as the motor carrier was poised to roll down the new interstate highways straight from one loading dock to another with precisely the service the customer required. It was as if the very soul of the railroad was wasting away.[6]

The Crying Towel Years

Most Americans remember the 1950s fondly. The country was booming. Life was good: television, cars with fins, rock 'n' roll. But for railroads, these became the crying towel years. The Golden Glow faded once the savings of the diesel were largely realized. Railroad executives had no other trick to pull out of their hat and did not know what to do. If railroads could not haul passengers at a profit, what, exactly, could they haul at a profit—besides coal? The express business was mostly gone. Less-than-carload (LCL) traffic was virtually gone, mostly taken by motor trucks: 13 million carloads a year were transported by the railroads in 1928, but carloads decreased to only 5.5 million in 1945, to 1.8 million in 1960, and to 205,000 in 1968. LCL was everything that moved in small lots, the products of small businesses, going to other small businesses. The paired "team" tracks of every metropolitan center, where LCL was delivered, where lorries and panel trucks and flatbeds pulled up to boxcar doors to pick up their goods, were once the scene of frenetic commercial activity, the American version of an oriental bazaar. Now they were silent.

Just about every category of traffic was either declining or threatened. Raw petroleum moved by pipeline. Railroads had less than 1 percent of that traffic by 1960. Livestock was gone—less than 12 percent of it moved by rail in 1958. Fresh-vegetable traffic was holding up, but fresh fruits, especially from Florida, were moving by truck. In 1950, 45 percent of the southern crop moved by truck; in 1963, 72 percent. Many finished manufactured goods were shifting to trucks because of faster door-to-door service and gentler handling. Shippers found that it was worth the higher price to get their goods on time and in one piece. Was any traffic safe? Coal? What if oil replaced coal? What if a coal slurry pipeline were built? That was a scheme to pulverize coal, mix it with water, and move it through a pipe; the plan was never widely used, but it hung like a Sword of Damocles.

How productive was the freight train? It could sprint down the main line at a pretty good clip, but cars waited at every junction point for reclassification into outgoing trains and waited for delivery to the customers' sidings. If a car had to be interchanged with another railroad, it waited for classification in the first railroad's yard, often for 24 hours, then waited for a transfer run to the connecting railroad, often for another 24 hours, then for reclassification in the second railroad's yard. Loading dock to loading dock, it was not much better than an ox cart—specifically, 19.5 mph in 1960, up (barely) from 16.7 mph in 1940 and 12.9 mph in 1928.

The 40-foot hopper or boxcar was not cost-effective, not when it required heavy underframes and four-wheel trucks to negotiate North America's relatively poor track. Most of this heavy equipment was without roller bearings. It had what were called friction bearings: a lot of oily fiber "waste" was wadded into the journal box with the hope that it would not catch fire. Low oil prices made all this heavy drag and enormous tare weight endurable, saving the railroads from the capital cost of lightweight, free-wheeling cars and good track. But what if oil prices went up?

The freight train required a full crew of at least five, and in some states six, every 100 miles. Most contentious was the fireman in the diesel, a machine that had no fires. Wages were going up. Good wages meant purchasing power, which meant national boom, which was good for business. However, rising wages hurt labor-intensive industries like the railroads. The labor productivity question was deeply embedded and would probably require one really nasty national strike, but Congress would never allow it. It would shut the whole economy down. But the question could not be postponed forever.

On June 26, 1959, with trumpets and pipe bands, President Eisenhower, Prime Minister Diefenbaker, and Queen Elizabeth II formally opened the St. Lawrence Seaway in ceremonies at St. Lambert, Quebec. The queen gave some of her address in the French language of Quebec, and so did Ike. Now the 120 miles of rough and shallow water between Montreal and Ogdensburg, New York, that had kept blue-water ships out of the Great Lakes, was open. The navigational (as opposed to the hydroelectric) portions of the project cost $400 million, $130 million of it from the United States. The tonnage in the early months of operation ran ahead of estimates, and everyone was thrilled. Railroads had their fingers crossed. Not all of them were going to be hurt; after all, James J. Hill, the empire builder himself, conceived the Great Northern Railway as multiple routes converging at the head-of-lakes at Duluth, for lake shipment eastward. But government had intervened massively to alter traffic patterns in the Great Lakes region. The future of the North Atlantic ports, particularly New York, and the Great Lakes–to–the–sea rail routes between New York and Buffalo seemed very much in question. The Seaway turned out to be too shallow, too narrow, and its locks too short for ships large enough to make money in the 1980s and 1990s. It was obsolete within a decade after it opened. But for railroading's most critical season, it was a public enterprise that did a number on the private.

Government had always altered the equations of transport. Railroads were the beneficiaries once upon a time. Giant projects like the Seaway or the interstates meant huge contracts and lots of jobs and had powerful support from both Democrats and Republicans, liberals and conservatives. Could the railroads not get in on this? Passenger and commuter problems were an obvious place to start. But railroads did not want that kind of help; they feared that even the appearance of a partnership with government was the back door to nationalization. They freaked over the nationalization of the British Railways after the war and led a public campaign to make sure that did not happen here. They were not going to climb aboard the public-private cooperative bandwagon. For an extra kicker, railroads paid taxes to build these projects for the other modes. They were often the largest single taxpayer in American small towns, and their yards and terminal facilities were usually on high-tax urban land.

Despite all that government was doing for competing modes, railroads still had powerful advantages. They could move tonnage at a lower cost than trucks and were more convenient and flexible than barges. But rate regulation now barred them from cashing in on their natural advantages. The question had shifted away from maximum rates, for which rate regulation was originally designed, to minimum rates. Could railroads set rates low enough to reflect their natural advantages? Applicable laws seemed to indicate that Congress did not want one mode artificially protected over another mode, so long as rates were fully compensatory (in other words, no price wars), except that section 305(c) of the Transportation Act of 1940 did give some special protection to barges. But beginning in the early 1950s, when railroads came to the ICC proposing lower rates that reflected their low cost, they were usually rebuffed. The commission seemed to want rates at a level where all modes could share in all traffic, meaning all modes were handling traffic inefficiently and the public was paying a higher cost for all transportation.

Individually, railroad executives of the era felt a terrible sense of frustration, as though stymied at every turn. Collectively, through the Association of American Railroads, their frustration came out as a massive whine; they cried in public about the unfairness of life. Advertising and press releases, notably the *Railroad Hour* radio program sponsored by the AAR, carped on the unfairness of government aid to competitors and the property taxes railroads paid that helped pay for the aid. There was little the general public could do or wanted to do about it. Railroads set up "public interest" lobbies in state capitals to get restrictions put on truckers, particularly on the size and weight of rigs. They even infiltrated state PTA organizations and distributed comic books through the schools about how unfairly the world treated the Little Engine That Could. Some of this got rather silly. One day, a young woman who felt that she had been badly treated by the Eastern Railroads Presidents' Conference walked into the American Trucking Association with a suitcase full of documents and suggested that they might be interested. The papers chronicled falsifications and dubious tactics in the antitruck campaign and led to multiple lawsuits and much embarrassment.[7]

The crying towel era was the most troubled in all of railroad history. In the depression, everybody was in the soup; this time, the railroads were alone. The economy was roaring, but railroads only managed to survive. Self-doubt seemed to express itself in a stifling timidity—they were afraid of their unions, afraid of government, afraid of the competition, afraid of the future, and afraid of any bold initiative.

Even on the matter of consolidation, which would soon become the panacea for all their troubles, they were timid. Robert Young put a bold Chesapeake & Ohio–New York Central affiliation on the table. It had real merit, but the industry was too timid. Young was a gadfly, and nobody wanted to see beyond the personality. The Lackawanna–Nickel Plate proposal had real merit, on a more modest scale, but certain classes of investors were too concerned with making their five points and found allies in managers who were too comfortable with the status quo.

Two Faces of the Crying Towel: Deramus and Barriger

Two railroaders who were prominent in the 1950s, though for different reasons, illuminated the mind-set of the crying towel years and the pall it cast over creative management. One was William N. Deramus III, whose Scroogian cost-cutting cut productivity and drove business away. The other was John Walker Barriger III, railroading's philosopher-king, who dreamed of super-railroads that lowered cost by investing capital and becoming more productive but could conceive them only within circumscribed limits.

Deramus III was the son of Bill Deramus, Jr., who was a major investor in, and a reasonably able executive of, the Kansas City Southern. Deramus III came to the presidency of the Chicago Great Western in 1949 after a group of investors that included his father bought a big chunk of it. The weakest of the midwestern granger roads, it probably was one railroad too many. Deramus understood that this marginal railroad had to be run a lot more efficiently or it was going to die.

He did some things right. He hacked off the passenger trains; they did not amount to much. The Mill Cities Limited and the Minnesotan had once aspired to greatness, but they were too slow to be of interest to passengers who valued their time. He embraced technology—the diesel, of course, and radio communication. Sometimes that backfired. For example, the new communications system made it easy to call headquarters to get a reversal of a division superintendent's ruling—"fishing expeditions" they were called—until morale at the divisional level collapsed.

Deramus understood, as did all railroad executives, that union work rules forced an unproductive use of labor and had to change. He was willing to endure a strike for it, for 42 days in 1953. He felt that he was fighting the good fight of all railroads and was disappointed that not a single officer of another railroad called him during the strike. He thought they were timid; they perceived him as a loose cannon and not the man to lead an industry-wide battle. But so far, it can be argued, Deramus was only being realistic.

There was a point where cost-consciousness began to cut into muscle and lowered productivity rather than raising it. He cut operating costs by running long, long trains, holding every train until it was filled out to maximum tonnage, often running only a single train a day over main routes. These trains operated with eight or ten diesel units up front. To those who knew no better, watching one of these monsters roll by, it looked as if business was booming on the CGW. But one train a day meant horrible service. Trucks provided the customer with service that the railroad had to match. One train a day, which stopped to switch cars along the way, making the through freight do the work of a way freight, was such godawful service that most shippers never came back. These long trains, and the utter collapse of all semblance of a schedule, were the root of his labor problem. Crews had to be away from home for exceptionally long periods at utterly irregular intervals. Morale dropped to zero.

Deramus slashed his staff—for example in car accounts and billing—until customers complained and other railroads complained and the people who remained on the job were overworked and morale collapsed. Deramus would just fire people, for example, one who apparently did not have a big enough smile for him one day when he came in—such as receptionist Rosalie O'Hara. He strode straight back to Personnel and said "fire her." That got him in trouble with her union.[8] In contrast, real leaders find ways to make people want to do their job well. Cutting, slashing, and browbeating usually did not have the intended results.

Deramus moved on to the Katy Railroad in 1957 to work his magic there. His first order of business was to have all the company's records in its St. Louis general office boxed up and moved out in the dark of night. Employees arrived for work the next morning and found it padlocked, with a notice that if they wanted work, they could report to Parsons, Kansas. The Katy was expelled from the St. Louis Chamber of Commerce after that stunt, amid mountains of ill will, and it was castigated as an outfit respectable shippers would never want to do business with. Deramus slashed employment—just slashed, until there were not enough people to get the job done. The operation looked shabby and was shabby. Shippers were not going to entrust their valuable commodities to an outfit with so little pride in itself. They began to leave, and this became an excuse to make more slashes. Labor relations were abysmal. Service was abysmal. The Frisco, the Katy's partner in the operation of the Texas Special streamliner between St. Louis and Texas, dropped the train abruptly in January 1959, because the Katy's incompetent maintenance and sloppy operations had turned it into an embarrassment. In the merger era, nobody who was anybody knocked on the Katy's door. It was a terrible railroad and Deramus III was most of the reason. Then he moved on to his daddy's railroad, the Kansas City Southern, in the 1960s, and it began to fall apart.

It has been written that Deramus III was a great railroader because he "saved" the Great Western and "saved" the Katy. But he did not save the Great Western. It died. There is almost nothing of it left. The Katy and the Kansas City Southern did survive, but not until they were reconceived by leaders with the imagination that Deramus III lacked. Deramus III was an extreme, and his wretched interpersonal skills made a bad situation worse. But all railroad executives of the crying towel years contained a little Deramus III in them—cut, slash, retreat, retrench, then cut some more. Cut people until there are not enough to get the job done, so that customers leave and revenue falls, and then you can cut more. It was a disastrous legacy that dominated the industry through the 1960s and the 1970s. It lingered dangerously into the 1980s and 1990s, when the situation changed drastically but the state of mind did not.

In contrast, Barriger was the grand old man of quality railroading, a different stripe altogether from Deramus III but the other side of the crying towel legacy. Once he was a rising star of the Pennsylvania Railroad. He left in 1927 to be a railroad analyst and technical expert for security holders who had come to question the data they were getting from management. It was for them that he did the technical studies for the Prince Plan (see chapter 2). After that he was a railroad technical expert for the government, first at the Reconstruction Finance Corporation, then at the Office of Defense Transportation. It has been suggested that because he did this service for "the enemy," the industry, perhaps the PRR, blackballed him from ever leading a major railroad. He led the Monon after the war, and when he had done all he could do there, he was a vice president of the New Haven. Then he led the New York Central's densely trafficked Pittsburgh & Lake Erie subsidiary. After that he tried to put the Katy back together, after Deramus had left it a ruin. In 1970 he went on to lead the profoundly troubled Boston & Maine.

Barriger was a proponent of super-railroads, a view expounded in his book *Super Railroads for a Dynamic American Economy,* which was published by Simmons-Boardman in 1956. It was a slender thing—only 73 pages plus a statistical appendix. It advocated physical excellence, especially for the right-of-way and especially in regard to grades and curvature. The railroad was the low-cost mode of transportation, he argued, and was as much the foundation of a productive economy in the twentieth century as it was in the nineteenth. But if it was to fulfill this purpose, it had to operate more

productively. Deramus would cut and slash. Barriger would build. Technical excellence would cut railroad costs and provide the cost-efficient transportation to underwrite a thriving national economy. This, in turn, would
bring more business to the railroad.

But it was a vision fenced in by the way things were. Passengers were a
given; regulation was a given; union work rules were a given. Barriger was
frustrated by these factors but accepted that they would never go away
and would just have to be dealt with. Freight would move in boxcars, the
way it always had. Railroads would deliver the boxcars to individual sidings, the way they always had. He conceived of no better distribution system. Salvation lay in physical excellence. To attain that excellence, railroads must raise their capital internally—that is, out of earnings, since
their ability to borrow was limited and they must never take money from
government. In other words, Barriger stood for the status quo, except that
he wanted to maintain the status quo effectively and efficiently.

If he had headed up the Union Pacific or the Southern Pacific, Barriger
might have had a real laboratory for super-railroads. But the Monon was
not built very well in the first place, especially at its southern end toward
Louisville. It could not raise enough money for a meaningful upgrade of
its right-of-way. He initiated a couple of projects—better alignment
around a bog at Cedar Lake, Indiana, and a better bridge over the Wabash
River at Delphi, Indiana. These helped but did not make the Monon a super-railroad. Economist George Hilton thought Barriger's experience on
the Monon proved two things: super status was probably beyond the
reach of all but the strongest roads, and Barriger was an excellent traditional railroad man.

"Traditional" was the killer qualifier. It was a limited vision that he had.
At the Katy, Barriger did begin to reconceptualize the whole purpose of
that railroad. He put money into its Kansas City–Fort Worth–San
Antonio–Houston main line and forgot the rest. But it was the Whitman
management, which succeeded him, that actually junked the loser
branches. Barriger could not quite cut the knot of intertwined shipper, labor, and regulatory and political interests that kept the railroad running a
few carloads a day up long branches, a distribution system that was neither labor efficient nor fuel efficient. The rail revolution that was coming
would require that the very idea of the railroad be reconceptualized and
reconceived. Barriger could not do that.

Abandonment

Railroads had been abandoned before: the Colorado Midland in 1918,
for example, because no railroad should ever have been built over Hagerman Pass. The Missouri & Arkansas quit in 1946. It was a road that never
had a purpose, and floods and labor troubles finished it off. The Pittsburgh,

Shawmut & Northern in northwestern Pennsylvania and southwestern New York gave up in 1947 because the forests were cut over and the mines played out. But beginning in the late 1950s, three railroads that had been on the fringes of genuine importance gave up the ghost. None of them were serious losses to the overall system, but their death cast a pall.

In 1957 the New York, Ontario & Western (O&W; known wistfully as the Old Woman) succumbed after a long illness. In days gone by, it had carried milk from upstate farms to New York City and city folks to the "borscht belt" resorts in the Catskills. Back in the Roaring Twenties, its trains were packed, especially on Jewish holidays. Before the war, it even got the renowned industrial designer Otto Kuhler to dress up one of its trains in black and maroon with orange accents and called it the Mountaineer. The crew were dressed in uniforms to match. It was a budget job but it all looked quite spiffy.

The O&W hauled some anthracite coal out of Scranton, although that business was on the skids. It went all the way to Oswego, New York, at the eastern end of Lake Ontario, missing both Syracuse and Utica and crossing every mountain range at right angles. Lakes-to-the-sea traffic never developed (mainly because Oswego was below Niagara Falls), and the west end

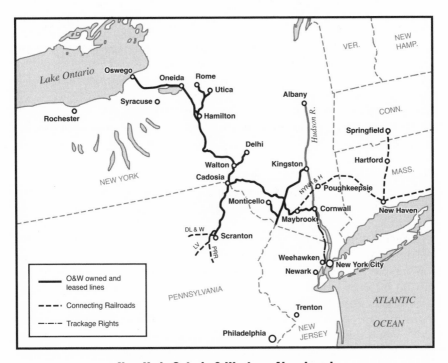

New York, Ontario & Western, Abandoned

of the railroad was streaks of rust. The O&W survived in modern times by ferrying traffic from the Lackawanna and the Lehigh Valley over its Scranton branch to a connection with the New Haven at Maybrook Yard. This was a through route to southern New England, but the 145-mile haul for the O&W was too short to make enough money.

It was a railroad that should never have been built, but it had some of the trappings of the big time: double track in places; some big Mohawk-class steam locomotives; then FT diesels in a rather striking livery of gray, yellow, and orange; and a miniversion of centralized traffic control. But the new diesels hauled manifest freights that sometimes had only 12 cars. New York State hoped the line might be declared essential to national defense. Right up to the end, rumors circulated along the line that the "civil defense" department had come up with a million dollars to keep it going. A million dollars would have bought another six months. There was no point. The same day the New York Central opened its new Frontier Yard in Buffalo, March 14, 1957, a bankruptcy judge in New York declared that O&W creditors had had enough and could liquidate.

On March 29, 1957, the final trains began arriving in Middletown, New York, O&W's headquarters, bringing in all rolling stock for disposal. The almost-new diesels were sold to the L&N and others. The *Middletown Times-Herald* wrote, "It is never pleasant to watch anything go through its death throes. The O&W has been a good friend, and its passing should be marked with regret. But death should not be mourned too long, for the loss will not be too great" ("Except in matters of the heart," added *Trains* in its "Obituary to an Old Woman" in July 1957).

Lingering labor troubles on the Rutland Railway through central Vermont caused it to shut down for good on September 25, 1961. Tower operators' desks were left just as if the next shift were about to take over, but not a wheel ever turned again on the Rutland. The application for abandonment was a shock to Vermonters. The line had been a wheezer, but with good management under Gardner Caverly in the 1950s, it showed a modest profit by 1957. He replaced 58 steam locomotives with 15 new diesels from Alco, paid for by the scrap from bucolic but unused branches. He bought 450 new freight cars, the first since 1925. The Rutland's passenger trains, the Mount Royal and the Green Mountain Flyer (which most certainly did not fly), had been the quaintest way to travel from New York to Montreal. It was a delightful ride, hopping from island to island in Lake Champlain between Burlington and Rouses Point, on the border. Caverly got rid of passengers. But labor troubles were the final straw. The Rutland could not afford to pay national wages, and the brotherhoods did not want the precedent of an exception to the national scale.

The Rutland was one too many railroads in thinly populated, short-distance Vermont, and that was why it finally quit.[9] Frantically, Sen. George Aiken of Vermont inquired of the Pentagon if the Rutland was in any way

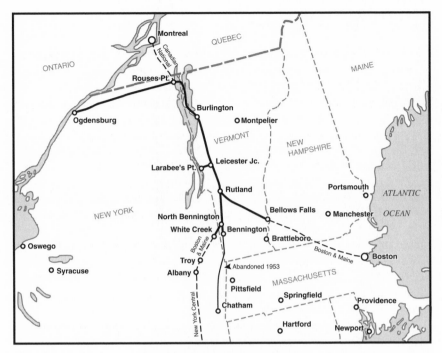

Rutland Railway, Abandoned

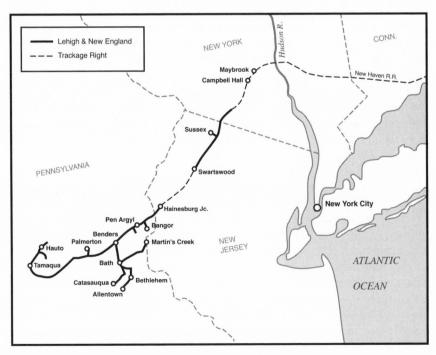

Lehigh & New England, Abandoned

essential for the national defense. The answer was no; it had handled only 75 cars of government cargo in its last year of operation, and all but 12 of them could have been rerouted. The 12 cars had carried Vermont marble for monuments and tombstones. Portions of its main line were bought by the state of Vermont and operated as the Vermont Railway, and another portion was reconstituted as the Green Mountain Railway, a prototype of the new short lines that would devolve from former Class I railroads. But another familiar name was gone.

The Lehigh & New England (L&NE) was abandoned in 1961. This was not lingering starvation. It was built to carry coal into southern New England via Maybrook Yard. When the mines closed, its owner, Lehigh Coal & Navigation, abandoned it without going through bankruptcy. The Jersey Central picked up a few segments; the rest was torn up. But another name vanished.

These roads were bit players in the grand scheme of railroading. The L&NE's death had an identifiable cause, but the O&W and the Rutland died because all the problems pressing on the whole railroad industry finally crushed its two weakest members. Among railroad executives throughout the country, there was a palpable chill. Abandonment was a possibility. Who was next?

The Transportation Act of 1958

In midsummer 1957 a recession began. It was more serious and more persistent than the one of 1954. For railroads, it continued without interruption into the 1960s. Carloadings on the New York Central in February 1958 were lower than in any month of 1932 or 1933. As usual, high fixed costs meant that a marginal drop in revenue (4% in 1957) produced a major drop in net earnings (17%). It was worse in 1958. The New York Central and the Pennsylvania reported declines in gross earnings of $100 million each, and their return on investment fell to 0.6 percent. The Jersey Central, the Lehigh Valley, the Erie, the Lackawanna, the New Haven, and the Boston & Maine all suffered net losses on operations (see table 1).

Of the figures seen in table 1, the rate of return is probably the most significant. Even in the best of years, it was less than what it cost to borrow money, which was about 6 percent. Thus, railroads were not earning enough to pay for improvements to their fixed plant. Railroads could make some improvements out of current earnings. They could borrow at above-market rates, representing the risk borrowers felt they were taking. But the rate-of-return figures spell slow starvation. This was the wall that Barriger's concept of super-railroads ran up against. The interstate highways were already under way. They would be state-of-the-art rights-of-way. Unless railroads could make similar improvements to their own rights-of-way, they could not continue long once the new roads were opened. The end would not be a cinematic fireball but a slow, lingering death; and when it came, what was left of the railroads would be too unimportant to matter.

Table 1   Basic Statistics for All Class I Railroads, 1928–1959

	1928	1940	1943	1950	1955	1959
Operating Revenues ($ billions)	6.3	4.3	9.0	9.4	10.1	9.8
Rate of return (%)	4.7	3.05	5.8	4.3	4.2	2.7
Ton miles (billions)		379.2	734.8	596.9	631.4	582.0
Share of total (%)		61.3	71.2	56.2	49.4	45.6
Passenger miles (billions)		23.7	87.8	31.8	28.5	22.1
Employees (millions)	1.7	1.0	1.35	1.2	1.1	.8
Ave. wage/hour	$.63	$.75	$.92	$1.58	$2.00	$2.59

Source: figures extracted from *Moody's Transportation Manuals* based on data reported to the ICC.

In January 1958 Sen. George Smathers (D-Fla.) and his Senate Subcommittee on Surface Transportation began hearings on an administration bill to ease the latest railroad crisis. Company presidents who came to testify were all pessimistic—posturing, perhaps, but it seemed as if doubts about the very future of the railroad, doubts that recent prosperity had barely glossed over, came welling up from the depths of frustration.

The resulting Transportation Act of 1958 dealt with peripheral problems of rate making, credit, and passenger service. There was no vision, no effort to deal with fundamentals. No one thought it was going to help very much. Perry Shoemaker of the Lackawanna, in his outgoing speech as president of the New York Chamber of Commerce, said it was "distressingly full of compromise, concessions and inertia." Earl Moore of the Jersey Central said it would help the roads ride out the storm but little more. Walter Tuohy of the C&O lambasted the ICC for being so negative about consolidation. ICC commissioner Howard Freas, himself in favor of consolidation, shot back that the initiative belonged to the railroads and that for all their talk, they had come through with precious few concrete proposals. Benjamin Fairless of U.S. Steel said that if Congress did not hurry up and do everything business wanted, the country would fall to the communists. In the end, the senators were left with a low opinion of the railroad executives, and the railroad executives with a low opinion of senators. An opportunity was lost. But the door was left open a crack. The bill ordered further studies, perhaps for future legislation. A panel was appointed, headed by retired Air Force general John P. Doyle. Perhaps the Doyle Report could cut the knot.

We can only wonder what might have happened if railroads had come to Congress united, with some bold ideas, such as (1) an end to rate regulation, so that the railroads could compete; (2) an "Amtrak" solution for passengers; (3) a comprehensive plan of their own for consolidation, since they did not want government planning; and (4) a proposal for meaningful

Table 2 *Fortune* Top Fifty Transportation Companies, 1959

Rank	Company	Gross Revenue ($ millions)		Net Income ($ millions)		Rate of Return[a]
1	Pennsylvania RR	888.2	(992)	16.6	(53)	0.9
2	Southern Pacific	787.7	(678)	69.8	(46)	4.8
3	New York Central RR	773.1	(872)	13.2	(43)	1.0
4	Santa Fe Ry	633.8	(590)	65.8	(70)	5.2
5	Union Pacific RR	515.8	(514)	64.8	(79)	5.3
6	Baltimore & Ohio RR	395.2	(465)	14.8	(30)	2.1
7	American Airlines	377.7	(291)	21.0	(20)	14.0
8	Pan Am World Airways	356.8	(289)	7.4	(14)	5.4
9	Trans World Airlines	348.5	(240)	9.4	(-2)d	7.9
10	Chesapeake & Ohio Ry	347.6	(419)	45.7	(67)	7.4
11	United Air Lines	330.2	(263)	13.8	(15)	10.0
12	Missouri Pacific RR	303.4	(305)	15.6	(20)	6.0
13	Eastern Air Lines	298.3	(228)	11.4	(15)	9.7
14	Greyhound Bus Lines	285.9	(245)	21.4	(14)	17.2
15	Southern Ry	271.9	(275)	33.1	(39)	6.3
16	Illinois Central RR	271.7	(298)	15.0	(24)	3.3
17	Burlington RR	263.1	(257)	17.7	(22)	3.1
18	Great Northern Ry	254.6	(281)	26.6	(32)	4.1
19	Norfolk & Western Ry	247.0	(240)	60.7	(42)	8.5
20	Milwaukee Road	242.0	(254)	5.9	(8)	1.7
21	Louisville & Nashville	229.8	(212)	13.4	(25)	3.7
22	Rock Island RR	219.5	(200)	8.3	(16)	2.8
23	Chicago & North Western	213.4	(193)	-2.9d	(-5)d	—
24	Northern Pacific Ry	183.6	(188)	23.8	(21)	3.6
25	Seaboard Air Line RR	161.4	(162)	17.0	(20)	7.6

Source: Data from *Fortune* (August 1960): 141.
Note: 1956 figures, rounded to the nearest million, are shown in parentheses.

public help to build super-railroads, to install CTC, and to build state-of-the-art classification yards, the way the government was funding capital improvement for other modes of transportation.

But the railroads themselves were not united. Frankly, they probably liked rate regulation more than they were willing to admit. Ending it would mean they would have to compete with each other as well as with other modes. They would have to develop marketing tools, and they were not sure they could do that. Marketing decisions would have to take precedence over operating convenience, and operating departments would no longer run the railroad, as they always had in the past. That would set off internal turf wars. Direct public aid would bring government in on certain managerial decisions, and the railroads were afraid of where

Table 2 continued

Rank	Company	Gross Revenue ($ millions)		Net Income ($ millions)		Rate of Return[a]
26	Atlantic Coast Line	156.1	(167)	11.8	(12)	3.5
27	Erie RR	154.3	(176)	-5.7d	(+5)	—
28	Nickel Plate Road	150.4	(175)	13.3	(16)	5.5
29	New Haven RR	143.9	(162)	-10.8d	(0.2)	—
30	United States Lines	136.5	(127)	8.2	(16)	8.8
31	Frisco Ry	133.6	(137)	6.6	(9)	4.1
32	Northwest Airlines	126.0	(77)	5.7	(3)	10.9
33	Wabash RR	119.6	(120)	3.8	(11)	2.1
34	Delta Air Lines	109.2	(67)	2.6	(5)	6.9
35	Capital Airlines	108.5	(64)	-1.8d	(-1)d	—
36	Reading Co.	107.0	(138)	1.8	(12)	0.7
37	Matson Navigation	101.5	(86)	3.1	(4)	6.3
38	Consol. Freightways	88.8		2.6		8.3
39	Amer. President Lines	82.4	(79)	6.5	(7)	10.0
40	Gulf, Mobile & Ohio RR	82.1	(84)	2.8	(5)	4.0
41	Rio Grande RR	75.4	(81)	8.7	(12)	7.4
42	Texas & Pacific Ry	74.5	(81)	3.5	(8)	2.1
43	Braniff Airways	74.3		2.5		6.8
44	Kansas City Southern	72.9	(77)	10.2	(12)	5.8
45	Boston & Maine RR	72.0	(88)	-3.8d	(0.7)	—
46	Lackawanna RR	71.9	(89)	-4.3d	(5)	—
47	National Airlines	70.9			(0.7)	—
48	Associated Transport	70.0		1.2		11.6
49	Pacific Intermountain	70.0		1.9		11.2
50	Moore-McCormack Lines	69.8		2.3		2.4

[a] As a percentage of invested capital

this might lead. What they wanted was for the government to stop building highways and airports. They had no positive plan of their own.

From Congress's perspective, it was a can of worms, certainly if the industry that needed help was not united. Shippers wanted the railroads clamped under tight regulation. States and communities did not want to lose any existing rail service as a result of consolidation, whether they were using it or not. Labor was watching like a hawk over anything that might cost jobs. No congressmen of either party wanted to wade into such murky waters.

The problem was that the crisis was not big enough. The attic was on fire, but the whole house had not gone up in flames yet. A real solution would require some important constituencies to swallow some bitter medicine. Recalcitrant railroad managements might have to be pushed with threats of eminent domain. Democratic friends of labor (Democrats ran the show in those years) would certainly have to tell the railroad unions in no uncertain terms that it was time to be realistic. Government money would be required, probably a lot of it. Everything on that plate was controversial. As great as the American system is, it is not good at dealing with distant problems before they become a full-blown calamity, not if they require short-term pain in the hope of achieving long-term good.

By the time the Doyle Report came out, the recession had eased and there was even less incentive for bold action. (The first edition of this book called the report "silly," but that was unfair.) The Doyle Report made good proposals, several of which were eventually implemented. It proposed a Department of Transportation at full cabinet level to instigate some kind of coordination between the competing modes of transportation. It advocated a national pooling of passenger service, what Amtrak eventually became, although it called for the railroads to run it, not the government. It called for a national pool of freight equipment so that cars could be available anywhere anytime, which one railroad executive at the time called asinine but which, ten years later, began to look like a very good idea. General Doyle spent the rest of his career as a professor of transportation at Texas A&M University, and as time went on, he felt that his recommendations had been right on the money.

Window on a Troubled Time

Fortune magazine's Top Fifty list in transportation was a handy window on the status of an industry. In 1959 it showed that railroads were clearly troubled, especially in the East (see table 2). Note that the rate of return on invested capital is usually lower even for the best of the railroads than the cost of borrowing money. Two of the best performers are coal haulers—the Norfolk & Western and the Chesapeake & Ohio. Looking at rates of return on truckers and airlines and steamship companies, one sees quickly what an advantage it is not to have to build, maintain, and pay taxes on your own right-of-way. Even among the supposedly high-flying competition, it was comforting to know there were a few dogs, such as Capital and National Airlines. The list does not reflect the importance of the trucking industry because it was decentralized into small units. Most of the nation's many truckers were not big enough to make the list, although a few began to appear at the bottom of it by 1959. The rise of the airlines and the decline of most railroads is obvious.

A few important railroads did not make the *Fortune* Top Fifty list; they are listed in table 3. In the case of the Soo Line, this was because it reported figures for its subsidiary the Wisconsin Central separately. Of interest is the cataclysmic skid of the once-great Lehigh Valley and Jersey Central roads.

Table 3 Selected Railroads Not on *Fortune*'s Top Fifty List, 1959

	Gross Income ($ millions)		Net Income ($ millions)		Rate of Return[a]
Soo Line[b] (CP)	81.6	(90)	0.4	(5)	—
Long Island (PRR)	69.3	(65)	0.3	(0.8)	2.0
Cotton Belt (SP)	65.4	(68)	9.5	(11)	11.76
Missouri-Kansas-Texas (Katy)	58.4	(74)	-2.9	(2)	—
Grand Trunk Western (CN)	56.4	(63)	-11.7d	(-5)d	—
Lehigh Valley	54.4	(72)	-1.6d	(4)	—
Western Pacific	52.9	(54)	4.7	(5)	6.5
Jersey Central (B&O)	52.6	(62)	-2.9d	(0.4)	—
Delaware & Hudson	46.2	(57)	5.4	(9)	13.7
Western Maryland	44.9	(52)	5.8	(8)	8.0
Central of Georgia	44.2	(45)	2.3	(3)	4.5
Elgin, Joliet & Eastern	44.2	(54)	5.4	(9.1)	7.0
Virginian	42.0	(56)	9.2	(14)	8.3
Chicago & Eastern Illinois	36.4	(38)	1.4	(2.3)	4.2
Chicago Great Western	34.1	(36)	2.7	(3)	6.4
Florida East Coast	32.8	(38)	-4.7d	(-0.3)d	—
Duluth, Missabe & Iron Range	32.4	(47)	-0.7d	(6)	—
Pittsburgh & Lake Erie (NYC)	30.6	(42)	8.1	(10)	—
Spokane, Portland & Seattle[c]	30.2	(29)	2.7	(3)	—
Maine Central	24.6	(27)	0.8	(1.4)	5.3
Richmond, Fredericksburg & Potomac	23.9	(27)	3.1	(4)	23.3
Detroit, Toledo & Ironton	21.6	(20)	3.9	(4)	10.8
Clinchfield (ACL)	21.1	(25)	5.3	(7)	—
Minneapolis & St. Louis	21.0	(21)	1.1	(2)	5.8
Bessemer & Lake Erie	20.4	(26)	2.8	(5)	—
Monon	20.2	(23)	0.6	(1)	2.9
West Point Route[d] (ACL)	15.9	(17)	0.4	(0.4)	—
Alaska	14.5	(18)	0.2	(2.0)	—
Bangor & Aroostook	13.2	(16)	0.1	(1.1)	—
Ann Arbor (Wab)	8.7	(10)	-0.3d	(0.6)	—
Pittsburg & West Virginia	8.0	(9)	-0.1d	(0.9)	—
Toledo, Peoria & Western	7.8	(8)	0.9	(1)	—
Chicago, S. Shore & S. Bend	7.8	(9)	-0.02	(0.3)	—
Akron, Canton & Youngstown	5.9	(6)	0.3	(0.4)	—
Central Vermont (CN)	5.9	(7)	d	d	—
Rutland	4.6	(5)	0.04	(0.5)	—
Lehigh & Hudson River	3.3	(3)	0.1	(0.2)	—
Chicago & Illinois Midland	3.0	(3)	1.0	(1.1)	4.2

Source: Moody's Transportation Manual, 1960 ed.
Note: 1956 figures, rounded to the nearest million, are shown in parentheses.
[a] As a percentage of invested capital.
[b] Includes Wisconsin Central and Duluth, South Shore & Atlantic.
[c] Includes Oregon Trunk.
[d] Includes Georgia; Atlanta & West Point; and Western of Alabama.

five

Solutions
1947–1964

In the gloom of the crying towel years, several solutions began to emerge. One was "intermodal," the carrying of truck trailers or containers on rail cars. In the 1950s it was known as "piggyback." In the 1960s and 1970s, it was known as TOFC or COFC (trailers or containers on flatcars). By 1960, it held forth a great deal of promise, though technical problems remained to be solved. By 1970, in spite of continuing technical problems and although it was not making much money, it was popular with shippers. Much later, it saved the railroads.

Another solution was productivity. That involved making more efficient use of labor, which meant renegotiating the work rules of union contracts. There would be a social cost because people would lose their jobs. There would be the possibility of a national strike that could bring the national economy to a halt. This story begins at the end of 1959 over the issue of firemen on diesels. By 1970, not much progress had been made. Eventually, productivity saved the railroads.

Merger was another solution. By 1960, rail executives saw it as the panacea. Merger was something they might actually be able to pull off, and if they did, it would be their monument. During the 1960s, the panacea set states against railroads, the federal government against railroads, labor against railroads, and most of all, railroads against railroads, and ended in the worst business debacle in American history. As late as 1968, it was still regarded as the panacea, but from 1961 on, problems were evident.

Piggyback

Back in 1935 the Chicago Great Western, the wheezy Corn Belt Route, bankrupt and desperate, struck a deal with the Chicago-Dubuque Motor

Transport Company to carry its trailers on flatcars from Chicago to Dubuque for $42 a trailer.[1] The CGW modified the apparatus used by Ringling Brothers–Barnum & Bailey to tie down circus wagons on flatcars and came up with a system of chains and a screw jack, which it patented. It worked well enough that, into the 1960s, other railroads paid the CGW a royalty to use the screw jack system. Chicago-Dubuque was not satisfied and withdrew its business, but Great Western found other customers. The next year, the New Haven began carrying trailers for both common carrier truckers and shippers who owned their own trucks, Sears and Pepsi Cola. Piggyback was launched.

In 1953 the Southern Pacific was the first to solicit piggyback on its own, to move railroad-owned trucks on rail flatcars. Would this violate the Motor Carrier Act of 1935, which required a wall of separation between the modes? The SP was not sure, and so its first service was intrastate, Los Angeles to San Francisco. Soon, the pigs were common sights zipping out of town on the tracks beside San Fernando Boulevard. In 1953 the New Haven filed the famous "Twenty Questions Case" with the ICC for a declaratory ruling on what was and what was not legal. The ICC determined that the intercity movement of highway trailers by the railroad was not on a public right-of-way, which would have been illegal, but on a private right-of-way. Out of the case came the various piggyback plans:

—Plan I. The trucker dealt with the customer. The shipment moved at the rail rate for the commodity shipped. The trucker owned the highway rig.
—Plan II. The railroad dealt with the shipper. The shipment moved at the rail rate for the commodity involved. The railroad owned the highway rig.
—Plan III. The shipper dealt with the railroad. The rig moved over the rails at a flat rate regardless of the commodity—FAK (freight all kinds). The shipper owned the highway rig.
—Plan IV. The shipper dealt with a freight forwarder.
—Plan V. The shipper dealt with the railroad or the trucker. The shipper handled the loading at one end, the railroad or the trucker at the other end.

After the war Gene Ryan, whose early career was at Chevrolet and General Motors Acceptance, did some independent transportation consulting, witnessed piggyback on the CGW and the New Haven, and decided it had a future if technical problems could be overcome. First, a single trailer on a single flatcar was too heavy to lug around at a profit. An eight-wheel flatcar weighed 26 tons. Second, the loading was too slow. Each trailer had to be backed down a cut of flat cars, one at a time, and unloaded the same way in reverse order. It was called "circus loading" because circus wagons were loaded that way. It just plain took too long, while expensive rail crews and truck drivers stood around and watched.

In 1952 Ryan founded Rail-Trailer Company, and with old friends at GM's Electro-Motive Division (the largest manufacturer of diesel locomotives), he designed a flatcar to carry two 35-foot highway trailers and be loaded by a modified forklift. But the system required tracks to be depressed so that the truck parking lot was level with the top of the flat car. That meant capital investment, and the railroads hesitated. But in 1955 Ryan found backing from the Pennsylvania and the Norfolk & Western Railroads, financing from New York Life, and the operating expertise of the PRR's vice president for operations, Jim Newell, to create TrailerTrain, a pool of standardized 75-foot flatbed cars, each capable of carrying two 35-foot highway trailers.

No sooner had TrailerTrain taken its first delivery of cars than highway rigs went to 40 feet and the rail cars had to be redesigned. The PRR's mechanical department wanted to retreat to a single 50-foot flatcar for each trailer. Ryan and Newell understood that though this might be desirable from an operating point of view, it would flop commercially because of the cost of toting around all that tare weight. The push to design a safe 85-foot flatcar was critical to the success of the venture. In 1956 the Boston & Maine, the Burlington, the Katy, the Wabash, the Frisco, and the Missouri Pacific joined TrailerTrain; in 1957, the Chicago & North Western; in 1958, the Baltimore & Ohio, the first PRR competitor allowed in; in 1959, the Illinois Central, the Atlantic Coast Line, the Seaboard, the Nickel Plate, the Louisville & Nashville, and the Western Pacific; in 1960, the Santa Fe, the Southern Pacific, the Union Pacific, the Great Northern, the Northern Pacific, and the Chesapeake & Ohio.

Ryan himself was TrailerTrain's emissary to Jimmy Hoffa of the International Brotherhood of Teamsters. The Teamsters could sink the whole experiment. Ryan convinced Hoffa that piggyback would create more jobs for Teamsters, and Hoffa gave his okay so long as Teamsters loaded the rigs. But in the meantime, Ryan had a falling out with the PRR. They forced him out of TrailerTrain and forced him to give up his TrailerTrain stock. One did not cross the Pennsylvania Railroad.

Meanwhile, in 1957 Ryan, trailer manufacturer Roy Fruehauf, and Rocky Canzoneiro, who ran the New Haven's pioneering piggyback operation, teamed up to create a pool of trailers much as TrailerTrain created a pool of flatcars. They eventually linked up with Railway Express, which had a nationwide system of maintenance depots, and the result was Realco, created in 1960 as a trailer-leasing pool. Also out of the New Haven's piggyback unit, Carl Tomm and two friends from the Boston & Maine created another trailer leasing pool, XTRA, in 1957. XTRA pioneered "per-diem relief," which allowed a railroad to cut rental (per diem) charges by returning trailers, after unloading, to any of XTRA's nationwide depots. This eliminated the usual backhaul of railroad-owned boxcars and underscored the importance of nationwide pools of equipment.

After he was shoved out of TailerTrain, Ryan still had his Rail-Trailer Company. He and six truckers—Cooper-Jarett, Eastern Express, Denver-Chicago, Midwest Emery, Interstate, and Spector—formed TOFC Inc., named for *trailer on flatcar*. In 1960 TOFC Inc. contracted with the Erie Railroad to run solid piggyback trains between Chicago and New York at FAK rates (freight all kinds, a flat rate per trailer). The Erie was hungry for business and began building dedicated piggyback terminals at 51st Street in Chicago and Croxton Yard in New Jersey. What the venture proved was that railroads could roll solid trains of piggybacks over long distances very fast and very efficiently. If they stopped to fool around switching cars in and out along the way, the efficiency was lost, but an important concept was born.

There remained delicate equations to work out. Would piggyback win over new traffic or "cherry-pick" the most lucrative of the railroads' boxcar traffic? If it moved at a flat rate per trailer (FAK), it could mean a loss of revenue. Railroads with a short haul feared that long-haul roads would unload the trailers, deliver the cargo by road, and cut out the short-haul road altogether. The Long Island was especially touchy, and all the New England roads felt that they could lose a lot.

And there were problems. Hauling two sets of wheels added a lot to tare weight, even with 85-foot railcars. As long as oil was cheap, this was bearable, but if oil prices went up, the whole business could be rendered uneconomical in an instant. Loading and unloading remained a bottleneck. A crane that rode back and forth on its own wheels, designed to lift yachts out of the water, was modified to straddle a track. It could lift a highway trailer off a flat car, set it down, and move on to any other one in any random order. Drott Company bought the rights, and the crane was named the Drott Travelift. The PRR installed one at Kearny, New Jersey. It had a lot of promise, but it was experimental, and it was expensive. Railroads wanted to maximize the length of their haul and so built a lot of piggyback terminals. That required expensive switching, and as a result the service was no faster than for ordinary boxcars. If you were going to compete with trucks, you had to do a lot better than that.

So there were still problems. And there was not much profit yet. But it was such a promising idea that all kinds of experiments were under way. In 1957 the Chesapeake & Ohio introduced railvan, a highway trailer with a set of flanged wheels that could be raised when it was moving on the highway, lowered when riding the rails. On rails, the front of the trailer was supported by the trailer in front, so that each trailer rode on a single axle. Railvans carried mail on passenger trains in the C&O's Pere Marquette District, setting a speed record for mail between Detroit and Grand Rapids of three hours and 18 minutes in 1958. In 1958 the Portager was introduced by the Canadian Pacific and General Motors Diesel (Canada). It was a container on a four-wheeled railcar that solved the problem of a single-axle self-centering truck that did not scrape off the inside of the rails on curves. This involved complex axle-track geometry. Neither the Railvan nor the Portager was an immediate success, but both held enormous significance for the future. Shortly after, Al Perlman and the New York Central introduced Flexivan, manufactured by the highway trailer maker Strick. Flexivan allowed the truck trailer to leave its road wheels behind when it was loaded on a rail car. It was a brilliant idea with much promise, but for the moment, there remained bugs to be worked out.

The Merger Panacea

Consolidation appeared to offer great savings. It would be a shot of adrenalin just as the shot delivered by the diesel began to wear off. During the years of the crying towel, railroaders who had talked consolidation in the past but had done little about it now saw it as a way to retreat. It was presented as a bold plan to move forward, but it was retreat.

The purpose of consolidation at this point was not really better service, although words to that effect were usually thrown in. It was never for lower rates. It was to strengthen railroads by combining terminals and eliminating duplicate routes to save money. It was to be orderly retrenchment. Just about everyone since the World War I era thought consolidation was a good idea, but almost nothing had been done. All that had happened since the Transportation Act of 1920 had tried to foster consolidation amounted to baby steps around the edges. Developments since 1938 included the following:

—The Kansas City Southern bought the Louisiana & Arkansas in 1938. The L&A was a weedy route of light rails through a poor land, but its route from Dallas to Shreveport to New Orleans would someday make the KCS a major player.

—The Atlantic Coast Line completed acquisition of the Atlanta, Birmingham & Coast in 1945. It seemed to be just streaks of rust through a poor land. Probably no one could foresee that its routes from Birmingham and Atlanta to Waycross, Georgia, near Jacksonville, would one day carry some of the heaviest traffic in the South for CSX.

—The Denver & Rio Grande Western built a connection to the Denver & Salt Lake Railroad (the Moffat Road) from its own line at Dotsero, Colorado, 35 miles from a point on the D&SL called Orestod (Dotsero spelled backward). Completed in 1934 with Reconstruction Finance Corporation funds, it shortened the old route from Denver to Salt Lake City by 175 miles and meant that trains could tunnel under the Rockies through the six-mile Moffat Tunnel at Winter Park rather than cresting Tennessee Pass. The D&RGW began purchasing D&SL stock, and by 1947 the purchase was complete.

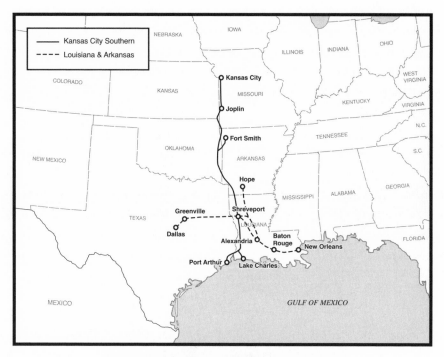

Kansas City Southern–Louisiana & Arkansas

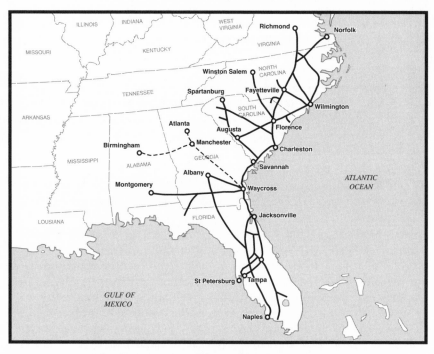

Atlantic Coast Line–Atlanta, Birmingham & Coast

—The C&O took the Pere Marquette in 1947; the Nickel Plate leased the Wheeling in 1949 (see chapter 3).

—The Gulf, Mobile & Ohio took the Alton in 1947. The GM&O was on the front edge of the panacea. It was a story of self-help and hope.

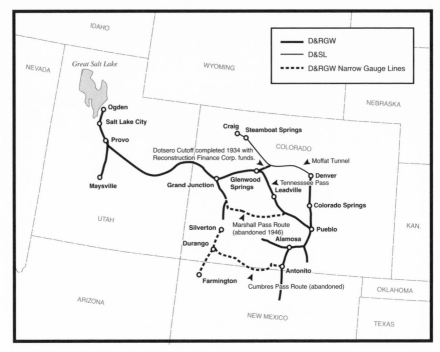

Denver & Rio Grande Western–Denver & Salt Lake

The Gulf, Mobile & Ohio

Back in 1941 the Gulf, Mobile & Northern (GM&N) merged with the Mobile & Ohio to create the Gulf, Mobile & Ohio. This was the vision of the GM&N's Isaac B. (Ike) Tigrett, and the success of the merger rested largely on Tigrett's energy. These railroads served the clay and pine hills of eastern Mississippi. That was not the cotton-rich Delta; it was a land of subsistence farms, cut-over forests, and, in those days, poverty of third-world dimensions. It was said that more broken-down cows per mile were run over by GM&O trains than by any other railroad, the dirt farmers hoping that the friendly judge would give them a little indemnity from the railroad's coffers, which to them must have seemed bottomless.

Tigrett's GM&N did not go north of Jackson, Tennessee. He made it viable by patching together dubious trackage arrangements with other railroads in order to reach friendly connections. He molded it into a modestly

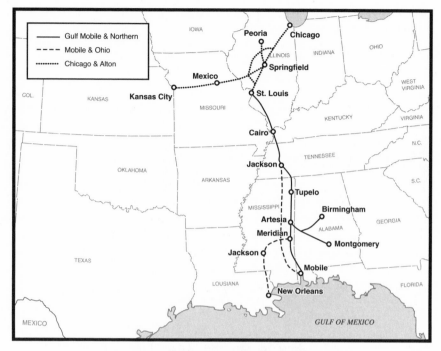

Creation of the Gulf, Mobile & Ohio

profitable entity in the 1920s. He even bought a little three-car shovel-nose streamliner in 1935, the Rebel. The Mobile & Ohio served the same area as the GM&N, but it also had a string line to St. Louis. Though it was bankrupt, Tigrett thought his stronger road coupled with the longer haul to St. Louis might give both roads a lease on life. These were railroads that had to expand or expire, said James Lemly, who wrote a history of the GM&O. It was a very modest merger. The GM&O never set railroading on fire, but it remained solvent and was able to buy diesels. Traffic through the port of Mobile picked up with the war, and things were looking up.

Tigrett was hopeful enough that in 1947 he merged the Alton into the GM&O. The Alton was a historic route between Chicago and Kansas City that was outstripped by later, straighter, shorter railroads. It was the straight-line speedway between Chicago, Springfield, and St. Louis, double tracked, fast, and busy. Its passenger trains were the Abraham Lincoln, the Ann Rutledge, the Alton Limited, and the Midnight Special, the last one a name that will forever live in the lore of railroading. They were not comfortable—mostly modernized heavyweight equipment—but they were pretty in their red and maroon paint, and they carried the crowds on a busy route.[2] It was not a long enough haul to make much money, passenger or freight. The line wallowed through the interwar years as an orphan of the B&O, which did not have enough money to invest in it. The GM&O did not have enough, either.

Tigrett did his best. Soon after the Alton merger, a St. Louisan wrote to tell him his trains to Chicago stank. He wrote back wistfully:

> Thank you for telling us about our poor service. We're trying mighty hard to improve things as best we can. Investors in Alton securities have lost $100 million over the last 35 years. Equipment has deteriorated and we have on order millions of dollars of new engines, new coaches and new freight cars. We hope you'll try us once more. We have a big job to do and we need your support.[3]

Tigrett wanted to sell the Alton's line to Kansas City. Then he could concentrate on north-south traffic and forget the east-west business, where Alton was a weak player anyway. The Santa Fe and the Burlington offered to buy the line. The Burlington wanted a better route into Kansas City, and the Santa Fe wanted to get into St. Louis. But other railroads went into a frenzy. The Missouri Pacific, the Frisco, the Rock Island, and the Cotton Belt could not abide the idea of the Santa Fe in St. Louis. They convinced the ICC to turn down the joint application. The Burlington went ahead and built its Brookfield Cutoff into Kansas City, and the GM&O line wallowed in obscurity.[4] Economist William Leonard lambasted the commissioners for ignoring what he thought were obvious economies. Most railroads, worried by how easily a worthwhile realignment was derailed, agreed with Leonard. Of course, the ICC was blamed, not the four railroads that had stirred up the ruckus.[5]

Labor: The *New Orleans* Conditions, 1948–1952

Labor thought consolidation was a code word for job reduction. Labor believed that capital would arrange the mergers to suit itself and working people would pay the cost. Management did not want strikes if it decided to merge, so it was willing to pay a price to have labor agreements in place to ensure that labor would go along, even if it went along only grudgingly.

By the terms of the Washington Agreement of 1936, workers who had to settle for less desirable jobs as a result of merger would receive a monetary allowance to make up the difference. Those who lost their jobs received separation pay of 60 percent of their previous salary. The protection lasted five years and began the day the person was actually affected (so long as that was within three years of the official date of consolidation—anything after three years was assumed to be caused by something other than consolidation). Since workers were subject to recall and would lose all benefits if they did not return, a provision was made for a lump-sum settlement. The company paid moving expenses, including losses on hastily canceled leases or hastily sold property.[6]

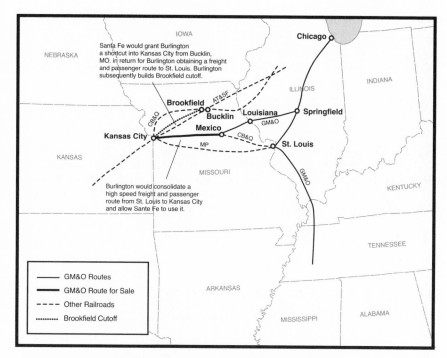

The Struggle over Alton's Kansas City Line

The Washington Agreement was a private collective bargaining agreement, not a law. It provided no protection at all for nonunion employees. There was no statutory protection, although the ICC had imposed protective conditions that had been upheld by the Supreme Court.[7] Most labor leadership did not want the Washington Agreement written into the Transportation Act of 1940, preferring collective bargaining to rigid codification. But during the floor debate in the House, Rep. Vincent Harrington of Iowa asked that all consolidation or coordination be prohibited if it resulted in the "impairment of existing employment rights of . . . employees." "If you want to pave the way for ghost railroad towns," he thundered, "if you want the blue envelope and the pink slip going out to 200,000 railroad employees, then do not vote for my amendment."[8]

The ICC was furious over the Harrington amendment. It had received days of testimony from brotherhood leaders and had written a bill that included everything they asked for. Only one union president, Alexander F. Whitney of the Brotherhood of Railroad Trainmen, wanted this ironclad prohibition, and Harrington was his mouthpiece. The House passed the amendment. The Senate refused. Now an interunion fight threatened to wreck the whole bill. Finally, a compromise was reached by imposing a time limit. The law would require 100 percent protection for four years from the date of the merger for every railroad wage earner affected by consolidation.[9] Thus, workers with union membership had two kinds of protection: by law, four years of 100 percent protection beginning the day the ICC gave its approval; and by collective bargaining agreement, five years of 60 percent protection beginning the day they were actually affected.

It took the ICC a few tries before it found a way to meet the new requirement and not bring all consolidation to a standstill. Under the so-called *Oklahoma* conditions of 1944, railroads were allowed to rearrange their workforce to suit themselves so long as employees' compensation remained the same for four years.[10] The *Oklahoma* conditions became routine, usually imposed for the benefit of nonunion employees. In the Pere Marquette and Wheeling & Lake Erie consolidations, for example, labor and management preferred the Washington Agreement, which they were free to substitute under the terms of the law.

When the railroads of New Orleans petitioned to build a new consolidated passenger terminal in 1948, a situation arose with which the *Oklahoma* conditions could not cope. The new station would not be completed until four years after the ICC gave its approval, during which time every old job would remain unchanged. Then, just as statutory protection ran out, there would be massive dismissals. The following solution emerged and was called the *New Orleans* conditions: workers received full protection under the *Oklahoma* conditions for four years. After that, any protection that might still accrue under the terms of the Washington Agreement was imposed as a matter of law. The *New Orleans* conditions were the standard protection for labor as the merger movement got under way.[11]

Management accepted this as a cost of consolidation. Labor was guaranteed that their lives would not be disassembled to suit the whim of the companies. Labor was free to oppose mergers before the ICC and before the courts; but after it had its say, it was bound by collective bargaining agreement and by law to accept the outcome. The companies were assured that there would be no general strikes as a result of consolidation.

The Florida East Coast, 1954

The bid by the Atlantic Coast Line to acquire the Florida East Coast set a significant legal precedent. What *Trains* called "Mr. Flagler's pretty railroad by the sea" carried tourists and citrus fruit between Jacksonville and Miami (and, until the hurricane of Labor Day 1935, to Key West).[12] It was such a logical extension of the ACL's Richmond-Jacksonville main line, and the two ran so many through passenger trains, that many people were unaware that it was a separate entity. Nonetheless, the FEC was also a friendly connection for the Southern Railway. The FEC had been in receivership since 1931. Florida businessman Edward Ball snapped up a majority of its bonds at bargain prices. Together with his brother-in-law,

Alfred I. DuPont, he put together an empire consisting of the railroad, several of Florida's major banks (the Florida National Group), and the big St. Joe Paper Company. The conglomerate was important in Florida commerce, and its roots sank deep into Florida politics. Ball loved Florida and wanted the FEC to remain small, independent, Florida-oriented, and (some thought) a big Lionel for him to play with.

The ICC thought a merger with the Coast Line made good operating sense and made such an affiliation a condition for the FEC's emergence from bankruptcy. Did that smack of a forced consolidation? Ball thought so, and he got the Supreme Court to agree.[13] Any kind of forced consolidation was out. If anything frightened the railroads about consolidation, it was the threat of being forced. Florida East Coast remained independent.

The Legal Prerequisites

The ICC and the railroads may have been in a go-slow mood, but all the legal prerequisites for consolidation were in place. The law, the Transportation Act of 1940, encouraged consolidation and allowed the railroads to plan it themselves, subject to approval. The Florida East Coast affair affirmed that there would be no coercion from government. The *McLean* decision set aside antitrust laws. The *Schwabacher* decision set aside restrictions by the states, including charter restrictions. The *New York Central Securities* decision provided a simple test for the term *public interest*. A railroad need only show that its proposal had a "direct relation to the adequacy of transportation services and to its essential condition of economy and efficiency."[14]

And the *DT&I* conditions, stemming from a request by the PRR to control the Detroit, Toledo & Ironton line, once a Henry Ford property, specified that merging railroads must maintain "all routes and channels of trade via existing junctions and gateways" and "all present traffic and operating relationships."[15] Railroads might merge, but they must continue to quote through rates and provide the same service with their old friendly connections as they had before. This muted objections from what could be consolidation's most effective opposition—other railroads. Since no real provision was made to enforce the *DT&I* conditions, merging railroads would be quite free to rearrange traffic patterns as they saw fit. Timidity ruled, nevertheless, and what action there was, was still on the fringes.

The Minneapolis & St. Louis, 1957

The Minneapolis & St. Louis Railway wanted to take over the Toledo, Peoria & Western (TP&W). The M&StL, called the Louie, though it did not go near St. Louis, was a little granger road, originally built by Minneapolis interests as a "rate breaker," to keep the rates charged by Chicago-based roads in line. It had one route west from Minneapolis to Aberdeen, South Dakota, and two routes south, one to Des Moines and one to Peoria. The Minneapolis-Peoria route formed a convenient bypass around the congestion at Chicago for traffic moving from the Northwest to the East. Quite a bit of traffic moved that way.

The M&StL was led by Lucian Sprague. Sprague improvised with new technology to find out what worked. He pioneered rail-highway and rail-waterway coordination (the latter on the Mississippi via Keithsburg, Illinois). He pioneered the use of IBM electronic calculators to keep track of cars with punched cards, very new in the 1950s. He bought diesels. The M&StL survived in the postwar age because of diesels, which compensated for its light rail and light bridges. Like Tigrett on the GM&O, Sprague got the most out of a marginal property. Unfortunately, he also had his hand in the till—they were petty thefts: a junket to Europe, a mink coat for his wife.[16] Described alternately as a visionary and a big fat crook, he was pushed aside by dissident stockholders led by Chicago lawyer Ben Heineman in 1954. Heineman provided very good management in the person of Pat Schroeder, brought in from the Chicago & Eastern Illinois. As with the GM&O, it was heartwarming to see a gutsy little company making it. But it lacked the capital to become a great railroad.

It was Heineman who sought to have the M&StL acquire the Toledo, Peoria & Western. The TP&W ran straight across Illinois, ferrying traffic from the Pennsylvania at Effner, Indiana, to the Santa Fe at Lomax, Illinois, allowing east-west traffic to bypass Chicago. It was a freight line, though one that ironically had had one of the worst passenger wrecks in American history: 82 excursionists bound for Niagara Falls were killed at Chatsworth, Illinois, in 1887. In the 1940s, the TP&W wrote a turbulent chapter in the history of industrial relations, which culminated in the 1947 assassination of its president, George P. McNear, Jr.

Heineman bid $69.50 a share for its stock. With the TP&W, the M&StL would form a giant 700-mile arc south and west of Chicago, but for no real purpose. "Tippy W" depended on the Santa Fe and the PRR. The big roads outbid the M&StL, and the ICC awarded it to them jointly. The affair seemed to indicate that big boys got what they wanted.[17]

The Nashville, Chattanooga & St. Louis, 1957

The Nashville, Chattanooga & St. Louis Railway from Memphis to Nashville, Chattanooga, and Atlanta (known locally as the N&C) had been controlled by the Louisville & Nashville since 1880. The two were operated separately and had quite different traditions, but the corporate linkage was well known. The L&N was controlled by the Atlantic Coast Line. In 1957 the N&C was merged into the L&N. Some have called this

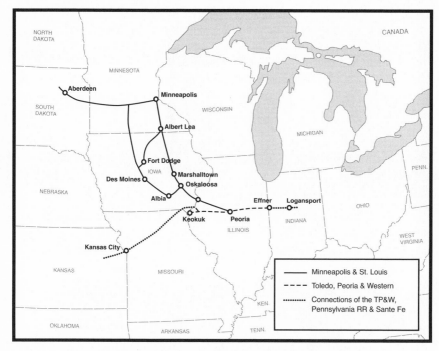

Minneapolis & St. Louis–Toledo, Peoria & Western Affair

the first of the modern mergers, but others thought it was merely a structural streamlining within the Coast Line family. Yet both the motive for merger and the obstacles that stood in its way anticipated things to come. If not a merger of truly separate entities, it was in many ways the prototype for all that followed.

The merger was meant to save money, in this case $3.75 million annually in operating expenses. Not much of this would come from the elimination of duplicate track; only a small segment of the N&C's line into Memphis would be eliminated, with trains rerouted over the L&N. The savings were going to come from the elimination of duplicate facilities and staff, money that could be spent on new capital improvement. It was the first merger whose principal objective was retrenchment.

The pattern of opposition would become familiar. Other railroads protested, in this case the Illinois Central and the Central of Georgia, for they would lose interchange traffic. The city of Nashville protested because all competition would be eliminated at this large and growing city except for the wheezing Tennessee Central. Stockholders of both roads protested because each group believed the other was getting a better deal. Labor protested that a total of 550 jobs would be lost, mostly in Nashville and surrounding Davidson County.

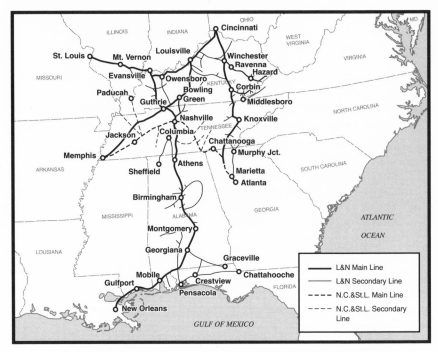

Louisville & Nashville–Nashville, Chattanooga & St. Louis Merger

The ICC faced the issues head-on. The L&N was ordered to retain all joint routes according to the *DT&I* conditions, but the IC and the CofG were advised that they might have to pay a price for the strengthening of railroads as a whole. Nashville was told that the benefits outweighed the damage of lost competition, as per the *McLean* decision. Stockholders were denied reconsideration, with the implication that they had tried to turn the merger to their own advantage. Labor was told that existing agreements gave it all the protection it was going to get.[18]

Furthermore, though it went down in popular wisdom that the ICC dragged its feet and created endless delays, the commission finished this case with reasonable dispatch. The misperception came from those who do not understand, or do not want to understand, the concept of due process, which attempts to balance the desires of those who want to move ahead with the fears of those who believe they have something to lose. Due process is designed to give every interested party an opportunity to present its case and then to respond to the cases of others.

Here is how it actually worked: the two roads agreed to merge on November 28, 1954, but did not submit their proposal until January 28, 1955. Hearings were held in August 1955, giving all parties time to prepare their cases. Then briefs were filed in which all parties had the opportunity to state their interpretation of the proceedings. The hearing examiner prepared a report for the full commission that outlined everyone's position and made a recommendation, in this case favorable to the merger. All parties were given time to file exceptions (rebuttals) to his report. The commission listened to oral argument, at which time each party could present a statement of its position in person before the full commission. After that, briefs were filed again and a report was prepared. Further exceptions were filed. A final decision was handed down on March 1, 1957. The L&N dropped its "Old Reliable" slogan and took the NC&StL's "Dixie Line." The merger was a success, and the L&N's position as a big player in southern transportation was strengthened.

Railroads that wanted to merge always said the process was too slow. Delay was an enemy of consolidation, for if the fortunes of one of the merger partners underwent a significant change in relation to the other while the case was in progress, the ratio at which they agreed to exchange their stock might have to be renegotiated or the whole deal might have to be called off. But those who believed their ox was being gored, including fellow railroads, expected due process, and that took time.

Deep in the mass of technical exhibits presented by the L&N lay a curious item. The NC&StL's locomotive repair shops at Nashville were to be phased out and all work transferred to the L&N shops at South Louisville. But the cost of repairs per unit, as revealed in such available sources as *Moody's Transportation Manual,* were less at the shop being phased out than at the one being retained. That was a small detail, but it caused some to wonder whether the people planning these mergers knew what they were doing or just had their fingers crossed.

Merger Talk

Two weeks before the L&N and the NC&StL made their first announcement in 1954, the Milwaukee Road and the Chicago & North Western announced that they were going to study coordination. Said David Morgan in *Trains,* "The slim statement handed out to the press was hazy in exact meaning but immense in its implication."[19] Early the next year, Patrick McGinnis, a gadfly in the mold of Robert Young, who had won control of the New Haven in a similar kind of proxy fight, said he would seek control of the Boston & Maine. William White, who had gone to the Delaware & Hudson after Young ousted him from the New York Central, proposed that the B&M join his D&H and, together with the Lackawanna and the Nickel Plate, form a new trunk line in the Northeast. The Lackawanna, in the meantime, announced that it would boldly abandon 70 miles of its main line and use the parallel tracks of the Erie. Although no mention was made of merger, the names of the two roads were linked from that day on. Consolidation had suddenly undergone a revival.

Why? Coincidence, perhaps, for none of the proposals were related. But the time was right. Traffic levels and profits were good during the Korean War. Even the New Haven was paying dividends and ordering new equipment. The gap between strong roads and weak ones was not so great. Then came the recession of 1954. It was short, but it was a jolt. In an industry with high fixed costs, even a mild recession brought a big reduction in earnings. The weak roads suddenly stood in stark contrast to the strong ones. The impact of the diesel had about run its course.[20] As soon as the jolt from 1954 was over, it was time to move. Mergers, like any bold change, take place smoothly when conditions are stable and differences blurred, a balm for all points of friction. The moment might never come again.

The initial spate of merger proposals washed out; a new management on the North Western in 1955 discontinued talks with the Milwaukee Road; Pat McGinnis was ousted from the New Haven; the Nickel Plate spurned the Lackawanna. But general talk about consolidation continued in the trade press; and in 1956 there was a whole new series of proposals. In the west, the Great Northern, the Northern Pacific, and the Burlington announced that they would re-create the Northern Securities empire. In the South, the Frisco said it would take the Central of Georgia. In the East, Perry Shoemaker of the Lackawanna prodded William White to substitute the Erie for the Nickel Plate and proposed an Erie-Lackawanna-D&H merger.

David Morgan in *Trains* was the first to sense the significance of all this upheaval. Commenting on the Milwaukee–North Western proposal, he noted that 1954 was not a good year for either road and that when the directors began their studies, "they would see parallel lines in thinly trafficked territory, two yards handling the tonnage of one. All railroaders," he said, "have much at stake. . . . A great many of them will be looking over the shoulders of this committee of directors as they sit down to study coordination." As for the Northerns, he recalled the *Northern Securities* decision of 1904 and asked who was right after all—Teddy Roosevelt, the trustbuster, or James Hill, the empire builder? Hill was accused of immoral and illegal action, but what he tried to do back then seemed like the right thing to do now. It was time to recall the words of banker Frank Spearman, back when "Northern Securities" was a tainted phrase: "That which will be incredible to men fifty years from now is that [Hill] should have been assailed as a wrongdoer. It should console Mr. Hill that in the canonization of really great men, the first appropriation is for faggots, the quarry of the marble being left to the third and fourth generation."[21]

The First Announcement of the Penn Central

On November 1, 1957, the Pennsylvania and the New York Central announced their "mutual intent" to make "further studies" into the possibility of merger. It was a thunderclap that shook all railroading. The next day, the *New York Times* called it the "best kept secret in financial circles." These were railroading's superpowers, two of the most intense and historic competitors in American business. They dominated the East. Together they would overshadow any other combination that could be put together in the region. The press settled down to a recitation of superlatives: assets of $5 billion, tenth largest of U.S. corporations, revenues of $1.5 billion, 80 million passengers a year, 378 million tons of freight, 184,000 employees. No small road thought it could survive against a combination like that. Yet for all their size, the Penn and the Central earned less than 1 percent on invested capital. They were marginal operators, said Robert Bedingfield in the *New York Times*. They were not sleek, powerful lions waiting to pounce, but dinosaurs—big, obsolete, and dying.

Robert Young of the NYC and James Symes of the PRR made the announcement separately from New York and Philadelphia. They said a merger would save $100 million a year. Then they appointed a committee to find out whether that was actually so. The *New York Times* said many railroaders doubted it would ever come to pass and thought the Penn and the Central were equally unsure themselves. George Alpert of the New Haven thought it was a gimmick to dramatize the plight of the eastern railroads. John S. Tompkins in the *Nation* thought it was all Young's doing, a way to blame his troubles on his "whipping boys of Wall Street" and fight the battle of the front pages for his legion of "Aunt Jane" stockholders.[22] After Young's death, some wondered whether his successor, Alfred Perlman, cared about merger at all. Perlman and Young differed on practically every other way to run a railroad, but for the time being, Perlman still wore a button in his lapel that said "merge."

The Penn Central proposal threw all other merger talk in the East into a state of panic, distorting it and compromising it. Whenever executives of the smaller roads met, at directors' meetings of the Association of American Railroads or at the Eastern Railroad Presidents' Conference, they would huddle over lunch and dinner to plan strategy. They came from a wide assortment of railroads: the wealthy C&O; the rather swaggering Nickel Plate; the Jersey Central, all weighted down with commuters, short hauls, and New Jersey taxes. Nobody quite knew how to treat the roads that the PRR kept in its stable—the Wabash, which it controlled, and the Norfolk & Western and Lehigh Valley, in which it had a dominant stock interest. Were they going to be part of a Penn Central? Even their own officers had no idea. Could confidences be shared with them or were they in the enemy camp?

In January 1958 Howard Simpson of the Baltimore & Ohio casually mentioned to Walter Tuohy of the Chesapeake & Ohio that their railroads "ought to get together."[23] The C&O, in the meantime, extended feelers to the Nickel Plate. The Nickel Plate was lean, busy, and quite debt-free, and it was not very big, so it would likely be the subordinate partner in a merger.

That made it a real catch. The B&O was in contact with the Nickel Plate as well, and some of the Nickel Plate's financial officers actually went to Baltimore to look the B&O over. They "put on their double bifocals when they looked at our financial reports," Simpson said ruefully later on.[24]

The public read about these mergers, looking at maps to see who connected which dots. The real substance of who could merge and who could not lay below the waterline, so to speak; it was a matter of how deeply a railroad was in debt and what bond issues were coming due, not what dots it connected. In deepest secrecy, the Norfolk & Western was in contact with the Nickel Plate. Those two did not connect any dots at all—there was no physical connection between them. But they were both big earners with minimal debt. All this was very secret, and no agreements were reached.

The outcasts—everyone outside the Penn-Central—felt that they had to assume the worst, that the Penn-Central studies would be completed soon and the case would go to the commission. Should they oppose it separately or together, and if so, on what grounds? Should they acquiesce and hope for the best or should they submit counterproposals of their own? In the second week of November 1958, they met in Cleveland in a kind of summit conference of the "outer seven"—the Erie, the Nickel Plate, the Lackawanna, the D&H, the B&O, the C&O, and the Reading. William White was thought to be the instigator.[25] No commitments were made, but channels of communication were open.

The same month, the New England roads held their own summit in Portland on the initiative of the Maine Central's E. Spencer Miller. Those roads were not compatible either. The Bangor & Aroostook and the Maine Central were wiry enough to stand alone or to merge with trunk lines, but the Central Vermont was Canadian-owned, the New Haven was heading toward bankruptcy, and the Rutland was closer to liquidation than anyone guessed. It was said that George Alpert, the violin-playing president of the New Haven, and Pat McGinnis, who had gone to the Boston & Maine after Alpert ousted him from the New Haven, loathed the very sight of each other. One "Wall Street observer" in the *New York Times* wondered, "How are these railroads going to sit down and work out a merger when they can't even work out the freight charges between them on a bushel of potatoes?"[26] Nevertheless, the Portland gathering put Spencer Miller in charge of a committee to study consolidation and hire consultants if need be.

The Transportation Act of 1958 did not touch on consolidation, but it was a subject of interest at the hearings. Senator Smathers thought it might be the answer to the railroads' problems and wrote an article about it in *This Week* magazine in which he called for four regional railroad monopolies, one in each quadrant of the nation, an idea *Trains* dismissed as "old as the hills."[27] The only way such a thing could come to pass would be to cram it down security owners' throats, because owners of strong railroads' securities were not going to see their equity watered down by weak railroads. The lawmakers kept repeating how we must strengthen the private enterprise system, but they clearly did not understand its nuances.

By the time of the Outer Seven and New England conferences, rumor was rife that the New York Central was no longer interested in the PRR. Perlman was still wearing his "merge" button but otherwise seemed strangely silent. Then on January 8, 1959, he said simply that he thought merger would be unwise at this time, although coordination short of merger might be worth looking into. "Before we marry the girl," he said a few days later, "we want to make sure there is no other heiress around that might fall into our lap." The Outer Seven and the New England talks ended abruptly. Perlman proposed that all eastern railroads get together and plan a series of rational mergers. *Trains* thought the idea was statesmanlike. "Railroad merger talk to date has been remarkable for its disregard of industrywide implications."[28]

Some thought Perlman was just weaseling out of a merger in which he and his company would play second fiddle. If that seemed selfish, he thought the PRR was downright grasping. After the deal was off, the PRR said it was not interested in coordination short of merger no matter what the savings might be. Perlman said the merger was the PRR's idea in the first place, that James Symes was its only real proponent, and that the PRR people had badgered him about it ever since.

The Virginian Railway, 1959

What was bothering Perlman, and it bothered him mightily, was that he thought the PRR had double-crossed him when, late in 1958, the Norfolk & Western announced that it would merge with the Virginian Railway. The Virginian was the Central's friendly connection to the West Virginia coalfields. The PRR controlled the N&W, or at least Perlman and just about everyone else thought so.[29] If the N&W gobbled the Virginian, the PRR would be stronger and the Central would be stripped. In a chess analogy, the PRR would have just taken the Central's bishop.

The N&W-Virginian merger was textbook perfect. Both roads went from the coalfields of West Virginia to tidewater at Hampton Roads. Both roads were very busy, so this was not a case of retrenchment. It was a case of building one super-railroad out of the best pieces of two that had heavy grades. The two roads crossed the same three mountain ranges. The Virginian had better grades over the Allegheny and Blue Ridge Mountains, whereas the N&W had better grades over Elkhorn Mountain. If connections were built at Roanoke and at Kellysville, West Virginia, trains could take advantage of the best grades over all three ranges, and helpers could be eliminated on the N&W. If all coal was routed to the N&W's Lamberts Point Terminal in Norfolk, the tonnage would justify the finest of automatic unloading equipment. After combining yards, shops, and executive staffs, the merger could save $14 million a year.[30]

The United Mine Workers and every community along the two lines endorsed the merger. West Virginia bituminous coal was used for coking (making coke for steelmaking) and for fueling steam plants for generating electricity. There was still a growing demand for it, but it was threatened by oil, gas, nuclear and water power, and perhaps by fuels yet unknown.[31] It was important for these communities and for the miners to get the coal to market as cheaply as possible to forestall the development of substitutes.

Stuart Saunders, the ambitious president of the N&W, prepared a pep talk on merger that he delivered to citizens' meetings in school gymnasiums up and down the line. He was very persuasive. He even dispelled the doubts of the Virginian's principal owners, Eastern Gas and Fuel Associates, a division of Koppers. He told Koppers that the Virginian had no traffic but coal; linking up with N&W, which did have some general traffic, would insulate it against the collapse of the bituminous market.

Railroad workers were not nearly as enthusiastic as the miners. When Saunders delivered his pep talk to the lawyers of the Railway Labor Executives' Association, he added as a finishing flourish that no railroad employees would lose their jobs as a result of the merger. That was more than labor ever asked for in collective bargaining. The labor lawyers were taken by surprise and asked if he would put that in writing. He said he would have to talk to his lawyers and scurried out of the room. When he returned, he said yes.

The result was the first "attrition agreement." Anyone whose job was rendered obsolete by merger could be transferred to other parts of the system, at company expense and at no loss of salary. When they retired or died, they would not be replaced if the position was not needed. But no person then employed by either the N&W or the Virginian would lose his or her job.[32] Probably not even Stuart Saunders realized what a major victory labor had won without even going before the ICC or the courts.

The N&W-Virginian merger was approved October 8, 1959. Work began immediately on the new connections at Roanoke and Kellysville. A parallel merger for the purpose of concentrating traffic was a reality, and Stuart Saunders was a man to watch. But Perlman was steamed, and relations between the NYC and the PRR were frigid.

Warnings on the Eve

On the surface, the Virginian merger seemed to be a smashing success. The ICC was able to demonstrate that it looked favorably on merger. Management, labor, local communities, and even other railroads seemed to emerge in harmony. Perlman kept his anger to himself; few knew how profoundly this had queered the Penn-Central relations. On the surface, merger was the

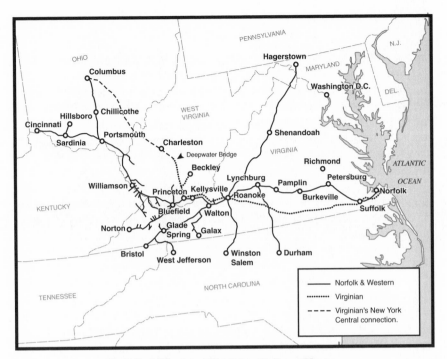

Norfolk & Western–Virginian Railway Merger

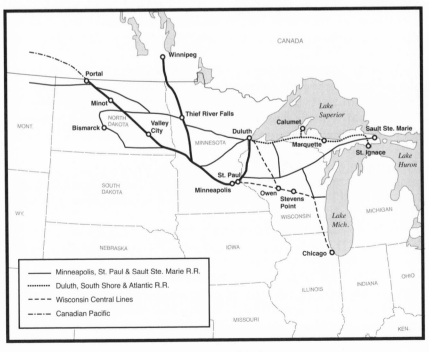

Soo Line Consolidation

salvation of railroading, the great panacea, the solver of all problems.

Down the track, yellow caution signals flickered. Capital sent one of the messages. In 1960 the Canadian Pacific merged its three subsidiaries in the midwestern United States—the Soo Line, the Wisconsin Central, and the Duluth, South Shore & Atlantic (DSS&A)—all under the Soo Line banner. (The Soo Line and the Wisconsin Central had operated as a single unit for some time.) Opposition was minimal except over the loss of jobs at DSS&A facilities on Michigan's Upper Peninsula. But the price of Soo Line bonds fell abruptly after merger. The Soo Line's president, Leonard Murray, insisted that it was because of poor grain harvests brought on by bad weather. If so, the euphoria that was supposed to accompany a merger did not last long.[33]

Labor sent up a warning. After Ben Heineman left the Minneapolis & St. Louis and won control of the Chicago & North Western, he bought the railroad properties of the M&StL, which was integrated into the C&NW. (The old M&StL corporation, now an empty shell, restructured itself as a holding company conglomerate, called itself MSL Industries, and went primarily into hardware and finished steel products. It was eventually bought out by Alleghany Corporation.) Despite the agreements between labor and management, carrying them out required specific "implementing" agreements, which meant that each lodge (local) of each brotherhood had to consent to, among other things, the merging of seniority rosters. The engineers in this case refused to sign and threatened a strike. An eleventh-hour settlement did not disguise the fact that labor might not docilely accept management's merger decisions.[34]

Shippers sent up a warning. The little M&StL had a legion of loyal shippers on the Albert Lea Route, where it connected with the Illinois Central for a through route between the Twin Cities and Chicago. Despite the *DT&I* conditions, the North Western effectively closed the Albert Lea Route by making sure trains were scheduled to miss the IC connection. Shippers did not like it and told the Minnesota Railroad and Warehouse Commission.[35] The *DT&I* conditions turned out to be ineffectual, and merger had resulted in a deterioration of service, contrary to what the railroads had said but consistent with what had happened in the past when competition was reduced.

The Frisco began to buy stock in the Central of Georgia with intent to seek control. The Alabama and Georgia Public Service Commissions fell in line immediately, in what would become a pattern for southern state agencies. Only the Illinois Central seemed to object, fearing the loss of a friendly CofG connection at Birmingham on the City of Miami route between the Midwest and Florida. (The IC had controlled CofG before CofG's receivership during the depression.) The commission approved the Frisco bid in July 1957, mainly because of CofG's inability to generate income for capital improvements.

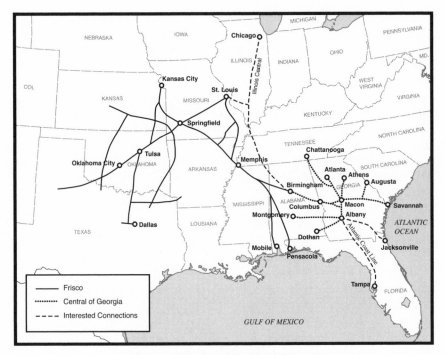

Frisco–Central of Georgia Affair

Then there came to light evidence that the Frisco actually had effective control before permission was given. It had kept secret the full extent of its purchases of CofG stock. Even while hearings were in progress, it borrowed money to buy more CofG stock until it had 66 percent. Fearing that this would be discovered sooner or later, it put the stock in a trust that the ICC believed was phony. "The public interest is concerned not only with improvements in transportation service," said the ICC, "but with . . . respect for and observance of the law."[36] The Frisco's permission to control was revoked.

The commission got very little criticism about this from other railroads. It was apparent that the moment for consolidation had come, and it was no time for preemption and piracy like there was in the 1920s, especially not from middle-weight players like the Frisco. When the stakes were high, railroads, like everyone else, wanted the regulators to keep order.

"I hear a lot more serious talk about merger than I can remember," said *Railway Age* editor Jim Lyne in December 1959. "People doing the talking were not serious advocates of it in the past. The head of a medium-sized road told me he had no enthusiasm for mergers until recently, but changed his mind because the growth of competing transportation was forcing railroads to concentrate traffic on low-cost routes."[37]

John Barriger, veteran of the Prince Plan studies in the 1930s, by now a New York Central lieutenant as head of its Pittsburgh & Lake Erie subsidiary, suggested transcontinental systems like Canadian National and Canadian Pacific. All the American railroad builders of the nineteenth century thought in transcontinental terms and were frustrated by accidents, not economics, he said. Consolidation began in the 1950s as a plan for orderly retreat, but it would become an advance in force if pursued according to his plan. He suggested that the carriers hold their own "Congress of Vienna" to get the process going.[38]

"What's holding up railway mergers?" asked *Railway Age*.[39] In the *New York Times*, Robert Bedingfield concluded that "when something everyone loudly asserts should be done is not done, there are two possible answers. Either it can't be done or some vocal advocates have their fingers crossed." After a year of talk since the "fuse was lit on Penn-Central, it was as firmly anchored to its launching pad as when it started." The usual progress in merger, he said, was "dramatic announcement, long 'study' and nothing."[40]

The Doyle Report (as mandated by the Transportation Act of 1958) did not help much. It called for consolidation planning but said no carrier should be forced to do anything against its will.[41] That had not worked in the 1920s, and there was no reason to think it would now. Without compulsion, railroad star performers would seek out other star performers, and wallflowers would have to be content with other wallflowers. The report was quickly buried and forgotten.

The decade coming was not going to be kind to the railroads. Recession would pass. After 1962, the economy was expansive and boomy. But for the railroads, absolute gains were small and market share dwindled (see table 4).

On April 22, 1959, the Erie and the Lackawanna, two wallflowers, announced that they would merge without the D&H. The hearings began in September.

On March 18, 1960, Stuart Saunders made the first carefully hedged announcement that the Norfolk & Western would seek to merge with the Nickel Plate. Having just pulled off the Virginian merger, Saunders was bullish. His negotiations with the Nickel Plate's chairman, Lynn White, and its president, Felix Hales, were done in deep secrecy, and the details of their arrangements were not finalized on the day of their announcement. If merger was supposed to be for the purpose of combining parallel lines, then what was the point of merging these two? Their rails did not meet anywhere. How would they connect? There was talk that the Nickel Plate might extend a secondary line from Fort Wayne to Muncie, Indiana, into Cincinnati. Would the ICC allow new construction? Indiana was crisscrossed with underused railroads. How could anyone justify building another one? There was talk that the N&W might acquire the Detroit, Toledo & Ironton, Henry Ford's old railroad for hauling coal to the River Rouge plant in Dearborn, Michigan. At the moment, DT&I was controlled by the

Table 4 Basic Statistics for All Class I Railroads, 1961–1971

	1961	1963	1965	1967	1969	1971
Operating Revenues ($ billions)	9.3	9.7	10.4	10.6	11.7	12.2
Rate of Return (%)	1.97	3.12	3.69	2.46	2.36	2.49
Ton Miles (billions)	569.9	629.3	708.7	731.2	780.0	744.0
Share of total (%)	42.96	43.02	43.02	41.43	41.07	38.6
Employees (thousands)	715.9	679.8	639.9	610.2	578.3	544.9
Ave. wage/hour	$2.46	$2.82	$3.07	$3.36	$3.79	$4.52

Source: figures extracted from *Moody's Transportation Manual* based on data reported to the ICC.

PRR, so its acquisition by N&W would have to be with the acquiescence of the PRR. The PRR owned 34 percent of the N&W. Most people thought the PRR was behind the N&W–Nickel Plate.

On April 28, 1960, reporter Robert Bedingfield was covering the C&O annual stockholders meeting for the *New York Times,* and a remark by C&O president Walter Tuohy sent him scurrying to the telephone to call other railroad presidents. He deduced that the C&O was seeking to control the B&O. The *New York Times* scooped the story the next day. The moment for consolidation, at least in the East, had come. The New York Central was out in the cold. The Central's Alfred Perlman called on the ICC to investigate and to rethink the practice of approving railroad-initiated mergers on a case-by-case basis.[42]

Firemen on the Diesel

At the end of 1958, the Canadian Pacific forced the issue of firemen in the diesels and took a short strike, which led to the creation of a Royal Commission, which in 1959 allowed both the CP and the Canadian National to stop hiring new firemen. In the United States, after the disappointment of the Smathers Act, with no help coming from government, the railroads decided they could no longer be welfare agencies for unproductive work. Their labor contracts would expire on October 31, 1959. At an AAR meeting of railroad presidents, the Santa Fe's Fred Gurley asked the Burlington's vice president of labor relations, James "Doc" Wolfe, to report on the status of negotiations with the engineers. Talk turned to the fireman issue. Some of the railroads, admiring and rather jealous of the Canadians' breakthrough, wanted to tackle the problem immediately and alone. Wolfe suggested that there was a greater chance for success if the industry bargained as a whole, if they coupled the fireman issue with other work-rule problems, and if they aggressively enlisted the support of public opinion. The gathered presidents liked what they heard and chose Wolfe to head up industrywide efforts. On November 2, 1959, the railroads gave Section 6 notices under the Railway Labor Act of their intent to revise work rules, including the elimination of firemen.

To enlist public opinion, a tough tactical decision had to be made. This was not to demand the elimination of firemen on passenger trains for fear of arousing a public panic over safety. Wolfe knew it was a lose-lose choice. There was no safety need for firemen—New York City subways with a thousand or more people on a train operated on five-minute headway with only a single motorman. Accidents were rare. But saying that firemen made passenger trains safer opened a wedge for the unions to insist that safety required them on all trains.

The next decision to arouse public opinion probably backfired. It certainly left lasting mistrust and bad feelings. The decision was to use the word *featherbedding* to describe the work rules then in place. The word had been used before; the public was familiar with it. But it had never been used so officially in national negotiations. It was pejorative, implying not that the situation was the result of an institutional impasse but that the fireman himself was a lazy cheater. Firemen faithfully did their job, the job they were hired to do, on call day and night, in all kinds of weather. It was not a personal failing. The railroads did more than just say "featherbedding." They emblazoned it all over full-page newspaper ads, complete with cartoons of fat railroad workers asleep on their featherbeds. It was nasty.

The unions retaliated with management-baiting. Their advertisements accused management of incompetence, of "living in a dream world," of risking "unconscionable slaughter" over safety, and they suggested that if management pushed this thing, it was time to confiscate their property and nationalize the railroads.[43] Deep in its heart of hearts, labor may have thought that to avoid a crippling strike, the government would nationalize the railroads and keep labor peace by retaining all the featherbed jobs. The European countries had done it. They made a conscious decision to use railroads as a cover for patronage and workfare. Some of the U.S. rail unions were beginning to think the European model was a pretty good one.

Another work rule up for negotiation in the 1959 talks was the rigidities that were set up when mileage was used as a base for pay instead of hours. It led to serious inequities. Older workers who had the seniority to get regular assignments in passenger service were assigned regular hours on high-speed trains—a "day's work" done in three hours or less. Younger workers had irregular schedules that often extended to the limit of hours of service—16 hours in those days—and included layovers in distant bunkhouses. Since there was no clear retirement age, many of the engineers on fast passenger trains were over 70 years old, which backed up all the junior men who were waiting for their crack at a plush assignment.

Another problem was the stark division between road work and yard work, which required separate crews for each kind of work, or a compensatory "day's" pay if one had to do even a single operation of the other's work. This rigidity could be fatal to the railroads' future because it discouraged timely pickup and delivery of cars to customers' sidings. When trucks could move from loading dock to loading dock, and the railroad could not compete with that service because of union rules, the long, slow death of the railroad was the likely consequence. As the interstates opened and truck service improved, this service deficiency was going to be one of the most crippling.

The brotherhoods had telling points to make, too. Railroad service, certainly for younger men, meant being on call at all times. Trains arrived at crew points at any time of the day or night, and a fresh crew had to be ready to take over, rested and alert for up to 16 hours of duty. Those who have never done this kind of work do not understand. When a call can come at anytime, there is no time for a life: no time for a movie, no time to go to the store. The worker must wait by the phone, and some days no call comes and the time is wasted. And there is no body rhythm. It is not like shift work, even night shifts, where there is a rhythm and the body adjusts. There was no pay for layovers at the other end of the line, usually in a bunkhouse with little privacy—endurable for young men, very difficult for older men. Factor in the hardships, said the unions, and look at the whole compensation package, not just "days" of pay, and railroad pay was not out of line with commensurate skills in other industry. On this matter, they were correct.

Negotiations broke down in October 1960. Both sides agreed to ask for a special study commission appointed by the president with members from management, labor, and the public. One was set up. Most of the public members were academics. Federal Judge Simon Rifkind was appointed to head it. He was an old New Dealer and the key author of the Wagner National Labor Relations Act of 1935. Doc Wolfe's heart sank when he heard that Rifkind was appointed. But Rifkind understood the need for productivity. He wanted free enterprise to work fairly for all, not just the rich and powerful, but he wanted it to work.

The Rifkind Commission worked hard for 15 months. Safety was a burning issue, and Wolfe mounted a solid case that safety was not compromised by the proposed changes. When the unions brought in pictures of points where safety would be sacrificed by using smaller crews, Wolfe had supervisors operate with three-person crews at those very locations, filmed them in action, and showed the commission that there was no problem. The commission's 500-page final report, issued on February 28, 1962, was a reasoned set of recommendations that actually would have meant higher wages for most rail employees but at honest jobs of productive work. It would have loosened the rigidities of seniority to reduce the bizarre discrepancies in hours worked and money earned, but it would not have wholly abandoned mileage pay and road-yard demarcations. It rejected the harsher demands of both sides, management's demand that management alone determine the size of crews and labor's demand for an annual employment guarantee. It did recommend that no new firemen be hired. No one who had a job would be fired, but firemen could be transferred to other jobs on the railroad and the craft would die out, much as the Royal Commission had recommended in Canada three years before.[44]

Management was guardedly pleased with the report. Labor denounced it as class warfare. Commission member A. F. Zimmerman, assistant grand chief engineer of the Brotherhood of Locomotive Engineers, refused even to sign it. Collective bargaining resumed in a mountain of animosity. The brotherhoods said productivity was going up, that fewer workers were performing more work. That was statistically true, but it was still no excuse to retain useless jobs. In the public mind, the image of the fireman on the diesel became the metaphor for unions that no longer defended the working person but stood in the way of progress and hurt everyone.

On July 17, 1962, management again served notice under Section 6 of the Railway Labor Act to institute the recommendations of the Rifkind Commission in 30 days. Labor fought back. Collective bargaining deadlocked. The unions filed suit in federal court to block management and lost in district court, appeals court, and the Supreme Court. On April 2, 1963, the railroads served notice again. A strike loomed. President Kennedy ordered a Presidential Emergency Board, number 154, under the Railway Labor Act, to make a recommendation. On May 13, that board recommended the Rifkind Report with a few extra sweeteners for labor. In 30 days, on June 12, all the mechanisms of the Railway Labor Act would be exhausted, and a strike loomed again.

Willard Wirtz, Kennedy's secretary of labor, tried to get both sides to accept arbitration. His efforts bought time and almost a breakthrough. Management and most of labor were willing, but Charles Luna, the new head of the Brotherhood of Railroad Trainmen, balked hard. On August 27, 1963, with a strike set and traffic embargoed, Congress ordered binding arbitration on the issues of fireman and crew size alone. Wayne Morse, Oregon Democrat and a friend of labor, said on the Senate floor that the brotherhood chiefs had themselves to blame for the first compulsory binding arbitration ever in peacetime. Luna was sitting in the front row of the gallery when he said it.

The panel was Arbitration Board 282. Wolfe led the management delegation. H. E. "Ed" Gilbert of the Brotherhood of Locomotive Firemen & Enginemen led labor's. Kennedy named Benjamin Aaron of UCLA and James Healy of Harvard as the neutral members. Ralph Seward was chosen to head it. He was a professional arbitrator, a veteran of the National Defense Mediation Board and the War Labor Board, and a permanent mediator between the United Steel Workers and the steel industry. Again, Wolfe doggedly debunked claims that safety would be compromised, just as he had before the Rifkind Commission.

The board rendered its verdict on November 26, 1963. The nation barely noticed, because in the days just preceding, Kennedy was murdered and buried. The nation was utterly distracted. But it was a great breakthrough both for the railroads and for workers who served loyally but whose skills were displaced by time and technology. The railroads could eliminate firemen, but no one who had a job would lose it. As firemen retired or were transferred to other jobs, they would not be replaced, and the old profession would be swallowed by time. There was a generous severance package for those who wished to leave.

But the brotherhoods were furious and challenged the constitutionality of arbitration in court. On April 27, 1964, the Supreme Court refused to review a lower court's denial of the unions' argument. Then the union tried to divide and conquer by striking individual roads—first the L&N, then the Southern Pacific. Both were stopped by injunction. On the morning of April 8, 1964, they struck the Illinois Central without warning. Commuter trains did not operate. One hundred thousand people had no way to get to work. Wolfe said "I'll be damned" and told all railroads to serve Section 6 notices on all work rules issues. That forced matters back to the national level, and now a national strike was imminent.

President Johnson got a promise from all parties for a fifteen-day postponement. On April 11, 1964, he summoned them to the White House. He gave them the Johnson "treatment" of jawboning and touching—a slap on the back, a threatening tug of the lapel. He put them all in the Cabinet Room of the White House for round-the-clock bargaining. He dropped in on them often and rambled in long sentences, using words like *seizure* (which scared the pants off management) and *arbitration* (which scared the pants off labor). He never quite spelled out what he would do if they failed to come to an agreement. The poet Carl Sandburg was visiting the White House, and Johnson took him into the Cabinet Room to show him industrial democracy at work. On April 22, Johnson had an agreement, pretty much along the lines of the recommendations of Presidential Emergency Board 154.[45] The big item was that no more firemen would be hired for freight or switching operations.

Johnson was jubilant. When he learned that it would take more than an hour to get microphones set up in the White House, he ordered a motorcade to take him to the CBS studios in Washington. CBS would feed the announcement to the other networks.

> Good evening, my fellow countrymen. Tonight the nation can celebrate an agreement that has been reached between the railroad companies and the men who operate the trains. This settlement ends four and a half years of controversy. I tell you quite frankly there are few events that give me more

faith in my country and more pride in the free collective bargaining process. . . . This is the face of American industrial democracy that we can proudly show to the world.[46]

Wolfe was a hero. He had begun on the railroad as a coal-chute operator, then moved to engine wiper, switchman, and clerk before studying his way into labor relations. He was a tough guy through the whole long ordeal, and he played his trumps well. His drink was boilermakers. But in creating Arbitration Board 282, Congress mandated that its decisions were for two years. Ed Gilbert of the Brotherhood of Locomotive Firemen promised that he would be back and the process would start from scratch.

In 1966 Gilbert demanded not only that firemen be reinstated but that they get cost-of-living adjustments and night-shift differentials. Doc Wolfe said of the firemen, "They make no worthwhile contribution to our operations." He was right, of course. It was an honorable profession that time had rendered useless. "What can I do?" asked Gilbert. He was elected by his men to defend them. He felt that he could not sign their jobs and union away. Jimmy Paddock of the Order of Railway Conductors offered the possibility of a merger of the two unions, but Gilbert could not bring himself to that. Gilbert and his union had been given a fig leaf to leave the field with a semblance of dignity. The issue was far from over.

SIX

The Erie Lackawanna
The Agony of the
Perfect Merger,
1960

On September 17, 1960, the Interstate Commerce Commission approved the merger of the Erie Railroad and the Delaware, Lackawanna & Western, to take place in 30 days, on October 17, 1960. The new company would be called the Erie-Lackawanna.[1] It was the first major merger of competing railroads that did not have a prior corporate linkage.

Everyone smiled. Erie president Harry Von Willer and Lackawanna president Perry Shoemaker smiled and shook hands in front of a big wall map of the new company. Erie fireman Truman G. Knight of Stow, Ohio, smiled as he was presented with 20 shares of Erie Lackawanna stock for designing its new diamond-shaped emblem in a contest. Painter Harold Johnson smiled as he applied the new emblem to the nose of an Erie diesel. Passenger agents smiled as they met to design the new public timetable. Freight agents smiled as they unveiled the new gray and maroon boxcars. The Erie-Lackawanna was front-page news in the *New York Times* and the *Cleveland Plain Dealer* and in papers up and down the system.

In that fleeting moment everyone pretended that the future was bright. Two busy freight and passenger haulers, regardless of their very different histories and traditions, hoped that by combining they would overcome temporary weakness and be made strong again. The Erie and the Lackawanna provided vital service to millions of people, starting with 100,000 New Jersey commuters, who rode the trains every workday. They were run by technocrats who loved the railroad and wanted it to be able to perform those services, trying to solve the railroad's problems without government help.

Forty years later, it all seems pointless. Very little is left of the Erie Railroad west of Hornell, New York. Hardly anything is left at all of what was the Lackawanna Railroad, except for commuter lines in New Jersey run by New Jersey Transit and a portion between Scranton and Binghamton. It was one of the very first super-railroads, built to engineering excellence for high speed and high capacity; now there are only ghosts.

Two weeks after the ICC decision and shortly before the actual merger, some of the company's unions got a restraining order to stop any substantive changes in operations pending a settlement of grievances. The company could go ahead and call itself the Erie-Lackawanna but otherwise had to remain unmerged. The smiles began to fade. It was the beginning of the long travail of the Erie Lackawanna.

Trains magazine said at the outset that the merger "was like a man in a leaky boat lending a hand to a man in shark-infested waters."[2] Ultimately, the savings that the merger promised did not amount to much. Merging one troubled railroad with another troubled railroad produced a bigger troubled railroad. The Erie Lackawanna would demonstrate why consolidation was not a panacea, although before it was all over and the Erie Lackawanna was folded into Conrail, it also showed how an honest little underdog could run circles around the dinosaur—the Penn Central—that would become its main competitor.

Two Traditions

In popular lore the Erie was poor and known as the "weary Erie." It was completed across southern New York State, the counties along the Pennsylvania border known as the Southern Tier, in 1851. It was financed on a shoestring and plunged into its first receivership in 1857. The infamous Erie ring of Drew, Fisk, and Gould watered its stock in one of the seamiest business scandals of the robber-baron age and pushed it into a second receivership in 1875. Depressions in the 1890s and the 1930s forced it twice more into receivership. It was said that hell would freeze over before the Erie's common stock paid a dividend. The Erie was a vaudeville joke: "I need to get to Chicago in the worst way." "Take the Erie." Four bankruptcies never wrung out the excessive debt. The interest on the debt ran around $5 million a year in the 1950s, consuming virtually all of the railroad's net income by the late 1950s. The Erie might have been a great railroad if it had not been for the debt.

The Erie's main line was double tracked with troublesome but not impossible grades across eastern Ohio. Its track was laid with heavy rail, and the Erie could roll a lot of fast freight. It generated only about 32 percent of its own freight traffic, receiving 68 percent from connections. A healthy 60 percent of its traffic was high-rated manufactures; another 14 percent was products of agriculture, much of it western perishables received from connections at Chicago for the long haul to New York and New England. On the downside, its main line missed just about every major city between its terminals at Chicago and Jersey City. Akron was the largest intermediate point; Rochester, Buffalo, Cleveland, and Cincinnati were reached over branches. It was easy to forget how rural much of the Northeast was until one rode the Erie.

The Erie ran a major commuter service from its Jersey City terminal through northern New Jersey, as far west on the main line as Port Jervis, New York. This accounted for much of the 13 percent of its revenues that came from passenger service. But the heart of the Erie was small towns, not metropolitan centers. It ran an unflashy but most adequate passenger service for the small and unflashy cities along its route. The Erie Limited, introduced in 1929, briefly with an extra fare, was its flagship. Leaving Chicago at suppertime, it reached the Pennsylvania panhandle by breakfast and rolled on through the classic Currier & Ives towns of the Southern Tier—Jamestown, Olean, Salamanca, Wellsville, Hornell—and on down the Canisteo Valley, then the Chemung, then the Susquehanna, then the Delaware, all of it a delight of Americana. The Erie had a rapport with people in those communities that may have been unique in American business. Those smaller cities had the same relationship to regional centers, such as Buffalo or Pittsburgh, as the Erie had to its big rivals, the New York Central and the Pennsylvania. The volumes of unsolicited letters to the ICC at the time of its merger, offering support and advice, attested to a genuine love for the Erie and a suspicion of the haughty Lackawanna.[3]

The Erie had generally mediocre management, the result of promoting from within, which eventually created a web of nepotism and cronyism. Robert Woodruff, for example, Erie's president 1941–1949 and chairman 1949–1956, presided over the "Erie Family" in a fatherly way, shutting down the whole general office on nice Friday afternoons so everyone could play golf. He believed that people's physical characteristics indicated their performance potential. Blonds made good salespeople, he thought, and a convex forehead indicated a keen observer and a quick thinker. Those ideas had currency early in the century but had long since been discredited, though not for Woodruff. He believed that IQ tests gave solid indications of who would be a good railroad officer—never hire anyone below average, but never hire the top scorer, either, because "where a man was too intelligent, we found he didn't make a good employee." This may have explained a lot about Erie management. Erie people did have an esprit. The sense of being an Erie family was real, not just a figment of headquarters' imagination. Erie people rather swaggered in Erie towns like Hornell and were known to give of themselves in crises. But the record also shows that they did not work very efficiently and that management was slow to innovate. Nevertheless, Woodruff was immensely proud of the show he ran and put his philosophy in a little booklet, *The Making of a Railroad Officer*.[4]

Once upon a time, the Delaware, Lackawanna & Western was rich. That was the salient fact of its history. The fortune came from hauling anthracite coal, and until the commodities clause forced divestiture of its coal subsidiary in 1911, most of it was mined in the railroad's own mines. The fortune enabled the railroad to pay handsome dividends— about 20 percent annually in the years between 1908 and 1916 and an incredible 50 percent in 1909 when the special Christmas bonus was figured in, making its stock the prototype of widow-and-orphan issues.

The fortune allowed it to reconstruct its original mountain routes and turn itself into one of the best-engineered railroads in the world. The first of its notable engineering feats was its extension to Buffalo, completed in 1882, a magnificent double-tracked speedway that slipped from valley to valley across western New York with nary a helper district. The second was the Slateford Cutoff, opened in 1911 to eliminate curves, grades, and 11 route miles across northwestern New Jersey. This area had been one of the original line's principal bottlenecks. A graceful Romanesque viaduct across Paulin's Kill was included in the project; and the Pequest Fill, a massive embankment four miles long and 110 feet above the valley floor, provided a level bed for a double-tracked, 80-mph railroad. The third was the Nicholson Cutoff north of Scranton, Pennsylvania, opened in 1916, which carried the railroad high along the ridge between the Delaware and Susquehanna valleys to eliminate curves and grades. The project included the construction of the 1,600-foot Martin's Creek Viaduct and the 2,600-foot-long, 240-foot-high Nicholson Viaduct, both of Romanesque concrete arch design, so appealing that for years they were pictured in basic civil engineering texts as the quintessence of the bridge-builder's art.

This technological excellence made Lackawanna a formidable competitor for Great Lakes–to–the–sea traffic against the likes of the older Erie, the larger New York Central, and the Johnny-come-lately Lehigh Valley (completed to Buffalo in 1892). In 1903, to advertise the soot-free cleanliness of its anthracite-burning locomotives, the Lackawanna dressed a young woman in sparkling white finery of the Gibson girl style, named her Phoebe Snow, and sent her off for a day on the train. Of course, she arrived without so much as a cinder to soil her gown.

> Said Phoebe Snow, about to go
> Upon a trip to Buffalo:
> "My gown stays white from morn to night
> Upon the Road of Anthracite."

The Phoebe Snow campaign was a public relations masterpiece. It marked the coming out of the Lackawanna as a super-railroad. The dignified woman in white forever embodied the aristocratic elegance that was the soul of Lackawanna.

The Lackawanna financed its improvements by borrowing money. It also bought a network of branchlines in central New York State by guaranteeing dividends on the stock of their predecessor short lines. All of this constituted ominous fixed charges. No one thought of it in quite the same terms as the Erie's fixed charges—the Erie was thought to be a poor railroad whose fixed charges went not for money-earning improvements but to line the pockets of robber barons. The Lackawanna was thought to be a rich railroad that borrowed for capital improvements to enable it to earn more money. That was partly true; but the branches in central New York, though not unimportant, were probably never worth what the railroad paid for them.

And the ability to pay these fixed charges always depended ominously on anthracite coal. Anthracite carloadings remained high until after World War II. After the war, the Lackawanna's old coal properties, now Glen Alden, still sponsored the popular radio show *The Shadow* with its Blue Coal brand anthracite. But oil and natural gas were becoming cheap and available. Anthracite carloadings on the Lackawanna fell from 116,639 cars in 1947 to 32,296 in 1959.

In 1937 the Erie was forced into receivership. It had weathered the worst of the depression, but a sudden downturn of traffic coupled with a bond issue about to mature put it at the mercy of the courts. Reorganization, accomplished in 1941, consolidated a hodgepodge of debt issues, some of them dating back to the nineteenth century, into three principal bond series, the first one not due until far-off 1964. In compensation, old bondholders were given 80 percent of the new common stock. The new stock wiped out the Chesapeake & Ohio's dominant interest, which dated back to Van Sweringen days. The C&O fought to hold on to the Erie and even hired a young consultant by the name of William Wyer to do a study of consolidating the two roads. The study indicated that consolidation would be worthwhile to all sides, but the bondholders wanted compensation now, not vague promises of savings in the future.[5] Henry Sturgis of the First National City Bank (Citibank) helped spurn the C&O, and when it was all over, he was so proud of what he had done that he wrote a booklet praising the 29 percent reduction in the Erie's funded debt.[6] But it was not nearly enough. The Erie still had one of the highest debt-per-mile ratios of all U.S. railroads, a legacy of nineteenth-century greed that four reorganizations had failed to correct. These sins would be visited on the Erie and its customers and its employees and the towns and cities along its route and go a long way to sabotage rational consolidation in the Northeast.

The Lackawanna was never forced into receivership, but William White, its new president in 1941, understood that unless fixed charges were reduced, every bit of net income would go for debt service, leaving nothing for the modernization of physical plant. It was not easy to convince holders of Morris & Essex stock, with dividends guaranteed at 7 percent, to take instead DL&W bonds with a lower rate of interest. White was a master of persuasion, and he managed to convince enough of the holders of these old widow-and-orphan securities that unless they did, their cash cows would go dry. But the Lackawanna had the highest debt-per-mile ratio of major American railroads.[7] For a prospective merger partner, that was not an attractive dowry.

However incomplete, these reorganizations, coupled with World War II, helped the Erie and the Lackawanna begin the postwar era with optimism. The Erie was able to dieselize. It had to. Its only modern steam power was the S-class Berkshires of the Van Sweringen era, the first batch built by Alco in 1927, the second by Baldwin in 1928, and the third, the last steam locomotives built for the Erie, by Lima in 1929. They were state-of-the-art machines when they were new, but they were obsolete now. A steamer in mainline service was rare after 1949, and dieselization was complete by 1952.

With its heavily ballasted track and wide clearances dating from its original construction to a 6-foot gauge, the Erie attracted high-rate traffic, merchandise and perishables, most of it long-haul, Chicago to New York or New England. It pruned its passenger service: Rochester Division service ended during the war, and Buffalo Division service ended at the beginning of 1951. What remained was lovely. It bought some lightweight sleepers, but most of the rest of its cars were rebuilt heavyweights. This service, especially along New York's Southern Tier, remained popular long after the New York State Thruway and American and Mohawk Airlines decimated New York Central's Great Steel Fleet. The Erie was paying dividends now, and its bonds were selling close to par.

In 1951, to celebrate its centennial, the Erie sent a special train all over the system. It included the original train that made the inaugural run in 1851, riding on modern flatcars. There was the actual flatcar where Daniel Webster had perched in his rocking chair on that inaugural run, to better view the new engineering wonder. The Erie was happy to host the public that year. It was a company with a sense of tradition and community spirit. It was busy, needed, well maintained, and proud, serving customers, bringing in new industry, providing livelihood for thousands of its own employees and for thousands more in plants along its routes. One could stand beside its double-tracked main line that curved through the gentle river valleys of southern New York and watch train after fast train of box and refrigerator cars pulled by sparkling four-unit black and yellow diesels. The Erie's fortunes never rode so high. It would be a fleeting moment.

Over on the Lackawanna, diesels also took over. Freight traffic volume through Buffalo was still immense in this last decade before the St. Lawrence Seaway. The Lackawanna perfected its freight connections with the Nickel Plate to an art form of cooperation. President William White did not allow for too many indulgences, but he did persuade his board to buy some new sleepers for the Buffalo–New York and

Syracuse–New York night trains, and a daylight streamliner—resplendent in gray and maroon with yellow accents, with coaches, a diner, and a full-length tavern-lounge at the rear—to replace the dowdy Lackawanna Limited. It was christened the Phoebe Snow after the famous lady in white. The original Phoebe had said, "I won my fame and wide acclaim / For Lackawanna's splendid name."

About ten o'clock each morning, a crowd would gather at the Lackawanna Terminal in Buffalo to wait for the departure of the Phoebe Snow. The Phoebe was favored by many travelers over its principal rival, the Empire State Express on the New York Central, because of its earlier departure. A ticket to New York on the Phoebe cost $13.42 in 1953, $24.35 round trip—less than half the cost of one on American Airlines. The crowd, especially on summer holidays, could number 250 or more. Once out of town, the quiet clickety-clack coupled with a ride so smooth it barely rippled a glass of water indicated traditional jointed rail that was superbly maintained. Every 45 minutes or so, the tranquility was punctured by a long freight slamming by on the westbound track—some out of the New York waterfront, some out of New England via connections, some from the Jersey Central at Taylor Yard near Scranton. The dining car opened at Bath. After Binghamton the train ran the ridges of the Nicholson cutoff, and after Scranton it slowed for the Pocono Mountain grades. The scenic highlight was the Delaware Water Gap, where the Delaware River broke through the mountains and the train entered New Jersey.

The electric catenary (overhead wires) for the commuter locals began at Dover. Phoebe Snow plunged on through the bedroom suburbs that Lackawanna itself had made possible with the clean, frequent commuter trains. Next came the industrial environs of Newark and then Newark itself, an inner city that the mostly middle-class passengers on the train found increasingly threatening. The train ride ended at Hoboken, and passengers boarded the railroad's own ferry for the last lap to New York. It was an awesome sight—the great metropolis on the New York shore, lights ablaze in the distance. The harbor was alive with ferries, freight car floats, tugs, fire boats, tramp steamers, and sleek ocean liners arriving from or heading to Europe and the Mediterranean.

The mighty double-tracked railroad that ended so triumphantly at the world's mightiest port seemed so vital a part of American commerce, American might, and American progress, that it was incomprehensible it would not always be there. But in fact, this was the eve of cataclysmic change.

During the second week of August 1955, Hurricane Connie swept north and battered the Jersey Shore. A second storm, Diane, following a few days later, sliced briefly into the Carolina coast and returned to sea. On Wednesday, August 19, morning sun shone brightly across New Jersey, but by noon, a heavy cumulus bank appeared over the Delaware

Valley. It began to rain at Trenton shortly after noon, and hard rain was soon falling in a wide arc around New York City from Asbury Park, New Jersey, to Newport, Rhode Island. The torrent continued into the night. Even by late afternoon, water was sweeping down the Pocono hillsides, the ground saturated from Hurricane Connie unable to hold it. Mountain streams left their banks and the Delaware began to rise ominously. By midnight, hillside homes were being ripped from their foundations, and their inhabitants were sent fleeing into the uncertain night.

East of Tobyhanna, at about 7:00 P.M., the signals flashed red for Lackawanna train 44, the afternoon local from Binghamton to Hoboken. Unknown to the engineer or the 89 passengers, the track was already washed out both ahead of and behind the train. At Cresco, Pennsylvania, the engineer of the Twilight, westbound out of Hoboken for Buffalo and Cleveland, noticed the sporadic operation of the signals, and at 8:00 P.M., with visibility zero and sections of the track underwater, he stopped his train to await orders. The 235 passengers bedded down as best they could as rain pounded the silent cars.

Early the next morning, the railroad announced that all service on the main line east of Binghamton was suspended indefinitely. President Shoemaker and Chief Engineer Bush flew by helicopter over the disaster area and discovered the worst. Seventy-five miles of the main line were obliterated. An order for 3,000 tons of rail went to Bethlehem Steel, which gave it the emergency designation "rights above everything."[8]

On August 22, 1955, the Phoebe Snow picked its way into Scranton over temporary trackage, but it was a month before normal operation was resumed. The Lackawanna lost $5 million in revenue and paid $8.5 million for rebuilding. No money was borrowed; it was paid entirely out of cash on hand. Like a disease-ravaged patient, the road was left vulnerable to the slightest economic infection. But it was nothing that time could not heal—five prosperous years would have done it. The year 1956 was a good one: revenue was up 8 percent; ton miles climbed above the Great Lakes Region average; anthracite revenue was up 7 percent and bituminous up 9 percent; merchandise was up 8 percent, passenger revenue up 7 percent. The net income for 1956 was $5.5 million.

But after that, everything went wrong. In 1957 a long cement strike cut bulk loadings, and a longshoremen's strike closed the Port of New York for most of February. Refunding the Morris & Essex bond issue strained credit; another $5.5 million had to be found to replace the Hackensack River Bridge, where the Army Corps of Engineers found a faulty foundation. Anthracite traffic declined precipitously; conversion to oil and gas was nearly complete. There was a recession. Ton miles in 1958 were only 68 percent of their postwar high, and there was a $4 million deficit at the end of the year. In 1959 the St. Lawrence Seaway opened, threatening all traffic through the New York port, and a prolonged steel strike sent the deficit to $4.5 million.

Like a caged animal, the Lackawanna struck out at its tormentors. After wage increases in 1959, it pared employment to a subminimum, which created a morale problem. It angrily intervened in a Mohawk Airlines application for increased mail pay.[9] Syracuse passenger service was discontinued and two Buffalo trains were combined. On December 8, 1959, it advised New Jersey authorities that it "would move as quickly as a statistical case could be prepared to eliminate commuter service on the electric line."[10] Perry Shoemaker distributed a pamphlet to his own commuters about the situation; for most, it was the first time they had even thought about the economics of elaborate high-density, high-speed facilities that earned money only at rush hours, only five days a week, and the first time they knew that Hudson County taxed railroads at grossly higher rates than it taxed anyone else. Governor Robert Meyner simply said freight rates were designed to be high enough to enable railroads to absorb these losses, and he walked away from the problem.

Over on the Erie, the decade was ending almost as badly. Hurricane Diane had inflicted only moderate damage, and anthracite never had been that important, but the recession had cut into the merchandise traffic on which the Erie depended. Steel strikes in 1956 and 1959 were disastrous, as were rising production costs in the rubber industry, which caused it to decentralize out of Akron. The Erie reported its first deficit since the depression in 1957. The next year, its executives took a pay cut of 10 percent.[11] (The Lackawanna, with younger, more mobile management, felt that such a move would hasten a departure of its most talented people and hesitated for over a year to make a similar cut.)

Despite hard times, not all amenities were dropped. The Erie still brought strings of its Stillwell commuter coaches to Buffalo or Rochester on autumn weekends for excursions through the Southern Tier. The long conga lines of revelers bunny-hopped down the aisles as the train rumbled and swayed over the Buffalo Division. But innovation was on the Lackawanna side, evident in the experiment with guaranteed rates (on crushed stone moving from Janesville to Vestal, New York, for the manufacture of asphalt) and on Plan V piggyback, which established joint rates with truckers and allowed delivery beyond the railroad terminal.

Coordination

The boldest move was coordination. During the short recession of 1954, the Erie and the Lackawanna agreed on two projects—joint use of a single passenger terminal on the Hudson River and joint use of 70 miles of main-line trackage in southern New York State. Both of these projects were fraught with possible misunderstanding, but in the brief good period of 1955 to mid-1957, the details were worked out. The Lackawanna's Hoboken Terminal was an elaborate affair with 18 tracks; ferries to Barclay and

Cortlandt Streets in Manhattan; buses to the Port Authority Bus Terminal near Times Square; and tube trains, one line to Hudson Terminal in the financial district and the other to 34th Street near Penn Station. It had a restaurant, a bar, a newsstand, and a delicatessen. Half a mile away, in Jersey City, the Erie operated a similar but less pretentious facility, a wooden structure with only a bar and a newsstand; it had ferries to Manhattan but fewer buses and no tube trains. A study showed that the Hoboken station could handle all of the Lackawanna's 292 daily trains and the Erie's 154. These trains carried a weekday average of 85,000 people. Similarly, the Lackawanna ferries could absorb the Erie traffic because, unlike the Erie boats, they could load two decks at a time. The changes in track connections would be a one-time cost of $2,211,956, but the estimated annual savings were $2,297,594.[12] The first Erie Limited from Chicago entered the Lackawanna terminal on October 13, 1956.[13]

There were pitfalls to sharing main-line trackage, but the need for savings was paramount. The only major expense was the installation of a common signal system, a one-time cost of $816,000. The annual savings were expected to be $488,000, for a first-year return of 66 percent. In addition, tearing up one of the lines would yield salvage of $2.3 million. The multipage contract gave a glimpse of the dangers. It was filled with minute detail on the sharing of expenses and liability; and even then, it was suggested, a great deal was left to good faith.

An immediate problem was the selection of a route. In many ways, the Lackawanna was the superior line. It was newer and thus skirted the perimeter of towns, whereas the Erie went through the middle. The Erie route was two miles longer. It was parallel to New York highway 17 along a geologically unstable bank of the Chemung River. However, most of the local industry was on the Erie, and that made the difference.

Opposition in the city of Elmira was intense, mostly out of fear that doubling traffic on a line close to commercial and residential areas would destroy property values and endanger schoolchildren. Frantic letters came from small businesses close to the Erie—the Foothills Motel, the Del Motel, the State Line Cabins, and the Paramount Diner. Trains rumbling all night would wipe out their investments. The railroad said that 60 trains a day would use the line, 14 of them fast passenger trains. That was less than the number of trains handled by either line during the war, which raised another question—what if there were another war? The railroad said that would be no problem—trains could run on a five-minute headway, which worried the little businesses even more.

Nonetheless, the ICC gave its approval.[14] It was 1958 now, and the Lackawanna had a hard time coming up with the cash for the physical changes. But on August 31, 1959, it was done. The last train over the old Lackawanna (number 15, the westbound Owl), arrived at Corning at 9:42 A.M. Two years of planning culminated in a major coordination project.

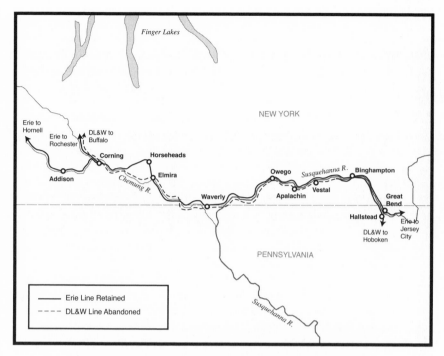

Erie and Lackawanna Coordination on the Southern Tier

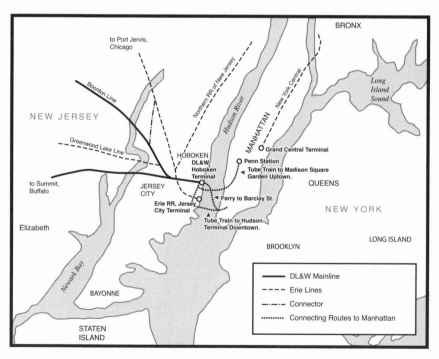

Erie Joins Lackawanna at the Hoboken Terminal

Once those tracks were gone, there was no going back, whether someday the companies merged or whether they remained forever in rival camps.

A Merger Is Negotiated

Neither coordination project was complete when the Lackawanna, the Erie, and the Delaware & Hudson made their first announcement of a merger on September 10, 1956. William White, former president of the Lackawanna (ousted from the New York Central in the famous proxy fight) went to the D&H in October 1954. He was close to Perry Shoemaker and the Lackawanna team; he knew Paul Johnston, the Erie's former president and now its chairman, and Harry Von Willer, its current president; he was a strong personality. He saw an opportunity to create a railroad large enough to be player in a changing competitive situation.

The three roads retained Wyer, Dick & Company, a famous partnership of railroad consultants, to determine what savings were possible. William Wyer was a veteran of the Prince Plan studies in the 1930s, known as a troubleshooter for sick railroads. It took two years to study the physical plants and the traffic patterns, but when the report was finished early in 1959, it looked so good that all three managements could hardly wait to conclude the deal.

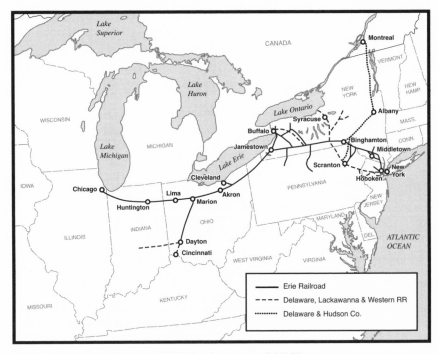

Proposed Erie–Lackawanna–D&H Merger

But there was trouble. The recession was on, and it hit the Erie and the Lackawanna much harder than the D&H. The little D&H might be only one-third the size of the Erie, but it had almost 12 times the net income. William White at the D&H sensed trouble and brought in financial consultants, the investment house of First Boston Company, to see if a three-way exchange was still possible. When it was all over, Harry Von Willer said, "We knew First Boston was having a hard time coming up with an answer, but no one expected a wholly negative report."[15] But negative it was. Given the differences in net income and outstanding indebtedness, and especially given that Erie and Lackawanna shares were selling at less than half their highs of 1956, the only fair division for D&H stockholders would be for them to get a 67 percent interest in the merged company, Erie shareholders 27 percent, and Lackawanna shareholders 13 percent. It was certain that neither Erie nor Lackawanna shareholders would approve. So, in the second week of April 1959, the three-way merger fell apart.

Anticipating what was coming, the Erie and the Lackawanna asked Wyer to extract figures from his report to see what advantages there would be in a two-way merger, leaving out the D&H. He was instructed to keep the cost of consummating a merger to a minimum. Plans for a new general office building in New Jersey, an electronic hump yard at Binghamton (impractical without the D&H), and an insurance subsidiary to handle all company insurance were dropped. This was called the "quickie" report, and the decision to merge was made on that.[16]

On the night of April 21, 1959, barely a week after First Boston shot down the three-way merger, DL&W business cars were attached to the rear of train 17, the Westerner, and the Lackawanna merger committee began its journey to Cleveland to meet its counterpart on the Erie. All evening, as the train climbed into the Poconos, they planned strategy for the next day. Perry Shoemaker explained that after living side by side with the Erie for so many years, knowing the Erie was twice as large, with twice the revenue and twice the employees, he pretty well expected Erie stockholders to hold twice the stock of the Lackawanna's. The final ratio agreed upon was 65 percent Erie, 35 percent Lackawanna.

The meeting in Cleveland lasted all day. No minutes were kept. A few penciled notes by Perry Shoemaker were later destroyed. Erie director John Thompson described it this way:

> We didn't develop any formula of 65-35 by taking these various factors and adding them together or anything like that. We had a number of things before us in our discussions. . . . A half a dozen of us were on one side of the table and half a dozen on the other, and we talked about expenses and earnings and where-do-we-go-from-here, and stock prices and all sorts of things. . . . And with a composite of all that discussing and thinking . . . we agreed to the 65-35 relationship.

There was discussion of whether future development would be more in the territory west of Buffalo than east of it. There was discussion of the anthracite coal situation. There was discussion of the possibility of additional traffic because of electric power development east of Buffalo. Everybody on both sides had the right to bring up whatever he wanted and it was discussed.[17]

Shortly after 6 P.M., April 22, 1959, the roads made a press announcement that they had agreed on terms. On July 1, the formal petition went to the ICC, and by August 6, a full report by Wyer was submitted as the principal exhibit. Stockholders' meetings were held on September 22, and they gave overwhelming approval. The ten largest stockholders of each company, including the New York Central, which held 114,000 shares of the Lackawanna, were unanimously for merger.[18]

Everyone with an interest in this merger, either pro or con, who cared enough to hire a lawyer certified to practice before the ICC gathered at the Hotel Buffalo on September 29, 1959. Merger hearings got under way before ICC examiner Hyman Blond.

The Proceedings

The first item of business was the presentation of the Wyer Report.[19] It determined that, through merger, the Erie and the Lackawanna could save $13 million annually that could not be saved in any other way. The report itself, compiled from a condensation of working papers and data sheets, appeared to be thorough. There were details right down to such minute items as the savings that would accrue from supplying less steam heat to parked sleeping cars when passenger services were combined. This detail showed that the $13 million was not going to drop from heaven. It was an important point to grasp. The savings were going to come from many small categories and were going to take a skilled management team to realize.

Wyer himself suggested two shortcomings to the study. First, the data on which it was based were collected in 1956. By the time they were presented, there were significant changes in traffic flow and volume. Second, the two men who worked with the Wyer engineers and supplied them information—Stanley McGranahan of the Erie and Philip Jonas of the Lackawanna—were both retired by the time the study was implemented; there was no one who could interpret the decisions they had made.[20]

In another sense the Wyer Report was unsatisfying. It cited cost figures, for example, of $1 a mile per 1,000 gross tons on the Erie line between Hornell and Buffalo but gave no hint how these figures were calculated. At major terminals, a certain number of crews were to be eliminated and a certain number of dollars saved, but there was no indication of why those crews were chosen or how the cuts were calculated. There was assurance under oath that all this had been carefully worked out. The Wyer Report, the prototype for future merger studies, was presented as hard numbers, a rock upon which decisions could be made. But there was a thinness to it. This is not an accusation. Nobody can predict the future, including Wyer. It is just important to keep in mind that behind the hard figures lay assumptions and guesses.

According to the Wyer Report, the most significant savings would come from yard and terminal consolidation. On the New Jersey waterfront, the Erie's Croxton Yard would become the principal classification point, and a new coal dock for anthracite on the site of the old Jersey City passenger station would concentrate all marine operations close by the Hoboken Terminal. In Buffalo, the combined traffic of the two roads would make feasible the construction of an electronic classification yard. This would sort incoming cars onto the proper outgoing tracks at twice the speed with half the labor of ordinary flat yards. The New York Central already had such a yard at Buffalo.

But as parallel and as duplicating as Erie and Lackawanna may have looked, there were not many routes that could be abandoned. Between Buffalo and Binghamton, the Erie route via Hornell was thought to be the low-cost line, but the Lackawanna route through Dansville could only be downgraded (reduced to branchline status), because it served on-line industries. An Erie branch parallel to the Lackawanna up the Cohocton Valley, a branch the Erie itself had nearly abandoned without a merger in 1945, could be dropped.[21] Between Binghamton and New York, there could be no meaningful abandonments or downgradings. The Erie line was thought to be better for through freight, and it provided the vital connection to the New Haven Railroad at Maybrook, New York, for New England–bound traffic. The Lackawanna had most of the on-line industry, served what was left of the anthracite business, and was the superior passenger line since it served the city of Scranton and the more populous of the New Jersey suburbs. So consolidation was not a vehicle for much route abandonment. Nor would many trains be consolidated, as both railroads were already operating most trains close to capacity. Nor could one administrative staff take on the work of two; Wyer calculated that only 18 percent of the combined managerial staff could be cut. The department to take the most severe cuts was traffic (sales).

There were three principal adversaries to the merger—labor, other railroads, and a small group of dissenting Lackawanna stockholders, each exhibiting the kinds of obstacles all mergers would have to overcome. Aside from what the merging railroad chose to tell the ICC, all it would learn about the merger, all it would know about whom the merger would help and whom it would hurt, would come from these opponents.

More than half of the projected savings were going to come from jobs consolidated or eliminated. Labor was going to pay a high price. There was no surprise in this. It had been an undertow to consolidation since

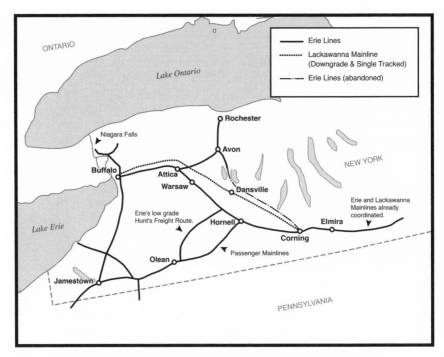

Proposed Erie Lackawanna Line Changes in Western New York

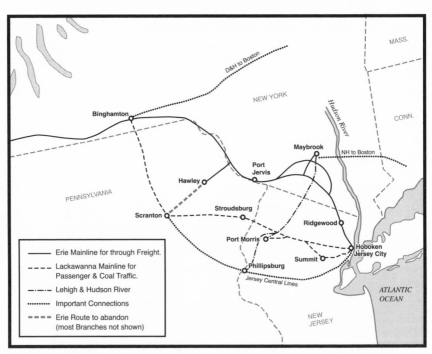

Proposed Erie Lackawanna Line Changes East of Binghamton

the days of the Ripley Plan. Assuming that a final settlement would be based on the *New Orleans* conditions, Wyer attempted to calculate the cost of a labor settlement. He was not stymied, but the equation had so many variables that the final result could only be regarded as a good guess. For example, precisely which job reductions were going to be the result of merger and which were the result of other causes? Wyer could figure with precision the number of crews that were going to be abolished, but he could not know how many of those employees would be taken care of by attrition, how many would take other jobs on the railroad, or how many would take a lump sum settlement. In metropolitan areas, where there was a variety of job opportunities, a higher proportion would probably take lump sum settlements. In a railroad town like Hornell, more would probably take settlement benefits, but he could not be sure. Eventually, he came up with a figure of $3 million as the cost of a settlement, less 52 percent for savings in federal income taxes, which left it under $1.5 million.[22]

By the time the hearing began, labor had already won an attrition agreement in the Virginian merger and would have liked to get one here. The Erie and the Lackawanna refused. For the N&W, already in top physical condition, where merger savings could be translated quite immediately into higher dividends for stockholders, there was a sense that labor should not be made to pay the full price. For the Erie and the Lackawanna, job reductions would make capital available to keep the roads competitive and to save the jobs that remained, and they were the only hope for creating sound jobs in the future.

Labor remained quiet through the hearings, preferring to go to court instead. After the hearings, its lawyers thought they had found a novel way to read section 5(2)(f) of the Transportation Act of 1940, the so-called Harrington Amendment, which governed merger settlements. It said that no employees shall be put "in a worse position with respect to their employment." Since 1940, that had been interpreted to mean that compensation would substitute for a job.[23] But on the premise that a job (work) must be provided and mere money was insufficient, labor went to court. It took seven months, but the Supreme Court threw out the premise, and the *New Orleans* conditions as traditionally interpreted governed the Erie Lackawanna settlement.

In approaching this issue it is important to understand that here were two proud railroads that, by 1959, were fighting for their lives. If they could not remain competitive, they were going to go the way of the Ontario & Western or the Rutland, not tomorrow perhaps, but soon. Every job, therefore, had to be a productive job. And yet, in the ICC's "docket" (its record of the proceeding) it is hard not to be touched by the letters—a bound volume of them—from "little" people: citizens, some of them employees or former employees of the railroad. Most of the letters were handwritten, many in pencil. These were people who loved the railroad deeply, many of whom had given their lives to it, who felt terribly, terribly displaced. One letter said:

> We are trying to find employment for people, not unemployment. By this merger, more than 100 men will be put out of work regardless of what they promise.
>
> Our country was built upon railroads. What should happen . . . if we should have another war . . . with all the railroads that have been taken up. Stations have been closed. People stand out in the cold and stormy weather. No way to tell whether trains are late or even running.
>
> Why not let these high salary people take a cut rather than sit in offices and figure out how to take trains off and raise rates. What man is worth $19,000 a year plus a private car and an expense account? I am for the railroads with some good service and reasonable rates. I am not a stormy day passenger. I use railroads for all my traveling.
>
> Sincerely,
> A friend of railroads,
> but not of unemployment caused by merger.[24]

Erie's president Harry Von Willer actually made a salary of $103,000. "A friend" would have been shocked.

Justice William O. Douglas dissented from the Supreme Court's decision on the Erie Lackawanna. This was a minor episode, he thought, of an important chapter in modern industrial history, the effect of technological change on workers. It was not the first instance "of a controversy settled in Congress by the adoption of ambiguous language and then transferred to the courts," but he would resolve it in favor of the people:

> Many men, at least, are not drones. Their continued activity is life itself. The toll which economic and technological changes will make on employees is so great that they, rather than the capital which they have created, should be the beneficiaries of any doubts that overhang these legislative controversies when they are shifted to the courts.[25]

By Wyer's estimate only 7.5 percent of the total savings would come from the diversion of traffic from other railroads, yet the other railroads were prepared to fight. Their opposition was formidable because they had lawyers on staff who could always be present at the hearings, who had staff to prepare elaborate exhibits. Due process worked best for those who could afford to make their voice heard. There was nothing sinister in this, but it is important to note.

The point of contention was how much of the Lackawanna's westbound traffic, formerly delivered to the Nickel Plate or the Wabash at Buf-

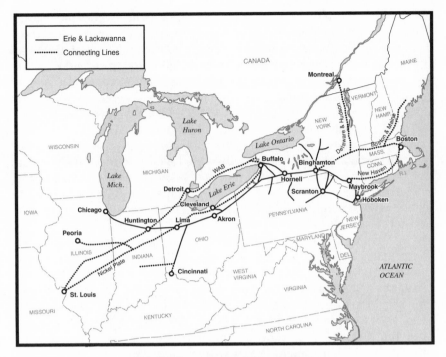

Erie & Lackawanna
Connecting Lines

Erie Lackawanna and Connections

falo, might be diverted to an all–Erie Lackawanna route. The converse was whether the Nickel Plate and the Wabash, on eastbound routings, would continue to turn cars over to the Erie Lackawanna at Buffalo or retaliate for what the Erie took away. Wyer analyzed each car separately.[26] He concluded that the Erie Lackawanna stood to gain a net of $1.3 million in additional revenues, whereas some other railroads would suffer net losses, for example, a $3.6 million loss for the Nickel Plate.

The study was done with a computer, which was rather new then, and everyone was very proud of how up-to-date this was. But it became apparent that each car (each computer card) represented a guess. Some of the guesses rested on such factors as which railroad's traffic agent was friendlier with a plant's traffic manager. That was probably realistic, but it raised eyebrows. Ultimately, a guess was a guess, no matter how scientific the computer made it look. When the other railroads demanded that the cards be rerun through the computer, the tabulations came out differently, which got a red-faced explanation that some of the cards must have gotten stuck, either the first time through the machine or the second.[27]

Assuming that it could not stop the merger, the Nickel Plate wanted ironclad guarantees that service would be as good into Buffalo as it had been before. Though it had shunned the Lackawanna in 1948, the Nickel

Plate always worked hard with the Lackawanna to develop traffic. Nickel Plate trains pulled right to the Lackawanna interchange, locomotives were changed, new crews swung aboard, pressure pumped in the air brakes, and the train was on its way with less than 28 minutes of split-second railroading. That was almost as fast as the New York Central could put a train through the city. If traffic were diverted to the Erie route, then fewer trains would come up to Buffalo to make the Nickel Plate connection. The Erie and the Lackawanna insisted that their plans to build the electronic Bison Yard was proof of their commitment to Buffalo. But then, everyone knew that the purpose of merger was to rearrange traffic patterns as the controlling railroads saw fit. As the ICC told the Nickel Plate, it was "part of the everyday risk of railroading in highly competitive territory." One question on everyone's mind was, Might this trigger retaliatory mergers by the Nickel Plate or others?

The Wabash and the Lehigh Valley wanted more than a guarantee of service. They wanted to use the proceeding to get trackage rights over the Lackawanna in Buffalo so as to improve their connections with each other. Perry Shoemaker of the Lackawanna and Harry Von Willer of the Erie were summoned to a meeting with Herman Pevler of the Wabash. There they were given an ultimatum: give the trackage rights that would make the Wabash-Lehigh route competitive with the Erie Lackawanna or face prolonged harassment.[28] When the hearing was over, Shoemaker could barely disguise his rage:

> The opposition of the Wabash and Lehigh Valley . . . reflected no credit upon the industry. . . . I know of no precedent for the price of merger being the supplying of property investment to improve a competitor's product, even if it is a product badly in need of improvement. It was a phony issue having no part in the merger proceedings.[29]

The Erie and the Lackawanna then proceeded to make a deal. On April 26, 1960, in a letter to Shoemaker and Von Willer, Pevler confirmed that the trackage had been made available "on terms mutually satisfactory," whereupon the two railroads withdrew from the case. "Both of you know," he added, "that we on the Wabash feel that your merger is for the good of our whole industry."[30]

In the midst of the hearings, James Symes, president of the Pennsylvania Railroad, dropped by to say—officially, on the record—how important mergers were for railroading. *Trains* magazine recognized that Symes never did anything without a purpose. It was quite in character, it thought, for a man of his stature to offer theoretical support and give credence to consolidation orthodoxy while his lieutenants, who were closer to the cash register, should oppose it.[31] Pevler was one of those lieutenants, for the Wabash and the Lehigh Valley were both in the PRR's sphere. Since the days of the Ripley Plan, the PRR always seemed to get what it wanted.

One last obstacle lay in the path of merger—a shadowy group of ten speculators, who never appeared in person at the hearing, whose purpose was never to block the merger but simply to get a better price for their shares. They owned 14,950 shares of Lackawanna common. It was never clear whether they bought the stock thinking the hoopla of merger would make it go up, or whether they intended from the beginning to use the threat of litigation to blackmail the company into paying off. Commission files were full of pathetic letters from people who had bought, or inherited, DL&W stock back in the glory days of anthracite and held on to it because all their lives they were told "it was really valuable." But these ten speculators were not old-line stockholders. "They are new," said Shoemaker after they disrupted the 1960 stockholders' meeting, "and they have as their purpose the harassment of the company."[32] Both the ICC and the courts dismissed their case.[33] The following letter in ICC files is self-explanatory:

LACKAWANNA

140 Cedar Street, New York, N.Y.
August 12, 1959
Mr. Fein:

You suggested at our meeting that a "deal" could be made by which you and your associates would withdraw your opposition to the merger of the Erie and the Lackawanna. That "deal," according to you, would involve the purchase by the Lackawanna, or some concealed entity on behalf of the Lackawanna, all of the Lackawanna stock owned by you and your associates at a price based on the average 1956–1957 value, "take a point or leave a point." You stated that for this purpose, your group had about 20,000 shares in Lackawanna stock and that the purchase could be covered up in some way.

Despite your threats of a suit through retention of an attorney on a contingent fee basis of over $20 per share if the Lackawanna refuses to accede to the foregoing arrangement, I can only repeat what Mr. Shoemaker stated at our meeting: the Lackawanna will not be a party to such a transaction at that or any other price. We do not believe it to be either ethical or legal. With respect to any such suit, I am sure your attorney is aware of *Schwabacher v. United States* (334 US 182). Under this case, the appraisal statutes of New York and Pennsylvania are rendered inapplicable to the proposed merger, and if the merger is approved by the necessary vote of the stockholders and by the Interstate Commerce Commission, the terms are binding on all stockholders.

I do not believe that further discussions will serve any useful purpose.

Rowland L. Davis, Jr.
Vice President and General Counsel[34]

Since the company would not deal, the speculators sent their lawyer to do battle at the hearing. Day after day, he put the company witnesses through grueling cross-examination, trying to prove that the Lackawanna was worth more than it was getting and that its management had conspired for motives unknown to sell it off cheaply to the Erie. Nothing seemed to stick. For example, had it not sold off valuable real estate, perhaps in a plot to cannibalize itself? No was the answer. It had sold land to General Foods and the Post Office Department and others who built facilities that produced traffic for the railroad. This was a wise use of its real estate.

The cross-examination reached its climax in questioning about the Lackawanna's sudden sale of its Nickel Plate stock without warning to its merger partners, on March 2, 1959. This was the stock it had purchased beginning in 1947 in hopes of a Nickel Plate merger, which the ICC had ordered to be put in trust. Though the Lackawanna could not vote it, it was valuable, paying dividends to the Lackawanna of $1.2 million in 1958. There was speculation that the D&H pulled out of the three-way merger because of the sale of this stock. Erie people denied that they had a hand in it, particularly over insinuations that it was the Erie, not the Lackawanna, that had an urgent need for cash. The questioning kept coming back to the point that, after the terms of merger were announced, the price of Erie stock pulled ahead of Lackawanna stock and stayed there, implying that the terms favored the Erie. Frustrated by the unsubstantiated insinuations and at the end of his patience, Perry Shoemaker stopped the line of questioning with what became an obituary to the Lackawanna Railroad:

> The purpose of that sale was to make one last desperate effort to put the Lackawanna's financial situation on an even keel before we found ourselves in bankruptcy. I think it is important that you understand the seriousness of our situation. We did not come to the decision to sell the Nickel Plate stock lightly. It was a hard decision to make. It was the last big liquid asset the Lackawanna had.
>
> What was our situation? We had more than $3 million in unpaid bills, some of them several months old. We had suppliers indicating doubt they would continue to give us material on a credit basis. We had just taken down, on February 1, the last million of the [Hackensack River] bridge loan, and were under obligation to have the first million paid back by August 1 of this year, and the income to accomplish it just was not in sight.
>
> We had the normal tax load to meet for this year. We were behind in our tax accounts, seriously behind. We were not taking advantage of any discounts in the buying of supplies because we couldn't do it. We couldn't pay for them quickly enough.
>
> We were in a very unhappy and serious situation, with no traffic upturn in the immediate prospect to change it quickly. All of these things, together with the realization that we were building up deferred maintenance, the real-

ization that we had put our supervisory people on a psychologically bad basis, certainly with the pay cuts that went into effect January 1 of this year—
all of these things were considered by the Board, and we came to the conclusion that we had one opportunity to put our house in order, and that was to
dispose of the asset, to clean up our bridge loan, to pay our back bills and to
restore our cash position and net working capital.[35]

That was the climax of the hearing and the record on which the commission gave its approval.

Merger

The Erie's practice of promoting officers from within had served it reasonably well in an earlier day but failed it now. Its president, Harry Von
Willer, had been in the top post only since 1956. He was remembered as a
good traffic man and an awfully nice guy, but he was neither foresighted
nor aggressive, and neither was the management team that he had assembled.[36] He became the president of the merged company. The Erie was
twice the size of the Lackawanna, and its directors were a majority of the
new board, so this was no surprise. Von Willer was nearing retirement,
and Perry Shoemaker of the Lackawanna assumed that he would be Von
Willer's successor. Von Willer stepped down in November 1960, but Shoemaker was passed over in favor of the Erie's Milton McInnes.

McInnes was remembered as competent but without a burning desire
to lead; "a good lieutenant but not a commander," said one who was
there. His vice president for operations, Garret (Gary) White, younger
brother of D&H president William White, did want to lead, but those who
knew him recalled that he was too dim a light to pull it off. His ace was
the solid backing of one of the dominant personalities on the board of directors, Harry Hagerty. Hagerty represented Metropolitan Life, which had
been a large Erie investor for many years. Many of their colleagues saw
Hagerty and White as bullies. "Slippery," "manipulative," and "egoma-
niac" were words used by former associates to describe White; "swelled
head" and "unethical as hell" was how an associate remembered
Hagerty.[37] White's staff meetings were described as endless and boring and
nothing but vehicles for him to strut around to show how important he
was. He even made McInnes sit on a camp chair on the side.

Some described a bad smell about the Erie's corporate culture—a dangerous nepotism, rampant cronyism, and perks (such as country club
memberships not for the purpose of entertaining customers but just for
being someone's buddy). Executives made "inspection" tours of the railroad in well-stocked executive (rail) cars with blinds tightly pulled, bottles
uncorked, and the poker chips on the table. The former Lackawanna men
were horrified by the lack of integrity at the Erie. At the depths of it, Perry

Shoemaker told the remnants of his team, "I feel terrible; I sold all of you down the river."[38]

The Lackawanna executives who moved to the Erie headquarters in the Midland Building in Cleveland felt excluded and shunned. Afraid to be seen together, they ate alone or met clandestinely away from headquarters. Perry Shoemaker was given the silent treatment. Even the Erie men who liked him were afraid to be seen with him, for fear of retaliation of the Hagerty–Gary White crowd. White and Hagerty barred him from access to many of the company's records, though he was officially the second in command.

The Erie people thought the Lackawanna people had chips on their shoulders because they did not get to run the show. In any case, most of the Lackawanna's good management team left. Its former general counsel, Rowland Davis, who had handled the dissident stockholders and had emerged as the star of the merger hearings, was very talented, had other offers, and left. Its former vice president for operations, William G. White (not to be mistaken for William H. White of the D&H) had an offer from Consolidated Freightways and left. He was soon its CEO. Shoemaker served briefly as chairman of the board, but he had little executive power and left to be CEO of the Jersey Central in 1963, taking two more ex-Lackawanna men with him, one of them James Barngrove, its traffic manager, whose friends were the railroad's best customers.

Then some of the premerger planning went awry. For example, the plan for accounting was to concentrate all revenue accounts at the Erie facility in Cleveland and all disbursements at the Lackawanna facility in Scranton. But in Scranton, both revenue and disbursement clerks were on the same seniority roster, and rather than move to Cleveland, where they already knew Lackawanna people were not being treated too well, senior revenue clerks bumped younger disbursement clerks. The result was that 70 percent of all disbursements were being handled by people inexperienced in that side of the business. The bungling became epidemic. Even the lingo of receivables clerks and disbursements clerks was different and entirely foreign even to skilled public accountants. Bills went unpaid. Suppliers were beginning to demand cash. One New Jersey trucker called Perry Shoemaker personally to get the $110,000 the company owed him. "This was a hell of mess, and took a long time to straighten out," said Shoemaker later on.[39] The same thing happened in locomotive repair: it was expected that 75 skilled Lackawanna mechanics would move to the Erie facility in Hornell, where all heavy repairs were to be concentrated. But many of them had homes and family in Scranton, so only a fraction of them made the move; thus, there was a shortage of skilled mechanics in Hornell while men in Scranton were getting benefits.

Elsewhere, premerger planning had failed to take account of the very different ways of running a railroad. The big difference was that the Erie had a strong divisional structure and the Lackawanna a strong departmental structure. So, for example, on the Erie, operating, mechanical, maintenance, and engineering staff reported to the superintendent of their division; on the Lackawanna, each of those areas reported separately to a vice president at system headquarters. At a more mundane level, the two railroads drilled their rail differently, so different kinds of angle bars were needed to fasten it to cross-ties. Erie locomotives used electric devices to spray sand under their wheels (for traction in getting a train started); the Lackawanna's had pneumatic devices; fleets began to mingle, but the Erie units could be paired only with other Erie units, and vice versa. It was a mess. The Lackawanna's former chief of purchasing, Curtis Bayer, told the New England Railroad Club in 1962 of 16 different ways the two companies ran purchasing and stores—different chains of command, different procedures, different controls.[40]

Losses on operations were $26.5 million in 1961, $16.6 million in 1962. In 1963, $7.6 million in notes were coming due and another $11.6 million in 1964. Was this the beginning of the final erosion of traffic in the East? The St. Lawrence Seaway was taking a toll on Great Lakes–to–the–Sea traffic through Buffalo. Other eastern roads were suffering losses too, but not (proportionately) like this. Labor's short-sighted litigation prohibited the company from realizing any savings that might come from merger for seven critical months, during which time other railroads treated it as if it were merged and diverted traffic away.

The Erie Lackawanna's efforts to capture traffic from others had mixed results, especially given its deteriorating service. Fourteen percent of its freight cars were out of service awaiting repairs, and the cost of renting cars from other railroads was a hemorrhage of cash. Shippers could not get the cars they needed and deserted, mostly for Alfred Perlman's lean New York Central. For example, Norwich Pharmaceuticals in Norwich, New York, liked and relied on the joint Lackawanna–Nickel Plate piggyback service, but it was so annoyed by EL salespeople badgering them about the long haul, so horrified by the new railroad's service, that the company called in the New York Central.[41]

In 1962 153 new traffic-producing plants were located on the railroad, proving that not all shippers had lost confidence. Cash was found to start work on Bison Yard, the new electronic hump yard in Buffalo. The Nickel Plate agreed to go in with them on the yard, picking up half the construction cost, and bring in the Wabash Railroad as a rent-paying tenant. This gave hope that the Lackawanna's old Buffalo connections were not going to desert it. This was the only good news the company had.

Meanwhile, the situation at Hornell was described as a nightmare. Hornell was the junction of the old Erie main line to Chicago and its branch to Buffalo. Now all of the Lackawanna's traffic was crashing in on Hornell, where it had to be split into Buffalo trains and Chicago trains.

The congestion was snarling the entire railroad. Woodruff Yard in Hornell, opened in 1953, was a budget job, not a hump yard, not electronic, and remained a point of congestion to the end of the railroad.

The Lackawanna's beautiful Buffalo passenger terminal was closed in 1962, and passengers boarded trains in a temporary freight shed. No sleepers or diners operated all the way from New York to Chicago on the main line. The rock bottom came in 1962, on a pre-Christmas Erie Lackawanna Limited. There was standing room only because the railroad did not have enough functional cars, because it did not have enough money to repair them; no food was left in the diner; water from leaking toilets flooded the floors; the heat failed utterly on this subzero Indiana night; the toilet water finally froze on the floor; some people were forced to flee the freezing train to seek the shelter of a hotel; train personnel were alternately humiliated by the tools they were given to do their job with and worried that the sullen, cold, and unfed passengers might mutiny. The train was eight hours late into Hornell because of repeated mechanical failure, where most people gave up and got a bus.[42]

Of the dark forces that were gathering about the Erie Lackawanna, none was darker than the growing encirclement of the Pennsylvania Railroad. In March 1960 came the first rumors that two of the PRR's satellites, the Norfolk & Western and the Wabash, would merge with the Nickel Plate. A year later, the PRR announced it would seek control of the Lehigh Valley. A firm link between the Lehigh Valley and the Lackawanna's old Buffalo connections was the Erie Lackawanna's worst nightmare. Interchange with the Nickel Plate dropped precipitously, from 150,000 cars in 1960 to 99,000 in 1964, by which time the Nickel Plate and the Lehigh were operating run-through freights. The Erie Lackawanna had no choice but to seek inclusion for itself in the PRR sphere. Its own merger had been a stark disappointment, and now other mergers threatened to engulf it.

William White

To be included in another merger, the Erie Lackawanna would have to make itself attractive. New leadership was the first requirement. Over at the Delaware & Hudson, William White watched the EL with growing concern. He was still close to ex-Lackawanna people, notably Robert G. Fuller. Fuller was the senior vice president of Citibank, a former member of the Lackawanna board, now a member of the EL board, and a member of its executive committee. Citibank had a big investment in EL securities. In the fall of 1961, White asked Perry Shoemaker to meet him secretly at Washington's Mayflower Hotel. They were old friends. Shoemaker told him the house was on fire.

By early 1963 Fuller and others on the executive committee persuaded White to help them. White would not give up his post at the D&H.

Would the ICC let him be chairman of two railroads at once? "I did not seek the position," said White, "but on Erie Lackawanna's board are old friends and associates who thought I could help them. One doesn't easily refuse a request from those with whom he has always had pleasant relations."[43] By then, even Harry Hagerty came around to support White; it was said to be out of raw panic that Metropolitan Life was going to lose its entire investment.

In May 1963, just before White arrived, the railroad needed to borrow money just to pay current bills. Somehow, a creditor was found. The New York Teachers' Retirement System was willing to loan the money at 4.75 percent if the ICC would guarantee it. White had arrived in the meantime and had barely gotten a grip on the situation when the ICC said it would not guarantee, because, it said, it saw no way the company could repay. It was a body blow. There were already $2.5 million in unpaid bills. In December, $4.5 million in New Jersey taxes was due, as was $1.5 million in interest charges. On the next October 1, $11.5 million of Erie Railroad Consolidated Mortgage bonds was due, and default was at more than even odds. As if that were not enough, the entire locomotive fleet was rapidly approaching the end of its service life. Diesel units last about 15 years before maintenance becomes uneconomical. The Erie and the Lackawanna had dieselized early, mostly before 1949, and so a crisis of major proportions was rapidly approaching.[44] "How would you like to be in the shoes of William White?" asked David Morgan in *Trains*. "Luckless Erie Lackawanna, the problem child of the east . . . is the road for which merger has yet to underwrite a miracle."[45]

Some thought White chose an odd place to start. He ordered the Phoebe Snow's old tavern-observation cars out of storage—the very cars he had wheedled out of his Lackawanna board in 1947—and put back in service. The traditionless Erie Lackawanna Limited was rechristened the Phoebe Snow. The cars were fixed up and the train made lovely again. It was a master stroke. The train proudly flew the company's flag, and the morale of employees, customers, and creditors rallied.

White had to make two painful personnel changes. The road's general counsel, M. Cayley Smith, Jr., an Erie man, was fired because he was too drunk to appear before ICC hearings in the Penn-Central merger case, a matter critical to the Erie Lackawanna.[46] Gary White, White's brother, resigned. Wyer Dick & Company was retained to make detailed productivity studies for the purpose of reducing manpower. Gary White fought this, but when Charles Shannon of the Wyer staff moved his desk into Gary White's office, it was clear who had his brother's backing.

The taxes were paid, though this momentarily drew working capital down to the danger level. Holders of the mortgage bonds, Citibank and Metropolitan, expressed a willingness to negotiate an extended deadline. Equipment trusts were secured for new cars and locomotives. The next year, White found a competent lieutenant, Gregory Maxwell, former troubleshooting ace on the New York Central and then CEO of the Terminal Railroad Association of St. Louis. He took over first as senior vice president and then as president under White's chairmanship.

Next, White turned to the single most terrible cash drain on the railroad and the factor that made it unattractive as a merger partner—the commuter service. Nothing could make commuter trains profitable, Shoemaker told the ICC, not if every seat on every commuter train were filled. The day was rapidly approaching when new equipment would have to be purchased, as the ancient Stillwells on the Erie routes and the electric cars on the Lackawanna were already past their service life. Raising capital for this was beyond the remotest capability of the company. New Jersey politicians bellowed, then decided that if the railroad could earn a profit, they could put the squeeze on it for more taxes:

> Senator Ozzard: I would interject at this point, Sen. Stamler and Sen. Hillary, that if we take over the passenger service and the freight service is profitable, that the railroad might assist us very easily through increased taxes.
> Senator Hillary: That was on my mind, too.[47]

New Jersey did finally agree to allow some trains to be taken off and to partly subsidize those that remained. In the early 1970s it financed equipment, and in 1982 it took over the operation entirely as New Jersey Transit. But in the spirit of Bill White, once help was on the way, the integrity of the Erie Lackawanna shone through. In the blizzard that struck New York on Monday, February 11, 1969, for example, the only railroad in the metropolitan area to report a normal schedule was the Erie Lackawanna. On Saturday night, as the storm settled in, EL crews came out on their own time and ran the trains back and forth over the tracks to keep them clear. White also persuaded New York and Ohio to repeal their "full crew" laws, which required a third brakeman on all trains.

Bill White turned the Erie Lackawanna around. In 1965 it reported a net income of $3.8 million, not much, but the first since 1956.

> In mid-1963, when we set for ourselves the goal of getting in the black by 1965, we knew it would be difficult to accomplish . . . and there were times in late 1963 and early 1964 when we feared bankruptcy could not be avoided because the cash available was one million dollars less than the bills the treasury was holding unpaid. We weathered those bad times, and favored by good business conditions and running a tight ship, the company in 1965 turned a profit. It is a big boost to the morale of our entire staff.[48]

After two successful seasons of shuttling people to the New York World's Fair, with possible merger partner Norfolk & Western demanding that the EL extricate itself from the passenger business as a price of inclusion, the Phoebe Snow had to go. So many people came for the last trip on the Sunday after Thanksgiving 1966 that it had to operate in two sections. White's business car was attached to the rear of the first section. It was a glowering day. A band played "Auld Lang Syne" as it left Hoboken Terminal. Hundreds of people came down to the stations along the way, many waving signs saying "Goodbye, Phoebe. We will miss you." Many brought their children for a last look.

But there were troubling omens for this fragile recovery. Bill White died suddenly of a massive heart attack in the Midland Building, company headquarters in Cleveland, on April 6, 1967. The company surgeon tried to revive him but could not.

In the boarded-up Lackawanna Terminal in Buffalo, the sweeping marble staircase was smashed. The vaulted ceiling had fallen in. Ugly graffiti had been spray-painted on the ticket counters where people once lined up to book passage for one of the world's great travel experiences. Dead rats and pigeons lay on the floor. It was the apocalypse of Erie Lackawanna.

seven

The Chessie
System and the
Norfolk & Western
1961–1964

On January 7, 1960, Alfred Perlman of the New York
Central, Allan P. Kirby of Alleghany Corporation, which controlled the
Central, and Cyrus Eaton and Walter Tuohy, the chairman and the president of the Chesapeake & Ohio, met to talk about the general trend of
mergers. The four men were old acquaintances from the days of Robert
Young. Kirby was Young's old bankroller at Alleghany. Eaton was a coal
magnate who succeeded Young to the chairmanship of the C&O; he was
nearly as controversial as Young. During the World War II alliance, Eaton,
like many other American businessmen, looked forward to postwar trade
with and investment in our ally, the Soviet Union. Eaton alone kept the
hopes alive long after the cold war began, and some of his favorable remarks about the Soviets raised eyebrows. Tuohy had been the C&O's aggressive vice president for coal traffic when Young raised him to the C&O
presidency in 1948. One of the few railroaders who continued to express
admiration for Young into the 1960s, he had been Young's personal emissary to Denver to persuade Al Perlman, then executive vice president of
the Rio Grande, to run the New York Central for Young. But in January
1960, the four were not as close as they had been, and nothing concrete
came of the meeting.

If the C&O men knew of the Norfolk & Western's plans to merge with
the Nickel Plate, they did not reveal it to Perlman. Perlman knew nothing
until he read about it in the paper on March 19 while vacationing at Palm
Beach. He called Tuohy. "I knew of this, Al," Tuohy told him, "I knew of
this before. I couldn't tell you because of confidences with Bill Daly of the
Nickel Plate, who is a friend of ours and who had negotiations with us."
As Tuohy described the conversation, "Al said well, I think this is very im-

portant and I think you and Howard [Simpson of the Baltimore & Ohio] and I ought to get together as soon as we can."[1] Tuohy and Simpson were already planning to have dinner, and Perlman was invited to join. Perlman could not make it, but he stopped by Tuohy's office in Cleveland a few days later, unannounced. In Tuohy's absence, he talked with Eaton, who thought the C&O was more interested in diversification outside of railroading than mergers within.[2]

Tuohy and Simpson had dinner as planned at the Statler Hilton in Washington on March 29, 1960. Tuohy said the C&O was ready to go ahead with consolidation with the B&O. He said the C&O was interested only in control, not a merger, because of the B&O's debt, and that the C&O was interested only if it could get at least 80 percent of B&O's stock. That was the requirement for filing a consolidated balance sheet with the IRS, which would allow B&O losses to reduce C&O taxes. He said there was no time for extensive studies. The C&O wanted to move now, and if it could not be done now, it had other prospects under consideration. Tuohy and Simpson met twice again in April to discuss the matter.[3]

That was when Robert Bedingfield of the *New York Times* picked up the story. He called Perlman, who was "not in," and the Central had "no comment." Simpson chattered like a magpie, because news that the B&O had such a handsome suitor would boost the price of its stock and raise its price. On May 17, 1960, the B&O accepted the C&O's offer. The next evening, Simpson and Tuohy had dinner with Perlman in Washington. This was the first Perlman knew their deal was final. Releases had gone to the press, and the Central was left out.[4]

The following week at a crowded and panicky meeting of New York Central stockholders at the Palace Theater in Albany, Perlman said he had been assured by Tuohy and Simpson that three-way talks would be held. In Cleveland, Tuohy said he was not altogether opposed to three-way talks, but the B&O's board of directors said it was opposed. On June 12, under pressure to make good on his bluff, Perlman demanded that the ICC make a general investigation of mergers to see if they were in the public interest. Said one railroad president to Robert Bedingfield, "It's the first time I ever heard *him* talk about the public interest." Another said it was "sour grapes. . . . Perlman was asleep at the switch when C&O and B&O moved without his permission."[5]

Perlman and Simpson had lunch together on June 16, and Simpson was urged to disavow the C&O offer. But Perlman could not make him a firm counteroffer. A week later, the Central board met in a stormy six-hour session to debate what it could afford to do. Four days later, it made an offer: one and one-half shares of New York Central plus nine dollars in cash for each share of the B&O until it had 1,550,000 shares or 60 percent of the B&O's voting stock. Based on the previous day's closing price, that was about $42.50 a share. The C&O's offer amounted to $35 a share, but the

C&O was paying dividends of four dollars a year with ease, whereas the Central was having a hard time paying one dollar. But Wall Street observers seemed to agree that the Central's offer was attractive and would probably keep the C&O from getting its 80 percent, or maybe even 51 percent. They wondered how a railroad like the Central, which had asked the government to guarantee a loan for $40 million because it could not raise the money, could spend $13 million in cash for another railroad.[6]

The B&O Proxy Fight

By July the scene shifted to Switzerland. A large block of B&O stock, perhaps 40 percent of it, was held through Swiss banks, which alone knew the names of the owners. Walter Grant of the Central and E. Bates McKee of Bache & Company flew to Zurich to recommend the Central's offer. Then Walter Tuohy and C&O vice president John Kusik flew over on a similar mission. On August 13, the bankers endorsed the C&O. "I don't know who misled them," said Perlman.[7] He flew back to Switzerland, then announced that he had persuaded the Swiss to remain neutral. But the general director of Crédit Suisse, J. J. Kurz, said that was not so: customers were urged to make up their own minds, but if they asked for advice, they were told to favor the C&O offer. "We don't see what grounds Mr. Perlman has for his neutrality statement."[8] But the Central was able to produce a telegram from Bank Hoffman, a small bank, not a large broker in B&O shares, giving it unequivocal support.[9]

Howard Simpson, in the meantime, was becoming disillusioned with the C&O and suggested that three-way merger talks would be a good idea after all. Tuohy demurred, but Perlman thought it was a great idea and appointed his vice president, John Kenefick, to supervise the project. Having displeased the C&O, Simpson conveniently left for his vacation. On his return, he gave a luncheon for Tuohy and Perlman, which lasted four hours, but the impasse remained. *Trains* rated it one of the social disasters of the season, "its words lost in the roar of jets leaving Idlewild for Switzerland."[10]

When the C&O's offer expired in September, only 29 percent of the B&O's stockholders had accepted, but the C&O thanked them anyway for their "hearty response" and announced that the offer would be extended for a while longer. Simpson was furious. If the C&O sought a merger rather than control, it would not need 80 percent. His fear was that control would guarantee the B&O nothing, and the C&O could loot it and leave it helpless. So Tuohy dispatched to Simpson what *Trains* called a "Dear Howard" letter in which he offered to investigate the possibility of a complete merger. The two men were supposed to meet in New York at the Eastern Railroads Presidents' Conference and later at a board meeting of the Richmond, Fredericksburg & Potomac Railroad, of which both were directors. At the last minute, Simpson canceled. On September 21, the B&O

board voted to begin merger studies with the New York Central.

The studies anticipated $23 million in savings from a full merger with the C&O. But the C&O wanted only control, and that would produce no more than $10 million in savings and guarantee the B&O nothing. With only control, if the going got rough, the B&O could be cast off to sink like a stone, as the C&O cast off the Erie in the 1930s. The B&O turned to the Central in desperation. Why had the B&O not tried to strike a better bargain from the C&O in the first place? "They forced us," said B&O's general counsel, Jervis Langdon. "They threatened to cancel their offer unless we gave in absolutely."[11] A number of B&O shareholders, visions of fat C&O dividends dancing in their heads, were none too pleased with their own board for making overtures to the Central. At the stockholders' meeting, one of them said he was amazed at the B&O's change of heart. One said to Simpson, "You are charging the C&O management with complete bad faith." In so many words, Simpson said yes. "They have talked merger in public and to the stockholders, but have not come through with an offer."[12]

The C&O was stamping the B&O shares tendered to it, meaning they remained committed to the C&O even if they changed hands. The Central was not stamping and (unlike the C&O, which published running tallies) would not reveal how many shares were committed to it. It was thought to have no more than 20 percent. At a stormy Central stockholders' meeting in Albany, Perlman was questioned about the B&O, about passenger losses, and about certain unpleasant developments within the Alleghany Corporation.[13] He would not discuss any of it. Aboard the Empire State Express returning to New York, the Central's officers read in the evening paper that the C&O had invited the B&O shareholders to a series of weekend parties and champagne balls at its posh golf resort, the Greenbrier, at White Sulphur Springs, West Virginia.[14]

On December 15, 1960, the C&O announced that it had 53 percent of the B&O's stock tendered to it and stamped. But on December 23, there was a startling offer for a block of 75,000 B&O shares at $47 a share. The price that day was $37.25. Trading in the B&O was temporarily halted. "We were convinced," said Tuohy, "that Central or Alleghany was buying on the open market."[15] On January 17, 1961, at 9:15 A.M., Walter Grant of the Central offered $46 a share for a block of 50,000 B&O shares. Its price at the moment was $34.50. At 11:15, the party called back to say the C&O had offered a better price.[16] The next day, B&O shares shot up six and one-eighth points, and the morning after that jumped another four points immediately after the opening bell. At 11:15, with a flood of sell orders pouring in as B&O shareholders rushed to unload at a high price, trading was suspended. The Central was purchasing any share, stamped or not. Even if it was stamped, the C&O could not vote it if it was in Central's hands. Shortly before trading was suspended, the stamped shares actually commanded a higher price than the unstamped.[17]

When it was all over, Kirby said that Alleghany had bought into the B&O to protect its interest in the Central. The Central said it had bought to protect its position in eastern mergers. The C&O said it had bought in response to the Central. The Central and Alleghany paid $13 million for 369,775 shares, while for $29 million, the C&O got 489,720 shares, which together with its remaining stamped shares, gave it 64 percent.[18] Nevertheless, even as the final exchange offer expired at midnight on February 2, 1961, the morning papers carried full-page advertisements by the C&O to the B&O stockholders deceptively titled "Merger at Midnight." It told B&O holders that they would be "connecting up with financial strength and earning power. Act now. If your B&O shares are held by your bank or broker, call them and have them sent to the C&O agent, Morgan Guaranty Trust Co." The C&O wanted the B&O very, very much.

Triumphant, the C&O prepared to send its case to the ICC. Wyer, Dick & Company made formal studies like those for the Erie Lackawanna. In March, the C&O said it was also buying the stock of the Western Maryland; it already had 7.31 percent. The B&O already owned 42.8 percent of the Western Maryland.[19] The State of Maryland sold $18 million in bonds to expand general cargo facilities at Baltimore and thus encourage the C&O-B&O relationship. Defeated, with no merger partner in sight, the Central flailed about helplessly. In April, it submitted a rather embarrassing petition for inclusion in the N&W–Nickel Plate merger, and then it issued a series of white papers to explain its behavior.

Wall Street had been treated to another railroad proxy spectacular, the second in a decade and the second to involve the New York Central. As it approached its climax, several other bolts of lightning struck the New York Central, all coming from Penn Center in Philadelphia.

When the Norfolk & Western and the Nickel Plate first announced their intent to merge on March 18, 1960, more questions were raised than were answered. How were these two railroads going to connect? They did not have a single common junction. They had nothing in common except that they both made money. What was the role of the Pennsylvania Railroad, which owned 34 percent of N&W's stock and named four directors to its fourteen-member board? What was this going to mean for other railroads in the region, particularly those who were not being invited to mergers? What was it going to mean for shippers and communities that depended on the railroads that were not being invited to mergers?

On June 13, 1960, the N&W and the Nickel Plate finalized their plans. Each Nickel Plate share would be exchanged for 0.45 shares of the N&W. The Nickel Plate shareowners would own about one-fifth of the combined company. All this was dependent on the willingness of the Pennsylvania Railroad to sell its Sandusky line, a money-making coal route running north and south through the middle of Ohio from a junction with the N&W at Columbus to coal piers on Lake Erie at Sandusky. It crossed the Nickel Plate main line at Bellevue, Ohio, also the Nickel Plate's principal marshaling point. So the Pennsylvania Railroad was involved.

On November 30, 1960, a very big deal was made. The Pennsylvania would sell the Sandusky line, 111 miles for $27 million. It would also lease the Wabash Railroad, which it controlled, to the N&W. The lease was for 50 years, but anytime after six years, the N&W had the option to buy the PRR's Wabash stock in exchange for N&W shares. This would create a railroad of 7,371 miles from Kansas City to Norfolk that would have been the most profitable transportation company in the country—air, highway, or rail—if it had been merged in 1959.[20] And there was no mistaking the key role of the Pennsylvania Railroad.

The Lehigh Valley

On December 16, 1960, the Lehigh Valley announced that its board had endorsed a plan for the Pennsylvania Railroad to acquire all of its stock and seek control. The PRR would exchange one share of its stock for every four and one-eighth shares of Lehigh stock not already in PRR hands. Between the Pennsylvania Company and the PRR, it already had 44 percent. By the terms of the Agreement of 1941, a treaty of peace between the PRR and the New York Central, all that stock was in a voting trust. The New York Central's nightmare of a PRR-dominated east-west route through the Central's Buffalo heartland was on the table again.

Symes said the Lehigh would not survive on its own, and he was probably right. Speculation was that the PRR's real interest in a railroad that a *New York Times* Wall Street column noted had "little freight and no passengers" was to ensure its leverage on the Norfolk & Western.[21] The Pennsylvania Company's interest in the N&W had been reduced from 45 percent to 34 percent by the Virginian merger (by which Koppers Corporation also became a major N&W holder). The enlarged N&W now on the drawing boards would be without a route from Buffalo to tidewater. It would want the Lehigh to fill this most obvious gap in its system. The PRR could sell it for an interest in the N&W.

There was a time when the Lehigh Valley was a great railroad. Its origins went back to the canal and inclined-plane schemes of the 1840s to get anthracite coal out of the area around Mauch Chunk, Pennsylvania (later renamed Jim Thorpe). It completed its own line across northern New Jersey to Black Tom Island in Jersey City in 1875. Two years later, it bought the Tifft farm south of Buffalo for a future terminal; and in 1892, it finished its long-expected line to the Great Lakes. It was a no-frills railroad that served the coal mines, the steel mills of Bethlehem and Buffalo, the flour mills of Buffalo, and a rich manufacturing region of New York

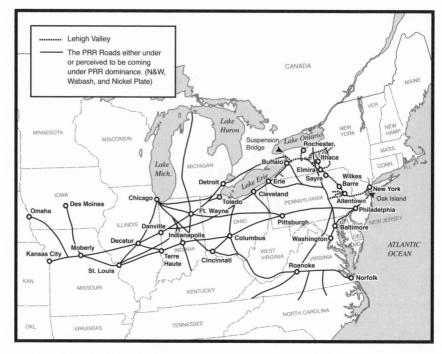

Lehigh Valley and the Emerging PRR

and Pennsylvania. It was the first to lay its entire double-track route with 136-pound rail—ultra heavy duty for the era, a gritty symbol of the glory days of coal and steel and heavy industry in the Northeast. Its decline foreshadowed the waning of those glory days.[22]

Even in the best of times, there was an aura of bad fate about the Lehigh. It had serious labor problems in the 1890s and again in the 1920s. On the morning of July 30, 1916, its Black Tom Terminal, packed with contraband munitions destined for the war in Europe, was blown up by German saboteurs.[23] The explosion rocked all of New York Harbor. The railroad sought indemnity from the Weimar and Nazi governments; the Bonn government finally settled in the 1950s, though probably not for what it cost the railroad in legal expenses. And the Lehigh was always a pawn in someone else's empire-building dreams—first the Reading in the 1890s, then the fifth-system schemes of the 1920s, and then the PRR.

But when the decline began after 1956, it was cataclysmic. The decline of anthracite and the opening of the St. Lawrence Seaway played a role, but so did the Lehigh's conservative management. For example, though it was clear from World War II onward that anthracite would decline and the future of the railroad was in general merchandise traffic, it failed to remedy its deficiencies in the Buffalo terminal. Its connection to the Wabash required a 30-mile detour through Niagara Falls. Its connection with the Nickel Plate required a seven-mile, five-hour ramble through the warehouse district crossing the New York Central main line at grade.[24] It never purchased enough freight cars and ran an annual freight-car per diem deficit of $1 million. It reduced its bonded indebtedness in the 1950s but did so out of cash; when revenue dropped in the recession after 1957, its cash position was dangerously low. One consultant said the Lehigh had made a "bad guess" in counting on continued prosperity when it used its limited funds to buy back bonds instead of making physical improvements. The company was slow to adopt piggyback or radio communication and never experimented with the ideas such as guaranteed rates that excited other railroads in the 1950s. The last regular passenger train it ever operated, the Maple Leaf from Toronto on February 4, 1961, broke down in howling blizzards with repeated mechanical failures and limped into Newark eight hours late, where the PRR refused to even accept it for its last lap into Penn Station.

By 1959, when it was clear that the Lehigh was in trouble and was not going to be invited to anyone's merger, its president, Cedric Major, arranged a series of meetings with Walter Tuohy of the C&O, Felix Hales of the Nickel Plate, and Stuart Saunders of the N&W to suggest that they include the Lehigh in whatever plans they might be making. They all turned him down. Discussions with the Wabash were more hopeful; and in the early summer of 1960, joint studies were authorized. Once the Wabash got an invitation from the N&W, talks with the Lehigh ended.

Lehigh wanted somebody to take it in but as usual was too timid to undertake an obvious coordination, what *Trains* called *the* most obvious coordination in the east. Between Wilkes-Barre and the sea, the Lehigh Valley and Jersey Central railroads were parallel—actually adjacent for a good part of the way, both double-tracked, neither carrying a fraction of its capacity since the demise of anthracite—but no merger was discussed. Nor was there coordination until 1965, when it was too late. Even then, it was only a jury-rigged patchwork of the two lines, and the first Jersey Central and Lehigh freights to use the coordinated trackage slammed in to each other head-on. The Erie and the Lackawanna thought briefly about bringing the Lehigh into their merger, but with all that Lehigh stock in PRR hands, it seemed pointless.

In mid-September 1960 Major asked Symes of the PRR for an appointment to discuss merger. The meeting was unproductive, but Major's board told him to try harder. So there were more meetings, and on October 14, Symes called to say the PRR was prepared to seek stock control. It drove a hard bargain on the exchange ratio, and the longer the haggling went on, the more the Lehigh's position deteriorated. In November, Symes made a final take-it-or-leave-it offer, and after a tumultuous meeting of the Lehigh board, it was accepted.[25]

The ICC would want to know how stock control would save the Lehigh from bankruptcy. After all, control was a far cry from the guarantees of merger. There had to be some kind of a report. The Lehigh was too poor to afford professional consultants, and the PRR never liked them, so the PRR sent two of its vice presidents, Walter Patchell from the operating department and Fred Carpi from traffic, to do the job. The Patchell-Carpi studies envisioned annual savings of $6 million, mostly by eliminating separate Lehigh management. There would be savings from yard coordination at Buffalo and from the abandonment of lighterage operations at Communipaw Terminal (Jersey City). The Lehigh could abandon its shops at Sayre, Pennsylvania, and the PRR would take over locomotive repair. The studies first drew a pessimistic picture of the Lehigh's traffic potential (to explain why the dubious help of stock control was essential) then said the future was bright (to explain why the PRR was interested). PRR geologists would study mineral deposits along the Lehigh. They might find something.[26]

On the eve of the Lehigh hearings, Robert Bedingfield said in a story in the *New York Times,* "Mr. Symes envisages for the Pennsylvania a series of consolidations in the next five years. He foresees in the same period combinations of other eastern railroads that may leave his system with one or at most two competitors in its territory. There are 34 today."[27]

To everyone but the PRR's lawyers, it seemed obvious that the Lehigh control and the N&W merger cases were related, that the PRR was finally moving to consolidate the empire it created in the 1920s. Symes was candid: the PRR had opposed the ICC's plan of the 1920s because it was a "squeeze play." "It is a matter of known fact," he said, "that the Pennsylvania acquired ownership in the Lehigh Valley to protect itself in the matter of mergers in eastern territory."[28]

In the midst of the hearing, Symes mentioned, perhaps by a slip, that the PRR would equip the Lehigh with centralized traffic control. But passenger trains were gone, and through freights were down to four a day each way; with Fred Carpi's traffic study giving little hope of an upturn, the CTC hardly seemed necessary, unless someone anticipated a major increase. The EL was fascinated. It suspected the traffic would come from diversions from them. The PRR's lawyers acted as though a cat had been let out of the bag and they were frantic to get it back in. Was it not true, they asked Perry Shoemaker, that Symes only "guessed" that CTC would be installed. "I have known Mr. Symes for many years," said Shoemaker, "and I have a great respect for his guesses."[29]

The Erie Lackawanna, with the most to lose, put forward a proposal of its own, a three-way merger of itself, the Lehigh, and the PRR. Wyer, Dick & Co. was hired to make a study. Neither the Lehigh nor the PRR would cooperate, so they had to resort to public information and clandestine interviews with Lehigh employees. A report was assembled that was more sophisticated than the Patchell-Carpi studies. Savings would be substantial; virtually the entire Erie and Lehigh main lines could be single-tracked. The report noted some savings that the Patchell-Carpi studies had overlooked and found some errors in Patchell's calculations.[30] This put Symes in a bind: to accept the proposal would make a minor control case the catalyst for a major realignment of railroads; to turn it down was to repudiate the savings that all railroad executives said was what they wanted.

Bankruptcy was a pretty bad thing, was it not? asked the PRR. The Erie Lackawanna had to agree; it was a likely candidate itself. Did the EL know that Lehigh shippers were getting nervous about that railroad's ability to continue to provide service? Bethlehem Steel, for example, noted that the Lehigh was constantly unable to supply adequate gondola cars for steel loadings and that its entire traffic policy was up for review as a result.[31] If the EL forced a delay, it would be responsible for all this, said the PRR. At the hearing, the PRR's lawyer questioned William Wyer of Wyer, Dick & Co.:

> Q: Is the Lehigh Valley headed for bankruptcy if the Pennsylvania does not get control?
> A: I think it probably is, yes.
> Q: What is your opinion of where the Erie Lackawanna is headed?
> A: Well, I think it is on the same road, but not as far down the road.
> Q: Even though it is currently losing money at three times the rate as the Lehigh Valley, you don't think it is headed for the drain as fast?
> A: No.[32]

The C&O-B&O Case

Hearings in the C&O-B&O case got under way in June 1961. The principal argument of the C&O had a familiar ring: unless a favorable decision was reached immediately, the B&O would be in bankruptcy. Only the expertise and credit of the C&O could save it. Part of this was true. The B&O was in terrible trouble.

The cataclysmic descent of the Baltimore & Ohio began in the third week of October 1957. From a 1956 high of $465 million, gross revenues fell to $359 million by 1961; that year, the net operating loss was $31 million, the worst showing of any railroad. The effects of recession were compounded because the B&O was in the middle of capital improvement projects that had already consumed cash but had no earning power until they were finished. Some, such as the new Hawkins Point Marine Terminal in Baltimore, were well enough along that they continued to receive funding. Others had to be put on indefinite hold, including the half-completed yard at Cumberland, Maryland, and the new coal docks at Curtis Bay (Baltimore). Low tunnel clearances on the main line across West Virginia made the use of piggyback equipment impossible. "Here we were, the shortest route between Baltimore and St. Louis," said Jervis Langdon, "and

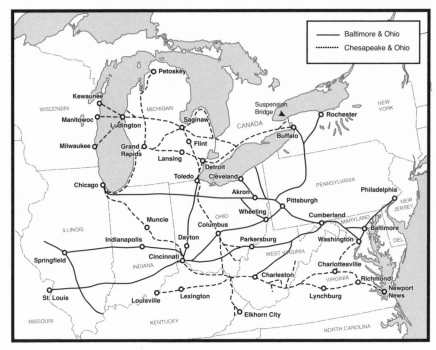

C&O/B&O, 1962

we were not competitive because we couldn't handle the equipment."[33] Plans to raise the clearances had to be canceled, and a million dollars' worth of bulldozers bought for the purpose were useless.

There were other projects that needed attention they could not be given. Most of the mechanical interlocks and semaphores, installed between 1900 and 1923, needed immediate replacement, as did thousands of angle bars installed during World War I when there were restrictions on their size and steel content. Much of the track was due for reballasting, especially in the mountains, where heavy sanding by the locomotives and leaking coal dust contaminated it and shortened the life of rails and ties. Most of the early F and FA model diesel locomotives were at the end of their service life, as was more than half the freight car fleet. Of its 86,000-car fleet of cars, 26 percent were bad-ordered (inoperable) by 1960 and hundreds with antique Duryea underframes could not be repaired.[34]

To cut costs, the passenger service was hacked to bits and the traffic department dismembered. John Kerslake, vice president for traffic, told how it took place:

Q: Are your sales people effective?
A: . . . the officers are stripped of help. We don't have enough clerks.

Q: When was the last general reduction?

A: We are having them all the time. The last one was last week.

Q: Was it a general one?

A: No, but it was substantial. We didn't furlough anyone. We retired them. Not that I didn't feel we should fill their jobs. We just couldn't afford it.

Q: When was the last general reduction?

A: About 18 months ago. . . . Some of them were furloughed and some were retired. . . . Over the last six months we have cut our traffic force, I would say, 34 or 35 percent.[35]

Like the Lehigh, the B&O had tried to repurchase its outstanding debt out of cash. In 1955 it refunded a number of debt issues into a single consolidated mortgage, which enabled it to reduce fixed charges by $2 million. But one of the series of bonds found no buyers. That meant that the B&O had exhausted its credit. "I am not sure if the B&O wanted to borrow any sizeable amount of money, such as $50 million, it could do it on any basis," said Winthrop Lenz of Merrill Lynch. "The Chase Manhattan, which has the existing loan, is practically on 24-hour call they are so worried about what may happen to this railroad."

Q: Would it be desirable to pay 10 percent or 15 percent for improvements that would pay for themselves in three years?

A: It would destroy what little credit is left. Bonds now selling in the 80s would sink to the 50s.[36]

Why should a railroad with these terrible problems be such a desirable partner? Despite the grim picture, the B&O's problems were temporary. Recessions were bad for everyone, but there were better and there were worse times to be caught in one, and the B&O had been caught at the worst. It was a highly leveraged company, meaning that the bulk of its capitalization was in funded debt, in bonds rather than in stock. Interest has to be paid on bonds every quarter, regardless of net income, in contrast to stock, or equity, on which dividends might be high in good times but do not have to be paid at all in bad times. To be leveraged as the B&O was means that in good times, fixed charges were a small part of a solid net income; in bad times, they were overwhelming. In other words, the B&O ought to snap back as soon as the recession was over. Besides, it had taken $27 million in extraordinary write-offs, which made the 1959 results look worse than they were.[37]

Even though the B&O and the C&O served a number of common points, their routes were entirely different and served different customers. As in the Erie Lackawanna merger, combining the C&O and the B&O would not permit line abandonment or terminal consolidation. The C&O insisted that this was an end-to-end combination of connecting roads, not duplicating roads. Both railroads hauled coal, for example, but the B&O's was mostly high-volatile coal used in steam plants, whereas the C&O's was mostly low-volatile coal used for coking. The B&O's automobile traffic came from St. Louis and Ohio, the C&O's from Michigan. The B&O's steel traffic came from Pittsburgh and eastern Ohio, the C&O's from Buffalo, Detroit, and Chicago. The B&O's chemical traffic came from Cincinnati and points in Illinois and Maryland, the C&O's from Charleston, West Virginia, Niagara Falls, and Ontario points. In the traffic of food products, paper, scrap iron, soda, glass, pipe fittings, and fluxing stone, each railroad served substantially different customers.

Not so, said the New York Central. Make a list of the 60 largest customers of the Central, the C&O, and the B&O, it said, and 15 of them would appear on all three lists—Allied Chemical, Armco Steel, Bethlehem Steel, Continental Can, Detroit Edison, Dow Chemical, DuPont, Eastern Gas & Fuel, General Motors, Jones & Laughlin, Owens-Illinois, Republic Steel, Union Carbide, the U.S. Government, and Youngstown Sheet & Tube. That was competition.

The C&O said control would produce great savings. Hardly, said the Central. The C&O's Wyer Report claimed only $13 million a year, not a lot for railroads that size.[38] If savings were the name of the game, much greater savings could be obtained from merger with the Central. The C&O said studies for this would take too long and the B&O would probably collapse in the meantime. "We will make studies," said the Central. "How can you afford studies like that? We thought [you] were poor," said the C&O. "We have enough to see that the public interest is considered," said the Central.[39]

The C&O promised that it would underwrite the remainder of the B&O's improvement program. It would not loan the money directly but would guarantee loans. This was the single most powerful argument for approving control. But what would compel the C&O to do as it promised? It was not a charity. Presumably, it acted in its own interest. The C&O said it never would have invested so heavily if it did not intend to protect that investment by rehabilitating the B&O. But when Walter Tuohy said he would commit $34 million with no assurance that the C&O or its stockholders would ever see it again, the opposition was incredulous. Had not the C&O once had major investments in the Erie and the Chicago & Eastern Illinois, and had it not refused them credit and let them go into bankruptcy? Prof. John Frederick of the University of Maryland offered scholarly sanction of the C&O's plan but did not know about this. "Then how are you so certain, Doctor, that it will help if you haven't explored the history of the C&O's past actions?"[40] Walter Tuohy said he felt no compulsion to rescue two other railroads that were already controlled by the B&O—the Jersey Central and the Reading. Why was the C&O so selfless about the B&O yet it recoiled in horror that it should do something for the Reading and the Jersey Central? The C&O's distinction between philanthropy and motivating self-interest seemed a little muddy.

Finally, the C&O promised the B&O its miraculous know-how, what it believed was the managerial excellence that made it rich. The C&O invested its profits wisely in an impressive assemblage of young graduates. It had engineers to study railroad problems and geologists to locate coal deposits along its lines, efficiency experts to streamline its business methods, and even a department of golf, headed by Sammy Snead, headquartered at the Greenbrier, to sell coal to visiting Japanese industrialists (although the golfers had just returned from Japan without selling a single carload).[41] More successful were the recent demonstrations of the efficiency of coal by C&O fuel engineers at government installations planning to convert to gas as well as the engineers' work with electric utilities to design plants that took best advantage of the burning qualities of C&O coal.[42]

There was a certain smugness about the C&O people, perhaps a holdover of the swagger of Robert Young, that did not seem to characterize other successful railroads, such as the N&W. John Barriger, then at the Pittsburgh & Lake Erie (P&LE), said he thought the C&O people ought to be proud of their accomplishments just as the P&LE people were proud. "But we know," he said, "that is in large part our favorable position for moving bulk commodities. I observe no deficiencies in B&O management that require C&O know-how."[43] It was true that the C&O's cost for locomotive repair was about two-thirds that of the B&O, and its cost for track maintenance was well below the national average. But its passenger deficit was out of control, it had no electronic yards, it had lagged in the development of piggyback, and its coal cars averaged only 16 round trips a year from mine to delivery, barely more than a trip a month.[44]

> Q: What are those magic procedures you're going to give the B&O?
> A: Did you say magic?
> Q: Well, I assume they are going to be magic.[45]

This swagger about superior management was not going to endear the C&O to B&O people. Charles E. Bertrand, later the president of the Reading but then the B&O's vice president for operations, saw it this way:

> Q: Do you assert the B&O is an unsafe railroad?
> A: No, we maintain safety.
> Q: Do you feel yourself qualified to run it?
> A: Yes.
> Q: Do you need C&O direction?
> A: No, I need money.[46]

John Barriger had been involved in consolidation matters since before most of the men at the hearings had received their first Lionel. Author of the Prince Plan of the 1930s and now president of the Pittsburgh & Lake Erie, he was not impressed with what the younger men had wrought. The C&O-B&O was a bad combination because it was end-to-end. Such affiliations could reduce expenses by only 10 percent at most, and he had plenty of historical evidence to prove it. Their principal effect was to damage competition, and they did not provide any of the textbook justifications, such as the concentration of traffic on fewer lines or in solid trains. Even if such affiliations were coupled with capital improvement, they could never solve the fundamental problems of excess capacity and declining traffic volume. As for the C&O's generosity in helping a sick railroad, it had never been generous before. Robert Young, for example, used to brag that the C&O saved the Nickel Plate from bankruptcy in 1941 when the Nickel Plate could not meet a maturing bond issue. Young never added that the funds came from the Reconstruction Finance Corporation, but Barriger knew. He had been the chief of the railroad bureau of the RFC, which authorized the loan.

Barriger talked in depth and with ease about all phases of railroading and presented sophisticated exhibits, such as a logarithmic chart of the peaks and valleys of competitive commodity shipments. He knew everyone at the hearings; he knew many of their fathers. He told C&O counsel Edward Wheeler how he had worked with his father, Sen. Burton K. Wheeler of Montana, shaping the Transportation Act of 1940. What the law intended, he thought, was nothing like the proposal before them. To some, he was an eccentric grandfather taking the juniors by the hand. But he was not reminiscing about the way trains used to be. His history was vital, the past speaking to the present. And unlike most of them, he even had a sense of humor:

> Q: Have you ever worked for the C&O?
> A: No. Are you offering me a job? I've been quite a boomer, you know. Maybe after this is over, I'll need one.[47]

The New York Central pursued its case against the C&O-B&O through the fall of 1961. It demanded, and was granted, hearings on the road, in Boston, in Syracuse, in Detroit, in Indianapolis, in Cleveland, and in Chicago, finally ending back in Washington on October 9, 1961. The very next day, hearings began on the N&W–Nickel Plate merger. Many of the people who had taken part in the one would take part in the other, and they were in a state of emotional exhaustion.

The N&W–Nickel Plate–Wabash

As the law read, railroads could not be compelled to merge, but if a merger were sought, and if a third road could demonstrate that its inclusion was required by the public interest, such inclusion could be required as a condition of approval. Whether the ICC was ready to face up to it or not, the C&O and N&W cases were going to restructure all of eastern railroading, and they were going to have a profound effect on every other railroad in the region. There was a domino effect at work: one merger could require another, and so on, so that none of these proposals could be evaluated in isolation. Too many states, cities, ports, factories, entire industries were all going to be affected, and the matter transcended the question of savings from consolidating a yard or downgrading a line. So states, cities, ports, shippers, and other railroads all showed up to try to make this clear. The N&W case became so weighted down with the worries of third parties that the question of whether it was a good idea on its merit became secondary. The only protesters to attack it on its merit were a group of communities on the St. Louis line of the Nickel Plate, a route that was going to be downgraded to local service.

The N&W had an impressive case for at least part of its proposal. Studies were dazzling, with tallies that anticipated savings of $27 million a year.[48] Stuart Saunders ticked off examples of improved freight schedules—15 hours faster for certain traffic moving east out of Chicago, and 12 to 15 hours faster for traffic moving east out of St. Louis. Total train

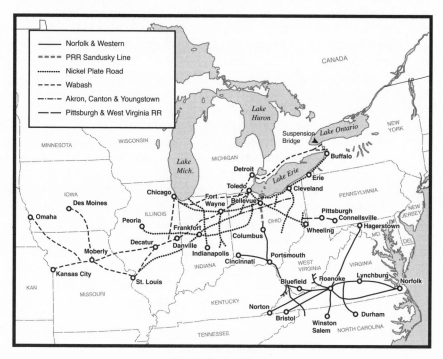

N&W–Nickel Plate

mileage would be reduced by 1.3 million miles a year. Eventually, Examiner Lester Conley would recite these same examples in his report, and the commission would accept them as evidence that the merger served the public interest "beyond question."[49]

Combining the Nickel Plate and the Wabash had always made good sense. Two railroads could hardly complement each other more. They connected the same points. Where one was weak, the other was strong. From Chicago to Buffalo, the Nickel Plate was a fast, flat railroad, but the Wabash had to ferry its trains across the Detroit River and then use trackage rights on the Canadian National. Toward St. Louis, the Wabash was a powerhouse whereas the Nickel Plate was an undulating line originally built to narrow gauge standards. Every one of Saunders's examples of improved service had to do with the Wabash and the Nickel Plate, not the N&W. The 15-hour reduction in Chicago-Buffalo schedules, for example, was nothing more than rerouting Wabash traffic over the Nickel Plate. There was no need for a merger to do this. All shippers had to say was "Nickel Plate," and they got the faster service. Dramatic statements of vast improvements that looked convincing in a press release were often quite hollow.

The question was what the N&W was going to bring to this. It was in the N&W's corporate interest to diversify out of coal and have single-line distribution for its coal in the Midwest. But was that in the public interest? When the hearing was over, the ICC had no basis for its assertion that the public would get better service specifically as a result of this merger. It was, said Commissioner William Tucker in a stinging dissent, "a wholly inadequate record."[50]

What was the public interest? Who was the public? Who spoke for it? How were conflicting interests among different sectors of the public to be resolved? The debate was old, and it was not going to be settled here. The commission's precedent in the *New York Central Securities Case* of 1932 had held that a railroad need only show that its proposal had a "direct relation to the adequacy of transportation services." To show that, the commission accepted the word of shippers and local communities, provided there were no corresponding objections from other shippers and communities. The N&W brought in several dozen shippers. The exercise did not prove much. Some of them said the merger would improve their supply of cars, particularly air-slide grain cars. "Has it been indicated the new system will acquire new grain cars?" The answer was no.[51] Some said it would improve service. Was it deficient now? No.[52] Some said it would increase transit privileges. Did they have assurances? No.[53] Some said it would reduce rates. Had they been told so? No.[54] Some said single-line service would be an improvement over interchange. Was interline service by any of these railroads deficient now? No. Some even thought their interline service was better than some other railroads' single-line service.[55] Others admitted after stating their glittering generalities that their distribution patterns would not change because of a merger.[56] Nearly all of the shippers indicated that railroads were collapsing and only mergers could save them. They had read about troubled railroads in the paper, or their daughter told them how decrepit the passenger train was when she came home for spring break. Their ill-informed comments implied that the N&W was going to be the first to collapse if it failed to get this merger.

More than a struggle between railroads, this case was a struggle between states and regions. Two railroads—the Wabash and the Nickel Plate—historically served as conveyors to the ports of New York and Boston (and in the case of the Nickel Plate's participation in the Alphabet Route, Baltimore). Now they would be linked to a railroad serving the Port of Norfolk. This struggle began to take shape in the C&O-B&O case, when Gov. Nelson Rockefeller of New York bumptiously arrived to offer his observations. The New York Central and the Erie Lackawanna served the Port of New York, and he was opposed to their being excluded from mergers meant to funnel traffic to other ports. Since he always liked to think positively, he offered a three-point program to solve the problem: (1) create a Federal Department of Transportation, (2) repeal the 10 percent tax on passenger tickets, and (3) take a coordinated approach to mergers.[57] It was easy to sneer at the governor's simplifications, and he nearly got himself politely excused as an incompetent witness. He understood that the Port of New York was in trouble, that in addition to its labor and cost problems every one of its railroads to the interior was in trouble. New York would do what it could to get the C&O to include the New York Central, and the N&W to include the Erie Lackawanna.

The N&W mustered political celebrities of its own. Governors Barron of West Virginia and Combes of Kentucky each made perfunctory appearances. Terry Sanford of North Carolina could not make it; he sent a substitute who was abysmally ill informed. For example, he said single-line service was a good thing, then was not able to define what it was.[58] The star performance was left to Gov. J. Lindsay Almond of Virginia. "I have heard no opposition from any representative source in Virginia," he stated. Naturally not. Virginia stood to be the big winner. His point was that if the N&W was not permitted to do what it wanted, railroads would have to be nationalized; that would be tragic, because he had just come back from South America where "the deplorable state of railroad transportation in those countries owned by the government [was] deplorable." Railroads, he continued, "were absolutely essential in peace and direly essential in war, and in my judgment, the only answer is for these railroads to merge to meet the age of progressive automation in which we find ourselves."[59]

The N&W merger could do for Virginia what the opening of the Erie Canal had done for New York in 1825—raise it triumphantly ahead of old rival ports. When the governor was asked about the devastating effect this might have on other states and ports, he said, "Well, the attitude of

Virginia has always been one of live and let live. I cannot conceive of any serious impact to other transportation systems outside the areas of this merger." When the situation was explained to him, he said, "I cannot accept your hypothesis. However, the attitude of Virginia would not change because of its faith in the American system of freedom of enterprise and fair competition in all areas of industrial endeavor."[60]

Having affirmed his faith in the sanctity of private enterprise and the horrors of nationalization by government, he announced that the state of Virginia would pick up the tab for new coal docks at Hampton Roads for the use of the N&W, to encourage movement through the Port of Norfolk. In contrast, and to their sorrow, the supposedly wild-spending "liberal" states of New York and New Jersey did not spend money on their railroads. Once upon a time they had invested in such things—the Erie Canal, for example—and it had paid off. Now they taxed them, required them to assume a massive urban transit burden with no public help, and (in New York's case) required a useless third brakeman on all trains.

From the moment of the first announcement of the N&W–Nickel Plate merger, the Erie Lackawanna perceived it as the single greatest threat to its existence. Its own merger was as yet undigested, but it felt compelled to devote the energies of its executive and legal talent to fight what it assumed was encirclement by the PRR. Therefore, it made an elaborate study of a four-way merger of the EL, the N&W, the Nickel Plate, and the Wabash. It anticipated $34 million in annual savings and an electronic classification yard at Huntington, Indiana, the EL's junction with the Wabash.[61]

This put Saunders and the N&W on the spot. Here was a proposal for genuine savings, exactly what railroads said their mergers were for. But the N&W security holders would never approve a merger with the Erie Lackawanna, even if Stuart Saunders could be convinced it was for the good of the industry. The EL's debt was too massive, and it served a territory that was not growing. But nationalization is what everyone said they feared the most; nationalization would be the most horrible thing they could think of, so hurry up and approve these mergers. But exactly what *was* going to happen to the leftovers if they remained left over? Was not this whole process hurtling toward some kind of government bailout, for the industry or for parts of it?

Saunders swung into the kind of action he loved best—deals. On October 12, 1961, the EL signed an agreement whereby it withdrew from the case. In return, the Nickel Plate would immediately join the EL in building the new Bison Yard at Buffalo, sharing the construction costs and ensuring that the EL would continue to be the route of preference for interchange coming off the Nickel Plate route.[62] Then, upon consummation of the N&W–Nickel Plate merger, the N&W and the EL would begin good-faith consultation to see if "some form of affiliation would be mutually advantageous." Disputes could be submitted to an arbiter, but they were limited to the question of whether each was acting in good faith. A failure by either party to reach an agreement would not be evidence of a lack of good faith. Any agreements had to be submitted to the security holders of each company. If either company should enter bankruptcy, the agreement could be canceled unilaterally. But to show its good faith, the N&W promised to buy $1.5 million of EL securities.[63] Paul Johnston, Erie's former president, negotiated this for the EL. He said it was the best deal he could get. But it was not very good.

> Q: Will you agree sir, that $1.5 million of EL securities is not a significant proportion of ownership?
> A: To a man brought up on the Erie Railroad, it is a lot of dollars.[64]

Others worried. Erie stockholders, for example, wired the ICC asking it not to let their company withdraw. Whatever it was doing was not in their interest, they said. Having permitted the EL to withdraw, even the examiner had second thoughts that he might have made a mistake.[65] New York and the New York Port Authority continued to fight the EL's battle in the belief that it was unable to fight for itself. Said Austin Tobin of the Port Authority:

> A: I am singularly unimpressed with the agreement of October 12, 1961, and to my mind it is a very flimsy piece of tissue paper indeed, and I see no commitment on the part of anyone to do anything that really means anything.
> Q: Is it your objection as to whether we will negotiate in good faith? [This question from John Fishwick of the N&W.]
> A: No. You are pledged to do that. We think if the heart were there, it could be done now.[66]

Saunders explained it this way:

> Q: Did your agreement with the Erie Lackawanna require stockholder approval? [This question from the examiner.]
> A: No.
> Q: But a merger would?
> A: Yes.
> Q: Then your contact with Erie Lackawanna is meaningless?
> A: Oh, no! I am shocked to hear you say that.
> Q: What did you contract to do with them?
> A: We will sit down in good faith.
> Q: There remains the possibility that nothing will be accomplished?
> A: Yes.
> Q: And the ICC is asked to consider this merger proposal on the basis that Erie Lackawanna may be left out in the cold and might not be included in

any arrangement that will provide security for Erie Lackawanna or the public? Is that what you are proposing?

A: No, sir. I have already stated this before. We think and we hope that we can work out an arrangement. It is absolutely certain that if we don't go that way, nothing is going to be done. . . . We are not going to accept the Erie Lackawanna regardless of what the commission says. . . . We are not going to do it. So you don't accomplish a thing. . . . Mr. Examiner, I cannot state too strongly on the record, we will not accept an order of the Commission to make us take Erie Lackawanna. We cannot do it.

Q: Under any arrangement?

A: No sir. And furthermore, the Commission has not the authority to require it.

Q: So what you are suggesting is a take-it-or-leave-it proposition?

A: I have said that flatly, and we think it is in the public interest.[67]

Labor got an attrition agreement, somewhat modified from the one in the Virginian merger. It withdrew its opposition.[68] The little Akron, Canton & Youngstown Railroad, an east-west line across central Ohio, mostly serving the rubber industry in Akron, was promised that the N&W would seek to control it. It would complement the merger in a minor way, but its tax base was too high for outright absorption, and it was said that the "rubber people" liked having it more or less independent. It withdrew.[69] The Pittsburgh & West Virginia Railway, the central link between the Nickel Plate and the Western Maryland in the Alphabet Route, was a healthy property as long as the Alphabet Route was healthy. It received the promise of a lease and withdrew.[70]

Making a deal with the Western Maryland Railway was tough because the WM was 42 percent owned by the B&O, and as we know, the C&O was buying its shares as well. There could be no deal here, and the Maryland Port Authority was giving the WM backbone. The Western Maryland and the Nickel Plate both participated in the Alphabet Route, and now it appeared that the eastern and western ends of that route would fall into different railroad groupings. Would not the N&W solicit against the old Alphabet Route in order to get the long haul to Norfolk instead of Baltimore? The N&W said no, not necessarily. It thought the Nickel Plate already had so many satisfied customers on the Alphabet that it would not want to risk losing the business altogether. There were hints that the N&W had offered transit privileges to large-scale shippers if they would choose Norfolk over Baltimore, but the lease of the Pittsburgh & West Virginia, plus a written promise to actively solicit for the Alphabet Route, seemed to be satisfactory.[71] The Port of Baltimore and the Western Maryland Railway withdrew.[72]

The New York Central kept a low profile in this case, though it was still fighting for inclusion in the C&O-B&O. Beginning in midautumn 1961, rumors were rife that it had resumed talks with the PRR. On January 12, 1962, it was official. The PRR and the NYC signed a merger agreement. On January 15, the Central withdrew from the N&W case. On January 17, it withdrew from the Lehigh Valley case. On January 29, it withdrew from the C&O-B&O.

The only remaining opponents were those noisy folks from the Nickel Plate boondocks. They would have to pay a price for progress. With no powerful opposition, the N&W–Nickel Plate was a done deal, except for Robert Kennedy.

Robert Kennedy and the Justice Department

In the middle of the brawl for the B&O, when Al Perlman began to realize that the Central was going to lose, he raised a serious question that embarrassed every railroad with merger on its mind. If the well-off roads grabbed only those pieces of the national system that struck their fancy, what would become of the leftovers? The commission had to be made to see through the cries of imminent nationalization by the roads that were well off. The best way to do this, said Perlman, was to combine the dockets into one huge case. Then there could be no choice but to find a home for everyone. "The continuation of the present piecemeal approach," he said, "will result in a chaotic situation based on the survival of the fittest." *Trains* continued:

> When the 1957 Penn Central talks collapsed, Al Perlman asked eastern presidents to review the whole merger question and produce a logical, voluntary blueprint that would . . . reduce railroading's cost, preserve essential competition and ensure the strong did not get stronger and the weak weaker. . . . Railroading is vulnerable to the charge of a lack of statesmanship when the president of the number two road feels compelled to call in the regulators to keep order.[73]

The predator roads—the PRR, the N&W, and the C&O—would hear none of this. Such talk was "planned" consolidation, they said, and planning was discredited. They offered no suggestion as to what was to become of the leftovers but insisted that what they wanted to do—and only what they wanted to do—was in the public interest.

The ICC knew it had failed in the 1920s. If it delayed mergers now, it would be accused of obstruction. Some of the commissioners honestly believed the proposed mergers were in the public interest. If dockets were combined and some of the weaker roads dropped over the brink while the hearings dragged on, the commission would be blamed. If the combined docket became too complicated and encumbered with take-it-or-leave-it conditions, the strong roads would walk away. Then there would be no consolidation and the commission would be blamed. But if the C&O–B&O and the N&W–Nickel Plate were approved, then a Penn Central combination was inevitable, whether it was a good idea or not, because the Central was too big to be left out. Everyone could see this. The dominoes were falling.

By the end of 1961, the Lehigh Valley case was moving to a decision. The Lehigh was visibly going down, and something had to be done quickly. Besides, all opposition had mysteriously melted away. The Erie Lackawanna had its vague promise to be included in the N&W. The Central had its agreement with the PRR. The *New York Times* thought everything had worked out: "The merger minded eastern railroads have finally settled family squabbles."[74]

But late in 1961, the Kennedy administration became alarmed about the ultimate designs of the PRR and whether or not it was moving to create a monopoly. It was alarmed that everything that stood in its way was bought off with a deal. Robert Kennedy, the attorney general, had the antitrust division of the Justice Department investigate. In February 1962, it filed a preliminary brief in the N&W case in which it attempted to show that the Pennsylvania Railroad did, in fact, control the Norfolk & Western. The Justice Department's work had been hindered by the refusal of Wyer, Dick & Co. and Coverdale & Colpitts, the two consulting firms capable of studies, to do work for the department. Presumably they feared displeasing their corporate clients. Congress was slower to react, but a few senators were beginning to speak out. The consensus seemed to be that the commission ought to wait before approving anything, to give both Congress and the administration time to sort things out.

On April 5, 1962, President John Kennedy was scheduled to deliver a message on transportation that, among other things, would touch on questions of consolidation and monopoly. On April 4, 1962, the day before, almost in contempt of the president, the ICC let the PRR take control of the Lehigh Valley. The domino was not big enough to knock over the others, but it meant there was one less option, and nothing but trouble lay ahead.

eight

The West
1960–1962

Consolidation in the West was going to travel a rocky road. The two kinds of railroads in the region were the grangers between the Mississippi River and the Rockies, which were by midcentury mostly marginal earners, and the transcontinentals, which had a long haul and tended to be strong earners. Anyone trying to plan consolidation would match a transcon with a granger and balance the assets with the liabilities. But as was usual in railroad affairs, the match was not perfect. And, as is obvious by now, the security holders of a strong, profitable company were not going to vote to dilute the value of their securities by taking on a weak road. It was not going to happen even if it made sense. A bit simplified, that was the dilemma of the West. The real problems come shortly. First, there was a hostile takeover bid.

The Southern Pacific–Western Pacific

In 1961 the Southern Pacific petitioned to take over the Western Pacific. The Southern Pacific was at the top of its game in the early 1960s. A railroad of technological excellence, it had the largest gross revenue of any transportation firm in the United States in 1963. Californians still thought of the SP with anger and awe. It was the company that had created for others the great fortunes of the Golden State. It was the SP that had figured out how to transport California fresh fruit to eastern markets, for example. That was back in 1886, and it set the stage for the richest, most productive agriculture in the world. But the SP was an ominously large landowner in California. Memories of the days when it paid off politicians, named the commissioners to the state's feeble Public Service

Commission, and pretty much did as it pleased were not forgotten. Frank Norris captured the feelings in his 1901 novel *The Octopus,* where the SP appears as the "Pacific Southwestern," a soulless corporation of power and greed. An onrushing train—"terror of steel and steam, with its single eye, cyclopean red"—never even attempts to slow for a flock of sheep that wander onto the track; it kills them all—"merciless, inexorable, cries of agony, sobbing wails of infinite pain, heartrending, pitiful."[1]

The Western Pacific was the last transcontinental railroad, completed between Salt Lake City and Oakland in October 1909. It was the work of George Gould, who was trying to fulfill his father's dream of a true transcontinental system. With the WP, his empire extended from San Francisco to Baltimore with only one small gap in the vicinity of Pittsburgh.[2] The day the WP passenger service began—August 22, 1910—Oakland had the biggest celebration in its history. A WP train chugged under a triumphal arch built for the occasion that proclaimed "Gateway to the Orient." Far Eastern trade got off to a good start. The WP even handled some of the famous silk trains that rushed live, spinning silkworms to New York.

The SP fought the construction of the WP. Harriman, who still controlled the SP, thought the SP could handle all the traffic there was. He saw the WP as a rate buster that would drive rates down until no one could make money. The WP had to seize a tiny harbor slip in Oakland at gunpoint. Five hundred armed men were landed from the waterside by night until the company could show in court that the SP's property extended only to the high-water line of 1852, not to the tidal waters drained since. For 170 miles across northeastern Nevada, geography forced the WP to use the same Humboldt River Canyon as the SP. The SP blocked the WP over one 14-mile stretch west of Deeth, Nevada, where both would have to be on the same side of the river, until the state of Nevada slammed heads together and mandated a three-track railroad, one for each company and one that both could use for passing in between.

The WP's crossing of the Sierras at Beckwourth Pass, north of Reno, was 2,000 feet lower than the SP's at Donner Pass and less exposed to the monstrous snowdrifts. Its route down the Feather River Canyon was spectacular for its sheer cliffs and raging waters hundreds of feet below the tracks. It held grades to a maximum of 1 percent, far better than the SP's route. It was a rough run in the early days, before the rocks settled and the cliff stabilized. As Bruce MacGregor and Ted Benson put it, an engineer coming up on a rockslide had just a moment for a word with God before he and his train slammed into the drink.[3]

The WP was completed just as the federal trustbusters were about to swoop down on the Southern Pacific. They were convinced that the SP's control of both the overland and the southern transcontinental lines was anticompetitive. In December 1912, the Supreme Court ordered divestiture of its Oakland-Ogden route.[4] The Court also said that nothing should

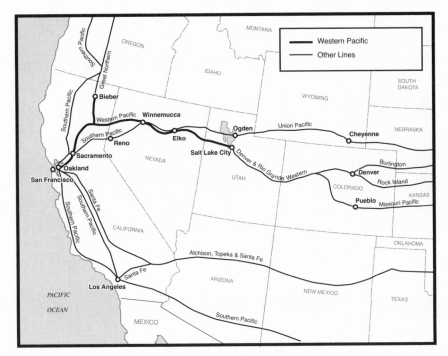

The Western Pacific Affair

prevent the "continuity of operation" of the Overland Route as intended by the Pacific Railroad Acts of 1862, which had created it (and paid for it). It looked as if the SP would be forced to give up its ownership of the Central Pacific to the Union Pacific.[5]

A strange thing happened. California rallied behind the SP, which it had heretofore regarded as the Octopus. The *San Francisco Chronicle,* which had led the charge against the SP; the state government, which was in the hands of railroad-busters; even the Western Pacific, all came to the SP's defense. The state and the *Chronicle* wanted the line "western" owned. The WP was afraid it would never see a carload of traffic if UP rails extended all the way west. With a little help from its enemies, the SP kept its stake in the Overland. To make sure the SP was not tempted to divert traffic away from the Overland to its southern transcontinental route, where it got a much longer haul, the ICC ordered the SP to route all traffic originating in Oregon and northern California bound for the East to the Overland.[6] Perhaps it would have been wiser to have the Overland Route under single UP ownership. On other transcontinental routes, single railroads stretched all the way from the Pacific to the Mississippi. On the Central Corridor, on two competing routes, ownership was divided. It was one of the odd quirks of the American railroad system.

At first, competition from the Western Pacific was not much for the SP to worry about. It was 146 miles longer than the SP from Salt Lake City to Oakland. It could not afford heavy rail, and it had no captive traffic of its own, such as coal. It was dependent on connections, and the ones it had were not very reliable. The Santa Fe in California had its own line all the way to Chicago and was not going to solicit for the WP. The Rio Grande at Salt Lake City was a natural ally. It was a Gould property in the early days—the D&RGW had underwritten WP loans—but in those days the D&RGW could barely put enough trains over its own tracks to make money, let alone feed traffic to someone else. It was expected that the Chicago & North Western, already at Lander, Wyoming, would build on through South Pass and enter Salt Lake City and that the Denver & Salt Lake would do the same. Neither ever did. So, for example, in 1926, in eastern Nevada, where the WP and the SP were parallel, the WP's president, C. M. Levey, was riding his business car behind the Atlantic Coast Mail, the WP's "flyer" on its 94-hour crawl to St. Louis. An SP cattle train began to overtake it on the other track. It happened that an SP division superintendent was riding a business car at the rear of the cattle train. He and Levey were able to exchange a few pleasantries before the cattle train eased on by. Said MacGregor and Benson, "the smell hung around Levey's car like a bad skin rash for the next twenty miles."

In 1926 the WP came under the control of Arthur Curtiss James, by some accounts the last swashbuckling railroad entrepreneur. He had inherited large amounts of stock in the Hill lines (the Great Northern, the Northern Pacific, and the Burlington). He bought into the WP and immediately began a line northward to meet the Great Northern, which was building south from Oregon. The GN and the WP met at the little hamlet of Bieber, California, on November 10, 1931, and there was a big celebration. Aside from a few cutoffs, it was the last new railroad route built in the United States.

The Bieber Extension was difficult construction for the WP. It branched off its main line at Keddie, California, on a Y-shaped trestle high above Spanish Creek; and then for the next six miles, it was cut into a sheer canyon wall. Dubbed the Inside Gateway because of its inland passage into California, it was the first competition for the SP's Shasta Route between San Francisco and Portland. With the Great Northern in the north, the WP in the middle, and the Santa Fe to the south, there was for the first time north-south rail competition for the SP on the entire West Coast. The SP fought this all the way, but the line hung on through the deepening depression.

Despite the depression, James managed to complete a six-year rehabilitation of the WP's main line in 1933. It bought big 2-8-8-2 Mallet locomotives that could handle heavy freights without helpers. It acquired feeder lines in northern California, most notably an electric line, the Sacramento Northern.

With the inauguration of the Exposition Flyer for the San Francisco

World's Fair at Treasure Island in the summers of 1939 and 1940, the WP was ready to compete seriously in the transcontinental passenger haul in connection with the Rio Grande, the Missouri Pacific, and the Burlington. Then came the war, and the WP was in good shape to expedite war trains to Pacific ports. After the war, the California boom began in earnest. Major industries located plants on the WP route, notably Ford at Milpitas, California. Because of the housing boom in southern California, a lot of lumber came down the Inside Gateway. In 1949, along with partners the Rio Grande and the Burlington, the WP inaugurated the California Zephyr, the flashiest of the postwar streamliners, all stainless steel with Vistadomes. Its owners boasted that it was "the most talked-about train in the country." The Korean War, and then the Vietnam War, boosted the WP's freight traffic to Pacific ports.

The WP fed traffic to the Rio Grande at Salt Lake City, which in turn fed it to the Missouri Pacific at Pueblo and to the Burlington and the Rock Island at Denver. That meant that if anything happened to the WP's independence, it would have reverberations for roads all the way to Chicago. The Western Pacific—once one railroad too many, once barely two streaks of rust across Nevada—was now a good railroad that easily covered its fixed charges. This was proof that competition worked and, for the time being, that a small railroad could be successful.

Without warning in September 1960, the Southern Pacific began to buy Western Pacific stock. It moved with lightning speed and had 182,000 shares, or about 10 percent, within five weeks. On October 12, 1960, Donald Russell of the SP called Frederic Whitman of the WP to request the pro forma information required by the ICC to file an application for control. This was the first Whitman knew what had happened.[7] He walked the six blocks down the street to the SP headquarters. Russell, a physically big man, up from the ranks of the SP's mountain lines in Oregon, was a contrast to the Princeton-educated, slender, silver-haired Whitman. Russell, it seemed, had the trumps.[8]

It can only be guessed what anger and frustration reigned at the WP those October days. It did not want to be controlled or consolidated. It was a successful railroad on its own. It was proud of what it had built. Its operating ratio was low, its net income was up, its fixed charges were under control, and its morale was high. Shippers loved it; the California Zephyr brought it national recognition and enormous popularity. It seemed to thrive on competition. Maybe that was what made it such an affront to the SP.

The WP board fought back. In a formal resolution, it said control by the SP was contrary to the best interests of shareholders, employees, and the public and demanded that Donald Russell be subpoenaed for oral interrogation.[9] But just in case, it sought shelter, specifically from its big connection to the south, the Santa Fe. On October 25, the Santa Fe announced that in the previous two weeks, it had also bought WP shares and filed for control. It said it was only reacting to the SP. It did not even seem to take the coordination "studies" that it made very seriously.[10] Most of what the two roads could coordinate, they had already coordinated. The Great Northern backed the Santa Fe, while the Union Pacific backed the Southern Pacific, both with further stock purchases.

The SP and the Santa Fe strong-armed support for their proposals. One group of southern California cities (which eventually backed the Santa Fe) said, "Seldom have our chambers been flattered with the attention and effort that was extended by both roads to acquire support in this proceeding." The SP convinced dozens of shippers, city and town councils, and chambers of commerce not just to write letters but to file pleas of intervention. Each was identically worded, indicating that it came not from the heart but from the SP.

Managers of small plants who actually had to worry about the availability of rail cars or whether delivery of raw materials was going to be on time needed to think twice about opposing the mighty SP, especially when their bosses traveled in the same social circles as SP executives. A California distribution manager for Armstrong Cork wrote a letter to the ICC praising competition. "In areas where the Southern Pacific has competition," he said, "we find our customers receive better service not only from competing lines but from the Southern Pacific as well. . . . Generally speaking, we get better help from railroads like Western Pacific." His bosses were not pleased. Two weeks later, he wrote frantically that the first letter had been written as an individual, not as a representative of his company, even though it had been on company letterhead:

> On further consideration of this entire matter, I do not believe that I have sufficiently strong feelings on the subject, but I would not want my comments to influence the thinking of the Commission. . . . I would appreciate your returning my letter of December 22, and deleting my name as an interested party in these proceedings. It would likewise be appreciated if the California Public Utilities Commission and the Western Pacific Railroad would return their copies of the same letter.[11]

The real economies had already been achieved without control. Where the routes were parallel across eastern Nevada, the SP and the WP coordinated operations and had done so since 1924—not just on the 14 miles in the Humboldt River Canyon where the State of Nevada ordered them to, but on 178 miles between Wells and Winnemucca as well. The result was that two single-track railroads operated as a double-track railroad (the WP eastbound, the SP westbound). To make this work, the mechanical, engineering, and operating departments of the two roads were in daily contact with each other. And it worked well; it was probably the best single example in the country of two arch rivals coordinating their operations when it was to their mutual advantage.

Donald Russell insisted that control would have "no substantial effect on the competition Southern Pacific is today encountering in providing transportation service," meaning that the real competition was from other modes, not other railroads. He insisted that railroads, including his, were down for the count and had no choice but to unite against nonrail carriers. "If such measures are carried out, I foresee a good future for railroads; if they are not, I can foresee only a continued shrinkage in the railroad's total share of transportation."[12] But tonnage on both the SP and the WP was increasing, not decreasing, including tonnage of high-rated manufactured goods. Both could handle more traffic, but neither was suffering from underutilization. Neither was having trouble raising capital. This was not the urgent problem that consolidation was supposed to solve.

In January 1961 the Department of Justice—Eisenhower's Justice—intervened in opposition to both the SP and the Santa Fe. It contended that control by either would reduce competition in violation of the Clayton Act. Justice thought control was an especially cheap way to get rid of competition. A merger would at least force the predator roads to pay a decent price for the WP securities. This was Justice's debut in the railroad merger cases of the 1960s. Its typed briefs looked amateurish against the elaborate, printed entries of the railroads, and even those of the California Public Utilities Commission. But its efforts would grow in sophistication as time went on.

California papers reported the case in detail. The stories always pointed out that the WP was the route of the California Zephyr. That was what interested people. The WP had poured its heart and soul into that train, and it was immensely popular. It was beginning to lose ominous amounts of money, because labor costs were going up and because it did not have the capacity to carry enough people to make money. The SP, in contrast, had sized up the economics of the passenger train earlier than most roads. Its City of San Francisco, competitor to the California Zephyr, was a businessman's train, scheduled for speed, not scenery, stocked with the best Scotch in the house and lots of single-berth roomettes for executives. But it had already lost its clientele to the airlines. The SP began to downgrade all of its trains, eliminating diners, eliminating sleepers, providing little more than basic transportation. So naturally California public opinion thought the WP was the way to run a railroad and the SP was the way to run it into the ground.

Hearings went on through most of 1961. Examiner Paul Albus recommended for the Santa Fe, but a majority of the commission finally decided neither road made much of a case and threw out both applications. Some speculated that the real reason the WP kept its independence in the face of the merger movement was not because it was a strong, healthy independent but because it was lucky to get caught between two equally powerful big boys who neutralized each other. But the panacea of consolidation had received a setback. Not every proposal was going to fly.

Looking into the future, the WP did need to join someone. Its luck was going to run out. It lost an important transcontinental rate-division case that began in 1963 and wandered for six years through the ICC and the courts. The WP would have to share about 15 percent more of the revenue on transcontinental traffic with other railroads, and it had to pay it retroactively from the time the case began. The California Zephyr was going to lose more and more money as costs rose. Its deficit was $1 million a year for the WP alone by the mid-1960s. There was a fierce political outcry to save it. Nobody much cared about the SP trains anymore because they were so terrible, but don't take *this* train off, said newspapers and citizen's groups and politicians. Make the little railroad preserve it, like a museum, forever and ever. The WP was now penalized for having run the train so well. The California Zephyr was finally discontinued on the WP on March 21, 1970, after three tries before the ICC. The story is told in gruesome detail in Bruce MacGregor and Ted Benson's book *Portrait of a Silver Lady*, the best biography there is of a single passenger train. Previously, the winter of 1968–1969 had been brutal in the Sierras. Multiple avalanches had sent all kinds of freight cars loaded with valuable goods hurtling into the Feather River Canyon. On March 28, 1970, the brakes failed on a WP freight train at 60 mph, and it slammed into the rear of an SP train on the shared track. The engineer who was killed was G. H. Hardy, engineer of the last eastbound California Zephyr. Two others died, and there were huge damage claims.

The WP's comfortable net income of around $8 million a year throughout the 1960s was cut in half in 1968 and became a small loss in 1969 and a $6 million loss in 1970. Its fortunes did turn around after Al Perlman came to run it. But, as in the stories of the Lackawanna and the Lehigh Valley, time was running out for bantam-weight railroads that depended on connections for most of their traffic, even nice ones that people liked and wanted to succeed. Nevertheless, the ICC had not made a mistake. Merging the WP with the Rio Grande and the Missouri Pacific, re-creating the old Gould empire, made sense. Joining it to the SP only eliminated competition.

The Concept of the Burlington Northern

In 1956 the Northerns—the Great Northern, the Northern Pacific, the Burlington (BN), and the Spokane, Portland & Seattle—announced that they would try to put together a mighty regional railroad. The Burlington's president, Harry Murphy, may not have had his heart in it—he loved the Burlington—but with the GN and the NP each owning 48 percent of his railroad, he had no choice but to go along. This was the Northerns'

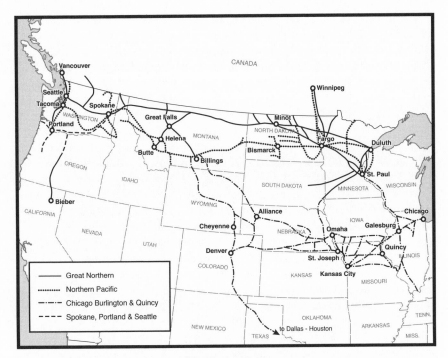

Northern Lines

third try. The first was the Northern Securities affair (see chapter 1). The second occurred in the 1920s, when the ICC said the Great Northern and the Northern Pacific could merge but could not take in the Burlington.

Now in the mid-1950s, the time seemed right again. All four railroads were profitable. It was believed that stockholders would see merger as a way to enhance their equity, not dilute it. They hoped that competition from the Milwaukee Road, and in places from the Canadian Pacific–Soo Line and the Union Pacific, plus motor carriers, protected them from charges of monopoly. All four of the merging roads were popular because of their excellent passenger services. They hoped this would temper opposition from states and communities. They hired Wyer, Dick & Company to make studies, and the studies showed an estimated $46 million in annual savings.

Their internal negotiations broke down over stock exchanges. The problem was the value of the NP's forest and mineral resources that were its land-grant dowry from the American people. A powerful group of NP security holders held out for better terms. These differences were resolved in the summer of 1960: on July 16, 1960, the roads announced their intent to merge into a new company to be called the Great Northern Pacific & Burlington Lines (GNP&BL). In January 1961, stockholders voted approval, although an NP dissident group held out to the last. On February 17, 1961, the application went to the ICC.

But the Burlington Northern would not be a reality until March 3, 1970. Something that took that long obviously stirred a lot of controversy. To say it was just bureaucratic delay is a statement of ignorance. Many people, from both the private and the public sectors, had misgivings about this proposal.

Putting these strong railroads together into a stronger whole was a good idea. It would not be a monopoly even for rail-captive commodities as long as the Milwaukee Road was there to compete. But such a merger would, in time, choke off the Milwaukee Road, whose presence in the Northwest was none too secure. Merging three strong railroads to make them even better railroads would leave the Milwaukee Road and other weak midwestern roads even weaker, perhaps condemning them to nationalization or death. Taken alone, the proposal for GNP&BL promised more efficient transportation and thus was in the public interest. Taking a broader view, it threatened other railroads whose services were vital to many people and provided the competition that alone makes the market system work. It would therefore not be in the public interest.

The Great Northern fairly glowed in the 1950s, consistently earning around five times its fixed charges. It had excellent leadership, first from Frank Gavin, who invested wartime profits in diesels and heavy rails, and then from John Budd, who kept the railroad up to date with centralized traffic control and a big UNIVAC computer. It ran a perfect passenger service that served all its markets with clean, reliable service. It streamlined its famous Chicago-Seattle-Portland flagship, the Empire Builder, in 1947, then reequipped it in 1951. That freed up the 1947 equipment for the second train, christened the Western Star, which ran via Great Falls. The GN ran three trains a day between Seattle and Vancouver, a good overnight train from the Twin Cities to Winnipeg, and the Red River, which carried folks from Grand Forks and Fargo into the Twin Cities in the morning and brought them home at night. But all these beautiful trains were a public service provided at a loss. GN freight traffic remained strong, but it was not growing; it fell off ominously in the recession of 1958 and 1959. As the good ores of the Mesabi Iron Range began to play out, the GN's extensive ore operations were threatened. Labor productivity per man hour was rising, but per dollar of compensation it was falling, from 234 ton or passenger miles per dollar of compensation in 1939 to 143 in 1951.[13] That was why Budd saw merger as a requirement for the long-run viability of the company.

The Northern Pacific of the 1950s was a mirror image of the GN in many ways. It did not have the iron ore operations; it was 109 miles longer from St. Paul to Seattle; it carried about two-thirds the traffic and had two-thirds the revenues. But it earned a consistent three times its fixed charges through the 1950s. Its president was Robert MacFarlane, one of the talented but unheralded railroad leaders of the era, who dieselized and installed CTC. Its flagship, the North Coast Limited, was one of the great but often unpublicized trains of the United States. Only one postwar generation was privileged to enjoy the North Coast Limited's warmth and bright lights as a noisy crowd would toast the new year and sing "Auld Lang Syne" in the Lewis & Clark Lounge. The train would roll through the windswept North Dakota darkness before spending the morning rolling down the majestic Yellowstone Valley. Snowbursts licked at its wheels as it climbed the spidery trestles around Spire Rock and up to Homestake Pass, before it finally approached the twinkling lights of Butte below.

The Burlington was a granger road. Although its revenues ran only a little higher than the next largest granger, the Milwaukee Road, they were far more secure, covering fixed charges nine times over in 1953, four times over in recession 1959. It blanketed the Midwest, with a special concentration in southern Iowa and southern and eastern Nebraska; those lines were all built to haul grain. But it also hauled coal from southern Illinois. It had a line that would be of monumental importance in years to come (because of coal) going from Kansas City across the Nebraska sandhills to Gillette, Wyoming, and Billings, Montana. At Billings it met the main line of the NP and an important branch of the GN. The Burlington controlled the Colorado & Southern Railway (C&S), giving it a second route out of Billings, this one to Denver and on to Texas. The C&S in turn controlled the Fort Worth & Denver Railway, which took Burlington rails on to Fort Worth, Dallas, Houston, and Galveston Bay.[14] All of this gave the Burlington a better traffic balance than most grangers had. Its Zephyr streamliners were a classy fleet of popular passenger trains, Chicago-Denver, Chicago–Twin Cities, Chicago–Kansas City, and Denver-Dallas. Riding a vista-domed Morning or Afternoon Zephyr to the Twin Cities at high speed for 300 miles along the bank of the Mississippi River was one of the world's finest travel experiences.

What set the Burlington apart from other grangers was consistently good leadership, from Ralph Budd (1932–1949) and then Harry Murphy (1949–1965). There were no revolutionaries such as Alfred Perlman on the New York Central or D. W. Brosnan on the Southern, but Burlington's leaders kept their railroad on the cutting edge of innovation and always kept their track in good repair so that expensive equipment and costly crews were earning revenue, not waiting around. Ralph Budd—the president of the GN in the 1920s and father of John Budd, who was the GN's president in the 1950s and 1960s—was one of the industry's statesmen. He was invited to advise the Soviet Union on railroad technology in the 1930s. He introduced the Zephyrs in the 1930s. Upon his retirement, Northwestern University asked him to be a professor of transportation, but he did not think he was qualified. He spent his retirement in pro bono work, heading up the Chicago Transit Authority and untangling both its operational and its political messes. Harry Murphy continued to keep high standards. He even put money into the Chicago commuter service with the purchase of stainless steel double-deck gallery cars (not the push-pulls that Ben Heineman would install on the C&NW), the first new private investment in commuter service since the Lackawanna's electrification in 1932. The Burlington was a respected and beloved railroad.

Spokane, Portland & Seattle, the fourth component of GNP&BL, deserved more attention than it generally got. It was medium-sized and beautifully engineered, a railroad of tunnels and high bridges, among them the Celilo Falls Bridge, more than a mile long over the Columbia, and the Crooked River Bridge in Oregon, 320 feet above the water. It was a high-speed line through some of the most beautiful scenery in America— the Columbia River Gorge into Portland and, over its subsidiary Oregon Trunk, down the Deschutes River Canyon to Bend. Hill, the empire builder himself, accepted the cheers of the crowd when the railroad arrived in Bend on October 5, 1911. It was his last great hurrah. The SP&S carried Portland folks out to the beaches at Astoria, Seaside, and Clatsop. Its subsidiary Oregon Electric ran the interurban down the Willamette Valley to the capital at Salem and the university towns of Covallis and Eugene. It fielded the heaviest of steam power, Baldwin 4-8-4 Northerns and Alco 4-6-6-4 Challengers, the last of them put in service October 20, 1944. Profitable but never independent, it was built by the GN and the NP and controlled by them. But it called itself "the Northwest's Own Railway" and deserves its place among the great and colorful components of the American rail system.

One other railroad figures in the situation. The Milwaukee Road struggled. Its existence gave credibility to the assertion that a GNP&BL would not be a monopoly across the Northwest. But what was the nature of this competition? Wartime prosperity enabled the Milwaukee Road to upgrade its Pacific Extension enough to put its crack Olympian Hiawatha on a hot 45-hour schedule from Chicago to Seattle, competitive with the Great Northern's Empire Builder. But for freight, one train a day could usually handle all the business there was. It was a long train, but on most days the only one. The elaborate electrification, state-of-the-art when it was installed in 1918–1919, was antiquated now. The wires could not carry enough juice to pull a freight train long enough to make money. Everyone understood that the Milwaukee Road hung by a thread.

No one questioned that merger could save the Northerns a lot of money. The Wyer, Dick & Company studies estimated $46 million a year in savings, and even the ICC commissioners who opposed the merger acknowledged that there were at least $29 million of potential savings. Of the original estimates, $15 million would be saved by the consolidation of yards, 91 percent of that figure from just seven points—the Twin Cities; the Twin Ports (Duluth-Superior); Fargo-Casselton, North Dakota; Billings; Spokane; Seattle-Tacoma; and Portland-Vancouver, Washington. At the Twin Cities, for example, the NP's Northtown Yard would be expanded to 63 classification tracks. That would permit the abandonment of the GN's Como and Lyndale Junction yards and Burlington's Dayton's Bluff yard. It would expedite traffic through the cities and free up land, which could be developed for traffic-producing shippers.

Another $10 million savings would result from combined administration. Responsibility in the new company would be divided between a chairman, who would run corporate matters, and a president, who would run the railroad. Accounting, treasury, and law departments would report to the chairman; traffic, operations, and purchasing would report to the president. The railroad would be divided into four semiautonomous districts, an idea later modified into six regions—Chicago, the Twin Cities, Omaha, Billings, Seattle, and Portland.

But the grand concept of the Burlington Northern was the creation of a single transcontinental main line. Between the Twin Cities and Fargo, the double-tracked NP main line was chosen over either of the GN's two single-track routes. At Casselton, outside Fargo, all through traffic would move to the GN and travel via New Rockford to Minot, North Dakota. All traffic to and from the head-of-lakes at Duluth-Superior would move via the GN rather than the NP and join the main line at Minot. The GN's sprawling Gavin Yard in Minot would consolidate cars from these routes. Westward, the trains would take the GN route over Marias Pass. For a short distance between Sandpoint, Idaho, and Spokane, the NP was considered the superior line. At Spokane, all Seattle traffic would move via the GN, and all Portland and California traffic would move via the SP&S.[15]

All traffic moving to and from the Burlington at Billings—both from Kansas City and from Texas and Denver over the C&S— would take the NP via Helena and the Mullan Pass. The NP routes to the Twin Ports (across North Dakota and Montana as far west as Billings, and across Washington over Stampede Pass) could be downgraded, although at the time of the hearings, no one foresaw how important the NP main line east of Billings, across North Dakota, would become as a coal mover. A total of 480 miles of track, mostly small segments, could be abandoned. This would reduce train miles and car miles—a savings of 400 million ton miles a year on Twin Cities–Seattle traffic and 107 million ton miles on traffic moving through Billings. Concentrating traffic would permit the upgrading of key routes with full centralized traffic control and welded rail.[16]

On the surface, this was an impressive case. But at this juncture an opposition, more intense than had been encountered in mergers so far, coalesced to fight. The extent and intensity of the opposition by states trying

to represent the broader public interest of their citizens as they saw it—
Minnesota, North Dakota, South Dakota, Montana, Washington, Oregon,
and the Province of British Columbia—was something that had not been
seen before.

Railroad consolidation might be good in the abstract, but there was
something wrong with this one. Two mighty questions loomed. The first
was, What would this merger do to competition in the Northwest? This
uncertainty was the reason the Northern Securities was broken up. Had
anything changed now? The Milwaukee Road was very much a part of the
question. If the Milwaukee Road was competition for the merged lines,
could it withstand the onslaught of their combined might?

The other question was, What would happen to competition in granger
country? Joining the Burlington to two transcontinentals would do nothing to solve the problem of weak roads in that region. The Milwaukee
Road was a part of this equation, too, and so was the C&NW. Saving
money for the merging railroads was very nice; and if it went for new investment, that was nicer still. But these Northerns were already profitable
companies. Who was going to be hurt by their merger? Who was going to
pay the price for their savings? How could the pluses and minuses be balanced to determine a public interest?

The merging railroads thought that to show a public interest, all they
needed was to get shippers to testify that merger would provide better
transportation for their needs. Shipper after shipper testified that the
merger would be good for them. It would allow better schedules, more reliable car supply, and an array of new transit privileges. But did this show a
public interest? Almost all of these shippers made identical points, usually
in the same order, often with the same key phrases, which coincidentally
were the phrases used in the booklet *Consolidation, Key to Progress,* which
the merging applicants distributed to them.[17] The Minnesota Railroad and
Warehouse Commission thought the exercise hardly proved a "public" interest in merger. "There was not a deviation as witness after witness pa-
raded to the stand, monotonously told his story on direct, stood cross ex-
amination showing the utter lack of facts he had available to him when he
made his conclusion, and then departed from his moment of glory."[18]

Opponents pointed out that on the matter of car supply, nowhere had
the merging roads committed themselves to buying more cars; they had
merely implied to NP shippers that they would have access to GN cars and
vice versa. The merging roads said merger was the only way to improve
service, specifically to speed up schedules. But when the Milwaukee Road
cut its freight schedules by 18 hours in 1963 with the inauguration of its
Thunderhawk and XL Special services, the unmerged Northerns followed
suit immediately, though admittedly with shorter trains that required
more trains to do the work.

Some of the ICC commissioners wondered why, if savings from the merging of yards was as spectacular as the merging roads said, and if their need for savings was as great as they said, they did not undertake coordination short of merger? The Erie and the Lackawanna had made it work. Why could the Northerns not do the same? Was this an indication that they had overstated the savings or their need for savings?

A total of 8,072 jobs were calculated to be lost in this merger, and 2,900 others would have to move to a different location. Perhaps as many as 80 percent of those displaced might be rehired within one year as a result of natural attrition. Nonetheless, of the $46 million in savings, almost $32 million would come from fewer paychecks.[19] Employees of the former NP would be affected the most because of all the downgrading intended for their railroad. The NP shop towns of Auburn, Washington, and Livingston, Montana, would be hit hard, and both were in areas of strong union activity that went back to the IWW years early in the century. Livingston was particularly sensitive, located between Red Lodge, where the IWW organized in the coal mines of Carbon County, and Butte, where it organized the hard-rock miners. Feelings were so intense in 1917 that IWW organizer Frank Little was dragged from the Finn Hotel in Butte by an anti-union gang, was towed behind a truck until his knee caps tore off, and was then castrated and hanged on the trestle where the Milwaukee Road crossed the NP. Thousands lined the route to the cemetery, and songs and poems were written to the martyred hero. In other words, Montana unionism had an edge to it. By 1961 these memories were old but not forgotten, and the NP unions were bitterly against merger.

But the primary issue in the Northern merger case was always competition. In the years since the *Northern Securities* decision, the Milwaukee Road had arrived, and so had the motor truck, but the issue never went away. The Northwest was a region where the haul to market was a long one, one of the longest rail hauls in the world, and this made traffic unusually captive to the rails. The merging roads insisted that competition between railroads no longer mattered; they served up an exhibit showing the amount of traffic they claimed they had irretrievably lost to the motor carriers.[20] The ICC dismissed this as specious because it failed to differentiate between traffic lost forever and traffic lost because of cyclical downswings; the ICC introduced a table of its own showing much more mixed results. Many of the merging roads' own witnesses, shippers of heavy extractive and agricultural commodities, said that 80 percent, even 100 percent, of their shipments went by rail and were captive to rail because of cost. Some of them, including G.E., Rayonier, A. O. Smith, and Zenith, said specifically that competition was what kept rates down and kept railroads eager to supply the kinds of cars they needed and supply them on time. John Budd of the Great Northern said, "We compete with the Northern Pacific as vigorously as we know how." Robert MacFarlane of the Northern Pacific said, "Great Northern is Northern Pacific's greatest competitor."[21] So they were well aware that competition between railroads did matter.

If the Great Northern and the Northern Pacific ceased to be competitors, the Milwaukee Road would be left as the only rail competition across vast areas of the Northwest. Could the Milwaukee compete? Was it strong enough to stand against the combined might of the Northerns? This merger, some thought, would leave the Milwaukee isolated, unable to afford capital investment, which would inevitably lead to its elimination as a competitor.

The market system works miracles, but it depends on the ability of buyers and sellers to bargain freely. If one side is a monopoly, the price does not reflect a true bargain. The system does not work. Adam Smith knew that. He was the one who first explained the beauty of the market philosophy back in 1776, but he warned sternly against monopoly. The merging roads said all they wanted to do was to provide the very best service at the lowest possible price to their shippers. But that is not normal behavior when there is no competition to force it.

The Department of Justice entered the case in opposition to the merger and cited 11 cases where the weaker Milwaukee Road had instituted service improvements first, and the Northerns had followed. The Milwaukee initiated faster schedules and piggyback and cut rates on Montana grain. The leaner and hungrier competitor was the one most likely to offer shippers the service they needed, said the Justice Department. Making the Northerns more solidly entrenched was not a likely way to increase their efficiency or capital investment. Justice pointed out that this proposal came just when railroads were beginning to break away from their worst shortcomings—noncompetitiveness and inflexible rate making—and just when the public was beginning to enjoy the fruits of competition.[22]

What should President William Quinn of the Milwaukee Road have done? He could have opposed the merger. The prevailing wisdom on the ICC was that mergers were a good thing, so the chances of this strategy working were not great. If somehow he did manage to persuade the commission not to allow the merger, his Pacific Extension would still be as marginal as ever and would probably die 10 or 20 miserable years down the road. Preserving the status quo was not a likely way to preserve the Milwaukee Road.

He could have demanded inclusion for his railroad in the merger. That could have paved the way for a lot of route consolidation and elimination of trackage down in Burlington country on the Omaha and Kansas City routes. This was the region that needed this kind of route rationalization the most, but it was not going to get it from this merger. It would have made operating sense and would have done what many thought mergers were supposed to do—eliminate marginal routes and shore up weaker roads. But there was no way that could happen. The Milwaukee was barely covering its fixed costs. It would stop covering fixed costs altogether in

1967. The security holders of the stronger roads would never approve taking Milwaukee unless its debt were canceled, which Milwaukee's investors would never consent to. Besides, that course of action would eliminate Quinn's job and the jobs of all his colleagues.

Quinn took a third option. He supported the merger if the GNP&BL would open 11 new gateways to the Milwaukee Road west of the Twin Cities. This would mean it could get the long haul on the traffic it generated, which at present had to be turned over to the Northerns at St. Paul. It demanded trackage rights on routes of the merging roads to give it access to Portland, Oregon, and to Sumas, Washington, on the Canadian border, where a connection was made with Canadian roads. It demanded access to Billings and that Billings become an agency station on the Milwaukee.[23]

Quinn knew this was a risk. If the conditions produced a whole 100-car train for the Milwaukee each day (or better yet, multiple trains), that would be great—if the aging electric wires could carry enough juice, or if the old jointed rail could withstand the added pounding. What if the conditions only produced 50 cars a day? That would require a second train over the line, but it would be too short to make money. It would add to costs but not to profits. Quinn said later that he truly believed getting these gateways and trackage rights was the only chance the Milwaukee had to keep its Pacific Extension alive, but he knew it was a gamble.

Then he left the Milwaukee to join the enemy as president of the Burlington. Which side was he on? His successor on the Milwaukee, Curtiss Crippen, had serious doubt that the 11 gateways and the trackage rights would produce enough traffic to be profitable. The Northerns claimed that Milwaukee's conditions would cost them $20 million a year in revenue, but Crippen could count at most $8 million in additional revenue to the Milwaukee, and since the gains would add to cost, he thought they would be "a wash." Lawyer Leon Keyserling, speaking for labor, said the Milwaukee could not compete against the combined Northerns even with its conditions, that it would be like a merger between General Motors and Ford and claiming there would still be competition from a few Packard dealers that were left around.[24]

The Northerns would not concede a point to the Milwaukee. They would fight its demands; they would keep it isolated. It was not their problem that the Milwaukee gambled and lost on a Pacific Extension that should never have been built in the first place. If loser railroads wanted to work out their own mergers, that was fine, but the purpose of merger was to preserve an industry, not an individual company. Yes, the Northerns were profitable railroads now, but their pie was not growing. How long would they be able to make capital investment to stay competitive with interstate highways if they did not take advantage of natural economies? Over the next ten years, two revolutions would overtake the Northern Lines, one in the technology of hauling grain (the rise of "Big Johns"; see chapter 11) and the other in the marketability of low-sulphur western coal. Both would require massive capital investment.

For the time being, the fear of monopoly outweighed the perceived need for capital investment. Protection from monopoly required either stopping the merger or ensuring the preservation of the Milwaukee Road. The Department of Justice, the Railway Labor Executives' Association, and six states all came to the Milwaukee's aid. The Minnesota Railroad and Warehouse Commission put on the most vigorous case of all.

There is a powerful story in the comparison of the case the merging railroads were able to mount and the case of the opponents—a story about how the regulatory process worked. The Northerns budgeted $5 million to get their merger through. There was plenty of money to bring in witnesses, prepare exhibits, and most of all to employ high-powered outside counsel. The railroads' own law departments took part, of course, but they had other routine matters to look after. So, when the hearings moved to Washington, for example, a Washington law firm that knew the ropes of government was hired. They dressed in Brooks Brothers suits and looked and acted sublimely corporate. In contrast, the Justice Department and the state bodies could not be single-minded; they had other cases, and they had tight budgets. Paul Rassmussen of the Minnesota Railroad & Warehouse Commission described how it looked from the perspective of someone representing a mere sovereign state, as opposed to a vast corporate interest:

> In the state of Minnesota, there is a revolving fund controlled by the legislative advisory committee, made up of the governor, two members of the senate and two members of the house. We found it necessary to go before the committee and request that $5000 be allocated to our commission in order that we could participate in the Northern Lines' proceeding. At the end of the 3-month period, the money was spent, and we had to ask for an additional $5000 to carry on for the next three months, and as of this June 26, I will have to appear before this same body and request another $3000 or $4000 in order to continue.
>
> At the present time, there are about 12,000 pages of testimony at 60 cents a page. That transcript would cost the state at present about $7200. Before it is over, there will probably be 20,000 pages, about $12,000. You try and go before a state appropriation committee to get $12,000 for a possible need in connection with purchasing a transcript.[25]

Eventually, the Milwaukee Road let Minnesota share its transcript.

As the hearings came to an end, a most serious question was raised about the fairness and impartiality of the ICC examiner. The examiner's job was to run a hearing openly and fairly, gather relevant information, prepare a report for the full commission, and make a recommendation either for or against. The function resembled that of a judge, and the hearings in many ways resembled courtroom proceedings, although there were differences. Although in a routine rate case, examiners might be little more than chairpersons, in big merger cases, they had to make many on-the-spot decisions on rules of order, admissibility, and so forth. Examiners were hired from a civil service list, and after a training period were assigned in rotation, though exceptions were made when a particularly sensitive or complex case was coming up. From the very beginning, from the volume of letters that came pouring in to the ICC, much of it relayed through members of Congress or the White House, it was clear that this was going to be a sensitive case.

The examiner who came up in rotation for this case was Robert Murphy, who had recently retired from the army; he had presided over a number of trucker rate cases but had no experience at all in railroad cases. He was not a patient man. He did not tolerate repetition, incompetence, or unfamiliarity with the rules. And it appeared that he had made up his mind on the case before he heard the evidence. Paul Rassmussen of the Minnesota Railroad & Warehouse Commission said that

> applicants' counsel were treated with normal courtesy, but opposition counsel were always put on the defensive . . . reminded that repetition would not be countenanced. He allowed petitions in support of the merger at all stages of the hearing, but when it came to petitions in opposition, a different rule was followed, and the attorney in opposition was put through the ordeal of explaining the nature of the petition, the nature of the organization supporting it, and so on.[26]

Rassmussen did not think the merging railroads intended for Murphy to be this way. He said:

> I personally observed that the legal staff of the applicants were extremely disturbed by the tendency on the part of the examiner to show prejudice in their behalf. There was every indication that they counseled with him and urged that he reverse his rulings, because they were apprehensive that if he did not do so, bias and prejudice would be so conspicuous that on appeal to the courts, the [opponents] might prevail to such an extent the entire proceeding would be discarded.[27]

In Murphy's defense the case was long and repetitive. Shippers, chambers of commerce, cities, counties, trade union locals, all had the right to say the same things over and over. Hearings were held all over the West, far from the comforts of everyone's home base, and living out of suitcases day after day got on everyone's nerves. Some shippers at the Seattle hearings, which seemed to emerge as the most contentious of all, detected no unfairness. The examiner, they thought "was firm and decisive, and at times, abrupt and curt. He reversed himself after reconsideration when he felt a previous spontaneous ruling was wrong, but he did give every party a full right to present its case."[28] Even the Milwaukee Road, with a tremendous stake, thought it had a fair hearing.

But two Department of Justice field staffers talked with the examiner on November 5, 1964, after he issued his report, and this is what he told them:

> When a person went to a doctor to have an ailment analyzed, that person didn't question the doctor's judgment but accepted his advice . . . and if I went to a dentist to have my teeth fixed, I would place the care of my teeth in his hands and not question his judgment. . . . Finally, we must have the same confidence in the applicants' witnesses.
>
> These railroads should merge because the railroads in the Northwest are in the shadows of the New England roads, and if they don't merge, the same thing is going to happen to them that happened to the New England roads.
>
> How could witnesses scheduled to testify at Spokane possibly be harmed when the applicant railroads have offered assurance that no one will be adversely affected?
>
> You don't think I'm going to sit on this hard bench for six months and listen to witnesses who don't know what it's all about?[29]

Later, said Justice, Murphy added that he "could not understand why people would oppose a rail merger." Justice thought this amounted to a "shocking, extreme and undisciplined personal bias in favor of the merger." "The examiner pictures himself and the ICC as the sick patient in need of ministrations from the railroads. But the ICC is supposed to probe; the public looks to it to do that. Bitter experiences with the abuses of industry experts who, through the years, sought rail consolidation in their own interests, was what gave rise to regulation in the first place."[30]

The hearings on the Northern lines' merger case lasted from October 1961 to July 1962. It took two years for briefs to be filed and for the examiner to prepare his report. It was served August 24, 1964, and recommended for the merger. By this time, the matter had the attention of Congress. Everyone awaited the commission's decision.

nine

Kennedy, the Kefauver Hearings, and the ICC

In 1960 consolidation was hailed as the solution to nearly all railroad problems. Only labor had said otherwise, and labor was easily dismissed as an interest group that wanted to preserve jobs that technology had made useless. By April 1962, consolidation, the panacea that was supposed to save an industry, had raised a lot of doubts in a lot of people.

What the public (primarily shippers) thought it was going to get was not what it was getting. It expected that existing channels of trade would be preserved, but without duplicate routes, and that the weaker railroads would be shored up so that everyone would be assured of continued service. What it was getting was combinations to strengthen the stronger carriers, reduce competition, eliminate jobs, and exclude the weaker carriers, paving the way either for their abandonment or for nationalization. It occurred to some that these mergers might be just a prelude to nationalization.

A Burlington Northern proposal was on the table that threatened to create a monopoly across the Northwest. A Norfolk & Western proposal was on the table that would do little to consolidate lines, do nothing to shore up weaker carriers, and do a lot to reorient traffic away from the Port of New York and toward the Port of Norfolk. A C&O-B&O proposal was on the table that would do nothing at all to eliminate duplication and would throw even those smaller lines that were in the B&O's sphere, the Reading and the Jersey Central, to the wolves. A Penn-Central proposal was in the works that looked like a monstrosity. Most of the New York congressional delegation came out against it.[1] Meanwhile, the Milwaukee Road, the Rock Island, and the North Western were dying. The New Haven was in rigor mortis, although its packed passenger trains still raced at close intervals and at high speed over visibly deteriorating track, their journal boxes occasionally catching fire, sometimes in the Park Avenue tunnels into Grand Central Station. Consolidation was not doing anything about this.

The public and public officials looked to the ICC to do something. It approved the Pennsylvania's control of the Lehigh Valley on April 4, 1962, as though that case stood in isolation from the others, as though all that needed to be addressed was how to preserve the Lehigh Valley Railroad. Did it not see that even if this was a minor case, it had implications for all the others in the East, that delivering this critical but troubled little railroad to the PRR might make any kind of competitive balance for the PRR impossible?

Commissioner William Tucker explained to an audience at Boston University on November 16, 1961, that the commission did not decide these cases on a matter of ideals nor, as some thought, on a whim. It decided them as a matter of law. The law in this case was the Transportation Act of 1940, or more properly, section 5 of the Interstate Commerce Act as revised in 1940. Under this law, the commission was directed to approve consolidation that was *consistent* with the public interest. That was quite different, he said, from the previous law, the Transportation Act of 1920, which directed approval only for those proposals that *promoted* the public interest. Despite what appeared to be the neutral language of the 1940 act, its legislative history indicated that Congress intended it to encourage consolidation. All the railroads had to show to get a merger through was that, on balance, a proposal was not harmful. The law was passed in the wake of a depression when there seemed to be excess plant in all industries, when contraction seemed like a good idea. Furthermore, the 1940 act virtually eliminated any government or public input into the planning of consolidation. Tucker himself was having misgivings about the wisdom of some of the proposals the commission had before it. But if times and needs had changed since 1940, Congress—and Congress alone—could change the law and give the ICC new direction.[2]

President Kennedy recognized the inadequacy of the existing law. His message to Congress on April 5, 1962, the day after the Lehigh decision, called for sweeping new transportation legislation. He wanted transportation to remain privately owned and unsubsidized, "operating under the incentives of private profit and the checks of competition."[3] Five days later, Kennedy denounced U.S. Steel and specifically its chairman, Roger Blough, for raising steel prices after he thought he had a promise from them not to, after he had strong-armed the United Steelworkers into not hiking wages. He felt betrayed and was angry. "My father always said businessmen were sons-of-bitches," he said, "and now I know what he meant."[4] After that, business perceived him as antibusiness. But at the time of his railroad message, he was clearly on the side of *competitive* private enterprise.

His suggestions were favorable to railroads. At least they included a number of things the Association of American Railroads was lobbying for. One was an end to minimum rate regulation, which would allow the railroads to get the benefit of their cost advantage over trucks. Another was a free hand to institute intermodal routes and rates. That was piggyback and container traffic that both truckers and some railroads wanted to keep severely regulated. (Small railroads, the Long Island, for example, feared that large railroads would deliver piggybacked goods by truck and bypass them.) Another was an end to subsidies for trunk airlines. They were not a pioneer industry anymore; it was time for them to fly on their own. Another was user charges for government-maintained facilities, such as air traffic control and inland waterways that the government had dredged for free. User charges meant that those who used them had to pay a fee, as motorists paid a toll on a toll road. As for railroad mergers, Kennedy said that the administration had a responsibility to recommend more specific guidelines than were available and more specific procedures for applying them.

The president assigned an interagency task force with representatives from the Commerce, Justice and Labor Departments and the Council of Economic Advisors. They were to examine each merger to make sure competition, efficient services, and labor welfare were maintained. He chose Clarence D. Martin, undersecretary of commerce for transportation, to head it. The task force held its first exploratory meeting in late May 1962. Eventually, it submitted a report that echoed the president's ideas and otherwise retraced conventional ground. It was never heard of again.[5]

Kennedy was not associated with trains for campaigning or presidential travel the way all of his predecessors since Lincoln had been. He rode a train only once as president, home from an Army-Navy football game in Philadelphia in 1961. "Yet of all the presidents, Kennedy alone explored the railroad dilemma in a message to Congress which point by point recommended legislative ways to reconcile it," wrote David P. Morgan in *Trains*. It was a paradox, he thought, that the young liberal president, often at odds with businessmen, should speak for the rails. "For the life of me, I don't know why the Kennedy people supported us," said a rail executive to Morgan. "We're not politically attractive like a tax cut. Helping the rails upsets all the vested interests in other transport. Ours is a complex problem to understand, yet they argued for us on the Hill. They cared." All trains in the United States stopped for two minutes on November 25, 1963, at the hour of John F. Kennedy's funeral.[6]

The Kefauver Hearings

Congress showed no great eagerness to act on any of Kennedy's suggestions. Sen. Estes Kefauver of Tennessee—a former presidential hopeful and a Democrat from a state that had benefited mightily from the New Deal—

introduced a bill to put a moratorium on mergers until December 31, 1963. It was offered as an amendment to the Clayton Act, which meant that hearings would be conducted by his own antitrust subcommittee. Mergers that did not reduce competition and would therefore not come under the Clayton Act would not be affected. Mergers of roads with less than $200 million in gross assets or in bankruptcy would be exempted.

The purpose was to give the president's task force time to make its study and Congress time to contemplate. Since most of the major cases before the ICC still needed briefs, examiners' reports, and exceptions (rebuttals), and since each commissioner had to digest all the testimony, running 20,000 pages per case or more, plus the briefs and the exhibits, it was not likely that this bill would delay mergers very much. Having no practical effect, then, its purpose was to test the political winds.

Opponents to Kefauver's motion affirmed their faith in the ICC's ability to do its job. They believed that things had been studied to death already and thought if more study was needed, it should be done by the Commerce Committee, not the Judiciary. These opponents tended to be people who deplored the *idea* of a regulatory ICC, but since it seemed poised to ratify everything the most powerful railroads wanted, they backed it. The vote to hold hearings was along party lines, Democrats for it, Republicans against.

A wide cross-section of experts were summoned, including railroad executives, labor leaders, state utility commissions, the ICC and its staff, and scholarly experts, some of them employed by particular interest groups and representing the gamut of opinion.[7] Most of those who testified did not embarrass themselves. Some thought it was inappropriate for Paul Rassmussen of the Minnesota Railroad & Warehouse Commission to bring up the grisly details of the examiner's deportment in the Northern lines' merger case, especially since he did it with such intensity. He and Sen. Roman Hruska (R-Nebr.) had an unpleasant exchange over that, which eventually boiled down to whether it was best to let railroads do whatever they pleased. Kefauver came to verbal blows with James Symes of the Pennsylvania Railroad. Symes said a Penn-Central merger would not diminish competition. Kefauver grilled him as to why, if he was so sure of this, he was so opposed to this legislation. It exempted mergers that did not diminish competition. These were the only dramatic moments. But there was substance.

The promerger forces were led by James Symes and Prof. Merrill Roberts of the University of Pittsburgh, testifying for the Association of American Railroads. They argued that the railroads' financial situation was serious because railroads were not sharing in the expansion of the national economy. The situation varied from carrier to carrier, but overall, their return on investment was low, the lowest of any major industry except commercial air transport.[8] As a result, the railroads were unable to attract capital. The new interstate highways were going to be more technologically advanced rights-of-way, which would compensate powerfully for the inherently higher cost of motor transport. Railroads needed capital to stay abreast. Merger would increase profits, which would increase capital reserves; and for the first time in a long time, railroads might become a genuinely attractive investment. There was nothing evil about profit. The purpose of merger was not to reduce rates. That would be a paltry, short-term gain for the public compared to a revitalization of the capital structure.

Furthermore, if railroads were to continue as private enterprises, they could not underwrite social goals: (1) they were not welfare agencies for unnecessary employment, and (2) they were not transit authorities to run passenger services to maintain the vitality of urban centers. This meant commuters. Ultimately, railroads could serve long-run goals best if they were slimmer and better able to attract capital. Roberts pointed to the Kilday Report prepared for the House of Representatives in 1959 on the transport needs for mobilization in the event of war. It said that railroads were not ready for a national emergency; they would be better prepared if they got rid of branch and duplicate lines and invested capital in state-of-the-art main lines, as the Soviet Union had done.[9] Any change as big as the mergers was bound to hurt some, and the benefits would not be realized overnight. Pluses outweighed the minuses, they thought, but it would be unrealistic to think there were no minuses at all.

Symes limited his remarks to the Northeast. He understood that controversy swirled about the Northern lines' merger, and he had enough controversy of his own. He pointed out that the eastern railroads had not even earned enough to pay income taxes because of the deteriorating traffic volume, and the blame went to Congress for creating a monumental oversupply of transport facilities, topped off with the St. Lawrence Seaway and the Interstate Highway System. It had not necessarily made the carriers using those facilities profitable, but it had gutted the eastern railroads. Many of those roads' lines were built to serve light manufacturing of the nineteenth and early twentieth centuries, often sending branches up both sides of a given valley. It was not retrenchment to trade in the nineteenth-century investment for new, necessary, twentieth-century investment. He thought soundly conceived mergers were the best means. "I think," Symes said,

> there is only one danger of monopoly in railroad transportation and it is this. Many railroads cannot long survive present conditions as private enterprise. Today in the East, we are actually looking down the road to nationalization. To my mind, that is the most dangerous monopoly of them all, a subsidized national railroad system. One railroad, the New Haven, has already gone into bankruptcy and others are close behind. A series of bankruptcies in the railroad industry could very well cause the nationalization of all roads. Unless railroads in deep trouble such as the major ones in the East are permitted to use the self-help which the Senate subcommittee urged on us four years ago, the public is likely to see the very ultimate in monopoly in transportation, namely, government ownership and operation.[10]

However, Symes raised as many questions as he tried to answer. He did not mention that railroads had survived bankruptcies before—waves of them—without nationalization. Was merger necessary to abandon branchlines? Was it even a way to abandon branchlines? It had not been so for the Erie Lackawanna. Why were the railroads that Symes himself cited as the weakest not being invited to mergers, such as the New Haven? Even George Harrison of the Brotherhood of Railway and Airline Clerks, a man not given to favorable talk about mergers, thought some consolidation might be necessary in New England. And what about Symes's favorite phrase, "soundly conceived mergers"? What was a soundly conceived merger? He offered no definition but seemed to assume that if he planned it, it was soundly conceived. Some people thought the eastern mergers were the result of an accidental chain reaction; others saw them as merely an effort to reduce competition and fix prices. Unfortunately, neither the senators nor their staff were familiar enough with the story to ask the right questions.

These questions weighed heavily on Prof. William Leonard of Hofstra, whose *Railroad Consolidation under the Transportation Act of 1920* was still the standard history of the subject. He believed in consolidation, the Albert Cummins–Joseph Eastman style of planned consolidation. He thought it was dangerous that capital should be the only planner, with no real input from shippers, labor, or the public. He thought some of the proposals before the commission were bad ones and that the commission was not getting good information. It relied mostly on opposing railroads that had high-priced legal firms and came only to get concessions, then faded away without a trace. State public service commissions were no match, as the experience of Paul Rassmussen and the Minnesota Railroad & Warehouse Commission in the *Northern Lines* case had indicated.

Nor could the Justice Department be very effective. Lee Loevinger from Justice testified that for five railroad mergers and the American-Eastern Airlines merger case, the department had available a total of six lawyers.

> Senator Kefauver:Frankly, half a dozen lawyers for all those mergers sounds like you're spreading it mighty thin.
> Mr. Loevinger:They are spread mighty thin, Senator.[11]

Into this void, said Prof. Leonard, swept the determined vested interests:

> The present rash of rail mergers has reached what might be termed the peril point, where there will be real damage to competition and the adequacy of rail service to the public unless the federal government acts in a broad and statesmanlike fashion. . . . I urge Congress to assume leadership in this matter . . . and not wait until we have giant rail systems crushing smaller and weaker lines in their territory or until one large combination dominates the country.[12]

The ICC, which was now under attack, sent three of its members—Chairman Rupert Murphy and Commissioners Kenneth Tuggle and William Tucker. Tuggle spoke favorably of mergers in the past, and Tucker sounded that early alarm over the need for new legislation, but it was not known at the time that these two represented opposite poles of merger thinking. Commissioners, like everyone else, had disagreements. But they did agree that the ICC was equipped to do the job properly and that input should come from sources other than just railroads. For example, when all the opposing roads withdrew from the *N&W–Nickel Plate* case, the ICC ordered its Bureau of Inquiry and Compliance into the case to develop the record. The bureau had already begun a study on its own and would be assuming a larger role in future cases. Furthermore, the commission's procedures were neither sacred nor cast in concrete. They could and would be modified to meet varying situations. It was inappropriate for any of them to comment on particular mergers they would have to decide, but they assured the subcommittee that they knew what was going on, had good staff input, knew which cases were related to which, had legal precedents for determining public interest, and could tell who was exaggerating and who was bluffing. In short, they had things under control.

Nonetheless, the Lehigh Valley decision—not the decision as much as the timing of it, the day before the president was to speak on the subject—called the commissioners' confidence into some question. And the Bureau of Inquiry and Compliance never did play a very active role. Its initial study, "Railroad Consolidation and the Public Interest—A Preliminary Study," reprinted in *Rail Merger Legislation,* the hearings of the Kefauver hearings, was supposed to be the first of several installments, but it was all there ever was. Its participation in the merger proceedings was sporadic and amateurish compared to the presentations of others. Even after it was reorganized as the Bureau of Enforcement, its role was minimal.

Labor led off for the antimerger forces. Railroads were financially strong, it said. Most were paying dividends. They had reduced their outstanding funded debt, even in the recent years that they claimed were so bad. Their earnings and net incomes were as high as they had been in the late 1940s and far higher than in the 1930s, when things were much bleaker than they had ever been since. Merger was not necessary then and it was not now, they said. Railroads and banks represented a web of interlocking interests. As in the days of Northern Securities, it was the banks who stood to make the real profits from these mergers by selling and manipulating the securities to finance them.[13] There was no evidence that any of the alleged savings had ever been brought down to net in mergers of earlier years. The public would pay in the form of reduced service and reduced employment (which reduced consumer spending). Finally, the public should not have to pay for the fact that many railroads were incompetently managed. If they were well managed, how could General

Motors report a half-billion-dollar profit on sales of $2.5 billion in diesel locomotives? Somebody, it would seem, struck a mighty poor bargain.

For the first time since the Clayton Act era, the antimerger side had strong intellectual expression. Prof. John Meyer of Harvard asserted that mergers treated a symptom, not a cause. Traffic volume was the real problem, and merger could do nothing about that. He had helped to set the field of economic history ablaze with his and Alfred Conrad's econometric study "The Economics of Slavery in the Antebellum South." He had done some economic studies of railroads as well and had found that in the absence of competition, costs always tended to rise to the level permitted by earnings. Competitive innovation nearly always came from the smaller, less entrenched railroads. Furthermore, with increasing size, railroads experienced clear and measurable difficulties in managing their unwieldy organizations. It was not an accident that well-managed compact companies were turning in some of the best records in the industry—the Rio Grande, the Frisco, the Nickel Plate, for example. "A great deal of wishful thinking would appear to exist in both transportation and banking circles on the beneficial effects that might be achieved from merger."[14]

There was no point in blaming railroad management, Meyer thought. They had to meet weekly payrolls and were therefore prone to grasping at straws. They could not be expected to think in the long term. But among the private reasons for merger, not often talked about, was the desire of well-managed roads to cash in on their managerial skills by taking over less-well-managed ones. He considered railroading remarkable for the mediocrity of its management, rather typical of heavily regulated industries where there was little room for innovation. Innovators became frustrated and tended to move on. A wider dispersion of good management was the greatest benefit that could come from the mergers.

He was worried, though. The experience of other countries was that the creation of huge regional systems that turned out to be inherently inefficient was an evolutionary step toward nationalization. Prof. James Nelson of Washington State agreed. If the giants began to falter, nothing could save them. Certainly, the mechanics and (therefore) the attractiveness of national operation would be greatly simplified by the mergers.

The sternest warning about these mergers was the testimony of Prof. Kent Healy, Thomas DeWitt Cuyler Professor of Transportation at Yale, based on his paper "The Effects of Scale in the Railroad Industry." It had been published in pamphlet form the year before by Yale and had received limited circulation.[15] It used sophisticated techniques of partial correlation analysis. Some who tried to read it could not understand it. But its conclusions challenged all the thinking about consolidation of the previous 50 years, and they were buttressed with statistical evidence more powerful than the guesses and hopes on which the conventional thinking rested.

Healy first eliminated from a list of Class I railroads certain special cases, namely short-haul roads (the Reading, the Maine Central, the C&EI); roads on which passenger traffic constituted more than 55 percent of train miles (the New Haven, the Boston & Maine, the Jersey Central, the Lackawanna, the Long Island, and the Florida East Coast); industrially owned roads (the U.S. Steel–owned Bessemer & Lake Erie and the Duluth, Missabe & Iron Range); and predominantly coal roads (the Norfolk & Western, the Chesapeake & Ohio, the Western Maryland, and the Virginian). Then he ranked the 37 remaining roads by size according to their number of employees. These were plotted on spreadsheets measuring such variables as administrative expense, transportation expense, labor cost, and capital requirements per unit of output. Standard deviations were calculated to measure how much above or below the norm a road stood. There were differences between regions (the adverse effects sometimes not setting in for western roads until a larger scale was attained). If the Pennsylvania and the New York Central were removed, the trend was still the same.

Healy's study showed that for railroads with more than 10,000 employees, there were no further economies of scale to be obtained from increasing size, and for roads with over 19,000 employees, positive diseconomies of scale set in. The larger roads required higher wages and higher transportation expenses and earned lower rates of return per unit of output than medium-sized roads. Only in administrative expense did unit costs seem to decrease with larger size. There was no relationship between traffic density and capital requirements, and at densities over $50,000 per revenue per mile, wages and transportation expenses increased per unit of output. Since the number of employees seemed to be crucial, the evidence suggested that the reason for this was the inability of management to oversee the larger organization. In short, economies of density or economies of scale would not materialize in the larger mergers. The companies would be worse off than they had been before.[16]

Nobody who advocated consolidation liked the implications of Healy's work. Healy commanded enormous respect. An engineering graduate of MIT, he was responsible for solving both the technical and the economic problems of main-line electrification for the New Haven and the Pennsylvania Railroads in the 1920s and 1930s. His merger study was so mathematically complex that no one was equipped to challenge it. The best Hruska could do was to chide him for taking so long to complete his work (two years). "We are going to do our study in two weeks," he said. "We are much more expeditious than you."[17]

Healy was correct for his time. Small mergers produced some good; gargantuan ones brought trouble; and in the Penn-Central's case, the result was a debacle. Looking further ahead, computers and communications technology would make it possible in the 1980s and 1990s to manage what was unmanageable in the 1960s. Healy's hypothesis spoke for its time but not necessarily for the ages.

The last day of the hearing was marked by an exuberant note of optimism, struck by Leon Keyserling, an economist and formerly the chairman of Truman's Council of Economic Advisors. He was now a paid consultant for the Railway Labor Executives' Association, which had just published in pamphlet form the study on which his testimony was based—*The Move toward Railroad Mergers, a Great National Problem.* At first glance, it looked sophomoric—a conglomeration of funky graphs of economic statistics illuminated with little drawings of people in overalls, happy farmers with pitchforks, cornucopias, and so forth. But what he had to say was straightforward, easy to understand, and backed up by the numbers; it underscored how the railroads' own pessimism had captured everyone's minds.

The economy was going to grow, and railroads were going to grow with it. After ten years of pre-Keynesian economic policy, he said, the economy had failed to grow as it could have if a policy of Keynesian high employment and fiscal policy had prevailed. But the economy was poised to take off under the policies of Kennedy's top economic advisor, Walter Heller, and of Kennedy himself. Railroads had a bad break after World War II, when they had to adjust to the presence of new forms of transportation that could do some jobs better. Nevertheless, their ton miles, the measure of work actually performed, were not significantly lower than at any other time in their history, and some roads were at their highest level ever. Many of those ton miles might be in low-value commodities, so were not always translated into net income. But the period of difficulty was largely behind.

In the next ten years, the need would not be for contraction but for expansion. Railroads handled 563 billion ton miles in 1961. By 1970, Keyserling predicted, they would handle 820 billion. (He missed by a few years. In 1970 they actually handled 764 billion but by 1973 were at 851 billion.) All this talk of duplicate facilities was based on an unwarranted pessimism; it would be a disaster if railroad capacity were carelessly junked. Since the history of cartels was always one of investment contraction, he was convinced that the best way to ensure the necessary expansion in the future was the preservation of vigorous competition. The fastest route to nationalization was cartelization. He thought the mergers that were on the table were nothing more than proposals for cartels.

There was irony here. Business executives, who lived in a fortress of expense accounts and health plans and fringe benefits, thought only of continued recession, retrenchment, and decline. Labor looked forward to growth, to an economy that produced traffic and jobs. It believed in competition and had faith in private enterprise to do the job. It was optimistic about the future—if business could deliver the leadership, which, in railroading, Keyserling thought it had failed to do so far, despite some high salaries in the executive suites.

Everyone looked good at the hearing except the senators. Estes Kefauver did his homework. His cross-examination was generally to the point, though in his effort to avoid discussion of any particular merger, he failed to pin anyone down. Hruska also came prepared and took an active part. He and Kefauver were at opposite poles, but no points would have been satisfactorily clarified without their conflicting approaches. Philip Hart (D-Mich.) was a freshman that session. Perhaps that excused his lack of familiarity with the subject. Everett Dirksen (R-Ill.) came in occasionally, siding with Hruska in opposition to the bill and contributing bits of Dirkseniana along the way. The others—Carroll (D-Colo.), Dodd (D-Conn.), Long (D-Mo.), and Wylie (R-Wis.) took no active part. Kefauver alone had the interest and the courtesy to listen to Leon Keyserling. Even the subcommittee could not grapple with the tough problems. It could hardly be expected that the full Senate or the full Congress would.

The Kefauver bill was never reported out of committee. It died at the end of the session and was not renewed. Congress did not deal further with railroad consolidation until the debacle, and then it was too late. The railroads had thrown down a terrible gauntlet: mess up our consolidations, and if we go bankrupt, you—Congress—will be to blame. Maybe Congress was frightened. It had more urgent things on its mind—civil rights, the Vietnam War, civil unrest. Railroad executives were acting in their companies' interest and in their own personal interest, as they would be expected to do. The ICC was trying to enforce the law as Congress had written it, trying to adjust the law's ambiguities as best it could. It was not a big enough crisis yet, and there were too many forces pulling in different directions. Congress was not able to focus, not yet. But if either the railroads or the ICC needed further legal guidance, it was up to Congress and Congress alone to provide it.

The B&O and the Cuban Missile Crisis

On October 22, 1962, President Kennedy first revealed the presence of Soviet missiles in Cuba. In what would be 45 years of cold war, the Cuban Missile Crisis was the closest the two superpowers came to direct nuclear war with each other. Many Americans thought that by nightfall the next day they would be at war or dead.

It happened that oral argument on the C&O-B&O case was scheduled for the next day. Jervis Langdon, now president of the B&O, took the unusual step of delivering his company's summation personally. If we go to war, he said, the men and women of the B&O are ready to do their part, but it was going to be a close call. Just a few more months' deterioration, and the B&O would be too weak to fight a war. Control by the C&O was essential, immediately. The B&O could not survive without the freight cars, the capital improvement, and the financial security of the C&O. The commissioners were as scared that day as everyone else. Some think that this single bravura performance linking the C&O-B&O control to the survival of the country in the face of nuclear attack dispelled all remaining doubt among the majority of commissioners. The ICC had to do its part to win the war against communism by approving this consolidation. The C&O-B&O was approved on December 17, 1962.[18]

Vice Chairman Abe MacGregor Goff wrote the majority opinion. As open and public a body as the ICC was, the weight individual commissioners gave to various arguments, and the give and take between them as they debated among themselves, is unknown. The collective wisdom of the majority was to accept nearly at face value the railroads' case and to reject the arguments of the opposition. (The contention of the New York Port Authority, for example, that diversion from the New York Central would bring that road to its knees, was dismissed as having "no weight," with no further explanation.) The B&O was in mortal danger, they said, and C&O control would save it. Ideally, perhaps there could be better combinations, and the commission was aware that the case was less than water-tight, for the report was peppered with little phrases of doubt, but on the whole it was persuaded that the C&O had behaved honorably in its dealings with B&O, that it would rehabilitate the B&O, and that the anticipated savings would become real.

But the decision was not unanimous. "I do not agree that these applications should be approved on this record at this time," began Commissioner William H. Tucker's long and eloquent dissent. In the first place, the case was much too weak, like that interminable testimony on car supply (how the C&O was going to lease cars to the B&O to ease its shortages). It was a short-run solution to a short-run problem, perhaps even a nonexistent problem.

> The evidence consists of impressive *post hoc* rationalizations, prepared by a corps of engineers, economists, accountants and traffic and financial experts, employed to justify a prior managerial decision. Neither the examiner nor any interested party to the proceeding, public or private, was endowed with the peculiar knowledge and the ample resources to challenge evidence of this character. The necessary findings could have been made if the general public had been represented by members of the Commission's staff and consultants retained by the Commission. We shall never know the answer . . . because the Commission's role has been passive from end to end. No such passive attitude existed half a century ago when the Commission retained Mr. (later Mr. Justice) Louis Brandeis as its special counsel in the *Five Percent Case* of 1914.[19]

Tucker found it incredible that the majority should trust to the C&O's self-interest to rehabilitate the B&O when the historical record of aid by parent roads was so abysmally poor. Nothing indicated that the B&O was in so much trouble that a decision could not wait until an adequate record was developed. The B&O's own president said it would operate in the black in 1962, and at the very least the commission ought to consider

B&O's good financial showing in the first three quarters of 1962.

The stakes were high, Tucker said. This was the first of a series of related cases that would reshape the eastern railroads. Since each would affect the other, they could not be decided in isolation.

> In a narrow, literal sense, the transaction proposed is the control of the B&O by the C&O. What these parties actually propose, however, is to become one of the giant rail systems of the East. The proposed three-rail system . . . presents one fundamental issue: what kind of railroad system should the present generation leave to the generations that follow? If there are any who maintain that only the owners are empowered to shape the device, I need only say that the properties have been duly entailed, first by the states, and later by the Interstate Commerce Act. The answer provided by the Commission majority seems to be that whatever the carriers show to be good for themselves is good for the country.[20]

Tucker was joined in his dissent by Charles A. Webb, and in part by John W. Bush. They saw where this decision was going to lead. If it was approved, the others would have to be approved for balance, even if they were not very good ideas, and then the final leftovers that nobody wanted would have to be nationalized, or something like that. "The decision to isolate this case from the others," they said, "is going to haunt the Commission for many days to come if the [New York] Central and to a lesser extent the N&W are not allowed to strengthen their lines in the remaining merger cases." Railroads knew this, said Tucker and Webb. This was why they engaged in a reciprocity of silence. They felt they must not impede the C&O-B&O so that the C&O-B&O would not impede them. "If the Commission is going to open the gates on all eastern merger applications, so each successive one becomes one of the basic reasons for requiring approval of the next, . . . we may end up as creators of another Frankenstein's monster, far more ruinous than its fictional counterpart."[21]

Labor drew attention to the ambiguities of the C&O-B&O record. Disappointed by the commission's decision, given hope by Tucker's and Webb's dissent, it led the remaining opponents to court. But the district court, the appeal courts, and the Supreme Court all refused to reconsider the case on its merits. The courts limited themselves to questions of ICC procedure. Affirmation of the method was affirmation of the decision. The Supreme Court upheld the lower court and the ICC in October 1963.[22] Consolidation would go forward.

Divestiture of the N&W

When a Norfolk & Western official was asked why his company had not protested the Penn-Central merger early, in light of how vigorously it protested later on, he answered bluntly: We couldn't; they controlled us. "They" was the Pennsylvania Railroad. The question of whether or not the PRR controlled the N&W came to dominate the N&W–Nickel Plate merger. It was public knowledge that the PRR owned about 33 percent of the N&W's common stock. It was public knowledge that four PRR officers (its president, James Symes; its first vice president for finance, David Bevan; and former presidents Walter S. Franklin and Martin Clement) sat on the N&W board of directors, while N&W president Stuart Saunders sat on the PRR's board. It was obvious that the N&W–Nickel Plate merger needed at least a blessing from the PRR; the decisions to lease the Wabash and sell the Sandusky line could have been made only by the PRR. Nonetheless, everyone connected with the companies vigorously denied having the power to control.

Throughout the hearings, Examiner Lester Conley made it clear that he was aware of the situation and kept asking tough questions. Where did the N&W hold its board meetings? (Philadelphia). Were N&W affairs or Penn-Central merger affairs discussed at a particular meeting of the PRR board? (Saunders: "I don't know, I purposely stayed away.") Regarding Saunders's concurrent directorships of the PRR and the N&W:

> Q: I would assume, sir, by your occupying those two very distinguished positions on two different railroads, it would indicate there is a relationship between those two roads? Am I correct in that?
>
> A: It doesn't necessarily indicate that.[23]

With no time to spare, the Department of Justice gathered dozens of scraps of evidence and wove them into a meaningful whole. On countless occasions in the past, the PRR or its officials had acknowledged the power to control the N&W—in its official history, *The Centennial History of the Pennsylvania Railroad,* in statements by A. J. County in the consolidation planning of the 1920s, in statements before the Wheeler Committee in 1938, and in statements in various court proceedings. Threats of antitrust action would occasionally frighten it into selling a few shares, but it would always buy them back when the threat passed, either directly or through Kuhn, Loeb & Company. In the period after 1938, the PRR cast sometimes as much as 62.5 percent of the votes for N&W directorships, and never less than 50 percent. Even in 1960, after the Virginian Railway was absorbed and PRR holdings were diluted, it cast 37.5 percent of the votes. Before the Virginian absorption, no other stockholder held more than 2.2 percent of N&W's stock, the wide distribution giving the PRR disproportionate clout in company affairs. Since Virginia law required approval by two-thirds of the stockholders of each issue of stock for certain kinds of corporate transactions, including merger, the PRR had an effective veto even after the Virginian was taken in. The PRR held a quarter, sometimes more than a third, of N&W directorships and always a quarter to a half the seats on its executive committee. Room 1034 of Penn Center Plaza in Philadelphia, on the same floor as the PRR's top executive offices, was inscribed as the office of the president of the N&W Railway and was adjacent to the offices of Walter Franklin and Martin Clement. On December 28, 1960, the PRR board of directors passed a formal resolution that it approved, authorized, and consented to a merger of the N&W and the Nickel Plate.[24]

Tie all that together, said Justice, and it constituted effective control, especially in light of the legal precedent set in the *Rochester Telephone* case (in which the court directed that the extent of control should be determined not by artificial tests but by the special circumstances of each case).[25] The PRR saw the danger immediately. Previously silent before the ICC in the big eastern mergers, it filed petitions to intervene as a precautionary measure.

This may have been the ultimate test for the ICC. Like many a federal regulatory agency, it was often thought to be influenced, and probably dominated, by the most powerful of the entities it was supposed to regulate. It came out of the C&O-B&O case looking as if the C&O had led it by the nose, accepting at face value the technical points raised by railroad attorneys and ignoring the broad regional issues that seemed obvious to everyone else. David Bevan raised a last-ditch technicality on the N&W question, the kind on which the commission was so prone to stumble. The PRR's N&W holdings were divided between the PRR itself and the Pennsylvania Company, the railroads subsidiary holding company; they could not be treated as a single block and therefore could not constitute control.

But the ICC rose to the occasion. The press release went out on April 17, 1963. Examiner Conley found that the PRR did in fact have the power to control the N&W. He recommended that full divestiture be required as a condition of a N&W–Nickel Plate merger. Admittedly, there would be problems. It was not possible for $300 million of N&W stock to be dumped on the market without a resulting collapse in its price and dislocations to other securities; furthermore, much of it was already pledged as collateral for various PRR loans. But the PRR immediately began to cast about for other high-yield investments to replace its N&W stock.[26]

The ICC approved the N&W–Nickel Plate merger on July 13, 1964. Tucker alone dissented on the merits of the case. As before, he thought the railroads had failed to make a positive case for consolidation. He thought the record inadequate, the need for hurry spurious, and the protection for other railroads, the Erie Lackawanna in particular, inadequate.

The N&W did not come through as unscathed as the C&O-B&O. Appendix O of the decision required that the record be kept open for five years, during which time the Erie Lackawanna, the Delaware & Hudson, and the Boston & Maine could petition for inclusion. In the meantime, and until such time as PRR influence was entirely gone from the N&W, the newly merged company was ordered to solicit traffic through the Buffalo gateway for the Erie Lackawanna. Consummation of any part of the merger constituted irrevocable assent to these conditions.[27] Furthermore, the PRR was given 90 days to submit its plan for complete financial and managerial divestiture.

Now the awful decision lay with the Pennsylvania Railroad. Its dream of having price-setting control in the East was dashed. Should it stick with the N&W or hope for a Penn-Central merger? The $11 million it received annually in dividends on its N&W stock had made the difference in whether it even had a net income in some recent years. If it kept the stock, the eastern mergers would come to a halt. If it pinned its hopes on a Penn-Central merger, there was no guarantee that such a merger would be approved, and even less that it would work. It had 90 days to make up its mind.

ten

The Rise
of the
Penn Central

In June 1964 the Boston & Maine Railroad filed for the discontinuance of all passenger service.[1] An impending railroad calamity in New England could no longer be ignored. In 1958, when Congress gave the ICC jurisdiction over passenger service, it was thinking about branch-line locals that nobody used, which state public service commissions and local politicians required to ply their lonely ways. These trains were not required by public convenience or necessity and were therefore a burden on interstate commerce. In New England, the B&M was going broke. Passenger trains were not the only problem, but they were a big one and therefore were a burden on interstate commerce. But the B&M's trains were reasonably well patronized, and there was no substitute service, so they were required by the public convenience and necessity. This was a situation that the law conveniently sidestepped. When there was finally no alternative for the Boston & Maine, Massachusetts came to the rescue of the Boston commuter service, and the ICC found a way to skeletonize the intercity trains. So once again, Congress and the states were able to postpone coming to grips with the real problem.

The Looming Crisis in New England

Distances were short in New England. The average haul on the B&M in 1964 was 174 miles and on the New Haven 154, well below the national average of 263 miles though not as short as a glance at a map of the small states might suggest. The greater problem was that so much of the traffic was terminating. The B&M made final delivery on one-third of all the traffic it originated and two-thirds of what it received from connections. The

New Haven delivered 50 percent of the traffic it originated and 84 percent of what it received. That required labor-intensive switching, and the New Haven bore the cost of collecting and distributing the revenue. Raw materials came in by rail, but most of the finished goods of New England's factories went out by truck, which meant moving empty rail cars and not enough of the high-tariff merchandise traffic to pay the bills.

In New England, because the railroad came after industrialization had begun, railroads followed rather than shaped industrial development. Hence, there was an unusual number of branches and secondary routes. Traffic filtered on and off branches through dozens of junctions and gateways, rather than whole trainloads moving to a few destinations. So much interchange and switching resulted in slow service: in 1920 it took three days to move a car the 40 miles from Nashua, New Hampshire, to Beverly, Massachusetts, and five days for the 165 miles from Nashua to Meriden, Connecticut. The situation was so bad that all interchange with the B&M was embargoed two out of every three days between 1916 and 1918 during the operating breakdown of World War I. This inability to move traffic, made public in the *New England Division* case of 1921 at the dawn of the motor-carrier age, indicated a classic vulnerability to motor-carrier diversion.[2]

Getting rid of the B&M passenger losses would help a little, but it was not a long-term solution. Merger was. Coupling short-haul New England roads to long-haul trunks might keep rail service viable in the region. When the public, and certainly politicians, heard railroads say they must merge to avoid nationalization, New England was the most obvious place to think it might work. But no one invited the New England roads to merge. And they would never be invited if passenger and commuter losses were piled on top of all their other problems.

The *New Haven Passenger Discontinuance* Case

On October 11, 1965, the New York, New Haven & Hartford posted discontinuance notices for all of its 273 daily interstate passenger trains.[3] These trains were required by the public necessity. The private automobile could not substitute for the work they performed, not without tripling turnpike mileage and tearing up downtowns for parking space.

The New Haven represented the worst-case scenario for all of the changes that were overtaking railroads in the Northeast, both passenger and freight. Its first problem was unstable management. In 1948 textile magnate Frederick Dumaine of Fieldcrest manipulated New Haven preferred stock and seized the road as it emerged from Depression-era bankruptcy. He sold its real estate, chopped maintenance, and fired so many people that morale was ruined. After his death, he was followed by his son, Buck Dumaine, Jr., who invested rather than cut back. He was ousted in a 1954 proxy fight by Patrick McGinnis, a raider very much in the mold of Robert Young. Like Young, McGinnis appealed to nonrailroad directors and the public with promises of snazzy passenger trains. His talk fooled *Trains* and the *New York Times* for a short while. He introduced a moderne color scheme of black, white, and orange trapezoids on the road's locomotives that at the time was said to have been designed by his wife, Lucille, but was actually the work of Swiss industrial designer Herbert Matter. McGinnis posted a nice net income in 1955.

The price for his net income was to chop everything, not for efficiency but simply to chop. The most serious effect was on maintenance, which went from an annual expenditure of $54 million in 1953 to $42 million in 1954 to $36 million in 1955. He bought his snazzy passenger trains, which were low-slung and articulated, but they did not begin to address the problem of moving 120,000 people into New York and 41,000 into Boston every day. They were mechanical catastrophes and a waste of money. One derailed and caught fire on its inaugural press run. The money spent on them was wasted.

In the McGinnis era New Haven commuter trains came to be notoriously dirty, cold, and late. Budgets were slashed so drastically, facilities so undermaintained, breakdowns so frequent, morale so poor, that even safety was in question. This railroad ran crowded trains at close intervals at high speed on track that rattled martinis off the bar on the five forty to Larchmont. Complaints poured in; McGinnis was the subject of editorials in the *New York Times* and the butt of cartoons in the *New Yorker*, particularly after he began charging commuters a fee to park their cars at the stations.

At the very end of 1954, three of McGinnis's associates bought shares of the B&M until between them, they held almost a third of its stock. McGinnis talked about creating a long-contemplated New England regional railroad. The matter—and McGinnis—was so politically explosive that Massachusetts' two senators, Republican Leverett Saltonstall and Democrat John Kennedy, demanded an immediate ICC probe. By 1956, a faction of New Haven security holders had had enough and prompted a former McGinnis ally, George Alpert of Boston, to lead a boardroom coup. McGinnis assumed the B&M presidency the day he was fired from the New Haven and signaled the revolutionary change of style and philosophy at the stodgy New England carrier by giving its locomotives a moderne color scheme of black and blue. He was eventually convicted of pocketing the money from the sale of B&M passenger cars and sentenced to 18 months in prison.

On the New Haven, Alpert probably meant well. He was a good man, a "father" of Brandeis University and a benefactor of Einstein Medical College at Yeshiva University. He was a cultured man, an accomplished violinist, although some thought he was too interested in the three-hole golf course on his New Hampshire estate. By the time he took over, matters may have gone beyond the ability of any management to solve them. The railroad could not afford freight cars, so it ran a deficit in per diem (daily rental paid to other railroads for the use of their cars) of nearly a million dollars a week. Hurricane Diane in 1955 and the opening of the Connecticut Turnpike in 1959 were severe blows. In 1960 the New Haven had to take out a government-guaranteed loan just to meet payroll.

Alpert said he would put safety first; and in fact, there were no major accidents on the New Haven in those years despite its deteriorating condition. But its trains broke down a lot, or caught fire, often in the Park Avenue tunnels at the peak of the commuter rush, constricting the movement of all trains on both the New Haven and the New York Central Railroads. After one such breakdown on January 4, 1960, Alpert said, "either the losses must be eliminated or the service must stop" and demanded an immediate 10 percent hike in commuter fares, which he did not get. Bankruptcy was declared on July 7, 1961, the first one by a major railroad since the Depression.[4]

The New Haven's discontinuance application in 1965 put the New England problem on the table. The trains could not be eliminated, but things could not go on as they were, and merging the New Haven into a trunk line was one solution short of nationalization. ICC commissioners Tucker and Webb saw the crisis coming as early as the C&O-B&O decision. Without dwelling on New England in particular, they recognized that among the eastern railroads there were winners and losers. The strong roads wanted only to pluck off the winners, but eventually they would have to do something about the losers, because neither the politicians nor the public was ready for nationalization. In the case-by-case approach, the losers were going to be dumped on the last merger, which, as things were turning out, was going to be the Penn Central. That was why they regarded the PRR's James Symes's talk of "soundly conceived mergers" and "balanced competitive systems" as so much prattle: it did not take into account the obvious problem of the losers.

Symes saw the problem coming, too. Actually, he could not pretend to ignore it, since Governor Powell of New Hampshire summoned him and the Central's Al Perlman to Concord and told them to come up with a plan for New England or he would do everything in his power to wreck their merger.[5] Symes's solution was to combine all of New England's railroads, including the New York Central's Boston & Albany, into a New England regional railroad. He assumed that the Norfolk & Western was eventually going to have to take the Erie Lackawanna, so that it would connect with New England. Only the C&O-B&O would have no access; he offered them the Lehigh Valley at scrap value, as if to say that they were expected to take some responsibility. The C&O would not bite. It had no interest in New England and said the Lehigh was never competitive to New England points anyway.[6]

Symes was not the only advocate. Maine Central's E. Spencer Miller had hosted a conclave of New England roads in 1959 to explore the idea of one big regional road. Those talks broke off, but not before studies were ordered from the J. G. White and Arthur D. Little firms of Boston. Their studies were complete and offered dozens of suggestions for coordination.

A stumbling block to Symes's idea was the New York Central's presence in New England in the form of the Boston & Albany. The B&A served the big cities of Worcester and Springfield, but it had tough grades over the Berkshire Mountains. The parallel Fitchburg Division of the Boston & Maine did not serve any intermediate points that large, but it was a good, double-track railroad with the 4.7-mile Hoosac Tunnel under the mountains. Alfred Perlman said that whenever he approached the B&M's Pat McGinnis about coordinating the two routes, McGinnis would respond, "Why don't you rip up the B&A?"[7] and drop the subject. In Perlman's view, though the B&A lost money by itself, it was a valuable feeder for the Central as a whole. But New England politicians annoyed him. Massachusetts, for example, refused the Central permission to install CTC on the B&A and rip up one of the two tracks, even though CTC worked everywhere else on the system. He had contempt for politicians who threatened to cut off any state aid to New Haven passenger services if the NH abandoned so much as a single branch. And incidentally, he had no respect for the New Haven's management, either—he thought it had been asleep at the switch when it failed to use its grandfather rights to blanket all of southern New England with joint rail-highway container services.[8] (The New Haven had been one of piggyback's pioneers.)

The idea of a New England regional railroad was not new. Just as Symes was pushing it now, the Pennsylvania Railroad had pushed it before. And it was not a very good idea. Charles Mellen of the New Haven, with the backing of J. P. Morgan, had tried to put such a system together early in the century (see chapter 1). The legacy of Mellen was an extraordinary burden of debt on the New Haven and a series of passenger wrecks. The episode fired public opposition. New England business and political interests developed a remarkable insularity after that to keep non–New England banks and non–New England railroads out. In 1923 a committee of New England governors, the Storrow Committee, declared public subsidy to New England railroads preferable to outside domination. (This suggestion for "socialization" came just shortly after the Plumb Plan hysteria of 1919–1920, which made it quite remarkable.)

In the early 1920s the issue of outside domination was academic, because the New England roads had such a low rate of return that no one was interested. It was in the late 1920s, when things began to look up, that the PRR made its moves on the New Haven. In 1931 another committee of New England governors recommended, rather hysterically, the expulsion of the PRR and the creation of an all–New England regional railroad. The

New York Central's presence on the B&A, or even the Canadian National's presence with its control of the Central Vermont, did not matter to them. Only the PRR had to be driven out. To make sure there was competition for a rail monopoly, they would subsidize coastwise steamer routes, using rail revenues, which would force rail rates higher. The steamers had long since ceased to play a viable role. James Nelson said that trying to keep them alive would maintain the form of competition though not the substance and that they reminded him of tales of ghost ships with ghost crews, condemned to ply the seven seas forever without cargo and without destination.[9]

In the New England governors' report of 1931, only the Rhode Island delegation perceived the weakness of a regional-terminal railroad. Though the word *piggyback* had not yet been coined, the concept of a rail-truck service was not unheard of. What would stop trunk lines from off-loading trailers at their own terminals and delivering the goods over the short New England hop by highway?

New England had reason to worry, because it was difficult to get traffic into the region: all traffic from the south or the southeast had to be ferried across New York Harbor or run in a wide arc around the city to Maybrook, New York, to cross the Hudson on the New Haven's Poughkeepsie Bridge. And trains could not move through Boston. There was no connection between the New Haven at South Station and the B&M at North Station. Passengers had to take a taxi. (The State of Maine, a famous through train between New York and Portland, did not pass through Boston but left the New Haven's Shoreline at Providence and passed through Worcester and Lowell to join the B&M's main line at Lawrence.) Freight had to follow the same circuitous route. All this, thought the Rhode Islanders, might make it convenient for the trunk lines to bypass a line haul on a New England regional railroad and deliver the goods by truck. They thought it was best to give the trunk lines a vested interest by letting them into New England. In their statement, they even used the word *container,* quite novel in 1931.

There were remarkable service improvements in the years that followed. In the 1920s, the B&M took 83 hours to deliver cars from Boston to the New York Central at Rotterdam Junction (near Schenectady). By the 1930s, it advertised fourth-morning delivery all the way to Chicago, by the 1950s third-morning, and by the 1960s second-morning. (Boston-Chicago schedules via the Canadian Pacific remained at 77 hours in 1965, which explained the diminishing significance of the once-important Canadian connection.) The New Haven pioneered the piggyback concept in the 1930s and under Buck Dumaine's leadership filed the petition with the ICC in 1954 to open vast new opportunities for piggyback service and rate making.[10] Many customers who had the classic New England pattern of distribution—raw material in by rail, finished goods out by truck—liked the new Plan I piggyback introduced that year, by which trailers were hauled at a uniform rate and moved on a motor-carrier bill of lading. But the McGinnis management on the New Haven did not follow up. As if to affirm the predictions of the Rhode Islanders in 1931, the two major trunk lines refused to work with the New Haven. The New York Central did not introduce piggyback until 1958 and then did it with its Flexivan container system, which was incompatible with the New Haven's piggyback system. As late as 1961, piggyback interchange with the Pennsylvania required an over-the-road haul through New York City streets, which encouraged shippers to take delivery directly from the PRR at Kearny, New Jersey, and bypass a New Haven line haul altogether.[11] That was precisely why the idea of a terminal railroad was a bad idea and why another conference of New England governors in 1963 recommended trunk-line affiliation.

Thus, once again, merger was not quite doing what it was supposed to do, which was solve the railroad problem. Alfred Perlman of the New York Central would stand in front of a hearing examiner and say with a straight face that he saw no way a Penn-Central merger could hurt the New Haven, even though one of the principal "savings" to be derived would come from rerouting interchange between the PRR and the New Haven via the Boston & Albany.[12] No one else had the nerve to be quite that bald-faced.

Hotboxes, derailments, electrical fires were now the norm on the New Haven. Both the New Haven and the B&M were unilaterally settling per diem accounts at $2 a day instead of the standard $2.88 because they did not have the money, a short-run saving that ran a terrible risk of retaliation and back indemnities. A B&M official almost bragged how his road resourcefully created its own cash flow by holding bills 45 days before paying them.[13] It was a problem, and somebody had to find a solution. Everybody recoiled from the idea of government operation, but Symes was beginning to suspect that that might be the only solution for the New Haven. The justification of the Penn-Central was that it was the only way to avoid government operation. It was a little awkward to suggest that what was a horror for Penn-Central was good for someone else. Just as the PRR was to be stripped of the Norfolk & Western, it began to appear that it was going to inherit the New Haven. The *New Haven Discontinuance* case was the vehicle that would tie the fortunes of the New Haven and the Penn Central together, to the death.

Symes, Saunders, and the Culture of the Pennsylvania Railroad

James Symes took personal credit for conceiving the Penn-Central merger. It was a bold idea when he first suggested it in the 1957 recession. His predecessors had built the railroad: they tamed the Alleghenies with the mighty Horseshoe Curve, tunneled under the Hudson to build Penn

Station, and electrified the lines east of Harrisburg. They made the PRR a mighty transportation enterprise that hauled 71 million tons of freight in 1944 to help win the war. On Christmas Eve 1943, on the New York–Washington corridor alone, it carried 379,000 people home to their families for a wartime Christmas.

The PRR was a troubled railroad after the war. Competition, regulation, shifting patterns of commerce in the Northeast, the very things that swamped the Erie Lackawanna, engulfed the Lehigh Valley, and killed off the O&W, spared the PRR only because of the unique importance of its routes and its mammoth size. *Fortune* picked up on its troubles in March 1948, warning a business generation that grew up in a railroad age, when the PRR was a corporate Rock of Gibraltar, that times were changing.

A series of horrendous passenger wrecks brought the railroad's troubles to public attention. Two in 1950 were on the Long Island Railroad, which the PRR then controlled: 31 died at Rockville Center on March 17, and 78 died at Richmond Hill on November 22. Those accidents set in motion the move by New York State to declare the LIRR a redevelopment corporation and wrest control from the PRR.[14] On February 6, 1951, the PRR's Broker on the North Jersey Shore Line hit a temporary trestle at Woodbridge, New Jersey, at excessive speed and killed 83. The railroad had failed to put up proper speed warnings. New Jersey authorities indicted it on 83 counts of manslaughter. On January 15, 1953, just as crowds were building for Eisenhower's inauguration, the brakes failed on the Federal from Boston; it careened into Washington Union Station, and the GG-1 electric locomotive crashed through the floor into the basement below.

Symes took the PRR's helm in 1954. He was the son of a PRR baggage master in Pittsburgh and had taken no more than a couple of secretarial courses after high school. He was the last of a breed of bright, talented kids plucked from the lower ranks in a business culture that still found experience more important than college degrees. On his way to the top, he was the architect of the PRR's dieselization. This may not seem important in hindsight, since we know the outcome was inevitable. But it was a big deal on that railroad at that time and could doom the career of anyone who stuck his neck out too soon. Steam, and steam men, ruled on the Pennsylvania Railroad. The PRR's mechanical department regarded itself as the standard mechanical department of the world. It was a matter of pride and tradition, although its penultimate efforts in new steam power design—the S2 turbine and the Q and T class four-cylinder piston locomotives—were disappointing. The coal industry was one of the PRR's biggest customers. In Philadelphia, President Clement leaned to coal but was torn, not so much by the diesel's efficiencies but by the stranglehold of John L. Lewis's United Mine Workers in a coal strike. According to legend, it was Lucian Sprague of the little dieselize-or-die Minneapolis & St. Louis who loaned Symes one of his new diesels for a couple of weeks. Symes tried it, and the week after that, the order went out from Philadelphia for $15 million in new diesels.[15] Clement made Symes his vice president of operations. Symes would have to wait for Walter Franklin, the executive vice president, to take a lackluster turn at the presidency before he got the top job.

The tradition of in-house promotion had given the Erie its down-home corporate culture but had not served it well. Fuddy-duddy was the operable concept. On the PRR, the same tradition was a product of pride and smugness, as though nobody from the outside could measure up. This tradition had not yet served it badly, but there were lurking dangers of arrogance and a lack of fresh input. Symes was a good railroader and a good manager, popular with subordinates and more informal than his austere predecessors. He assumed his assigned role in the country club culture of Philadelphia society with ease and grace. On becoming president, he convened the railroad's entire management in the grand ballroom of the William Penn Hotel in Pittsburgh and told them to stop using the slogan "standard railroad of the world" until the PRR was again, in fact, the standard railroad of the world. Everything on this railroad, he told them, would be pointed toward that goal. He set about making Conway, the PRR's mighty marshaling yard outside Pittsburgh, into the operating hub of the system. But the big railroad never responded.

So merger would be Symes's monument. He would conquer the arch rival New York Central for the enduring glory of the Pennsylvania Railroad and the Philadelphia culture from which it sprang. He took a humiliating rebuff when Al Perlman broke off merger talks in 1959. He then forgave everything instantly when Perlman, his Central an outcast everywhere else, came knocking at the door.

As he approached mandatory retirement age in 1963, Symes pushed the board hard to bring in outside blood to head the railroad, specifically the man with a reputation for getting mergers through, Stuart Saunders of the Norfolk & Western. They certainly knew Saunders at the PRR. The PRR controlled the N&W, and Saunders was on the PRR board. Saunders was respected in the financial community. He had a high profile in civic affairs as chairman of the Virginia Association for Independent Colleges, a trustee of Hollins College for Women in Roanoke, and chairman of the trustees of Roanoke College, his alma mater. And Saunders was socially acceptable, a matter of more than passing interest to the men who ran the PRR. On Symes's list to his board of the reasons why Saunders was a good choice was number 11, "Good family life with charming and capable wife who would fit into the Philadelphia picture quite well. He has four children."[16] This left serious broken noses in the PRR command. One was that of Jim Newell, vice president of operations, who quit and headed up TrailerTrain (of which he was a cofounder). The other was David Bevan, vice president of finance, who stayed, smarting and chafing under Saunders's command.

Saunders was an active Democrat. In an era when it seemed the Democrats would be the government party for years to come, this would compensate for the PRR's long-standing and well-known preference for the Republican Party. After all, there was a reason why Democratic presidents always rode the B&O. Kennedy, eager to cultivate businessmen who were Democrats in the wake of the Steel Crisis of April 1962, appointed Saunders to head the President's Advisory Board on Labor-Management Relations and named him to the board of the National Cultural Center in Washington, later known as the Kennedy Center. In 1965 Johnson named him to the National Alliance of Businessmen, which was meant to involve business in solving the problem of the chronically unemployed. Johnson called on him to persuade "detachable" Republican congressmen from Pennsylvania to vote for the Equal Opportunity Act, the War on Poverty, the centerpiece of the Great Society.

Saunders arrived in Philadelphia acting every bit the role of the CEO of a very blue-chip firm. He was invited to the boards of directors of U.S. Steel, Chase Manhattan Bank, Georgia-Pacific, First Pennsylvania Banking & Trust, and Pennsylvania Bell. He bought an estate in Ardmore next to the Merion Golf Club, which he joined. Ardmore was on the Mainline, the very plush western suburbs of Philadelphia, so called for its proximity to the railroad. Mainline was synonymous with Protestant heritage, social grace, and lots of money. All PRR executives lived there, and many had named estates, for example former president Martin Clement's Crefeld and David Bevan's Treverigge. Reporter John Gunther once wrote about the Mainline: "it doesn't matter on what side of the tracks you are. These are very superior tracks."[17]

Saunders was a patron of the arts, an exquisite dancer, and a connoisseur of fine wine. He played bridge and enjoyed French cooking. He cultivated close friendships with Walter Annenberg, publisher of the city's newspapers and *TV Guide,* and John Dorrance, a member of his board and chairman of Campbell Soup. He was invited to the city's most prestigious clubs, including the Philadelphia Club. This amounted to affirmation that high society found the railroad's new CEO scintillating company. Saunders was driven to work in a limousine, which did not endear him to the riders of the "red rattlers," the PRR's antediluvian commuter cars.

Soon after his arrival in Philadelphia, Saunders became fascinated with diversification. That involved investing what paltry profits the railroad was earning and borrowing against the railroad's credit to acquire high-yield enterprises outside of railroading. Conglomerates were all the rage on Wall Street in the middle to late 1960s. Jim Ling had started a tiny electronics firm and by means of the leveraged buy-out turned it into the giant Ling-Temco-Vaught. It was a major electrical cable manufacturer and a major defense contractor. It owned Wilson & Company, the nation's third-largest meatpacking company. It bought Braniff Airways and National Car Rental and was going after Jones & Laughlin Steel when the Justice Department became interested. Other famous conglomerates were Litton Industries, Textron, TRW, and Gulf+Western. They left Wall Street in awe, at least until they started to come unglued.

Saunders set out to make the PRR a high-flying conglomerate, too. The PRR acquired Florida, Texas, and California land developers, amusement parks, and a very dubious little airline, Executive Jet Aviation. (See chapter 14 for more about diversification.) Milton Shapp, a Philadelphia industrialist in TV antennas and later governor of Pennsylvania, told reporters Joseph Daughen and Peter Binzen that Saunders wanted to get out of the railroad business, that after a few drinks he would talk about Litton Industries and the good returns they were getting and how he wanted to put money in real estate instead of the fucking railroad. "That's what he said," said Shapp, "the fucking railroad."[18] The PRR needed leadership from a master railroader. What it had in Saunders was a lawyer who knew little, and apparently cared little, about how to run trains. The people he had to run them were mostly in-house, inbred PRR men, steeped in tradition and wary of new ways of doing things—and wary of Saunders. There was trouble ahead.

Perlman and the New York Central

Values were entirely different on Alfred Perlman's New York Central, although this did not seem to make much difference on the bottom line. In contrast to Symes, Perlman had a college degree (from MIT) and a master's degree in business and transportation (from Harvard). The effect in terms of running a railroad was that Perlman was constantly experimenting with new ideas and new ways of doing things.

The young Perlman rose quickly on the Northern Pacific in his native St. Paul to become assistant vice president for operations by age 32. He was such a whiz that the Reconstruction Finance Corporation borrowed him to make engineering studies of troubled roads to which it had loaned money, notably the New Haven. In 1935 Ralph Budd, president of the Burlington, borrowed him to manage reconstruction on the Denver line when floods washed it out in western Nebraska on the plains northeast of Denver. Perlman used off-track vehicles to tote supplies and lay the track. This was unheard of. Old-time railroaders brought cranes and supplies by rail; they thought using rubber-tired vehicles was betrayal. But the line was reopened in record time and the trains were rolling and making money; that was what counted.

In 1938 Judge Wilson McCarthy, supervising the reorganization of the bankrupt Denver & Rio Grande Western, invited Perlman to Denver to be the Rio Grande's chief engineer. The Rio Grande was broke, and the standard approach would be to scrimp and live within limited budgets. But

Perlman did the opposite. He figured out how to open up the mountain railroad so it could run enough trains to make money. He made the Rio Grande into a formidable competitor for the Union Pacific. He arrived at the New York Central in 1954 and immediately made plans to rip out the nearly sacred four-track main line and replace it with double-track centralized traffic control, a much more efficient way to run more trains faster. He was not bound by tradition or sacred cows.

At the New York Central, Perlman surrounded himself with bright, educated lieutenants. Walter Grant (Wharton School), vice president of finance, was an executive for Hotpoint and Studebaker-Packard before coming to the Central in 1955. John Kenefick (Princeton), vice president for transportation and an ace operating man, was a Buffalo native who was broken in on the Central, went to the Union Pacific and the Rio Grande, and returned to the Central with Perlman in 1955. Wayne Hoffman (University of Illinois), executive vice president, was a lawyer from the Illinois Central who came in 1957. Ace operating men Robert G. (Mike) Flannery (Purdue) and Richard Hasselman (Yale) were Central men but were young and had worked all over the system.

Perlman was determined to unkink the worst bottleneck of railroading, namely classification yards. What good was it to roll trains at reasonably high speed only to have cars delayed for hours at every junction while they were regrouped into outgoing trains? With the cost of labor going up, sorting cars with switch engine crews in flat yards was out of the question. In traditional hump yards, where cars were cut loose to roll by gravity down a hump to their correct outgoing track, freight cars slammed into each other at a pretty good clip. This was all right for coal, but slamming a carload of television sets meant the railroad would not be carrying television sets much longer. Electronic yards employed sensing devices that calculated the weight and speed of a car rolling down a hump, applied pressure to its wheel flanges, and guided it to a safe, sure, gentle coupling. The result was that whole incoming trains could be resorted and regrouped into outgoing trains for different destinations in a fraction of the time with a fraction of the labor and a fraction of the damage claims.

These yards were expensive. The PRR built one at Conway, which was Symes's bid to make the PRR a modern transportation machine. Perlman built a whole series of them—Frontier at Buffalo, Collinwood at Cleveland, Young Yard at Elkhart, Big Four Yard at Indianapolis, Junction Yard at Detroit, and Selkirk near Albany, which was not opened until shortly after the merger in 1968. The technology was cutting-edge and there were bugs to work out. These were not instant miracles. But not far in the future, these yards would make all the difference in whether railroads retained time-sensitive business or not. There was a time coming when shippers would want to keep overhead low with "jit" (just-in-time) delivery—not too soon so it would have to be carried as expensive inventory, but never, never late so that production was disrupted. Only railroads that had invested in rapid classification could hope to compete for this business.

Less tangible than the giant classification yards but perhaps more significant was Perlman's marketing revolution. The railroad's inherent advantage was the low coefficient of friction of steel wheels on steel rails, resulting in low cost; its inherent disadvantage was its inability to provide the specialized, customized door-to-door service that many shippers wanted and were willing to pay for. Traditional railroad pricing and marketing was to charge a low rate but to offer minimal service—one could ship whatever could be stuffed in a boxcar but could expect it only when it got there. This was designed to maximize tonnage over the railroad; the railroad would make its money on volume. Regulation, which set minimum as well as maximum rates, robbed railroads of some of their cost advantage, but still most railroad marketing (to the extent that they even understood marketing) rested on the concept of low service for low rates. That was how the PRR marketed its services.

It was Perlman's idea to offer the shippers precisely the service they wanted, even buying specialized equipment for their special needs, so long as the railroad got a price that was profitable for the railroad. It was a higher price, of course, than the price of basic service. Tonnage, thought Perlman, was of no value to the railroad if it did not produce a profit. This concept was the secret of motor-carrier success. Of course, only a railroad that could offer precision service could hope to pull this off, so CTC and electronic yards had to precede a marketing revolution.

When it was necessary to increase revenue, the PRR favored ex parte (across-the-board) rate increases. Shipments of mostly bulk commodities that had no choice but to go by rail paid more, but across-the-board increases tended to drive away traffic that had options, certainly if the price increase was not accompanied by an improvement in service. The New York Central preferred instead to be more selective in its pricing, raising rates when extra service was performed but posting 846 targeted rate reductions between May 1960 and May 1961, to retain business that was still profitable but that it feared it would lose. Perlman said he thought the marketing revolution would make the New York Central depression-proof. The idea was that it would make the railroad much less dependent on bulk raw materials, whose volume dropped dramatically in recessions, and more reliant on finished products, which were less volatile. There was no statistical evidence that the Central was depression-proof, but it was a good idea.

The Central's marketing revolution was still brand new at the time of the merger. It did not really take hold until James R. Sullivan became vice president of marketing in 1967 and brought in a number of up-and-coming young professionals, such as David DeBoer. Sullivan's accession represented the victory of the new idea over the old. The concept required a rate low enough to get the business but high enough to make a profit. A precise knowledge of costs was needed, in an industry wherein most costs were shared among other traffic on other trains, freight and passenger. Sullivan and his skunk works had computers to help figure this out, of course, but the technology was primitive. Although the marketing revolution was pointing the way to the future, it was far from an instant fix to anything.

Not all of Perlman's ideas worked out. For example, as piggyback service became more important to railroads, allowing them to offer door-to-door service, Perlman opted for a Flexivan system designed and built by Strick. It was more like latter-day container technology in that the trailer was detached from its highway undercarriage before it was put on a rail car. This lowered the center of gravity and vastly reduced the tare weight by eliminating two sets of wheels that in a later day of high fuel prices made traditional piggyback uneconomical. But the Flexivan system required specially equipped highway tractors at both ends, the sending and the receiving, and thus would be effective only if it became universal. Perlman never understood why other railroads failed to adopt it, but none ever did except the Milwaukee Road. And so Flexivan became something of a millstone.

Perlman was fascinated with cybernetics (he eventually served as chairman of the World Cybernetics Conference). Cybernetics is the study of human control systems with the idea of replacing them with electronic or mechanical devices. Perlman struggled with the first generation of mainframe computers for business, with decidedly mixed results (see chapter 14). And Central field offices in his era were a bizarre mixture of the new and the antique—the latest teletype machines clattering out the consist of incoming trains beside crank telephones for interoffice communication. And strangely, for all Perlman's passion for control systems, his critics thought he spent too much time troubleshooting in person around the railroad, which limited him to seeing only what was in front of him.

Perlman never was able to establish firm lines of managerial control at the bottom levels. For example, Niagara Falls, New York, was a major industrial point that produced electrochemicals (Olin, Hooker, DuPont, Stauffer, and North American Cyanamid), abrasives (Carborundum), carbon rods (Union Carbide), alloys (titanium, vanadium)), aircraft (Bell), auto parts (GM's Harrison Radiator in Lockport, N.Y.), paper (Kimberly-Clark), batteries (Autolite), compressed gas (Linde Air), food processing (Nabisco Shredded Wheat), and food-processing machinery (Chisholm-Ryder), all of which required the transport of bulk raw materials by rail. The trainmaster at Niagara Falls was an old-fashioned railroader: he was hired by the railroad before he finished high school, spent his life on the railroad, saw his job as running trains, and did it exactly as he had been taught to do it in the years around World War I. He had no managerial skill and did not inspire those who worked for him. He did not frighten them; he just avoided them. He had no concept of how to please a customer or even how to deal with a customer. His clerks were left alone to take the customers' wrath and to deal with them as best they could.

I went to work as a clerk and car checker in that office on Perlman's New York Central while still in high school in 1958, determined to make good in my first real job at a company that I cared about. I was hired and trained, not by management, but by agreement employees (employees covered by union contracts), who set my work assignments and schedules. So it was with them, not management, that I had to curry favor. The union men's morale was none too good. They taught me all the tricks of how to take shortcuts in the work, how to do a poor job and get away with it. They expected me to do just as they did. Indeed, there could be real penalties for attempting to do a good job. Only once did anyone from management visit the yard office: a perspiring young business school graduate who was visibly different from everyone else because he wore a necktie but who instantly revealed that he knew nothing about trains. Perlman came through the yard once and found an empty Canadian National boxcar that someone had forgotten and left on a remote siding for two months (which cost the railroad per diem charges every day it sat there). The irony was that it was only a half-mile from its home rails across Suspension Bridge. Perlman was furious. He went into the trainmaster's office and slammed the door, and the air turned blue clear over to Ontario Avenue. The poor old coot kept his door tightly shut after that. None of us clerks ever saw him again.

The brotherhoods had regular lodge meetings (and summer baseball leagues) where strong loyalties quickly developed. Management's only contact was the *Headlight,* a run-of-the-mill house organ. There was no point in trying to do a good job, because there was no one from management to see or hear. Agreement employees, at least those at Niagara Falls, regarded the railroad as an everlasting cow whose purpose in life was to be milked. Their security lay in seniority, which rewarded those who kept their mouths and their minds shut. Management abdicated leadership to soviets of workers in a way that few leaders of American unionism ever intended or wanted.

Niagara Falls was one of the worst-case scenarios of Perlman's New York Central. After the Penn Central crashed in flames, Peat, Marwick & Mitchell, the railroad's auditors, observed "two agency locations with probably the worst working conditions we have ever seen—Kalamazoo and Niagara Falls [both former NYC points]. It is inconceivable that personnel working under these conditions can perform quality work commensurate with the rest of the system."[19] They suggested that even the most rudimentary custodial services would be a major boost to morale.

In 1979 William Gale, who had been the DL&W's Philadelphia traffic agent and became Erie Lackawanna's agent and trainmaster at Niagara Falls, said he remembered the NYC as being so incompetent at that point that taking traffic from it was like taking candy from a baby. It was strange, he thought, since the NYC was such a formidable competitor at other points. He told how merely sharing information with his own yard employees on how much extra revenue was received when they put out some special effort made them eager to work extra hard.[20]

In Perlman's fascination for technology and systems control and new marketing tools, one clearly sees the super-railroad of the latter twentieth century struggling to be born. He was hampered by all the problems of railroads generally and by the inadequacy of early computers and the programs that ran on them. He was also hampered by characteristics of his own temperament. The forgotten boxcar, for example, demanded a search for some procedure to make sure it never happened again, not a temper tantrum that shot everyone's blood pressure out of control and shredded what little morale was left. And as the Niagara Falls story shows, the ancient inertia of the old-fashioned railroad and old-fashioned railroad men (they were mostly men in those days) was a residual problem he was never able to quite solve.

But even though there were troubles, there was a deep sense on the management team Perlman assembled that the New York Central had a better fix on the future of transportation than the PRR had. At the top levels, there was an esprit on Perlman's Central. Many thought they were on the threshold of turning the railroad's fortunes around, but not just the Central; they thought of the Central as a model for the whole industry. Many of them thought the PRR men were too interested in their country clubs and their personal investments.

The Concept of the Penn Central

In the grand sweep of the disaster that lay ahead, it is sometimes forgotten that there was more rationale to the Penn-Central merger than perhaps any other. Although the two mighty roads were built to compete, and although every attempt at planning consolidation made them the nucleus of rival systems, no other proposal rested on such a sweeping rationalization of physical plant. The two greatest railroads in the East would be redesigned as specialty railroads to do what they could do best.

Squarely in the path of the Pennsylvania Railroad lay the backbone of the Allegheny Mountains, a defiant wall astride this four-track artery of commerce. On its 924 miles between New York and Chicago, 25 percent was on grades of more than 0.5 percent; on the tortuous passage between Altoona and Johnstown, around the engineering feat known as Horseshoe Curve, 36 miles were on grades greater than 1 percent. It was a dangerous bottleneck. Stephen Meader wrote a yarn about it called *Long Trains Roll*, set in World War II. German saboteurs infiltrate the crews that guide the squealing, smoking trains down the mountain, filling secret notebooks with vital statis-

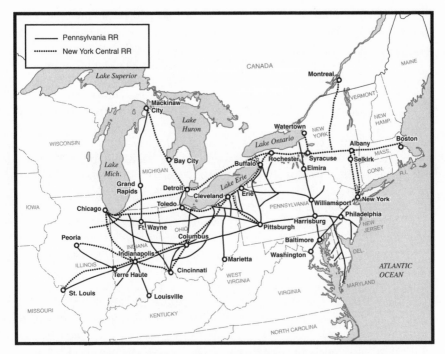

Pennsylvania–NYC Transportation Company as Originally Proposed

tics of traffic moving over this jugular of the American war effort. It was railroading that made the heart beat fast but kept efficiency factors low.

If all railroads were operated as one, no dispatcher would make New York–bound merchandise climb that mountain. Such traffic would be winged eastward over the Water Level Route of the New York Central that paralleled lakes and rivers for nearly its entire length. Only 16 of its 949 miles from New York to Chicago were on grades over 0.5 percent. Yet as long as these roads were separate, the vast traffic-generating mechanism that was the Pennsylvania Railroad had no choice but send it all up and around the Horseshoe Curve.

The situation was even more absurd for traffic bound for New England on the PRR. The PRR hauled it to the New Jersey waterfront, to Greenville Yard in Bayonne, New Jersey, and ferried it across the Upper Bay to the New Haven's Bay Ridge Yard in Brooklyn. The ferries were frequently delayed by tides and by fog over the headlands. At Bay Ridge cars were reassembled for dispatch across the Hell Gate and on to Connecticut. It would have been much better for New England traffic from the west to roll over the Water Level Route to Selkirk Yard, near Albany; New England traffic from the south would roll up Central's River Division, the old West Shore Railroad, to Selkirk. From Selkirk trains would be assembled for New

England destinations, free of ferries, free of fogs and tides, and free of labor disruptions on the waterfront.

Some said this plan would gut rail service across Pennsylvania. Potent political forces would mobilize in that state to stop the merger because of the diversion of these trains and the jobs they entailed. But the trains in question did not serve Pennsylvania; they just passed through. The PRR main line would be cleared to do the job it was meant to do—serve the steel district with the vast tonnage of raw resources that went into its maw. It would be cleared to serve the heavy industry of the Schuykill and lower Delaware Valleys. It would serve the ports of Philadelphia and Baltimore. New York Central's traffic to these ports, not inconsequential, moved over a circuitous route from Lyons, New York, to Newberry Junction, Pennsylvania, and a connection with the Reading Railroad. It would take the direct PRR route. The NYC would concentrate on the ports of New York and Boston.

Merger would allow the magnificent transportation mechanism that was the Water Level Route to realize its full potential. Selkirk Yard outside Albany would be the heart of the new system. The merger would succeed or fail on Selkirk. Add to this the savings from 160 common points, including all the major cities of the Midwest. No one was naive enough to think one yard could always do the work of two, but there would be vast opportunity for yards to specialize. Electronic yards would be assured the volume to operate at peak efficiency. Duplicate lines crisscrossing the area between Cleveland and St. Louis, Cincinnati and Chicago could be downgraded or abandoned. The original prediction was $81 million of savings a year. That was later increased to $100 million.

These were deeply troubled railroads, and their continued existence as private enterprises was not a foregone conclusion. Yet they had good routes and performed vital services. Despite the changes that were sweeping both transportation and the Northeast, if even a portion of these savings were real and could produce the capital for revitalization, there seemed to be a golden opportunity. In addition to the $100 million in savings, there would be combined sales forces and combined routings. It was reasonable to think that all might turn out well. But problems were also on the table.

There was deferred maintenance. Symes admitted on the first day of the hearings that the PRR had accumulated $304 million in deferred maintenance as a matter of policy and was shrinking plant in order to avoid the purchase of new material. Maintenance on a railroad is vital. If a year is bad, some maintenance can be deferred for a time. There is no problem at first. Then low points develop on a section track, and train speed has to be cut to 40 miles an hour. This is called a *slow order*. Then trouble develops on another section, maybe some rotted cross ties, and speed drops to 40 there. Then the first trouble spot gets worse, and speed goes to 30. Pretty soon, trains are missing connections and missing promised delivery times, sometimes derailing if things are bad enough. The productivity of the train crews falls because trains are moving so slow. Labor costs rise. Connecting railroads complain. Shippers complain. Shippers begin to divert traffic and revenue begins to fall. With revenue falling, the railroad is less able to make up the maintenance it deferred. A cataclysmic downward spiral begins. This is called the "point of no return."

The PRR was not at the point of no return. Its main line was good enough. Its secondary mains, Chicago to Louisville, for example, or Chicago to Cincinnati, were beginning to show dangerous signs of deterioration. The PRR had a high accident rate in 1963, and the system was dotted with slow orders. Fifteen percent of its freight cars were bad-ordered, meaning they were out of service in need of repair. Twenty percent of its locomotives were awaiting repair. Both the PRR and the Central had a poor record of equipment and labor utilization and a high frequency of shipper complaints. These were all signs that the point of no return was lurking like death. In retrospect, all one had to do was look out the window of a PRR train to see a dying railroad—shabby facilities, abandoned facilities, yards and sidings choked with weeds, stations with broken windows and coated with pigeon droppings. But until 1967, this was, on paper, disguised because good trends mingled with the bad. When the statistics for 1967 were posted early in 1968, just as the merger took place, there was no way to hide the desperate situation.

Then there was the nagging question raised by the Healy Hypothesis. Would merging railroads of this size and complexity of operation create an efficient dynamo, as Penn-Central wanted everyone to believe? Or would size and complexity swamp it in diseconomies, beyond the ability of management to control? After all, problems of management control at the lower levels was already evident.

Once a merger was consummated, there was no going back. If management had misdiagnosed its ills and if the merger faltered, government would be all that could save it. What the ICC was being asked to determine had shifted almost imperceptibly from their task in previous cases. It was no longer simply trying to find out who would be helped and who would be hurt, but whether or not merger was the correct medicine for the fundamental ills of the industry. In 25,000 pages of testimony and 100,000 pages of briefs, exhibits, and correspondence, the right questions somehow never got asked.

For example, the railroad's operating studies were not adequate. They concentrated on the grand sweep of rerouting traffic over the Water Level Route and the importance of Selkirk and conveyed a dazzling illusion of vast efficiencies. They were remarkably different from the Wyer studies of other mergers, which focused on detail. Walter Patchell of the PRR was in charge of Penn-Central studies and stood cross-examination for a grueling two weeks. He seemed to defend them brilliantly. Some of the exhibits were a little obscure or a little technical, lacking something in the way of concrete decisions, but they did not seem any more deficient than exhibits in other mergers. No one in previous mergers had asked the merging railroads precisely what they were going to do first, who was going to do it, and how employees were going to be instructed. It was just assumed that executives would not be where they were if they did not know how to execute things like this.

The Penn and the Central probably did themselves a great disservice by relying entirely on expertise from within. First, they were limited by the intellectual capacities of people already imbued with a company's way of doing things. Second, they had no one to arbitrate disputes, of which there were plenty because these were two very different corporate philosophies coming together. The result was that the studies never went beyond the theoretical level. When the Penn or the Central disagreed, the matter went unresolved. Later investigations revealed glimpses of this—a memo from a PRR executive who returned from vacation to find mountains of technical data piled on his desk. "I am searching desperately for some concrete evidence of progress," he wrote, "completed projects, approved networks, etc., but finding little. Nevertheless, everyone seems to be working very hard, and I am sure there is as much progress being made as can be expected at this time."[21]

The *Wall Street Journal* had already revealed some of the chaos of implementing a merger that occurred with the Erie Lackawanna, and that was a smaller and more manageable property. The Erie Lackawanna witnesses were forced to say—on the Penn-Central record—that their plans had been inadequate and their merger had produced few of the savings anticipated.[22] An indication that planning in the Penn-Central was less than comprehensive came from Fred Carpi, PRR vice president for sales. When asked to give a single example of more efficient routing that would come as a result of merger, he chose traffic from Buffalo to Rochester, where the Central had a direct main line of 66 miles and the PRR had to drag it over a circuitous route involving a scenic but soon-to-be-abandoned branch of 167 miles. He admitted that the PRR did not get much of the business—only when both the shipper and the receiver had sidings on the PRR. Everyone was appalled that it got any of the business at all. "I have a couple of oxen down on the farm," said one of the lawyers, "and I think they can beat that schedule from Buffalo to Rochester."[23] What was appalling was that when he was asked to give one example, that was all Carpi could think of. Nonetheless, no one picked up on the idea that the planning for this merger was thin.

R. F. Ventrella, Michigan representative for the Brotherhood of Maintenance of Way Employees, made one of the most prophetic comments of the hearing. "As to merger, we have heard here this morning, and we heard at Kalamazoo . . . shippers and a lot of others testifying on behalf of merger, and it was all guesswork of what can happen. Nobody knows. I don't believe the railroad companies themselves can testify as to what will happen." He was very humble, not encumbered with a law degree, he said, and he did not always know what the lawyers were talking about. He thought the technicians had a language all their own so ordinary people could not understand them. He hoped they could understand each other. "I would urge the ICC to look back and get all the facts on all the mergers they approved and see what the result was."[24] But it slipped by—just another labor guy who did not understand what it was like to run a big corporation.

Six years passed between the time the first studies were presented to the commission and the time they were implemented. They were updated and refined, resulting finally in the Master Operating Plan, but that document was not distributed to general managers before the merger, and when it was, after the merger, it proved to be of no help.[25] Every study of the Penn Central debacle agreed that premerger planning was inadequate and that it was the direct cause of the operating breakdown after the merger. But in all the hearings, no one asked the right questions.

One reason the hearings missed their mark was that opponents, who asked most of the questions, asked only about what directly concerned them. Opposing railroads never challenged the Penn-Central on its merits. They just wanted to get something for themselves. The New Haven demanded inclusion. So did the Erie Lackawanna, the Delaware & Hudson, and the Boston & Maine *if* they were not included in the N&W. The Western Maryland wanted its friendly connection, the NYC subsidiary Pittsburgh & Lake Erie, detached from the NYC before the merger. The Monon wanted out of a contract for using the Indianapolis passenger terminal. The Chicago & Eastern Illinois wanted to make sure its rental for trackage rights on the NYC did not increase. The Chicago & North Western wanted better interchange arrangements in Chicago. State authorities defended railroads in which they had a special interest—Maryland the Western Maryland; New York and New Jersey the Erie Lackawanna; Massachusetts, Rhode Island, New Hampshire, and Connecticut the New Haven.

Penn and Central lashed back at their pursuers. For example, Al Perlman on the subject of the New Haven (which stood to lose its single most important friendly connection, the PRR):

> Q: Do you believe the New Haven would be competitively disadvantaged by the formation of a Penn-Central system?
> A: No.
> Q: You testified that the Central would be hurt by C&O-B&O?
> A: That was entirely different.
> Q: You find nothing in the relations of the Pennsylvania and New York Central which would cause you to believe there would be any disadvantage at all to the New Haven?
> A: None at all.[26]

Or Fred Carpi on the Erie Lackawanna:

> Q: Let me test your judgment. The Erie, based on figures given here, last year lost something like $25 million. I ask you to assume that in the next two years, it only loses $15 million a year. Your testimony is that Erie Lackawanna can continue to provide good service, strong competitive service losing money like that?
>
> A: Sure.
>
> Q: If that is so, Mr. Carpi, why can't the Pennsylvania Railroad and why can't the New York Central keep doing a splendid job for the public losing Niagaras of dollars in the same way?
>
> A: Why should we?[27]

Politicians were mostly uninformed. A few, such as Rep. William Ryan (D) of New York City, spoke with dignity and eloquence. He was sympathetic to the railroads' problems, he said, but he thought they had been crying for more opportunity to compete, and that was what President Kennedy's message offered them. Now they just seemed to want less. As he saw it, merger would require more regulation to replace the lost competition.[28]

Others were neither eloquent nor enlightening. Mayor Hugh Addonizio (D) of Newark, for example, thought the PRR should help out with Newark's urban renewal problems before it was allowed to merge and was angry that it had not established a station stop in South Newark.[29] Rep. Thaddeus Dulski (D) of Buffalo, a northern ethnic Claghorn, got all the information he cared to get from labor. He never bothered to find out what other constituencies in his district might think, such as shippers. He had never even heard of the Nickel Plate—the name did not ring the foggiest bell—so of course he had no idea whether it served his district. He settled on what he thought was a really substantive issue, the PRR's night passenger train from Buffalo to Washington, which he thought was crummy. It was not the world's best: the track was so bad it could jar one's teeth out. But it still carried sleepers with roomettes and bedrooms, and it had breakfast service into Washington. Nobody rode it much except in blizzard season when the airports were closed and the highways were blowing with drifting snow. Then everybody wanted to ride it. That was when he wanted to ride it, which was why he could not get space, which was why he was mad.[30]

Milton J. Shapp appeared pro bono publico. That was all anyone could think to call it. He made a fortune in television antennas. He wanted to be governor of Pennsylvania or to win Hugh Scott's seat in the U.S. Senate. He wanted to make the Penn-Central merger his issue. But he had not been elected to anything yet, so he appeared only on behalf of himself. He stuck with it from beginning to end, with a higher caliber of input than most of the politicians. Unfortunately, he latched onto an unimportant facet of the case and would not let go. The merger, he said, would be the greatest disaster to Pennsylvania since the Erie Canal; it would "penalize today's citizens and future generations of unborn citizens, condemning them to a loss of opportunity, low wages and poor education," all because 31 trains a day were going to be diverted from the PRR to the Water Level Route. He was not dissuaded by the explanation that these trains only passed through Pennsylvania and clogged Pennsylvania rails for Pennsylvania commerce. But it was his straw horse, and he rode it right into the governorship in 1970.

The Railway Labor Executives' Association, representing the combined brotherhoods and represented by its attorney, William Mahoney, put on a thoughtful case with no banker-baiting and no political posturing; but like the rest, it missed the boat. It was based on the Keyserling Hypothesis that railroads needed to expand to meet the needs of an expanding economy, not retrench through merger. Keyserling himself came and testified for five days in April 1963; most of his testimony was what he had presented to the Kefauver Committee. It was reasonable and intelligent. Railroads suffered from a mentality of retrenchment. He thought that constantly thinking in terms of how to trim here, cut there, eliminate this, discontinue that, was hardly the mentality they needed to go to customers with a menu of new services and new ideas so that the business might grow.

The Penn and the Central thought they were expanding. PRR stockholders were told in the 1963 annual report that the railroad had "entered a progressive phase of restored financial health and growth." Perlman bragged about how the Central was expanding in a pamphlet, *A Decade of Progress on the New York Central, 1954–1964*. But these investments, more real on the Central than on the Pennsy, did not seem to do much for the bottom line. The roads of the Burlington Northern merger liked to portray themselves as worse off than they were so the commission would grant their merger; they needed a blast of the Keyserling thesis. The PRR and the NYC had more profound troubles and were desperately trying to portray themselves as better off than they were; the Healy thesis of diseconomies would have been a fruitful line of inquiry.

The Healy thesis was on the minds of many who were at the hearings. Symes was so concerned that he felt compelled to rebut it in his opening remarks. He pointed out that the PRR and the NYC each had more employees during World War II than the combined company would have now, so there was no danger of unmanageability. (James Nelson, in his New England study, asked to what extent previous large and perhaps unmanageable size contributed to subsequent decline.) Perlman lashed out when Healy's thesis came up—that "non-sensical idea," he said, was thought up by a man who never ran a business in his life.[31] (Healy was a classmate of Perlman's at MIT.) The reactions of both Symes and Perlman indicated that the Healy thesis bothered them.

The most controversial presentation came from an unexpected quarter, the Pennsylvania Federation of Labor, represented by Albert Brandon of Pittsburgh. His technique was to fire verbal shotguns at key witnesses and see if anything stuck. His questions were based on scraps of evidence— hearsay from the people he represented or rumors that appeared in the press. Most of what he asked produced denials or just came to a dead end, though one wondered, if there was that much smoke, was there fire?

Brandon asked Symes whether, despite the PRR's complaints of a heavy tax burden, it was true that in the state of Pennsylvania the PRR paid no property taxes except in the cities of Philadelphia and Pittsburgh, and then only in the 1905 boundaries of those cities. Symes stated that it was true. Under Brandon's questioning, Symes confirmed that although the PRR complained it suffered from politically motivated regulation, it had never been denied permission to remove a passenger train by the Pennsylvania Public Utilities Commission (PUC). Brandon asked whether the PUC had ever denied the PRR a rate change in Pennsylvania. It had not. He noted that although the PRR claimed the PUC discriminated against it, the bus lines and the streetcar lines had to go before the same PUC when they wanted to cut service. Symes said he did not know about them.

Brandon asked if it was true that the PRR's policy of favoring ex parte rate increases was costing a lot of business. Symes denied it. He also denied knowing that the PRR lost seven cars a week from the Iron City Brewery in Pittsburgh to Fairmont, West Virginia. Brandon charged that because Symes's list of the ten largest stockholders of the PRR was mostly brokerage houses—anonymous street names—holding stock for somebody else, it was not really known who owned the railroads. Symes agreed. When asked whether the comptroller (whose office was granted a lot of authority) determined the amount spent on maintenance, Symes got huffy: "I see all these railroad lawyers coming down here and not one of them is opposing the merger." Brandon shot back, "Maybe it's because they're all afraid."[32]

Brandon played with Perlman, too, and shined a little light in the inner sanctum of the New York Central. Brandon asked if, after Robert Young waged an expensive proxy fight, he turned around and gave Perlman full control of the railroad. "He certainly did," said Perlman. "The chief financial officer even reported directly to me." Brandon asked who Mr. Allan P. Kirby was. (Kirby was one of Young's old cronies and bankrollers at Alleghany Corporation.) "Mr. A. P. Kirby is an industrialist or financier or whatever the heck you want to call him. I don't know. He's got a lot of money, anyway." He was asked about John Murchison, one of his directors and son of Clint Murchison who was one of Young's bankrollers: "He has a lovely wife and he dances well." Brandon asked if, in the first Penn-Central talks, Mr. Barriger had done most of the studies for him. Perlman insisted no, but admitted that he had helped. Brandon asked whether, in those studies, Mr. Barriger had indicated a low opinion of PRR management. Perlman answered no. Brandon repeated, "You are telling me that Mr. Barriger did not indicate to you a very low opinion of the competency of Pennsylvania Railroad management?"

"He did not."

Brandon asked whehter the Pennsylvania had better equipment. Perlman didn't know. He thought their equipment was OK. "Well Mr. Barriger found out for you, didn't he?"

"He did not."

"And so from November 1957 to January 8, 1959, you had under active exploration a merger between the Pennsylvania and the New York Central and you never got a written report of it?"

"That's just what I've said three times before."

Neither Brandon nor Mahoney believed that and wanted to see those earlier studies, which they never got.[33]

Saunders Deals for His Merger

James Symes was past retirement age. Stuart Saunders took over on October 1, 1963, the day before the hearings closed. He understood that it was his job to get the merger through. So he began to work the magic he had worked in the N&W's mergers with the Virginian and the Nickel Plate. One by one, opponents to the Penn-Central either withdrew or scaled back their demands. Saunders was a remarkable man, and it was a virtuoso performance. His technique was to be generous with adversaries, too generous, perhaps, for any railroad but the coal-rich N&W. If generosity failed, he could pour on social charm or political pressure, in just the right combinations.

Labor knew that Saunders would come through with an attrition agreement as he had done in the Virginian and Nickel Plate mergers, so it demanded, and got, a little more in the Penn-Central. The Luna-Saunders Attrition Agreement was executed on May 20, 1964.[34] Its additional concession was that it applied to all employees *on the date the agreement was signed,* not the date the merger actually took place. No one could foresee that four years would pass before the merger took place. On the day it did (February 1, 1968), the Penn Central had to take back into its employ every person who had worked for it since May 1964. Some thought that was the merger's death warrant. The ICC hearings were reopened to review the labor settlement. Saunders said his arrangement was cheaper for the company than the *New Orleans* conditions. He said it would give management the flexibility to transfer people from one point to another as needed (although he implied they might be transferred across seniority and craft lines, which labor lawyers firmly scotched). Saunders's testimony on his labor agreement dealt in vague generalities and fell apart on cross-examination. It is doubtful that he understood—or cared—about such mundane issues as how to calculate the rate of attrition or how his agreement was going to be implemented, or how it was going to play out at the bottom levels. Symes, who remained on the PRR board, understood and warned of trouble. For Saunders, the important thing was that labor and its political allies withdrew their opposition.[35]

On the day that Saunders took the chairmanship, just as hearings were drawing to a close, the previously dormant Justice Department read a statement denouncing the merger on its merit, on its destructiveness to competition, and on the harm it would do to innocent parties. It advocated a four-system East, so that in case things did not work out, there would still be maneuvering room for more mergers. The timing of its action was curious. Justice had put on no witnesses. It had been quiet in railroad mergers so far except in the politically sensitive *Northern Lines* case. It was believed that the Kennedy administration was bending over backward to avoid antagonizing business more than it already had in the Steel Crisis in the spring of 1962. But it was also rumored (by Drew Pearson) that Justice's late entry in the Penn-Central was to "save the Kennedy family's favorite railroad," the New Haven. Justice reiterated its complete opposition to the Penn-Central in its brief of June 1964.

Negotiation with the New Haven's trustees for inclusion in the Penn Central began on June 16, 1964. Only Saunders showed any enthusiasm for it. Perlman was opposed, and so was Symes. Determined to extract the best price they could, the New Haven's trustees came prepared with some heavy ammunition, namely a report from Wyer, Dick & Company that showed that the property was capable of generating enough income for fixed charges. The first sessions began with book value (the value of its financial obligations) as a starting point, but different methods of calculation, particularly over what weight to give the common stock, led to an impasse. The New Haven's trustees claimed that the property had a valuation of $84 million; the Penn-Central acknowledged only $41 million.

In July the ICC approved the N&W–Nickel Plate merger, giving the PRR 90 days to make up its mind on divestiture of the N&W. Saunders had to have assurances that if the PRR gave up the N&W, the Penn-Central merger would go through. A meeting was arranged with Attorney General Robert Kennedy on August 24, 1964. Kennedy said he would be leaving office soon and could not bind his successor, and it would be unseemly to retreat too soon from positions taken on the June brief. But he said he would recommend to his successor that Justice drop its opposition if the ICC approved the merger and if terms were reached for the inclusion of the New Haven that were acceptable to the New Haven's trustees. Within two weeks, Kennedy left office. The new attorney general, Nicholas Katzenbach, told Saunders he concurred with Kennedy's recommendation.[36] Saunders updated Katzenbach on negotiations with the New Haven in face-to-face meetings the following January (1965) and again in

April. Both times, Katzenbach reaffirmed the understanding.

Beginning in September 1964, the New Haven trustees introduced the concept of liquidation value[37] as a means of determining fair price. This was considerably greater than book value. Perlman was annoyed; liquidation had been a fiasco in settling the affairs of the Ontario & Western, he said, because it precluded anyone's attempting to operate it as a railroad. Nevertheless, on the basis of liquidation value, the New Haven trustees demanded $161 million. The Penn-Central reluctantly offered $128 million, and the New Haven trustees accepted immediately.

The agreement was signed on January 5, 1966. This entailed operation of the New Haven's freight service only; exactly what was going to happen to the passengers was not clear. The feeling was that the Penn Central had been generous; in place of a cadaverous railroad running annual deficits of $15 million, the New Haven got 95,000 Penn Central shares, $23 million of Penn Central bonds, and $8 million in cash.[38] This cleared the most serious obstacle to merger. Connecticut, Massachusetts, Rhode Island, and New York continued to push for the inclusion of the New Haven's passenger service in the deal, but the opposition of New England had been diffused. Whether the New Haven was the millstone that would ultimately sink the Penn-Central merger was another question.

Other critical opposition vanished as well. In Pennsylvania, Gov. David Lawrence, a Democrat, had initiated the original opposition to the merger. When Republican William Scranton took over in 1964, he was willing to reach an understanding: Pennsylvania would withdraw its opposition in return for guarantees of service to the Port of Philadelphia. New Jersey withdrew its opposition. It was never clear whether its attorney general, William Gural, got anything in return. Reporters Joseph Daughen and Peter Binzen thought Saunders had merely dangled the railroad's historic Republican leanings in front of Scranton, and Saunders's own personal commitment to the Democratic Party in front of the New Jersey Democrats. Saunders seemed to have worked his personal charm, which was great, on Philadelphia mayor James Tate. Tate had been adamant in his initial opposition, fearing not only that the port might suffer but also that the railroad's headquarters might be moved out of the city, causing a massive loss of both jobs and prestige. But the mayor had a dramatic change of heart, and Saunders thanked him for his support in the most glowing terms.[39] Daughen and Binzen said the mayor admitted he had found Saunders "most persuasive."

Milton Shapp was in a predicament. He had assumed that the PRR's old-line Republicanism could be converted into an issue for the Democrats, but he had not counted on Saunders, an active Democrat with close connections to President Johnson. Former governor David Lawrence underwent his conversion when Johnson brought him to Washington as chairman of the Committee on Equal Opportunity in Housing. After that,

Lawrence let it be known in state Democratic circles that it was time to back off on the railroad. Shapp did manage to get the gubernatorial nomination in 1966, but Johnson sent Secretary of Commerce John Connors to campaign for him, and Connors kicked things off by saying the merger would be good for Pennsylvania and the nation. *TV Guide* publisher Walter Annenberg, a Republican but a good friend of Saunders, brought the full weight of his near monopoly of Philadelphia communications to bear against Shapp—the *Philadelphia Inquirer,* the *Philadelphia Evening Bulletin,* and WFIL-TV. Day after day, they ran stories with damaging inferences that slammed him. Annenberg told the *Philadelphia Magazine* that Shapp was using Saunders and the merger as his *shtick* (gimmick), and he did not like anyone using his friend that way. In April Saunders brought Arthur Krim, finance chairman of the Democratic National Committee (DNC), to Philadelphia and arranged a luncheon for the three of them alone— Shapp, Saunders, and Krim—at the Warwick Hotel. Krim told Shapp that President Johnson favored the merger, and if Shapp would drop his opposition, his campaign was in for a big infusion of cash, and so was the DNC, which was what seemed to interest Krim.[40]

But Shapp did not back down. In fact, he uncovered a very haunting piece of evidence but never could get anyone to take it seriously. Saunders had traveled up and down the smaller cities of Pennsylvania, speaking before city councils and civic groups in school gymnasiums, in an effort to placate local interests. He had been at his persuasive best, and most of them came on board. At New Castle, he held up two unwieldy volumes and said they contained new data on the operational plan of the merged railroad that the ICC did not even know about. "We have taken every department, every operation of our railroad, we've studied 43 different railroad yards—none of this was done in 1961—as to how we are actually going to operate this railroad."[41] This was an admission that the companies had misled the ICC, since they had certainly implied they already had this data. Should the ICC not take a look at these studies, to see what the railroad did, or did not, know about what it was doing? Shapp thought so, but the railroads replied it was "just a study of implementation . . . nothing of substance." Whatever was or was not in those studies never became public.

M-Day—April 27, 1966

The ICC got a very black eye in the way it handled the N&W–Nickel Plate announcement. It had reached its decision on June 24, 1964, but did not make it public until July 13. In the interim, word leaked out that set off a last-minute speculative rush in Nickel Plate securities.[42] This kind of gaffe was common at other regulatory agencies but was a rarity at the ICC. It was important that it not happen again. Nevertheless, it was almost impossible to stop rumors, especially when the commission was sitting on so many controversial cases and when so many people, from 11 commission-ers and their secretaries and staffs to typists and printers, knew about it. As early as November 19, 1964, Drew Pearson wrote in his *Washington Merry-Go-Round* column: "You can write it down that the biggest railroad merger in history . . . will soon be given the green light."

The PRR went ahead and divested the N&W, and its N&W stock was put in a trust as a preliminary step to its sale. The N&W–Nickel Plate merger was consummated on October 25, 1964. Wabash president Herman Pevler, once a PRR lieutenant, had already taken over as N&W president after Saunders left for the PRR. As far as was known on the outside, the N&W merger went smoothly. Only the question of whether or not the Erie Lackawanna and a few others might have to be included seemed to cast a shadow on its horizon.

Throughout 1965, three cases—the Northern Lines merger, the New Haven passenger discontinuance, and the Penn-Central merger—were the big cases still pending. By the spring of 1966, the ICC had wrapped up the Northern Lines and New Haven cases; the examiner's reports were in and oral arguments were finished. When the commissioners began their closed-door deliberations on the Penn-Central and they saw how things were likely to go, they realized that a common thread of reasoning entwined all three cases. That being so, it seemed wise to hand down all three decisions together so that everyone would see the entwining logic.

M-Day, the day of the big combined announcement, was set for April 27, 1966. Two days before, on April 25, a press release explained that in two days, three of the most far-reaching decisions in ICC history would be rendered simultaneously. Preparations were elaborate. Microphones and a battery of press telephones were installed. Special preannouncement briefings for the press began at 9:30 A.M. The official announcement at noon was to be coordinated with a statement by Sen. Edward Kennedy of Massachusetts to the people of New England regarding the New Haven.

At noon on M-Day, the blows fell. By a 6-to-5 vote, the Northern Lines merger was denied. The New Haven Railroad was permitted to drop 21 of the 37 trains on the shoreline and 19 of the 37 trains on the Springfield line. All other trains, including its commuter trains, would remain in operation. By an 11-to-0 vote, the Penn-Central merger was approved on the condition that it include all the services of the New Haven Railroad, both freight and passenger.

Webb's majority report in the *Northern Lines* case concluded that a need for merger had not been demonstrated, that it would violate the antitrust laws and be harmful to other railroads. The dissenters (Tuggle, Freas, Walrath, Murphy, and Goff) seemed astonished that a merger was turned down. They thought preserving the status quo was not going to save the Milwaukee Road with its one freight a day over 1,500 miles of mountain railroad.

The Penn-Central was approved *only* because it was the *only* way to

solve the problem of the New Haven Railroad short of government operation. That was why it was approved and the Northern Lines merger was
not. Even so, it was approved on the condition that the Erie Lackawanna,
the Delaware & Hudson, and the Boston & Maine be indemnified for
losses from diversion that a Penn-Central merger might cause. Reimburse-
ment was to be calculated on a complicated formula and would end upon
inclusion of those roads in the N&W system.[43] The commission believed it
had dispatched its duties well and even put out a little brochure to pat itself on the back for the "uncommonly accurate reporting of the complex
issues" of M-Day.

But it was not over. In June, the Norfolk & Western, previously silent in
the *Penn Central* case, petitioned that it be reopened. Its statement was a
brutal denunciation of the Pennsylvania Railroad. Among other allega-
tions it said that, despite the trusteeship of the PRR's N&W stock, the PRR
still had the power to control the N&W indirectly by its influence over the
stock's trustees. This included private meetings of PRR officers with the
trustees for the purpose of giving them instructions. It further believed the
PRR was going directly to N&W stockholders in an effort to turn them
against the policies of the N&W management.[44] In light of this, the ICC
postponed the effective date of the Penn-Central merger from August 12,
1966, to September 30. The Erie Lackawanna, the D&H, and the B&M
went to court over issues of indemnity and inclusion if the ICC did not reopen the case immediately. In July, at what was probably the merger's
most sensitive moment, without consulting the PRR, the New York Central announced it would petition to end all passenger service. Instant
wrath came down on its head from just about everyone. Was this stupidity, or was it Perlman's own way of derailing the merger? On September 8,
1966, civil suits were filed to block the Penn-Central merger.

In July and August the Northern Lines petitioned for reconsideration.
The states of Oregon, South Dakota, and Iowa, previously opposed,
switched sides and now approved the merger. The Milwaukee Road and the
Chicago & North Western announced that the Northerns had capitulated
on all their demands for open gateways and trackage rights. Labor unions
notified the ICC that they were in the process of working out attrition
agreements, which the Northerns had earlier sworn they would never accept no matter what. Labor was expected to withdraw its opposition shortly.
Everything was settled. Nothing was settled.

eleven

The South
1960–1972

Mergers seemed to go easier in the South than elsewhere, mostly as a result of good luck. The Atlantic Coast Line and the Seaboard Air Line, the twin railroads of the southern coast, were roughly equal in financial strength and were able to pair off nicely. Their merger into the Seaboard Coast Line (SCL) on July 1, 1967, was the first of railroads that were both hotly competitive and financially strong. It indicated that the ICC would permit parallel consolidation, which reduced competition without the roads' being at death's door.

Elsewhere in the South, strong carriers were able to absorb weak carriers without endangering their own strength and to no one else's stark disadvantage. The Southern took the Central of Georgia; the Illinois Central took the Gulf, Mobile & Ohio to create a virtual monopoly in Mississippi; the Missouri Pacific took the Chicago & Eastern Illinois; and the L&N took the Monon. These mergers merely grouped the pawns for the big moves later on.

The larger southern roads were blessed in those years with good top executives. Bill Brosnan of the Southern helped to revolutionize the whole industry. The path of consolidation was made easier because southern roads were mostly free of the industry's deadliest problems. There were almost no commuters.[1] Passenger losses were bearable (with a few trains on the Florida run probably earning a profit, depending on what fixed costs were charged to them).

The "sunbelt" of rapid economic growth in the regions of sunnier climes did not really reach the old Confederacy until after 1970, after segregation came to an end and the stigma of injustice was no longer attached. Before 1970, corporate America moved low-level manufacturing into the South to take advantage of cheap labor. It was after 1970 that white-collar, managerial, professional, and executive jobs came as well and gave the Sunbelt its luster. Most of the events of this chapter take place just before the Sunbelt boom got under way.

But already in the 1960s, the eagerness of southern state governments for economic development caused them to support and encourage railroad mergers, in contrast to states elsewhere that were fighting them. The South's probusiness environment was a complex package of letting corporations do as they pleased and helping them get what they wanted—an updated version of seventeenth-century mercantilism. This included building infrastructure for them, giving them tax rebates, providing technical training for workers at state expense, helping them with their battles against federal regulators, and passing laws to discourage unions or weaken their effectiveness. The latter was a powerful incentive for manufacturing to relocate to the South. It worked, and it worked for the railroads. It was in sharp contrast to the old days of southern populism when state governments harassed railroads and targeted them as Yankee-owned bloodsuckers. (In 1902, for example, South Carolina mandated one brakeman for every two cars on a train.)

Southern railroads did have problems. For one, geography was not kind. The coastal plain that stretched 100 miles or more inland from the Atlantic and Gulf coasts and included the entire state of Florida allowed for straight and flat rights-of-way and fast running but required lots of bridges, culverts, and close attention to drainage. Elsewhere, the eroded uplands of the Piedmont and Cumberland Plateaus, split by the Appalachian Mountains, made for tough railroading. It lacked the drama, perhaps, of grinding up the high mountain passes of the West, but there was one hilly obstacle after another that required curves and grades. The best examples were the Nashville, Chattanooga & St. Louis's tough climb up Cowan Hill over Cumberland Mountain or the Southern's nearly 5 percent climb up Saluda Mountain between Spartanburg, South Carolina, and Asheville, North Carolina, the steepest main-line grade in the country—steep enough that if it were an interstate highway, there would be big signs saying "truckers beware, check brakes."

For another, the traffic mix of southern roads was changing. Much of their traditional traffic was agricultural products. As late as 1946, the Atlantic Coast Line listed citrus, watermelons, tobacco leaf, and fresh vegetables among the major commodities it hauled. The Georgia peach crop and the Alabama potato crop would soon be moving by truck. Citrus, once shipped as fresh fruit from many stations around Florida, would soon be shipped as concentrate from a few plants, rendering a lot of Florida branch mileage redundant.[2] When Sunbelt industry came, it moved into industrial corridors along the interstate highways, which happened to be along major rail lines. Off the interstates, where weedy branchlines trod, there was no development and no Sunbelt. There was poverty. Railroads in the South did not have a lock on any traffic the way Pocohontas roads did on coal; nor could they sit back and wait for the Sunbelt to happen. They were going to have to help create it.

The Seaboard Coast Line

For all the troubles of railroading at the end of the 1950s, the Atlantic Coast Line and the Seaboard Air Line did not seem to be a part of them. They were competitors, mile for mile, from Richmond to Jacksonville. Both served Atlanta and Birmingham. Both blanketed Florida. These were fast-running railroads, freight and passenger. Their long, fast passenger trains on the Florida run were popular and packed to the very end of private operation in 1971. Hurtling through a frosty Carolina night on a train of 18 to 20 silvery cars through Rocky Mount, Florence, and Charleston on the Coast Line, or through Raleigh and Columbia on the Seaboard, was one of the thrills of the American rails. Speed may have given an illusion of greater stability than was the case, but these roads were profitable and successful, as good an example as one could find for the lesson of Adam Smith that private initiative worked wonders when it was checked by competition. Their ton miles took a little hit in the recession of 1958, but not much of one. They were earning record net incomes. They had good management that was highly respected in the industry.

Nevertheless, pessimism hung like a pall. Agricultural traffic was waning. Branches meandered everywhere, not unlike the New England picture. Many of them were originally intended as main lines, built before or just after the Civil War when it was assumed that traffic in the South would flow east and west, from hinterland to port, the way it did in the North. But for the first three-quarters of the twentieth century, it flowed mostly north and south, and the result was a lot of light-density lines. In Florida, the two competing railroads each built passenger branches to every resort, so the state was crisscrossed with light-density lines. There was a pervading sense that even if the present for these roads was okay, the future was not going to support the rail structure the way it was.

Some say that Prime Osborn, then the ACL's vice president and general counsel, was the man who conceived the Seaboard Coast Line. The way the Seaboard's John Smith told it, the idea to merge came just after the Smathers Committee hearings in Washington in 1958, where railroads poured out their troubles and thought Congress would come through with solutions. When it did not, he realized that self-help was the only alternative. He just happened to be having lunch one day with Tom Rice of the ACL. "I don't know who originated it, but it was a simultaneous acceptance of merger."[3]

A special meeting was held for officers and stockholders in July 1960 in Jacksonville (where the Atlantic Coast Line had recently relocated its headquarters from Wilmington, N.C.)—a time to plan and celebrate the everlasting joy of union. Delegates were given a kit entitled "Your Plan for Progress." Tom Rice of the ACL told the crowd how he racked his brain to think of ways to describe the new day that was dawning—"Ceiling unlimited" had crossed his mind, and so had "The sky's the limit."

> We could sit here and dream for hours and be unable to foresee what is possible under a happy union of these two railroads that have run side by side. . . . I'll tell you a story. I've told it to the Coast Line folks, but I'd like to tell it for the benefit of the Seaboard, because I think it is appropriate when you think of what this merger can mean. During World War II, there was a little boy standing in a field near London on a heavy foggy day with his hands held in front of him, with a string going up in the fog, and an American Army officer walked by and said "son, what are you doing?" and he said "I'm flying a kite." The officer asked "well, why are you doing that? You can't see it?" and the boy replied "no, mister, but I can feel the pull." And I hope as you gentlemen sit here for the next two days and listen to some of these talks on the planning of merger, that you can feel the pull, and you will go away from here as enthusiastic and as jubilant over the possibilities and opportunities as I am. Thank you so much.[4]

The stockholders approved the merger in August 1960, and an application was filed with the ICC. Some who thought their ox was going to be gored—Southern Railway, the Florida East Coast, the Illinois Central, the big paper companies and labor, all eventually joined by the Justice Department—thought the Seaboard and the Coast Line were testimony to the effectiveness of competition. Like the N&W–Nickel Plate, they thought these were precisely the kinds of railroads that did *not* need merger. Cynical about the syrupy harmony of the Jacksonville meeting, they would forever dub it "the Jacksonville love-fest."

The two roads had Wyer, Dick & Company prepare a report on merger savings. A total of $39 million annually was advertised. The ACL's double-tracked main line between Richmond and Jacksonville would become the new railroad's main line. The Seaboard's freight main line through Charleston (distinct from its high-speed passenger main line through Columbia) could be downgraded and portions abandoned. Much of the Seaboard between Savannah and Jacksonville would be redundant. However, the Seaboard main line through Raleigh and Columbia to Savannah would still have to be maintained to high-speed passenger standards. So only 20 percent of the savings would come from line elimination. On the surface, this merger looked like the elimination of competition without much rationalization of railroad plant.

These two prospering railroads had not known prosperity for long, particularly the Seaboard. Neither was conceived as an integrated system;

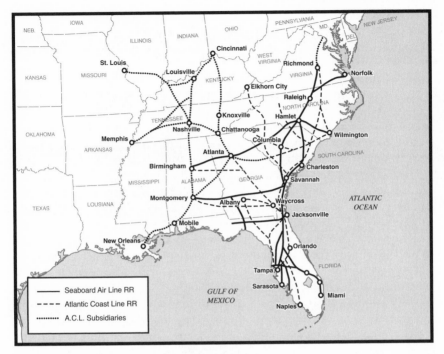

Seaboard Coast Line

both were pieced together from pioneer roads, many of them local projects planned before the Civil War. The Atlantic Coast Line, the senior of
the two roads, was put together out of local lines by William Walters of
Baltimore and later his son Henry. These "Baltimore interests" eventually
lodged in the Mercantile–Safe Deposit Trust Bank of Baltimore, which
would retain its dominant interest in the merger. To make ACL a viable
north-south route, an air-line cutoff through Fayetteville was built from
Wilson, North Carolina, to Pee Dee, South Carolina, which shortened the
original route through Wilmington. It became the main line, and the
Wilmington routes were abandoned in the 1980s.

The ACL was still evolving deep into the twentieth century. In 1902 it
bought the Plant System. Henry Plant put together a rickety network of
lines to the west coast of Florida that included hotels, in a pale imitation
of Henry Flagler's Florida East Coast railroad and hotel empire. The Plant
System was anchored in the north by an awkward U-shaped east-west
route from Charleston to Montgomery by way of Waycross, Georgia. Another cutoff at Folkston in southern Georgia made this a viable north-
south route for the ACL. In the 1920s, the ACL bought into the wheezy
Atlanta, Birmingham & Coast, which had been completed only in 1910,
but the purchase was not completed until 1945. It also took the

Charleston & Western Carolina, which gave it a connection at Spartanburg, South Carolina, to one of its key subsidiaries, the coal-hauling
Clinchfield Railroad. The ACL completed its own last route construction
in 1928 with the opening of the Perry Cutoff, now abandoned, which provided a direct entrance to the Tampa–St. Petersburg area from the west
without going through Jacksonville.

The ACL called itself the "Standard Railroad of the South" and remained solvent through the depression. In some of those depression
years, it would have earned as little as 62 percent of its fixed charges had it
not been for the dividends on the controlling block of Louisville &
Nashville shares that it owned. The ACL only began laying 130-pound rail
during World War II. In the 1950s, although the ACL earned a healthy 3.1
times its fixed charges, it was showing little capacity to grow and was being surpassed by its distinctly junior rival, the Seaboard.

The Seaboard was pasted together by joint Richmond and Baltimore interests from even more components—some before the Civil War, some after. It was not until 1892 that it managed to string a through line from
Portsmouth, Virginia, to Atlanta via Hamlet, North Carolina, which is
more east-west than north-south. It purchased routes from Columbia
south to Florida, but only in 1900 was it able to complete 91 miles of new
construction between Columbia and Cheraw, South Carolina, which created what became its Richmond-Jacksonville main line. That was the year
it formally adopted the name Seaboard Air Line. But it was struggling. It
went into a year-long receivership in 1908.

On November 21, 1925, at the height of the Florida land boom in the
1920s, it introduced one of the truly memorable trains of American railroading in the heavyweight era, the Orange Blossom Special. It began
building a new line from a junction at Coleman, Florida, for 275 miles
along the northeastern shore of the Everglades, to West Palm Beach, Fort
Lauderdale, and Miami. The triumphant Orange Blossom Special entered
Miami for the first time on January 8, 1927. Unfortunately, the Florida
boom had become the Florida bust. Then the depression hit and the
Seaboard was busted again.

In March 1938, when the *Miami Daily News* began asking why the western roads built streamliners for their passengers but the Florida roads did
not, it was the bankrupt Seaboard that bit. It inaugurated the Silver Meteor on January 25, 1939. The ACL countered with the Champion that December. These were so successful for both roads that more streamliners
were bought. Thanks to the two railroads, Florida began to be an all-year
destination for the coach crowd, not just a winter destination for the Pullman crowd. It was one of the most successful passenger operations in the
country, right up to the coming of Amtrak.[5]

After the war the Seaboard was auctioned off to its bondholders, and in
1952, it came under the leadership of John Walter Smith. Smith belongs

in the ranks of great railroaders. He was not the pioneer of any great technological breakthroughs as Alfred Perlman was on the New York Central or as D. W. Brosnan was on the Southern. Smith simply ran a very, very good railroad, as classy with its freight trains as it was with its passenger trains. The Seaboard was quick to adopt promising technology without being hard-nosed or ruthless. It earned record net incomes. By 1958 the junior Seaboard posted a higher gross income ($154 million) than the senior ACL ($149 million) and a much higher return on investment—6.9 percent, compared to 3.1 percent. Smith was also 12 years older than the ACL's Tom Rice. By the time merger talks began, he was beginning to look forward to retirement. That meant that the Seaboard had no problems with Rice running the merged company. That was one of those often overlooked but critical details in successful merger negotiations.

Looming over the merger proceedings was the ACL's controlling interest in the mighty Louisville & Nashville Railroad. The L&N served the central south, the Cumberland Plateau to the Gulf. It was bigger than either the ACL or the SAL (1958 gross revenues of $227 million). The ACL got the L&N pretty much by accident. In 1902, suspecting there had been short sales of L&N shares, John "Bet-a-Million" Gates cornered the market. When, in the ensuing uproar, J. P. Morgan arranged to auction off the whole block, Henry Walters of the ACL was the high bidder. The ACL and the L&N were managed and operated separately, although they took joint control of the West Point Route, an informal name for the combined Georgia Railroad, Atlanta & West Point Railroad, and the Western Railway of Alabama, which formed an important route from Augusta through Atlanta to Montgomery. The L&N was not a party to the ACL-SAL merger proceedings, but the corporate linkage was a silent presence. Everyone knew it was there and knew that the L&N could not join in any railroad combination without the approval of the ACL, or really of Mercantile–Safe Deposit.

The hearings for the Seaboard–Coast Line merger were conducted by Examiner Hyman Blond starting on November 28, 1960, in Richmond, Tampa, Miami, Savannah, Atlanta, and Montgomery and ending in Washington on July 28, 1961. They did not go swimmingly well. Some shippers endorsed the merger, but some very important ones did not, notably the big paper companies—St. Regis, St. Joe, and Union Bag–Camp. St. Regis was finally bought off with the promise that the Southern Railway could serve its plant at Quinlan, Florida. Big boys got what they wanted. Some political entities endorsed the merger—the governor of South Carolina fell all over himself with laudatory praise of free enterprise and self-help and the "get the government off our backs so corporations can do whatever they want" line.[6] Others did not. The Georgia Public Service Commission was an opponent, and there was a lot of opposition in the Tampa area. Eighty-eight counties in six states, including most of Florida, were going to lose all rail competition.

Nor were the Wyer studies given the blind acceptance they had received just a year before in the Erie Lackawanna hearings. The Coast Line presented its studies as definitive perfection. It said the use of a single year's data was the only valid way to do a study. But it was on record for having denounced a similar study done by the same single-year method by the same consultants (for the Florida East Coast, showing why the ACL should not control the FEC) as "superficial," "biased," "erroneous," "unsound," and a "euphonic fantasy."[7] This verbal overkill by executives, that what they proposed was sound transportation policy and the only path to a fulfilling life for all humankind and what anyone else proposed was trash, unworthy of a moment's consideration, persisted throughout the mergers, even into the 1990s. It was the reason business executives often had a credibility gap. Two commissioners, Tucker and Webb, said the studies were junk, "whipped together by paid consultants to justify a merger that management had already decided on."[8]

The ghost of the hearings was pessimism. Here were two very successful railroads. They had lost some kinds of traffic, but ton miles were up, except for a little nick during the 1958 recession. Everybody took a nick during the recession. Gross revenues were down during the recession, 6 percent for the Coast Line, 1 percent for the Seaboard, but net income was the highest ever and dividends were strong. Both railroads grew in all measurements (except passenger traffic) up to the recession and continued to grow when the recession was over. But they presented their case as though all was lost and only ruin lay ahead, with merger as the only hope of salvation. In 1950 they carried three times as many people to Florida as the airlines; now they carried only 40 percent. Citrus traffic was gone to the truckers and the new interstate highways were not even built yet. Truckers had forced them to lower their rates on Florida phosphates. They called that doom, but it turned out to be a false alarm. They had thought the bulky stuff was captive traffic and overpriced their service. Truckers called their bluff. The railroads got it back at a lower rate but were still making money at the lower rate.

Specters of doom were pervasive. Was it a ploy for the railroads to get what they wanted from the regulators? Or did it well up out of the paranoia of the cold war, as though no matter how strong and thriving they were, the forces of doom and destruction were at the gates? Listen to the The cold war vocabulary of ACL lieutenant Lawrence Jeffords's comments at the Jacksonville meeting: "I would view [merger] as a necessity for survival's sake if nothing else. . . . We are competing against each other when we should be fighting the common enemy. . . . What is more desirable than the achievement of security?"[9]

The examiner recommended approval on August 24, 1962. The full commission received briefs, heard oral argument, received further briefs, and approved the merger on December 2, 1963. This was pretty speedy, given that it had taken the Seaboard and the Coast Line more than two years to prepare their own case. Once they submitted it, they clamored incessantly to hurry things up, and for good reason: the Seaboard continued to outperform the Coast Line, and if things dragged on, Seaboard stockholders would almost certainly demand a renegotiation of the stock exchange ratio, and Mercantile–Safe Deposit might lose its dominant interest. But many parties felt that this merger could hurt them and required a forum to present their side. The Florida East Coast, for example, said it was going to have a major impact on them, and they had only a small legal department that was already busy with other matters and could not just throw everything else overboard to devote full time to this. The Southern said it was not possible for the Seaboard and the Coast Line to save $39 million a year without a "violent and far reaching impact on transportation service in the region." They demanded the engineering data and work sheets of the Wyer report but were denied on the grounds that it would delay things.[10]

Approval came with a blistering dissent from Commissioners Tucker and Webb. They thought that on the record, the railroads had failed to make a case, except that the merging railroads and Mercantile–Safe Deposit might make more money by eliminating competition. For example, the roads said they were operating at only 25 percent capacity to show why traffic needed to be concentrated, and the commission accepted this figure as correct. But it was wholly unsupported, said Tucker and Webb, and the term *capacity* was undefined. "The figure is therefore meaningless, phony. It dangles in mid air. Of all the straws clutched at by the Commission to justify this merger, this is the most fragile."[11]

They thought it was unseemly for the commission to depart so quickly from President Kennedy's call for the restoration of market forces, not the elimination of them. "In viewing the unfolding rail merger scene," they said, "one cannot fail to be impressed by the sense of inevitability that hovers over it. . . . By this decision, the Commission has given consolidation a virtually unobstructed green light. . . . After this current wave of unification has receded, some merged companies will no doubt, in turn, seek to combine with other merged companies."[12]

> I do not say that the undesirable consequences of this merger will be experienced overnight. The merged company will enjoy for a time the enlightened management of the separate companies. Competitive instincts will not atrophy immediately. The aggrandizement spawned by monopoly is likely to develop by imperceptible degrees.[13]

They thought the commission's confidence in its own ability to provide checks and balances through regulation that would normally be provided by competition was wishful thinking. "The ICC, conceived in the sweat and tears of the Granger Movement [76 years ago], finds today that there is a great public benefit in the ability of shippers to deal with one railroad rather than two. *Sic transit gloria mundi.*"[14]

Armed with this dissent, the Florida East Coast and most of the other opponents headed off to court. They convinced a circuit court that insufficient weight and improper interpretation had been given the antitrust laws, following much the same reasoning as Tucker and Webb. The Supreme Court did not agree. It thought the commission had put a correct interpretation on the *McLean* decision.[15] If Congress wanted to change the law, Congress could do so, but as it stood, the mergers would go through exactly as management had planned them. There was nothing to stop them.

The Southern Railway and the Illinois Central went back to court specifically to get the L&N detached from the Coast Line. The L&N was not a party to the merger and was not going to be merged into the Coast Line—not yet. The courts eventually denied the plaintiffs' pleas, but it took time. It should be clear that this delay was not because of regulatory foot-dragging but because private parties tried to use the proceeding to extract something for themselves.

The Seaboard–Coast Line merger took place on July 1, 1967. The new company should have been a success. It had good management and plenty of cash to make the necessary physical changes, and traffic volume continued to grow. But it was not a success. It was not a catastrophe, either, but shippers throughout Florida were screaming before long, and it had a lot of wrecks. The merged company never had the luster or the popularity of either of its components.

The Strike on the Florida East Coast

One cannot appreciate the forces that would change railroading without knowing what happened on the Florida East Coast Railway in 1963. On January 23, 1963, while the Seaboard–Coast Line merger was still in the works, 11 nonoperating unions on the FEC went out on strike. The national unions had just reached a settlement with other railroads for a 4.5 percent wage hike. The FEC was not a party to the national negotiations. Just two years out of receivership, it was not making money. A freeze across much of Florida dented citrus loadings. The rise of Castro in Cuba cut off the Havana car-ferry traffic, which had been substantial. The FEC told its unions it could not afford the raise, not right away. It offered them some alternatives, ten different proposals, including a boost totaling 5 percent in three increments, which, ironically, would have made them the best-paid workers in all of railroading within a little more than a year. A number of the men did not want to go on strike, but the national unions wanted not so much as a crack in the concept of a single national settlement.

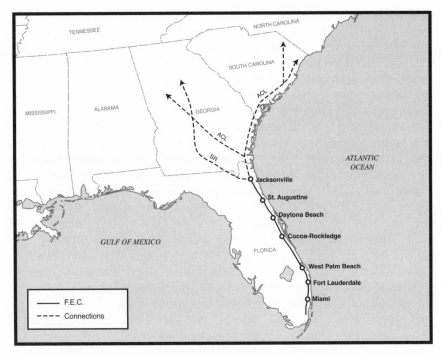

Florida East Coast

For ten days, not a wheel turned on the FEC. The fleet of ACL passenger trains to Miami was hastily rerouted over the Seaboard. This was a big fleet. What David P. Morgan called Mr. Flagler's Pretty Railroad by the Sea was built for carrying people to the American Riviera. The parade was the Florida Special and the East Coast Champion from New York, the Vacationer from Boston, the Havana Special (recently renamed the East Coast Special because of Castro), the Everglades from Washington, and the South Wind and the City of Miami from Chicago. Rerouting left the important resort areas of St. Augustine, Daytona Beach, New Smyrna Beach, Cocoa-Rockledge, Melbourne, Vero Beach, Fort Pierce, and Stuart without passenger service.

After the ten days supervisory personnel began to operate a few through freights. After a couple of weeks, strikebreakers were hired—500 of them, including 75 former union members who quit the union and crossed picket lines. The new crews were paid for an eight-hour day with overtime, not the 100-mile day as before. A single three-person crew ran freights through from Jacksonville to Miami. Formerly, it had taken three five-person crews to do the same work. All distinction between road and yard crews was dropped, so that road crews could do switching work wherever and whenever it was needed. Seniority lists were simplified into one single consolidated list—starting from the day the person hired on. Pretty soon, the FEC was up and running. The Kennedy administration, not wanting to trigger a national walkout over this, put pressure on the FEC to settle. It did not.

Over the next year, the railroad suffered more than 200 incidents of vandalism. Many of them looked suspiciously like more than teenage pranks. Several involved spiked switches. One involved rifle shots into the cab of a moving locomotive. One involved the removal of a rail. Early in 1964 the track north of Miami was dynamited and 32 cars were blown off the track. The wrecker on its way to the crash site was sabotaged. Four days later, a bomb was discovered by four teenagers under the track near Titusville and was defused. A third freight was blown up at New Smyrna Beach. On February 9, 1964, two trains were blown up south of St. Augustine, one on the main line and one on the old main line via Palatka. President Johnson was 15 miles away at a dedication ceremony that day and was on his way to address the AFL-CIO. At first, he was shaken. Then he became livid because so little was being done to stop the sabotage. He helicoptered over the bombed trains and ordered the FBI into the case. Shortly, several embittered members of the former unions were caught trying to blow up a train at Vero Beach. They were indicted, convicted, and jailed. After that, the sabotage mostly came to an end.

In 1965, primarily to advance the political career of Miami mayor Robert King High, the state of Florida decided that charter obligations required the FEC to restore passenger service. It ran a two-car local train with stern warnings that patrons used it at their own risk because of strike conditions and acts of sabotage. A pilot car preceded the little train to test for bombs. The train was discontinued in 1968.

There were multiple court challenges to the FEC's right to run a nonunion railroad. The railroad was upheld, so long as its new employees did not vote for a union. There were efforts to prevent other railroads at Jacksonville from interchanging with it, but they failed.

In time FEC operations did return to normal, minus passengers and minus unions. It took the better part of ten years to restructure it from a double-track passenger road to a single-track high-speed freight road. By the time things settled out in 1973, a little more than 1,000 workers did about twice the work formerly done by 2,100. In 1977 the FEC spent 30 percent of each revenue dollar on wages, versus 53 percent for railroads nationally and 65 percent for Conrail in the Northeast. The savings went to lay the main line with 132-pound continuous-weld track on concrete ties and granite ballast. The line was equipped with CTC, automatic yard switching with radio-controlled drones, and automatic grade-crossing protection. (There is a public grade crossing every 1,200 feet in the 68 miles from West Palm Beach to Miami.)

New work rules plus good track meant fast, frequent service. In prestrike days, 90 workers ran three freights a day from Jacksonville to Miami. After the strike, 32 workers ran eight trains a day. As business increased, the frequency increased to ten, even twelve, trains a day in each direction. Rolling trains at high speed through to their destinations meant better car utilization. The industry in 1977 got about 59 revenue car miles a day, southern roads got 53 miles, but the FEC got 88, and that on a railroad where 100 percent of its traffic was either originating or terminating. The ability of road crews to switch cars on the spot provided service almost as good as trucks could do. Business that was lost began to return to the rails. The FEC performed 773 million ton miles of work in prestrike 1962. That more than doubled to 1.9 billion in 1973. And it put the lie to union claims that reduced crews sacrificed safety. Once ex-union men stopped sabotaging its trains, the FEC posted consistently excellent safety records, winning the coveted Harriman Award for Safety for roads of its size in most of the years of the 1970s and 1980s.

That was the prototype of the lean, mean, service-oriented railroad of the latter twentieth century. Indeed, it was a prototype of the downsized, globally competitive enterprise of any field. Its architect was Winfred (Win) Thornton, a Virginia Military Institute graduate who was broken in under Bill Brosnan on the Southern Railway and was vice president and chief operating officer of the FEC at the time of the strike. He probably deserves more credit than he has generally received as one of the vital revolutionaries of railroading, one who found the equation to keep the railroad alive and thriving.

The FEC might have been more of a model for both railroads and unions if it had shown a broader sense of social justice than it did. It might have treated its reduced and productive workforce well, like professionals and colleagues. They were making its productivity possible. But it did not. In 1973, for example, the FEC paid average wages of $9,986 a year to its people; the industry average was $13,627. It was authoritarian. A job at the FEC meant jump when management said jump, and there were no guarantees of anything. A worker's only freedom was to quit. In 1971 many of its employees did vote for a union and signed with the Florida Federation of Railroad Employees, which many regarded as a company union. In 1994 its employees voted to be represented by a real union, the United Transportation Union, and a contract was signed on March 1, 1995.

Other railroad executives watched Thornton and the FEC with envy. Some wished they had the guts to take a strike as he did and settle the work rules problem once and for all. But it was also thought that the FEC was a special case whose experience could not be universally applied. It was straight and flat. The highest elevations on its entire railroad in the old days were the overseas trestles on the Key West Extension, 30 feet above high tide. It had no blizzards. It had no complicated junctions or terminals.

There was such a hardness to the FEC after the strike that many drew back from making Thornton a hero. The price of its salvation had come so clearly out of the hide of those who could least afford it, even if they were people who had brought their troubles on themselves.[16] Efficient but not popular, it carried a stigma. But all of railroading after 1963, and all of railroad labor, lived in the shadow of what had happened on the Florida East Coast.

Bill Brosnan and the Southern Railway

The Southern Railway was the biggest railroad in the Southeast even after the creation of the Seaboard Coast Line. It did not take part in a major merger in this era. It absorbed the little Atlantic & East Carolina to the port of Morehead City, North Carolina, in 1957. In 1961 it bought the Interstate Railroad, a short line in the mountains of western Virginia that originated a lot of coal. In 1963 it absorbed the Georgia & Florida Railroad, a wheezer that went from Greenwood, South Carolina, through the onion country around Vidalia until it ran out of track at Valdosta, Georgia. Also in 1963 it took control of the midsized Central of Georgia. Central had a not-very-good network of lines to the east and south of Atlanta and a rather key line extending southeastward from Birmingham toward Jacksonville. It did not earn much, had no money for capital improve-

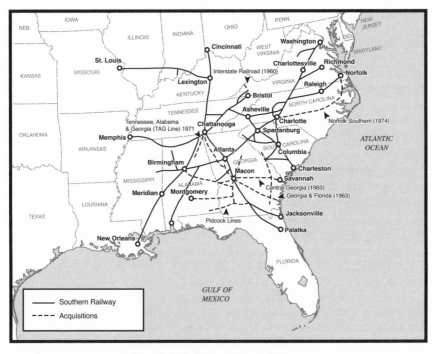

Southern Railway's Acquisitions

ment, and was more important as part of the big Southern than it could be on its own. With the Central came the Savannah & Atlanta Railroad, a property controlled by the Central. In 1971 the Southern acquired the Tennessee, Alabama & Georgia (the TAG line), a coal hauler in northeastern Alabama that was in decline. In 1974 it took the Norfolk Southern (not to be confused with the latter-day Norfolk Southern), which dropped south from Norfolk through the Great Dismal Swamp and across Albemarle Sound into North Carolina, eventually reaching Charlotte. It was best remembered for running the electric "big red cars" from downtown Norfolk to Virginia Beach.

The Southern, to paraphrase its motto, served the entire South. Its route structure was a distorted *X*, Washington to New Orleans on one leg and Cincinnati to Jacksonville on the other, crossing at Atlanta. It was not created until 1894, largely from two Morgan-controlled properties, both then in receivership, the Richmond & Danville Railroad from Washington to Atlanta and Birmingham and the Queen & Crescent Route from Cincinnati to New Orleans. The Southern never paid a dividend until 1924. It was far from a given that this would become a great railroad.

Most of the Southern's routes were on the broken uplands of the Piedmont and the Cumberland Plateaus. The line from Washington traversed the high Piedmont and encountered constant curves and grades. This is the line where, in 1903, the Fast Mail out of Washington, number 97, hit a curving trestle on White Oak Mountain (near Danville, Virginia) too fast and found its way to lasting glory:

> Well, they gave him his orders at Monroe, Virginia,
> Saying, Steve, you are way behind time.
> This is not thirty-eight, but ol' ninety-seven,
> You must put her into Spencer on time.
>
> He was going down grade doing ninety miles an hour
> When his whistle broke into a scream.
> They found him in the wreck with his hand on the throttle,
> He was scalded to death by the steam.[17]

The line's passage over the Appalachians between Atlanta and Birmingham was not easy, and its entrance into New Orleans was on a wooden trestle over Lake Pontchartrain, almost out of sight of land in spots, guarded at all times by railroad fireboats.

The line south from Cincinnati became one of the nation's great traffic arteries, but it crossed the Cumberland Plateau. The portion from King's Mountain, Kentucky, to Oakdale, Tennessee, is known in railroad lore as the Rathole Division. Engineered in the 1880s, it was a line of curves and tunnels, spidery trestles, and steep grades that was considered one of the

most difficult railroads to operate on the continent. Further south, between Chattanooga and Atlanta, the line was not as tough as the Rathole,
but it was tough enough and was the scene of another wreck set to song,
the head-on crash of the Florida limiteds Royal Palm and Ponce de Leon at
Rockmart, Georgia, in pouring rain on the day before Christmas Eve 1926.

Other components were historic roads that echoed vanished dreams:
the South Carolina Railroad ran the first scheduled passenger train in the
United States out of Charleston behind the famous Best Friend of
Charleston in 1830 and was the longest railroad in the world—136
miles—on its completion in 1836. Had it succeeded in its attempt to build
on to Cincinnati (it tried and failed in 1836 and again in 1857),
Charleston might have become everything that Atlanta became, the transportation and economic hub of the South. Such a line might have linked
the economic interests of the West to the southern ports before northern
roads linked the West to New York and Philadelphia, which in turn would
have made the West's alliance with the North in the Civil War more prob-
lematic.[18] Another component was the Memphis & Charleston, which was
the fulfillment of John C. Calhoun's pre–Civil War dream of an east-west
route anchored at the port of Charleston that would foster a self-sufficient
southern nation.

In time these routes became the South's premier industrial corridors. I-85
was built roughly parallel to the Southern's Washington-Birmingham line.
I-75 was parallel to the Rathole except that the highway passed through
Knoxville, the railroad through Chattanooga. I-40 across North Carolina;
I-26 across South Carolina; I-81 up the Tennessee River Valley from Birming-
ham to Chattanooga, Knoxville and a connection with the N&W at Bristol,
Virginia; and I-64 to St. Louis all were industrial corridors pioneered by the
Southern. The Southern built the industrial New South.

But at the end of World War II, it was not making much money. It had
huge debt maturities coming due that threatened its solvency. It was labor
intensive. It had branches chasing antebellum ghosts, and it had to make
capital improvements, including the reengineering of key routes, notably
the Rathole. Otherwise, it was going to die.

Harry DeButts was the president. His job was to raise the capital. He
turned operating authority over to his operating vice president, D. W.
(Bill) Brosnan, a 1923 Georgia Tech engineering graduate who came to the
Southern in 1926. Brosnan aggressively set about to replace unproductive
labor with technology. DeButts did not interfere in Brosnan's work. Brosnan became president of the road in 1962, although much of his most important work was done before that.

One cannot understand the future shape of the Ameri-
can railroad system, or of American transportation, without an apprecia-
tion of the legacy of the Southern Railway and Bill Brosnan. His biogra-

pher, Charles Morgret, believes that Brosnan was the person most responsible for creating the modern American high-tech labor-productive railroad, which in turn opened up new markets for all goods and which added substantially to the wealth of the region and the nation.[19] He was also a son of a bitch. It is a story of flawed genius.

Brosnan set out to solve the railroad's ghastly inability to get cars through marshaling points. The answer was automatic yards. The Southern was a pioneer, ahead of Perlman and the New York Central. The first was Sevier Yard in Knoxville in 1951; then Norris Yard in Birmingham; Citico (later DeButts) Yard in Chattanooga; and the mighty Inman Yard in Atlanta, which opened in 1957. At Brosnan's retirement, the new yard in Macon was named in his honor. The first computerized installation was Sheffield (later Claytor) Yard in Alabama, which guided traffic to and from the Memphis Gateway. It opened in 1973. Brosnan installed CTC, first on the Charlotte Division and then on all main lines; that nearly doubled line capacity, even with the removal of second (double) track. Eventually, everything was controlled from the Atlanta Control Center, opened in 1965. It dispatched trains across the system and received data on all car movements so that both the railroad and its customers had the information they needed for effective management. The Control Center was the culmination of Brosnan's work and represented the effective use of computer technology that would elude Perlman and the Penn Central.

Brosnan knew that good track was essential to reliable service and low-cost operation. He also knew it was the most labor-intensive aspect of a railroad. In an age of rising labor costs, it was an Achilles' heel. So he set out to mechanize track work. Some ideas he borrowed, although those he usually modified. Some were purely original, and those he patented. First came the Athey ballast cleaning machine, modified by him into what came to be called Gravel Gertie, which sucked the rock ballast from under the trains, cleaned it, and spewed it back down ready to support smooth-riding track. Then came the Matissa Tamper, which automatically tamped the ballast into a firm support for heavy trains. He invented a tie-renewal machine that unspiked an old cross-tie, shoved in a new one, and spiked it in place. This required several attempts. The first machine, built in the shops at Ludlow, Kentucky, required five men to operate and replaced only 300 ties in an eight-hour day. That was not good enough. A second attempt, the Tie Master, first built at Charlotte, did the job much better. It looked like classic Rube Goldberg, but it worked. He devised the idea of prespiked, preassembled track in sections that could be transported to a work site and laid like Lionel toy track, for new industrial sidings or to repair a wreck site, for instance. He devised a system for laying welded rail in mile-long sections: a train of flatcars could carry seven miles of track at a time, could offload two rails at a time, and could simultaneously pick up the old 39-foot sections of rail.

He pioneered the use of hotbox detectors. Nothing was more likely to cause a wreck than an overheated wheel bearing (hotbox) that could sear through an axle. An infrared heat detector was installed experimentally on track near Charlotte in 1960, its data transmitted on the new microwave communication network. It caught a hotbox just before the train was about to roll over a long bridge; after that, Brosnan ordered them installed all over the system. He invented and patented the SPOT system of jockeying freight cars in need of repair so that they came to the repair crew instead of the crew going to them. It substituted labor-free "rabbits" on pulleys to move the cars for switch locomotives (with crews) and cut repair costs to less than half their previous level.

He began a marketing revolution, perhaps ahead of, or at least contemporaneous with, Al Perlman on the New York Central. The railroad would work with shippers on rates and in the design and purchase of the right equipment. Salespeople were ordered to post in every Southern Railway sales office the acronym YCSFSOYA, "You can't sell freight sitting on your ass." He forced the operating and traffic departments to talk to each other and drink with each other and get along. This was an age-old rivalry on every railroad. The traditional attitude of operating people was that real men ran trains and sissies wined and dined customers. The attitude of the traffic people was that they worked their butts off to solicit the business that paid everyone's salaries, and then the operating people lost it or bonged it up or otherwise screwed up. Brosnan used the annual officer's retreat at Almond, North Carolina, to knock heads together.

In 1956 Al Perlman toured the Southern, mostly to size up Brosnan. He and Mrs. Perlman traveled in a private car, sometimes attached to regular passenger trains and sometimes run as a special. He liked what he saw and tried to hire Brosnan away. Brosnan liked Perlman and let him use his SPOT car system without paying royalties, but he did not want to work for the Central. When the Cotton Belt used SPOT without paying, Brosnan burned them; when Perlman let it slip off to the Central's subsidiaries, the matter was more delicate, and Perlman corrected it immediately.

In 1961 Brosnan began the task of opening up the Rathole. This required some delicate politicking. The line is unique in American railroading in that it is owned by the city of Cincinnati. The city paid for its construction after the Civil War when it feared it was going to lose out to Louisville and its L&N. Leased to the Queen & Crescent and then to the Southern, it was a perennial cash cow for the city, one of the best investments a city ever made. But if it was going to remain competitive (big trilevel automobile cars were coming on line, and so were larger container cars), it was going to need a lot of capital improvement to straighten curves, ease grades, and daylight (open up) the tunnels. The city was persuaded, and the work was completed in 1963, including a new 307-foot-high bridge over the New River at Helenwood, Tennessee. Even so, the

Rathole always remained difficult. As freight traffic swelled, the Southern hastened to get rid of the passenger trains, which bottled up the line. The last trains to use it, a sad remnant of the Royal Palm from Atlanta and a sad remnant of the Carolina Special from Charleston, were discontinued in 1968. It was said that one of the reasons the Southern chose not to join Amtrak at its inception in 1971 was fear that it would route a Chicago-Florida streamliner over the Rathole and gum up one of the most intense freight operations in the nation.

Those Brosnan innovations saved the Southern and were models for the railroad industry. Two others altered the national economy. One was the rolling gantry crane on wheels or treads that lifted containers or truck trailers on and off flatcars. The other was Big John.

The Southern was slow to offer piggyback service. Loading truck trailers on flatcars was seen as one of railroading's few bright rays of hope in the 1950s, but Brosnan perceived from the outset that it was not very economical. It was slow and labor intensive to load and offload the trailers, and hauling around two sets of wheels, the truck's and the train's, was expensive. For a long time Brosnan dismissed the whole idea as foolish.

Al Perlman was inaugurating Flexivan. It reduced tare weight by leaving the trailer's wheels behind, but it required Flexivan equipment at both ends, and it required a driver to jockey his rig in a precise right angle to the railroad car at precisely its center. That was slow. Rail crews pretty much sat around and watched the loading. Flexivan was a step in the right direction, but Brosnan did not think it was the answer.

Then he saw a crane, a gantry crane, the Drott Travelift, then on loan to the Pennsylvania Railroad at Kearny, New Jersey. It could pick up a trailer, or a detachable container, and set it on a flatcar. It could do it fast, in any order. Brosnan saw instantly that this crane was the solution to piggyback's problem. It both sped up the loading and left the truck wheels at home.

In July 1959 Brosnan summoned Drott's representatives to Southern's headquarters in Washington. He wanted four of the Travelifts immediately. Nobody had yet seen what Brosnan saw in that crane, including Drott, who was not remotely prepared to mass-produce them. So Brosnan went to work on his own crane. The Brosnan crane was a giant four-legged Rube Goldberg thing with hydraulic cylinders. It straddled a track and a roadway and could lift a trailer in the air and set it on a flatcar. It did not require the same equipment at the other end. It could hoist regular piggybacks or Flexivans or containers interchangeably and did not require skill on the part of the truck driver. And it was quick; that meant that railroad crews were not hanging around watching the loading or offloading process. The original revenue installation of the four cranes was in collaboration with the Florida East Coast Railroad on traffic moving from Port Everglades, Florida, to Jacksonville, Atlanta, and Cincinnati.

Eventually, the crane became universal, manufactured in several

designs by several manufacturers. It lowered the cost of intermodal shipment to the point where it had a clear advantage over much all-highway
shipment. This in turn had a dramatic effect on who was competitive in
what markets and forever changed American patterns of distribution. As it
began to challenge the truckers in the early 1960s, truckers—led ironically
by their principal union, the Teamsters—sought legislation to stop the
railroads from taking advantage of the technology. These were called the
Hoffa laws, for Jimmy Hoffa, the Teamster head and buddy to hoodlums
who pushed hard for them. JFK and Bobby Kennedy's Justice Department
thwarted Hoffa, not so much to help railroads but to keep the nation from
being held hostage to the thug union. Brosnan hated Kennedy—thought
he should have bombed the hell out of Cuba—but he admired him for
this action. Of the not wholly implausible theories of who was really behind the Kennedy assassination, revenge by Jimmy Hoffa over the Hoffa
Laws is one of them.

One cannot understand the resurgence of the modern railroad without
understanding Big John, a 100-ton-capacity covered hopper car for hauling
grain. Before Big John, grain was shipped in 40-foot boxcars that carried
barely 25 tons and were awkward to load and very awkward to unload.
And they leaked grain, feeding millions of happy rodents along the rail
lines. Big John enabled the Southern to drop the rate on grain moving
from St. Louis to Gainesville, Georgia, for example, from $10.50 a ton to
$3.97 a ton if it moved in 1,800-ton lots. What that meant was that for the
first time, cattle in large numbers could be raised and fattened on cheap
western grain in the mild climate of the South. For the first time, the South
would not have to import meat from other regions. It meant that giant
hog and poultry farms could use cheap western grain and sell a competitive product. In the case of poultry, this development was going to change
the American diet, because chicken, not all that inexpensive once upon a
time, would become so. The Southern even built an experimental farm in
Tennessee where week-long seminars were presented for farmers on how to
run feedlots that made use of the cheap wheat, buckwheat, corn, rye, oats,
barley, sorghum, and soybeans that could move in Big Johns.

Big John had enormous implications for the grain-producing end as
well. The jumbo cars did not necessarily need heavy rail, but they needed
good track with sound rail joints and sound structures underneath
(bridges and culverts). This meant that granger branches on, say, the Milwaukee Road or the Rock Island, which could barely roll 40-foot boxcars
and could not justify the improvements necessary for the big cars, would
die. That was no big problem for farmers; they had trucks that could take
the grain 40 or 50 miles further to a main rail line. But the co-op elevators, the little towns around them, and the little businesses in those towns
would vanish. Big John and its successors would change the face of the
prairie forever. The technology of Big John was so superior it could not be

denied; change was inevitable. Big John was only the forerunner of other jumbo cars that would change the world of other commodities as well.

Having been urged by Congress to be innovative, and having devised this superior technology, the Southern was astounded when the ICC denied them permission to post the new reduced rates on grain. Big John was nothing more than a big bin on wheels. But building a car this big that did not fall apart in normal operations required a structure that was complex. Big John cars were not prohibitively expensive, but they were not cheap. Everyone who was not able to compete ganged up on the Southern—the Gulf, Mobile & Ohio, who could not afford the cars; the L&N, who could but did not feel like it; the truckers on the highways paid for by the government; barge operators on the government-maintained inland waterways; the Tennessee Valley Authority, which had done so much to bring the South into the twentieth century but which now operated boondoggle waterways and had to justify its existence. Even some large-scale grain exporters fought the Southern for a while, specifically Cargill and Central Soya, which built loading facilities on the waterways. In 1961 the ICC denied the Big John rates, saying in effect that the public should pay more for food so as not to hurt inefficient carriers.

Brosnan was stunned. His privately owned, tax-paying railroad came up with a technology so superior that it beat the pants off subsidized carriers. The whole conception of the ICC, he thought, was to ensure the lowest possible rates to shippers and consumers. That was not quite the whole story: low rates were part of the equation, but so was reasonably equitable access to markets for all producers, not just those who, by no foresight of their own, happened to be located on the most innovative carrier. The opponents' argument was that the rates were noncompensatory to the Southern and therefore designed to drive out competition in order to jack up the rates later on. Nonetheless, the technology could not be denied. Brosnan knew it. Deep down, everyone knew it.

The ICC dug in its heels. Its powers over rate making, and hence its whole reason for being, were at stake. All other railroads except Al Perlman's New York Central and Ben Heineman's Chicago & North Western sided with the ICC. Brosnan was dumbstruck. He concluded that they were so accustomed to living in a regulated environment that their competitive instincts had atrophied. There were appeals; the case went to court, eventually reaching the Supreme Court once, then a second time. For the second round, the Southern hired Dean Acheson to present its case. Acheson had been Truman's secretary of state and one of the principal architects of the cold war and the military policy of containment. Brosnan hated him—thought he was a pinko, presumably for not bombing the Soviet Union to pieces. Graham Claytor, his vice president for law, had to reason with Brosnan using logic that Brosnan would understand. He patiently explained that the Supreme Court was made up mostly of pinkos, and it took one pinko to persuade the other pinkos.[20] This convinced Brosnan. It was not until 1965 that the Supreme Court, in a decision handed down in yet a third round, cleared the way for Big John rates.[21] President Johnson specifically commended the Court, saying its decision would save $30 million to $40 million annually in consumer food prices. The ICC found a way to drag out "administrative reconsideration" for another six months. Only then did the L&N begin to buy "Big Blues."

Many believe it was the sheer stupidity of the ICC's vendetta against Big John that set in motion the bipartisan move to deregulate transportation rates that would culminate in the Staggers Act, signed by Jimmy Carter in 1980. This in turn made the ICC superfluous and led to its abolition in a bill signed by Bill Clinton in 1995.

Brosnan's initial application of technology at the Southern substituted machines for labor. Each employee on the Southern in 1947 was responsible for 391,000 ton miles of work a year. At the end of Brosnan's reign, each employee produced 1.2 million ton miles.[22] Brosnan said at the outset that it was mandatory to cut the labor force. In 1952 the newly named vice president assembled his officers at the Henry Grady Hotel in Atlanta and told them, "The Southern is on the rocks. For all practical purposes we are broke. . . . We have to replace people, I mean people by the thousands, replace them with machinery and more efficient methods. There is no other way. . . . Many will be people we respect and admire, but there is no other way."[23] Naturally, the men who were going to be cut wanted to hang on to their jobs, and they turned to their unions. Brosnan was an autocrat and resented that the workers had somewhere to turn. He came to see the unions as the principal obstacle to progress, and he hated them.

At what point Brosnan's dislike of unions became a vendetta is hard to determine. According to Morgret, it started in 1951 in a settlement with the Brotherhood of Railroad Trainmen over the use of walkie-talkies. They had protested that the use of the gadgets was unsafe, but when the railroad kicked in an extra dime an hour for their use, they signed. Brosnan asked their chairman if it was still unsafe to use them? "Cap," said the chairman, "the dime just made it safe." After that, Brosnan regarded them as lying weasels.[24]

In the beginning he instituted his changes in track maintenance or radio communication or computers by surprise. The equipment was put in place secretly and the changes were made overnight, before the unions could react (or get a restraining order). And if customers were having labor difficulties and the Southern's unionized workers refused to cross picket lines, he had Southern officials switch the cars themselves to help bust other people's unions. In disgust he withdrew from national bargaining over the issue of firemen in diesels; the result was, ironically, that when the rest of the industry began to reach an agreement in the wake of Arbitration Board 282 in 1965, the Southern was not a party to it and had to keep firemen in place. Brosnan hired retired old geezers as firemen, to show that anyone could do this silly job. He pointedly hired African American geezers to throw a little extra fat in a southern fire. One was old Willie Glass, a retired Atlanta garbageman. They showed him where to sit and where to pee. That was all he needed to know. With a big smile, he told a reporter for *Time:* "I don't do nothin', I just set."[25] Brosnan openly admired Win Thornton on the Florida East Coast and the way he broke its unions, although Brosnan never risked the big showdown on the Southern.

Brosnan was an autocrat with his own executives and constantly threatened them with firing. His brother Ray was superintendent at Greenville, South Carolina, and over a delay to number 36, a local passenger train, he wired, "The delay was about as stupid as anything I have heard in a long time. Any more such performances and I will put you to picking peas. It was most embarrassing to me." Morgret points out that Ray knew as long as their mother was alive he would not be picking peas.[26] Others did not have mothers to protect them. At the annual retreat at Almond in 1963, a subordinate, who had just presented a very fine session, was handed a drink at the happy hour; he was jostled from behind, and the drink spilled on Brosnan. Cold as steel, Brosnan said, "Get your ass off my property." After Brosnan changed his shirt and calmed down, he got the man another drink; but in the meantime, no one rallied around the poor guy because no one dared, and that indicated that the Southern Railway was in a reign of terror.[27]

There was the *Newsweek* episode. *Newsweek* did a story on Brosnan and the Southern in 1965. It was a laudatory piece about a tightly run ship, but the reporter caught Brosnan being Brosnan and reported what he saw. In the tower at Inman Yard, there was a minor delay in switching cars, and Brosnan flew off the handle at the supervisor: "Is that the way you do things? A 12-year old with an erector set could do better. I'll run you off here at the drop of a hat." The reporter saw Brosnan in his private railroad car scratch out memos, drop them on the floor, and have an assistant on hands and knees gather them up.[28] Brosnan went into a frenzy when the article came out and these details were in it, saying that it misrepresented him, although it did describe what the reporter saw. All Southern Railway advertising in *Newsweek* was summarily canceled.

There was the pistol fiasco in Canada. On an extended trip west in the Southern's executive rail cars in 1964, Brosnan was told that Canada would not allow guns. The hunting rifles were declared in advance, and Canadian customs agreed that they could be transported sealed, though if the seals were broken when the cars left Canada, there would be trouble. Brosnan did not mention the two pistols, one kept under his pillow, presumably in case the Jesse James gang broke out again. At the border, Brosnan did not quite have the guts to lie about it to Canadian authorities himself; he let subordinates do that. One of them was willing; another was not. He would have committed a crime if he had done so. No, Canada would not allow the pistols, no matter what hotshot American company the guy was head honcho of. The pistols would be confiscated and destroyed. The pistols were finally retrieved, but Brosnan was determined to fire the assistant who squealed, but was at least talked out of it.[29]

Brosnan demoted Ross Martin, the superintendent at Sheffield, Alabama, and one of his closest hunting buddies of many years. There had been some complaints from shippers at Memphis, and one from the Southern Paper Company put Brosnan over the edge. Martin tried to explain. Brosnan wired him back:

> Frankly, I am disturbed by the panic that is evident throughout your letter. . . . Records at Memphis do not support your contention that freight business has so sharply increased. Your estimates of the number of men required are ridiculous.
>
> What is needed is for you to get your bottom out of the chair, quit being frantic and sympathizing with yourself, and go to work. . . . We will not continue to tolerate the kind of failures that have been constant at Memphis over the past several years. It is your job to run this and not let the men do as they are now doing.
>
> It pains me to write you in this vein, but frankly, I am at the end of my patience.[30]

Martin soon became an assistant to someone who had been an assistant to him.

Brosnan fired Macon Tolleson, his executive vice president, who many thought might have been his eventual successor. As Morgret told the story, it blew up over a passenger delay in Washington. There had been a broken catenary[31] on the Pennsylvania Railroad north of Washington, which backed up all traffic on the corridor, including the Southern's Peach Queen to Atlanta and Pelican to New Orleans (via Chattanooga). Two cars on the Pelican developed mechanical problems and could not continue south of Washington. Sleeping passengers had to be wakened in the middle of the night and asked to change cars. Brosnan was livid and demanded that Tolleson convene a meeting of the board of the Washington Terminal Company for the purpose of firing its general manager, Bill Johnston. Johnston thought he was falsely accused. The problem was a structural failure on the PRR outside of the Terminal Company's jurisdiction. The other members of the Terminal Company—the PRR, the B&O, the C&O, and the Richmond, Fredericksburg and Potomac—seemed to roll their eyes when they heard that the Southern was demanding an emergency meeting. When the vote was taken, it was four to one and Johnston kept his job. Then Brosnan fired Tolleson for not persuading the others to fire Johnston. "Hell, he's just a weak sister," said Brosnan. "He can't do the job and is not man enough to do the job."[32]

Railroading is unique in that to get a shipment from one customer's siding to another's, it is often necessary for different railroads to cooperate. Even the hottest competitors have to do business with each other on a daily basis. The Washington Terminal affair signaled other railroads that things on the Southern Railway were becoming bizarre.

Back in 1960 the L&N had opposed Brosnan over control of the Interstate Railroad. It was said that Brosnan hated the L&N after that. He never forgot anyone who ever opposed him. Retribution was immediate if he had the power. If he did not, he had to wait, but the grudge was never forgotten. The L&N's line between Chattanooga and Atlanta was owned by the state of Georgia. It was the pioneer Western & Atlantic Railroad (W&A), the scene of the famous locomotive chase of Civil War legend between the General (commandeered by Union forces) and the Texas (commandeered by Confederates) at Dalton, Georgia, in 1862. The W&A was leased to the Nashville, Chattanooga & St. Louis, of which the L&N was the successor. The lease had been made in 1917 for 50 years. Both the W&A through Cartersville and the Southern's own line through Rome had

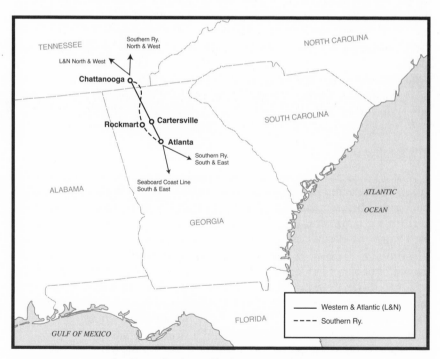

Southern Contests the Western & Atlantic

curves and grades, but the W&A was 20 miles shorter. Brosnan determined to wrest control of the W&A away from the L&N.

In 1964 Georgia had not yet thought about the renewal of the lease, but Brosnan pushed it. To sever the L&N on this critical route would severely cripple the Seaboard Coast Line–L&N system that was taking shape. What would be a competitive coup in other industries would be a diplomatic rupture in railroading. In Brosnan's view, without a competing bid, the L&N would get the W&A for a price that amounted to state subsidy, while the Southern's own line had to pay its way.

The matter went to sealed bids to the Georgia Property Control Commission. It turned out that the brother of Gov. Lester Maddox worked for the Southern. In 25 years, the brother had risen to be the senior man on a five-man switch crew, not exactly a blossoming career. Then suddenly he was named supervisor of all terminals and yards in Georgia. Lo and behold, the Property Commission threw out the L&N bid on technicalities. That attracted the attention of the Atlanta media and the legislature. One lawmaker said, "Jes' remember ol' Bill Brosnan shelled out a barrel of money for this fight and he wants some return." *Newsweek* reported that the L&N first offered to put a "Negro legislator" on the payroll (who must have been Julian Bond, because he was the only one). When that was refused, they offered Bond a cash bribe, which he turned down cold. W. H. Kendall of the L&N was apoplectic. He said that was not true. The L&N would never do such a thing. The editors reply: "*Newsweek* got its information from reliable sources and stands by the story."[33] The Southern's own directors finally told Brosnan to back off, and the L&N kept the Western & Atlantic. Over this episode, Brosnan's own board of directors began to sense that this mucking around in the industry was not in the Southern's long-run interest.

The Central of Georgia Fiasco

The Central of Georgia was a plain old railroad, too important to too many Georgia and Alabama industries to be abandoned, too poor to make the capital investment to be a great railroad. There was a good deal of affection for it in southern Georgia, the parts of that state where fortune had not smiled (the way it had on snazzy Atlanta). The Central's little streamliner, the Nancy Hanks II from Savannah to Atlanta, disgorged a crowd of people every day at Atlanta's Terminal Station who ran across the street to Rich's Department Store, filled huge shopping bags, and got back on the train and went home. The Central was the last railroad to advertise racial segregation: its timetables said that reservations would be made for white passengers only, until the ICC put a stop to it.

The Central was a major connection for the Illinois Central at Birmingham. The IC controlled the Central before the depression. The Frisco, also a major connection at Birmingham, tried to buy the Central in the mid-1950s, but it made the attempt in advance of proper authority and was ordered to put its Central stock in trust. The Southern applied for control in 1960. It would pay the Frisco $22 million for its Central stock. The application was made about the same time as the Seaboard and the Coast Line proposed their merger, and though the cases were separate, there was a sense that together they would maintain an equilibrium in the South. Tucker and Webb, in their dissent on the Seaboard Coast Line, referred to the Central case as creating a great "duopoly" and predicted that it would be much easier for the Southern and the Seaboard Coast Line to join in a "cozy cartel. Two can tango. It's much harder for three."[34]

Labor wanted attrition agreements like the one it got in the Virginian merger. The Supreme Court, in litigation stemming from the Erie Lackawanna merger, ruled that the *New Orleans* conditions were all that could be imposed as a matter of law. If the unions could negotiate a better deal privately, that was fine, but it would not be imposed as a matter of law.

The *New Orleans* conditions dated from 1952 and were getting a little creaky. They did not take into account fringe benefits—hospitalization, medical-surgical, and life insurance and vacation rights. Those were matters that had become issues in the years since. Another was protection for job losses that resulted from capital improvements *that were made possible by the merger itself.* The conditions had been difficult to implement. Specific implementing agreements had to be worked out with each lodge (local). Senior people who were going to be affected used their seniority to bump junior people, so a single dislocation might set off a chain reaction that affected a dozen people or more. The one who often got the boot was the one with so little seniority that the conditions offered little protection.

Disputes, and they were many, went to arbitration panels. They may have been the best machinery around, but they were far from perfect. In the case of those displaced by capital improvement, the burden of proving that it was the result of consolidation rather than of something else was on the employee. The employee, of course, could not afford the lawyers to carry the case further. Commission files were filled with pathetic letters from low-level workers who felt they had been let down and screwed by everyone—the company they devoted their life to, their union, and their government. These were usually handwritten, often in pencil, often with misspellings and grammatical errors, some dictated and signed with an X. Those who think only of productivity and bottom lines should read some of these letters and think about them.

Furthermore, even the possibility that these cases might be litigated was sealed off by three companion cases growing out of the L&N-NC&StL merger, which held that such cases were matters for arbitration boards, not judicial review.[35] Another decision ruled that neither individuals nor an individual union could block a merger by refusing to negotiate implementing agreements.[36] Years later, the Court would open a slender avenue of redress by ruling in the *Nemitz* case that an implementing agreement that did not meet the minimum protective standards could be litigated by an individual employee. But even that concession was wrung out of the Court by the slimmest of margins. Three justices dissented, and two Nixon appointees, Powell and Rehnquist, had not yet taken their seats.[37]

So as part of the Southern-Central case, the Railway Labor Executives' Association asked for clarification of the *New Orleans* conditions. It did not expect what it got. The commission rewrote all the protective conditions from scratch in the hope of updating and clarifying them. These *Southern-Central* conditions were drawn up with no input from railroad or labor lawyers. This was tricky business. To understand the *New Orleans* conditions, one had to have a command of the *Oklahoma* and the *North Western* conditions that preceded them, as well as the Harrington Amendment and its legislative history and the Washington Agreement. Just to mention the Washington Agreement, for example, was to invoke the entire body of decisions, interpretations, and conventions that had grown up around that agreement over 25 years. To write into a code what the Washington Agreement said, or what some bureaucrat *thought* it said, invited some very serious omissions. Nevertheless, the commission plunged ahead.[38]

The Southern would never have been interested in a declining property like the Central unless it could convert its obsolescent, labor-intensive operation into a productive, technology-intensive one like its own. But it had given early warning that it did not intend to be generous with labor. It calculated the cost of labor protection on the basis of the obsolete *North Western* conditions and was enraged when the examiner said the *New Orleans* conditions would be imposed. It claimed, rather hysterically, that this would cost it $20 million. The commission said this was absurd, that based on the number of people the Southern *said* would be affected, it had never cost any carrier that much before—unless the Southern was not telling the truth about how many were going to be affected.

After the *Southern-Central* conditions were drawn up, the Southern asked for declaratory rulings on how the commission would rule if it were an arbitration board. It was not an arbitration board and should have treated this request with caution. Arbitration boards are not bound by the rules of evidence, and it was regarded as crippling to their work if they were locked in by interpretations arrived at elsewhere. The commission said it could not pretend to be an arbitration board if it did not have the particulars of a case. So Southern offered some scenarios. Suppose it built a new classification yard at Macon, Georgia, a point served by both the Southern and the Central prior to merger. Would an arbitration board rule that this was the result of merger, entitling displaced employees to protection? Suppose it built a yard at St. Louis? Would a board say that was made possible by the savings from the Central merger?

The commission said it thought these "horror" scenarios were unreasonable. As for determining whether a certain capital improvement was the result of merger, it thought arbitration boards were equipped to handle that, "although with regard to the St. Louis yard we cannot conceive that an employee would be successful." It thought—and said this several times—that the company was unduly mistrustful of arbitration boards. "The industry generally has accepted them as a reasonable method for settling disputes of this nature, and we are not apprised of any situation where this has resulted in harassment or injustices to the railroads."[39]

Commissioner Webb was not so sanguine. He sensed that the *Southern-Central* conditions had been a mistake and that the company was laying a trap. "These opposing ideas cannot be reconciled by sprinkling comments throughout the report to the effect the applicant is unduly mistrustful of arbitration. . . . The befuddlement of all could not be more complete." And what the commission could not measure was Brosnan's hate for the unions on the Central of Georgia Railway. They had dared to cross him, to question a merger he thought was for their own good. Nobody crossed Brosnan and failed to pay. Brosnan was a hater.

And so with this unclear clarification, the day the Southern got permission to take the Central, it summarily dismissed 1,500 Central employees without prior notice, without implementing agreements, and without attempting to merge seniority rosters. To make sure the Central people did not get wind of this, officials were instructed to talk about it only through AT&T "outside" phones, never through the company's own microwave system, for fear that labor ears might be listening. Some Central people were run off the property by railroad police when they reported for work. Workers at the Central's headquarters in Savannah found the doors padlocked, and they were escorted one by one by railroad police to clean out their desks. Many who were dismissed were old and had given their life to the Central of Georgia. Many were barely literate and had no idea how badly they had been wronged. They lived in states with weak unemployment insurance systems and labor laws that generally favored management. Among those run off, along with track workers and clerks, was Allison Ledbetter, the chairman of the Central's board. He had once criticized Brosnan's purchase of specialized freight cars.[40] No one criticized Brosnan without paying for it.

Some of the Central people were offered lump-sum settlements if they signed on the spot a release waiving any further company responsibility. Some others were offered menial jobs in distant parts of the system and were eliminated from all other protection if they refused. Older men were given jobs they physically could not perform; and when they failed to perform satisfactorily, they were dismissed for cause with no further protection. No Southern employees were affected. The burden fell entirely on Central people. It was the worst case of labor relations to come out of the mergers. The Southern was a signatory to the Washington Agreement, but it chose not to honor its contract, taking the narrow view that the *Southern-Central* conditions were its only obligation.

The trouble seemed to lie in the fact that the new conditions did not include critical phrases from the Washington Agreement, notably clause 4 (requiring 90 days' written notice of contemplated changes) and clause 9 (permitting a lump-sum separation allowance in lieu of a coordination allowance). The *New Orleans* conditions included all this simply by citing the Washington Agreement. Omitting a reference to that document opened the door to an interpretation that abided by the letter of the law but not its spirit.

The unions asked the Federal District Court in Richmond for a declaratory ruling on whether the *Southern-Central* conditions were valid. Management won that round—they were upheld.[41] But the commission was instantly uneasy over an interpretation that held its new rules and the Washington Agreement mutually exclusive. So it issued a new clarification, explaining that it always assumed the Washington Agreement would be honored by those who had signed it.[42] The Supreme Court thought this was still insufficient and remanded the case to the commission with orders to clear up the confusion once and for all. Litigation continued for three years, but the final report, on November 15, 1967, was a rare instance of ICC anger toward a railroad carrier.

The Southern's own president, it said, had once testified that he would honor the Washington Agreement. The railroad then tricked the commission into clarifying certain issues while leaving others vague. It read the law in a novel way that no one in the history of protective conditions had done before. It exhibited a "callous disregard for the established rights and interests of the employees of the Central of Georgia." Straightening out the mess was going to be costly, but that was too bad. Back indemnities would have to be paid. (It was now more than four years since the dismissals. Merely contacting some of these people was going to be difficult.) Then seniority rosters would have to be merged with the Southern's, as they should have been in the first place, and that would involve a whole new category of people. Once that was done, all employees were to receive the full benefits of the *New Orleans* conditions *beginning the day the implementing agreements were signed.* As before, the Southern responded with hysterical claims that this would cost it $55 million and ruin it. The commission doubted that but otherwise did not give a damn. It said:

> Such self-serving interpretation is totally inconsistent with the purpose of railroad labor law. . . . In relying on an interpretation that almost assuredly constituted a radical departure from past employee benefits, applicants willingly assumed certain risks of subsequent judicial reversal. . . . Applicants knew, or should have known, the frailty of their position.[43]

Reflecting on the matter, Bill Dillard, who had been the Central's president and whom Brosnan liked and kept on, said the animosity toward the Southern was palpable in Savannah and all over southern Georgia. Thirty years later, he thought, it still stuck in people's craws. Graham Claytor, who would become the Southern's vice president for law just after Brosnan decided to fire the Central people, and on whose head the whole mess therefore came crashing down, said of Brosnan:

> There was no excuse for Bill's performance in the Central merger. I almost got fired for telling him "you can't do that." Because of his incredibly arbitrary and stupid action, the merger almost got blown out of the water when the ICC reopened the proceeding. The merger would have been set aside if Central hadn't been nearly bankrupt and had nowhere else to go. . . . He should have put the two rosters of employees together and over the next two or three years [most of what he wanted] could have been done. But he had to do it right away. Bang! That just made people mad, every politician, every ICC member, every labor leader livid, and they never forgot it. It took me until 1975 to try and overcome the damage.[44]

In Asheville a very talented Southern executive, Don Strench, crossed Brosnan and got fired. Brosnan cut his crews until he did not have enough people to keep the yard moving, and so he had to pay overtime. Brosnan would not tolerate overtime. Strench was snapped up immediately by the L&N, because he was very good. William H. (Bill) Moore, after 22 years at the Southern, decided he could not handle the tension anymore and left to head up the Terminal Railroad Association (TRRA) of St. Louis, which operated and switched the complex gateway. Moore was so valuable that Brosnan had to hire him back, but Moore came back only with a contract—he had the job five years no matter what. That gave him some leverage to try to reason with Brosnan that others did not enjoy. Graham Claytor had to roll with the punches, but he emerged as another stabilizing factor. The Western & Atlantic affair, the Washington Terminal Affair, the Central of Georgia affair all began to alert the board that something was wrong.

Brosnan would be 65 in 1968. That was the Southern's mandatory retirement age, although its previous presidents, Ernest Norris and Harry DeButts, had been granted waivers. A number of the Southern's top executives—and they were a very talented stable, as one would imagine—were ready to move to other railroads if Brosnan were kept on past age 65. In the early summer of 1966, the board reached an understanding that Brosnan could stay until his 65th birthday but not beyond. The former president and now board chairman, Harry DeButts, volunteered to break the news. "I was the one who hired him," said DeButts, "so I'll be the one to tell him," which he did on the way home from the board meeting in New

York on July 26, 1966.[45] DeButts put it gently, but clearly suggested the sooner the better. Brosnan dug in his heels for a time. He would be allowed to name his successor, and he chose Graham Claytor. He stepped down November 28, 1967, a date he chose in part for tax reasons. Only the *Wall Street Journal* detected that it may not have been voluntary.[46] An article there in 1976 saying that he had been dismissed early caused an uproar between Brosnan and the people at the Southern who had spoken to the *Journal* reporter.[47] Brosnan stayed on the Southern's board until 1983.

The prestigious journal *Modern Railroads* devoted its entire August 1966 issue to Brosnan and the revolution he worked at the Southern. In retirement, Brosnan served as a consultant to Iron Ore of Canada, which operates the Quebec, North Shore & Labrador Railroad (QNS&L), which moves iron ore from western Labrador to the St. Lawrence River at Sept-Iles, Quebec. He showed them how to make their railroad a conveyor belt for ore. Brosnan spent months at a stretch in Labrador, and at the peak of it brought a number of Southern people on loan to turn the QNS&L into an automated railroad. Like the Southern, the QNS&L suddenly had big labor problems. A memento of that liaison are passenger cars, veterans of the New Royal Palm, that the Southern sold to the QNS&L for its passenger train through its roadless wilderness. They were modified to put a big wood-burning stove in the middle, that being a part of the world where one takes winter seriously. Brosnan died in 1985, a deeply flawed genius but one who had changed railroading forever.

The MoPac and the Chicago & Eastern Illinois

Like the Southern in the 1960s, the Missouri Pacific was on its way to becoming a great railroad—not a pleasant one, but a great one, a kind of Southern Railway, Jr. The MoPac was two railroads in one. The original Missouri Pacific part of its system stretched west from St. Louis to Kansas City, up to Omaha, and out across the Kansas plains to Pueblo, Colorado, connecting with the Rio Grande. This was a granger railroad. Grain elevators were visible for miles on the high prairie—Scott City, Leoti, Tribune, Eads, and Chivington (named for the Colorado militia commander who wantonly massacred Black Kettle's encampment of friendly Cheyenne on the nearby banks of Sand Creek in 1864, in what was the most savage single incident of the Indian Wars). The railroad came in 1887, and soon the Scenic Limited carried white people by the massacre site to the wonders beyond— the Royal Gorge and the Feather River Canyon. The Colorado Eagle plied this line in the modern age. It was a popular train from Denver to St. Louis until new management reduced it to a nameless coach-only plug run in 1963. Nobody lives in Chivington anymore; there is just an abandoned schoolhouse. The railroad is gone, too, abandoned by MoPac successor Union Pacific in 1997, leaving nothing but the wind.

The other part of the MoPac was the St. Louis, Iron Mountain & Southern route and its connections southwest from St. Louis and Memphis to Little Rock, and on to Louisiana and Texas, known as the Sunshine Route in the old days for the great train that traveled it, the Sunshine Special. Included were routes to what became the petrochemical corridor of Louisiana and eastern Texas known as the "chemical coast" and routes to the Mexican border at Brownsville and Laredo. The Iron Mountain name was phased out in the World War I era.

The MoPac acquired preferred stock in the Texas & Pacific Railroad in 1923, and by 1957 it had 80 percent of the common stock, enough to file a consolidated tax return. The T&P was chartered to build westward to San Diego in 1871. Led by Tom Scott of Pennsylvania Railroad fame, it started with great promise but it was cut off at the pass, literally, east of El Paso, by the Southern Pacific. So it stretched from New Orleans and Dallas across the Permian Basin to West Texas with the SP as its only U.S. connection, and not a friendly one. The MoPac laid out all the pros and cons of a full merger with the T&P in a two-volume internal study in 1958 and decided it was not a good idea at that time. The T&P was finally merged on October 15, 1976, without fanfare.

The MoPac had an unusually rough receivership that began in 1933 and did not end until 1956. This was because Robert Young's Alleghany Corporation fought hard to preserve the rights of its MoPac stock bought by the Van Sweringen brothers in the 1920s. Along the way, Young pulled such stunts as full-page ads in the *New York Times* about how fat cat bondholders and crooked federal judges "trampled behind, naked and helpless, the tens of thousands of men, women and children" who owned MoPac stock.[48] Young's ad agency quit over that one, and the MoPac waters were hopelessly poisoned.

This had not stopped the MoPac from dieselizing after the war. It never met a diesel salesman it did not like, resulting in a hodgepodge fleet for which it never had the right part at the right place at the right time. Its modernization did not begin in earnest until Russell Dearmont took the helm in 1957. He was a former Missouri state senator and the chief company attorney through the reorganization. Dearmont may have been a politician, but he had a very good fix on the future of railroading. He pushed his railroad to make a commitment to containerization with a big investment in the new TrailerTrain Company. He pushed it into computerizing car records. And he was responsible for the first electronic yards, Neff Yard at Kansas City, which came on line in 1958, and North Little Rock, which followed soon after.

He also believed in the passenger train. He believed that if it died, the rest of the railroad would die soon after. That was prophetic. The MoPac was a big long-distance passenger hauler, especially on the Texas routes. The Texas Eagle, which replaced the Sunshine Special, streamlined in blue and silver and carrying "Planetarium" domes to view the southwestern sky, normally departed as two trains of between 16 and 23 cars each, one to Dallas, Fort Worth, and El Paso, the other to Houston, San Antonio, and Mexico City. Along the way, cars from Memphis and New Orleans were cut in, and cars for Monroe and Alexandria in Louisiana were cut out. As late as Christmas 1961, on December 22, the Texas Eagle left St. Louis carrying more than 1,500 people in three sections.[49] In 1962 MoPac came under the control of St. Louis magnate William Marbury and his Mississippi River Fuel Company, a pipeline, but one that encouraged the railroad's rebuilding.

The re-creation of the MoPac as a lean and taut railroad on the industry's cutting edge is really the story of Downing Jenks. He was the president of the Rock Island who was sent as an envoy to the MoPac in 1961 to inquire if it would like to merge. No, the MoPac was not interested in the Rock, but it hired Jenks to be its president. Jenks brought two of his top lieutenants from the Rock Island with him, a body blow to that railroad from which it never quite recovered. Jenks went to work on the top-to-bottom physical rehabilitation of the railroad, most notably its southern end, with welded rail and CTC. Now trains could run fast. He bought a standardized fleet of locomotives, and computers. Jenks will be remembered primarily as the man who made computers work in billing, in payroll, and in keeping track of cars. "How would you design a railroad if you were creating a new one using computers?" he asked his computer team. Historian Craig Miner called it a true "skunk works" of creative computer geniuses whom Jenks trusted to experiment on their own. The result was the Transportation Control System (TCS), which was a model for other railroads.[50]

Jenks slashed the passenger service as ruthlessly as it was ever done on an American railroad. The philosophy was to treat the public like dirt and make sure they never came back. All sections of the prestigious Texas Eagle were combined into one humongous train, sometimes 30 cars long. It was spliced in and out at various junctions until everything was late or lost and the passengers were driven off. By the end, in 1968, it was down to four cars—standing room only because the railroad refused to put enough cars on—late, waiting in sidings for multiple freights to pass, the dinette out of food, the toilets malfunctioning, mothers losing control of cranky babies because the train was so late. It sounded and smelled like a slow train through Bolivia, lacking only the live chickens. Then, getting off in San Antonio, the traveler arrived at a lovely, mission-style station with stained-glass windows—a last look at what had once been the graciousness of the Missouri Pacific–Iron Mountain, the Sunshine Route. The MoPac made it a policy into the Amtrak age to put slow freights in front of passenger trains. Amtrak had to take it to court to stop this. Jenks said of what he did to the passenger train: "Once we got rid of them, we started to make money."[51]

In a triangle-shaped area with Chicago at the apex and Pensacola and El Paso holding down the base, there were three dominant railroad empires, the Louisville & Nashville in the east (controlled by the Seaboard Coast Line), the Missouri Pacific on the west, and the Illinois Central up the middle. Except that neither the L&N nor the MoPac reached Chicago. They needed the little Chicago & Eastern Illinois to complete the triangle. The C&EI was like a three-pronged wishbone, one prong to an L&N connection at Evansville, Indiana, another to a MoPac connection at St. Louis, and a third, its own great traffic generator, to the "Little Egypt" coal country of southern Illinois. This route included what was to become a crucial link to the MoPac at Thebes, Illinois, (known as the "Thebes Gateway"). The MoPac's main freight line out of St. Louis (as opposed to its passenger line) came down the east side of the Mississippi, through the big Dupo Yard, on trackage shared with the Cotton Belt. It crossed back into Missouri at Thebes. So the Thebes route with C&EI could become a formidable southwest-to-Chicago route that bypassed St. Louis.

The C&EI was a free agent, and merger discussions of the past seldom paired it with either the L&N or the MoPac. Before 1920 it was controlled by the Frisco. The PRR coveted it as a Chicago–St. Louis link in the 1920s, but it eventually came within the Van Sweringen sphere. The Vans let it

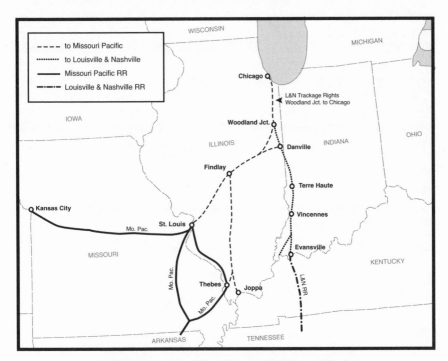

Dismemberment of the Chicago & Eastern Illinois

slip into receivership in 1933. The ICC's Final Plan of 1929 put it with the Chicago & North Western. In 1947 it had tentative three-way discussions with the Katy and the Chicago Great Western, and when the Katy backed out, it made overtures to the Monon. Later it asked to be included in a C&O-B&O-NYC combination if that should ever become a reality. What all this meant was that everyone, including the C&EI itself, thought of it as logically combined with someone else.

As small as it was, the C&EI had pulled off some competitive coups and had some trappings of the big time. It was a pioneer in piggyback. It aggressively marketed Illinois soft coal to supply 14,000 tons a day to the TVA's thermal plant at Childs, Kentucky. It did this by quoting joint rail-barge rates via Joppa, Illinois, and this caused something of a stir at the time from other railroads who wanted a higher all-rail rate that excluded the C&EI entirely. With that success it began to quote rail-barge rates via Chicago as well. For its efforts, it kept its operating ratio respectable.

Passengers knew it as the northern anchor of the Dixie Route through its connection to the L&N at Evansville. From Chicago to Nashville, Atlanta, and Florida, there was the Dixie Flyer, the Dixieland, the Dixie Limited, the Dixie Mail, the streamlined Dixie Flagler, and the lovely and popular Georgian-Hummingbird. Hugh Vierling, its general manager who went to C&EI's successor MoPac and MoPac's successor, the Union Pacific, recalled how in their heyday the Florida trains left in multiple sections and the C&EI had to borrow Pullmans from other railroads, as many as they could get their hands on. The C&EI even had its own little streamliners for the local folks, one from Evansville and one from southern Illinois, to Chicago in the morning and home at night.

The C&EI was called the all-American average railroad. If it could have raised the capital to stay technologically up to date, it might have opted to remain independent. It needed locomotives; it needed cars; and it needed bridges. Bridges were critical. Even a troubled railroad can borrow money for rolling stock; the creditors can repossess it and sell it to someone else if the borrower cannot pay. But bridges were another matter.

Several bridges on the Evansville line, notably the one over the Wabash River at Clinton, Indiana, were not strong enough to carry Big Johns or the L&N's Big Blues or the new jumbo chemical tank cars. These cars were 125 tons apiece when fully loaded. If the C&EI could not rebuild its bridges, it would lose the traffic—such as the shipments of Dow Chemical from Freeport, Texas, to Midland, Michigan, which earned a revenue of $400 a car for the C&EI. If it lost this traffic, it would be unlikely that it could ever earn the revenue to make the improvements to get it back. It would be beyond the point of no return.

The point of no return was where inadequate plant caused revenues to drop, which made even routine maintenance difficult, which caused revenue to drop more. The C&EI recognized that this could be a turning point for the railroad. It was the reason the B&O had to raise its clearances on the Baltimore–St. Louis line. It was suspected that some railroads, the Katy, the Great Western, and many routes of the Milwaukee Road, the North Western, and the Rock Island, might already be beyond the point of no return. By 1965 the C&EI was able to finance bridge improvement only by selling the bridges to insurance companies who contracted for the necessary work and leased them back. This involved an expenditure of only $3.7 million on the Wabash River bridge, for example, not a lot in terms of normal corporate borrowing. It indicated that the C&EI skated past its crisis on very thin ice.[52]

Recognizing the peril of the point of no return, the C&EI's David Matthews began merger discussions with the MoPac in the spring of 1960, and Wyer, Dick & Company was asked to make studies. Without some kind of liaison with the MoPac, the "Thebes Gateway" could never reach full potential because the MoPac would short-haul itself to turn traffic over to the C&EI anywhere south of St. Louis. With the Thebes Gateway, 14 hours could be shaved off Dallas-Chicago schedules, for example, and this would make a MoPac-C&EI route competitive with the single-line route of the Santa Fe. The MoPac was not quite prepared to buy it—a huge block of shares owned by Henry Hammack of Kansas City could be for sale if the MoPac offered. A true merger was complicated by the two classes of MoPac stock created as a result of its tortured reorganization. An exchange of stock would be difficult. Mississippi River Fuel, which controlled the MoPac, had mixed feelings. So Matthews went to the L&N. Another Wyer study was commissioned. The L&N was so sure it had the inside track that when Hammack died, it let the block of securities slip through its hands. Jenks, who had just arrived at the MoPac, understood their importance. The MoPac bought them.[53]

Did that constitute the power to control, which would be illegal since the ICC had not given an OK? When the fire got hot, the MoPac put the stock in trust but continued to buy more. The ICC's Bureau of Inquiry and Compliance and ICC commissioner Tucker thought the dealings were as shady as Frisco's dealing in the Central of Georgia back in the 1950s, but the full commission did not agree, nor did the courts.[54]

The MoPac formally applied to control. The hearings were long. The Illinois Central was not happy about a MoPac invasion of Chicago. That, plus litigation over the stock, postponed a decision into 1965. The C&EI did not collapse the way the MoPac had said it would. It bought new equipment and rebuilt its bridges and put a respectable net income on the bottom line.

David Matthews was proud of his railroad and did not want to see it swallowed up by something as cheap as stock control. Stock control did not obligate the MoPac to do anything if the going got rough. In the meantime, the MoPac said that control would bring the C&EI the blessing of superior MoPac management. Why, asked Matthews, did the MoPac just hire away three of his best young executives? Was that the superior management the MoPac wanted to give back?[55] All the schedule improvements that the MoPac touted via the Thebes Gateway were offered by the C&EI now, and southbound traffic developed just fine. The MoPac was the one dragging its heels over this. The MoPac said this was due to some obscure clause in its trackage rights agreement with the Cotton Belt on that route. So how was control by the MoPac going to solve this problem with the Cotton Belt?[56]

The L&N was electrified by the news of impending MoPac control. It began retaliatory purchases of C&EI stock until it had enough to block control. But it would support the MoPac so long as it could buy the line from Evansville to Woodland Junction, where the C&EI's Evansville line met its St. Louis line, and with trackage rights into Chicago.

So the C&EI was pulled apart like a wishbone. The ICC's approval in 1965 was predicated on the assertion that the C&EI would collapse without it. Commissioner Tucker thought the record showed just the opposite. The MoPac was required to submit annual reports on how well it was reaching the goals of control. Needless to say, they showed it was doing very, very well. Physical improvements were made. The MoPac put a lot of money into improvements on the Thebes line, believing it was either this or pay for a lot of derailments later on. Traffic via Thebes required three manifest freights each day in each direction by 1972.[57] Experiments with incentive rates seemed to work out. As the life of the Dixie Route passenger trains flickered out, most Chicagoans were unaware in 1969 when the last impediment was cleared and the L&N entered their city. The C&EI was formally merged with the MoPac on October 15, 1976.

The Illinois Central Gulf

The Illinois Central was two railroads in one. Its northern half blanketed Illinois and stretched across Iowa to the Missouri River. It was pure granger. Its southern half blanketed the Mississippi Delta to New Orleans, went as far as Birmingham on a key route to Florida, and flung an important east-west route from Meridian to Shreveport, which crossed the Mississippi at Vicksburg. It was a class act railroad. Freight traffic was anchored in coal and grain. The IC stuck with steam until the diesel became standardized and so wound up with an economical fleet of standardized black EMD general purpose units to haul an endless parade of freights. Its passenger fleet was headed by the all-Pullman Panama Limited on the Chicago–New Orleans run, complemented by the daylight City of New Orleans—the one in the song by Steve Goodman that Arlo Guthrie made famous:

Nighttime on the *City of New Orleans,*
Changin' cars in Memphis, Tennessee.
Halfway home and we'll be there by morning,
Through the Mississippi darkness, rolling down to the sea.[58]

The IC ran a big commuter service out of Chicago on an electric line physically separated from its intercity operations. Its main-line trains, including a fleet of secondary trains, were packed right up to Amtrak. I-57 parallel to the IC was completed late. It was much faster to go by train to Chicago from the university towns of Champaign and Carbondale than to drive—two hours as opposed to four from Champaign. The IC ran 18-car specials on weekends for students—old heavyweight equipment, modernized, clean, and painted the same orange and chocolate colors of the streamliners. It cost five dollars for the round-trip from Champaign, ten dollars from Carbondale. Beer cans began popping as soon as students were on board. Conga lines were an excuse to meet strangers of the opposite sex, mostly by conveniently falling in their laps. As late as Christmas 1967, local trains such as the Seminole and the Louisianne ran in two sections through Illinois because so many people still used them. Watching them roll to a station and stop at high speed, brakes squealing, sparks flying, was the quintessence of railroading.

Wayne Johnston, the IC's president in those years, belongs in the pantheon of great railroaders of the regulated era, running perhaps the most successful traditional railroad in the United States. He kept the IC abreast of some of the technological changes in railroading, including automated yards—Markham (Chicago), Nonconnah (Memphis), and Mays (New Orleans). He retired debt, cut the labor force in half, and tripled productivity. Strangely, there was little CTC. Johnston relied, like the old railroad man he was, on the IC's double track. In the old days, when you needed more capacity, you put down a second track. With the advent of CTC, double track meant extra expense with less capacity—unless every train operated at the same speed. At the time of Johnston's retirement, he was beginning to experiment with bulk rate making—"rent-a-trains" that charged a flat fee of $1 million a year to carry grain from Gibson City, Illinois, to the port of New Orleans for Cargill in a train that did nothing but shuttle back and forth as a solid unit. The ICC canceled the rate as "anticompetitive."[59]

The IC did not fare well in the merger wave of the 1960s. It was a good railroad, but its north-south route structure did not fit in anyone else's plans. The Union Pacific had held a block of IC shares since early in the century. There was talk of a UP deal, but the UP showed no interest. When other railroads demanded a probe of what they accused of being a conspiratorial interlocking web of interest between UP, IC, and the investment firm of Brown Brothers, Harriman, UP sold its shares.[60] The IC watched with concern when the Southern took the Central of Georgia, because the

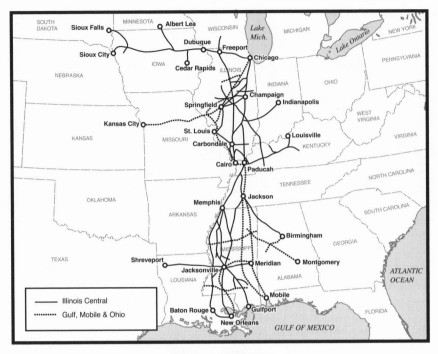

Illinois Central Gulf

Central was a key connection at Birmingham and part of the City of Miami passenger route to Florida. The IC had controlled the Central once upon a time. It was not happy at all when the MoPac took the C&EI. It offered to absorb the entire C&EI itself and was the one responsible for taking the MoPac to court over its acquisition of C&EI shares.

But the IC finally found a good merger partner in the Gulf, Mobile & Ohio. Johnston conceived the idea, although he died (in 1967) before the application was filed. The GM&O that Ike Tigrett put together in 1947 (see chapter 5) worked all right in the 1950s and into the 1960s, producing a decent net income. Its passenger trains between Chicago and St. Louis pounded high-speed rails, seen first in the rearview mirror of many a driver on the parallel Route 66 before they whooshed past. That was the closest the GM&O came to the big time, although its rate of return actually ran higher than the IC's in the 1960s, 4.55 percent to 2.93 percent in 1967, for example. But it was fragile. Down in Mississippi, where the IC served the rich delta in the western part of the state, the GM&O served the pine hills of the east, an area described (by Clyde Fitzpatrick of the C&NW) as so poor "even a rabbit would have to pack a lunch." It had no automated yards, CTC, welded rail, or jumbo cars. What historian James Lemly had said of the GM&O in 1940 was still true: it was a railroad that had to expand or expire.

This merger made a lot of practical sense. These were two north-south railroads who needed each other. Anticipated savings were modest ($12.1 million, two-thirds from office and administrative consolidation) which was odd given how parallel these two railroads appeared. One glitch was that together they would constitute a railroad monopoly in Mississippi, except for a nick by the Southern in the east and the L&N along the Gulf Coast. Mississippi did not care. What was good for corporations was good for Mississippi. The merger agreement was signed at a gala reception hosted by Gov. John Bell Williams at the governor's mansion in Jackson on December 28, 1967.[61]

The U.S. Department of Justice said it was unconditionally opposed. It produced an expert witness, Dr. George Wilson of the University of Illinois, who thought nonprice rivalry was an effective instrument of progress. The ICC was confident that regulation would keep a lid on prices, he said, but it could not compel innovation. Only competition could do that. Justice thought other modes of transportation were no substitutes for the railroads. Justice thought the savings were too inconsequential and the IC's case too shallow. The commission disagreed. It thought these two railroads, more than any others, faced the competition of barges on the inland waterways. It noted that, though overland distances of 800 miles or more were captive to the rails, these roads had average line hauls of less than 300 miles, and only one of their routes—Chicago to the Gulf—was over 800 miles.

There ensued a railroad catfight of monumental proportions, reflecting no credit whatsoever on an industry that wanted everyone to believe it could plan its own mergers. The railroads made fools of themselves over this case in that the stakes were so small compared to the bile expended. It is important to note that the Illinois Central–Gulf merger proceedings took place as the Penn Central crashed and burned (see chapter 14). The Penn Central's collapse in 1970 revealed an entire industry in deep and perhaps mortal danger, but in the IC-Gulf case, railroads were still fighting each other over the possible diversion of a few carloads of freight.

It was getting late in the merger game. The issue of whether or not the railroads were going to be restructured was already settled; the only question was how. Everyone knew by this time that merger studies were guesstimates. There were so many variables. The studies showed that six switching crews could be saved at St. Louis to handle the IC's daily 3,500 cars and the GM&O's daily 1,500 cars. The MoPac made detailed calculations to show that only one switch crew could be saved. Routing the GM&O's two to four freights a day between St. Louis and Jackson over the IC would require a new local train to run down the GM&O, because the GM&O's through freights used to handle the local business. Those making the studies had not thought of that. This was nickel-and-dime stuff. The MoPac demanded days of testimony over this. The IC had messed in the MoPac's control of the C&EI, so the MoPac messed back.[62]

It was true that in some instances, a particular shipper might not find daily service improved. Crown Zellerbach at Bogalusa, Louisiana, for example, would henceforth be served by one local train instead of two (one on each former railroad). Well, no, the merging railroads had not exactly pointed that out when they asked Crown Zellerbach to support their merger. They had stressed the better marketing potential the merged company would offer.[63] They had not made it clear to St. Regis Paper that service to their new $100 million plant on the GM&O at Wanilla, Mississippi, would involve a 27-mile longer haul via the IC. The representative from St. Regis even came to testify in favor of the merger, and then got that cold water thrown in his face.[64] And had the merging roads made specific promises that they would buy new equipment or lower rates? Well, no, they had not been specific. Promises had not been made in any other merger, either. Had they sworn on a Bible that they would never join in ex parte rate increases when they implied shippers would get lower rates? Well, no.[65] Nobody could do that.

But the Illinois Central had made sweeping and rather silly generalizations about service improvements that could not go unchallenged. It had asserted that the merger would cut transit time on traffic from Kansas City to Montgomery from 70 hours to 60 hours. That was nice, but it was purely a GM&O matter, since the GM&O was the only one that went from Kansas City to Birmingham. Service was slow because it did not even make connections with itself at Artesia, Mississippi. There was no reason to do so—it had no traffic to speak of between those points.

> Q: Couldn't the GM&O cut down the waiting time at Artesia now?
> A: They possibly could.
> Q: Well, is there any reason that you know of that they couldn't?
> A: Apparently the demands of service have not required it.
> Q: Well, why would the demands of service change because of a merger?
> A: We believe we could do a better job as a merged company by utilizing the routes and lines of a merged company.[66]

The Frisco wanted IC trackage in Birmingham. The MoPac denounced the Frisco. The Rio Grande made studies showing it would lose $835,597 a year from the merger. The Illinois Central said that was absurd. The Chicago & North Western and the Rio Grande thereupon set about to destroy each other's diversion studies.[67] The Rock Island thought it should be given access to the GM&O's Venice Yard in St. Louis. The Kansas City Southern wanted the case consolidated with other western merger cases because, in so many words, it wanted the GM&O for itself. It even went ahead and planned schedules. The Katy bitterly opposed the KCS. The Chicago & North Western said the KCS's demands were "nothing short of effrontery."[68]

The Illinois Central kept reminding everyone that the law said a merger did not have to *promote* the public interest; it merely had to be *consistent* with it. That was not much of a sales pitch. The arguments for merger in this case were no worse than in some previous cases. It was not a necessity; it would save a little money and it might result in capital improvement. There were no guarantees. One nice thing was that the Illinois Central Gulf (ICG) would be roughly equal in size to the other big southern systems that were emerging. This gave the appearance that there had been a plan for consolidation all along.

The ICC's approval was unanimous. Illinois Central Industries, the diversified holding company that controlled the IC, was declared a common carrier and subjected to full ICC regulation. The IC was ordered to take in three short lines, all with names that echoed of Mississippi lore—the Mississippi Central, the Bonhommie & Hattiesburg Southern, and the Columbus & Greenville. Last-minute legal maneuvering by the MoPac and the KCS delayed the merger for a while. It was consummated on August 10, 1972, after the Penn Central collapse. But in terms of trying to make sense of this broad canvas, the ICG merger belongs with southern mergers as a product of, and aftermath of, the mergers of the 1960s, not with the crisis of the 1970s.

But a funny thing happened, given that the railroads insisted that they alone could plan sound mergers. The Illinois Central–Gulf merger was a flop—not a debacle like the Penn Central, just a flop. The operating ratio climbed and net income fell. Track condition, even on the Chicago–New Orleans main line, got worse. By the spring of 1977, rumors were so rife that Illinois Central Industries wanted to dump the railroad that ICG chairman Stanley Hillman wrote a two-page piece in the *ICG News* to quash them, more or less. "What's in the long haul, in the merger program, or nationalization. . . . Who knows? What we do know is that the railroad is not currently for sale."[69] The ICG began to devolve almost as soon as it was put together. The first piece was the Columbus & Greenville. In 1975 on-line shippers, threatened with abandonment, petitioned for and got their railroad back as an independent. The rest of the devolution is outside the scope of this volume.

Those who contend that mergers were inevitable, or that management knew best, or that they all worked out for the best, have the Illinois Central Gulf to explain. Given the Illinois Central's solid performance in the Johnston years, probably no one could have seen it coming. What would the GM&O have become if it had found a better merger? David Morgan wrote its eulogy in *Trains:*

> The Gulf, at least, won that "G" in ICG. A letter in a reporting mark, a
> word on a letterhead—that's more than marks the last mile of Minneapolis
> & St. Louis or Wabash, or many others. . . . "G" in ICG—the late Ike Tigrett

would have enjoyed that—hanging his road's signature on the name of the carrier that tried to derail him in 1940.

We Americans sympathize with the underdog, yet we applaud the success story. For a season in railroading, we had both under one banner—and that's what the "G" in ICG is all about.[70]

The L&N–Monon

Two more items tidied up the South. At the end of August 1968, the Tennessee Central wound up its affairs and quit running.[71] It was the only railroad in Nashville besides the L&N, and Nashville was emerging as a national metropolis. The TC was broke, with no hope of reorganizing independently. The IC took the western portion, from an IC connection at Hopkinsville, Kentucky, into Nashville. The Southern took the eastern portion around Harriman, Tennessee. The L&N took the middle. Once, the little TC had played a stormy role in Tennessee politics. Now it was a memento that would not be missed.

Nor was there a place for the Monon. The Monon operated across Indiana from Louisville to Chicago. Indiana may have seemed like the land of eastern trunks, but the Monon's traffic flow was north and south. Its biggest interchange was with the Southern at Louisville. It was a natural extension for a southern carrier. In 1963 it purchased stock in the Chicago, South Shore & South Bend electric line, hoping to get access to the new Bethlehem Steel plant and the new Port of Indiana at Burns Ditch, but the C&O wanted the South Shore too and had more money. The Monon wanted to build coal docks on the Ohio River and Lake Michigan and run coal in unit trains between them, but the ICC said no. After the L&N took the Evansville line of the C&EI, the Monon clearly felt it had to get in somewhere. It approached the Southern. The Southern had just upgraded its line into Louisville and wanted to develop traffic through that gateway. Why it did not make a bid is anyone's guess. It is one of the mysteries of the merger movement.

Up and down the Monon, everything is fine,
'Cause that rootin' tootin' Monon, she's a Hoosier line.[72]

Back in 1946, when the Monon emerged from receivership, it got a new leader, John Barriger III. Barriger was one of the great railroad intellectuals of the regulated era, the advocate of super-railroads. For a few seasons he turned the little Monon into a success—even fashioned a couple of pocket streamliners out of used Army hospital cars from World War II. Hoosiers loved the "Hoosier Line." Thousands came to its centennial celebrations in 1947.[73] Even the singing radio commercials were good, which Monon offered for sale in a record album—78 rpm, of course:

All across this great big nation,
They're the epicures' sensation,
Oh—those—wonderful Monon meals.[74]

That was in a day when Indiana was full of independent railroads feeding traffic to the Monon through multiple junctions and gateways. When they were gone, eliminated by mergers, there was no place for a local road, even a nice little one that was run well. When the Southern Railway showed no interest, Monon petitioned, really pleaded, with the L&N to take it in. The L&N already had the C&EI route into Chicago, but the Monon was not going to cost much and offered it access to Indianapolis and the northern Indiana steel district. Monon, the Hoosier Line, became the Monon Division of the L&N on July 31, 1971.[75] By 1996 much of it was abandoned. That was a tragedy, because it was a reasonably good railroad that could have been a useful component of the latter-day Norfolk Southern. The L&N threw most of it away.

The L&N was a mighty railroad. It was buoyed by coal revenues from mines in eastern Kentucky. It connected the ports of New Orleans, Mobile, and Pensacola to the mighty Cincinnati Gateway. It

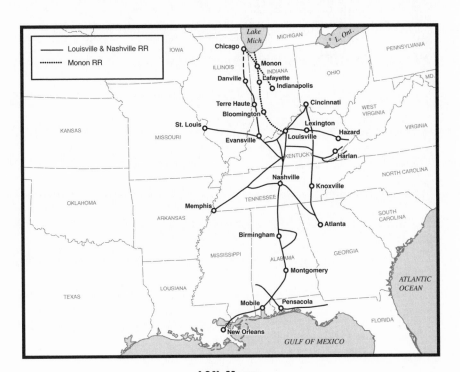

L&N–Monon

served the South's new burgeoning metropolises of Atlanta, Nashville, and Memphis. It was never flashy, always conservative, but emerged a well-engineered, physically sound railroad. The L&N would stumble in the 1970s. As Atlanta and Florida blossomed into the Sunbelt, it had difficulty supplying coal to customers south of the coalfields. It was built to carry coal north. The run from Knoxville to Atlanta was difficult, even after such kinks as the Hiwassee Loop were bypassed. But this was a problem of economic growth, not death, and there was money to fix it.

Riding the Hummingbird on the L&N out of New Orleans on a foggy winter morning was one of the great experiences of American railroading. In the diner, cooks fried up country ham and grits for breakfast, made red-eye gravy and fresh biscuits, and squeezed fresh Florida oranges. Outside, track signals flashed in the fog as the train rumbled over trestles in the deep bayous of this watery land, across Chef Menteur Pass and Great Rigolets Pass.[76] Then it rolled out along the Mississippi Gulf coast, the surf breaking in the fog—Waveland, Bay St. Louis, Pass Christian, Gulfport, Biloxi, Ocean Springs, Pascagoula. Steel on steel, rumbling through the wetness: it was a spectacular show of technology, commerce, and the elements.

After 1969 the Seaboard Coast Line began to buy the L&N stock that it did not already own. In 1974 the SCL, the L&N, the Clinchfield, and the West Point Route began calling themselves "the Family Lines." This was never a formal name, just an advertising device to show shippers there was a corporate linkage and that if you dealt with any one of those railroads, you would have access to a mighty system.

twelve

Stalemate
in the West
1963–1970

As the full effects of the industrial revolution fell into place in the nineteenth century, factory workers in the cities had to be fed. They were fed with grain from the rich prairies of central North America. The railroads that carried that grain made possible the vast division of labor that was the essence of the industrial revolution. Those granger railroads were very successful ventures.

In contrast, it was not a given that transcontinental roads were going to be financially successful. There were not that many people out west to be supplied. People on the West Coast itself could be supplied by sea. It was a long voyage around Cape Horn, but sailors were paid only a pittance and water transit was cheap. There was not much produced in the West that could bear the cost of an overland haul across the continent. That was why the transcontinental roads had to be built with a huge government subsidy—the land grants. Gross mismanagement and scandal plagued the first transcontinental, the Union Pacific, and plunged it into bankruptcy twice before the turn of the century. But then California grew. Trade with the Far East became important. This was the age of Dewey and the Battle of Manila Bay and the Open Door. The refrigerator car made it possible to sell fresh western produce in eastern markets.

Wall Street investor Edward H. Harriman perceived that the real money would be in the transcontinental haul and bought control of the UP after its second bankruptcy. He put money into it and made it a great railroad. Its rival to the south, the Santa Fe, built its own line to Chicago from Kansas City in 1888, an air-line straight as an arrow and avoiding population centers. Its rivals to the north, James Hill's Great Northern and Northern Pacific, chose the granger road Burlington to be their entrance to Chicago in 1901.

For a time the remaining grangers had dreams of building their own lines to the West Coast. The Burlington made surveys west of Denver in the 1880s. The North Western built to the very foot of the Wind River Mountains at Lander, Wyoming, and was poised to build on through South Pass. The Rock Island built west across the high plains to Colorado Springs and southwest to a connection with the Southern Pacific at Santa Rosa, New Mexico, in 1902. The St. Paul, later known as the Milwaukee Road, was the only one to complete a transcontinental line. Its "Pacific Extension" was finished in 1909. When that turned out to be a flop, it signaled all the grangers that the market was saturated and it was futile to dream transcontinental dreams any longer.

So the grangers had to be content with feeding at the trough of the Union Pacific at Omaha. The North Western was always the UP's favorite—158,000 cars in 1968. The North Western was the first railroad to Omaha from the east, arriving in 1867. It eventually had a good double-track route across Iowa and Illinois, with a bridge across the Missouri River north of Omaha carrying it to a shortcut junction with the UP at Fremont, Nebraska. It traditionally forwarded most of the UP's passenger trains to Chicago, the eastern anchor of what the world knew as the Overland Route. But in 1968 the Burlington (104,000 cars), the Milwaukee Road (76,000), and the Rock Island (24,000) all got a share of the traffic. The Wabash got most of its UP traffic at Kansas City (90,000 cars) but was a player at Omaha. And so was the Illinois Central. The IC route was 30 miles longer than the North Western and did not have the track capacity of the others. But part of Harriman's old investment empire was a 23 percent ownership of IC shares, which the UP retained through the years. This did not made the IC its favorite at Omaha, but it turned over 58,000 cars a year, and a relationship existed.[1]

But there was trouble at the mighty UP. Its corporate headquarters in New York, where the Harrimans, Robert Lovett, and Frank Barnett held sway, grew dangerously remote from operations headquarters in Omaha. Like the Pennsylvania, the UP was a railroad so proud of its traditions, with so much to be proud of, that it promoted only from within and only those who shared the corporate culture. The last of the great leaders this system produced was Carl Gray, who stepped down in 1937. His successor, William Jeffers, was a petty tyrant. Historian Maury Klein called him the czar. Jeffers terrorized subordinates, and the talented ones tended not to stick around. When Jeffers left, the best they had was George Ashby, who was in way over his head and started drinking. His UP was so unprepared for the blizzards that struck the West in January 1949 that he and his executive car had to be forwarded from Salt Lake City to Denver on the Denver & Rio Grande Western. Roland Harriman, his boss at the UP Corporation, invited him to dinner aboard his executive car to discuss "the blizzard." Ashby opted for the sauce instead, never told Harriman, and

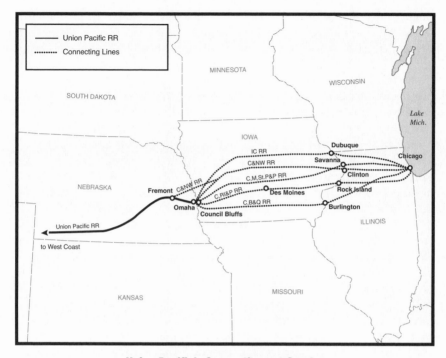

Union Pacific's Connections at Omaha

Harriman dined alone at a table set for two. A week later at a testimonial for Harriman in Salt Lake City, Ashby came late and fell asleep in his plate, snoring audibly while Harriman gave his speech.[2] Ashby was fired a few days later. Only two from the UP came to his funeral a year later.

Arthur Stoddard, who led the company through the 1950s, failed to keep the UP abreast of the industry's changing technology. According to Klein's account, Edd Bailey, who succeeded Stoddard, was better, but not by a whole lot. He is remembered mostly because the big marshaling yard at North Platte, built after he retired, is named for him. If the UP had had a healthier corporate culture in those years, the following story might have turned out much differently.

Ben Heineman and the Chicago & North Western

On the Chicago & North Western, the Williams and Feucht managements after World War II were just plain bad. Paul Feucht, president from 1952 to 1956, came from the Pennsylvania Railroad. He was dull. He required daily compliments from subordinates and never wanted to know anything bad that was happening on the railroad.[3] The North Western invested in no technology. It relied on manpower and had one of the worst wage-to-revenue ratios (56 versus an industry average of 47). It had obsolete yards. It bragged that its Proviso Yard at Chicago was the biggest in the world, but it was far too big for the North Western's needs. The property was littered with unused buildings and structures, many left over from steam operations, that were never sold or dismantled and so were taxed at full assessment. It had excessive double track and excessive branches, plied mostly by local passenger trains, of which there were far too many. Passenger losses absorbed 95 percent of its freight net income. As late as 1956, it operated one of the biggest commuter operations in the world—110,000 passengers a day into Chicago—entirely with teakettle steam locomotives. Its working capital, $27 million in 1947, fell to $1.5 million in 1955. And it had seriously deferred maintenance—about $60 million of it by 1955.

That was the year the UP summarily canceled its contract with the North Western to forward its West Coast passenger trains to Chicago. The North Western was constantly late delivering the trains to the UP. Its track was bad. Donald Russell of the Southern Pacific, the western anchor of the Overland Route, rode it, and it bounced him around so much that he said it was a disgrace. In October the UP lost its patience. The North Western said it was happy to be rid of the streamliners, said they were losing money and took track space away from the freights. In any case, it was a stunning blow to its prestige and morale.[4] The terrifying question was, Would freight traffic follow? The Milwaukee Road got the passenger contract and hoped it would get the freight. It invested a lot of money to bring its Omaha line up to speed, and it did not do it just for some passenger trains of dubious profit potential.

In January 1956 lawyer Ben Heineman, who had previously taken over the Minneapolis & St. Louis and who represented the owners of about 30 percent of the C&NW stock, walked into a C&NW board meeting and demanded representation. The upshot was that Heineman was named board chairman. He brought in the IC's ace operating vice president Clyde Fitzpatrick as president and Larry Provo, the finance expert from the M&StL, as comptroller.

Together they found enough diesels already on the railroad to end all steam operations. Provo, with help from Arthur Andersen & Company, mechanized billing and disbursements. Double-deck "gallery" commuter cars replaced some of the raunchiest old cars on American rails. These were the first trains to operate in the "push-pull" fashion with controls at both ends, which meant they could operate with equal ease in either direction and never had to be turned around. This required an investment of over $43 million, a breathtaking gamble; but by 1964 the North Western reported a profit on commuter operations. It was not a big one ($706,000), but all the others in the business were losing their shirts. The swelling complaints of Chicago commuters and the Chicago media turned to amazement and praise. The C&NW bargained with the state of Wisconsin to improve service on two passenger trains the public might actually use and eliminate 21 others that nobody used.

Surplus property was sold. Track work was mechanized. Payroll was reduced, in part simply by replacing crossing watchmen with automatic crossing gates and ending many one-man agency stations across the prairies, some where the agent did no more than 15 minutes of work a day. There were showdowns with labor, especially the Order of Railroad Telegraphers, but productivity was increased. And like Perlman on the New York Central and Brosnan on the Southern, Heineman wanted to market his product with targeted rate reductions, not just go along with ex parte rate increases. He had limited success with this, fearing to buck the rate bureaus by which the railroads fixed their prices.[5]

After 1963 Heineman made the C&NW the anchor of a diversified holding company, Northwest Industries. He engineered its acquisition of chemical companies (Velsicol and Michigan Chemical), Lone Star Steel, Fruit of the Loom (the famous underwear manufacturer), Acme Boot, and others. He was very publicly rebuffed in an attempt to take over B. F. Goodrich in 1968.

There was a hardness to Heineman's North Western that made it seem something of a bully. The long-distance passenger trains were unceremoniously axed. The train to Chadron in northwestern Nebraska came off in 1958, the Twin Cities–Omaha trains in 1959, the Chicago-Omaha and Chicago–Rapid City trains in 1960, the Chicago-Duluth trains in 1961, and the Chicago–Twin Cities trains in 1963 (leaving only trains to Green Bay and Michigan's Upper Peninsula). It should be remembered that passenger-friendly roads like the Burlington and the Santa Fe, which garnered so much public praise, lasted only a few years longer before they got out the unceremonious axes. The North Western bet correctly that it would keep the Union Pacific freight traffic. It could offer better schedules with its Fremont shortcut, so the chump Milwaukee Road got the loser streamliners and the North Western kept the good stuff.

The North Western played hardball with customers. It told coal customers in Wisconsin and the Michigan Upper Peninsula that if they did not use midwestern coal (as opposed to eastern coal shipped across Lake Michigan in barges and delivered a short hop by rail) or if the midwestern coal did not move entirely by rail (to shut out the Monon's plan to carry it to Lake Michigan docks for barge delivery), they could expect not to get much coal delivered at all. "Fitz made it crystal clear," they said on the record, referring to C&NW President Clyde Fitzpatrick, "that the C&NW is determined to eliminate the movement of coal into the [market] area via rail-Lake routes. He made it clear C&NW is not interested in hauling any coal, either eastern or midwestern moving from commercial docks on the west bank of Lake Michigan."[6]

When the North Western took over the Minneapolis & St. Louis in 1960, it shut down that little road's gateways if they short-hauled the North Western. Old M&StL customers were told to take a hike, particularly at Albert Lea, Minnesota. Giant meatpacker Hormel was not happy. When the North Western took over the Great Western (a story included in this chapter), Great Western customers were told that if the North Western did not get the long haul, they could expect lousy service. Land O' Lakes Creameries was furious, and so were General Mills and Masonite.[7]

The hardness showed up in stark relief in the North Western's massive interventions to block everyone else's mergers. In the Burlington Northern case, it put up almost as big a fight as the Milwaukee Road did. Whereas the Milwaukee had a lot at stake, the North Western had not much to lose—it only received 35,000 cars a year from the Northern Pacific in the Twin Cities and probably would not lose that. But it dreamed that new gateways could be opened up for it with the Burlington Northern at Oakes, North Dakota, the end of a fragile North Western branch, and Crawford, Nebraska, where its fragile Cowboy Line to Wyoming crossed the Burlington's line to Billings. Traffic would not actually move over these 30-mph routes with light rail and light structures, but rate divisions would be computed as if it did. That meant that the Burlington Northern would do the hauling while the North Western got the revenue. The Oakes and Crawford gateways took up days of testimony and filled multiple mountainous briefs, and, needless to say, the Northerns took it as an affront.

In the Rock Island case, the North Western did have a lot to lose, but it swerved violently from claiming that it had plenty of capital to rehabilitate the Rock Island to claiming that it was so poor it would collapse if a single carload of freight was diverted. The Rock Island vented its anger in a brief of January 27, 1969, in which it likened the North Western to Goldilocks, for whom one bowl was too hot and another bowl was too cold, and asked, Can anybody find C&NW a bowl that is just right?[8] In its merger plans with the Milwaukee, the North Western insisted that competition between railroads was no longer important—trucks were the only real competition. But in the Monon-L&N case, it said, "The shipping public wants, needs and receives substantial benefits from competition between railroads."[9] The North Western raised a terrible ruckus in the Illinois Central–GM&O merger and filed brief after brief to keep the merger tied up as long as possible. In the C&NW's own proposal to merge with the Milwaukee Road, it constantly hounded the ICC to hurry up and not wait for others to make their case. The C&NW became such a loose cannon that it got on the nerves of all the other railroads.

There is another side to the North Western's management. It is an important part of the whole picture. Ben Heineman was a high-profile civic leader as well as a railroader, a "can-do man with a conscience," said the

New York Times in 1966 when Lyndon Johnson asked him to chair a White House Conference on Civil Rights. He gave every single weekend that winter and spring to keep a dialogue between the races open. Some of the ideas that came out of it were incorporated in Great Society legislation.

In the summer of 1966, Martin Luther King Jr.'s Chicago campaign to end the infamous real estate practices of red-lining and block-busting was sputtering. King was jeered and spit on; the American Nazi Party was distributing swastikas as symbols of white power. The city seemed poised for the kind of explosion that had engulfed Los Angeles the year before and would engulf Detroit and Newark the year after. Heineman's own home was in the racially mixed (though affluent) Kenwood neighborhood on the South Side. Mayor Daley pleaded with him to cut short his vacation at his summer home in Wisconsin to chair a dialogue between the civil rights leadership and the real estate dealers. He returned to a tense city to chair explosive all-night sessions at the Episcopal Cathedral of St. James. Chicago did not explode, and Ben Heineman deserves a lot of credit for helping to steer it through a terrifying passage.[10]

In 1968 Lyndon Johnson called on him again, this time to chair a Blue Ribbon Panel on Income Maintenance, or welfare reform. The other businessmen on the panel were James Aston of the Republic National Bank of Dallas, Thomas Watson of IBM, Donald Burnham of Westinghouse, Henry Smith of Equitable Life, and Henry Rowan of the Rand Corporation. Their suggestion was a flat guarantee of $2400 for a family of four, an idea not much different from the Family Assistance Plan of a negative income tax that President Nixon would put before Congress the following year. The Nixon plan emphasized "workfare," which was popular with voters. The Heineman panel of businessmen argued that it was foolish to think business could pay living wages to individuals who, because of lack of ability or lack of education, were not productive. Heineman, like all railroaders, was sensitive on the matter of productivity. He thought people could not be left to starve and beg in the streets, but business could not shoulder an impossible responsibility. It had to be a collective, that is, government, responsibility. Neither the Heineman nor Nixon plans were enacted. As a result the country struggled with the "welfare mess" for years afterward.[11]

There were those in and outside of the railroad community who regarded Heineman as a son of a bitch—members of the incompetent management he replaced on the C&NW, partisans of the small roads his aggressive North Western gobbled up and discarded (the Minneapolis & St. Louis and the Chicago Great Western), and partisans of the two grangers that were going to be pushed aside by a resurgent North Western, the Rock Island, and the Milwaukee Road. This was a part of the world where there were too many railroads; some would survive and some would not. Heineman made sure the North Western was a survivor.

At the time the UP canceled the North Western's passenger contract, the North Western and the Milwaukee Road were discussing merger and even commissioned Wyer to see what was feasible. But after Heineman took over, the Milwaukee Road canceled talks. It said it had no idea that the North Western had so much deferred maintenance, which the Wyer studies uncovered, although a ride on just about any North Western train would have told them as much. One suspects that Heineman's style was too close to the fast lane for the hidebound Crowley management on the Milwaukee, whose chief goal in life was self-preservation. In 1957 there was a rumor that talks were revived, but Heineman said, "It's dead. I have no interest in it."[12]

In 1959 the Milwaukee opened negotiations with another granger road, the Rock Island. The Rock Island's Downing Jenks was the instigator. That winter, the two roads hired Coverdale & Colpitts to make operating studies and R. W. Presspritch to make financial studies. In 1961 Jenks left the Rock Island to head up the Missouri Pacific, and talks ended. There was a rumor that the two roads' biggest creditors, Metropolitan and Equitable Life, were pushing for a three-way merger of the North Western, the Milwaukee, and the Rock Island. Metropolitan's Harry Hagerty wanted action

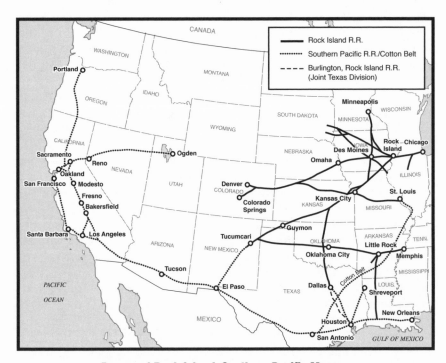

Proposed Rock Island–Southern Pacific Merger

and was tired of management's diddling. The Milwaukee Road–North Western merger talks were resumed, this time with no comment from either management. Patrick Lannan, a Milwaukee Road investor and director, said he would fight the financial terms that the insurance companies were attempting to dictate.[13]

On June 19, 1962, the Rock Island's president, R. Ellis Johnson, announced that he had spent the last five days discussing merger with Donald Russell of the Southern Pacific. A map of the proposed system was breathtaking in its geographic good sense. Using the emerging Port of Los Angeles as a base, the route fanned out like a cornucopia—the SP's own line to Houston and New Orleans, and the Rock's routes to Memphis, St. Louis, Chicago, and the Twin Cities. The Golden State Route from Los Angeles to Chicago over the two roads, the lowest crossing of the Continental Divide of any American railroad, without a single curve for 72 miles between Guymon, Oklahoma, and Dalhart, Texas, would reach its full potential at last.

That September the Union Pacific announced that it had joined the Rock Island–Southern Pacific talks. Johnson had no comment, except to say the Rock Island was cooperating fully with the Southern Pacific. On May 13, 1963, the Union Pacific announced that it would seek to merge with the Rock Island and, upon receiving approval, would sell the portions of the Rock Island south of Kansas City to the Southern Pacific. The story had a San Francisco dateline (the SP's headquarters).[14] The Rock Island stock, which had been in the $20 range, hit $26 and was the second most active issue on the New York Stock Exchange that week.

The Union Pacific's Choice

Thus began the most protracted and tangled railroad merger case of all time. It involved a test of wills between the Union Pacific and the North Western, followed by recriminations. The ICC made a futile attempt to straighten out the mess, but it took too long to do this. What could have been hammered out with common sense in an afternoon took 13 years. The railroads denounced and rejected the commission's efforts, and the whole idea went into the dumpster. Instead of seeing this as the result of a death struggle between the Rock Island and the North Western, everyone was content to blame the ICC. The collapse of the Rock Island merger led ultimately to the death and destruction of the Rock Island Railroad. It was a profoundly sorry exhibition by just about everyone.

The announcement of a UP–RI merger was a firebell in the night for the North Western. Its bread and butter was the UP interchange at Fremont, Nebraska. If it lost that interchange, it was as good as dead. In 1963 it was a viable railroad. It had aggressive management, its main lines were in reasonably good shape, and it was determined to fight for its life. So it made

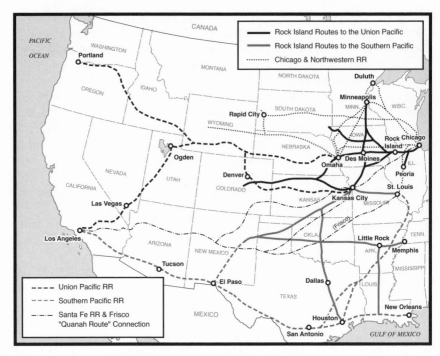

Union Pacific–Rock Island Proposal

a counteroffer to Rock Island stockholders, a package of C&NW collateral trust bonds, C&NW common stock, and five dollars in cash for each RI share. This was a most attractive deal. If you were a Rock Island stockholder who cared about the long-term viability of your railroad, the UP offer was the most promising. But if you were a speculator and cared only about short-term bucks, the C&NW offer was better. The C&NW did not have the earning potential of the UP, nor was it seeking a merger, only stock control, but it said this was preliminary to an eventual three-way merger that would include the Milwaukee Road.

Col. Henry Crown, the Rock Island's largest stockholder, liked Heineman and had tried to recruit him to head up the Rock Island. But he said he had given his word to the UP and accepted their offer and could not back out on this commitment. Asked if the RI would consider a merger with the C&NW, RI director Roy Ingersoll said, "We are not interested in mergers with someone whose future is so uncertain."[15] But in the short run, the North Western's offer was worth more than the market price of RI stock. It would likely be enough to keep the UP from getting the required two-thirds vote of RI shares.

The Union Pacific placed advertisements in a number of papers on July 26, 1963, suggesting that the North Western could not afford to make good on the offer it had made, since it could involve as much as $15 million in cash that it did not have. This amounted to a solicitation of proxies and had not been cleared by the Securities & Exchange Commission (SEC); the UP was sharply reprimanded. The UP hired Wyer, Dick & Company to study the condition of the Rock Island, and the report was horrendous. Shippers said RI service was a day slower than other lines. Congestion at major yards was serious. Tight curves and annoying grades rendered the Kansas City–St. Louis line out of all competition. Rehabilitating the Rock was going to cost a bundle. The UP had the money, but was it worth it? For whatever reason, the UP had decided it *wanted* the Rock Island.

Rock Island stockholders met for a vote in November 1963. A UP internal report indicated that only 47 percent would vote for the UP offer. Moments before voting was to begin, the UP rushed in with a restraining order. With victory in its grasp, the North Western committed a terrible gaffe. It failed to register with the SEC a pamphlet mailed to Rock Island shareholders pointing out the advantages of the C&NW offer. The pamphlet had been prepared by Pierre Bretey, the respected railroad securities expert at Hayden, Stone & Company, but it constituted an illegal solicitation of proxies. Heineman was described as "shaken" and seemed genuinely concerned that it would leave the impression that the C&NW had acted dishonorably. There was nothing for the Rock's shareholders to do but go home.

The Rock Island's R. Ellis Johnson thought most of the RI's big shareholders would have voted for the UP at the last minute. Almost 33 percent of all Rock Island stock was held by directors—with Colonel Crown holding the most. It was not until January 1965 that a vote was finally taken, and the UP won with 78 percent of the shares voted for it. The application went to the ICC, and hearings began on May 4, 1966. This was nearly three years after the first announcement. It had taken that long for the railroads themselves to sort the matter out.

And they had not sorted it out at all:

—The Milwaukee Road could not tolerate a UP line into Chicago any more than the North Western could. It had been starkly disappointed that the UP had sent it so little freight after it took the UP's passenger trains; but hope still burned, and it could not afford to lose what it had. It backed the North Western.

—The Santa Fe could not tolerate a Southern Pacific entry into Kansas City or Memphis if it should get the RI's southern half. It supported the North Western on the condition that *it* would get the RI's southern half.

—The Frisco could not tolerate the loss of its interchange with the Santa Fe if the Santa Fe should get the RI's southern half, so it backed the Southern Pacific.

—The Texas & Pacific–Missouri Pacific could not tolerate the loss of the SP interchange at El Paso if the SP should get the Rock Island, so it backed the North Western and demanded trackage rights on the SP all the way to the West Coast.

—The Rio Grande could not tolerate any further encirclement by the Union Pacific and demanded "affirmative relief"—the right to buy the Rock Island's lines from Denver to Omaha and Kansas City, including the Armourdale Yard complex at Kansas City.

—The Burlington could not tolerate the thought of Southern Pacific ownership of the line it owned jointly with the Rock Island between Fort Worth, Dallas, and Houston, now called the Joint Texas Division, formerly called the Burlington–Rock Island Railroad. It demanded full control of the Joint Texas Division.

—The Kansas City Southern could not tolerate further encirclement by the Southern Pacific–Cotton Belt and demanded routes over the SP to Houston and Dallas–Fort Worth and over the Rock Island to Chicago. It began to plan schedules and solicit traffic for these new services.

—The Missouri-Kansas-Texas, the Katy, could not tolerate any diversion by anyone and demanded inclusion in the plans of anybody who had money.

In the middle of all this, the Missouri Pacific bought three million shares (8%) of the much larger Santa Fe and asked for stock control.

Heineman offered to sell the entire C&NW to the UP. He offered to buy the entire UP in a deal that would leave UP stockholders in control of the C&NW. There were huddled meetings throughout the rest of 1966 and into 1967 between Heineman and Frank Barnett of the UP. Robert A. Lovett attended many of them. He and his father were partners of the UP's Harriman family. He and Averell Harriman were two of the foreign policy advisors to Harry Truman known as the Wise Men, the architects of the diplomatic and military policy of containment against the Soviet Union after World War II. Now he represented the investment house of Brown Brothers, Harriman. Ernest Marsh and John Reed of the Santa Fe attended some meetings, as did Benjamin Biaggini of the Southern Pacific. The best they could come up with was a four-way control of the Rock Island, which satisfied no one.[16] So the railroads were deadlocked, and the Rock Island was dying.

The Rock Island

What was this railroad that became the vortex of the most disastrous merger case ever? Huddie Ledbetter (Leadbelly) fixed it in the national folklore:

Oh the Rock Island Line, she's a mighty good road.
Oh the Rock Island Line, she's the road to ride.
Oh the Rock Island Line, she's a mighty good road,
And if you want to ride her,
Got to ride her like you find her,
Get your ticket at the station on the Rock Island Line.[17]

The Rock Island had promise in the beginning. It was the first railroad to bridge the Mississippi (in 1857). Then growth slowed. It was the second to reach Omaha, arriving on May 11, 1869, the day after the first transcontinental was completed. It served population centers at Rock Island–Moline–Davenport and at Des Moines but was hill-and-dale across western Iowa, where the North Western and the Milwaukee followed river valleys. In the late nineteenth century, it built across the recently conquered high plains to Colorado Springs and south to help open the Indian Territory (Oklahoma) for white settlement with a line following the Chisholm Trail. It pushed to a connection with the Southern Pacific in New Mexico in 1902, making it a through route to southern California that would be known as the Golden State Route for the famous train that traveled it.

In the year the Golden State Route was completed, the Rock Island came under the control of the brothers William and James Moore and their partner, Daniel Reid, what came to be known as the Moore-Reid Syndicate. They had previously put together Diamond Match (the kitchen match trust), Nabisco (the bakery trust), American Tinplate (the tin can trust), and had had a hand in the creation of United States Steel (the steel trust). By some lights, these were brilliant moves, for they permitted the integrating of new manufacturing technology and the stable business environment that could risk investment in that technology. They also aroused public animosity over the accumulation of monopoly power without public accountability.

At the Rock Island, the Moore's last big venture, their business acumen seemed to leave them. They added routes helter-skelter, notably to Memphis and deep into Louisiana through country that would be third-world poor for another 40 years. They loaded the railroad down with debt to speculate in the stocks of the Frisco and the Alton Railroads. These were eventually lost, and the Rock Island had nothing but debt to show for it.

What they did not do was reengineer the Rock into a modern railroad. This was the time when pioneer railroads rebuilt themselves into modern arteries of transportation. Pioneer railroads built as cheaply as possible, pretty much to the contour of the land. By the turn of the century, the crush of traffic was pouring in on them from the maturing industrial economy they helped create. They eliminated curves and grades and rebuilt bridges for heavier, faster trains. The window of opportunity was brief. It began about 1898, at the end of the depression that began in

1893. It ended sometime before World War I, some think because of regulation that took away railroads' ability to price their product (see chapter
1). The Rock missed out on this. The Moore-Reid regime was the subject of
federal investigations and legal challenges and was a good part of the reason that the public demanded regulation.[18]

That was how the Rock Island missed becoming a great railroad. When
the Southern Pacific took control of the St. Louis–Southwestern (better
known as the Cotton Belt) in 1932, it gave the Southern Pacific its own
route to eastern connections (at St. Louis and Memphis). This vastly reduced the flow of freight over the Golden State Route, sealing the marginal status of the Rock Island. Nevertheless, the Rock Island was an important railroad. It served vital routes and meant life or death to many
customers, especially on the plains. It ran cross-country trains and booked
passengers with through steamship tickets to Honolulu and Shanghai. It
was stuck in a twilight zone—essential, but on a fringe.

In the middle of the depression, bankrupt, the Rock Island's general
manager, John Dow Farrington, wheedled enough money out of the
trustees to buy silvery Rocket streamliners. These pleased the public and
boosted the company's own morale. War traffic was heavy, especially on
the Golden State Route to California. Farrington used wartime profits for
major construction projects after the war. The most famous was the high
bridge over the Cimarron River near Liberal, Kansas. It was 1,300 feet long
and 100 feet above the water. It eliminated a tortuous descent into the
floor of this gash on the plains, eliminated the danger of washouts, and
eliminated the need for helpers. Samson of the Cimarron, it was called. To
this day, travelers on U.S. 54 stop to admire it.[19] There were three major
line realignments on the Chicago–Kansas City line in the vicinity of El-
don, Iowa, that reduced mileage, curvature, and grades and permitted passenger train speeds to rise from 50 to 90 mph and freight train tonnages
to triple to 6,500 tons without helpers. CTC was installed on the route
from Kansas City to Fort Worth and on the main line across Illinois from
Rock Island to Chicago. The Rock Island built a testing lab at the 47th
Street Yard in Chicago, similar to Al Perlman's on the New York Central. It
built new yards, Armourdale at Kansas City and Silvis, near Rock Island,
Illinois. At Silvis, trains from Denver, California, Texas, and the Twin
Cities were broken down, regrouped, and preblocked for connecting rail-
roads out of Chicago.[20]

It is sometimes forgotten that Rock Island trains such as the Twin Star
Rocket (Minneapolis–Kansas City–Dallas–Houston) and the Rocky Mountain Rocket were fast and popular even into the late 1950s. On a summer
day in the midfifties, the Rocky Mountain Rocket left Denver with nine cars
and picked up five more at Limon that came out of Colorado Springs, all of
them packed with festive crowds fresh from mountain holidays. This train
ran on the track one sees driving along I-70 into Denver. The railroad is

plied only by a local freight of the short-line Kyle Railroad now, and the target signals are blind. But in those days, it ran like the wind across the high plains, the clickity clack of jointed rail, the classic doppler effect of highway crossing signals as the train raced through the farm towns—Stratton, Burlington, Kanorado—squealing to a stop at Goodland, Kansas, at twilight.

The postwar glow did not last long enough, and mistakes were made. One was to buy diesels from just about every manufacturer in just about every model. There were no standardized parts. The Rock Island was notorious for bizarre lash-ups of mismatched motive power in varying states of disrepair that even a casual observer could tell was a sloppy operation. It was the outward sign of an inward mess. There just were not many places the Rock went that some other railroad did not get to faster and straighter. It was not as though it had no purpose to serve. The RI carried seven billion more ton miles in 1970 than it had in 1960, which suggests that there was important work for it to do. But it could not earn enough to maintain itself. In 1964 it recorded a small net income after fixed charges. It was the last one the Rock Island Railroad posted—ever.

Henry Crown had bought bonds of the bankrupt Rock Island in 1946 at a fraction of their face value and had seen them triple in value when the road was reorganized. He effectively controlled it. He was an American rags-to-riches classic, the son of Arie Crown, who fled Lithuania's anti-Semitism for Chicago and worked the rest of his life in a sweatshop. Arie's sons got into the sand and gravel business in the 1920s, and Henry built his business into Material Service Corporation, the biggest supplier of construction materials in Chicago. In the tough world of Chicago's political machine and unions, Material Service could play with the toughest, and it made millions. Crown volunteered his services in World War II and was commissioned a colonel in the Army Corps of Engineers. Forever after, he was called "colonel." After the war, in addition to the railroad, he invested in Hilton Hotels on the eve of Hilton's great expansion that made it the world's largest hotel chain. He bought the Empire State Building in New York. In 1960 he merged his Material Service Corporation into General Dynamics. He arrived as the dominant force of the giant defense contractor just as the great Kennedy era weapons buildup began. Crown was instrumental in bringing in Roger Lewis as General Dynamic's CEO. In 1966 Lewis redeemed Crown's bonds, forcing the 70-year-old tiger out. Four years later, Crown had bought enough General Dynamics stock to go on the board and fire Lewis.

At some point while the Rock Island–Union Pacific merger negotiations droned on, Crown and his clique on the RI board decided not to put money back into the railroad. They assumed that the Union Pacific would soon be in control and would start rebuilding it from scratch to its own specifications. In the meantime, it was important for stock exchange purposes to make the Rock's finances look as cosmetically good as possible.

The concept of the "point of no return" was introduced in chapter 10 in regard to the deteriorating state of the Pennsylvania Railroad in the 1960s. Cutbacks in maintenance brought about slow orders—railroad lingo for speed restrictions—on bad stretches of track. Cutbacks also brought about delayed trains and reduced productivity, which caused customers to desert and costs to rise, which made it less likely maintenance deficiencies could be made up and more likely they would get worse, leading to yet another downward spiral. Eventually, costs would rise so high and revenues fall so low that the railroad could never pull itself up again. The Pennsylvania Railroad did not quite reach the point of no return before its merger. The concept came up again in chapter 11 as the Chicago & Eastern Illinois Railroad hurtled toward, but did not reach, the point of no return.

The Rock Island was headed squarely for the point of no return. It had 500 miles of track under slow orders in 1967. it had 2,300 in 1970. Trains lurched and swayed violently. Rolling stock was in disrepair and locomotives inoperable. This was a railroad that still carried 35,000 commuters a day into Chicago and the situation could obviously not continue.

The Chicago Great Western

On July 1, 1968, the Chicago & North Western took over the Chicago Great Western, the Corn Belt Route. There was little fanfare and little mourning. The Great Western had been one railroad too many from the start, having been conceived largely as a rate breaker to the established lines. The Deramus management in the 1950s proved one thing: running only one humongous train a day that was held out for more cars and did local switching along the way was *not* the way to cut labor costs. It was awful service and shippers deserted. Revenues declined every year after 1956, but costs rose. It had one important asset. It developed and served the Roseport Industrial Park south of the Twin Cities, and that produced a good volume of valuable traffic.

By the time of the North Western's offer, the CGW was not insolvent, but it was approaching the point of no return—"serious financial problems with an inability to solve them internally" as the court would put it. Aware from at least 1960 that it probably could not survive independently, it sought merger partners—first the Rock Island; then a favorite connection, the Soo Line (which the Great Western ultimately rebuffed); then the Frisco. No one was interested. The C&NW's offer in the summer of 1964 was a happy surprise.

There were local issues to settle. Employment at Oelwein, Iowa, site of the Great Western's shops, was going to be hit hard. It was the road's operational center and the point where its Chicago-Omaha and St. Paul–Kansas City routes crossed. But the real opponents with deep pockets who knew how to take their case to the ICC and the courts were other

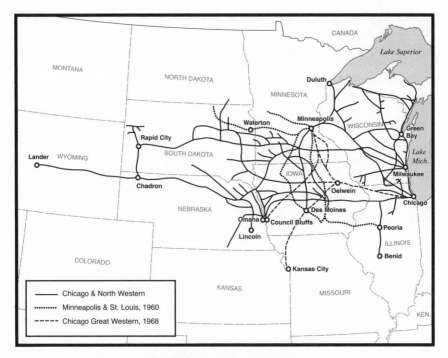

C&NW–Chicago Great Western

railroads, in this case the Soo Line. The CGW had favored the Soo Line, particularly on traffic bound north and west out of Roseport. How much of this would be lost was a matter of dispute; the C&NW was not necessarily hostile to the Soo Line, not north and west of the Twin Cities. Diversion studies reached probably their peak of absurdity in this case, as the Soo Line hysterically claimed that it would lose $1.7 million annually and the C&NW said, by its scientific calculations, that the sum could be no more than $13,000.

The ICC approved the merger in 1967 but threw up its hands over the diversion studies and simply said the truth must lie somewhere in between.[21] The Soo Line went straight to court, a very friendly court, it turned out. The court said it was not its place to substitute its judgment for the commission's, even if it thought the commission's judgment was bad. It then proceeded to substitute its judgment for the commission's. It said the Great Western case should have been combined with the Rock Island case. It thought Soo Line employees were entitled to job protection for layoffs that this merger might cause them, even though this merger did not involve the Soo Line. It found a precedent it liked better than the one the commission cited. It thought the Soo should have access to Roseport. Finally, it said the commission should come to grips with diversion

claims and not just throw up its hands.[22] So the case came back on re-
mand. The commission complained testily and thrashed around the diversion studies some more, though with no particular resolution. It accepted
the court's judgment in place of its own.[23]

The Great Western disappeared into the fold of the North Western. The
North Western had Roseport and a line to Kansas City. Over the next
decade, most of the rest of the Great Western was abandoned and the
track pulled up.[24] The last revenue train ever to run north from Oelwein
pulled out on November 6, 1981. Later, the North Western got a better entrance to Kansas City, and the Great Western's Kansas City line was pulled
up as well.

At the end of the nineteenth century, the CGW's builder, Alpheus B.
Stickney, positioned his railroad as "the people's railroad," meaning a rate
cutter that kept the rates of the big monopolies in check. This was at the
height of the "railroad question" (see chapter 1), and Stickney was glorified
as the honest working farmer's railroad man. Whether Stickney did it out of
altruism or because he had an inferior railroad and did not have a choice
has been debated ever since. But now the people's railroad was gone.

Those who earned a living from the Great Western over the years num-
bered in the thousands. Company C of the Thirteenth Railway Engineering Battalion, which helped keep the French railroads open in the terrible
winter of 1917–1918 was a Great Western unit. That same winter, national
security required the posting of the Illinois National Guard at the Great
Western's Winston Tunnel in the wilds of Jo Daviess County, to guard it
around the clock from German sabotage. The Great Western's little stations across Iowa and Minnesota were the front door, the window on the
world, to dozens of prairie towns in the days before improved roads and
television and the Internet. The sight of its monster 2-10-4 Texas-type
steam locomotives blasting a freight up the heavy grades out of the Mississippi Valley west of Dubuque was as pulse-pounding as anything in railroading.[25] The loss of the Great Western was catastrophic to Oelwein. Elsewhere, there would be little physical evidence that it ever existed.

The Burlington Northern

On M-Day, April 27, 1966, the ICC approved the Penn-Central, approved the New Haven passenger discontinuances, and denied the Northern Lines merger. "Chalk up one thoroughly constructive action [on Penn-
Central]," wrote *Fortune*, "and chalk up one outrageously bad decision, the
six to five rejection of Burlington Northern."[26] As we now know, the Penn
Central decision was going to end up a debacle. As for the Burlington
Northern decision, good or bad, the merger had powerful adversaries in
the private sector. This was not a case of stupid government; it was government trying to referee violently opposing private forces. The Northerns

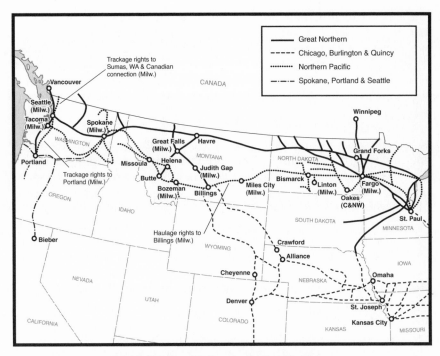

New Gateways for the Burlington Northern

just never made their case as to why profitable railroads had to merge to save themselves, while they excluded the one railroad in their territory that most needed to be merged—the Milwaukee Road.

So the Northerns went to work to make deals. They approached the Milwaukee Road and the North Western with an offer to open up the gateways and grant the trackage rights they swore they never would. The North Western got the Oakes, North Dakota, gateway. The Milwaukee Road got 11 gateways across the west,[27] plus trackage to Portland and to Sumas, Washington, on the Canadian border, and the right to serve Billings. Labor got an attrition agreement, something the Northerns swore they would never grant. All their antagonists came on board except the states of Minnesota, Montana, and Washington and the U.S. Department of Justice. Four ICC commissioners originally opposed to the merger left the commission, including the merger's two most intense opponents, Tucker and Webb. Perhaps a new commission would now change its mind.

It did. The case was reopened. The final report of the second go-round retraced the same ground as the first, approving what had previously been disapproved. The lesson? If one commission turns you down, wait for another. If your budget for legal and regulatory affairs is big enough, you can stick it out until you get what you want. Only two commissioners, Paul

Tierney and Virginia Mae Brown, remained unconvinced. Both believed that despite what the Milwaukee Road was now saying, a few gateways were not going to turn it into a viable railroad. At least, said Tierney, we should wait until the other western mergers are decided. That did not mean combine the cases, just wait. Keep options open. But Tierney and Brown stood alone. The Northern Lines merger was approved on November 30, 1967.[28]

There were petitions for reconsideration. The Northern Pacific Stockholders Protective Committee and the city of Auburn, Washington, filed suits and sought restraining orders. Both were turned down. On the morning of May 10, 1968, when all the legal roadblocks were supposed to be cleared, company operators began answering phones with a cheery "Burlington Northern." That stopped at 10 A.M., when Chief Justice Earl Warren issued a restraining order on behalf of the Justice Department. John Budd of the GN and Louis Menk, who had moved from the Burlington to the NP, were sitting with the final papers in front of them. Menk complained to the press that bureaucratic delays were costing the railroad $100,000 a day. Later, he clarified that what he meant was that the railroad was not getting started on the work to achieve merger savings that might in the future save it $100,000 a day. Most of the papers picked up the story the first way and never got around to the clarification.

Delay was all that was accomplished. The merger was upheld, first by a three-judge panel, then on February 2, 1970, by the Supreme Court by a vote of 7-0.[29] It was 14 years after merger planning began, 9 after it went to the ICC. The Burlington Northern began operation on March 2, 1970. The industrial design firm of Lippincott & Marguiles created new graphics for it, a big letter *B* with an *N* squirreled in the middle. It was the weakest of the anagram emblems that came in the wake of the Canadian National's striking CN "wet noodle" and weaker than the powerful heraldry of the GN's mountain goat or the NP's yin-and-yang monad. Happily, the clumsy name Great Northern Pacific & Burlington Lines was dropped. A new colossus had arisen in the West. The BN proudly introduced itself to a national public with a special advertising supplement in the Sunday *New York Times* for September 21, 1970.

Ultimately, the BN merger was a success, but it stumbled out of the gate. It profited from the experience of the Penn Central and planned carefully, not just cosmetically. Executive positions, and the people to fill them, for example, were designated in advance, and that seemed to give jealousies time to cool before it really mattered. In *Fortune,* Rush Loving, Jr., referred to the BN as the "merger that worked" but pointed out that very little implementation planning had been done in 1968 at the time Chief Justice Warren issued his stay. If the merger had been slammed together then, it would likely have ended in disaster just as the Penn Central did. Even so, the operating ratio climbed and shippers complained. One shipper came in person to the 1976 shareholders meeting and said his freight rates had doubled and the railroad was seldom able to supply cars on time.[30] This stagnant performance was a shock that culminated in top-level management's being bundled off to an isolated resort at Wickenburg, Arizona, and told to get a grip on themselves and their jobs before there was a disaster. Menk warned them that they would be held accountable.[31] In 1973 the ICC and the SEC launched investigations into the extent to which shareholders' equity had been diluted by the undermaintenance of track.

Louis Menk, by this time CEO, and Robert Downing, who was chief operating officer, were stung. The company was investing 16 cents of every revenue dollar in plant and equipment.[32] Two new technologies were consuming capital. One was new hopper cars for hauling grain—jumbo 100-ton-capacity air-slide cars like the Big Johns of the Southern Railway. These cars were hauled in unit trains that moved from one or two loading points as a solid train through to destination. That rendered obsolete granger branches where a car was picked up here, a car there. The BN was disinvesting in them, which is what the ICC and the SEC saw in their investigations. Most of those branches would be abandoned in the 1980s. But in the meantime, air-slide cars had to be bought. Heavy locomotives had to be bought. Rail had to be welded into continuous strips because trains that heavy would knock old jointed rail out of line in no time. Each of these trains carried the equivalent of 400 semitrailer trucks. More and more of them moved west, to West Coast ports for shipment to Asia and the Soviet Union. This was the same problem the L&N had with coal—a railroad built to haul it north now had to satisfy a growing demand to the south. The Northerns traditionally hauled western grain east. Now they had to add capacity over the Rockies and the Cascades to move it in the opposite direction.

The other project that consumed even more capital than the grain cars involved the movement of vast quantities of low-sulfur coal. This coal was in eastern Montana, near the ex-NP, and in the Powder River Basin of Wyoming, around Gillette on the Burlington's Kansas City–Billings line. Its low-sulfur composition resulted in less air pollution, which made it an ideal fuel for steam plants for generating electricity. But it was a long way from markets. To keep the business on the rails and forestall the construction of a coal slurry pipeline required the purchase of 100-ton coal cars in 100-car unit trains, heavy locomotives, opening up tunnels in northwestern Nebraska and southwestern South Dakota, the reduction of curvature and grades, and the installation of heavier welded rail and CTC. Ultimately, it would require the construction of a new line of railroad, 76 miles between Gillette and Orin, Wyoming.

The first unit coal train operated in 1967 for Minnesota Power & Light and required the cooperation of the as yet unmerged GN and NP. It originated at Forsyth, Montana, at the northern edge of the coalfields. The NP took it to Fargo, where it was turned over to the GN for delivery to the generating plant at Grand Rapids (Cohasset), Minnesota. Immediately after the roads were merged, the coal business took off, especially after the first Arab oil embargo in 1973. Robert Downing, who was the architect of the new coal operations, said later,

> It would have been extremely difficult to develop that coal business if merger had not put the routes of the Burlington and NP together. The financial strength of the merger was needed to finance the improvements for the coal business. In fact, for awhile in 1972 and 1973, we were spending money a lot faster than we were earning it. The BN board got rather nervous about having to borrow so much money without a clear indication that it was going to work out.[33]

On the day before Christmas Eve 1970, waiting on the windy platform of the station at Yakima for the Mainstreeter, watching the ticket agent going about his business in his bay-windowed office as agents had for more than a century, one could not help but wonder how this would change and how soon. The Mainstreeter was not a fancy train like the North Coast Limited. It was a train for ordinary folks going ordinary places. It was 16 cars long for the holidays, a mish-mash of Burlington silver, NP green, GN big-sky blue, and some BN Cascade green. It was standing room only, young folks, old folks, families, everybody hauling packages wrapped in ribbons and bows. The mood was cheery. Folks in almost every car broke into Christmas carols at some point during the evening. The "economy buffet" bar car stayed open past midnight, until the last chorus of "Jingle Bells" was sung, the liquor gave out, and everybody was tired of laughing. The next morning, the long train swung east from Garrison, Montana, and descended Mullan Pass into windswept Helena to be swallowed by the vastness of the eastern plains. So much was changing so fast.

The Chicago, Milwaukee & North Western

There was more to the Burlington Northern's deal with the Milwaukee Road and the North Western than gateways and trackage rights. The BN said that if the Milwaukee Road and the North Western wanted to merge, the BN would not interfere. It was rumored that the BN forced the Milwaukee and the North Western to promise it access to certain industrial sidings as a price of silence. The ICC was not impressed with this deal making.[34]

As this was occurring, the UP–Rock Island case had caused an implosion of midwestern railroads and was not likely to be settled soon. The Milwaukee and the North Western were in contact again, and the settlement with the Northerns was the catalyst to launch an actual merger proposal. The plan was to create a new company, the Chicago, Milwaukee &

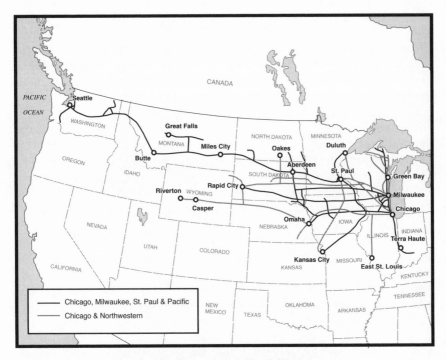

Chicago, Milwaukee & North Western

North Western Transportation Company. Employees were asked to rack their brains for a catchier name, something like Trans-Midwest Lines, perhaps. The North Western would name 8 of the 15 directors, and Northwest Industries, the holding company, would have control. Application for merger was filed with the ICC in June 1966.

The Milwaukee Road management was summoned to the auditorium at North Western's headquarters at 2 North Riverside Plaza in Chicago for seminars conducted by North Western's corporate planning department. The Milwaukee Road had no corporate planning department. It had no auditorium, either. The Milwaukee gang was instructed in the application of the "Critical Path" method of management that some of them recalled as a rather chilling version of New Truth.[35] Two corporate cultures were colliding here: one that worked on the newest concepts of systems analysis and the other just plain old duct-tape railroad.

The Milwaukee–North Western proposal had a lot of support from communities and industries along both lines. Rep. Gaylord Nelson of Wisconsin told the commission, "All of my mail has been unanimous in support of the consolidation."[36] Except for the Northerns, who were silent, every railroad in the region took part, their law departments expending vast resources compiling briefs as thick as telephone books. The Union Pacific was mightily annoyed that the North Western was trying to block the Rock Island merger and simultaneously trying to silence all who opposed this merger. The UP wanted the two cases combined. The UP's lawyer thundered for an entire day on this. Those who were there said he spoke for eight hours without coming up for air. When he had finished thundering, the examiner, looking neither right nor left, said in a quiet monotone, "Petition denied. Next?"

One controversy swirled about the "Lyle" condition demanded by the Illinois Central. That was trackage rights for the IC from its own branch at Lyle, Minnesota, to the environs of St. Paul, to replace the friendly connection it lost when the C&NW took over the Minneapolis & St. Louis. The Minnesota Railroad & Warehouse Commission took up the IC's cause. Its involvement seemed to have been prompted by several well-connected agribusiness shippers in southern Minnesota, notably Hormel, but it wanted to make its case sound as though it was a plea for the small-scale farmer and the small-scale grain operator. Arguments of monopoly profiteering simply did not apply to marginal roads that were too poor to borrow money for capital investment. An additional rail route from Chicago to the Twin Cities was hardly what the country needed.

Another controversy was the demand of the Soo Line for access to the industrial district of the city of Milwaukee. The Milwaukee Road served 576 sidings in the city, and the North Western served 208; and they already had a reciprocal switching agreement between them, meaning that each could serve all sidings. The Milwaukee Road had already granted the Soo Line trackage rights into the city with full rights to serve all sidings, but not to solicit traffic competitive with the Milwaukee Road, which very specifically included traffic to Chicago. The Milwaukee Road had 51 percent of the city's traffic; the North Western 33 percent; the Soo 5 percent; and, via Lake Michigan car ferries, the C&O had 8 percent and the Grand Trunk 3 percent.[37] The Soo said the merger would give the new company a virtual monopoly; the Milwaukee and the North Western said that granting the Soo its demand would give it the benefit of investment it never made and wipe out one of the few real trumps the new company had.

The ICC began prehearing conferences almost as soon as the application was filed on July 6, 1966, because these complex cases needed a roadmap. Actual hearings began in July 1967 and ended January 12, 1968. They took up 19,000 pages of testimony, some of the briefs running over 400 pages. The Milwaukee and North Western's joint brief was prepared to look like, and read like, the examiner's report they would like to see. The Soo Line's brief was eye-catching in four colors, with elaborate charts, diagrams, and maps. The Department of Justice opposed the merger on the grounds of loss of rail competition. Its brief was typed. It appeared to have been done on a manual typewriter and looked like a student's term paper. Admittedly, this was not a big case for Justice, but it represented the government and the people of the United States. Its entry was a popgun beside those of private vested interests, even of a relatively small one such as the Soo.

Examiner Henry Darmstadter recommended approval on December 18, 1968. His report was a monster—290 pages of text and more than 700 additional pages of appendixes. It tried to come to grips with the nature of competition, both between railroads and other forms of transportation and between railroads themselves. He broke down competition between railroads into several categories. This went on for one eye-glazing page after another and left the issues hopelessly confused.[38]

Everyone then vented their spleen on Darmstadter. There were more briefs, angry ones, accusatory ones, and petitions to reopen the case. Any number of cliches applied: "Tempest in a teapot," "Fiddling while Rome burns," "Deck chairs on the Titanic." The railroads said they were capable of self-help if the government would let them. The government was ready to let them, but they turned on each other. The Soo Line and its ally, the Minnesota Railroad & Warehouse Commission, were especially whiny. The opposing railroads thought of their traffic as a finite pie; any deviation from the status quo would diminish that pie. The idea that in a growing economy the pie will grow eluded them.

The worst was yet to come. Some dissident Milwaukee Road stockholders accused their own company of selling out to the North Western. They noted that the Milwaukee's net income was higher than the North Western's in 1967. The Milwaukee's preferred holders were going to lose the tax-exempt status of the dividends on their stock; that was the reason they had bought the stock in the first place. And they believed the deal on gateways with the Northern Lines would permanently make the Milwaukee the stronger railroad. That was what their own management was saying. They noted that the Milwaukee Road management had not informed stockholders of the gateways deal in its most recent proxy solicitation, and for that indiscretion they filed a class action suit.[39] What they wanted, however, was not to block the merger but simply to renegotiate the stock exchange ratio.

The situation got worse yet in 1969 after Northwest Industries' attempt to acquire B. F. Goodrich backfired. Goodrich was a big boy and had plenty of money to fend off a takeover. Goodrich bought a small trucking outfit deliberately to complicate ownership by a railroad holding company. Northwest Industries had been a high flyer up to this point, with earnings approaching a billion dollars in 1968, but these plummeted 50 percent in 1969, and it omitted a dividend altogether in the first quarter of 1970. Its stock dropped from a 1968 high of $60.625 to a 1969 low of $10.625. At that point, renegotiation with the Milwaukee Road was a necessity. Everybody knew it, and the ICC ordered it.

Heineman refused renegotiation. He said that if one was forced, he would cancel the whole merger proposal. Whether he could do that, whether the merger agreement was a binding contract subject only to ICC approval, was a question that would likely end in a court case. A plan for Northwest Industries to sell the C&NW to its own employees was already being hatched, but as Heineman told Milwaukee Road attorney Tom Ploss years later (in 1981), he felt he had a moral if not a legal obligation not to leave the Milwaukee Road with nothing.

The Milwaukee Road's president, Bill Quinn, was considered one of the bright new breed of lawyer-executives when he assumed the Milwaukee's helm in 1958. He was the father of eight wonderful children, a civic leader, a good man. Heineman took him to lunch at the Chicago Club and offered to sell him the C&NW on the same terms being hatched in the employee deal. It was a very attractive offer that would involve almost no cash, just a new equity issue for the Milwaukee to exchange for C&NW shares. The advantage to Northwest Industries was a huge tax loss that would offset its horrendous federal tax liabilities. At lunch, apparently all Quinn could talk about was what a great deal the tax loss was for Northwest. Heineman recalled that Quinn never said a word about what a great railroad the combined Milwaukee–North Western could be, what opportunity there was to combine parallel lines and 140 common stations. All he could think about was the Northwest's tax benefit. Heineman was stunned that Quinn could be so dense and gave him 30 days to think it over.

Ploss recalled that there was much consternation in the C&NW management. They of graduate business school systems analysis and Brooks Brothers' suits had always assumed that they would run departments and that the Milwaukee Road's boiler-plate gang in horn-rimmed glasses would be their underlings. Now it was going to be the opposite, and apparently some of the back-pedaling was quite humorous. But when the 30 days was up, Quinn said he had no interest, because the cost of physically merging the railroads would create a negative cash flow for the next five years. That would have been true only if the two railroads were slammed together at once. There was no reason they had to be slammed together at once. Heineman told Ploss years later that he thought Quinn was a nice enough fellow but was no businessman and was too scared to take the risk.[40] That is an opinion, of course. Quinn may have thought the Milwaukee just could not afford it, even at a good price. He certainly knew there was a problem with his preferred stockholders, who were grandfathered in with a very sweet deal; they might have blocked it anyway, or at least put up an expensive fuss.

There is no way to know how such a merger would have played out. Ploss thought the merged company would have been a sufficient tower of strength in the Midwest to funnel enough traffic to the Milwaukee's Pacific Extension for that line to fulfill its destiny. Perhaps. Perhaps the merger of two marginal roads would have created a bigger marginal road, just like the Erie Lackawanna, perhaps too big for absorption into one of the megasystems that would emerge in the 1980s. It is best for historians not to speculate "what if."

With 100 percent certainty, the opening of gateways to the Milwaukee Road in the West as a result of the Burlington Northern merger, and the new trackage rights to Portland and Canada, would not be enough to save the Milwaukee. There had to be something more. Quinn's decision not to accept Heineman's offer was the road's death warrant.

The Black Hole of the Great Rock Island Case

Meanwhile, the Rock Island case became the great black hole of railroading. Everyone regarded the stakes as being too high to lose. "The weapons are coldly legal, but the personal bitterness among railroading's biggest names is at white heat," wrote Dan Cordtz in *Fortune*.[41] The UP's Roland Harriman and Frank Barnett thought Ben Heineman of the C&NW was impossible to reason with. Heineman thought the Union Pacific "spoke only to God." The Rock Island's officers, led by Jervis Langdon, were publicly committed to the UP merger but were privately infuriated by the UP's condescension toward them. They had to solve problems with ingenuity, not with buckets of money, the way the UP did, and they thought they deserved a little credit.

For all its massive volume, the *Rock Island* case boiled down to a series of violently conflicting studies on traffic diversion. They were the products of electronic computers—everybody had access to them now—and the computers made things hopelessly complex and confused. The complexity required ever more elaborate cross-examination to untangle. Everyone selected a different method of computation. Some took random samples; some took "typical week" samples; some did car-by-car analyses. Some included all traffic; some excluded certain kinds of traffic, for reasons that constantly varied. Some used judgment early in their calculations, others not until the very end. The method chosen produced the results desired. The discrepancy between what one railroad said it would lose to diversion and what its opponent said it would lose ran between 200 percent and 2,000 percent. The ICC was under court order to take this seriously and try to reconcile it, and not roll its eyes.

Then came briefs that were enormous, running in some cases to 1,000 pages, with lovely charts and maps, sometimes in color, costing thousands of hours by legal staff to prepare. It took untold lawyer hours to read them, and they still did not clear the issues. The exercise truly raised questions about the effectiveness of the adversary system.

The man who wound up in charge, Administrative Law Judge Nathan Klitenic, did a yeoman's job of trying to sort it all out. It is important to understand that, up to this point, it was the railroads themselves that had tangled this case in nit-picking and delay. But then the fault shifted to

Nathan Klitenic. From him, there was silence. What was he doing? What was taking so long? The UP announced the merger in 1963. Now it was 1968. It had taken the railroads long enough to sort out their own little jealousies. What was the holdup now? Suspense began to turn into a bad odor as the Rock Island began to rot in the sun. Henry Crown refused to put any money into it. He had figured the UP would have it by now. What in blazes was going on?

While Examiner Klitenic thrashed around for the perfect solution, Martin Luther King, Jr., and Robert Kennedy met violent deaths, the Civil Rights Movement ended with the final orders for desegregation, the student protests and hippie movements of the 1960s ended, the Middle East went to war twice, Nixon opened up new relations with China and the Soviet Union, the Arabs embargoed oil, the economy roared off to hyperinflation, burglars broke into Democratic Headquarters at the Watergate complex, Nixon resigned, Saigon fell and the Vietnam War ended, the Penn Central crashed in flames, and the whole railroad industry stared at possible liquidation or nationalization. But Klitenic seemed hypnotized by the chessboard of the western railroads.

The Klitenic Plan

With the drip, drip of a Chinese water torture, Klitenic finally began to pull his thoughts together. His report came out in three installments, running around 1,000 pages each. In the first (September 1971), he analyzed the nature of the railroads involved and their traffic patterns. In the second (March 1972), he discussed the demands each railroad was making and the repercussions those demands would have on others. In the third (February 1973), he tried to reconcile the traffic studies.

In his third installment, Judge Klitenic recognized that either the applications of the Union Pacific to take the Rock Island and sell the Rock Island's southern half to the Southern Pacific had to be denied, or a complete restructuring of the railroad system west of the Mississippi was required. There was no middle course, most certainly not the Union Pacific's demand to have its merger with the Rock Island with no strings attached. That would condemn to death too many other railroads and would jeopardize too many industries located on those railroads, too many communities on those railroads, too much investment, and too many jobs. Perhaps it was wise, he thought, to let the Rock Island slide into receivership, since that was clearly where it was headed, at which point a court could order its disposal. But he rejected that idea on the grounds that the ICC should not condemn a still-solvent carrier to a receivership that might end in liquidation.

Given all that, he introduced his ground-breaking thesis. The very existence of independent granger roads was obsolete and was the cause of railroad problems in the West, he said. The idea that a few transcontinentals can feed enough traffic to a half-dozen grangers who in turn feed it to a few eastern trunks was, as he put it, as old-fashioned as the steam locomotive. Transcontinentals must be combined with grangers. So he rejected the North Western's bid for the Rock Island to create a giant granger. The Rock Island would go to the UP. A granger would be combined with a transcontinental. But that was not all.

Here are the strings he attached: if the Union Pacific took the Rock Island, then

—The Union Pacific must sell the southern portions of the Rock Island to the Southern Pacific.

—The Southern Pacific must give trackage rights over these routes to the Santa Fe.

—The Southern Pacific must sell to the Santa Fe the Rock Island's Choctaw Line from Amarillo to Oklahoma City, Little Rock, and Memphis.

—The Southern Pacific must give the Burlington Northern sole control of the Joint Texas Division, formerly known as the Burlington–Rock Island Railroad, between Fort Worth and Galveston, now jointly owned by the BN and the RI.

—The Union Pacific must acquire the Chicago & North Western.

—The Southern Pacific must sell, and the Union Pacific must buy, the Central Pacific between Ogden and Oakland, giving the Union Pacific sole ownership of the Overland Route.

—The Santa Fe must acquire the Western Pacific, the Denver & Rio Grande Western, and the entire Missouri Pacific–Texas & Pacific system.

—The Texas & Pacific must sell, and the Southern Pacific must buy, the line from El Paso to Fort Worth.

—The Southern Pacific must sell, and the Santa Fe must buy, the Modoc Line from Flanigan, Nevada, to Klamath Falls, Oregon.

—The Southern Pacific must acquire the Katy and the Kansas City Southern.

—Holding companies, specifically the Union Pacific Company, the Southern Pacific Company, and Santa Fe Industries were to be considered common carriers by rail and come within ICC jurisdiction.

—The record was to be held open to determine whether the Milwaukee Road should be included in the Union Pacific System.

—The record was to be held open to determine whether the Frisco should be included in a system of its choice.

A look at the map shows what this plan would do. It would create four competitive balanced systems west of the Mississippi—the Burlington Northern, the Union Pacific, the Santa Fe, and the Southern Pacific. If the Milwaukee Road were put into the UP system (which is what the "open record" was expected to recommend unless the Milwaukee's obstinate

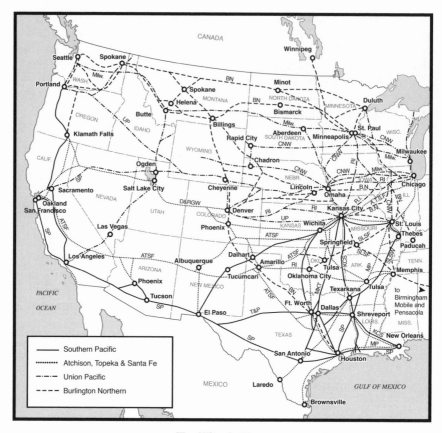

The Klitenic Plan

preferred stockholders decided to shoot themselves in the foot), each of
the four systems would serve two of the major gateways to the East: the
BN and the UP would serve Chicago and St. Louis; the Santa Fe, Chicago
and Memphis; the SP, Memphis and New Orleans. There would be two
competitors on each of the three major corridors—the BN and the UP on
the northern, the UP and the Santa Fe on the central, and the Santa Fe and
the SP on the southern. The competition would not necessarily be equal
on the corridors, but the weaker competitor would have compensating areas of strength. For example, the UP with the former Milwaukee Road
route would be weaker than the BN on the northern corridor but would be
the stronger on the central. The Santa Fe would be weaker than the UP on
the central (the ex-WP-D&RGW-MoPac route) but would have more complete feeder lines in California. No weak carriers would be left over except
perhaps the Soo Line, although it was assumed that it was part of the
Canadian Pacific empire. No one would be left with long string lines into

hostile territory and without friendly connections.[42] The only weakness was that three of the main lines between Omaha and Chicago (the RI, the C&NW, and the Milwaukee) would be in UP hands. Giving the Santa Fe the Rock Island's Denver-Chicago line would have neatly balanced this.

Just as Professor Ripley said in 1921, this kind of balance would not be possible without dismembering at least one of the existing major systems. Circumstances cast the Rock Island as the blood sacrifice. In an imperfect world, the balance of the Klitenic Plan was remarkable. If there had been some provision for compulsion, with one big oomph, with the big railroads and their investors getting untold opportunity along with a few bitter pills (and not many, really) the West would have had a damn good railroad system with no one being unduly violated. The railroads eventually created for themselves essentially what the Klitenic Plan envisioned, except they failed to retain competition on two important corridors. The Klitenic Plan offered better balance and effective competition, without tearing up and abandoning useful lines of railroad.

However, the western railroads saw nothing remarkable in the plan. Nobody was going to make them do what they did not believe to be in their immediate, short-term corporate interest, and the stronger roads were in the driver's seat. Only the North Western and the Milwaukee Road seemed to accept that what had happened was probably no surprise given the furious and contradicting ultimatums the commission had been presented with. Of course, it was not the first time weaker roads looked to the ICC to protect them.

The stronger roads rejected the proposal. Their reaction was immediate and hateful. The UP and the SP filed exceptions that refuted every condition of the Klitenic Plan point by point. The Santa Fe, the SP, the C&NW, the MoPac, the Rio Grande, and the Soo asked to have the entire case dismissed immediately. The Rock Island, which had been diddled by everyone for 11 years, was in no mood for that and denounced the petition as the most "arrogant and cynical document ever filed with the Commission."[43]

So what choices did the ICC have? To insist on implementation of the Klitenic Plan would accomplish nothing because it did not have the power to compel and the strong roads were going to walk away from it. That would leave the Rock Island hurtling toward bankruptcy. The Rock Island did not have a large funded debt, so receivership that merely protected it from creditors was not likely to save enough money to keep it alive. Receivership, therefore, would probably mean liquidation. Perhaps Amtrak would take the Chicago-Omaha line through Des Moines. Perhaps the "cram down" provisions of the bankruptcy act could be used to force reluctant parties to take some responsibility. Such an end for the Rock Island was a shame. No one who ever rode the Rocket streamliners could look on this without sadness.

The ICC backed down and pushed the Klitenic Plan aside. On November 8, 1974, it said the UP could have the northern Rock Island and the SP the southern Rock Island. But then, even the fallback plan got immensely complicated, which underscored how devilishly complex the West was. The Rio Grande could have the western Rock Island from Denver and Colorado Springs to Omaha, but not Kansas City, because that would hurt the MoPac. (The Rio Grande had previously offered to buy the MoPac's Pueblo–Kansas City line if it wanted to sell.) The Burlington Northern would get several nice presents—access to industrial areas in Portland previously served only by the UP, access to the Canadian Pacific over the UP subsidiary Spokane International Railroad, and sole control of the Joint Texas Division.

The Santa Fe could have the Rock Island's Amarillo-Memphis "Choctaw" Line but must also acquire the Katy Railroad, which at the moment was a booby prize. (The Katy's owners, Katy Industries, who used the railroad mostly for tax loss purposes, would in turn be ordered to negotiate sale on the basis of scrap value or earning power, not on outstanding debt, which was largely in the hands of speculators.) To protect the midwestern grangers, the UP and the SP would be ordered to deliver as many cars to them in interchange as they had in the past, for a period of five years. If traffic fell short, there was a formula for indemnification. If shipper routing made it difficult to comply, the big roads would be ordered to change those routings so they would comply. If the protected roads failed to provide adequate service, the UP and the SP could complain to the ICC. Holding companies would come under ICC regulation.

Commissioners Tuggle, Deason, and Clapp sensed that even this was more than the big roads would accept. The game had to be played their way, or it would not be played at all. If the purpose was to save the Rock Island, they thought, it would not, because the big roads were still going to walk away.

Only Commissioner Brown stood by the Klitenic Plan. She thought a grand opportunity to restructure the western railroads so as to bring permanent prosperity and stability had been allowed to slip by. She wondered what was going to happen to the protected roads in five years when the protective conditions expired. She thought the majority was opting for a middle ground that solved nothing.

The Union Pacific, grumbling loudly that businesses were not allowed to run their own business anymore, withdrew from the proceeding entirely on August 4, 1975, and the ICC formally dismissed it on July 10, 1976. The big case was over and there was nothing to show for it. Track conditions were so bad between Omaha and Chicago on all three of the granger roads involved in the case (the North Western, the Rock Island, and the Milwaukee) that the Union Pacific began sending more and more traffic east on the Burlington via Grand Island, Nebraska, for fear of losing customers if it did not. The North Western began removing the second (double) track on the western end of its Chicago-Omaha main, assuming that its loss of Union Pacific interchange was permanent.

In 1975 John Kenefick, now in charge of the Union Pacific, asked the Rock Island if it would like to be the UP's "best friend" at Omaha. Presumably, if the Rock Island accepted, some loans would be arranged to rehabilitate its Omaha-Chicago line. The UP had never quite gotten over Ben Heineman's frontal assault. The North Western's service was deteriorating badly. But the Rock said no, if it was not going to be a part of the UP, its interests were in the long haul to Denver and Tucumcari, and its long-haul connections with the Rio Grande and the Southern Pacific. By this time, Larry Provo was in charge at the North Western, and the UP and the North Western began to work together to develop coal traffic from the Powder River Basin. The Rock Island was doomed.

It was standard wisdom to blame the ICC for what happened. For years, those wishing to prove that regulation was bunk said the Rock Island would have survived if only the ICC had not screwed everything up. That was not right, or at least it certainly was not the whole story. It was another railroad, the North Western, that believed that if the Union Pacific got the Rock Island, it was doomed. It was a duel to the death between the C&NW and the RI. The C&NW won. Judgment on the ICC therefore really depends on which railroad you root for.

The story of the Great Rock Island Case spanned the years 1962 to 1975. This makes telling the story of the whole railroad industry with any semblance of chronology very difficult. However, to split the story for the sake of chronology would only be confusing. The reader must bear in mind that the story has extended well beyond the Penn Central disaster and also beyond the chronological scope of this book.

thirteen

The Eastern Inclusion Crisis
1966–1968

Until the late 1960s, the ICC chairmanship was a rotating office, which shortly after M-Day passed to the commission's chief dissident, William H. Tucker. Tucker, a Kennedy campaign organizer in Massachusetts in 1960 and a Kennedy appointee to the commission in 1961, opposed the mergers, not because he thought mergers were intrinsically bad but because, in his view, the railroads had planned them badly. It was said that once the majority reached a decision he disagreed with, he never twitted them when events proved him right and them wrong. For that reason, he was able to impart some of his thinking to them.[1] Tucker was the driving influence behind the denial of the Northern Lines merger on M-Day. His colleague Charles A. Webb, who frequently joined him in dissent, held his tongue in the Penn-Central decision. So Tucker alone, concurring separately, said "I told you so." When the ICC approved the C&O-B&O and the N&W–Nickel Plate without really thinking of the implications for other railroads, the creation of this monstrosity was inevitable. Once the C&O-B&O was approved, the Penn-Central had to be approved, for they were as interlocked as if they were on a single docket.

Everyone said they believed Penn Central was going to be a juggernaut of power. It was going to blanket the East. If there were such things as merger savings (and railroad executives wanted to believe there were), the Penn Central was going to have somewhere between $60 million and $80 million a year for new capital investment, which would turn it into a sleek technological machine that would drive all others to the wall. It would be the dominant railroad voice in statehouses and in Washington and would dominate the Association of American Railroads. Powerhouses like the

C&O and the N&W claimed to feel the hot breath of the Penn Central; for outcasts like the Erie Lackawanna, it was dragon fire.

John Fishwick, then the general counsel of the N&W, saw the problem clearly:

> For over a generation, we have had an eastern railroad problem that has been a source of concern and frustration for the industry and the public. Its symptoms are pockets of poverty in an age of plenty. Penn Central, with all its promise, is no answer to this. It will shift the woes of the New Haven to the Erie Lackawanna, the Delaware & Hudson, the Boston & Maine and the Jersey Central.[2]

These were the leftovers that had to be put somewhere. The much-ballyhooed three-system plan had been no plan at all because it did not take these leftovers into account.

The Bison Yard and the Erie Debt

When the Erie Lackawanna sealed its Agreement of October 12 (1961) with the N&W, it gave no hint that it was dissatisfied or that it had signed at the point of a loaded gun. The N&W–Nickel Plate would join in the construction of the Bison Yard at Buffalo, which would assure the continued flow of traffic over the old Nickel Plate–Lackawanna route. Ground was broken, construction began, and all appeared to be well.

Then relations between the EL and the Nickel Plate turned ice cold. There was a persistent rumor around the Buffalo yards that the Nickel Plate had tried to build a siding from the far end of the yard to a connection with the Lehigh Valley a few hundred yards away, and the EL said no. That was one reason the Nickel Plate would lose interest—it was committed to help pay for the yard but not necessarily to use it. When the yard opened, and for years afterward, there was not a Nickel Plate or an N&W train in sight. N&W said only that the Bison Yard "wasn't working out." Years later, John Fishwick said the real reason was that the Erie Lackawanna kept them out (by refusing to negotiate proper labor agreements).[3]

When the Nickel Plate and the Lehigh Valley failed to get a connection by way of Bison, they went to the PRR, which had a spur line around the southern outskirts of the city. Trackage rights were arranged and approved by the ICC: freights soon began to roll off the "Abbott Road" interchange, 100 cars long, usually with Nickel Plate locomotives and always with Nickel Plate crews, running through from the Nickel Plate's eastern marshaling point at Conneaut, Ohio, to the Lehigh's western one at Manchester, New York. Service began in February 1964 with one train each way,

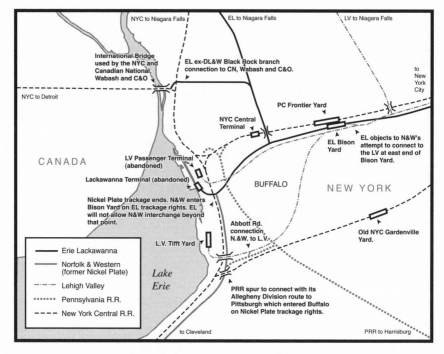

Bison Yard and the Abbott Road Connection

and it was so successful that a second train was added in July; together they averaged 200 loaded cars a day eastbound and 160 westbound.[4] But it was against the law for Nickel Plate crews to operate on Lehigh Valley tracks without authorization, and it was against the law not to have air brakes tested at the exact point where a train was received in interchange. So the folks at the Erie Lackawanna hurried down to Abbott Road to catch the action on their Kodaks.

If you were from the Erie Lackawanna standing down there at Abbott Road in 1964 in a Buffalo chill, this was the deepest winter in your railroad's history. The Nickel Plate was about to merge with the N&W, which the PRR had been found to control. The N&W's top officers were all former PRR officers. The PRR controlled the Lehigh Valley directly. Was it not obvious that the PRR intended the Lehigh to be the N&W's route to the East Coast? The Erie Lackawanna merger had not been successful. Robert Fuller, the chairman of its executive committee, was saying so publicly. If it had no friendly connection at Buffalo, then its investment in Bison Yard had been a waste of money. Appendix O of the N&W–Nickel Plate merger required the N&W to solicit preferentially for the EL, and this run-through service with the Lehigh was not only a breach of good faith but a breach of ICC orders.

Is it not true, asked an EL attorney of the Lehigh's general manager,

Howard Kohout (a former PRR man), that the more traffic diverted from the EL the less it will be worth and the less someone will have to pay for it? That someone was the N&W, already under agreement to negotiate in good faith. That is not the point, said Kohout. Look at the EL's debt, almost $320 million (counting equipment trusts). Most of it was due in the near future. Everybody knew about that $320 million. The Lehigh Valley, he said, had only $70 million of outstanding debt, with maturities spread out to the year 2000. "If the N&W's objective is to reach the seaboard, they can do it a damn sight easier by acquiring the Lehigh Valley."[5]

From the Lehigh's perspective, this was the last chance to save itself. It was in such disarray that it could hardly be considered a major railroad anymore. When quizzed on how sweet it must be to be comfortably ensconced in the PRR empire, Kohout, who came to the Lehigh from the PRR, almost shouted that the Lehigh was getting no help from the PRR at all. The PRR has given us no clue whatsoever of what it intends to do with us, he said.

He was just trying to run a railroad and stay afloat. Everyone was up against the deadly competition of Al Perlman's New York Central, which had become especially aggressive with high-value, high-speed, high-rate commodities. The new run-through service with the Nickel Plate allowed the Lehigh to reduce terminal time in Buffalo by seven hours. Closing time for the piggyback out of Oak Island Yard in Newark was competitive with the Erie Lackawanna and the New York Central for the first time ever. The reasons were technical, but if crews were changed or air tested at any other spot, much of that time advantage would be lost. He was negotiating with the unions to run crews through from Connneaut to Manchester, but so far no agreement had been reached. The new, young management at the Lehigh wondered why something like this had not been done years before; but then, there was a lot to wonder about with regard to past Lehigh managements.

The Nickel Plate may have been in the driver's seat, but it had gripes of its own. The old Lackawanna was its right arm, it testified. The two roads solicited traffic together. That meant the EL knew all of the Nickel Plate's customers and went to them and tried to solicit business for the EL's long haul. The Nickel Plate knew for a fact that the EL had gone to some of its customers and told them that the Nickel Plate service out of Buffalo had deteriorated and that they should route EL all the way, via Hornell. The Nickel Plate had approached the EL on the matter of run-through service, but the EL said it was committed to Bison Yard and was not interested in run-throughs. "We leaned over backwards for the Erie Lackawanna," said John Fitzpatrick of the Nickel Plate, "admittedly for selfish reasons, because Lehigh service was so deficient. But it wasn't deficient anymore." The change, said Fitzpatrick, was due to the persuasiveness of the Lehigh's young traffic man, George Wallace, who "was out making friends where the Lehigh was never known before . . . and gee whiz, we wanted to be in their picture, too." Wallace was a Yale graduate and a former PRR man. He was a real gift to the LV.

The state of New Jersey admitted that the only reason it was intervening on behalf of the Erie Lackawanna was to make sure the EL was profitable enough to save the state from having to subsidize the EL's suburban passenger service. Most of the railroad executives regarded New Jersey as a little weasel of a state whose citizens refused to pay taxes for the services they required. Would you be here opposing the Erie Lackawanna if it wanted to cut five hours off its schedule? asked the Nickel Plate attorney of the New Jersey witness. The answer was no.

> Q: But you are here opposing the Lehigh Valley for doing the same thing?
> A: You didn't let me finish.
> Q: No further questions.[6]

Nickel Plate signed the Agreement of October 12, 1961, with Erie Lackawanna because Stuart Saunders of the N&W told them to. Saunders was a savvy enough businessman to know about Erie's $320 million debt, but he wanted his (Nickel Plate) merger so much that he practically ordered poor old Paul Johnston of the Erie down to Washington to sign the agreement and deliver it to the ICC before the ink was dry. When it dawned in the cold light that the N&W might be saddled with this whopping Erie debt, Saunders ordered a study put on his desk to see the extent of the damage. Hobart L. Scott of the N&W and James M. Moonshower of the EL worked on the study and had a preliminary draft ready by August 1963.[7] That coincided with the nadir of the Erie Lackawanna's fortunes. The property was visibly decaying, the treasury held $6 million in unpaid bills, and morale was at rock bottom. A wave of derailments caused by undermaintained track and lax discipline was the most visible symptom of the mess.

In the meantime Saunders left the N&W for the PRR. The PRR divested the N&W. The N&W merged with the Nickel Plate. The Lehigh runthrough service began. With regard to the EL, the silence from Roanoke, the N&W headquarters, was deafening. So, in August 1964, the EL board decided to do a little prodding. Its optimum plan was to saddle the N&W with the EL's debt and leave EL stockholders in possession of $84 million of prime N&W bonds, a package worth $16.64 a share, a price Erie stock had not commanded since 1957. Speculators immediately moved into EL stock—there was a 100 percent turnover in 1965.

In Roanoke the idea met an icy reception. The N&W's new president, Herman Pevler (formerly of the Wabash and before that of the PRR), did nothing about it until the next spring and then said only that it would have to be studied some more. The EL thought it could tell when somebody was stalling, especially after John Fishwick told N&W stockholders at their annual meeting that with the EL's excessive debt, it would *never* find a home in the N&W. Did that constitute a violation of the Agreement of

October 12, a breach of good faith?[8] Fishwick said that as a prerequisite to further talks, the EL would have to demonstrate that it could help itself by slimming its long-distance passenger service and getting New Jersey at long last to take responsibility for its mass transit needs.

Meanwhile, Scott and Moonshower were proceeding with the studies, but not altogether harmoniously. Differences seemed to settle on the N&W's reluctance, even refusal, to make any capital outlays in order to integrate the Erie and the N&W's refusal to admit that EL lines west of Hornell had any value.[9] When the studies were complete, there was renewed silence. On November 1, 1965, Scott arrived unexpectedly in Moonshower's office with a proposed report that he wanted signed immediately so he could take it back to Roanoke that night. "I saw at a glance that it was a major departure from our joint plan," said Moonshower. "It was little more than coordination. . . . I saw that he had signed it already. When I said three or four times that I would not sign, he said he would buy a razor and stay overnight or however long it took."[10]

If on the surface this seemed as if the N&W was not negotiating in good faith, there was another side to the story. In August 1965, the N&W negotiating committee confronted the EL on its debt. Fishwick said that $270 million of nonequipment trust debt was absurd for a railroad of the size and earning power of the EL. It had to be reduced to the $120–140 million range, comparable to other railroads' debts. The N&W was not going to be responsible for the past profligate managements of the Erie and the DL&W. Even Robert Fuller, chairman of the EL's executive committee, seemed aware that sooner or later a major write-down was going to be necessary. But the day of reckoning was at hand. The EL had barely made it past its maturity of $12 million of consolidated mortgage bonds in 1964 and had done so only by extending the maturity date to 1969 and paying double the interest. More issues were due in 1971 and 1973. This was on a railroad with a net working capital that equaled less than a month's expenses. Neither the N&W nor anyone else could take a risk like that. "It's too bad," said John Fishwick. "Without that debt, Erie would be valuable."[11]

It was within the power of the EL bondholders to do something about it. They included the most prestigious insurance companies in the land, and Fuller made sure they understood the seriousness of the situation. But their response, on at least two occasions, was that they would rather see the company go under than have a write-down.[12] If that were the case, said Fishwick, there "would be little possibility they would be agreeable to modify those securities after N&W had an $84 million investment to protect."[13]

The Chessie's Orphans

When the Baltimore & Ohio became part of what would soon be called the Chessie System, it brought with it a dowry of mixed distinction. It owned 43 percent of the outstanding stock of the Reading Company, and although it did not exercise formal control, its influence in the form of dual executives was great. The Reading had one of the heaviest freight traffic densities in the nation and one of the heavier passenger densities, mostly commuter service into Philadelphia. But distances were short, its anthracite was gone, some of its industrial base was showing signs of erosion, and it was not making much money. The Reading controlled the Jersey Central, a giant terminal railroad, stripped of the anthracite that once made it a lot of money but not of its commuters, which lost a horrendous amount. Its main line was busy across northern New Jersey from Jersey City to Phillipsburg on the Delaware River, but it was only 73 miles long. Both the Reading and the Jersey Central desperately needed to be a part of a railroad with a longer haul. They needed merger. Needless to say, they were not going to get it, not unless the big roads were compelled and not unless the state picked up the tab for commuter losses.

The B&O also owned 43 percent of the outstanding stock of the Western Maryland Railway. The WM carried West Virginia bituminous. It was a tough haul over the Black Fork grade west of Thomas, West Virginia, one locomotive for every ten loaded coal cars in steam days. But the WM was one of the great coal and general cargo delivery systems to the seaboard at Port Covington in Baltimore. The B&O could not touch the WM or vote that stock because of Clayton Act proceedings in the 1930s. Back then, it was an open-and-shut case. The WM and the B&O had routes that intertwined like snakes. Of course they were competitors, and of course having them both under single control would be a violation of the Clayton Act. But the C&O had a peculiar passion for the WM and began buying WM stock on its own account even before it got control of the B&O in the summer of 1964. Then the B&O sought permission to exercise formal control over the WM. It expressed no interest whatsoever in control of the Reading or the Jersey Central.

It made good operating sense for the B&O to control the WM. At Cumberland, Maryland, the B&O already had a sophisticated yard for westbound traffic, and the WM yard could easily become its eastbound equivalent. At Baltimore, the B&O's new automatic coal unloading facility at Curtis Bay would work at peak efficiency only if both the B&O and the WM funneled into it. The WM had superior eastbound grades over the Alleghenies, the B&O superior westbound grades. Predicted savings came to $6.2 million a year, substantial for a road the size of the WM.

The proposal was mainly in the corporate interest of the emerging Chessie System. Not only did the WM compete mile for mile with the B&O, but it also served as a prime connection for the B&O's competitors—the famous Alphabet Route, mentioned earlier, in connection with the Nickel Plate—soon to be in the N&W system, and with the Pittsburgh Dispatch Route in connection with the Pittsburgh & Lake Erie and the New York Central, soon to be in Penn Central. The Chessie said there was no

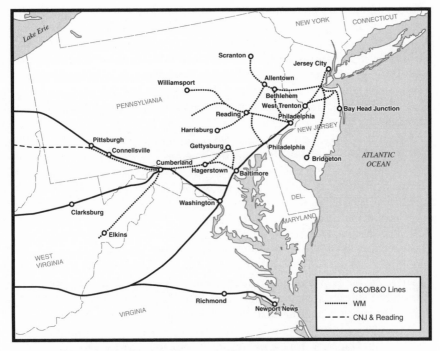

Chessie, Western Maryland, and Reading/Jersey Central

place for a little railroad like the WM now that mergers had surrounded it with hostile competitors, and for the long run that was probably correct. But the WM was still profitable and had a legion of satisfied customers. There was no sign yet that its traffic was threatened.[14]

When the case was laid out before the ICC, it struck some of the commissioners that a golden opportunity had come along to take care of at least two of the trouble spots in the East. On one hand, here was a consolidation that made a good deal of sense and which the wealthy C&O wanted very much. On the other hand, here were two outcast roads, the Reading and the Jersey Central, already in the Chessie sphere, which needed a secure and permanent home. Why not make the C&O take the outcasts as a price for getting the WM?

One reason was that Jersey Central and Reading made no official requests of their own. Jersey Central sent only a single letter to the commission suggesting that it was hemorrhaging and needed help. The Reading's board specifically refused to take official action. (The author was told, off the record, that the reason for both roads' silence was that Chessie was now in control and that it refused to let them ask for help.) The Reading's case was presented to the commission by minority stockholders who were horrified that those in control of their company seemed to prefer to watch it die. Despite this inaction, the commission wrote a report requiring inclusion of Reading and Jersey Central as a price for getting Western Maryland. Just then came word that Jersey Central would default on a government-guaranteed loan. After that, only two commissioners, Tucker and Tierney, were left in the hardliners' camp. So the Western Maryland case passed, and nothing was done about the Reading and the Jersey Central. The C&O got the WM on February 21, 1967, without a shred of obligation for the broader problems of the East.

Five weeks later, on March 27, 1967, the Jersey Central with its jaunty Statue of Liberty emblem threw in the towel. The CRRofNJ was known to New Jerseyites as "the Central Railroad." It was to the credit of Perry Shoemaker, who had been its president since he left the Erie Lackawanna in 1962, that it lasted as long as it did. It was such a small railroad, with every railroad's worst problems in concentrated form—short hauls, terminal operations, marine operations, obsolete terminal facilities at a declining port (Jersey City), a principal commodity that no one wanted anymore (anthracite coal), passengers, commuters, and crushing taxes. Shoemaker thought he had a promise from New Jersey governor Richard Hughes for a $2 million subsidy for commuter operations that would pay the bills until June. But the governor backed out, assuring the road's 13,000 commuters that they would continue to be served, though by what miracle he did not make clear. The New York Port Authority put the railroad on a cash basis for stevedoring services, which was like a sign saying "no personal checks." Others then did the same, and that was the last straw.

How will the Jersey Central be remembered? It only had 633 miles of track, 410 of it in New Jersey, but the traffic on its short main line was unusually dense, especially east of Bound Brook, New Jersey, where the Reading's line from Philadelphia joined for the final sprint to Jersey City. It was a parade of ceaseless movement—local freights, transfer hops, long coal trains, merchandise trains off the Reading or the B&O, or the Lackawanna at Taylor Yard near Scranton. There were commuter trains and Philadelphia and Harrisburg passenger trains, and until 1958 and the demise of the Royal Blue Line, there were B&O streamliners like the Capitol Limited to Chicago, the National Limited to St. Louis, and the Royal Blue itself to Washington.

Its Jersey City Terminal (now the headquarters building for Liberty State Park opposite Ellis Island and the Statue of Liberty) is clearly visible on the New Jersey shore from Battery Park at the tip of Manhattan. It was the quintessential waterfront terminal, which unloaded ferry boats two decks at a time into a 300-foot-long concourse, with 20 tracks for its 140 or more trains a day. It was protected by a signal bridge that was the classic symbol of railroading in a complex metropolitan terminal. A picture of it was frequently reprinted in encyclopedias and appeared in *The Boys' Wonder Book of Trains*. Leaving the terminal, the line dropped south through Bayonne, then turned west to cross the mighty Newark Bay

Bridge, twin trestles of two tracks each, two miles long, with vertical lift spans over the navigation channels.

The most haunting memory we will have of the Jersey Central is the Newark Bay Bridge disaster of September 15, 1958. A commuter local from the North Jersey Shore made its scheduled stop at Elizabethport. At about that same moment, the lift span on the bridge began to rise to let a dredger, the *Sand Captain,* pass through. After its station stop, the train slowed as it approached the first signal warning of the raised span. It appeared to be preparing to stop, as was the proper procedure. But once past the signal, it inexplicably began to speed up. It rumbled past a second stop signal and then a third, now hitting 45 mph. Ped Pedersen, the skipper of the *Sand Captain,* saw the impending disaster and began blasting his warning horn. This was enough to alert some the passengers on the train that something was wrong, but not the men in the locomotive cab. The train hit the final safety device, the automatic derail, and began smashing over the wooden ties. Then, 26 feet from the open span, somebody in the cab managed to slam on the brakes. It was too late. The locomotive and the first three cars plunged into the bay. Some passengers managed to swim out through open coach windows. Forty-eight died.

Had the brakes failed? There was no sign of trouble at Elizabethport. The locomotive's black box, recovered from the bay, showed that they worked properly when they were finally applied. Warning signals all functioned as they were designed to do. What had gone on in the locomotive cab in those final moments? The autopsy indicated that the fireman was dead before he hit the water. Had the engineer rushed to his aid and then realized he had put himself and his passengers in mortal danger? The official conclusion was that both men apparently suffered some kind of incapacitation, but one of them somehow, belatedly, managed to slam on the brakes.[15]

Shoemaker guided Jersey Central to a solution of one of its major problems—the Jersey City Terminal. On April 29, 1967, after much planning, the Aldene Plan was implemented, by which Jersey Central passenger trains would turn onto the Lehigh Valley Railroad at Aldene, New Jersey, and terminate at the PRR station in Newark. Passengers could travel on to Manhattan via Hudson & Manhattan tube trains. This eliminated the ferry service and the Jersey City Terminal, but unfortunately not the Newark Bay Bridge, which remained for freight.

The Jersey Central had once been a proud railroad. It still carried 23,000 commuters into New York every day and carried them home at night. It served more than 400 New Jersey industries directly, most visibly from Manhattan, the big Colgate-Palmolive plant in Bayonne with its giant clock by which many New Yorkers downtown told the time of day. It was also a microcosm of problems that were coiling to engulf most of railroading. The troubles were deeper than poor management. The Jersey Central was the canary in the coal mine, and it just dropped dead.

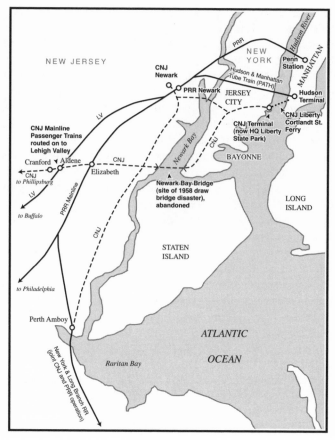

The Aldene Plan

John Fishwick and the N&W–C&O

Early October 1964 was an exciting time at N&W headquarters in Roanoke. Would the PRR divest the N&W? Though the N&W's Fishwick once argued before the ICC that the PRR did not have the power to control the N&W, he now described the PRR as a thumb on the N&W. "The Pennsylvania always had a thumb, and I think anybody on the N&W knew that thumb would be exercised if we did anything they really didn't want us to. . . . In a great many ways, the N&W ran by itself, but there was always—to use Justice Holmes' phrase—the brooding omnipresence in the sky."[16] He doubted that the PRR ever thought it could merge with the New York Central and keep the N&W too. "It was a risk they knew they were taking." But he said, "I think they were playing for high stakes— domination of the East."[17]

The PRR had 90 days to make up its mind about the N&W. The first day of October came and went, and there was no word, and so a delegation from Roanoke paid a visit to Philadelphia. "We wanted them to divest," said Fishwick, "but there was no question it was their business judgment." We tried to tell them that "giving you half the East is alright, but at least give the rest of us the other half."[18]

That coincided with the moment of decision on the Western Maryland. The C&O wanted to know what position the N&W would take regarding the WM, and that led to several meetings between delegations of the two roads. One night after one of those meetings, and just after the PRR decided it would divest, Fishwick lay awake in bed thinking about it:

> This was going through my mind, and I woke up in the middle of the night and I kept turning this thing over, and finally, the idea of a merger of the N&W and the C&O seemed like a good one. The next morning, I went to see Mr. Pevler, and with some trepidation, because it seemed like quite an idea in view of all the propaganda that had been spread about the other alignments, and I told him it just seemed to me we were focusing on the Western Maryland problem and this didn't really solve the situation, and we ought to start talking.
>
> Mr. Pevler seemed quite surprised, but then we talked about it, and a couple of days later, when we were driving over to the Greenbrier about the Western Maryland situation, we talked about it some more and agreed we ought to throw this idea out, and we did. When we did, it seemed to generate a spark, and they picked up, and it didn't seem like such a radical idea.[19]

Fishwick's reasoning was that, sooner or later, someone was going to be made to take responsibility for the outcast roads. They were too important to be abandoned. Neither federal nor state authorities would ever allow that. If they had to be nationalized, it would prove that private enterprise could not solve its problems, and nationalizing the whole system would probably be not far behind. The Penn Central was probably going to get the New Haven, leaving the Reading, the Jersey Central, the Erie Lackawanna, the Delaware & Hudson, and the Boston & Maine. The rich roads were almost certainly going to have to bear that burden. Each of the two had its own crosses to bear, what with the C&O's linkage to the Reading and the Jersey Central and the N&W's legal obligations to the other three. A merger of the coal giants would have enough financial strength to privately shoulder the burden of $650 million of these roads' debts and not wind up in receivership itself. So the N&W-C&O was to be the vehicle to bring the outcasts home.

Even a company as powerful as this giant would have to be insulated from a risk this size, so a holding company dubbed "Dereco" was to be the device. (Originally it was DERJCO, *D* for the D&H, *E* for the EL, *R* for the Reading, and *J* for the Jersey Central. "Dereco" was pronounceable.) The

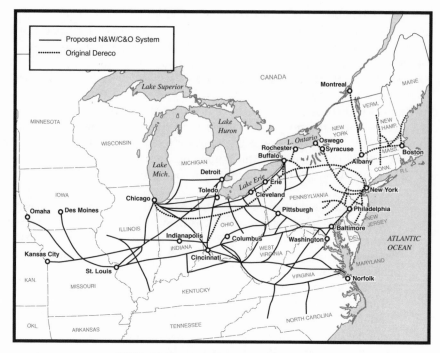

N&W–C&O and the Original Dereco Plan

underwriting firm of R. W. Presspritch Company, whom the N&W trusted to keep the plan secret, was given the task of working out details. The plan was complicated. It was meant both to serve as a circuit breaker in case there was trouble and to take advantage of tax-loss carry forwards on losses. Modification of the federal tax code to permit losses of the loser roads to reduce the tax liability of the profitable roads was an essential part of the plan.

The old loser railroads would be merged into new loser railroads—thus the Erie Lackawanna Railroad would become the Erie Lackawanna Railway. All stock of the new railroad would be owned by Dereco, a holding company controlled by the N&W-C&O. Dereco would issue its own stock to the stockholders of the old railroads, and in five years that Dereco stock would be convertible into N&W-C&O stock. If one of the loser roads defaulted, the immediate strain would be on Dereco, not on the N&W-C&O. "We had to have the N&W-C&O merger to meet the onslaught of Penn Central," said Fishwick, "and we had these losers. They were having speculators move into their stocks and we felt we could not deal directly with them."[20]

These plans were being made in secret through the spring and summer of 1965, just when the Erie Lackawanna was flailing about on its own for inclusion and the Scott-Moonshower studies were proceeding. The first public announcement was on August 31, 1965. The next day the EL and N&W delegations met again for another of their continuing round of talks, but this time Walter Tuohy and Gregory Devine of the C&O were there. The EL was presented with the idea and the terms. "We asked if it was take-it-or-leave-it," said the EL's Robert Fuller. "Mr. Pevler said it was. We asked Mr. Fishwick if the N&W would continue to bargain in good faith as required by Appendix O. He said the proposal for the N&W-C&O plan constituted compliance with that obligation and there was nothing more to negotiate."[21]

Fishwick was disappointed and perturbed.

> We were looking at this as some sort of a jigsaw puzzle. If we looked at each of the items separately, it wouldn't have been a workable deal for us, but looking at these things as part of a whole . . . we saw a great risk, but a great opportunity to do something that was good for us, but would also be in the public interest. . . . It was a program for hope. We had no studies. All we were saying was "Let's take a look as to what's in it for us and for the Dereco people."

He said he expected "the boards of the Dereco roads would jump up and say 'Hurray, we have found a savior.'"[22]

In Philadelphia the PRR had a very dim view of this Dereco business and was bitter at the thought of an N&W-C&O merger. Fishwick had been a protégé of Stuart Saunders, who was the godfather of Fishwick's children. Now the relationship had soured. "You are going to regret your action," Saunders told Fishwick when they met one day by chance at the ICC.[23] It was said that the two men did not speak to each other again for years.

On the Dereco Roads

The Dereco roads did not jump up and say "Hurray!" The Erie Lackawanna gave up on the N&W's good faith and asked to have the N&W–Nickel Plate merger case reopened for the purpose of requiring its inclusion. It had five years to ask for this, and the ICC expressly warned the N&W that consummation of its merger constituted irrevocable assent to whatever inclusion might be ordered. The N&W insisted that its Dereco proposal was the only means for this, and a merger of the N&W and the C&O would have to come first. But the word *merger* no longer rang the old bells of panacea for railroading, and the N&W surmised, probably correctly, there was a lack of patience at the ICC and among the public for the plight of the rich. The Delaware & Hudson and the Boston & Maine joined the EL for the showdown.

The EL was not unaware of its liabilities, and William White and his team set out to remedy what they could. The company aggressively and successfully solicited piggyback business, now increasingly called TOFC (trailer on flatcar). It hauled TOFCs from Chicago to New York in twenty-six and a half hours—an hour slower than New York Central but an hour and a half faster than Central States Dispatch (B&O–Reading–Jersey Central), six and a half hours faster than the N&W–Lehigh Valley, and seven and a half hours faster than the C&O–Lehigh Valley. It moved to trim long-distance passenger service. The Phoebe Snow made its last run the Sunday after Thanksgiving 1966, which left only the Lake Cities on the New York–Chicago run, a connecting train to Cleveland, and no trains to Buffalo.

The EL tackled the commuter service, determined "to solve the damn thing" once and for all, in the words of Charles Shannon of Wyer, Dick & Company, which did the key studies on avoidable costs. The EL had wheedled approximately $14 million out of New Jersey between 1960 and 1965, but aid was constantly held political hostage and covered less than a third of the railroad's losses. This time, the EL was armed with hard numbers, counting only those costs that would be eliminated if the suburban service were eliminated. They were substantial. The high-speed Morris & Essex line via Morristown—almost entirely for passengers—could be single-tracked and downgraded, the Hoboken Terminal could be abandoned, and the electrification could be ripped out. The railroad also went armed with high-powered counsel—Harry Silleck from the New York firm of Nixon, Mudge, Guthrie, Rose & Alexander. Hearings before the New Jersey Board of Public Utility Commissioners began in January 1966. The EL was allowed to drop service on some routes, notably the Northern Branch, and to reduce the number of daily trains overall from 298 to 155, a move quickly affirmed by the New Jersey Supreme Court. Gov. Richard Hughes convinced his legislature to protect what was left by entering into long-term contracts with the railroads through the Commuter Operating Agency, which would eventually metamorphose into New Jersey Transit.

On the possibility that it might be involved with Dereco, the C&O went secretly snooping on the EL in the fall of 1965 and was reasonably pleased with what it saw, a 50-mph railroad with generally on-time service and satisfied customers. After the commuter breakthrough in 1966, the EL was able to show a profit. *Value Line Survey*, a financial newsletter, said, "This is not an impressive profit by most standards, but for Erie it is nothing less than sensational." *Inside Story*, a publication of International Stanley, said, "The resurgence . . . cannot help but bring a sigh of relief and a blush of pride to railroaders everywhere."[24]

The D&H was in good physical condition, was still profitable, and its debt was reasonable. It would have been an attractive merger partner. But it was like a rich kid in a poor neighborhood. It was separated from a connection with the N&W or the C&O by 200 miles between Binghamton and Buffalo, bridged most competitively by the Erie Lackawanna. Unless the EL could make itself acceptable for inclusion, the D&H was sunk.

Time was working against the D&H. In the midst of national prosperity, and before the Penn Central onslaught, the D&H held its own but showed no capacity to grow. Its anthracite traffic was largely gone. It was sustained by bridge traffic from the Erie Lackawanna at Binghamton and the PRR at Wilkes-Barre to the Boston & Maine at Mechanicville, New York, or the Canadian roads at Montreal. But all the traffic coming off the PRR was soon going to be routed to the Penn Central via Selkirk. It was not even certain that the Penn Central would keep the Wilkes-Barre line, or at least keep it in a condition suitable for competitive service. The D&H desperately wanted to get that line. It wanted PC trackage rights to Hagerstown, Maryland, to a connection with the Chessie System (the Western Maryland) and the N&W coming up from Roanoke. The N&W doubted that this could ever be a viable service route because it would be in the Penn Central's interest to delay and harass the D&H trains.[25] So the D&H's plan for inclusion by itself got a lukewarm reception.

The Boston & Maine's reception was as frozen as a New England winter. It had lost money every year since 1957 in substantial amounts, only some of which could be traced to passenger losses. Its freight revenues had declined 30 percent since 1957, a fact that the B&M countered with boosterish projections about growth in New England in the next five years. The B&M had made similar projections in other cases. The N&W looked up the record. It found that the B&M's "experience in crystal ball gazing has been calamitous. B&M has barely been able to predict revenues for three months, let alone five years."[26] Huge blocks of B&M securities were reaching maturity in the immediate future—$46.5 million in 1967 and $19 million in 1970. Both issues were already selling at substantial discounts, so refunding was out of the question.

As if that were not enough, there had been a distressing amount of speculation in B&M stock shortly before it petitioned for inclusion, much of it by the company's own officers, at prices only a fraction of what the B&M claimed it was worth to the N&W. A grand jury had just handed down a 30-count indictment against the B&M's president, its former president, and other officers. The charge, not technically embezzlement, was "improper sale at known unadvertised prices to fraudulent middlemen with the defendants intending acquisition and retention of the proceeds." The B&M president, Pat McGinnis, was fined $5,000 and sentenced to 18 months in prison for fraudulently selling B&M passenger cars and pocketing the money. His executive committee expressed its "deepest respect and confidence in his ability," but stockholders were complaining about his $75,000 salary and initiated seven civil suits over the profiteering.[27] In short, the waters around the B&M were so murky that the N&W could hardly be blamed for wanting to steer clear.

In March 1966 the N&W sent a special train to inspect the Dereco roads firsthand. Clarence Jackman, vice president of engineering for the C&O, was in charge. The train traveled the EL main line, stopping overnight at Youngstown, Binghamton, and Hoboken. It returned to Scranton and entered the D&H at Wilkes-Barre. It spent a night in Albany, then went on to Montreal. It traveled the B&M from White River Junction to Springfield, then went to Boston and Portland and returned through Lawrence to Mechanicville. The D&H forwarded it to Binghamton and the EL to Buffalo. The D&H got relatively high marks, though Jackman noted virtually no new material had been installed since 1960. The B&M was described as "rundown." It had put a veneer of ballast over the main line and mud was already pumping through. The speed was 45 mph. The EL's maintenance had deteriorated since 1960. Less than a mile of new rail per year had been installed, 30 percent of the ties were rotted, and speed on the main line was 50 mph. "In summary," Jackman wrote, "EL has been held together for the past several years by the installation of used material made available through the retirement of track since the merger." On the three roads, 43 percent of their locomotive fleet was overage, and the freight car fleet had been reduced 27 percent since 1960.[28] The B&M denounced the tour as a "whirlwind." No one from the ICC was invited to go along.

That left the problem of debt, particularly the Erie Lackawanna's. The next move was up to security holders. If the poor roads had no debt and no fixed charges, they could earn money. How much of their outstanding debt would carry over to Dereco? Put another way, it was a question of how big a write-down the old security holders were willing to take in return for the promise of a brighter future. Five of the EL's principal creditors— Metropolitan Life, John Hancock Life, Prudential, Woodmen of America Life Insurance, and Aid Association for Lutherans—were gearing up for a showdown in the courts to make sure they got every red cent. Was it greed? Or would the same people who would be hurt if these railroads shut down be more hurt if their life insurance company got in trouble by a write-down of serious proportions?

Ever since John Fishwick had confessed that the idea for an N&W-C&O merger came to him in the middle of the night, there had been a number of guffaws "about this dream or this vision of yours." "It was not a vision as I tried to tell you," he answered. "I was awake. It happened in the middle of the night when I was thinking about this. It was my best attempt to be honest . . . and I resent it being called a vision."[29]

Vision or not (and it was the most promising idea on the table), there was plenty of room to be cynical. Both the N&W and the C&O cried that their proposal was essential for survival. But they had cried wolf before, the first time they merged. Back then it was supposed to be a three-system East, the industry's plan for balanced competition. Now it was asserted that the Penn Central would create imbalance, so the N&W and the C&O had to be allowed to merge. But month after month, all through the Penn-Central hearings, the N&W and the C&O said nothing—not a word to hint they had anything to fear from the Penn Central. The N&W now said they were silent because the PRR had controlled them and they had no choice.[30] That meant some very important executives had lied on record when they said the PRR did not control the N&W. What else in their testimony was a lie? When you destroy your own credibility, there should be no surprise when it comes back to bite you. The C&O had no excuse at all. If it were true that the C&O believed the Penn Central would unbalance the East, then its silence was an attempt to deceive the ICC. There never had been a three-system plan at all. Managements simply played it by ear, making up rationales as circumstances came along. Practically any two railroads could rattle off a list of savings and service improvements that might come from merger, especially if nobody could check up (especially after the fact) to see if any of the predictions came true.

That was not quite fair, said Fishwick. The PRR and the NYC were staggering giants in the early 1960s, and talk about a Penn-Central merger was not really very frightening back then. Now they had "shifted from two sick railroads to two that were growing stronger, and this growth had been slow, but it was accelerating." On what statistical basis he said this was far from clear, but he continued. Unlike the N&W-C&O, the Penn Central had the advantage of a balanced freight traffic, not dependent on (money-making) coal. It would have better coverage of the region with greater ability to make through rates, extend transit privileges, and attract new industry. It alone had sufficient concentrations of traffic to justify large capital investment in railroad facilities.[31]

Take any of the indices that really count, said Robert Minor of the New York Central—net income, operating ratio, transportation ratio, carload traffic, fixed charges, passenger deficit—and the Penn Central was going to be way behind either the N&W or the C&O, let alone those two combined. The PC might have better routes across the industrial heartland, but the N&W-C&O would get more traffic because they alone could afford the specialized equipment. As to PC service, which they said was going to crush everybody, train AJ-1, the Reading–Alphabet Route manifest out of Philadelphia every day at 7:35 P.M. already beat the PRR's best schedule to St. Louis by more than two hours. The whole purpose of the Penn-Central merger was to balance the financial strength of the coal roads. Would the PRR have divested the N&W if it thought the N&W was going to turn around and merge with the C&O? "I don't know," said Fishwick. "I can't read their minds." But he did not think they divested for any altruistic feelings toward the N&W. It was a business judgment, what they believed was best for them and their stockholders.[32]

Would a merger of the N&W and the C&O not create a monopoly in the transportation of eastern coal? All private parties, shippers, receivers, and transporters said no. The way the N&W-C&O explained it, the N&W and the C&O originated most of the coal headed into the Northeast, but they terminated only a portion of it, so the Penn Central would still be very much in the coal business. The N&W already dominated the low-volatile coalfields and the C&O the high-volatile ones. There was not much competition to begin with, so nothing would be lost, would it? (Roughly this same argument had been used to justify the C&O-B&O.) A number of the big coal producers—Island Creek Coal, Valley Camp Coal, and Southern Pocahontas—all said a merger would improve service. But every single state whose industry depended on an uninterrupted flow of coal from the Pocahontas fields felt a deep concern. Coal was more bound to rail transportation than just about any other commodity. Most iron ore had a long water haul, but only the railroad could get the coal out of every mountain hollow. Once this rail monopoly was created, there was no going back. It was either stick with it or nationalize it in anger. Every public body thought it was unnecessary to play with dynamite like this.

The one great public benefit of the idea was that it would provide a home for the Dereco roads. Or would it? Nobody had promised anything of substance.

> Q: Would approval of these terms fulfill your obligation under Appendix O?
>
> A: Yes. If the Commission approved everything as we say, then we could merge and make an offer to the five, and if they didn't take it, we would have fulfilled our obligation. After all, nothing can make those railroads merge with us.[33]

But then, could they be blamed? Speculators were playing with the Dereco stocks, and the Penn Central would soon be breathing down everyone's neck. Maybe the merger was going to be a roaring success just as the Penn and the Central said it would. The hearing examiner recommended approval of the N&W-C&O merger, although not until March 29, 1969. It was a long, straightforward report that laid out the case in detail for the commissioners. The ramifications were far too deep to be prejudiced at a lower level.

The Inclusion Cases

Although the railroads as a whole had insisted all along that they could plan consolidation and do a better job of it than the government, they were winding up this first phase of the merger movement divided, mutually distrustful, even hateful. They never came up with a plan that met even their own needs, let alone those of their customers or the public. They had swept the ICC along with arguments of savings and service improvements that were significant only when taken in isolation. That led directly to the inclusion crisis. ICC commissioners, a majority of them, went with the flow, swept along by the argument that whatever managements wanted to do was the same as the public interest. There were never enough commissioners willing to hold managements' feet to the fire and make them come up with a solution. Congress could not focus its attention. Kefauver tried and failed. So now, as in so many other areas of American life, it was up to the courts. In broad outline, there were three sets of cases: one to halt the Penn-Central merger; one to force the N&W to take three of the Dereco roads (the EL, the D&H, and the B&M); and one to force a merged Penn Central to take the New Haven, including passengers and commuters. The cases had the generic title "the inclusion cases."

The first set began over Appendix G, the protective conditions imposed on the Penn-Central merger for the benefit of the outcast roads, including the controversial indemnity payments. The protests came in such a chorus from everyone on all sides that the commission surmised it was the novelty of the conditions that had everyone spooked, rather than any demonstrable grievance. But it reopened the hearings anyway, noting that it believed the conditions were self-enforcing. Any attempt by the Penn Central to frustrate the purposes of protection automatically invited terrible retribution by the ICC, to which consummation of the merger constituted irrevocable assent. So, it said, while the hearings went on, the merger could go forward as well, and everyone had better be happy. But the Erie Lackawanna's nerves were at hair-trigger. With the N&W giving it

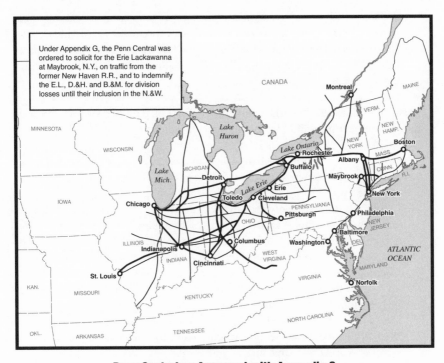

Penn Central as Approved with Appendix G

the cold shoulder in the summer of 1966, with the brooding anticipation of a hotly competitive Penn Central, it led the pack to court.

The outcasts lost the first round in district court. On October 4, 1966, the court found:

> We do not suggest that the country will perish if [the PRR and the NYC] which have lived apart for more than a century . . . must continue to do so pending reconsideration. . . . but what is in the public interest eventually is in the public interest now unless there are truly significant considerations by the other side. No suggestion has been made . . . by the plaintiffs of a willingness to post bond to indemnify PRR and NYC against loss from what may prove to be an unjustified postponement of the anticipated savings.[34]

On October 18, 1966, Justice John Harlan granted a stay of the lower court's ruling. Argument on the stay was held the following January, and a decision was handed down January 27. A minority (Harlan, Abe Fortas, Potter Stewart, and Byron White) was willing to uphold the lower court. But the majority found Appendix G neither self-enforcing nor adequate, and they ordered consummation of the Penn-Central delayed until it was reconsidered.

> We do not believe this is too high a price to pay to make as certain as human ingenuity can devise, a just and reasonable disposition of this matter. After all, this is the largest railroad merger in our history and if not handled properly, could . . . irreparably injure the entire railroad system in the northeastern section of the country.[35]

Justice William O. Douglas went much further. The decision in favor of a merger was irresponsible from the start, he said:

> Now the panic button is being pushed and we, in turn, are being asked to act hurriedly and become the final instrument for foisting this new cartel upon the country.
>
> What is the nature of this cartel? . . . Only one of the largest stockholders of the applicants is known. The remaining largest stockholders are brokerage houses and Swiss banks holding nominal title for their customers. The beneficial owners are unknown and apparently of no concern to the Commission.
>
> . . . Nor did the Commission consider it relevant that, through interlocking directorates, the proposed directors of the merged company are the directors of . . . corporations which deal with the railroads, or that the control of the railroads is steadily being concentrated in the hands of banks, insurance companies and other large financial interests.
>
> This merger, like the ones preceding it, apparently is a manipulation of fi-

nanciers and not part of the regional planning which is the ultimate function of the Interstate Commerce Commission. Yet if the imprimatur of the Commission is to be put on the plans of the financiers, much more should be known about them.[36]

As for the problem at hand, he asked: If the Penn-Central merger was justified on the grounds of saving the New Haven, why was it permissible to destroy the Erie Lackawanna and the rest of the outcasts?

Under court order for reconsideration, the commission decided it was time to bring the reopened N&W–Nickel Plate case to a conclusion. The N&W was ordered to take in the Erie Lackawanna, the Delaware & Hudson, and the Boston & Maine immediately, under the Dereco holding company plan but without a prior merger with the C&O. Terms, including stock exchange ratios, were prescribed. The N&W went straight to U.S. District Court in Roanoke to have the order set aside, while the Erie Lackawanna went to District Court in New York to have it enforced. In a combined decision, the ICC was upheld.[37] The N&W was going to have a network of routes east of Buffalo whether it wanted one or not.

On M-Day the Penn-Central was required to take over the New Haven. Dickering over the terms continued through the summer of 1966, during which time the New Haven was kept pasted together by various state subsidies, most of which were going to run out on January 1, 1967. After this date cash began to hemorrhage at such a rate that by summer it would be impossible to meet payroll. Negotiations with the Penn Central were contentious, coming down to arguments over the liquidation value of individual items of property. Take the New Haven's 40 parlor-bar cars, for example. The NH trustees said they were worth $23,000 apiece. The Penn-Central said that was ridiculous. Those cars were at the end of their service life. There was no significant market for them anywhere in North America, certainly not if they were all dumped on the market at once. It offered $5,000 apiece, top.[38] But some New Haven bondholders still thought the trustees were selling them out. A pack of them led by one Oscar Gruss brought suit.[39] The haggling was bitter. They insisted that a freight-only New Haven would be capable of earning a return. All this time the derailments, the hotboxes, the electrical fires, the power failures got worse on the New Haven. The ICC hurried its deliberations, winding them up in November 1967, but the derivative suits went on. On January 15, 1968, the Supreme Court ended all debate on all issues. As for the dissenting New Haven bondholders:

> While the rights of bondholders are entitled to respect, they do not demand Procrustean measures. They certainly do not dictate that rail operations vital to the nation be jettisoned. . . . The public interest is not merely a pawn to be sacrificed for the protection of a class of security holders.[40]

Despite the ability of the privileged rich to keep these matters in almost endless litigation for their own benefit and entertainment, capital was reminded that investment implied a risk and that those who put their money in the New Haven Railroad knew, or should have known, the extreme risk they were taking. They had gambled and lost, and the Court was going to give them no insulation from that risk. The Penn Central, upon merger, would acquire the New Haven for the $90 million package agreed upon (of which only $8 million was in cash).

That was it. This final installment of the inclusion cases reaffirmed the N&W's obligation to pick up the three outcast roads and the desirability of a Penn-Central merger. What the industry and the ICC and Congress had failed to do, the Supreme Court did in one sweeping decision. There are many who fret about judicial activism, but when everything else deadlocks, what else can cut the knot?

The N&W sent John Fishwick to head up the Erie Lackawanna. "Sending one of our top men to Cleveland to restore Erie Lackawanna's earning power should be solid evidence we are dead serious about forming Dereco," said Herman Pevler, noting, "I didn't tell Jack that he had to go out there. I asked him if he wanted to go and he said he did." Fishwick knew that if he made a success of the EL, big things would open up for him on the N&W. It was not going to be easy. His family was less than eager to leave civilized Roanoke for the icy inconveniences of a northern city that was then approaching the nadir of its rust belt decline. He kept a stiff upper lip: "I'm selling my house in Roanoke. We're moving to Cleveland to do the job given me by the N&W to look after the interests of the Erie, and it is my intention to make it the best competitor of the Penn Central and the N&W and the trucks and the waterways and do the best job I can for Erie Lackawanna and its security holders."[41]

As much as the EL wanted into the N&W, there had been no love lost between the officers of the two companies. The N&W was sophisticated and technology-oriented, with computers and big budgets for more computers. The Erie was just plain old railroad. It was impossible to disguise the contempt of the N&W people and the jealousy of the EL people. But the Dereco plan went ahead, and the Erie Lackawanna Railroad became the Erie Lackawanna Railway on April 1, 1968. The haggling over Bison Yard at Buffalo ended. A Buffalo Terminal Division was established, including the N&W and EL lines in the area. Not long afterward, arrangements were made for the C&O (Pere Marquette District) to use the yard as well, making it the focus of nearly all non–Penn Central activity in the city.[42] The Delaware & Hudson joined Dereco the following June, but the Boston & Maine held out for more money (which the Supreme Court made clear it was not going to get).

The Pennsylvania–New York Central Transportation Company

In December 1967 the New York Central virtually went out of the long-distance passenger business. The Twentieth Century Limited, the Empire State Express, and the Wolverine began their final runs on December 2. After that, trains 62 and 63 carried most of what was left of the Great Steel Fleet (with dysfunctional sleeping cars to Chicago, Detroit, and Toronto) in a single, monstrous, unreliable train. Service that was once the Southwestern Limited to St. Louis and the Ohio State Limited to Cincinnati was reduced to all-stop locals, without connections and without amenities. Perlman coupled this retreat with a new idea for a passenger service that might actually serve a useful purpose. Called Empire Service, it had trains leaving New York for Albany every two hours, five of them continuing on to Buffalo. Unfortunately, the equipment was so shabby and unreliable and the cavernous and empty stations so spooky, located in parts of town where nobody went anymore, that it was not much of a success.

The PRR signed on with the U.S. Department of Transportation to build Metroliners for the New York–Washington corridor. They were designed to go 160 mph and be faster than air travel in terms of getting someone from where they were to where they wanted to go. It was going to take more than new trains, for such speeds were not remotely possible on the PRR's track, not in the condition it was in. Elsewhere on the system, the Broadway Limited soldiered on, still a respectable train but the only one on the system that was. Everything else was bareboned and threadbare, two or three decrepit cars behind a single diesel unit, heat and air conditioning either malfunctioning or nonfunctioning, paint peeling, stations decrepit, and station lavatories too horrible to even think about.

The Penn Central was born at one minute past midnight on February 1, 1968. After daylight, the new board of directors gathered in Philadelphia for its first meeting and unofficial photographs. They tried to smile as warmly as they could, given that some of them hated each other's guts. There were press conferences later, the podium decked in Penn Central bunting. The new emblem was unveiled, an anagram of the letters *P* and *C* intertwined, an obvious imitation of the Canadian National's brilliant anagram CN, called the "wet noodle." All railroads, really all industry, had wet noodle envy. Stuart Saunders and Alfred Perlman posed in front of a Lionel toy boxcar painted green with the new PC emblem. The two smiled the smile of let's-get-this-over-with. It was made expressly clear that the shade of green on the little boxcar was *not* the New York Central's old jade green, but a new green, a tealish green, a distinctly Penn Central green. "Long courtship makes for eternal bliss," said Saunders, explaining that the companies had taken advantage of the long delay in consummating their merger to work on new studies so that the merger would go more smoothly. There were going to be new superunit trains,[43] and the Metroliners were going to be a great success.[44] Everything was going to be wonderful.

The Penn Central headquarters would be in Philadelphia. Stuart Saunders would be chairman and was in charge of corporate affairs, diversification, and politics. He was on the cover of *Time* and was named *Saturday Review*'s businessman of the year. Perlman was president and would run the railroad. David Bevan, the railroad's chief financial officer, whose job it was to get the credit from the banks to keep the merger afloat, was not on the new board, though he had been on the PRR's old one. Once, he was in line to be the PRR's CEO; then the board fell all over itself to woo Saunders and his Democratic Party connections and his lovely wife and all that. No one asked Bevan to join in the smiley photograph in front of the toy boxcar. He was mad. Perlman did not stick around for the champagne toasts or to soak up the ambiance of Philadelphia Society that was the soul of the PRR. He had a railroad to run. He got on his private railroad car and went back to New York. That was how the biggest adventure in modern railroad history began.

Four months later, on June 8, 1968, the Penn Central was asked to operate Sen. Robert Kennedy's funeral train from New York to Washington. Kennedy had been shot soon after winning the California presidential primary. After the funeral at St. Patrick's Cathedral in New York City, burial was to be at Arlington National Cemetery beside his brother. The railroad was thrust center stage into a national nightmare. All that Penn Central could assemble was a train of mismatched old and older equipment. It carried 1,146 passengers. At least there were no hotboxes or electrical fires, but *Newsweek* noted that it was a "rolling catalog of the physical discomforts that have turned U.S. passenger railroads into the nation's most unpopular form of mass travel."

At that time the railroad was rapidly fading from public consciousness. Harry Reasoner, reporting for CBS aboard the train, even said it was "as anachronistic as the horse."[45] This was the last time that a railroad remotely seemed a natural part of the lives of Americans. The crowds poured out to wave goodbye. Many saluted the rear observation car *Philadelphia* that carried the coffin. Many reached out to touch the *Philadelphia* as it passed. As the train rumbled through the station in Baltimore, the crowd broke spontaneously into the "Battle Hymn of the Republic." The clickety-clack of the train's wheels picked up by television microphones sent shivers at multiple levels. The country was drifting closer to anarchy than at any time since the eve of the Civil War. The railroad was drifting closer to dissolution than anyone realized.

fourteen

The Fall of the Penn Central
1968–1970

In November 1967 the PRR's vice president for finance, David Bevan, wrote that the Pennsylvania Railroad required average cash balances of $45 to $50 million to cover normal activities. "We have not had balances in this area at any time this year, and at the end of October, our cash balance amounted to roughly eight and one half million dollars." He pointed out that money had been borrowed just to maintain balances, that in spite of this, at the rate accounts were being drawn down, they would reach zero by the end of the year and be $22 million in the hole by February. February 1968 was the month the PRR merged with the New York Central.[1]

The merger anticipated $100 million in annual savings. The Penn Central, particularly the Penn side of that equation, had to have $100 million immediately. And so it decided to slam these two giant railroads together immediately, in the pyrrhic hope that somehow $100 million would come miraculously floating down to net income.

It should have been expected, since it had happened in previous mergers, that connecting railroads would deliver cars to whichever facility (whether former PRR or former NYC) was convenient for them. At Chicago, for example, the Penn Central pleaded with connecting roads to designate "PCP" if cars were to go to the old PRR's 59th Street or Colehour Yards or "PCN" if they were to go to the former NYC's Kensington or Englewood Yards. But connecting roads had problems of their own. It was not their job to save the Penn Central.

No effort was made to train the more than 5,000 routing clerks in the new routes, junctions, and stations for which they were responsible on the merged road. "They'd get a car bound for Harrisburg," said a supervisor at

Selkirk on the old NYC to reporter Rush Loving, Jr. "They'd never heard of Harrisburg because it wasn't on the Central. And they'd say 'where the hell is Harrisburg? I know where Pittsburgh is. Shit! I'll send it to Pittsburgh.'"[2]

Waybills, the paperwork that explained what was in those cars and where and to whom they were going, could easily be delivered to the facility of the other former railroad. That rendered the cars effectively lost— "no-bills" they were called on the railroad. No-bills by the thousands began floating around yards, until frustrated yardmasters rounded up whole trains of them and sent them off to somebody else's yard. They had to get them out of the way. These were the legendary "lost trains" of the Penn Central. Needless to say, the shippers of every one of those lost cars were going to be on the telephone to headquarters in the morning, not feeling very pleasant about it.

No time was taken to complete track connections or yard alterations before rerouting began. That caused delays. Delays meant that locomotives and crews were tied up longer and were not available for new trains. Crews on the job more than 16 continuous hours by law had to "book off"—take 8 hours' rest. If crews were close to home at the moment they had to book off, they might just call a cab and go home, leaving their train on a siding somewhere. Loving reported that one 100-car coal train was left outside of Syracuse for ten days before anyone remembered it. "It was just a goddamned operating mess," one crew member told Loving. Here are some of the things that happened after this "soundly conceived" merger.

Trouble Spots: Selkirk and Big Four

Construction of the new Selkirk Yard near Albany was begun before the merger. It was opened on September 25, 1968, and officially named the Alfred E. Perlman Yard. It was to be the focal point of the new railroad where all the traffic rerouted over the Water Level Route would be funneled to New York City, the New Jersey ports, and New England. The budget for the project was $20 million, but cost overruns exceeded 100 percent. By July 1968, only 70 of the 90 classification tracks were in place, but management wanted the yard open, and no one dared tell them it was not ready.

Traffic poured in on clerks and crews that were unrehearsed, to a yard that was half-completed. Lost loaded cars wallowed at Selkirk for sometimes up to 27 days. Routing instructions changed almost weekly. As one set proved unworkable, new ones were issued. One of the ICC's inspectors asked a clerk what his instructions were. "Yesterday's, today's or tomorrow's?" was the reply. "They're all different."[3] Meanwhile, fully staffed work trains waited to complete construction, but day after day they could not get into the yard because the entrances were blocked by the crush of traffic. The crews, ready to work, drew their full wages for the hours and days that were lost, and the construction that might relieve the congestion could not be finished.

All traffic delivered by the PRR on car floats to the New Haven's Bay Ridge Yard in Brooklyn was ordered rerouted through Selkirk. Lighterage operations in New York Harbor were expensive, so it was important in terms of "savings" to get Bay Ridge closed. That meant that cars bound for destinations even in Brooklyn or Queens were sent all the way up to Albany on the West Shore, then all the way back down the east bank of the Hudson, resulting in delays of up to six days, further aggravating the situation at Selkirk.

Nor was the River Division, the old West Shore Railroad up the Hudson, ready for this new crush of traffic. In the heyday of West Shore passenger trains, with their picturesque stop at West Point, the line was double tracked. In the 1950s, when the passenger trains were gone and freight dwindled to three trains a day, the track was reduced to single track without many passing sidings. No sidings were added after the merger, although the number of trains tripled and many of them were too long for the sidings anyway. Trains often had to wait "in the hole" (on a passing siding) more than six hours for trains in the opposite direction. Average over-the-road time, as calculated from the dispatcher's log, was 6 hours and 11 minutes for the 128 miles, but 13 percent of the trains took more than 11 hours and some as long as 18 hours. The sixteen-hour rule kicked in frequently, and crews had to "book off" en route, blocking the line while they rested. Police at Bogota, New Jersey, for example, received repeated complaints about diesel engines idling all night in residential neighborhoods.

South of Alsen, New York, nine racks of new Cadillacs flipped over on a broken rail and lay beside the track in a mangled heap for 18 months. Wrecked boxcars lay along the track at Lake Katrine, at Esopus, at Cornwall, and at West Point. The speed was 10 mph on the temporary track installed after each of these wrecks, and since the line was so congested, there was no downtime for the work crews to get in to clean up the mess.[4]

At the time when Bay Ridge was shut down, proper track connections were not completed between the NYC's River Division and the PRR's Waverly Yard, where the route to the car floats to Bay Ridge diverged from the main line. In fact, the connection had not even been started. Trains had to make a tortuous backup around Newark using a portion of the Lehigh Valley and crossing the Jersey Central's main line at grade. Add that to the routine delays on the River Division and at Selkirk, and transit time to New England was increased by five to six days. Shippers were not happy.

On the drawing boards in Philadelphia, Buffalo's Frontier Yard was supposed to have a capacity of 2,026 cars per shift. But those who knew it knew that it began to congest at 1,100 cars a shift, and if a strong west wind was blowing off Lake Erie, it could reasonably expect to dispatch no more than 900 cars. Frontier was never meant to handle industrial traffic.

The plans called for the old PRR's Seneca Yard to do that. But all former PRR facilities were ordered closed, so everything was dumped on Frontier. Frontier broke down. Overflows were sent to nearby yards, which were having problems of their own.

At Toledo, the PRR's Outer Yard was closed in favor of the NYC's Stanley Yard. Before merger, Stanley was used mostly for coal. It was so deteriorated from that track-busting tonnage that the Central had thought of closing it, especially after derailments began to average more than 50 a month. Even so, Stanley was more efficient than Outer. Stanley could switch an (appalling) 83 cars per locomotive shift; Outer could do only 72. When Outer was closed and its crews moved to Stanley, Stanley's efficiency fell to 42 cars per shift. A year later, it was back up to 57 cars. That was mostly because sales in the Toledo region fell off 30 percent, shippers having given up in disgust and taken their business elsewhere. At Stanley, the weight scale broke and no one could come up with the funds to fix it. So cars that had to be weighed had to be classified separately, taking up a whole track of precious yard space, then sent to the half-abandoned Airline Yard nearby, weighed, and sent back and reclassified for a delay of three to four days.

The same thing happened at St. Louis. The PRR's Rose Lake Yard could not handle the combined traffic of two railroads, so some of the cars had to be taken back to the Central's old yard. That was the worst of both worlds—one congested, the other half-abandoned—but with the expense of operating them both. The NYC line between Indianapolis and St. Louis was to be downgraded in the merger. Cars for local points on that line were sent up the PRR all the way to Indianapolis for classification and then sent back down the NYC line, some of them almost all the way to St. Louis. Needless to say, those shippers took their business elsewhere.

Before merger the NYC averaged one derailment a week in its St. Louis yard, for an average delay of three to four hours and an average cost of $100. The PRR averaged two derailments a week, with an average delay of four hours and an average cost of $470. Now, thanks to the magic of merger, there were four derailments a week with an average delay of seven hours and a cost of $500.

The NYC's Big Four Yard at Indianapolis was to be the Selkirk of the west.[5] Cars from all over the Midwest were to be gathered there, grouped into solid blocks for common destinations for dispatch as far east as Selkirk. Premerger planning called for the installation of extra tracks when the PRR's Hawthorne Yard was closed, but a second study purported to show that the extra tracks were not necessary. "I was told by a Penn Central employee that management didn't want to incur the extra expense and the second study was tailored to fit that decision," said an ICC inspector.[6] Big Four was so jammed with lost and misclassified cars that trains were backed up down the main line waiting to get in. Sometimes, just to

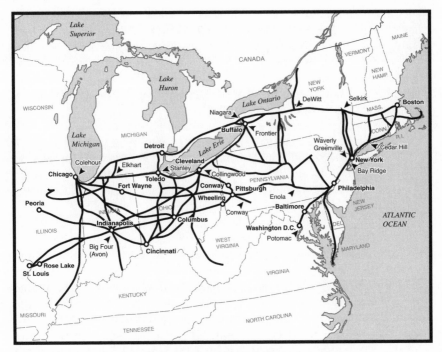

Penn Central Trouble Spots

clear space, batches of cars were sent out to be classified somewhere else, and many had to be returned to Big Four to be handled a second time. ICC inspectors thought Big Four was the classic example of trying to force savings out of merger before it was physically possible to do so.

The armrest story was typical of the lack of planning. The labor contract between the NYC and the Brotherhood of Locomotive Engineers required that locomotive seats be equipped with armrests. The PRR's agreement had no such requirement, and its locomotives had no armrests. It was not long before NYC and PRR units funneled into Big Four and became intermixed. But NYC crews stood on their rights and refused to operate units not properly equipped. That required endless switching and turning, which added to the overall chaos. On one ICC inspection to the ready track (where fueled and serviced locomotives stood ready for their next assignment), there were only PRR units and NYC crews available for service, so everything was at a standstill.

Stories like this usually provoked disgust at the shortsightedness of the union rather than at the incompetence of management. But these contract differences were well known before the merger and required only minor modifications to the locomotives, which were never performed. Because of the shabby maintenance of the locomotive fleet, a lot of units were out of service altogether. The problem of power shortages quickly became critical. In the third quarter of 1969, 624 trains were delayed for lack of power; in the fourth quarter, 1,817 trains were delayed, and in the first quarter of 1970, 2,993 trains were delayed because no locomotive was available to pull them.

ICC inspectors watched the chaos at Big Four and surrounding territory and thought these stories were typical:

—One day at Terre Haute, there was a burst of activity to call a crew and a locomotive to send out some badly delayed cars. When the crew reported for duty and the locomotive was attached, it was discovered that no caboose would be available for several hours, until incoming trains arrived.

—At Big Four, 79 cars of coal for local delivery to the Indianapolis Union Railroad were reported arriving on the next train, and so a transfer crew and an appropriate switching locomotive were called up. When the train arrived, it was not 79 cars for local delivery but 129 cars for Chicago. So the local crew was paid its day's wages and sent home, and a road crew was called. Two hours later, the 79 cars showed up, and the same crew had to be recalled and paid a second day's wages.

—One day at Big Four there were 300 empty hopper cars clogging things up, waiting for dispatch over a single track line to Ashby in southern Indiana. Two trains were ordered to forward them immediately, without taking into account that three trains were, at that very moment, headed up the line. The line had only two passing sidings. It was instantly jammed. Three of the trains suffered delays of more than six hours.

—One day at Anderson, Indiana, nearly 70 loaded and badly delayed cars were waiting to be picked up by a passing train. Despite telephone calls, Big Four had no idea when a train could be expected. Local people were frantically discussing what to do when four locomotives and a caboose came rolling down the track. They tried to wave it down. The crew cheerfully waved back and rumbled on into the afternoon sun. The dispatcher at Big Four said another train might be along in four hours, but it would have room for no more than 20 cars.[7]

Unhappy Customers and Connections

"Shippers are dissatisfied with our service," said an understated memo of November 1968.[8] There followed a list of some of the railroad's most prestigious customers—Allied Chemical, International Paper, Uniroyal, Shell Oil, National Distillers, National Starch, Stauffer Chemical, Hooker Chemical, and the New York Perishable Dealers' Association. Complaints from each were attached. A year later, nothing had changed; there was a similar memo with similar attachments, but the list was much longer. Kodak piggyback vans, for example, were missing connections in St. Louis 75 percent of the time on their way from Rochester to Dallas. More than 40 percent of St. Louis–New England traffic was suffering delays of more than three days. "We have lost a sizeable amount of fresh meat traffic to Erie Lackawanna. Shippers have said it was the far greater reliability of their service."[9]

> I keep getting reports of the success of our sales people, only to have the business taken away due to our poor service. Attached are two sheets of specific instances. It is by no means complete, as we don't always learn of lost traffic until long after the fact. This business listed represents $800,000 in revenue. Attachment showing Truc-Train performance. Only two operated on an acceptable basis. Maximum weekly performance was 35 percent on time. Many cars of western perishables are being misclassified. During April, 2000 cars were improperly blocked.[10]

In Cincinnati Chevrolet was complaining, Delco was complaining, and March Foods was complaining. Anchor-Hocking Glass reported 110 cars due but not delivered, which interrupted their production. Thatcher Glass supplied empty bottles to Seagrams; Seagrams then reloaded with filled bottles. They required clean cars, but since the car-cleaning track was discontinued in a cost-cutting move, they were not available. They switched to motor carriers. Armco Steel reported no deliveries for five days in April 1968, causing a backup of 209 cars. Supervisors explained every instance as a special case. Special cases were epidemic.

> We always have published second morning delivery schedules to the East. It was always sent in two trains from Rose Lake to Enola [near Harrisburg] and arrived in time for evening market trains. It is now taking five days to move over the line.
>
> DuPont is complaining. Publicker is complaining. Rohm & Haas is complaining. Tenneco is complaining. The auto industry is complaining. These are just a few of the patrons who were promised good service when we merged, but instead, service has deteriorated.[11]

Other railroads were getting annoyed. On run-through service with the Cotton Belt, cars were taking 6 to 11 days longer just to reach the Cotton Belt. "We have lost a major amount of business between New Jersey and the West Coast," said the Cotton Belt. "Can you get it back?" "Responsibility for this rests in your region," said headquarters to supervisors in St. Louis. "Our reputation with connections has suffered." "My first reaction is that it is not that simple," came the reply from St. Louis. "On further reflection, I still think it's the same. . . . Let's wait and see what happens."[12]

Reluctantly, the Cotton Belt and the Missouri Pacific agreed to do some of the Penn Central's blocking (grouping of cars bound for common destinations), but the PC still missed its principal Missouri Pacific connection three out of four days. "This is the record of BF-3," said headquarters to Rose Lake. "Needless to say, it isn't very good. Would you review your entire operation and hopefully show a marked improvement in the performance."[13]

Things were no better at Chicago. Following former NYC practice, trains from all over converged on Elkhart, Indiana, where they were broken down and regrouped for Chicago-area destinations and individual connecting railroads. They were arriving late in Elkhart, frequently bunched up, clogging the yard. They were constantly missing connecting trains of western roads, and those roads began to get short-tempered in return. "Eastbound deliveries are not being made properly to our yards [by western roads]," wrote a beleaguered local official. "Chicago & North Western is the worst offender, delivering traffic randomly to Englewood and 59th Street with no blocking. Illinois Central is also bad."[14] A delegation from headquarters was dispatched to smooth things out with those roads. But a year later, Jervis Langdon of the Rock Island wrote Perlman, "Our Rock Island run-through must make Union Pacific connections. You are so late, we run a special make-up if there is any possibility we can overtake at North Platte [Nebraska]. If not, we add your cars to mail-express train #1, but even so, connections are terrible."[15] By that time the Santa Fe and the Milwaukee Road were also complaining.

Of 71 shippers contacted by ICC inspectors in Baltimore, 5 said they detected some improvement in service since the merger, 43 said service was worse, and 22 thought it was about the same, usually noting it was none too good before. Chrysler and General Motors said they would divert if they could but were stuck with sidings on the Penn Central. Scott Paper, Philco, and Crown Cork switched to motor transport. Downingtown Paper said erratic deliveries of coal caused it to convert to fuel oil. Lukens Steel switched to the Reading. Hotpoint switched to the Central States Dispatch (the Reading-B&O). The Indiana Grain Cooperative switched 75 percent of its business to the N&W. Its new unit train to Baltimore would go B&O.

"It took them ten days to get one of our cars out of town," said Central Soya in Indianapolis, "then another seventeen to get it to Louisville, then it was returned to us still full of feed. After that, we divert all we can. Even if service improves, we're not returning to Penn Central. 85 percent of inbound traffic is now diverted and 100 percent of outbound." Kroger Supermarkets of Indianapolis advertised a special on fresh cantaloupes. The cars went to Pittsburgh instead, and by the time they got back, the fruit was rotten, a total loss of $9,000. Kroger said the damage to its customer relations was "severe." At Syracuse, a carload of live hogs was left in the yards over a hot summer weekend, with no provision to water them. Upon arrival, 54 of the animals were dead, the others unusable. Said the shipper, "The carrier says the number of damage claims causes this kind of traffic to be a loser, but it seems to be the carrier's fault." At Indianapolis, Stokely-Van Camp noted that a batch of fresh fruit from California was misclassified as "empties" and sent back to California. The contents were a total loss and production came to a halt. Cannery workers had to be paid and sent home. The company had planned to build a new warehouse and distribution center on the Penn Central but were going to build it on the N&W instead. Eli Lilly, the manufacturer of pharmaceuticals, reported that a car containing frozen animal glands going from Davenport, Iowa, to its plant in Indianapolis, arrived 27 days late and thawed. The contents were a reeking mess and a total loss of $15,000.[16] At about this juncture, the advertising department wanted to kick off a new campaign with the theme "Have you tried Penn Central service lately?" The campaign was shelved as ill-timed.

Don't Blame It on Computers

If you were a shipper and wanted information about your delayed shipment, it was best to be patient. More likely than not, the railroad had not the foggiest idea where it was. Partly because of understaffing and partly because of embarrassment, it did not answer its telephones. Kroger Supermarkets in Indianapolis said it took an average of seven employee hours a day by its own staff to trace lost cars on the Penn Central Railroad. Allied Chemical thought it was no wonder: the Baltimore switchboard was taken out in a cost-cutting move. Customers were asked to route calls through the Philadelphia switchboard, but the railroad's Philadelphia operators did not know the Baltimore people or their numbers. Armstrong Cork said it did not care what switchboards the railroad took out; when it wanted information, it made a person-to-person collect call to Bossler or Flannery at Philadelphia headquarters. A New York shipper noted that it took several days and many calls to reach the New York tariff office, and when he got through, they did not have the information and told him to go bother the Erie Lackawanna for it. Said an ICC inspector:

Nearly all shippers said the attitude of station employees, which was none too good prior to merger, became almost intolerable within a few months after the merger. It was my experience, when making agency checks, that these employees were flooded with requests to trace delayed traffic. When this became almost impossible, they had to face, day after day, irate shippers and receivers, and suffer the caustic comments made toward them and their company. This, plus the failure of their railroad to provide any semblance of the service they had known on their separate lines prior to merger, dropped their morale to near zero. It was not confined to station employees, but happened to sales people, yard police, and any other department that had contact with the general public.[17]

Even shippers were probably unaware of how totally management had lost control of car tracing. In one test, computers were asked, on the basis of existing data, to locate 20 cars known to be on the system. They could not find any of them.

One of the first revelations after the debacle was that the two railroads had incompatible computer systems. Both used IBM 360s, but the NYC fed information with punched cards and the PRR with punched tapes. So the systems could not exchange information. It looked all the worse because this hardware was purchased after the decision to merge. These computers were the basic tools for car tracing, billing, and statistical data for management, the data on which crucial decisions would be made. The two railroads, poised to merge, could not agree on something so simple yet so fundamental as how to feed information into their computers. Some reports suggested that computer failure was the reason the railroad failed. Certainly, as it strangled in lost cars, its customers deserting in droves, this was a matter that demanded investigation.

Both railroads used essentially the same method of car tracing. A complete report showing every car on the system was prepared by computer between 3:00 and 5:00 A.M. and delivered to management at 5:30 A.M. It was possible to get selective updates every two hours. It was fairly sophisticated computer technology when it was developed in 1959 and had been improved since then, especially with the installation of the 360s. But unlike newer systems being used on other railroads, it had a fundamental flaw in that it could not detect errors fed into it, even to the basic logic of car movements. If erroneous data was entered into the system, it stayed there. Data could be checked to see whether it was consistent within itself, but not to see whether it was consistent with previously reported data. Before the merger, both the PRR and the NYC computer people were aware of these problems and agreed that a new system was in order, but they could not agree on which one, so decisions were postponed. While the Southern Railway and the Southern Pacific went ahead with new sophisticated systems, the NYC and the PRR stagnated, and on merger day had to struggle to make the old systems function at all.

The breakdown of the computer billing system not only irritated customers, who did not need further irritation, but also cost the railroad timely payments of accounts receivable. The NYC's old treasury accounting control (TAC) system was abandoned in favor of the PRR's station revenue accounting (SRA) system. This was a bad decision because TAC gave weekly reports and showed every account unpaid for eight working days as delinquent. SRA gave only a monthly report. It required a large amount of manual preparation and allowed only minimal control on the accuracy and adequacy of the information fed into it. There was no way to ensure that all movements got into the billing system. It could not provide information that sales people needed in order to resolve customers' problems.

At the start of an audit in March 1968, there were in Detroit, for example, 140 unidentified checks on hand amounting to $306,768 in revenue, the result of lost paperwork and inadequate computer controls. By May, only 83 of these checks had been identified; the remainder, some of them up to five months old, included one check for $32,158. Machine errors were found in 104 items, totaling $45,875 in collectible revenue. Twenty-three more bills totaling $97,938 in collectible revenue had incorrect due dates; collection would be delayed at least a day. On hand in excess of 48 hours were 1,490 statements with unbilled revenue of $372,000. In Chicago, an auditor found a file cabinet of switching orders for which switching bills had not been prepared. These were a month old and totaled $10,000 in revenue. After preparing the remittance of January 13, 1969, said the auditors, there were still on hand 23 checks totaling $7,125. Auditors found serious arrears of unanswered correspondence on the coal desk, the rate desk, and the cashier's desk. Across the system, unsettled accounts went from $57 million shortly after the merger to $87 million in January 1970, to $101 million in March 1970. "In freight billing," concluded ICC inspectors, "delay in forwarding the data to the billing centers and inexperienced personnel were the primary cause of the problem."[18] At Indianapolis, which had not been a billing center before the merger, it was necessary to bring in billing clerks from other parts of the system. Although 80 jobs were authorized, only 20 experienced billing clerks transferred; most preferred a lump-sum severance rather than to move. About 60 percent of the people working in that office were hired off the street. So 20 experienced people were left to cope with accounts amounting to $100,000 a day. Functions such as corrections, revisions, and overdue notices pretty much lapsed.

Errors were common. "Patrons get no bills, or wrong bills, or pay their bills and get threatened with legal action for non-payment because it was entered in the wrong account. Agents are continually trying to assist patrons in obtaining correction and relief from these errors, and it is frustrating when they can't get it." Auditors noted that examples of triple billing on accounts that were already paid resulted in "stronger than normal commentary from the most reputable of patrons."[19] The company's auditors, Peat, Marwick & Mitchell, clearly alarmed, concluded, "The present system is totally dependent on the quality performance of agreement personnel. Management control over the quality and promptness of rendering bills is too late in the system and otherwise inadequate."[20]

Agreement employees can be no better than the management that directs them. Firm lines of authority were never laid down at the bottom levels. Hence, noted auditors, station agents in charge of accounts reported to trainmasters whose responsibility was the operation of trains, who usually did not understand nor appreciate the importance of paperwork; nor were they sensitive to the feelings of those loyal workers who did jobs other than jockeying boxcars. At Niagara Falls, New York, the agent was made to do the trainmaster's operating reports to the neglect of agency work. At Watertown, New York, the agent was used as an extra brakeman. Auditors found him riding on top of boxcars. "We found poor morale existing throughout most the agencies. It was primarily the result of recent budget cuts being applied to personnel performing functions related to revenue processing or revenue control at the agency level."[21]

Even the computer reports needed by management for effective control and budgeting failed because they were studded with errors, which led either to wrong decisions or false hopes. Inspectors again cited the lack of training at the bottom. One inspector visited the office of Jonathan O'Herron, executive vice president of finance under David Bevan. On his desk the inspector found confidential memos describing the planned reduction of forces from 95,000 in 1969 to a projected 91,000 in 1970, yet employment charts also on his desk showed that employment had risen from 94,000 in mid-February 1969 to 95,792 in mid-June. "The confidential memo painted a rosy picture while the house was burning down."[22]

"If you looked at the 'T' report [a major report on train movements] this morning," said vice president David Smucker, "you would wonder what happened to the Pennsylvania Railroad."[23] Information was missing, sometimes from whole regions in old PRR areas. The information that was there was unreliable. An ICC inspector at Chicago explained that, for years, "the FT-3 report was known to be less than factual since it was believed by personnel to be the basis for the elimination of yard crews. Yardmasters would add a few hundred cars, trainmasters some more, and so false figures were made up to compare with past false figures."[24]

An example of how good ideas came to naught was the demurrage inventory car control system (DICCS). Cars delivered to a customer's siding had to be unloaded in a specified amount of time or else the customer owed a fee (demurrage) for every day the car remained unavailable for reloading. Also, if switching movements were performed within a plant, the customer had to pay. Both were important sources of revenue. Previously, clerks had to check each individual siding, but DICCS provided a simple method for conductors on the switching runs to record the information and feed it into the teletype. However, conductors were never taught how to do it, or precisely what constituted a demurrage day, or what constituted a chargeable switching move. So the record was incomplete, with many cars omitted. At Toledo, for example, $3,812 was collected in June 1967 for demurrage, whereas in June 1970, for approximately the same work, only $1,601 was collected. Many of the clerks, rather than checking for errors themselves, let the customers do it, which they did, though not very cheerfully. Forty percent of the demurrage bills were being returned for correction. The conclusion of ICC inspectors:

The mere fact that computers couldn't talk to each other was not that serious. At worst, it should have meant that two telephone calls might be necessary to get any given information. Long delays in transit, misdelivery of cars, improper blocking of trains, misrouting and congested yards, were not the computer's fault. It was only the recorder of information. Problems of computer incompatibility, when examined, usually revealed it was other problems underneath. Such fault as there was seems to have been the inability of field personnel to report information due to their inexperience or the fact that their attentions were constantly being diverted elsewhere. The system depended absolutely on operations personnel giving it the right input. They were so harassed, or so inexperienced, the information didn't get in, or it was the wrong information.[25]

Don't Blame It on Labor

The Luna-Saunders Labor Agreement of 1964 required the railroad to provide a job for everyone who worked for it from the day the agreement was signed until the merger. No one dreamed it was going to take four years to consummate. Many people were hired during that time, and many were laid off, but on merger day jobs had to be offered to all of them; 2,967 accepted, and the railroad was saddled with what appeared to be an impossible burden. The 2,967 who were taken back were ordered to be kept idle, as a spectacle of the unreasonableness of the unions.

In 1964, when the agreement was made, the railroad estimated that this labor agreement would cost $78 million over eight years, based on wage scales of the early 1960s. Like many things in the merger, these estimates were never updated. Within 18 months of the merger, $64.7 million was spent (or was claimed to have been spent) in implementing the labor settlement. Insurance executive E. Clayton Gengras, who was a Penn Central director and a former Republican candidate for governor of Connecticut, said the Luna-Saunders Agreement was the merger's "death warrant," and the idea was repeated so often that it became common in some quarters to blame the debacle on labor.

Despite the 2,967 employees taken back on merger day, total employment fell in the first year of merger (February 1968–February 1969) from 106,000 to 102,000, and it fell further to the 95,000 range by early 1970. So it was not as though the railroad was stuck with a permanently inflated workforce. Recalled workers used different-colored time cards to make sure they were paid from a special fund that was categorized as a nonrecurring expense of merger, not a regular operating expense. It helped to disguise the railroad's many real problems to charge as much to this account as possible. The railroad was so eager to keep a full contingent in that category that substitutes were added to the recalled category when recalled people were transferred to the active labor pool.

Officially, recalled labor was to remain idle or be assigned make-work projects "such as cleaning up facilities that would not otherwise be cleaned, and so forth."[26] But field inspectors of the company's auditors, Peat, Marwick & Mitchell, reported that

> recalled employees do not, in fact, stand around idle. All are given work and integrated into regular work teams, especially at Altoona, which had the greatest number of recalled employees. . . . In our audit work thus far, we have made visits to the shops, and from visual observation, could not distinguish regular workers from recalled personnel. All seemed to be doing the same work.[27]

When the ICC's Bureau of Enforcement visited Altoona in 1971, it was told by the local supervisor that there were no nonproductive employees at Altoona and never had been. "Those called back were put to work. Wages of 767 men were charged against the special account. While their time-cards designated them as non-productive employees, they performed productive functions on car lines and normal shop activities."[28]

Saunders insisted that his labor agreement was a good agreement because the company had the right to transfer employees wherever they were needed. But many who had the skills most needed by the railroad took a lump-sum settlement rather than move. In 1969, a year after the merger, 61 percent of all trainmasters, 81 percent of all transportation superintendents, and 44 percent of all division superintendents had been at their jobs less than one year. These were positions that can be compared to noncommissioned officers in the military. As any military officer knows, the success of a unit depends on the skills and experience of its noncommissioned officers. They are the ones who translate strategies and concepts into a nuts-and-bolts operation.

On the railroad these positions required critical skills and experience; without them operations broke down. Perhaps it is worth a thesis by a social historian to quantify who transferred and who did not. Anecdotal evidence suggests that those who were experienced and skilled, valuable to any employer but still young enough to find new jobs, were the ones who took the lump-sum settlement and moved on to other employment. It is known that, in the wake of the merger, the railroad developed a terrifying gap of employees with between 5 and 15 years' experience. That is a bracket of enormous value to any industrial operation. Clearly, the Luna-Saunders Agreement did not guarantee that the railroad would have the individuals it wanted with the skills it needed at the place it needed them, as Saunders said it would.

By 1970 the Penn Central was paying out 59 percent of its revenue in wages. The industry average was 44 percent. It paid overtime that was 12 percent of its gross payroll. That was double what it had been for the NYC and the PRR separately. The productivity per employee was 87 percent of the industry average.[29] An ICC inspector calculated that had it remained close to the industry average, the Penn Central would have saved $377 million in wages plus an additional 15 percent in fringe benefit costs. This indicated a breakdown of management, not of labor's protection agreement. Citing Niagara Falls, New York, and Kalamazoo, Michigan, as the two most incompetently run stations on the system, ICC inspectors noted the hundreds of cars moving through these stations on illegal "memo" waybills that left no duplicate record in case the car and its paperwork should become separated. They attributed this to lax discipline. An extraordinary number of mistakes and omissions in yard records had been made by untrained or undisciplined personnel.[30] They suggested that even the most rudimentary custodial services—such as providing toilet paper in the lavatories—would vastly improve morale.

The way labor saw it, the railroad pleaded poverty but never missed a dividend. Its officers were paid very handsome salaries—$279,000 for Saunders in 1970, for example (which was indeed very handsome in 1970). Little things—Saunders's chauffeured limousines and his memberships in fancy Philadelphia clubs—fueled a sense by labor that no, it was not going to make concessions so that people like that could save face. Saunders made the Luna-Saunders Agreement. He could have gotten a better deal if he had not wanted his merger at any cost. Now he would have to live with it.

This did not excuse labor: its lobbying had resulted in laws requiring excessively large crews in three Penn Central states—New York, Ohio, and Indiana. But on a railroad where so much work needed to be done, where there were not enough clerks or telephone operators or freight-car repairmen, where over a quarter of the late trains in 1969 were late specifically because of the unavailability of crews, it was hard to make a case that the railroad collapsed because shortsighted unions forced it to pay workers it did not need.

The Red Team and the Green Team

People from the old New York Central were called the Green Team, after that railroad's jade-green boxcars. People from the old PRR were called the Red Team, after that railroad's Tuscan-red passenger cars. At the time of the collapse, it was suggested that antagonism between the Green Team and the Red Team wrecked the merger. It probably played a significant role. But not all relations were bad. ICC inspectors thought friction was minimal at Detroit, where the old NYC was dominant, and at Pittsburgh, where the old PRR was dominant, and at Rose Lake (St. Louis)—that was surprising, since there was so much trouble there. Even at York, Pennsylvania, deep in old PRR country, an ICC inspector noted that the only

Green Team person around there was trainmaster Bill Armand, who was regarded as "a gentleman all the way around and very respected."[31] In other places, the rivalry was poisonous.

At the employee level, it seemed to be petty, but it could run deep. Despite the long period prior to the merger, when agreements could have been worked out and minor contractual differences reconciled, few were. In Chicago, only yardmasters and company police worked out agreements before the merger. Everyone else worked under old agreements with the separate railroads that preserved minor contractual differences. So, explained a local supervisor, Employee A, a former NYC clerk, works in an office with Employee B, a former PRR clerk. Both hold identical positions. Both are called up for jury duty. The railroad pays Employee A full salary because of her former agreement with the New York Central, whereas Employee B gets nothing. Imagine how they are polarized. Former NYC passenger crews that laid over in Chicago were put up at the Fort Dearborn Hotel, which was not exactly five-star. Former PRR crews were bunked at the 16th Street commissary or in the basement of Union Station. Ironically, said ICC inspectors, "both crews claimed it constituted favorable treatment of the other."[32]

At lower and middle management levels, the rivalry was severe. ICC inspectors noted that a common remark was "It wasn't a merger, the so-and-so's took us over, and the so-and-so's get all the choice assignments."[33] Another inspector said:

> I found the relationship after the merger between the employees of the former PRR and the former NYC to be strained and suspicious. You always heard derogatory remarks about the other group. I have been seriously questioned by the officers of both former Penn and former Central as to the competency of officers and employees of the opposite railroad. I was always told that bankruptcy was caused by the Penn or the Central people depending on who I was talking to. . . . The policy of mixing officers [he continued], however well-intentioned, meant that a Central man always reported to a Pennsylvania man who always reported to a Central man. They did not understand each other, or if they did, were at odds with the instructions, or the procedures, or both. The tendency of a supervisor was to bypass his superior to get the ear of a friend from his road. So countermanding orders were frequent, with ill feeling all around. Pennsylvania people ate lunch with other Pennsylvania people, and so forth. The feeling was that "we were doing all right until the Red side (or the Green side) took us over."[34]

Some examples: A shipper of fresh meat at Albany said he was visited by three salesmen for the Penn Central Trailvan service. Each of them made it crystal clear, repeatedly, that they were former NYC men, not idiots from the PRR. At Philadelphia, a former NYC trainmaster was brought to the PRR's Greenwich Yard; another NYC man was superintendent of the district. An ICC inspector noted that not one former PRR trainmaster had a good word for either of them. They said the superintendent showed extreme partiality to that one trainmaster, that when that trainmaster needed extra cars, he always got them, even if they did not have enough cars for regular evening placements (the cars regularly placed at a customer's sidings ready for loading). They believed members of the Green Team would bend over backward to keep each other from looking bad.

Every merger disturbed top-level management, for everybody wondered what the merger was going to do to their careers. The longer the merger was postponed, the more corrosive was the effect. Neither the NYC nor the PRR designated who would hold top posts in each department until the merger actually took place. The thinking was that, if it never came about, a person passed over would be forever damaged in front of subordinates. So, on merger day, the assignments fell across the senior management with surprise and shock.

Except in the financial area, which was all Red Team, it looked as if Red and Green had been spread evenly through the top ranks. Nonetheless, the Green Team believed the Red Team held the real power, and much of the young and aggressive management that Perlman had assembled panicked and fled. Wayne Hoffman went to Flying Tiger, eventually to be its CEO; John Kenefick went to Union Pacific, eventually becoming its CEO, and was brilliantly successful; Walter Grant went to Consolidated Edison. Nearly 100 of the NYC's marketing staff, the brains and energy of the marketing revolution, were gone by 1970.

Rivalries that smoldered in other mergers apparently set off explosion after explosion at the Penn Central and paralyzed decision making. Some of the evidence is hearsay and must be used with caution. It was collected by reporters and ICC inspectors, and some of it was self-serving to the Green Team, which increasingly gave the impression that the New York Central would have survived if it had not been swallowed by the monumental incompetency of the Pennsylvania Railroad.

It was known that the Red and the Green Teams had found it almost impossible to reach any agreements of significance prior to the merger. A key issue was the inability to reconcile the decentralized organizational structure of the PRR with the top-down structure of the NYC. Upon merger, said ICC inspectors, rather than the management's adopting one system or the other, lines of authority just got muddled. On the PRR, for example, budgets were worked out at lower levels and passed upward for review and were meant to monitor performance; on the NYC, they were handed down from above and meant to allocate resources. After merger, both systems were used, and both ineffectively.

Rivalry showed up in two philosophies of railroading that were embodied in the Central's marketing revolution. The rate structure of the PRR was designed to maximize volume and encourage movement—minimum rates for minimal service. That had been standard railroad thinking for generations. The reasoning was that pricing services low enough that traffic would move and contribute *something* to fixed costs was better than not having it move at all. Marketing research existed only to justify charges, not determine them. On the Central, the new idea was to provide shippers with precisely the service they wanted, but only at prices that made money for the railroad. This emphasized service over volume.

The marketing revolution was new on the Central, and its young turks had to fight against entrenched rate-making philosophies on their own road to bring it about. They were not about to have it undone by the Red Team, who, as they saw it, never had a new idea at all. James R. Sullivan, one of the architects of the marketing revolution on the NYC and vice president for marketing on the Penn Central, who tried in vain to hold his marketing team together, said, "If we lose this battle and they prevail, we can paint this whole thing nationalization green."[35] But of course, marketing a product that promised service and charged a price for it would work only if the railroad could provide the service, which the merged Penn Central clearly could not.

This led to one of the top-level confrontations that rocked the railroad, between Perlman and Henry W. Large, who was vice president for sales and a member of the Red Team. At a sales staff meeting in Tarrytown, New York, early in 1969, for which Large worked hard preparing sessions, Perlman delivered a blistering diatribe against the low-rate philosophy and against Large personally.[36] Daughen and Binzen, in *The Wreck of the Penn Central,* described it as a brass-knuckled attack that the Red Team received in stunned silence. Later, when Perlman was again urging Saunders to dump Large, Saunders, according to Rush Loving, Jr., in *Fortune,* said, "You just don't like Henry Large." "I do like Henry Large," said Perlman. "He's a great big lovable St. Bernard. No one can help but like him. But he's giving away the railroad." "But shippers like him," countered Saunders. "Who doesn't like Santa Claus?" observed Perlman.[37]

Perlman did not get along with another Red Team senior vice president, David Smucker, described as an autocratic PRR traditionalist; he was known as "Mother Smucker" to his subordinates. The two men apparently just hated each other. "You run a wooden-wheeled railroad," Perlman is said to have told Smucker shortly before the merger. Perlman did not think Smucker was out on the road enough and did not show enough enthusiasm. Several of the sources for Rush Loving, Jr., and Daughen and Binzen saw it as a personal vendetta and believed that Perlman was unable to adjust to being number two under Saunders. Perlman thought he was effectively under Smucker as far as operations went, for Smucker was Red Team and had the support of Saunders and a majority of the board. Smucker vetoed many of Perlman's demands for funds for the capital improvements necessary to make the railroad work, even chiding Perlman that the only ideas he had were to spend money like a drunken sailor on electronics and cybernetics. Perlman perceived, correctly, that he would be blamed for the operating snafu even if the fault was Saunders's unwillingness to spend money in order to make money. Pushing Saunders to purge the Red Team became a fixation.

Smucker was finally kicked out and replaced by the Green Team's R. G. (Mike) Flannery. But Smucker's swan song was the memo of November 13, 1969, in which he told Saunders the extent of the operating disaster and blamed it on Perlman. Whatever Saunders did or did not know about it before, he could not pretend to be ignorant after that.

At the very top, Saunders was the chairman and the chief executive officer; Perlman was the president and the chief administrative officer; Bevan was the vice president of finance. Saunders attended to diversification and politics. Bevan controlled the purse. Perlman ran the railroad. The three never met, much. It was as if there were three separate spheres at the top that seldom communicated and never shared common goals, but each had access to friendly ears on the board of directors. Perhaps if there had been enough money to physically merge the railroad properly, at a deliberate pace, paths might never have had to cross, but Perlman felt he was made to look bad because the Red Team, in tight control over finances, never gave him the money or the time or the authority to run the railroad right.

None of them liked each other. Maybe it was not quite mutual contempt, but it came close. Saunders said, "I like Perlman, I really do, And he's got a lovely wife. She's a nice woman. A real lady. And he's got nice children. I like Perlman. I really do."[38] But his testimony left no misimpression: Perlman's job was to run the railroad, and if it was an operating disaster, then it was Perlman's problem. Saunders told a Senate investigating committee:

> Mr. Perlman and I—I have the highest regard for him and I think he is an excellent operating man, and I have no great difficulty getting along with him. We don't want rubber stamps or men that don't have convictions at the top of this railroad. We had disagreements, and that was natural. But they weren't of any critical nature, and Mr. Perlman *had complete authority to do whatever he wanted to do,* and he is an excellent operating man.[39]

Perlman was just steely:

> Mr. Saunders came from one of the wealthiest railroads in the country [the N&W] and his outlook on problems may be entirely different from mine. A lot of people say "well here are two men of different philosophies." Well, sure, when a man comes from one side of the tracks, he may have a different philosophy from the other.[40]

> Q [by Senator Hartke]: Mr. Saunders . . . left the impression, at least with this senator, that you had complete authority to run the operation and you were given everything you needed to run it. Is that true?
> A: It was not true.
> Q: In other words, it was not true in personnel, was it?
> A: No, sir.
> Q: Was it true in regard to money, for these projects you were talking about?
> A: No, sir.[41]

Perlman's style of management was to recruit professionals and treat them like professionals with respect and encouragement. The PRR managed essentially through fear—do as you are told or be fired. It was autocratic, a style rooted deep in the company's history. It both terrified the Green Team and invited their contempt. To them, great companies were run by mutual respect. Terror was for second-raters. To the Red Team, Perlman and the whole Green Team were insufferably smug, swaggering with feelings of superiority. The Green Team did swagger. Wayne Hoffman, the one who went to Flying Tiger, told Daughen and Binzen, "I had no regard for PRR management or their philosophy. I felt they had to be changed."[42] Robert Odell, a Penn Central director and former New York Central director, told the board in a highly charged meeting of November 26, 1969:

> As to some background. The New York Central was in excellent condition before merger. . . . To say the merger has been a tragic mistake to date is an understatement. Central had a smooth-running, efficient organization with teams of capable and enthusiastic executives. Discord among management or directors was practically non-existent. Many of the outstanding executives resigned because they correctly anticipated the existing discord in Pennsylvania management would be increased after the merger.[43]

He called the NYC "depression-proof," meaning that the new marketing techniques made it less reliant on commodities whose volume fluctuated wildly in recessions. "Depression-proof" was Perlman's term. Statistics bear out that the Central was a better-run railroad but not that it was really depression-proof. But members of the Green Team never got over the feeling that once upon a time they had run a great railroad and the Red Team came and wrecked it.

As early as the spring of 1969, Saunders was planning to get rid of Perlman. In March, he entertained Louis W. Menk, then of the Northern Pacific, in an effort to recruit him. The Menks were even guests in the Saunders's home in Ardmore and did some preliminary house-hunting of their own. In September, he found Paul Gorman to take the job. Gorman was the retired president of Western Electric, an able manager, known as a cost-cutter—what would later be called a "downsizer." Saunders did this without consulting the full board. Perlman was kicked upstairs. He had a year before his contract was up, so he was paid but was stripped of power and whiled away his hours in a lonely office under a kind of house arrest.

The differences were probably deeper than different philosophies of running a railroad. There was a social and cultural gulf between the two executive teams that they never were able to bridge. The PRR's leadership had been a self-perpetuating elite since the railroad's founding in the 1840s. The NYC had gone through a revolution in the Robert Young proxy fight of 1954 that severed its connection to its founding family, the Vanderbilts, and their self-perpetuating management. The PRR's senior officers were mostly in their late fifties or early sixties, had spent their whole careers with the PRR or its farm clubs—the N&W, the Wabash, or the Lehigh Valley. They lived in the plush western suburbs of Philadelphia, were members of the city's social elite and prestigious clubs, were Protestant, and were Republicans—except Saunders, of course, a prominent Democrat. Senate investigators concluded: "It appears that the Pennsylvania Railroad responded substantially to the people its management met socially. Its direction was determined more by the social ethos of Philadelphia and its own traditions than by the demands of the market or the concepts of the business community at large."[44]

The Green Team had been assembled by Perlman from careers on other railroads, even other industries. They were in their forties or early fifties, lived in respectable suburbs of New York but were not part of the city's social elite and were more mixed religiously and ethnically. Perlman was Jewish in an industry that Senate investigators acknowledged was not noted for its tolerance.[45] One Green Team member of Irish extraction told Daughen and Binzen, "I was brought up to hate Protestants and the Pennsylvania Railroad. After this [merger], I am supposed to love them both."[46]

There is no way to measure the effect of cultural differences. There are many who would be more comfortable to limit the story to the hard statistics of car loadings and bottom lines. Others dismiss the infighting of the two teams as "politics" and give up trying to analyze the situation. But railroads, like all other businesses, are human endeavors. If one cannot give at least some account of the human side, one has failed to tell the story. It may have been a cultural gulf that doomed this merger to failure.

Pitfalls of Diversification

At the time the Penn Central collapsed, a lot of press attention focused on its investments outside of railroading. Some of them were inexplicably bizarre. They were supposed to bring money into the railroad; instead, some of them at least seemed to drain cash away. On balance, diversification earned about the same as the railroad; it was certainly not the dazzling fountain of cash flow it was supposed to be. The spectacle of the hide-bound Pennsylvania Railroad wheeling and dealing with flashy real estate developers from the Sunbelt was either amusing or pathetic, depending on one's point of view. In addition, diversification brought executive suite intrigue, unaccounted funds, posh clubs, beautiful women, saunas, money laundered in Liechtenstein banks, and a lot of very bad judgment. Needless to say, this made prime copy for reporters.

Once it was clear that the PRR would have to divest its dividend-paying Norfolk & Western stock, it had to make a decision. It could put the proceeds into the railroad—into electronic yards, CTC, welded rail—to restore the PRR to its traditional physical excellence. It could pay off PRR debts that would free up about $40 million a year in fixed charges that could then be put into the railroad. Most of the $40 million in fixed charges that debt redemption might eliminate went to the banks and insurance companies represented on the PRR's board of directors. They were not thrilled by the idea of debt redemption.

They agreed with Stuart Saunders that putting money into the railroad was the same as putting it in 1 percent securities. It should be put in something earning a lot more, and in businesses whose return did not fluctuate as much as the railroad's did in recession. The idea of insulating the railroad from recession was the primary justification of diversification.

Diversification would not necessarily have been a wrong decision if it had paid off, but one senses, right out of the gate, that a certain conflict of interest was at work as concerns the financial institutions represented on the board. Eventually, the House Banking Committee and lots of others would want to know about this. They also wanted to know if the real intent of management and the board was to starve the railroad of capital and then dump it on the government, while they, like a snake shedding its skin, went on to a new life in a much faster lane. The men who made these decisions tucked many of the diversified acquisitions into holding companies separate from the railroad, so that in case the railroad crashed and burned, they would still get to keep the acquisitions.[47] They took out an insurance policy for $10 million from Lloyds of London to protect themselves from breach-of-trust lawsuits over this.[48] They misled their board of directors on the success of diversification. Some of them appear to have bought shares in the same diversified companies as the railroad, trading on inside information and using the railroad's credit to get themselves better rates of interest.[49]

Both the merger partners had been in businesses other than railroads for years, mostly real estate on railroad land. The PRR owned the Penn Center Complex in Philadelphia and Madison Square Garden adjacent to Penn Station in New York City. It owned a dominant interest in two sports teams that played there, the New York Rangers hockey club and the New York Knicks basketball club. The New York Central virtually owned New York's Park Avenue as far south as 42d Street, for that had been the railroad's right-of-way until the tracks were put underground with the construction of Grand Central in 1913. It owned the skyscrapers on that land and five hotels—the Commodore, the Biltmore, the Barclay, the Roosevelt, and the Waldorf Astoria. In the days when the Great Steel Fleet hauled thousands of passengers to Grand Central every day, owning hotels near its stations was a logical extension of its business. By the late 1960s, these were "has-been" hotels, a leftover of passenger glory days long gone. Investments after 1963 were different in that they required an outlay of cash, and except for Buckeye (a pipeline laid along some PRR right-of-way) and Strick (the manufacturer of the highway trailer equipment for the NYC's Flexivan service) were unrelated to railroad operations.

Paying for these acquisitions was not simply a matter of selling N&W shares and buying other shares. The N&W stock had a market value of $289 million, but much of it was pledged as collateral on loans and could not be sold. That which was sold netted only $37.6 million for the railroad. The sale of the Long Island Railroad to New York State for $65 million actually netted more. The rest of the $201 million sunk into diversification was borrowed, much of it from the financial institutions represented on the board of directors. Any dividends the railroad might receive from these subsidiaries had to be balanced against the interest it paid out on the loans.[50] What some called investments others thought was gambling with borrowed money.

If diversification had been a roaring success, there may never have been a fuss. Overall, it broke even, with distressing segments that were losers and one that was a fiasco of nuclear proportions. Strick and Buckeye turned out quite well and made regular contributions to net income. Arvida Corporation was a Florida land development company with choice holdings in the Miami and Sarasota areas. It was building condominium complexes. In 1968 it began construction of Boca Raton West, a $500 million residential development with an 18-hole golf course, close by its Boca Raton Hotel and Club. Arvida was beginning to get into environmental trouble, especially in Sarasota, for sub-sea-level sewage systems. It made money, paying dividends to the railroad of 2 percent a year, but there was trouble ahead.

Great Southwest Corporation was developing industrial land around Dallas and the Six Flags amusement parks near Dallas and Atlanta. Macco Realty Company, later merged with Great Southwest, developed residential land around Los Angeles. Neither paid a single cash dividend to the railroad. Sen. Vance Hartke (D-Ind.) was incredulous that a businessman like Saunders was so nonchalant about the fact that these supposedly flashy investments were doing worse than the railroad.

Q: You have the Great Southwest Corporation on page seventy-seven?

A: Yes.

Q: Does it show a loss of $330,473 for 1968?

A: See, the Great Southwest has a number of subsidiary companies. This only includes part of them. If you look at the annual report and what reflects there, through earnings, the Great Southwest Corporation and subsidiaries—and the figures that I gave you are the consolidated earnings—and they are the only things that count.

. . . .

Q: Lets go through a couple more and then I have a question. Do you want to comment on the system's investment in the Capistrano Highlands?

A: That's nothing but a subsidiary of Macco Corporation.

Q: Losses to the extent of $740,000?

A: Macco Corporation is a corporation that has some acres in California, very fine property, and they have a number of—

Q: Very fine property, right?

A: Yes.

. . . .

Q: What about the Great Southwest Golf Club, Inc., assets of $2 million and a $120,000 loss in 1968?

A: . . . Now you can go through and pick out individual companies and find this.

. . . .

Q: Now L-A-G-U-N-A, how do you pronounce that?

A: Laguna.

Q: The Laguna. They had assets of $2 million and a loss of $286,000. Pent Land Home, assets of $28.6 million, losses of $142,000. Another one here, total of $5 million in assets, losses of $187,000. . . . You needed cash in hand rather than these losses right?

A: But if we were going to sell anything, what we ought to sell is Great Southwest Corporation, not these little nits and lice.[51]

There was a reason why companies like Arvida and Great Southwest had an interest in the stuffy old railroad. There were advantages to being linked up with a transportation company whose securities were regulated by the ICC and therefore, under the Investment Company Act of 1940, not subject to the full disclosure law of the Securities and Exchange Commission.[52] This was true only so long as the investment company did itself hold a substantial ownership in ICC-regulated companies. So when the NYC's old holding company, Alleghany Corporation, had its railroad holdings fall to less than 22 percent of its assets after the Penn Central merger and the ICC revoked its status as a common carrier, it hastily bought a motor carrier, Jones Motor Freight Lines, and petitioned to have its ICC regulation restored.[53] When the Pennsylvania Company's railroad holdings were reduced after it sold its Wabash Railroad stock to the N&W, it hastily pointed out that it still held control of the Detroit, Toledo & Ironton Railroad and had joint control of the Toledo, Peoria & Western; nonetheless, the ICC had expressly ordered in 1942 that "unless and until otherwise ordered, said Pennsylvania Company shall be considered a carrier subject to the provisions of Section 20 (1) to (10) inclusive . . . of the Interstate Commerce Act."[54] That's what attracted these developers to the railroad. Why the railroad was attracted in return was a tougher question, since they were not earning as big a return as it was.

There was no conclusive evidence, but there was circumstantial evidence to which both the House Banking Committee and the Senate Commerce Committee investigations gave great weight. David Bevan was vice president and chairman of the finance committee. His good friend was Charles J. (Charlie) Hodge, who was a retired army general and now chairman of the executive committee of Glore, Forgan & Company, investment brokers. Hodge helped arrange the early acquisition of Buckeye Pipeline and otherwise cultivated a close relationship with PRR officers. He staged an elaborate dinner party for Saunders at the Links Club in 1963, with a guest list mostly of prominent bankers.[55] He arranged a gala trip to Europe for Stuart and Dorothy Saunders in 1965. The relationship of Hodge and Bevan grew warmer, particularly through a fishing club that they called the Silverfish, whose members were 12 men with successful careers in finance. In that way, Hodge, and Glore, Forgan & Company became virtually the sole financial advisor to the PRR and later to the Penn Central. Hodge was an ardent promoter of the land company deals, and his company received large brokerage fees in the transactions.

The significance was that, because of this social relationship, objectivity in making investments may have been obscured. It may have been further obscured by Penphil, an investment club composed of members of the Silverfish plus PRR treasurer William R. Gertsnecker (who left the PRR in 1969 to join Provident National Bank in Philadelphia, Bevan's old bank) and four other PRR vice presidents, all in the area of finance or investments. Eventually, it included executives of Arvida; Great Southwest; other PRR holdings such as Executive Jet Aviation, National Home, Kaneb Pipeline, and Tropical Gas; and subsidiaries of these holdings, including the First Bank of Boca Raton. Thomas Fleming of First Bank, who was invited late, wrote, "I am thrilled and delighted and want to take all the stock [in Penphil] that is left. I am so happy to join this exalted group of gentlemen investors about whom I have heard so much."[56] Members put up around $16,000 (a little more than $72,000 in today's dollars), which later prompted Bevan to testify that it was only "a very small affair." Much more was borrowed from the Chemical Bank, which made loans to the group at the prime rate, based on the railroad's credit and compensating balances.

Penphil invested in companies in which the railroad had an interest, often just before or during the railroad's purchases. For example, it bought shares in Great Southwest after the railroad started to buy, held its shares while the railroad bought more (which raised the price), then at a propitious time sold its shares to the railroad at approximately twice what it paid for them. Bevan and Hodge made all the decisions regarding the placement of Penphil investments. So the possibility of trading on inside information and of conflict of interest was great.[57] They did not disclose their interest in Penphil to Saunders or the railroad's board of directors.

Of all the railroad's investments, none was stranger than Executive Jet Aviation. EJA was an air shuttle service—essentially corporate jets for hire—though it had dreams of becoming a regularly scheduled airline, perhaps a big one. It was illegal at that time for a railroad to own or control airlines or any company engaged in commercial aviation. The PRR said it thought that its investment solely in nonvoting securities of EJA would insulate it from criminal charges, or the Civil Aeronautics Board (CAB) would rule in its favor, or Congress would act in its favor. In fact, the CAB ruled against the PRR (and fined it $65,000 to make sure the point was clear). But the railroad, or specifically Bevan and Gertsnecker, not only continued to bankroll EJA, but they also authorized it to acquire large aircraft—two Boeing 707s and two 727s—and to sign a letter of intent with Lockheed for six jumbo L-500s, the civilian version of the military C5-A transport. The Lockheed deal could have cost the railroad $136 million if it had been finalized.[58]

EJA had no CAB authorization to operate any of these aircraft, so it attempted to buy a small European airline, Transavia. The Transavia deal eventually required a loan indirectly from the railroad, $10 million, which was laundered through a Liechtenstein bank. EJA was also negotiating with International Air Bahamas, not then an operating airline but one that had landing rights in Luxembourg. At this point, airline giant Pan Am, not eager for a fly-by-night rate cutter and knowing that railroad involvement was illegal, went to the CAB to find out what was going on.

The funny thing was, for all this, EJA was not making any money. It had to beg the railroad for infusions of cash, and the railroad always came through. This was done by making "advances" through a subsidiary of the Pennsylvania Company known as the American Contract Company, which disguised where the money was going. EJA's founder and president was O. J. (Dick) Lassiter, a retired Air Force general. He liked celebrities. Gen. Curtis LeMay of Strategic Air Command (and in 1968 George Wallace's presidential running mate), actor Jimmy Stewart, and radio/television star Arthur Godfrey were on his board of directors. He also rolled up around $50,000 in 1969 dollars in annual expense accounts. Readers of *Car and Driver* discovered in April 1970 that he frequently escorted one Linda Vaughan on his junkets while she was on assignment for the Hurst Performance Products Company, a purveyor of racing car accessories. She was known in the trade as "Miss Hurst Golden Shifter" and rode around the track perched atop a large replica of a floor-mounted gearshift lever. Lassiter gave her a 10-carat diamond before he dumped her for other girlfriends. There was also enough money in the EJA till for a deluxe gymnasium-sauna complex; the head karate instructor was Wally Soga. The House Banking Committee could not help itself from burlesquing this one, entitling a section of its report the "Saga of Soga."[59]

That committee was so gleefully appalled by the rot it uncovered at Executive Jet that it filled 93 pages documenting it with memos, testimony, and tabulations. Needless to say, the details have only been touched on here. How was it that a man such as David Bevan, supposedly savvy in financial affairs, would pour $21 million of railroad money down this wretched little money hole, especially after the CAB ruling? The question, said House investigators, cried out for an answer.

They thought a document known as the Ricciardi Deposition was the clue. J. H. Ricciardi had been hired by EJA as a kind of social director, had been fired, and had sued for recovery of salary. In a deposition in that suit, Ricciardi said he had arranged trips for David Bevan and Charlie Hodge and had provided them, on more than one occasion, with female companions. Lassiter, in a deposition of his own, said he believed Bevan and Hodge felt threatened by disclosure of certain activities and directed investigators to the Ricciardi deposition.

Ricciardi said that Lassiter met Bevan and Hodge in Bevan's private Pullman car in Penn Station and then for dinner at Jose's.

> Q: Who was present?
> A: General Lassiter, General Hodge, Dave Bevan, myself and dates.
> Q: Everybody had dates? Do you remember their names?
> A: General Lassiter was with . . . Michelle ———. I had a young lady Carol ——— with me, and General Hodge and David Bevan had two young ladies. I don't recall their names.
>
> . . . .
>
> Q: Any other occasions in New York when you performed these functions?
> A: Yes, I once got a date for David Bevan with a young lady called Norma ———.
> Q: Did you pay for any of the dinners or drinks?
> A: No.
> Q: Did you pay any moneys to these girls?
> A: No.
> Q: To your knowledge, did anyone pay any money to these girls?
> A: I don't know. They all went their own way, so I don't know.[60]

Female companions may have been irrelevant; most of the money was squandered before Ricciardi ever came on the scene. But Bevan did his best to keep the EJA involvement secret. Memos eventually leaked, and the railroad began an internal investigation, directed by the PC's executive vice president, Basil Cole. The matter was sensitive for Bevan, who said about Cole: "They couldn't have picked a man on the railroad who hated me more." Cole wrote Saunders on March 13, 1970: "Doors in this building have been slamming ever since the accounting department was returned to Mr. Bevan. Now all the cracks are sealed."[61]

It finally took Congress to get as far to the bottom as anyone cared to go. The House investigation concluded: "Under the circumstances, consideration must be given to the possibility that public revelation of certain personal activities that might have been extremely embarrassing to Bevan is inevitably linked to the questions of why Bevan acted in the strange way he did throughout the deteriorating Executive Jet catastrophe."[62]

On July 1, 1970, Detroit Bank & Trust, the trustee of Penn Central's EJA holdings, voted the PC's shares to oust Lassiter. The bank's lawyer, Bruce Sundlun, accompanied by Pinkertons forced the lock on EJA's offices in Columbus one night and took possession. They seized records, including Lassiter's stack of photographs of himself with various young women. Three weeks later, Lassiter tried to forcibly regain possession of his office in a kind of shootout. He was repulsed by the Pinkertons, and the EJA revelations began shortly thereafter.[63]

To focus on Executive Jet, however, was to exaggerate the losses from diversification. Overall, the program did a little better than break even. At worst, it occupied the attention of management at a time when that attention was needed elsewhere. But on the balance sheets, it was deceptive enough to fool the board of directors and mesmerize management.

Statistically, it appeared that in the five-year period 1964–1969, diversification earned a net return of $146 million. But included in that figure was $115 million of "undistributed earnings," which were funds the subsidiaries had not declared as dividends, which meant they did not flow upward to the railroad. In fact, by the time fixed charges on money borrowed for diversification were subtracted, only $19.9 million flowed upward to the railroad. That was a rate of return of 14.27 percent in five years, or 2.85 percent a year.

Earnings Maximization and Imaginative Accounting

Bleeding subsidiaries for noncash dividends was one of the principal tools of a policy known as earnings maximization, which exaggerated consolidated net income. It was a deliberate policy on the PRR after Saunders became president, and then on the Penn Central. One memo called it "imaginative accounting."[64] Bevan described it this way in a memo to Saunders on November 21, 1966, underscoring that the idea was Saunders's own:

1. A policy may be instituted for attempting to keep, as far as possible, net income and cash flow as closely together as possible without regard to what the immediate effect is on earnings. Up to several years ago, this was basically the policy pursued by the Pennsylvania Railroad.

2. The policy may be instituted for maximizing earnings to the greatest extent possible within the limits of good accounting practices. In the last several years, this has been done on the Pennsylvania in accordance with your expressed desires. It does mean however, that we tend to create a wider and wider difference as between reported income and cash flow. Today, the cash flow of the Pennsylvania Railroad is substantially less than its reported income.[65]

Specific examples were difficult to explain without excessive detail. Two should suffice.

When the real estate subsidiaries (Arvida, Macco, and Great Southwest) sold land, purchasers normally made only a down payment, with the remainder due over time. Two methods of accounting could be used. One recorded a profit on an installment basis only as cash was received. On that basis, Macco and Great Southwest together earned $9.4 million in 1968. The other approach recorded the entire profit in the period in which the sale was made, regardless of the amount of cash received. That was how Penn Central chose to record it, and on that basis, it appeared to earn $30.7 million.

Another example involved the Washington Terminal Company. The Penn Central and the Baltimore & Ohio each owned 50 percent of the Washington Terminal Company, which owned Washington Union Station. In 1969 the station was leased to the Department of the Interior, and the Washington Terminal Company was liquidated. This had to show on the railroad's books as something, even though it represented no immediate cash income. The B&O chose to represent its share of the station at the conservative book value, derived from the original cost of construction, $3.1 million. The Penn Central represented it at its appraised value, a sum that would not be realized for many years, if ever, under the lease agreement—$13.7 million. It was a lowly stockholder who happened to own shares of both the PC and the B&O who saw this, wondered about the huge discrepancy, and blew the whistle.[66]

None of this was illegal. Was it calculated to be deceptive? That was another question. Much of the trouble resulted from differences between the ICC's accounting rules and the Generally Accepted Accounting Principles (GAAP) as promulgated by the Accounting Principles Board of the American Institute of Certified Public Accountants. The ICC's rules were written in the early years of the twentieth century when railroads were just railroads, not diversified holding companies, and were designed to be uniform and specific so as to keep tight regulatory control. Many people thought they needed updating. The GAAP allowed greater leeway and enabled investors to make fairer comparisons between regulated and nonregulated enterprises. Major differences were in depreciation, deferred taxes, the recording of noncash dividends from subsidiaries (whether on a cost or an equity basis), and the installation or improvement of nondepreciable property.

The ICC allowed railroads to report figures in GAAP to their stockholders so long as differences were fully disclosed. Differences were disclosed in footnotes, and although the PC always provided footnotes, could they be understood by investors, or even by its board of directors? "Financial statements are confusing enough to the average investor, and differences cited in the footnotes between alternative accounting methods quite probably do not clarify the report. Rather they tend to cloud the issue of the financial performance of the company by presenting too much conflicting and technical data," said a Senate investigatory report.[67]

Within the bounds of generally accepted accounting principles, there was opportunity to make many choices. This was necessary because there were so many varying circumstances in so many kinds of businesses. At every turn, the Penn Central chose the course that made net income look the biggest, even forsaking hard cash to preserve phantom figures. For example, it could have acquired hard cash by selling scrap from unused branchlines, of which it had many serving no useful purpose. But under ICC rules, that would have required a big paper write-down, and that had to be avoided. It was the practice of maximizing income at *every* juncture that made it deceptive.

After the debacle, when stories of the Penn Central's accounting began to appear as lurid articles in the press, the company's auditors, Peat, Marwick & Mitchell, were stung. After all, they had tried to flag management on the breakdown of revenue accounting in the field. One article—Rush Loving's excellent "Penn Central Bankruptcy Express" in *Fortune*—angered them so much that they forced *Fortune* to make a partial retraction. *Fortune* admitted that its interpretation of differences between ICC and GAAP accounting methods was in error in the several particular instances the company contested and apologized if anything in the article was construed to imply that the auditors violated professional standards. The problem was all in the choices. *Fortune* pointed to its editorial "Its Time to Call the Auditors to Account," which had appeared in its previous issue and which said, "The wide range of accounting options permits companies enormous leeway in handling transactions." It called for a hastening of the kind of reforms that many accounting firms—notably including Peat, Marwick—had been fighting for.[68]

There was good reason why Saunders wanted earnings maximized when he arrived at the PRR, even if he hesitated to use the precise phrase. The stock exchange ratio with the New York Central called for 1 share of the PRR for every 1.3 shares of the Central. But the decline in PRR earnings would probably have required the renegotiation of this delicate matter if there had not been a way to cosmetically inflate the PRR's earnings. Bevan added in a memo of November 21, 1966:

> In the short term today, the New York Central earnings as reported are much more real and tangible from the standpoint of an ability to pay dividends than are those of the Pennsylvania. Virtually all of their earnings are actually available for the payment of dividends. . . . On the other hand, much of the Pennsylvania Railroad's income is in the form of subsidiary companies, which in turn, have their own requirements for the plough back of money.[69]

When Saunders wanted something from the government, such as a loan guarantee, it was important to be able show that things were bad. He wrote in 1969, "I think our position is bleak enough to achieve most of the results we need from the point of view of legislation and regulatory agencies. . . . If we go too far in this regard, we get ourselves in greater trouble as far as financing is concerned."[70] In front of creditors, an absolutely rosy picture was essential. The greater the apparent earnings on the bottom line, the better the credit of the railroad. The railroad was living on borrowed money. It had to be able to keep on borrowing until somehow, by some miracle, the operating debacle could be reversed.

Only one director, Robert Odell (formerly a Central director), was willing to probe the gangrene. He was aware of the railroad's operating problems and knew of some of the troubles at Great Southwest–Macco. It was not just an insult but bad judgment, he said, that he was not consulted on a multimillion dollar land purchase by Macco within 20 miles of his Los Angeles home—land that was purchased without even the Penn Central being consulted. He warned Saunders that Great Southwest–Macco, by not consulting its principal owner, may have broken the law. Saunders was upset and sought legal advice, which confirmed that Odell was right. So Saunders went shopping for other lawyers until he got the opinion he wanted. In another "Dear Stuart" letter, Odell warned that self-serving legal advice was not fooling anyone and was typical of management's high-handedness.[71] It was no surprise to Odell that, a few months later, Great Southwest–Macco was forced to write down two-thirds of its assets, for a $130 million paper loss.

At the Penn Central board meeting of November 1969, Odell offered a resolution to restructure management, giving power of both operations and finances to the president and designating Perlman as the one man capable of filling that post. The minutes of the meeting read as follows: "The chairman of the board thereupon asked if the motion were seconded.

There was no second. The board then unanimously adopted a motion that Mr. Odell be thanked for his interest in the company's affairs and that his motion be tabled."[72]

The directors did not want to come to grips. Once upon a time, thrifty small-scale investors put their tiny savings into shares of stock that built great corporations. They became part owners, and they hired a management to run the shop, to be fired and replaced as they saw fit. The corporate form derived its strength from the fact that ownership and management were separated, so owners need not be restrained by any one management's limited ideas and vision. Everyone knew that, by the twentieth century, stockholders no longer played an active role in company affairs. If they did not like the way their company was run, they normally sold their shares rather than fight. Robert Young's proxy fight for the New York Central in 1954 was the exception, not the rule. But at least it was still assumed that the board of directors, who represented shareholders and large-scale creditors, would keep an eye on management for the benefit of investors generally. They were not there as a formality. They were not there as a gentlemen's club. They were there to do a job—to look after management. The Penn Central collapse was the first real indication of how totally the board-of-director system had broken down.

These directors—executives in their own right, usually for large banks and insurance companies—were each on the boards of several corporations. Perhaps they were spread too thin. Perhaps they had forgotten what an active role they were expected to play. Perhaps they socialized too much with management in Philadelphia's exclusive clubs. Perhaps they lacked guts. They were content to remain ignorant, even as the house was on fire, and were very surprised when the roof fell in.

That was why the railroad continued to pay dividends even as it hurtled toward bankruptcy. There was little discussion over paying one in the first quarter of 1969. By the second quarter, some warning flags were up, but Saunders was ebullient and persuaded everyone it was best to put on a good face, and the dividend was paid. He was gambling that somehow a confident front could be maintained, even in front of all the creditors sitting on the board, until problems somehow took care of themselves. But the puffery came to be peppered with phrases like "uphill fight" and "adverse conditions." By the third quarter of 1969, there was no possibility that a dividend could be paid. It was the first omission for the PRR since 1847.

Finally, at the terrible meeting of the Finance Committee on May 27, 1970, the information could no longer be bottled up. Cash losses for 1968 had actually been $140 million; for 1969, $220 million; for the first quarter of 1970, $100 million. Since the merger, $993 million had been borrowed, of which only $240 million had been repaid.

The Debacle

The final descent into the abyss began in the winter of 1970. Bevan knew there were going to be substantial debt maturities that year—$100 million of them—and the only way they could be met was to borrow more money. In December 1969, Bevan flew to Switzerland and secured a loan for $59 million, but it was denominated in Swiss francs, meaning it had to be repaid in Swiss francs. The dollar was poised to devalue against gold and foreign currencies, and this was going to be a very troublesome deal. Besides, it was not nearly enough. That year the railroad wrote off its long-haul passenger facilities west of Albany and Harrisburg for salvage value, which it set at $126 million. This showed as an extraordinary loss. As long as an investor's eye caught a big extraordinary number, it cosmetically disguised the other cosmetic disguises that had been used to fuzz a $193 million loss on railroad operations. Cosmetic disguises were running out.

In March 1970 Bevan suggested a new issue of $100 million of Pennsylvania Company debentures. Saunders, the board's finance committee, and the ICC all seemed receptive. Saunders and Bevan must have had an inkling of what the first-quarter earnings report was going to look like. The railroad was awash in problems. The winter had been brutal. Blizzards closed Selkirk and Frontier for days on end in January, with temperatures averaging 22 degrees below normal. More than $8 million was spent on snow removal.

But when the quarterly report came out on April 22, it shocked even those who expected the worst. The losses from railroad operations were $102 million. That was more than a million dollars a day. Saunders hurried off to Washington to see what could be done. His manicurist said the hands of this normally self-confident man shook uncontrollably.[73]

Bevan thought of offering 11.5 percent on the new debentures, but it was decided that this might frighten investors away. At 10.5 percent, it was hoped they would find buyers, despite the bad first-quarter report. But when the prospectus came out in mid-May, it contained, in the small print at the back, a notation that meant death. It said that between April 22 and May 8, "maturities and payments of commercial paper exceeded sales of commercial paper by $41.3 million." That was the same as a run on the bank. The depositors were bailing. There was no further chance that funds could be raised privately. On May 28, the news came over the Dow Jones wire at about 1:20 P.M.: "The Penn Central today withdrew its proposed offering of $100 million in debenture bonds. No reason was given."

There had already been massive sales of stock by company executives and by institutions represented on the company's board, suggesting that trades were made on insider information.[74] Penn Central stock had sold in the 80s in 1968. Its high in 1969 was $71.75. On June 2, 1970, it closed at $12.75, and three weeks later it went to less than $5. These men had already lost most of their life savings. The rush to sell continued.

Walter Wriston of Citibank, the bank most deeply involved in the Penn Central revolving credit loan of $320 million the year before, was furious. Now he was made to look like a fool. How could this have happened unless somebody had not been telling the truth? He summoned Bevan and Saunders to New York separately and was not impressed by their answers. Others were beginning to suggest that it was time for a change in management, but Wriston was apparently the chief protagonist. For the first time, said Daughen and Binzen, Saunders and Bevan were up against outside forces they could not control. That very day Bevan's friend and protector on the board, Richard King Mellon, heir to the Mellon fortune, who had once asked Bevan if he would head up the Mellon Bank, died. Bevan would probably now be the blood sacrifice. Saunders thought his own position was safe. Perlman knew none of this.

At a special board meeting on June 8, 1970, with Perlman and Bevan present, Saunders opened the meeting and turned it over to Gorman, who read a statement that the banks' willingness to loan money, even with federal guarantees, depended on a reorganization of management. Saunders, Perlman, Bevan, and Gorman were asked to leave the room. Franklin Lunding, chairman of the directors' executive committee, took over. Discussion raged for the next two hours. Voices raised and tempers flared. A motion was made to fire Perlman and Bevan and kick Saunders upstairs, stripped of power. There was discussion. Some thought Saunders should be sacked as well. Director William Day, president of the Pennsylvania Banking & Trust Company and a member of the same clubs as Saunders, kept murmuring "Oh no! Oh no!" Gorman was summoned. Did he think Saunders should go or stay? His answer was "Go." The resolution was unanimous. The meeting adjourned, and a delegation was dispatched to tell Saunders, Perlman, and Bevan they were fired. Perlman was not there. He was so furious that he had his private car attached to an afternoon train and was on his way to New York. Saunders turned an ashen gray.[75]

The Nixon administration desperately did not want the worst business failure in American history on its watch. Its worst fear was a Wall Street panic, and a bankruptcy of this magnitude could trigger one. Secretary of Transportation John Volpe worked on a loan guarantee for $200 million from Congress. Great hope was pinned on the Pentagon. The railroad served military bases, ports, and defense contractors. A shutdown would jeopardize national security and defense. Perhaps an arrangement could be made under the Defense Production Act of 1950.

Gorman told the House Banking Committee that $200 million was pretty small change compared to the amounts Congress normally threw around, that "in the wink of an eye" this amount would be voted for a highway or some other development. Wright Patman of Texas was the chairman. "Curmudgeon" was a good description of him, and he never trusted a railroad or a bank. He was the last of the old populists, as classic as they came, and he was not impressed with these rich folks from Philadelphia. But Gorman knew how Congress worked. That August, not quite in the wink of an eye, but almost, Congress voted a $250 million bailout for the failing Lockheed Aircraft.

Patman smiled and rubbed his chin at the administration's frantic pleas to bail out big bankers. The facts that the railroad's real estate holdings were carefully beyond the reach of a bankruptcy court and that the discredited officers were getting handsome pensions—$125,000 a year for Saunders—were fatally damaging as far as politics were concerned.

Somebody leaked transcripts of the closed-door session of the House Defense Appropriations Subcommittee to Jack Anderson, who published some of the morsels in his *Washington Merry-Go-Round* column. The $200 million was not going to be enough; $200 million would only see the railroad through the summer. At least another $500 million would be required to rehabilitate it. Undersecretary of Transportation James Beggs named a number of prominent congressmen who would sponsor the bill; but when they were contacted, they said no, they had not been asked, nor would they sponsor it. Undersecretary of Defense Barry Shillito admitted that the only security for the loan was accounts receivable, because the railroad's other assets were pledged and because otherwise there was no contingency plan in case the railroad defaulted. He assured them that the government was not expecting to have to make good on this loan. "An endorser never does," shot back Rep. Robert Sikes (D-Fla.). Where was this money going to go? Most of it was not to bail out the railroad but to bail out its security holders, including $59 million to Swiss banks.

The Department of Defense could still have made an emergency loan administratively. Secretary of Transportation John Volpe worked hard for it. Attorney General John Mitchell, Federal Reserve Chairman Arthur Burns, Secretary of the Treasury David Kennedy, and Secretary of Commerce Maurice Stans had all seemed to throw themselves into the business of securing the loan. But the Pentagon was skittish from the start. The Defense Production Act of 1950 was meant to help small-scale subcontractors in defense industries that were having liquidity problems, not to bail out large corporations and their bankers. Yes, continued service on the Penn Central Railroad was essential to the national defense, but bankruptcy would not mean the trains would stop running, at least not right away.

The politics were terrifying. Editorials and cartoons were already appearing about Nixon bailing out big railroads and big banks but skimping on school lunches for kids. Patman aroused opposition in Congress. And there was a web of conflicting interest between the administration and the railroad. The railroad was a client of Nixon's and Mitchell's former New York law firm of Nixon, Mudge, Guthrie, Rose & Alexander. Retaining the Nixon Mudge firm was Saunders's idea, and he meant it as a power play to enmesh the administration in the Penn Central. Nixon himself owned shares of Investors' Diversified Services, which had a large holding of Penn Central shares. John Mitchell owned shares in Great Southwest. David Kennedy once headed Continental Illinois, one of the banks that stood to lose a lot by a default. Walter Annenberg, now Nixon's ambassador to Britain, owned 189,000 Penn Central Company shares and had been one of its directors until 1969. All of this could be dynamite.

Still, it looked as if the government would come through. On Friday afternoon, June 19, 1970, the railroad delegation arrived at the Federal Reserve Bank of New York, where the actual package of credits would be arranged. Saturday morning at the Fed, they were waiting for a call from Secretary of the Navy John Chafee to say the loan was a go. But when the call came, it was not from Chafee but from an assistant at Defense who said the president had changed his mind and the deal was off. There would be no loan from the Department of Defense. That was it—just a few quiet words around the table in the Fed's meeting room. The railroad men packed their briefcases.

The Department of Transportation took Nixon's change of heart as a slap, and Volpe took it personally. He was not told in advance. He had resigned the governorship of Massachusetts to join the Nixon cabinet, and now it was obvious that Nixon regarded him as a nobody.

The railroad men took the Metroliner back to Philadelphia. It was Saturday afternoon and offices were closed, which added to the gathering gloom. In those offices in Penn Center Plaza, reporters were not allowed above the tenth floor, where public relations had its office. In New York, Walter Wriston was asked what was going to happen. The railroad had notes coming due. It had commercial paper that was due. "I just don't know what is going to happen now," he said.[76]

The Midnight Hour

There was, at the close of business on Friday, June 19, 1970, approximately $7 million in Penn Central bank balances. The payroll on the next Tuesday was $12 million, and on Thursday another $8 million. By the end of the week, $10 million in commercial paper was due for redemption. The board met in special session on Sunday, June 21. Most of them felt it was better to declare bankruptcy voluntarily than to have creditors force it. A motion to file under section 77 of the Bankruptcy Act carried unanimously. It was hoped that by taking the action on Sunday, financial markets would have a night to think it over before they panicked. Gorman pleaded with the company's 94,000 employees to please stay on the job and keep giving "the best possible service to the thousands of shippers and millions of passengers who are depending on us."[77]

Monday, Wall Street was described as shaken, but there was no panic.

The Penn Central stock dropped to $6.50 and its 6 percent bonds dropped to 50 cents on the dollar. But the Dow barely rippled. Even commercial paper markets—short-term financing secured only by promissory notes— remained calm. The Federal Reserve stood by to intervene in case any of the banks with major loans to the Penn Central faced a liquidity crisis. The big ones were Citibank, Chemical, Chase Manhattan, Mellon Bank of Pittsburgh, Marine Midland of Buffalo, First Pennsylvania of Philadelphia, and Continental Illinois of Chicago. Giving clear signals that credit was there if needed was enough, and the crisis passed. The discredited railroad executives continued to get their pension checks. Some banks refused to cash Penn Central payroll checks for the men and women who slugged it out all week trying to keep the trains rolling.

fifteen

The Turning Point
1970

The Penn Central was the big, thudding problem of railroading in 1970. Its collapse marked the rock bottom of the entire industry. The big problem at Penn Central was not the executive-suite scandals that made the lurid headlines. The real trouble was that there were fewer and fewer services that railroads could perform as well as their competitors for which anyone would pay enough for the railroads to make a profit. This was the same equation that spelled the death of the passenger train in the 1950s. Now it was reaching up to grab the freight.

Railroads could make a profit hauling coal. That was about it. If they were going to haul much else at a profit, they were going to have to reconceive what they did and how they did it. That would mean breaking out of some age-encrusted hierarchies of the operating and mechanical departments. They had to get rid of unproductive investment. That meant cutting off branchlines. They had to make more productive use of labor. That meant breaking out of productivity-crushing work rules, cutting the labor force in half, and using what was left for productive work, not make-work. They would have to invest in new technology, including CTC, welded rail, automated yards, and container terminals. And they had no capital to do that.

How bad was it? The Jersey Central was already in bankruptcy. Its demise forewarned all railroads and public officials that the wolf was at the door. The Boston & Maine entered bankruptcy six weeks before the Penn Central when it could not even find the cash to pay its 1969 taxes. The Lehigh Valley declared bankruptcy on July 24, 1970, a month after Penn Central. The Reading declared on November 23, 1971.

The Erie Lackawanna looked as if it might be the Cinderella of the East, wiry enough to capitalize on the Penn Central's lost business. But on the night of June 21–22, 1972, Hurricane Agnes dumped enough rain on the southern tier counties of New York State to wash out or structurally damage every bridge on its main line between Elmira and Salamanca. The railroad was inoperable for 135 miles. Bankruptcy was declared on June 26, 1972. All these railroads were beyond the point of no return. They could not borrow, obviously, nor could they raise the capital internally to renew obsolete plant. The Erie Lackawanna might not have been in that position if it had not been for Hurricane Agnes, but such is life.

At the time of the Penn Central's collapse, the Illinois Central–Gulf merger proceeding was descending into a pit of accusation and recrimination. Railroad turned on railroad out of raw fear that even a small diversion of traffic would ruin it. The Rock Island–Union Pacific merger, at this point, still lingered in limbo. The railroads had created this deadlock, but now the fault lay with the ICC for taking too long to make a decision. While the ICC dallied, the Rock Island was visibly dying, the Milwaukee Road was visibly dying, the Katy was visibly dying. These railroads also had passed the point of no return.

Here and there were pockets of financial strength. The coal roads were doing all right, and so were the long-haul transcontinentals, at least for the time being. If railroads outside the Northeast could no longer deliver cars to the Northeast, because all the roads in the Northeast were hurtling toward liquidation, it was not likely that any railroad would remain secure for long. The lights were blinking out on the whole industry, except maybe for hauling coal. Twelve years after Congress acknowledged that the railroads had a passenger problem, everything was sliding into the vortex.

In the years just around the corner, the oil embargo of 1973 would send railroad costs climbing. All that heavy tare weight they lugged around, none too economical before oil prices went up, would be intolerable after. Major breakthroughs in technology would have to work, or the railroad would be rendered uneconomical. But how would the railroads afford this technology? Those beyond the point of no return, by definition, could not afford it. Inflation, fueled largely by rising oil prices, would force wage rates to double, then triple, across the coming decade. Productivity issues that had simmered since the Shopmen's Strike of 1922 were on the table for all to see at the time of Arbitration Board 282, concerning firemen on the diesels. They could not be postponed any longer. Either some jobs would be lost or all jobs would be lost.

What were some possible outcomes? The market solution was to let the railroads die. But the utilities, the auto industry, the chemical industry, and agribusiness, among others, made it clear that this could not happen without causing the national economy to spasm mightily. If the railroads died, or if they ceased to function as a national system, then more expensive and less fuel-efficient transportation would have to be substituted. For the moment, the supply of oil was in the hands of nations that did not wish the United

States well; and in any event, the consumer would foot the bill of higher transportation costs. Prices, starting with utility rates, would go up—a lot.

The government could come to the rescue. But if the government came to the rescue, could it tell communities that an efficient, slimmed-down rail system would require them to lose their rail line? Could the government tell taxpaying workers that they would have to sacrifice their railroad jobs? Probably not. So nationalization would embalm all the inefficiencies of the old system within the federal budget. The taxpayer would pay. How would the American people like to pay—with higher taxes or higher prices? It was one or the other. Railroad investors were saying clearly they were tired of footing the bill and they were bailing out. Could there be a middle ground of government help without the inefficiencies? No one knew. Politics being what they were, it would take real stamina for the government to tell taxpaying citizens they could not have everything they wanted. A sound public-private cooperation like, say, the TVA, was not out of the question, but it would not be easy, not in a day when every interest group made demands and every suggestion was subject to violently clashing ideologies over what government should or should not do.

The Defining Moment

On July 11, 1970, two weeks after the bankruptcy, a Penn Central delegation was back in Washington trying for a loan. By this time it was no longer to bail out the bankers but just to keep the trains rolling through the summer. Jonathan O'Herron was sent to beg before the House Commerce Committee. O'Herron had been top aide to the ousted PC vice president of finance, David Bevan. Harley O. Staggers, a West Virginia Democrat, presided at the meeting. O'Herron took a take-no-prisoners approach. "I deplore the necessity, but there is a certain irony in the fact that we must seek aid from the very hand that has had at least a significant part in forcing us to our present posture," he told them. "In no small measure, our financial problems are the result of a long history of neglect of the serious difficulties facing America's railroads, over-regulation by government on all levels and a swiftly spiraling period of inflation that has coincided with our two years of merged operations."[1]

There were echoes of truth in O'Herron's thesis, but because it came from a company whose operating fiasco, breakdown of managerial control, laundered bank accounts, insider trading, misjudgment, and malfeasance were all on the table, the congressmen were not buying. Staggers was so furious that he was shaking before O'Herron had finished. He jabbed a pencil in O'Herron's direction and said, "I resent your coming here and saying the Government has put you in the position you are in. The whole tenor of your testimony was to attack the government, that we were to blame for everything that has happened on Penn Central."[2] Staggers wanted to know exactly what Penn Central's 25 vice presidents did for their fancy salaries, given that the whole world could now see how incompetently they ran the railroad? What exactly did Mr. O'Herron do for his fancy salary and his recent raise? The congressmen who the railroad now hoped would save its butt earned $42,000. How much did these men who screwed up the railroad earn? O'Herron was chastised. Later, he told reporter Robert Bedingfield, who was covering the hearing for the *New York Times*, that he had never testified like this before, but after nearly three hours of tough questioning, he thought he had learned a lot.[3]

But that confrontation before the Staggers Committee was the turning point for American railroads. O'Herron's tactical error put it all on the table: the crisis was here. The government would have to focus on railroad problems, and it would have to stay focused. There were no more Band-aids. Letting them discontinue a few passenger trains, granting a merger, and ordering up another study was not going to cut it anymore. It was time to make some hard decisions. Was it time to nationalize the railroads? Then everybody could have their railroad service and their railroad job, but it would cost a lot. Or was it time to rebuild the railroads, just as the government had built highways and developed aircraft for others, and then free them from rate regulation so that they could compete in a free market? That could mean some big rate hikes for some very important customers and the loss of a lot of railroad jobs. But it might salvage the railroads as bona fide private enterprises and efficient providers of transportation for a growing economy. What was it going to be?

It would be six years before the government figured out what to do with the Penn Central, the Erie Lackawanna, and all the others in the Northeast. It would be ten years before the coming of deregulation, which turned the industry around for good.

The American railroads would wander in the wilderness through the 1970s, but they were going make a historic turnaround. They were going to return as a vibrant economic force. When they returned, they would be changed utterly. Many branch and secondary lines would vanish. Some famous old companies, including the Rock Island and the Milwaukee Road, would vanish entirely. Only six super-railroads would rule the continent— the Union Pacific, the Burlington Northern Santa Fe, CSX, the Norfolk Southern, the Canadian National, and the Canadian Pacific, along with a few wiry regionals and a lot of new short lines. The boxcar would largely vanish. So would the caboose. Railroad jobs would disappear. In 1970 half a million workers (566,544) performed 765 billion ton miles of work. In 1996 less than a quarter million workers (181,511) performed 1,356 billion ton miles of work. With O'Herron's testimony before the House Commerce Committee, a chain of events was set in motion.

Epilogue for the Old Penn Central Gang

What happened to the gang that wrecked the old Penn Central and the sad corporate shell they left behind?

It was said that Mike Flannery was just beginning to solve the Penn Central's computer and operational problems as it crashed in flames. He was a hands-on railroader highballing his way up and down the system, said Rush Loving in *Fortune*, freeing bottlenecks, demanding more of his men, but always by encouraging them, challenging them, and instilling pride. If only he had not been hit by the horrible winter of 1969–1970. If only he had had more time.

Perlman, when his contract was up in November 1970, accepted the invitation of the Western Pacific to be its president and come to San Francisco and get that little carrier back on track. Flannery, his lieutenant from the heady days of the marketing revolution at the New York Central, went with him. Saunders's peace was interrupted by summonses to testify. He wound up in Richmond with Wheat First Securities as a consultant to coal producers.

Bevan and Gertsnecker were indicted on criminal charges for misappropriation of funds, specifically on the loan for EJA that wound up in the Liechtenstein bank. They were released on $50,000 bail. They pleaded not guilty. Charges were dismissed in 1977. There was talk of criminal charges against Saunders. In 1974 he signed a consent decree (neither an admission nor a denial of guilt) on allegations by the SEC that he had conspired to withhold vital information and defraud the public by misrepresenting the railroad's true financial condition, and for the improper diversion of funds to the Liechtenstein bank.[4] The investment brokerage house of Goldman, Sachs was included in the consent agreement for failing to inform its customers of the actual state of the financial affairs of the Penn Central. Auditors Peat, Marwick & Mitchell were found guilty of certifying financial statements that "it knew, or should have known, to be misleading." The auditors replied that the SEC had "no credible evidence" and that "once again, the Commission has seen fit to include auditors in its apparent program to offer scapegoats to the public."[5]

A group of plaintiffs including the railroad's trustees filed suit against Penphil, Bevan, Hodge, Gertsnecker, DuPont (F.I.) Glore Forgan, Inc., alleging that Penphil was an unlawful conspiracy. A group of plaintiffs that included the railroad and holders of Pennsylvania Railroad debentures charged Saunders, Perlman, Bevan, other former financial officers, and Peat, Marwick & Mitchell with dereliction of duty and issuing false financial statements and misleading proxy material. They reached a settlement of $12.6 million in September 1975. Of that, $2 million was covered by the $10 million breach of trust policy with Lloyds of London. It was known that of that sum, Perlman had to contribute $25,000; it was not known what share others were made to pay.[6] The court ordered the defendants to place full-page advertisements in major newspapers explaining the judgment.[7]

Judge John Fullam of the U.S. District Court for Eastern Pennsylvania was appointed to oversee the reorganization of the Penn Central. The financial structure was byzantine, with layer after layer of subsidiaries. These included component railroads that had lost their operating identity in the nineteenth century as the Pennsylvania and the New York Central grew into mighty systems. All of them had outstanding securities, many of which were pledged as collateral or otherwise encumbered. Many still had minority holders, who, of course, had legal rights. At some of the court proceedings, more than 100 lawyers were present, with legal fees costing the railroad nearly a million dollars in its first year of bankruptcy, nearly a million and a half in the second.[8]

In 1972 the railroad auctioned off its library and other memorabilia, the heritage of the Pennsylvania Railroad, and raised about half a million dollars. Items included a brass doorknob from the old Broad Street Station in Philadelphia, the station clock from Newark, and a treatise dated 1812 by John Stevens, one of the principal developers of the steam locomotive, on the feasibility of the railroad. Buffs paid two dollars to be admitted to the auction and one dollar for the program; they took everything. One of them even offered the railroad patrolman watching over the proceedings $50 for his Penn Central badge.

At first only the railroad was in bankruptcy. The Staggers Committee (House Special Subcommittee on Investigations) concluded: "The financial acumen of management, while it did not protect the railroad from bankruptcy, was able to insulate those other assets carefully beyond the reach of a government asked only to rescue the railroad, not the highly profitable non-railroad properties."[9] But briefly in 1976, primarily over the Swiss franc loan, the Penn Central Company (which included the real estate, the diversified investments, everything but the railroad) was forced into bankruptcy. It emerged shortly as Penn Central Corporation, a diversified investment company. It was awarded a $2.1 billion reimbursement from the government for its railroad properties. It acquired subsidiaries, mostly in real estate, recreation, energy, and technology, which it spun off and bought back, constantly churning the assets. There was money to be made in churning, and it made a lot of people a lot of money, though it was almost entirely a new crowd from the railroad days. By 1989 the Penn Central Corporation was regarded as a cash-rich investment hedge. In 1992–1993 it had a bitter dispute with New York City over building in the air space above Grand Central. Jacqueline Kennedy Onassis played a personal role in opposing this. It reached a settlement with the city. In 1994 it changed its name to American Premier Underwriters, headquartered in Cincinnati and moving mostly into insurance.

Perlman and his undying faith in technology and cybernetics brought the Western Pacific physically and financially to a level that made it an attractive merger partner. He retired in 1976 and was succeeded by Flannery. He lived to see the WP safely included in the Union Pacific in December 1982. He died in San Francisco on April 30, 1983. In railroad lore he was the pioneer of the technological wonder that was the super-railroad of the latter twentieth century. He is remembered for having a better fix on the future of railroading than anyone else of his generation. He is a flawed hero, but a hero.

After the Western Pacific entered the Union Pacific, Flannery became one of that mighty system's top lieutenants, sent out to run the Missouri Pacific, which the UP acquired at the same time as the Western Pacific. In 1983 he became president of the Union Pacific Railroad. He was brilliantly successful, one of the great railroaders of the century.

Saunders died on February 8, 1987, in Richmond, Virginia. In railroad memory he is not really a villain, just a painful memento of the industry's darkest hour, and otherwise forgotten. David Morgan eulogized him in *Trains:* "Seldom in the industry has a man risen so rapidly, rearranged the rail map more, or fallen from favor faster. . . . None can question Saunders' behavior after the fall from grace . . . in which he lost his personal wealth and made no excuses."[10]

Notes

Introduction

1. The *Official Guide of the Railways and Steam Navigation Lines of the United States, Porto Rico* [*sic*], *Canada, Mexico & Cuba*, published monthly by the National Railway Publication Company of New York, was a compendium of railroad timetables along with maps and station indexes. For those who worked with or loved railroads, it was regarded as a nearly holy text.

2. Delivering or terminating roads should not be mistaken for *terminal* railroads, short lines usually set up by one or all of the railroads in a metropolitan area to absorb the high cost of terminal switching, to open up all industrial sidings and loading docks to all carriers on a reciprocal basis, and to operate union passenger stations. The most famous one was TRRA, the Terminal Railroad Association of St. Louis.

3. Suspension Bridge, New York, was previously the village of Bellevue, then Niagara City, before being absorbed by the city of Niagara Falls in 1892 where it is now known as the "North End." It is located on the American side of the Michigan Central and Grand Trunk railroad bridges from Canada. It remained the official railroad and one of the great junctions of the East. Its importance waned significantly after the creation of Conrail in 1976.

4. Though it was always associated with the Southern, the original Crescent (not the Amtrak version) was handled west of Atlanta by the West Point Route and the Louisville & Nashville.

5. Hank Williams, "Pan Amercian," copyright © 1948 Acuff-Rose Music, Inc./Hardin Music, administered by Rightsong Music, Inc., BMI, as recorded on Sterling Records, 1947.

6. Ray Welch, "Sunshine Special," Acuff-Rose, Inc./BMI, recorded by Roy Acuff, Capitol Records, 1953.

7. Copyright © 1945 Johnny Mercer and Harry Warren, Leo Feist Inc., ASCAP, Capitol Records.

1: The Ambiguous Legacy of the Era of Reform

1. Ralph W. Hidy, Muriel E. Hidy, Roy V. Scott, and Don L. Hofsommer, *The Great Northern Railway: A History* (Cambridge: Harvard Business School Press, 1988), 85. This is an excellent history.

2. William Gilpin, *The Cosmopolitan Railway* (San Francisco: History Co., 1890).

3. Matthew Josephson, *The Robber Barons* (New York: Harcourt Brace, 1934), 449.

4. Theodore Roosevelt, speech given at Cincinnati on September 20, 1902, reproduced in *New York Times*, September 21, 1902, 2.

5. *Northern Securities Co. v. United States*, 193 U.S. 197, 230 (1904).

6. Jonathan Raban, *Bad Land: An American Romance* (New York: Pantheon, 1996), 315.

7. It was not the first North American installation of electric power by a railroad. The B&O's three-mile Howard Street Tunnel in Baltimore opened in 1895 for freight and passenger service. The New York Central began electric passenger operation into the as yet uncompleted Grand Central in 1906. The Grand Trunk's St. Clair Tunnel was electrified in 1908 with Baldwin-Westinghouse 3,300-volt single-phase AC for the heavily graded but short hop under the Saint Clair River between Sarnia, Ontario, and Port Huron, Michigan. See William D. Middleton, *When the Steam Railroads Electrified* (Milwaukee: Kalmbach, 1974).

8. A story of the Milwaukee Land Company homesteaders and their descendants, particularly in the area of Montana east of Miles City, is told in Raban, *Bad Land*.

9. The story is told in grizzly detail in Max Lowenthal, *The Investor Pays* (New York: Knopf, 1933).

10. *Consolidation and Combinations of Carriers*, 12 ICC 277 (1907).

11. Senate Committee on Interstate Commerce, *Railroad Combination in the Eastern Region: Hearings before the Committee on Interstate Commerce*, 76th Cong., 3d sess., 1940, S. Rept. 1182, serial 40-26367, 16–24.

12. Henry Lee Staples and Alpheus T. Mason, *The Fall of a Railroad Empire* (Syracuse, N.Y.: Syracuse University Press, 1947); Richard M. Abrams, "Brandeis and the New Haven–Boston & Maine Merger Battle Revisited," *Business History Review* 36, no. 4 (1962): 408–30; and Senate, *New York, New Haven & Hartford RR Co., Evidence Taken before the ICC*, 63d Cong., 2d sess., 1914, S. Doc. 543, serial 14-3085, 3.

13. House of Representatives, *Pere Marquette RR Co. and Cincinnati, Hamilton & Dayton Ry. Co.*, 65th Cong., 1st sess., 1917, S. Doc. 137, serial 6833, 217.

14. *Interstate Commerce Commission v. Alabama Midland Railway Company* 168 U.S. 144 (1897).

15. Albro Martin, *Enterprise Denied: Origins of the Decline of American Railroad, 1887–1917* (New York: Columbia University Press, 1971). A more conventional interpretation of this period may be found in I. Leo Sharfman, *The American Railroad Problem* (New York: Century, 1921). A leftist interpretation may be found in Gabriel Kolko, *Railroads and Regulation, 1877–1916* (Princeton, N.J.: Princeton University Press, 1965).

16. Ari Hoogenboom and Olive Hoogenboom, *A History of the ICC: From Panacea to Palliative* (New York: Norton, 1976).

17. "The B&S," *Hamburg (N.Y.) Sun Suburban*, July 7, 1960, 1. Portions of the B&S south of Wellsville, New York, that served Pennsylvania coal mines remained and eventually became part of the B&O. They were later spun off as a short line, the Wellsville, Addison & Galeton, and abandoned in 1979.

18. Senate Committee on Interstate Commerce, *Government Control and Operation of Railroads: Hearing before the Committee on Interstate Commerce*, 65th Cong., 3d sess., 1918, 124, 339.

19. Ibid., 123.

20. Ibid., 89.

21. Louis Brandeis's claim, famous but largely unsupported, was that scientific management could save railroads a million dollars a day. Senate, *Five Percent Case*, 63d Cong., 2d sess., 1915, vol. 14, pt. 6:5248.

22. The Royal Blue Line was named for the principal passenger train that traveled the route between Washington and New York. It consisted of the B&O between Washington and Park Junction in Philadelphia, the Reading from Park Junction to Bound Brook, New Jersey, and the Jersey Central from there to Jersey City, with ferry connections to New York. The B&O owned the Staten Island Rapid Transit Line and facilities at New York Harbor, even though its lines did not actually go to New York.

23. Senate Committee on Interstate Commerce, *Extension of Government Control of Railroads*, 66th Cong., 3d sess., 1919, S. Rept. 304, 12–15.

24. Ralph M. Sayre, "Albert Baird Cummins and the Progressive Movement in Iowa," Ph.D. diss., Columbia University, 1958.

25. Senate, *The Railroad Problem: Address by Albert B. Cummins*, 66th Cong., 1st sess., 1919, S. Doc. 19, vol. 14.

26. *Blair v. City of Chicago*, 201 U.S. 400 (1906); *Washington Evening Star*, August 2, 1922.

27. Glenn Plumb, "The Plan of Organized Employees for Railroad Reorganization," *Commerce and Finance*, July 23, 1919.

28. Undocumented clippings in the ICC Library; House Committee on Interstate and Foreign Commerce, *Return of the Railroads to Private Enterprise: Hearings on H.R. 456*, 66th Cong., 1st sess., 1919.

29. W. E. Simnett, *Railway Amalgamation in Great Britain* (London: Railway Gazette, 1923); Kimon Apostolus Doukas, *The French Railroads and the State* (New York: Columbia University Press, 1945); G. R. Stevens, *History of the Canadian National Railways* (New York, 1973). The French railroads were nationalized in 1937 and the British in 1945. See also Logan McPherson, *Transportation in Europe* (New York: Henry Holt, 1910).

30. Alfred Mierzejewski, *The Most Valuable Asset of the Reich: The German National Railway* (Chapel Hill: University of North Carolina Press, 1999).

31. Senator Lenroot had offered a bill to merge all railroads into a single national system, hence all the questions on its practicality. *Congressional Record*, 66th Cong., 2d sess., 1919, vol. 56, pt. 1:132.

32. One of the best analyses of the World War I and post–World War I railroad debates is K. Austin Kerr, *American Railroad Politics, 1914–1920* (Pittsburgh: University of Pittsburgh Press, 1968).

33. Samuel Rea, *Our Railroad Problem*, and Howard Elliott, *An Efficient Transportation Machine*, pamphlets at the ICC Library.

2: The Legacy of the Transportation Act of 1920

1. Hidy et al., *The Great Northern Railway*, 192.

2. *Consolidation of Railroads*, 63 ICC 455 (1921), contains the Ripley Report and the Tentative Plan.

3. *Congressional Record,* 69th Cong., 1st sess., 1926, vol. 67, pt. 7:7331.

4. Senate, Discussion to Promote the Unification of Carriers Engaged in Interstate Commerce, 70th Cong., 1st sess., 1928, S.B. 1175, vol. 69, 347.

5. Senate Committee on Interstate Commerce, *Railroad Combination,* 618–20.

6. Senate Committee on Interstate Commerce, *The Van Sweringen Corporate System,* 77th Cong., 1st sess., 1941, S. Rept. 714, serial 41-46481.

7. *New York, Chicago & St. Louis RR Co., Operation of Lines and Issue of Capital Stock,* 79 ICC 581 (1923).

8. Senate, *Railroad Combination,* ex. C-979, C-1015.

9. Albert J. County, *Consolidation of Railroads into Systems: A Review of Some of the Financial Considerations That Consolidation under the Transportation Act Imposes* (Washington, D.C., December 28, 1923), pamphlet in author's collection.

10. See Robert Kanigel's excellent biography, *The One Best Way: Frederick Winslow Taylor and the Enigma of Efficiency* (New York: Viking, 1998).

11. *Labor* (September 11, 1920, 1), pamphlet cited in Colin Davis, *Power at Odds: The 1922 National Railroad Shopmen's Strike* (Urbana: University of Illinois Press, 1997), 52. The following account of the Shopmen's Strike is condensed from Davis's excellent book.

12. Davis, *Power at Odds,* 77.

13. Report of Fred Davis, U.S. marshal, quoted in ibid., 128.

14. From Richberg's memoirs, cited in ibid., 128.

15. Ibid., 131.

16. Senate, *Railroad Combination,* 2027–38.

17. Senate, 1981; *Pittsburgh & West Virginia Ry. Co., Proposed Construction and Extension,* 138 ICC 755 (1928).

18. Senate, *Railroad Combination,* 1228–30.

19. *Norfolk & Western Ry., Proposed Acquisition and Control of the Virginian Ry.,* 117 ICC 67 (1926).

20. *Virginian Ry. Extension,* 162 ICC 552 (1930).

21. Senate, *Railroad Combination,* 2143.

22. *ICC v. Baltimore & Ohio RR,* 152 ICC 721 (1929); *ICC v. B&O RR,* 160 ICC 785 (1930).

23. *ICC v. Pennsylvania RR Co.,* 169 ICC 618 (1930); *ICC v. PRR Co.,* 291 ICC 651 (1934).

24. Senate, *Railroad Combination,* 2075–122.

25. *In the Matter of Consolidation of Railroad Properties in the United States into a Limited Number of Systems,* 159 ICC 522 (1929); Senate, *Railroad Combination,* ex. C-2821.

26. *In the Matter of Consolidation,* 185 ICC 401 (1932).

27. See Stuart Daggett, *Railroad Consolidation West of the Mississippi* (Berkeley: University of California Press, 1933).

28. Frederick H. Prince, "A Plan for Consolidating the Operation of the Railroads of the United States," March 15, 1933, mimeographed pamphlet in author's collection.

29. Earl Latham, *The Politics of Railroad Consolidation, 1933–1936* (Cambridge: Harvard University Press, 1959), 38.

30. Years later, the B&O Pittsburgh-Chicago line was busy with traffic as part of CSX, while Conrail, successor to the PRR, eliminated the parallel PRR route as a main line.

31. House of Representatives, *First Report of the Federal Coordinator of Transportation,* 74th Cong., 1st sess., 1935, H. Doc. 89.

32. House of Representatives, *Report of the Federal Coordinator of Transportation,* 74th Cong., 2d sess., 1935, H. Doc 89.

33. William Leonard, *Railroad Consolidation under the Transportation Act of 1920* (New York: Columbia University Press, 1946). He cites these studies as single copies at the Bureau of Railway Economics Library.

34. Latham, *Politics of Railroad Consolidation,* 57.

35. House of Representatives, *Omnibus Transportation Bill: Hearings,* 76th Cong., 1st sess., January 14–March 3, 1939.

36. *Congressional Record,* 76th Cong., 3d sess., 1940, vol. 86, pt. 11:11766.

37. See Frank N. Wilner, *The Railway Labor Act and the Dilemma of Labor Relations* (Omaha: Simmons-Boardman, 1988).

38. See David P. Morgan, "The Diesel That Did It," *Trains* 20 (Feb. 1960): 18–25.

39. Tom Lewis, *Divided Highways: Building the Interstate Highways, Transforming American Life* (New York: Viking, 1997).

3. Dead Ends with Pennroad and Robert R. Young

1. *McLean Trucking Co. v. United States,* 321 U.S. 67 (1944).

2. Senate, *Railroad Combination,* 2110.

3. *New York Times,* March 29, 1940, 31.

4. *Overfield v. Pennroad,* 113 F. 2nd 6 (1941), rev. 39 F. Supp. 482 (1941); 42 F. Supp. 586 (1942); 48 F. Supp. 1008 (1943); 146 F. Supp. 889 (1944). *Perrine v. Pennroad,* 28 Del. Chancery 342 (1945); 29 Del.Ch. 423 (1947). *Swacker v. Pennroad,* 30 Del. Ch. 495 (1947); 333 U.S. 862 (1948).

5. FD 14530, *Pennsylvania Co. Notes,* Shipstead to Paterson, May 26, 1944.

6. *New York, New Haven & Hartford RR Co. Reorganization,* 247 ICC 365 (1947); FD 13235, *Wabash Ry. Co. Control,* transcripts 192–204.

7. *Wabash Ry. Co. Receivership,* 247 ICC 581, 584 (1941).

8. FD 13235, transcript 40.

9. Ibid., transcripts 154–59.

10. Ibid., transcript 6.

11. Ibid., transcripts 156–64.

12. Joseph Borkin, *Robert R. Young, the Populist of Wall Street* (New York: Harper and Row, 1969), chap. 3; Matthew Josephson, "The Daring Young Man of Wall Street," *Saturday Evening Post,* August 11, 18, 25, 1945.

13. ICC docket 29085, *In Re Alleghany,* examiner's report, as recounted in Josephson, "Daring Young Man," and Borkin, *Robert R. Young.*

14. Quoted in Borkin, *Robert R. Young,* 47.

15. *Wheeling & Lake Erie RR Co. Control,* 249 ICC 490 (1941).

16. John A. Rehor, *The Nickel Plate Story* (Milwaukee: Kalmbach, 1965), is an excellent company history.

17. FD 15228, *Pere Marquette Ry., Merger,* transcripts 206–39, 361.

18. FD 15228, transcript 469.

19. The PM wanted the new C&O preferred stock that was to be issued in exchange for the PM's own preferred stock to be noncallable, since it was expected to be a prime dividend-paying issue. The C&O agreed to make it noncallable until

November 1, 1950. FD 15228, transcript 480.

20. FD 15228, transcript 37.

21. Ibid., transcript 1082.

22. Ibid., transcripts 39, 179, 337–38, 379.

23. *PM Ry., Merger,* 267 ICC 207, 237–38 (1947).

24. *Schwabacher v. ICC,* 72 F. Supp. 560 (1948); *Schwabacher v. United States,* 334 U.S. 182 (1948).

25. *W&LE RR Co. Control,* 257 ICC 713 (1944); 267 ICC 163 (1946).

26. FD 15685, *W&LE RR Co. Control,* transcript 40; FD 16308, *W&LE RR Co. Control,* transcripts 31, 38, 65, 164.

27. FD 15685, transcript 74.

28. ICC docket 12964, *In Re Consolidation of Railroads* (1925), digest of testimony and exhibits of eastern carriers.

29. FD 17803, *New York, Chicago & St. Louis RR Control,* transcript 259.

30. FD 17803, transcript 144.

31. *NYC&StL RR Control,* 295 ICC 131, 152 (1955).

32. FD 14692, *Chesapeake & Ohio Ry. Purchase,* transcript 1019.

33. *New York Times,* December 4, 1946, 49.

34. FD 14692, corres. vol. 1-C.

35. *New York Times,* March 4, 1946, 15.

36. FD 14692, transcript 1027.

37. Reproduced in Borkin, *Robert R. Young,* 2.

38. *New York Times,* July 9, 1948, 23; FD 14692, Estin corres., vol. 1-C.

39. *New Automobiles in Interstate Commerce,* 259 ICC 475 (1945); FD 14692, transcripts 538, 1089.

40. FD 14692, brief of Vgn. Ry., vol. 3, transcript 538.

41. FD 14692, transcripts 852, 909. The ICC was always reluctant to approve interlocking directorates. *In Re Boatner,* 257 ICC 369 (1944), based on *In Re Coverdale,* 252 ICC 672 (1942); *In Re Astor,* 193 ICC 528 (1933); *In Re Rand,* 175 ICC 587 (1931).

42. FD 14692, transcripts 1086–87.

43. Ibid., transcript 1036.

44. Ibid., transcripts 1083–84.

45. Ibid., transcripts 1027–28.

46. Ibid., transcripts 1065–66.

47. Ibid., transcripts 1149–268.

48. *C&O Ry. Purchase,* 271 ICC 5 (1948).

49. *New York Times,* December 11, 1947, 55.

50. Advertisements in *Time,* January 19, 1947, 67; February 2, 1948, 41; February 23, 1948, 41.

51. Memo to Robert R. Young. *Trains* 8 (Feb. 1948): 3.

52. *New York Times,* February 5, 1947, 32; May 21, 1948, 35; November 28, 1951, 45.

53. Quoted by John Brooks in the *New Yorker,* May 3, 1954, 44.

54. *New York Times,* July 12, 1954, 1.

4: Troubles

1. Bill Caloroso, *Pennsylvania Railroad's Elmira Branch* (Andover, N.J.: Andover Junction, 1993). The pictures and text of this excellent volume document well

what a railroad actually did for a living in the 1950s.

2. Thomas J. Gaffney, "The Changing Role of the Railroad and Its Effect on the Thumb Region of Michigan," master's thesis, Clemson University, 1999.

3. While diesel had the edge on heavy freight, steam seemed to have an edge in heavy, fast passenger service. See Bill Withuhn, "Did We Scrap Steam Too Soon?" *Trains* 34 (June 1974): 36–48, which is a good story of the economics and the history of technology. Had there been no diesel, steam technology would probably have advanced with such developments as "dynamic augment," which would compensate for the efficiency lost in the backward thrust of a piston rod on a forward-moving locomotive. After the oil embargoes of the 1970s, the price of oil jumped, the mix of cost factors changed again, and there was a momentary blip that steam might return.

4. There is nothing wrong with providing service for a luxury market if it can be done at a profit, but it needs to be a service separate from basic common carrier transportation.

5. Railroad slang for a fast, through freight train, derived from the red balls that once served as trackside signals—in low position, they meant "stop"; in high position, they meant "go," or "highball," which was the origin of that term also.

6. The title of this section, "Who Shot the Passenger Train?" was the title of a famous article by David P. Morgan that appeared in the April 1959 issue of *Trains*. But the commentary here is not a condensation of that article. The ideas that luxury private rooms and vista-domes were unproductive and that states and railroads should have worked together to build hub-and-spoke systems are my own.

7. *Noerr Motor Freight v. Eastern Railroads Presidents Conference*, 155 F. Supp. 768 (1957).

8. H. Roger Grant, *The Corn Belt Route: A History of the Chicago Great Western Railroad Company* (DeKalb: Northern Illinois University Press, 1984), 151.

9. Jim Shaughnessy, *The Rutland Road* (Berkeley: Howell-North, 1964).

5: Solutions

1. This section is condensed from the excellent book by David DeBoer, *Piggyback and Containers: A History of Rail Intermodal on America's Steel Highway* (San Marino, Calif.: Golden West Books, 1992).

2. The route is now operated by Union Pacific, with Amtrak passenger service.

3. Quoted by Freeman Hubbard in "The Expanding GM&O," *Trains* 8 (February 1948): 16.

4. *Chicago, Burlington & Quincy RR Co. Control*, 271 ICC 63 (1948). The line was still a part of the GM&O when that road merged with the Illinois Central. The IC later sold most of the GM&O's routes, and the Kansas City line was eventually operated as a short line, the Gateway Western.

5. William Leonard, "Decline of Railroad Consolidation," *Journal of Economic History* 9 (1949), 1–24.

6. Railway Labor Executives' Association, untitled compilation of documents relating to labor-protective conditions in consolidation cases (Washington, D.C., reprinted 1968).

7. *United States v. Lowden*, 308 U.S. 225 (1939).

8. *Congressional Record*, 76th. Cong., 1st sess., 1939, vol. 84, pt. 9:9882.

9. Ibid., 3d sess., 1940, vol. 86, pt. 6:5869.

10. *Fort Worth & Denver City Ry. Co. Lease*, 247 ICC 119 (1941); *Texas & Pacific Ry. Co. Operation*, 247 ICC 285 (1942); *Chicago, Milwaukee, St. Paul & Pacific RR Co. Trustees Construction*, 252 ICC 49 (1942); *Chicago & North Western Ry. Trustees Abandonment*, 254 ICC 820 (1944); *Oklahoma Ry. Trustees Abandonment*, 257 ICC 177 (1944).

11. *New Orleans Union Passenger Terminal Case*, 267 ICC 763 (1948); *Railway Labor Executives' Association v. United States*, 339 U.S. 142 (1950); *New Orleans Union Passenger Terminal Case*, 282 ICC 271 (1952).

12. David P. Morgan, "Where Did the Railroad Go That Once Went to Sea?" *Trains* 35 (February 1975): 22.

13. *St. Joe Paper Co. v. Atlantic Coast Line RR Co.*, 347 U.S. 298 (1954).

14. *New York Central Securities Co. v. United States*, 287 U.S. 12 (1932).

15. *Detroit, Toledo & Ironton RR Co., Control*, 275 ICC 455 (1950).

16. See the *New York Times*, April 18, 1954, 32; April 25, 1954, sec. 3, p. 1; May 13, 1954, 45; and Frank Donovan, Jr., "Minneapolis & St. Louis in the News Again," *Trains* 19 (March 1959): 16–19.

17. *Toledo, Peoria & Western RR Co., Control*, 295 ICC 523 (1957), affirmed *Minneapolis & St. Louis Ry. Co., Control*, 361 U.S. 173 (1959). Like the GM&O discussion, this is a departure from my conclusion in Saunders, *The Railroad Mergers and the Coming of Conrail* (Westport, Conn.: Greenwood Press, 1978), where I clearly rooted for the little road over the big ones. Little roads like the M&StL were what made railroading in the 1950s so fascinating, and it was fun to see an underdog make it. But joining the little M&StL to the little TP&W would only have made a bigger little railroad, still weak and still vulnerable.

18. *Louisville & Nashville RR Co., Merger*, 295 ICC 457 (1957).

19. David P. Morgan in *Trains* 15 (January 1955): 6.

20. Senate Subcommittee on Surface Transportation, *Problems of the Railroads*, 85th Cong., 2d sess., 1958, testimony of John M. Budd, 437–40.

21. David P. Morgan in *Trains* (April 1956): 6.

22. *New York Times*, November 3, 1958, 43; *Nation*, November 30, 1957, 406.

23. FD 21160, *Chesapeake & Ohio R. Co.—Control—Baltimore & Ohio R. Co.*, 317 ICC 261 (1962), transcript 62.

24. FD 21160, transcript 332.

25. *New York Times*, November 20, 1958, 49.

26. Ibid., November 14, 1958, 1.

27. *Trains* 19 (September 1959): 6.

28. Ibid. (March 1959): 5.

29. FD 21160, *C&O R. Co.—Control—B&O R. Co.*, transcript 2145.

30. *Norfolk & Western Ry. Co.—Merger—Virginian Ry.*, 307 ICC 401 (1959).

31. Perlman's evidence for PRR control of the N&W was the reduced coal rates requested in *Coal from Kentucky and West Virginia to Virginia*, 308 ICC 99 (1959); *Coal to New York Harbor Area*, 311 ICC 355 (1960); *Coal from Southern Mines to Tampa and Sutton*, 318 ICC 371 (1962).

32. FD 20599, *N&W Ry. Co.—Merger—Vgn. Ry.*, agreement of June 18, 1959, signed by Stuart Saunders for the N&W and Frank Beale and George Leighty for the RLEA, after which the RLEA withdrew from the proceedings.

33. *Duluth, South Shore & Atlantic RR Co.—Merger—Minneapolis, St. Paul & Sault Ste. Marie RR Co. and Wisconsin Central RR Co.*, 312 ICC 341 (1960); Senate Subcommittee on Antitrust and Monopoly, *Rail Merger Legislation*, 87th Cong., 2d sess., 1962.

34. *Chicago & North Western Ry.—Purchase—Minneapolis & St. Louis*, 312 ICC 285

(1960); *Brotherhood of Locomotive Engineers v. Chicago & North Western Ry. Co.*, 314 F. 2nd 424 (8th circuit, 1963).

35. Senate Subcommittee, *Rail Merger Legislation*, 1000–1010; *Enforcement of Conditions on Merger Proceedings*, 313 ICC 191 (1961).

36. *Central of Georgia Ry. Co., Control*, 295 ICC 523 (1957); 307 ICC 39 (1958).

37. Jim Lyne in *Railway Age* 60 (December 1959): 41.

38. John W. Barriger, "Why Consolidation?"—remarks before the Transportation Management Institute, Stanford University, Stanford, Calif., June 17, 1959; see also John W. Barriger, *Super Railroads for a Dynamic American Economy* (New York: Simmons-Boardman, 1956).

39. *Railway Age* 61 (January 1960): 28–29.

40. *New York Times*, October 26, 1958, sec. 3, p. 1.

41. Senate Committee on Commerce, *National Transportation Policy*, 87th Cong., 1st sess., 1961. Specifically, the Doyle Report recommended that (1) consolidation be approached on a national or regional basis, (2) competition between railroads should be preserved, (3) monopoly should be allowed only in restricted areas where traffic flow is limited, (4) no obstacle should be placed in the way of joint use of facilities, (5) no carrier should be forced to absorb a carrier it deems undesirable, and (6) overall public interest should supersede that of participants or opposing parties. There was no discussion of how (6) should be reconciled with (5).

42. *New York Times*, January 14, 1960, 49.

43. *Trains* 19 (October 1959): 5.

44. For a detailed summary of the findings, see *New York Times*, March 1, 1962, 18.

45. Marvin Hugo Zim, "Master Strategist of the Railroad Settlement," *Fortune* (July 1964): 164–66. See also Henry Hazlitt, "History of a Law," *Newsweek*, June 16, 1963, 75.

46. *New York Times*, April 23, 1964, 25.

6: The Erie Lackawanna

1. William White had the hyphen dropped in 1963.

2. *Trains* 19 (September 1959): 6.

3. The most elaborate was a pamphlet, *The Proposed Erie-Lackawanna and D&H Consolidation: Let's Stop, Look and Listen*, by an Erie stockholder, Charles Henkel. Some highlights:

> It is bewildering how the Erie is bailing out the Lackawanna. . . . It is difficult to understand why Erie management has retained Wyer, Dick & Co. to make a study . . . when its own operating, engineering and traffic departments should be able to tell there would be little or no benefit from consolidation. . . . Left to its own devices, the Lackawanna, which has the heaviest grades of any eastern trunk . . . is a dying industry and will probably follow the Ontario & Western to the junk heap. (FD 20707, *Erie R. Co.—Merger—Delaware, Lackawanna & Western R. Co.*)

4. H. Roger Grant, "Robert E. Woodruff: Railway Statesman?" *Railroad History*, bulletin 177 (autumn 1997): 78–86.

5. *Erie RR Co., Reorganization*, 239 ICC 653 (1940).

6. Henry Sturgis, *A New Chapter of Erie: The Story of the Erie's Reorganization*,

1938–1941 (New York, 1948).

7. *New York, Lackawanna & Western RR Co.—Merger,* 257 ICC 91 (1944).

8. *New York Times,* August 20, 1955, 8.

9. *Mohawk Air Lines Mail Rates,* 29 CAB 198 (1959).

10. *Railway Age* (April 13, 1960): 27.

11. Ibid. (May 5, 1958): 27.

12. FD 19182, *Erie R. Co., Trackage Rights,* reported 295 ICC 303 (1956).

13. *Erie R. Co., Ferry Abandonment,* 295 ICC 549 (1957); *Erie R. Co. v. Board of Public Utility Commissioners,* 395 U.S. 957 (1959).

14. FD 19989, *Erie R. Co. et al., Trackage Rights et al., Binghamton-Gibson, N.Y.,* reported 295 ICC 743 (1958).

15. FD 20707, transcript 853.

16. Ibid., transcript 664.

17. Ibid., transcripts 189, 787.

18. Ibid., transcripts 47–49.

19. Ibid., ex. H-48, August 6, 1959 (the Wyer Report).

20. Charles Meyers, executive vice president, Wyer, Dick & Co., telephone interview with the author, March 26, 1969.

21. *Erie R. Co., Abandonment,* 252 ICC 697 (1944).

22. Buffalo would be the hardest hit, with 136 operating and 121 nonoperating jobs eliminated. Total job loss in northern New Jersey would be 160. Projecting the employment records of 1956–1958 into the future, it was figured that 60 percent of those displaced would be taken care of by attrition. In metropolitan areas, it was estimated that 35 percent of those would have to move their homes; in nonmetropolitan areas, 60 percent would have to move—a total of 259 homes sold across the system at an average loss of $2,500 each. It was estimated that displaced employees in metropolitan areas would earn up to 80 percent of their former salary in other occupations; in nonmetropolitan areas, no more than 20 percent. The average length of service for displaced employees would be three years; therefore, average protection allowances would last 18 months. FD 20707, ex. H-48.

23. *United States v. Lowden; Interstate Commerce Commission v. Railway Labor Association,* 315 U.S. 373 (1942); *Railway Labor Association v. United States,* 339 U.S. 142 (1950).

24. FD 20707, corres. vol. 1-C.

25. *Brotherhood of Maintenance of Way Employees v. United States,* 366 U.S. 169 (1961). Labor's case rested on words spoken in the House of Representatives debate on the Transportation Act of 1940. In 1940, the House approved the Harrington Amendment; the Senate rejected it. When Representative Lea presented the House with the final conference committee report, he said: "The substitute we bring in here provides two additional things. First, there is a limitation on the operation of the Harrington Amendment for four years. . . . In other words, employees have protection against *unemployment* for four years" (emphasis supplied). *Congressional Record,* 76th Cong., 3d sess., 1940, vol. 86, pt. 9:10167.

In the Erie Lackawanna (EL) case, a majority of the court thought the following colloquy, spoken moments after the words above, was clarifying:

> Rep. O'Connor: As I want to see those who lose their jobs as a result of consolidation protected, I should like to have the gentlemen's interpretation of the phrase that the employee shall not be placed in a worse position with respect to his employment. Does "worse position" as used mean that his *compensation* will be just

the same for four years . . . as it would if no consolidation were effected?

Rep. Lea: I take that to be the correct interpretation. Our conference committee followed the instructions of the House in that respect. It gives railway labor generous protection against sudden and long unemployment. (*Congressional Record*, 76th Cong., 3d sess., 1940, vol. 86, pt. 9:10167)

A majority of the Court thought that since that was spoken moments before the final vote, it would have been the last impression on the matter left with the House.

26. Examples: a car of fresh meat from Omaha to Brooklyn routed Rock Island to Chicago, Nickel Plate to Buffalo, and Lackawanna to destination, was determined to be lost to the merged EL because it was believed that the Nickel Plate solicited it in the first place. Another car—of wooden products from Depew, New York, near Buffalo but on a Lackawanna siding, bound for Alabama, routed Nickel Plate–C&O to Cincinnati, thence L&N—would be routed EL to Cincinnati. The Lackawanna's $38 in revenue would become the Erie Lackawanna's $384. FD 20707, transcripts 381–95.

27. FD 20707, transcripts 1138–41.

28. Ibid., transcripts 1672–73.

29. *Railway Age* (November 16, 1959): 34.

30. FD 20707, corres., vol. 1-C.

31. Ibid., transcripts 821–22; *Trains* 20 (December 1959): 5.

32. FD 20707, exhibits.

33. *Fried v. United States*, 212 F. Supp. 887 (S. D. N. Y., 1963).

34. FD 20707, corres., vol. 1-C.

35. Ibid., transcripts 1067–73.

36. Charles Shannon, interview with Roger Grant, 1988, in H. Roger Grant, *Erie Lackawanna: Death of an American Railroad* (Stanford, Calif.: Stanford University Press, 1994), 75.

37. Interviews with former executives and board members by Roger Grant, in Ibid., 104.

38. Ibid., 111.

39. Quoted in ibid., 114.

40. Listed in ibid., 108–9.

41. FD 23422, *Erie Lackawanna v. Lehigh Valley,* reported 330 ICC 306 (1966), transcripts 131–39.

42. I was on board.

43. *Wall Street Journal,* June 14, 1963, 14.

44. EL Annual Report, 1963, interim report (University of Illinois Library, Champaign).

45. David P. Morgan in *Trains* 15 (January 1965): 9.

46. Grant, *Erie Lackawanna,* 135.

47. New Jersey Senate, *Hearings before a Special Committee of the New Jersey State Senate to Study Passenger and Freight Operations,* November 30, 1965, 50.

48. EL Annual Report, 1965, 3 (University of Illinois Library, Champaign).

7: The Chessie System and the Norfolk & Western

1. FD 21160, *C&O R. Co.—Control—B&O R. Co.,* transcript 138.

2. Ibid., transcripts 140, 1924.

3. Ibid., transcripts 28–30.

4. Ibid., transcript 1928.

5. *New York Times,* May 27, June 4, 1960; June 14, 1960, 49.

6. Ibid., June 26, 29, July 17, 1960.

7. Ibid., August 13, 1960, 22.

8. Ibid., August 31, 1960, 38.

9. Ibid., July 30, August 13, 26, 27, 31, 1960.

10. *Trains* 20 (October 1960): 5.

11. *New York Times,* June 26, 1960, sec. 3, p. 3.

12. FD 21160, minutes of meeting November 21, 1960, in vol. 4.

13. Among Young's former bankrollers, Murchison was trying to wrest control from Kirby.

14. *New York Times,* September 18, October 5, December 15, 1960.

15. FD 21160, transcripts 38–39.

16. Ibid., transcript 2525.

17. *New York Times,* January 20, 1961, 1.

18. Statements filed with SEC. *New York Times,* January 20, 1961, 1.

19. C&O Annual Report, 1962 (University of Illinois Library, Champaign).

20. *New York Times,* December 1, 1960, 51.

21. Ibid., December 20, 1960, 50.

22. See Robert F. Archer, *A History of the Lehigh Valley Railroad: "The Route of the Black Diamond"* (Berkeley: Howell-North, 1977).

23. The United States was neutral in 1916 though critical of others it accused of violating neutrality laws.

24. FD 23422, *EL v. LV,* transcript 30.

25. FD 21459, *Pennsylvania R. Co.—Control—Lehigh Valley R. Co.,* reported 317 ICC 139 (1962), transcripts 38–42.

26. FD 21459, transcripts 68–125.

27. *New York Times,* December 22, 1960, 33.

28. Symes quoted in FD 21459, transcript 167.

29. Ibid., transcript 427.

30. Ibid., transcripts 469–535.

31. Ibid., transcripts 199–207.

32. Ibid., transcripts 591–92.

33. FD 21160, transcript 3903.

34. Ibid., transcripts 520–21, 5696–98.

35. Ibid., transcripts 1261–62.

36. Ibid., transcript 1568.

37. Ibid., ex. H-9, H-21, transcript 2364.

38. Ibid., ex. H-98. Estimated savings for the C&O-B&O were common points, $6.97 million; duplicate lines, $37,346; duplicate passenger trains, $566,875; administration, $3 million; equipment pool, $3.73 million.

39. FD 21160, transcripts 576–77.

40. FD 21160, transcript 2879.

41. Ibid., transcript 93.

42. Ibid., transcript 847.

43. Ibid., transcript 2879.

44. Ibid., transcripts 847, 866, 1507.

45. Ibid., transcript 135.

46. Ibid., transcript 578.

47. Ibid., transcripts 2169–956. A boomer in railroad lore is a man who worked at many places on many railroads. In legend, a boomer was a happy-go-lucky person, perhaps with different wives at different junctions, never caring about stability or seniority.

48. FD 21510, *Norfolk & Western Ry.—Merger—New York, Chicago & St. Louis RR,* ex. H-30.

49. *N&W Ry.—Merger—NYC&StL RR,* 324 ICC 1 (18) (1964).

50. Tucker cited in 324 ICC 1 (53).

51. FD 21510, transcripts 821 (Kansas City Board of Trade), 835 (Hercules Powder), 912 (Missouri Farmers' Association).

52. Ibid., transcript 912 (Missouri Farmers' Association).

53. Ibid., transcript 810 (Cargill).

54. Ibid., transcripts 810 (Cargill), 898 (Ralston Purina), 944 (Spencer Chemical).

55. Ibid., transcript 760 (Detroit Steel).

56. Ibid., transcripts 792 (Continental Grain), 840 (Streitman Biscuit), 929 (Allied Chemical).

57. FD 21160, transcripts 2558–70.

58. FD 21510, transcripts 737–38.

59. Ibid., transcript 719.

60. Ibid., transcripts 715–25.

61. Ibid., ex. H-138.

62. Ibid., ex. H-120.

63. Ibid., ex. H-137.

64. Ibid., transcript 1231.

65. Ibid., transcripts 748–49.

66. Ibid., transcripts 1359–60.

67. Ibid., transcripts 1073–76.

68. Ibid., ex. H-177.

69. Ibid., transcripts 1023–62, ex. H-140.

70. Ibid., transcripts 1724–25, ex. H-121.

71. A transit privilege, most often pertaining to grain, is the right to stop a shipment en route and have it processed (milled into flour) and then continue its journey at the through rate.

72. FD 21510, transcripts 1514–21, ex. H-41.

73. *Trains* 20 (August 1960): 8.

74. *New York Times,* November 7, 1961, 47.

8: The West

1. The best history of the modern SP is Don Hofsommer, *The Southern Pacific, 1901–1985* (College Station: Texas A&M University Press, 1986); Frank Norris, *The Octopus* (New York: Doubleday, 1903): 50–51.

2. That stretch was the Connellsville Extension, which completed the Alphabet Route. See chapter 2, the section titled "Fifth Systems and the Scramble of 1929."

3. Bruce MacGregor and Ted Benson, *Portrait of a Silver Lady: The Train They Called the California Zephyr* (Boulder, Colo.: Pruett, 1977), 8–18.

4. *United States v. Union Pacific,* 226 U.S. 61 (1912).

5. *United States v. Southern Pacific,* 259 U.S. 214 (1922).

6. *Control of Central Pacific by Southern Pacific,* 76 ICC 508 (1923). The SP routinely flaunted this, however, because its entrance to Saint Louis was over a subsidiary, the St. Louis–Southwestern (or Cotton Belt). The Cotton Belt solicited freight in the Pacific Northwest for the long SP haul, and when the SP was questioned about this, it said only that the Cotton Belt had a right to look after the interests of its minority stockholders.

7. FD 21314, *Southern Pacific—Control—Western Pacific,* reported 327 ICC 187 (1965), transcripts 85–87.

8. MacGregor and Benson, *Portrait of a Silver Lady,* 24–25.

9. FD 21314, exceptions of the RLEA, vol. 1-L; transcripts 3402–3.

10. Ibid., transcript 3928.

11. Ibid., vol. 1-B.

12. Ibid., transcripts 91–92.

13. Hidy et al., *The Great Northern Railway,* 237.

14. Technically, the Fort Worth and Denver Railway, known as the Fort Worth & Denver City Railway prior to 1951, extended only as far north as Texline, Texas. Trackage south of Dallas was operated jointly with the Rock Island as the Burlington–Rock Island Railroad. The C&S was formally merged into the BN in 1981, and so was the FW&D a year later.

15. Eventually, the BN chose to retain the NP line between Spokane and Pasco, Washington. The former SP&S east of Pasco was ripped up in 1992. By most analyses, they ripped up the wrong one, as the newer SP&S line was better built, with fewer curves and lower grades.

16. The best summary is Robert Del Grosso, "The Wyer Report of 1957: BN Conceptualized," in Robert Del Grosso, *The Burlington Northern Railroad in 1993* (Bonners Ferry, Idaho: Great Northern Pacific, 1994).

17. A copy of *Consolidation: Key to Progress* is in Senate Subcommittee, *Rail Merger Legislation,* starting at 801.

18. FD 21478, *Great Northern—Merger—Northern Pacific,* reported 328 ICC 460 (1966), exceptions of the Minn. R&W Commission, January 15, 1965, 128.

19. *Great Northern—Merger—Northern Pacific,* 478.

20. Ibid., 517 (1966).

21. FD 21478, transcripts 810–11, 1320.

22. Ibid., exceptions of Dept. of Justice, 103.

23. The Milwaukee Road passed north of Billings. Access would require haulage rights on the NP.

24. FD 21478, exhibit of Minn. R&W Comm.

25. Senate Subcommittee, *Rail Merger Legislation,* 235–36.

26. Ibid., 239–40.

27. Ibid., 241. It should be noted, however, that Rassmussen could also be intemperate. For example, elsewhere in *Rail Merger Legislation* (1000–1010) an exchange of letters is reprinted between him and Ben Heineman of the C&NW. He had referred to hundreds of complaints received by him about the C&NW's service, but when pressed, he would not produce the letters; instead, he insisted that the inadequacy of the C&NW's service was well known and said that questioning the existence of these letters was "ridiculous" and "childish."

28. FD 21478, reply of 230 Pacific Northwest shippers.

29. Ibid., exceptions of the Dept. of Justice, January 15, 1965.

30. Ibid., brief of Dept. of Justice, appendix 10.

9: Kennedy, the Kefauver Hearings, and the ICC

1. Derounian (R), Dooley (R), Dulski (D), Healy (D), King (R), and Ostertag (R). Senate Subcommittee, *Rail Merger Legislation*, 1216–18.

2. William H. Tucker and John H. O'Brien, "The Public Interest in Railroad Mergers," in Senate Subcommittee, *Rail Merger Legislation*, 911.

3. "Message from the President of the United States Relative to the Transportation System of the United States," in Senate Subcommittee, *Rail Merger Legislation*, 718.

4. David Burner, *John F. Kennedy and a New Generation* (Glenview, Ill.: Scott, Foresman 1988), 146.

5. *Report of the Interagency Committee on Transport Mergers* (ICC-CAB—FMC), January 17, 1963.

6. David P. Morgan, "JFK: What He Meant to Railroading," *Trains* (February 1964): 49.

7. The railroad executives were James Symes (PRR), Leonard Murray (Soo Line), and Jervis Langdon (B&O). The labor leaders were Harold Crotty (Maintenance of Way), George Harrison (Clerks), George Leighty (Telegraphers), William Kennedy (Trainmen), and Paul O'Dwyer (Transport Workers Union). Harrison had served on FDR's Committee of Six in 1938. State utility commissions were represented by Walter McDonald (Georgia PSC) and Paul Rassmussen (Minnesota Railway & Warehouse Commission). The scholars included George Baker (Harvard), Kent Healy (Yale), William Leonard (Hofstra), John Meyer (Harvard), James Nelson (Washington State), and Merrill Roberts (Pittsburgh).

8. Symes's chart in Senate Subcommittee, *Rail Merger Legislation*, 339, included the following:

Industry	% Rate of Return	Industry	% Rate of Return
Drugs	19.7	Petroleum	10.4
Soap/cosmetics	17.2	Brewing	8.0
Soft drinks	15.8	Coal	7.5
Tobacco	14.8	Iron/steel	6.4
Automotive	14.2	Lumber	5.9
Finance	12.9	Meatpacking	4.7
Supermarkets	12.3	*Class I RR*	2.2
Chemicals	11.5	Air transpt	deficit
Construction	10.5		

9. Senate Subcommittee, *Rail Merger Legislation*, 337. The Kilday Report for the House Committee on Armed Services was titled *Transportation Systems in Support of the National Defense Effort in Event of Mobilization*, 1959.

10. Senate Subcommittee, *Rail Merger Legislation*, 371.

11. Ibid., 559.

12. Ibid., 305, 313.

13. Max Malin, "A Realistic Appraisal of the Financial Condition of Railroads," published by the Brotherhood of Locomotive Engineers and reprinted in Senate Subcommittee, *Rail Merger Legislation*, is much too detailed to summarize here, but it is

an important antidote to the railroad crying towel. Keyserling compiled a detailed chart of interlocking financial relationships (669–774). Derek Bok discounted this motive:

> While it is generally conceded that the great combinations at the turn of the century were the result of the desire to gain control of the market, the anti-competitive motive seems to have become increasingly rare in later years, having been replaced by a number of tax, managerial and commercial considerations of rather neutral effect from an antitrust standpoint. ("Section Seven of the Clayton Act and the Merging of Law and Economics," *Harvard Law Review* 74, no. 2 [December 1960]: 233)

14. Senate Subcommittee, *Rail Merger Legislation*, 26.
15. Kent Healy, "The Effects of Scale in the Railroad Industry," reprinted in ibid.
16. Ibid., 735.
17. Ibid., 58.
18. The commission even cited the "world crisis" as a reason for its approval. *C&O R. Co.—Control—B&O R. Co.*
19. Ibid., 298–99.
20. Ibid., 298.
21. Ibid., 331.
22. *Brotherhood of Maintenance of Way Employees et al. v. United States*, 221 F. Supp. 19 (E.D. Mich., 1963), affirmed 375 U.S. 216 (1963).
23. FD 21510, *N&W Ry. Co.—Merger—NYC&StL RR*, transcripts 136, 1150, 1738.
24. FD 21510, Dept. of Justice Motion for Dismissal, vol. 1-D.
25. *Rochester Telephone Corp. v. United States*, 307 U.S. 125 (1939).
26. David Bevan, memo, April 30, 1963, reprinted in Senate Committee on Commerce, *The Penn Central and Other Railroads*, 92d Cong., 2d sess., 1972, 389.
27. *N&W Ry. Co.—Merger—NYC&StL RR*, 148.

10: The Rise of the Penn Central

1. *Boston & Maine Discontinuance of Passenger Service*, 324 ICC 418 (1963); George W. Hilton, *The Transportation Act of 1958: A Decade of Experience* (Bloomington: Indiana University Press, 1969), chap. 4.
2. *New England Divisions: Bangor Aroostook RR Co. et al. v. Aberdeen & Rockfish RR Co. et al.*, 62 ICC 513 (1921).
3. *New York, New Haven & Hartford Trustees Discontinuance of All Interstate Passenger Trains*, 327 ICC 151 (1966).
4. Robert Bedingfield, *New York Times*, January 21, 1956, 1; January 6, 1960, 1; January 8, 1961, 1.
5. FD 21989, *Pennsylvania R. Co.—Merger—New York Central R. Co.*, reported 327 ICC 475 (1966) transcripts 194, 1061.
6. *In Re Consolidation of Merger Proceedings*, October 24, 1962, transcript 73.
7. FD 21989, transcript 1078.
8. Ibid., transcript 1164.
9. James R. Nelson, *Railroad Mergers and the Economy of New England* (Boston: New England Economic Research Council, 1966), 80. This is a most thoughtful analysis of New England railroad problems in the twentieth century, and my analysis draws heavily on it.
10. *Movement of Highway Trailers by Rail*, 293 ICC 93 (1954).

11. FD 21989, transcripts 18, 469, 6488.

12. Ibid., transcript 1104.

13. Ibid., transcript 11574.

14. The LIRR used the PRR's Sunnyside Yard on Long Island, PRR tunnels under the East River, and Penn Station on Manhattan. Complete separation of the two operations did not come until 1966.

15. David P. Morgan, "Is Pennsylvania Really Coming Back?" *Trains* 15 (December 1954): 21.

16. Joseph Daughen and Peter Binzen, *The Wreck of the Penn Central* (Boston: Little, Brown, 1971), 65.

17. Quoted in *Inside U.S.A.* (New York: Harper & Bros., 1947), 604.

18. Daughen and Binzen, *Wreck of the Penn Central,* 85.

19. Peat, Marwick & Mitchell to Hill, December 22, 1969, in Senate Committee, *Penn Central and Other Railroads,* 706.

20. Gale to the author, January 15, 1979.

21. Basil Cole to Ferdinand Kattau, August 30, 1965, in Senate Committee, *Penn Central and Other Railroads,* ex. 63. Some outside consultation was employed but only for technical advice with no discretionary power.

22. FD 21989, transcript 11044.

23. Ibid., transcript 5169.

24. Ibid., transcripts 6742–46.

25. David Smucker to Stuart Saunders, November 12, 1969, in Senate Committee, *Penn Central and Other Railroads,* ex. 65.

26. Ibid., transcript 1104.

27. Ibid., transcript 5893.

28. Ibid., transcript 8563.

29. Ibid., transcript 8949.

30. Ibid., transcripts 7082–95.

31. Ibid., transcript 1598.

32. Ibid., transcripts 571–75.

33. Ibid., transcripts 1397–508.

34. Charles Luna was the president of the Brotherhood of Railroad Trainmen (BRT).

35. FD 21989, transcripts 19639–44, ex. S-291, H-349.

36. Katzenbach to Saunders, September 4, 1964, in Senate Committee, *Penn Central and Other Railroads,* ex. 67.

37. This is what the railroad would bring if its rolling stock were sold, its rails sold for scrap, and its real estate auctioned off.

38. FD 21989, ex. NH-1, transcripts 24, 549–52.

39. Saunders to Tate, July 13, 1965, in FD 21898, vol. 1-K.

40. Daughen and Binzen, *Wreck of the Penn Central,* 88.

41. FD 21989, petition of M. J. Shapp, January 3, 1966, vol. 1-L.

42. See *Wall Street Journal,* July 20, 1964, 20.

43. FD 21989, *PRR Co.—Merger—NYC R. Co.,* 532–34, 561–63.

44. FD 21989, petition of N&W, June 13, 1966, vol. 1-M.

11: The South

1. The L&N ran a single train from stations on the Mississippi Gulf coast into New Orleans until 1965, and the MoPac ran a single train from Saint Louis's western

suburbs into Saint Louis until 1961.

2. FD 21215, *Seaboard Air Line—Merger—Atlantic Coast Line,* 320 ICC 122, 150–53 (1963).

3. FD 21215, 320 ICC 122 (1963), ex. 232 (not accepted in evidence), vol. 1-G.

4. Ibid., ex. 232.

5. See Joseph M. Welsh, *By Streamliner from New York to Florida* (Andover, N.J.: Andover Junction, 1994), an excellent account.

6. FD 21515, corres., vol. 1-A.

7. Ibid., brief of RLEA, vol. 18. Coverdale & Colpitts also did some of the Seaboard Coast Line (SCL) studies.

8. FD 21215, 320 ICC 122, 218.

9. Ibid., ex. 232.

10. FD 21515, petition of SR, August 23, 1960, vol. 1.

11. FD 21215, 320 ICC 122, 240.

12. Ibid., 218.

13. Ibid., 239.

14. Ibid., 329.

15. *Florida East Coast Ry. v. United States,* 242 F. Supp. 14 (M.D. Fla., 1965); *Seaboard Air Line R. Co. v. United States,* 382 U.S. 154 (1965).

16. Seth Bramson, *Speedway to Sunshine: The Story of the Florida East Coast Railway* (Erin, Ontario: Boston Mills Press, 1984), is an excellent history. See also David P. Morgan, "What's Going On in Florida?" *Trains* 14 (April 1964): 3; Morgan, "Where Did the Railroad Go?" *Trains,* 22–28; Luther Miller, "FEC: Florida's Productivity Showcase," *Railway Age* (May 8, 1978): 40–42; Jeffrey A. Harwell, "Florida East Coast: Survivor in the Sun," *Trains* 56 (July 1996): 34–43.

17. Attributed to Henry Whitter, Charles Noell, and Fred Lewey, claimed by David Graves George. Litigation nullified.

18. See Richard Saunders, "The Louisville, Cincinnati & Charleston Railroad and the Elusive Hope for Intersectional Unity" (master's thesis, University of Illinois, 1964; on deposit at the University of Illinois and at the Atlanta Historical Society).

19. Charles O. Morgret, *Brosnan: The Railroads' Messiah,* 2 vols. (New York: Vantage Press, 1996). This is a most important work on railroad history. The Brosnan family made Brosnan's personal papers available to Morgret, who organized this mountain of material in strict chronological order, so major stories like the Big John rate case dribble out over many chapters, all interspersed with details of Brosnan's personal life. Morgret provides no internal citation of documents that he uses. I have drawn heavily on Morgret for this account and have treated it as a semiprimary source, simply providing page references to it. A company-sponsored history by Burke Davis, *The Southern Railway: Road of the Innovators* (Chapel Hill: University of North Carolina Press, 1985), is pale and empty beside the Morgret work.

20. Morgret, *Brosnan,* 2:43. Morgret uses the term "leftist radical" instead of "pinko."

21. *Arrow Co. v. Cincinnati, New Orleans & Texas Pacific R. Co.,* 379 U.S. 642 (1965), remanding the case to the ICC. *Grain Moving in Multiple Car Shipments—River Crossings into the South,* 325 ICC 752 (August 10, 1965). Prior cases had been 318 ICC 641 (1963); 321 ICC 582 (1963); 229 F. Supp. 572 (S.D. Ohio, 1964).

22. The comparison is not quite accurate in that in 1947 many employees were in passenger service; by 1967 very few were.

23. Morgret, *Brosnan,* 1:207–8.

24. Ibid., 1:220.

25. *Time,* August 9, 1963, 16.

26. Morgret, *Brosnan,* 1:439.

27. Ibid., 2:64.

28. *Newsweek,* October 18, 1965, 89.

29. Morgret, *Brosnan,* 2:73–74.

30. Ibid., 2:78.

31. Catenary is the overhead wire that provides power to electric locomotives.

32. Morgret, *Brosnan,* 2:79–82.

33. *Newsweek,* March 13, 1967, 84; April 10, 1967, 12.

34. FD 21215, 320 ICC 122, 239.

35. *Arnold v. Louisville & Nashville R. Co.,* 180 F. Supp. 429 (M.D. TN, 1960); *Batts v. Louisville & Nashville and Louisville & Nashville v. Cantrell,* 316 F. 2d 22 (6th circuit, 1963). A subsequent decision on this issue was *Clemens v. Central Railroad of New Jersey,* 264 F. Supp. 551 (E.D. PA, 1967).

36. *Brotherhood of Locomotive Engineers v. C&NW Ry. Co.*

37. *Nemitz v. Norfolk & Western R. Co.,* 404 U.S. 37 (1971).

38. *Southern Ry.—Control—Central of Georgia Ry.,* 317 ICC 557, 588–91 (1962).

39. Ibid., 729, 730.

40. Morgret, *Brosnan,* 1:611.

41. *Railway Labor Executives' Association v. United States,* 226 F. Supp. 521 (E.D. Va, 1964), reversed and remanded 379 U.S. 199 (1964).

42. *Southern Ry.—Control—Central of Ga. Ry.,* 320 ICC 377 (1964).

43. Ibid., 331 ICC 151 (1967).

44. Morgret, *Brosnan,* 1:613.

45. Ibid., 2:270.

46. *Wall Street Journal,* November 29, 1967.

47. Ibid., August 30, 1976.

48. *New York Times,* November 28, 1951, 45.

49. From Fred Frailey's excellent account in *Twilight of the Great Trains* (Milwaukee: Kalmbach, 1998), 95.

50. See Craig Miner, *The Rebirth of the Missouri Pacific, 1956–1983* (College Station: Texas A&M University Press, 1983).

51. Frailey, *Twilight of the Great Trains,* 97. Frailey says that even in the Jenks era, MoPac trains continued to be clean. That was not my experience.

52. FD 21755, *Missouri Pacific R. Co.—Control—Chicago & Eastern Illinois R. Co.,* reported 327 ICC 279 (1965), affidavit of intervening security holders, May 5, 1965, vol. 1-D.

53. FD 21755, ex. H-1, H-78, H-79, exception of Bureau of Inquiry and Compliance, vol. 1-B.

54. FD 21755, *MP R. Co.—Control—C&EI R. Co.,* 316–21; *Illinois Central R. Co. v. United States,* 263 F. Supp. 421 (N.D. IL, 1967).

55. FD 21755, transcript 2596.

56. Ibid., statement of D. O. Matthews, vol. 1-A.

57. Ibid., ex. H-188, H-198.

58. Copyright © 1970 Buddah Music, Turnpike Tom Music, ASCAP.

59. *Urbana Daily Illini,* November 26, 1968.

60. FD 21503, C&NW motion for discovery of January 24, 1969, with supporting memoranda; 338 ICC 805, 866–873 (1971).

61. FD 25103, *Illinois Central Gulf R. Co.—Acquisition—Gulf, Mobile & Ohio R. Co., Illinois Central R. Co. et al.,* reported 338 ICC 805 (1971). Williams letter of October 10, 1968, in vol. 1-B.

62. FD 21503, transcripts 2062–63.

63. Ibid., transcript 2261.

64. Ibid., transcript 2210.

65. Ibid., transcript 3271.

66. Ibid., transcripts 1634–43.

67. Ibid., transcript 4215.

68. Ibid., brief of C&NW (March 23, 1970).

69. *Trains* 37 (August 1977): 7.

70. Ibid., 32 (October 1972): 3–4.

71. *Tennessee Central Ry. Abandonment,* 334 ICC 235 (1969).

72. "Up and Down the Monon," from Monon Centennial Music, by John A. McGee and Owen Haynes, copyright © 1947, Chicago, Indianapolis, and Louisville RR and Indiana Society of Chicago.

73. These can be seen on the video presentation *Monon, She's a Hoosier Line,* produced by Bill Warrick for Interurban Video, 1990, a gem of a production.

74. "Last Call for Dinner," from Monon Centennial Music, by John A. McGee and Owen Haynes, as performed by the Monon Waiters and the French Lick Springs Hotel Orchestra for Monon Records.

75. *Louisville & Nashville R. Co.—Merger—Monon RR,* 338 ICC 134 (1970). See also an excellent history by George Hilton, *Monon Route* (Berkeley: Howell-North, 1978). The Monon was officially the Chicago, Indianapolis & Louisville Railway until 1956.

76. The outlets of Lake Pontchartrain.

12: Stalemate in the West

1. Carload figures are from FD 22688, *Chicago & North Western R. Co.—Control— Chicago, Rock Island & Pacific R. Co.,* vol. 1-T, the Klitenic Report, vol. 1.

2. Maury Klein, *Union Pacific: The Rebirth, 1894–1969* (New York: Doubleday, 1989), 456–59.

3. See H. Roger Grant, *The North Western: A History of the C&NW Ry. System* (DeKalb: Northern Illinois University Press, 1996), 182–83.

4. *Trains* 16 (November 1955): 6.

5. See William D. Middleton, "What Are They Doing to the North Western?" *Trains* 18 (July 1958): 16–30.

6. FD 24182, *Chicago, Milwaukee, St. Paul & Pacific Ry. Co.—Merger—Chicago & North Western R. Co.,* not reported, transcripts 13524–26; Brief of Upper Lake Docks Coal Bureau, Inc., April 26, 1968, vol. 1-K.

7. FD 24182, Land O' Lakes Creameries et al., petition to reopen, March 26, 1969, vol. 1-K.

8. FD 22688, vol. 1-L.

9. FD 24182, brief of Soo Line RR, vol. 1-L.

10. *New York Times,* August 18, 1966, 19.

11. Ibid., November 13, 1969, 1 and 34.

12. Ibid., February 23, 1957, 25.

13. Ibid., February 25, 1961, 25. The terms were one and one-quarter share of a new company for each of the C&NW's 800,000 shares, and share-for-share for Milwaukee's two million. Both companies' stock was selling in the $15–$17 range and would descend over the next year to the $9–$10 range.

14. Ibid., May 14, 1963, 51.

15. Ibid., October 24, 1963, 45.

16. *Chicago Daily News*, April 30, 1968, 16.

17. Huddie Ledbetter (Leadbelly), copyright © Folkways Music Publishers, BMI.

18. Albro Martin wrote an excellent entry on William H. Moore in Keith Bryant, ed., *Encyclopedia of American Business History and Biography: Railroads in the Age of Regulation, 1900–1980* (New York: Bruccoli Clark Layman/Facts on File, 1988).

19. See Wallace Abbey, "Great Feats of Railroad Engineering," *Trains* 13 (February 1953): 48.

20. See S. Kip Farrington, "The Rock Island Story," in S. Kip Farrington, *Railroads of Today* (New York: Coward-McCann, 1949), 93–102.

21. *Chicago & North Western Ry. Co.—Merger—Chicago Great Western R. Co.*, 330 ICC 13 (1967).

22. *Soo Line RR v. United States*, 280 F. Supp. 907 (1968).

23. *C&NW Ry. Co.—Merger—CGW R. Co.*, 333 ICC 235 (1968).

24. Two segments in north central Iowa and a short one between Elmhurst and Franklin Park, Illinois, remain.

25. Vignettes from H. Roger Grant, *The Corn Belt Route*.

26. *Fortune* (June 1966): 106.

27. Fargo and Linton (N.D.); Miles City, Judith Gap, Great Falls, Bozeman, Butte, and Missoula (Mont.); Spokane, Tacoma, and Seattle (Wash.).

28. *Great Northern Pacific & Burlington Lines—Merger—Great Northern Ry. et al.*, 331 ICC 228 (1967); 331 ICC 869 (1968).

29. *United States v. Interstate Commerce Commission (Northern Lines Merger Cases)*, 396 U.S. 491 (1970).

30. Robert Klass to Menk, May 13, 1976, in "BN Second Quarter Report to Shareholders."

31. Rush Loving, Jr., "A Railroad Merger That Worked," *Fortune* (August 1972).

32. "BN Report on Sixth Annual Meeting of Stockholders," May 8, 1975.

33. Robert Downing, "Downing Recounts Merger Days," *Vintage Rails* (winter 1996): 69.

34. *United States v. ICC*, civil action 1132-68, November 20, 1968, 40. 331 ICC 228, 243.

35. Thomas Ploss, *The Nation Pays Again*, privately printed, 1983; ISBN 0-9613788. Ploss was an attorney for the Milwaukee Road. His insider's account has a number of keen insights but is clearly a personal observation.

36. FD 24182, Nelson to ICC, February 10, 1967, vol. 1-E.

37. Ibid., exceptions of applicants, January 31, 1969, vol. 1-J.

38. For a good summary of Darmstadter's findings, see Dudley Pegrum, "The Chicago & North Western–Chicago, Milwaukee, St. Paul & Pacific Merger: A Case Study in Transport Economics," *Transportation Journal* (winter 1969): 43–50.

39. FD 24182, corres., vol. 1-L, 1-M.

40. Ploss, *Nation Pays Again,* 75.

41. *Fortune* (June 1966): 140.

42. FD 22688, vol. 1-L.

43. Ibid., reply of CRI&P RR (March 22, 1973).

13: The Eastern Inclusion Crisis

1. *New York Times,* January 8, 1967, sec. 3, p. 3.

2. FD 21510, *N&W Ry.—Merger—NYC&StL RR,* supplemental report, 330 ICC 780 (1967), statement NW-1, vol. 13.

3. FD 21510, transcript 1386.

4. FD 23422, *Erie Lackawanna v. Lehigh Valley,* transcripts 30–50, 131–39.

5. FD 23422, transcript 89.

6. FD 23422, transcripts 122–23.

7. FD 21510, statement EL-3, vol. 9.

8. Ibid., statement EL-1, vol. 9.

9. Not to give the story away, but Conrail would eventually abandon most of the Erie line west of Hornell, affirming that it in fact had no value. From the N&W's point of view, it already had a route from Buffalo to Chicago that was technologically superior to the Erie route (it was flatter) and certainly did not need two routes.

10. FD 21510, statement EL-4, vol. 9

11. Ibid., transcript 1305.

12. Ibid., ex. NW-4, pp. 31–33, vol. 14.

13. Ibid., rebuttal of J. P. Fishwick, ex. NW-4.

14. FD 23178, *Western Maryland Ry. Co., Control by Chesapeake & Ohio R. Co.,* reported 328 ICC 684 (1967).

15. See Don Wood, "The Drawbridge Dilemma," *Trains* 20 (February 1960): 36.

16. FD 23832, *Norfolk & Western Ry. Co.—Merger—Chesapeake & Ohio R. Co.,* not reported, transcript 253.

17. FD 23832, transcript 262.

18. Ibid., transcript 630.

19. Ibid., transcript 249.

20. Ibid., transcripts 419–29.

21. FD 21510, statement EL-1, vol. 9.

22. Ibid., transcripts 1289, 1295, 1347.

23. *New York Times,* March 17, 1968.

24. Grant, *Erie Lackawanna,* 147.

25. FD 21510, statements DH-1 to DH-5, vol. 11.

26. Ibid., ex. NW-4, pp. 53–54.

27. Ibid., proxy statement at annual meeting of B&M stockholders, April 13, 1966, attached to ex. NW-4 and NW-45, vol. 15. See *Galcy v. United States,* docs. 6652–56, U.S. Cir. Ct. of Appeals; *United States v. Boston & Maine,* 380 U.S. 57 (1965).

28. FD 23832, ex. A-11, vol 8; FD 21510, ex. NW-9, vol. 15.

29. Ibid., transcripts 631–32.

30. Ibid., transcripts 251–52.

31. Ibid., transcript 249, ex. 146, rebuttal of John Fishwick, December 14, 1967, vol. 16.

32. Ibid., transcript 630.

33. Ibid., transcript 228.

34. *Erie Lackawanna R. Co. v. United States,* 259 F. Supp. 303 (SDNY, 1966).

35. *Baltimore & Ohio R. Co. v. United States,* 386 U.S. 372 (1967), 392.

36. Ibid., 442.

37. *Erie Lackawanna R. Co. v. United States,* 279 F. Supp. 303 (SDNY, 1967).

38. *PRR Co.—Merger—NYC R. Co.,* 331 ICC 643 (1967).

39. *Oscar Gruss & Son v. United States,* 261 F. Supp. 386 (1966).

40. *Penn Central Merger and Norfolk & Western Inclusion Cases,* 389 U.S. 486 (1968), 510–11.

41. *New York Times,* March 17, 1968; FD 23832, transcript 9826.

42. Ken Kraemer and Devan Lawton, "Buffalo Terminal," *Trains* 36 (February 1976): 29–43.

43. Trains dedicated to carrying one commodity from one point of origin to one destination.

44. FD 23832, Saunders's address to Security Analysts of San Francisco, November 9, 1967, vol. 16.

45. Reasoner quoted in David P. Morgan, "The Most Closely Watched Train," *Trains* 28 (August 1968): 10–12.

14: The Fall of the Penn Central

1. Bevan to Saunders, November 8, 1967, 559, in Senate Committee, *Penn Central and Other Railroads.*

2. Rush Loving, Jr., "The Penn Central Bankruptcy Express," *Fortune* (August 1970): 107. This was the first in-depth analysis of the disaster to appear.

3. FD 35291, *Investigation into the Management of the Business of the Penn Central Transportation Co. and Affiliated Companies.* Accused of being asleep at the switch, the ICC undertook this investigation in 1970–1971. It is a series of reports from field staff all over the PC system. Most of the material in the first five sections of this chapter is drawn from these reports.

4. Loving, "Penn Central Bankruptcy Express," 109.

5. The yard was named in honor of the "Big Four Route," the old Cleveland, Cincinnati, Chicago & St. Louis Railroad that was a component of the NYC. It is located at Avon, Indiana, just outside Indianapolis, and later on was usually called Avon Yard.

6. FD 35291, statement 16, John Michael, Indianapolis.

7. Ibid., statement 16.

8. Ibid., Henry Large to David Smucker, November 11, 1968.

9. Ibid., Large to Saunders, November 14, 1969.

10. Ibid., Large to Saunders, May 1, 1967.

11. Ibid., L.S. Bossler to H.E. Ring, December 3, 1968.

12. Ibid., William D. Lamprecht to Smucker, September 4, 1968; Richard Hasselman to Edwin K. Taylor, September 10, 1968; Taylor to Hasselman, September 10, 1968.

13. Ibid., Robert G. Flannery to Harrison, August 26, 1969.

14. Ibid., Smith to Schofield, May 7, 1969.

15. Ibid., statement 35, Langdon to Perlman, April 21, 1969.

16. Ibid., statements 16, 26.

17. Ibid., statement 16.

18. Ibid., statement 32, Claude A. Bowen.

19. Ibid., report of Peat, Marwick & Mitchell, December 22, 1969.

20. PM&M to Charles Hill, December 22, 1969, in Senate Committee, *Penn Central and Other Railroads,* 706.

21. FD 35291, statement of Peat, Marwick & Mitchell, December 22, 1969.

22. Ibid., statement 33 of Peter Starvu, ICC Bureau of Accounts.

23. Ibid., Smucker to Schofield, Smith & Kohout, October 9, 1969, in statement 35 of Hugh Lynch.

24. Ibid., statement 18 of Burke Tracey and Nicholai G. Sotor.

25. Ibid., statement 30.

26. Ibid., Walrath to Hill, December 23, 1969.

27. Ibid.

28. Ibid., report to J. F. Aigeltinger of the ICC Bureau of Enforcement after a visit to the Altoona shops on April 8, 1971.

29. Ibid., statement 33.

30. Ibid., statement 32.

31. Ibid., statement 23, Paul Macyauski.

32. Ibid., statement 18, Tracey and Sotor.

33. Ibid., statement 26, George Finn.

34. Ibid., statement 16, John Michael.

35. Sullivan quoted in Loving, "Penn Central Bankruptcy Express," 108.

36. Preparations for the Tarrytown meeting are discussed in FD 35291, Smucker to Perlman, October 1, 1969. The journalistic accounts referred to are Loving, "Penn Central Bankruptcy Express," and an account in Daughen and Binzen, *Wreck of the Penn Central,* 121.

37. Loving, "Penn Central Bankruptcy Express," 108.

38. Daughen and Binzen, *Wreck of the Penn Central,* 97.

39. Senate Committee on Commerce, *Failing Railroads,* 91st Cong., 2d sess., 1970, 324 (my emphasis).

40. Ibid., 396.

41. Ibid., 388.

42. Wayne Hoffman quoted in Daughen and Binzen, *Wreck of the Penn Central,* 102.

43. House Committee on Banking, *The Penn Central Failure and the Role of Financial Institutions,* 92d Cong., 1st sess., 1972, Staff Report, 156.

44. Senate Committee, *Penn Central and Other Railroads,* 343. The whole section entitled "Corporate Character" is filled with insight.

45. Being a Protestant, even being a Mason, had been virtually mandatory for advancement on many American railroads. "Catholic" railroads—meaning roads that had some Catholics in high executive positions and where advancement for other Catholics was possible, notably the Milwaukee Road, the Northern Pacific, and the New Haven—were rare. The classic quote on this matter was found by historian Roger Grant in his history of the Chicago Great Western, a statement by its outgoing president William Deramus III to his successor, Edward Reidy, a Catholic, in 1957: "I'll fry your ass if you give any mackerel snapper special breaks." D. Keith Lawson, interview by H. Roger Grant, in Grant, *The Corn Belt Route.*

46. Daughen and Binzen, *Wreck of the Penn Central,* 97–98.

47. Penn Central Company was a holding company that held the Penn Central Transportation Company as a subsidiary. Penn Central Transportation could go into

receivership without touching Penn Central Company. Many of the diversified acquisitions were made through a third entity, the Pennsylvania Company, the railroad's old wholly owned subsidiary, dating from the sphere-of-interest games early in the century. The Pennsylvania Company did not have to go into receivership just because the railroad did.

48. House Committee, *Penn Central Failure*, 280–84, discusses this with supporting evidence.

49. See ibid., 189–271, for a discussion of this with supporting evidence.

50. Most of the acquisitions were made by the Pennsylvania Company, not the PRR. The Pennsylvania Company was wholly owned by the railroad, but to imply that the railroad made the purchases is technically in error. For a description of the financing of diversification, see Senate Committee, *Penn Central and Other Railroads*, 387–430.

51. Senate Committee, *Failing Railroads*, 329–31.

52. For a full discussion of this, see House Committee on Commerce, *Inadequacies of Protections for Investors in Penn Central and Other ICC-Regulated Companies*, 92d Cong., 1st sess., 1971, Staff Study.

53. SEC Administrative Proceeding 3-2536, *In the Matter of Alleghany Corporation*, 1970, reproduced in House Committee on Interstate and Foreign Commerce, *Penn Central Transportation Company: Adequacy of Investor Protection: Hearings before the Committee on Interstate and Foreign Commerce*, 91st Cong., 2d sess., 1970, 56.

54. David L. Wilson (Penn Central) to Solomon Freedman (SEC), August 11, 1970, reproduced in House Committee, *Penn Central Transportation Company*, 40.

55. The guest list is reproduced in House Committee, *Penn Central and Other Railroads*, 527, and a discussion of the Hodge-Bevan relationship is at 404–6.

56. Daughen and Binzen, *Wreck of the Penn Central*, 170.

57. A lengthy discussion of Penphil, with supporting documentation, is in House Committee, *Penn Central Failure*, 189–254.

58. See ibid., 55–148, for a lengthy discussion of Executive Jet, with supporting documentation. See also Daughen and Binzen, *Wreck of the Penn Central*, 185.

59. House Committee, *Penn Central Failure*, 112–14.

60. The Ricciardi deposition is reproduced in its entirety in House Committee, *Penn Central Failure*, 130–42. This section is on 133–34.

61. Reproduced in its entirety in Daughen and Binzen, *Wreck of the Penn Central*, 180.

62. House Committee, *Penn Central Failure*, 129–42.

63. Daughen and Binzen, *Wreck of the Penn Central*, 176–77.

64. William S. Cook to David Bevan, October 5, 1967, in House Committee, *Penn Central and Other Railroads*, 732.

65. Bevan to Saunders, November 21, 1966, in ibid, 616.

66. FD 35291, Geza Weitzner to Saunders, December 10, 1969.

67. House Committee, *Penn Central and Other Railroads*, 359. A full discussion of differences between ICC and GAAP and the PC's use of them is found on 358–66.

68. *Fortune* (September 1970): 88.

69. Bevan to Saunders, November 21, 1966, in House Committee, *Penn Central and Other Railroads*, 616.

70. FD 35291, Saunders to William L. Day, December 8, 1969.

71. House Committee, *Penn Central Failure*, correspondence and memos, 163–67.

72. Ibid., minutes, November 26, 1969, 150.

73. Vignette in Daughen and Binzen, *Wreck of the Penn Central,* 128.

74. House Committee, *Penn Central Failure,* 318–20, gives a chronology of both the publicly known events leading to bankruptcy and those not publicly known and then continues with a discussion with supporting documentation of possible illegal trading by banks.

75. Perlman refused to resign until his contract was up in November 1970.

76. *New York Times,* June 20, 1970, 1. Other observations in this account are from Daughen and Binzen, *Wreck of the Penn Central.*

77. Linda Charlton in *New York Times,* June 22, 1970, 59.

15: The Turning Point

1. Robert Bedingfield in *New York Times,* July 12, 1970, 1.

2. Ibid.

3. Ibid.

4. *New York Times,* January 7, 1972, 41; July 30, 1974, 43.

5. Ibid., May 3, 1974, 1.

6. Robert Bedingfield in ibid., September 4, 1975, 1A. A full list of defendants is on p. 46.

7. Ibid., September 5, 1975, 39, 41.

8. Israel Shanker in ibid., January 22, 1973, 1.

9. House Committee, *Penn Central Transportation Company,* 5.

10. David P. Morgan in *Trains* 47 (May 1987): 9.

Bibliography

Selected Bibliography

The principal source for this book was the docket files of the now defunct Interstate Commerce Commission. The files consist of the testimony, briefs, and exhibits of each case and amount to anywhere from 20,000 to 200,000 pages each of typed or printed material. They are housed at the Federal Records Center at Suitland, Maryland. Merger cases (as opposed to rate cases) were designated as Finance Dockets. Hence, they are cited in the notes by the designation FD and a serial number as, for example, FD 20707, *Erie R. Co.—Merger—DL&W R. Co.* The first citation of each merger case in each chapter includes the full title of the case. Reports that were issued from these cases have a standard legal citation, consisting of the volume of ICC reports in which the case appears, the designation ICC, the page on which the report begins, and the page on which the particular information can be found. The first citation of each case in each chapter includes the full name of the case and the year it was decided as, for example, *Erie Lackawanna v Lehigh Valley*, 330 ICC 306 (1966), 310.

Additional sources were law cases, miscellaneous government documents, pamphlets (mostly from the ICC Library, now housed at the University of Denver), and news stories.

The following list of works cited includes the secondary histories, articles of special significance beyond simply news accounts, and the important Congressional reports.

Federal Government Documents

House. Committee on Banking. *The Penn Central Failure and the Role of Financial Institutions.* Staff Report. 92d Cong., 1st sess., 1972.

House. Committee on Commerce Staff Study. *Inadequacies of Protections for Investors in Penn Central and Other ICC-Regulated Companies.* 91st Cong., 2d sess., 1971.

House. Committee on Interstate Commerce. *Omnibus Transportation Bill*. Hearings. 76th Cong., 1st sess., 1939.
House. Committee on Interstate Commerce. *Return of the Railroads to Private Enterprise*. Hearings. 66th Cong., 1st sess., 1919.
House. Special Subcommittee on Investigations of the Committee on Interstate and Foreign Commerce. *Penn Central Transportation Company: Adequacy of Investor Protection*. Hearings. 91st Cong., 2d sess., 1970.
House. Subcommittee on Transportation and Aeronautics of the Committee on Interstate and Foreign Commerce. *Emergency Rail Services Legislation*. 91st Cong., 2d sess., 1971.
Senate. *First Report of the Federal Coordinator of Transportation*. 74th Cong., 1st sess., 1935.
Senate. *New York, New Haven & Hartford RR Co., Evidence Taken before the ICC*. 63d Cong., 2d sess., 1914.
Senate. Committee on Commerce. *Failing Railroads*. Hearings. 91st Cong., 2d sess., 1970.
Senate. Committee on Commerce. *National Transportation Policy*. 87th Cong., 1st sess., 1961.
Senate. Committee on Commerce. *The Penn Central and Other Railroads*. Committee Report. 92d Cong., 2d sess., 1972.
Senate. Committee on Interstate Commerce. *Extension of Government Control of Railroads*. 65th Cong., 3d sess., 1919.
Senate. Committee on Interstate Commerce. *Five Percent Case*. 63d Cong., 2d sess., 1915.
Senate. Committee on Interstate Commerce. *Government Control & Operation of Railroads*. Hearings. 65th Cong., 3d sess., 1919.
Senate. Committee on Interstate Commerce. *Pere Marquette Railroad Co. and Cincinnati, Hamilton & Dayton Ry. Co.* 65th Cong., 2d sess., 1917.
Senate. Committee on Interstate Commerce. *Railroad Combination in the Eastern Region*. Hearings. 76th Cong., 3d sess., 1940.
Senate. Subcommittee on Antitrust and Monopoly. *Rail Merger Legislation*. Hearings. 87th Cong., 2d sess., 1962.
Senate. Subcommittee on Surface Transportation of the Committee on Commerce. *Problems of the Railroads*. Hearings. 85th Cong., 2d sess., 1958.
Senate. Subcommittee on Surface Transportation of the Committee on Commerce. *Review of the Penn Central's Condition*. 92d Cong., 2d sess., 1971.

Books and Articles

Abrams, Richard M. "Brandeis and the New Haven–Boston & Maine Merger Battle Revisited." *Business History Review* (winter 1962): 408–30.
Archer, Robert F. *A History of the Lehigh Valley Railroad: "The Route of the Black Diamond."* Berkeley: Howell-North, 1977.
Barriger, John W. *Super Railroads for a Dynamic American Economy*. New York: Simmons-Boardman, 1956.
Bok, Derek. "Section Seven of the Clayton Act and the Merging of Law and Economics." *Harvard Law Review* (December 1960): 226–355.
Borkin, Joseph. *Robert R. Young, the Populist of Wall Street*. New York: Harper and Row, 1969.
Bramson, Seth. *Speedway to Sunshine: The Story of the Florida East Coast Railway*. Erin, Ont.: Boston Mills Press, 1984.
Bryant, Keith, ed. *Encyclopedia of American Business History and Biography: Railroads*

in the Age of Regulation, 1900–1980. Columbia, S.C.: Bruccoli Clark Layman/Facts on File, 1988.

Caloroso, Bill. *Pennsylvania Railroad's Elmira Branch.* Andover, N.J.: Andover Junction, 1993.

Daggett, Stuart. *Railroad Consolidation West of the Mississippi.* Berkeley: University of California Press, 1933.

Daughen, Joseph, and Peter Binzen. *The Wreck of the Penn Central.* Boston: Little, Brown, 1971.

Davis, Burke. *The Southern Railway: Road of the Innovators.* Chapel Hill: University of North Carolina Press, 1985.

Davis, Colin. *Power at Odds: The 1922 National Railroad Shopmen's Strike.* Urbana: University of Illinois Press, 1997.

DeBoer, David. *Piggyback and Containers: A History of Rail Intermodal on America's Steel Highway.* San Marino, Calif.: Golden West Books, 1992.

Del Grosso, Robert. *The Burlington Northern Railroad in 1993.* Bonners Ferry, Idaho: Great Northern Pacific Publications, 1994.

Donovan, Frank, Jr., "Minneapolis & St. Louis in the News Again." *Trains* (March 1959): 16–19.

Doukas, Kimon A. *The French Railroads and the State.* Ph.D. diss., Columbia University, 1945.

Elliott, Howard. *An Efficient Transportation Machine.* Pamphlet at the ICC Library.

Farrington, S. Kip, Jr. *Railroads of Today.* New York: Coward-McCann, 1949.

Frailey, Fred. *Twilight of the Great Trains.* Milwaukee: Kalmbach, 1998.

Fuess, Claude M. *Joseph B. Eastman, Servant of the People.* New York: Columbia University Press, 1952.

Gaffney, Thomas J. "The Changing Role of the Railroad and Its Effect on the Thumb Region of Michigan." Master's thesis, Clemson University, 1999.

Gilpin, William. *The Cosmopolitan Railway.* San Francisco: History Co., 1890,

Grant, H. Roger. *The Corn Belt Route.* DeKalb: Northern Illinois University Press, 1984.

———. *Erie Lackawanna: Death of an American Railroad.* Stanford, Calif.: Stanford University Press, 1994.

———. *The North Western: A History of the Chicago & North Western Railway System.* DeKalb: Northern Illinois University Press, 1996.

Harwell, Jeffrey A. "Florida East Coast: Survivor in the Sun," *Trains* (July 1996).

Hidy, Ralph W., Muriel E. Hidy, Roy V. Scott, and Don L. Hofsommer. *The Great Northern Railway: A History.* Boston: Harvard Business School Press, 1988.

Hilton, George W. *The Monon Route.* Berkeley: Howell-North, 1978.

———. *The Transportation Act of 1958: A Decade of Experience.* Bloomington: Indiana University Press, 1969.

Hofsommer, Don. *The Southern Pacific, 1901–1985.* College Station: Texas A&M University Press, 1986.

Hoogenboom, Ari, and Olive Hoogenboom. *A History of the ICC: From Panacea to Palliative.* New York: Norton, 1976.

Hungerford, Edward. *Daniel Willard Rides the Line: The Story of a Great Railroad Man.* New York: G. P. Putnam's, 1938.

———. *A Railroad for Tomorrow.* Milwaukee: Kalmbach, 1944.

Josephson, Matthew. "The Daring Young Man of Wall Street." *Saturday Evening Post,* August 11, 18, 25, 1945.

Kanigel, Robert. *The One Best Way: Frederick Winslow Taylor and the Enigma of*

Efficiency. New York: Viking, 1998.

Kerr, K. Austin. *American Railroad Politics, 1914–1920.* Pittsburgh: University of Pittsburgh Press, 1968.

Klein, Maury. *Union Pacific: The Rebirth, 1894–1969.* New York: Doubleday, 1989.

Kolko, Gabriel. *Railroads and Regulation, 1877–1916.* Princeton: Princeton University Press, 1965.

Latham, Earl. *The Politics of Railroad Consolidation, 1933–1936.* Cambridge: Harvard University Press, 1959.

Leonard, William. "Decline of Railroad Consolidation." *Journal of Economic History* (May 1949): 1–24.

———. *Railroad Consolidation under the Transportation Act of 1920.* New York: Columbia University Press, 1946.

Lewis, Tom. *Divided Highways: Building the Interstate Highways, Transforming American Life.* New York: Viking, 1997.

Loving, Rush, Jr. "The Penn Central Bankruptcy Express." *Fortune* (August 1970): 107–9.

———. "A Railroad Merger That Worked." *Fortune* (August 1972): 128–33.

Lowenthal, Max. *The Investor Pays.* New York: Knopf, 1933.

MacGregor, Bruce, and Ted Benson. *Portrait of a Silver Lady: The Train They Called the California Zephyr.* Boulder, Colo.: Pruett, 1977.

Martin, Albro. *Enterprise Denied: Origins of the Decline of American Railroad, 1887–1917.* New York: Columbia University Press, 1971.

McPherson, Logan. *Transportation in Europe.* New York: Henry Holt, 1910.

Middleton, William D. "What Are They Doing to the North Western?" *Trains* (July 1958): 16–30.

———. *When the Steam Railroads Electrified.* Milwaukee: Kalmbach, 1974.

Miner, Craig. *The Rebirth of the Missouri Pacific, 1956–1983.* College Station: Texas A&M University Press, 1983.

Morgan, David P. "The Diesel That Did It." *Trains* (February 1960): 18–25.

———. "Where Did the Railroad Go That Once Went to Sea?" *Trains* (February 1975): 22–28.

———. "Who Shot the Passenger Train?" *Trains* (April 1959): 14–51.

Morgret, Charles O. *Brosnan: The Railroads' Messiah.* 2 vols. New York: Vantage Press, 1996.

Nelson, James R. *Railroad Mergers and the Economy of New England.* Boston: New England Economic Research Council, 1966.

Pegrum, Dudley. "The Chicago & North Western–Chicago, Milwaukee, St. Paul & Pacific Merger: A Case Study in Transport Economics." *Transportation Journal* (winter 1969): 43–50.

Ploss, Thomas. *The Nation Pays Again.* Privately printed, ISBN 0-9613788, 1983.

Plumb, Glenn. "The Plan of Organized Employees for Railroad Reorganization." *Commerce and Finance* (July 23, 1919).

Raban, Jonathan. *Bad Land: An American Romance.* New York: Pantheon, 1996.

Rea, Samuel. *Our Railroad Problem.* Pamphlet at the ICC Library.

Rehor, John A. *The Nickel Plate Story.* Milwaukee: Kalmbach, 1965.

Saunders, Richard, Jr. "The Louisville, Cincinnati & Charleston Railroad and the Elusive Hope for Intersectional Unity." Master's thesis, University of Illinois, 1964.

———. *The Railroad Mergers and the Coming of Conrail.* Westport, Conn.: Greenwood Press, 1978.

Sayre, Ralph. "Albert Baird Cummins and the Progressive Movement in Iowa." Ph.D. diss., Columbia University, 1958.

Sharfman, I. Leo. *The American Railroad Problem.* New York: Century, 1921.

———. *The Interstate Commerce Commission: A Study in Administrative Law and Procedure.* New York: Commonwealth Fund, 1931.

Shaughnessy, Jim. *The Rutland Road.* Berkeley: Howell-North, 1964.

Simnett, W. E. *Railway Amalgamation in Great Britain.* London: Railway Gazette, 1923.

Staples, Henry Lee, and Alpheus T. Mason. *The Fall of a Railroad Empire.* Syracuse, N.Y.: Syracuse University Press, 1947.

Stevens, G. R. *History of the Canadian National Railways.* 2 vols. New York: Macmillan, 1973.

Sturgis, Henry. *A New Chapter of Erie: The Story of the Erie's Reorganization, 1938–1941.* New York, 1948.

Taylor, George R., and Irene D. Neu. *The American Railroad Network, 1861–1890.* Cambridge: Harvard University Press, 1956.

Vrooman, David. *Daniel Willard and Progressive Management on the Baltimore & Ohio Railroad.* Columbus: Ohio State University Press, 1991.

Warrick, Bill, producer. *Monon, She's a Hoosier Line.* Interurban Video, 1990.

Welsh, Joseph M. *By Streamliner from New York to Florida.* Andover, N.J.: Andover Junction, 1994.

Wilner, Frank N. *Railroad Mergers.* Omaha: Simmons-Boardman, 1997.

———. *The Railway Labor Act and the Dilemma of Labor Relations.* Omaha: Simmons-Boardman, 1988.

Withuhn, Bill. "Did We Scrap Steam Too Soon?" *Trains* (June 1974): 36–48.

Zim, Marvin Hugo. "Master Strategist of the Railroad Settlement." *Fortune* (July 1964): 164–66.

Cases

Arnold v. Louisville & Nashville R. Co., 180 F. Supp. 429 (1960).

Arrow Co. v. Cincinnati, New Orleans & Texas Pacific R. Co., 379 U.S. 642 (1965).

Baltimore & Ohio R. Co. v. United States, 386 U.S. 372 (1967).

Batts v. Louisville & Nashville and Louisville & Nashville v. Cantrell, 316 F. 2d 22 (1963).

Blair v. City of Chicago, 201 U.S. 400 (1906).

Boston & Maine Discontinuance of Passenger Service, 324 ICC 418 (1963).

Brotherhood of Locomotive Engineers v. Chicago & North Western Ry. Co., 314 F. 2d 424 (1963).

Brotherhood of Maintenance of Way Employees v. United States, 366 U.S. 169 (1961).

Brotherhood of Maintenance of Way Employees et al. v. United States, 221 F. Supp. 19 (1963), affirmed 375 U.S. 216 (1963).

Central of Georgia Ry. Co., Control, 295 ICC 523 (1957) and 307 ICC 39 (1958).

Chesapeake & Ohio R. Co.—Control—Baltimore & Ohio R. Co. 317 ICC 261 (1962).

Chesapeake & Ohio Ry. Purchase 271 ICC 5 (1948).

Chicago & North Western R. Co.—Control—Chicago, Rock Island & Pacific R. Co. 347 ICC 556 (1974).

Chicago & North Western Ry.—Purchase—Minneapolis & St. Louis, 312 ICC 285 (1960).

Chicago & North Western Ry. Trustees Abandonment, 254 ICC 820 (1944).

Chicago & North Western Ry. Co.—Merger—Chicago Great Western R. Co. 330 ICC 13 (1967), 333 ICC 235 (1968).

Chicago, Burlington & Quincy RR Co. Control, 271 ICC 63 (1948).

Chicago, Milwaukee St. Paul & Pacific RR Co. Trustees Construction, 252 ICC 49 (1942).

Chicago, Milwaukee, St. Paul & Pacific Ry. Co.—Merger—Chicago & North Western R. Co. ICC Finance Docket 13526, not reported.

Clemens v. Central Railroad of New Jersey, 264 F. Supp. 967 (1965).

Coal from Kentucky and West Virginia to Virginia, 308 ICC 99 (1959).

Coal from Southern Mines to Tampa and Sutton, 318 ICC 371 (1962).

Coal to New York Harbor Area, 311 ICC 355 (1960).

Consolidation and Combination of Carriers, 12 ICC 277 (1907).

Consolidation of Railroads, 63 ICC 455 (1921).

Control of Central Pacific by Southern Pacific, 76 ICC 508 (1923).

Detroit, Toledo & Ironton RR Co., Control, 275 ICC 455 (1950).

Duluth, South Shore & Atlantic RR Co.—Merger—Minneapolis, St. Paul & Sault Ste. Marie RR Co. and Wisconsin Central RR Co., 312 ICC 341 (1960).

Enforcement of Conditions on Merger Proceedings, 313 ICC 523 (1957).

Erie Lackawanna v. Lehigh Valley, 330 ICC 306 (1966).

Erie Lackawanna R. Co. v. United States, 259 F. Supp. 303 (1966) and 279 F. Supp. 303 (1967).

Erie R. Co.—Merger—Delaware, Lackawanna & Western R. Co. 312 ICC 185 (1960).

Erie R. Co., Abandonment, 252 ICC 697 (1944).

Erie R. Co., Ferry Abandonment, 295 ICC 549 (1957).

Erie R. Co., Trackage Rights, 295 ICC 303 (1956).

Erie R. Co. v. Board of Public Utility Commissioners, 395 U.S. 957 (1959).

Erie R. Co. et al., Trackage Rights et al., Binghamton-Gibson, N.Y., 295 ICC 743 (1958).

Erie RR Co., Reorganization, 239 ICC 653 (1940).

Florida East Coast Ry. v. United States, 242 F. Supp. 14 (1965).

Fort Worth & Denver City Ry. Co., Lease, 247 ICC 119 (1941).

Fried v. United States, 212 F. Supp 887 (1963).

Galcy v. United States, docs. 6652–56, U.S. Cir. Ct. of Appeals.

Grain Moving in Multiple Car Shipments—River Crossings into the South, 318 ICC 641 (1963), 321 ICC 582 (1963), 229 F. Supp. 572 (1964), 325 ICC 752 (1965).

Great Northern—Merger—Northern Pacific, 328 ICC 460 (1966).

Great Northern Pacific & Burlington Lines—Merger—Great Northern Ry. et al., 331 ICC 228 (1967), 331 ICC 869 (1968).

ICC v. Baltimore & Ohio RR, 152 ICC 721 (1929) and 160 ICC 785 (1930).

ICC v. Pennsylvania RR Co. 169 ICC 618 (1930) and 291 ICC 651 (1934).

Illinois Central Gulf R. Co.—Acquisition—Gulf, Mobile & Ohio R. Co., Illinois Central R. Co. et al., 338 ICC 805 (1971).

Illinois Central R. Co. v. United States, 263 F. Supp. 421 (1967).

In Re Astor, 193 ICC 528 (1933)

In Re Boatner, 257 ICC 369 (1944).

In Re Consolidation of Merger Proceedings (1962).

In Re Consolidation of Railroads (1925).

In Re Coverdale, 252 ICC 672 (1942).

In Re Rand, 175 ICC 587 (1931).

In the Matter of Consolidation of Railroad Properties in the United States into a Limited Number of Systems, 159 ICC 522 (1929) and 185 ICC 401 (1932).

Interstate Commerce Commission v. Alabama Midland Railway Company, 168 U.S. 144 (1897).

Interstate Commerce Commission v. Railway Labor Association, 315 U.S. 373 (1942).

Louisville & Nashville R. Co.—Merger—Monon RR, 328 ICC 134 (1970).

Louisville & Nashville RR Co., Merger, 295 ICC 457 (1957).

McLean Trucking Co. v United States, 321 U.S. 67 (1944).

Minneapolis & St. Louis Ry. Co., Control, 361 ICC 173 (1959).

Missouri Pacific R. Co.—Control—Chicago & Eastern Illinois R. Co., 327 ICC 279 (1965).

Mohawk Air Lines Mail Rates, 29 CAB 198 (1959).

Movement of Highway Trailers by Rail, 293 ICC 93 (1954).

Nemitz v. Norfolk & Western R. Co., 404 U.S. 37 (1971).

New Automobiles in Interstate Commerce, 259 ICC 475 (1945).

New England Divisions: Bangor Aroostook RR Co. et al. v. Aberdeen & Rockfish RR Co. et al., 62 ICC 513 (1921).

New Orleans Union Passenger Terminal Case, 267 ICC 763 (1948) and 282 ICC 271 (1952).

New York Central Securities Co. v. United States, 287 U.S. 12 (1932).

New York, Chicago & St. Louis RR Control, 295 ICC 131 (1955).

New York, Chicago & St. Louis RR Co., Operation of Lines and Issue of Capital Stock, 79 ICC 581 (1923).

New York, Lackawanna & Western RR Co.—Merger, 257 ICC 91 (1944).

New York, New Haven & Hartford RR Co. Reorganization, 247 ICC 365 (1947).

New York, New Haven & Hartford Trustees Discontinuance of All Interstate Passenger Trains, 327 ICC 151 (1966).

Noerr Motor Freight v. Eastern Railroads Presidents Conference, 155 F. Supp. 768 (1957).

Norfolk & Western Ry. Co.—Merger—Chesapeake & Ohio R. Co., ICC Finance Docket 23832, not reported.

Norfolk & Western Ry. Co.-Merger—Virginian Ry., 307 ICC 401 (1959).

Norfolk & Western Ry.—Merger—New York, Chicago & St. Louis RR, 324 ICC 1 (1964), 330 ICC 780 (1967).

Norfolk & Western Ry., Proposed Acquisition and Control of the Virginian Ry., 117 ICC 67 (1926).

Northern Securities Co. v. United States, 193 U.S. 197 (1904).

Oklahoma Ry. Trustees Abandonment, 257 ICC 177 (1944).

Oscar Gruss & Son v. United States, 261 F. Supp. 386 (1966).

Overfield v. Pennroad, 113 F. 2d 6 (1941) rev. 39 F. Supp 482 (1941), 42 F. Supp 585 (1942), 48 F. Supp 1008 (1943), 146 F. Supp 889 1944).

Penn Central Merger and Norfolk & Western Inclusion Cases, 389 U.S. 486 (1968).

Pennsylvania R. Co.—Control—Lehigh Valley R. Co., 317 ICC 1139 (1962).

Pennsylvania R. Co.—Merger—New York Central R. Co., 327 ICC 475 (1966) and 331 ICC 643 (1967).

Pere Marquette Ry., Merger, 267 ICC 207 (1947).

Perrine v. Pennroad, 28 Delaware Chancery 342 (1945), 29 Del Ch 423 (1947).

Pittsburgh & West Virginia Ry. Co, Proposed Construction and Extension. 138 ICC 755 (1928).

Railway Labor Association v. United States, 339 U.S. 142 (1950).

Railway Labor Executives' Association v. United States, 339 U.S. 142 (1950).

Railway Labor Executives' Association v. United States, 226 F. Supp. 521 (1964), reversed and remanded 379 U.S. 199 (1964).

Rochester Telephone Corp. v. United States, 307 U.S. 125 (1939).

St. Joe Paper Co. v. Atlantic Coast Line RR Co., 347 ICC 298 (1954).

Schwabacher v. ICC, 72 F. Supp 560 (1948).

Schwabacher v. United States, 334 U.S. 182 (1948).

Seaboard Air Line—Merger—Atlantic Coast Line, 320 ICC 122 (1963).

Seaboard Air Line R. Co. v. United States, 382 U.S. 154 (1965).

Soo Line RR v. United States, 280 F. Supp. 907 (1968).

Southern Pacific—Control—Western Pacific, 327 ICC 187 (1965).

Southern Ry.—Control—Central of Georgia Ry., 317 ICC 557 (1962), 320 ICC 377 (1964), and 331 ICC 151 (1967).

Swacker v. Pennroad. 30 Delaware Chancery 495 (1947) and 333 U.S. 862 (1948).

Tennessee Central Ry. Abandonment, 324 ICC 235 (1969).

Texas & Pacific Ry. Co. Operation, 247 ICC 285 (1942).

Toledo, Peoria & Western RR Co., Control, 295 ICC 523 (1957).

United States v. Boston & Maine, 380 U.S. 57 (1965).

United States v. Interstate Commerce Commission (Northern Lines Merger Cases), 396 U.S. 491 (1970).

United States v. Lowden, 308 U.S. 225 (1939).

United States v. Southern Pacific, 259 U.S. 214 (1922).

United States v. Union Pacific, 226 U.S. 61 (1912).

Virginian Ry. Extension, 162 ICC 552 (1930).

Wabash Ry. Co. Control, transcripts 192–204.

Wabash Ry. Co. Receivership, 247 ICC 581, 584 (1941).

Western Maryland Ry. Co., Control by Chesapeake & Ohio R. Co., 328 ICC 684 (1967).

Wheeling & Lake Erie RR Co. Control, 249 ICC 490 (1941).

Index

McCarthy, Wilson (judge; D&RGW), 255
McDonald, Walter (Ga. PSC), 437n
McGinnis, Lucille, 247
McGinnis, Patrick (NYNH&H), 141, 144,
  B&M, 247, 249, 251; convicted, 369
McGranahan, Stanley (Erie), 170
McInnes, Milton (Erie), 179
McKee, E. Bates (Bache & Co.), 188
McKenzie, Sir William (Canadian
  Northern), 28
McLean case, 78, 140, 284
McLean Trucking Co., 78
Meader, Stephen, 260
Mechanicville, N.Y., 369
Meet The Press, 97
Mellen, Charles (NYNH&H), 30–31, 249
Mellon, Richard King, 412
Mellon Bank of Pittsburgh, 412, 415
Melstone, Mont., 26
Memphis, Tenn., 6, 12, 138, 139, 290,
  291, 307, 308, 320, 328, 331, 333,
  349, 350, 352
Memphis & Charleston RR, 290
MeNear, George P., Jr. (TP&W), 138
Menk, Louis J. (NP), 340–41, 398
Mercantile-Safe Deposit Trust Co., 279,
  281, 283
Mercer, Johnny, 15
Meriden, Conn., 246
Meridian, Miss., 312
Merion Golf Club, 254
Mero, James, 59
Merrill Lynch & Co., 92, 197
Metroliners (passenger trains), 377–78, 414
Metropolitan Life Insurance Co., 96,
  179, 183, 328–29, 370
Mexico City, 12, 308
Meyer, John, 236
Meyner, Robert (N.J. gov.), 165
Miami, Fla., 27, 280, 281, 285, 286, 287
Miami Daily News, 280
Michigan Central RR, 10, 66
Michigan Chemical Co., 325
Midland, Mich., 310
Midnight Special (passenger train), 133
Midwest-Emory Motor Freight, 129
Miles City, Mont., 25
Mill Cities Limited (passenger train), 113

Miller, E. Spencer (Maine Central), 144,
  249
military, and railroads, 233, 437n
Milpitas, Cal., 213
Milwaukee, Wis., 344
Milwaukee Land Co., 25
Minneapolis, Minn. *See* St. Paul, Minn.
Minneapolis & St. Louis Ry., 14, 65,
  125, 137–38, 148, 252, 324, 326,
  327, 430n
Minneapolis, St. Paul & Sault Ste. Marie
  Ry. *See* Soo Line RR
Minnesota, and opposition to BN, 222
Minnesota Light & Power Co., 341
Minnesota Railroad & Warehouse Com-
  mission, 222, 226, 232, 234, 344–45
Minor, Robert (NYC), 371
Minot, N.Dak., 221
Mississippi Central RR, 317
Mississippi River Fuel Corp., 308
Missouri & Arkansas RR, 116
Missouri Farmers Association, 435n
Missouri-Kansas-Texas RR, 12–13, 66; and
  Deramus management, 114–15; and
  Barriger management, 116, 123, 125,
  310, 311, 316, 332, 349, 352, 417
Missouri Pacific RR, 5, 12, 54, 66, 74,
  76, 100, 122, 128, 134, 213, 216,
  275; history of, 306–8; and C&EI,
  309–12, 314, 315, 317, 328, 332; and
  Klitenic Plan, 349–52, 385–86, 422
Mitchell, John (attorney general), 413–14
Mobile, Ala., 12, 319
Mobile & Ohio RR, 66, 133
Modern Railroads, 306
Modoc Line (SP), 349
Moffat Tunnel Co., 130
Mohawk Airlines, 162
Moley, Raymond, 69
Moline, Ill., 333
Monon RR, 66, 115–16, 125, 265; and
  L&N, 318–20, 325, 326
Monroe, La., 308
Montana, and opposition to BN, 222
Montana Central RR, 17
Montana Power Co., 27
Montgomery, Ala., 279, 281, 316
Montreal, Que., 8, 28, 11. 118, 369, 370